Lecture Notes in Computer Science 15755

Founding Editors

Gerhard Goos
Juris Hartmanis

The series Lecture Notes in Computer Science (LNCS), including its subseries Lecture Notes in Artificial Intelligence (LNAI) and Lecture Notes in Bioinformatics (LNBI), has established itself as a medium for the publication of new developments in computer science and information technology research, teaching, and education.

LNCS enjoys close cooperation with the computer science R & D community, the series counts many renowned academics among its volume editors and paper authors, and collaborates with prestigious societies. Its mission is to serve this international community by providing an invaluable service, mainly focused on the publication of conference and workshop proceedings and postproceedings. LNCS commenced publication in 1973.

Panagiotis Katsaros
Editor

Model-Based Safety and Assessment

9th International Symposium, IMBSA 2025
Athens, Greece, September 24–26, 2025
Proceedings

 Springer

Editor
Panagiotis Katsaros 🆔
Aristotle University of Thessaloniki
Thessaloniki, Greece

ISSN 0302-9743   ISSN 1611-3349 (electronic)
Lecture Notes in Computer Science
ISBN 978-3-032-05072-4   ISBN 978-3-032-05073-1 (eBook)
https://doi.org/10.1007/978-3-032-05073-1

Preface

This volume contains the papers presented at IMBSA 2025: the International Symposium on Model-Based Safety and Assessment, held on September 24-26, 2025 in Athens.

IMBSA focuses on model-based and automated ways of assessing safety and other attributes of dependability of complex systems. This was the 9th edition of the symposium, which has evolved throughout its history into a forum where brand-new ideas from academia and industrial experiences are brought together. The objectives are to present experiences and tools, to share ideas and to bring together the industrial and academic community.

Another important focus in the latest edition of the symposium was the impact of AI techniques on system safety. In IMBSA 2025, the Program Committee selected 8 papers on machine learning techniques for system safety. The program also included a keynote on the Scaling Law Challenges for Digital Twins, given by Rajiv Ranjan from Newcastle University.

We received 39 submissions from authors in 11 countries. A single-blind review process took place. Each submission was reviewed by three members of the International Program Committee. The committee accepted all papers that had a clear consensus of acceptance, defined by a combination of only positive and neutral reviews - 28 in total.

As organizers, we would like to thank all the members of the International Program Committee. We also want to thank the General Chair, Kai Höfig from the Technische Hochschule Rosenheim, as well as all members of the Steering Committee.

On behalf of everyone involved in IMBSA 2025, I hope you will be joining us at the next IMBSA edition.

July 2025
Panagiotis Katsaros

Organization

Program Committee

Jose Ignacio Aizpurua	University of the Basque Country, Spain
Koorosh Aslansefat	University of Hull, UK
Stylianos Basagiannis	International Hellenic University, Greece
Lorenzo Bitetti	Thales Alenia Space, France
Marco Bozzano	Fondazione Bruno Kessler, Italy
Xavier de Bossoreille	Apsys, France
Kevin Delmas	ONERA, France
Ewen Denney	NASA, USA
Jana Dittmann	University of Magdeburg, Germany
Marielle Doche-Petit	Systerel, France
Francesco Flammini	Mälardalen University, Sweden
Lars Grunske	Humboldt University Berlin, Germany
Matthias Güdemann	UAS Munich, Germany
Michaela Huhn	Ostfalia University of Applied Sciences, Germany
Bernhard Kaiser	Ansys Germany GmbH, Germany
Panagiotis Katsaros (Chair)	Aristotle University of Thessaloniki, Greece
Leila Kloul	Université de Versailles Saint-Quentin-en-Yvelines, France
Nikolaos Matragkas	CEA, France
Till Mossakowski	University of Magdeburg, Germany
Thomas Noll	RWTH Aachen University, Germany
Yiannis Papadopoulos	University of Hull, UK
Jürgen Mottok	OTH Regensburg, Germany
Tatiana Prosvirnova	ONERA, France
Antoine Rauzy	Norwegian University of Science and Technology, Norway
Wolfgang Reif	University of Augsburg, Germany
Daniel Schneider	Fraunhofer IESE, Germany
Christel Seguin	ONERA, France
Ioannis Sorokos	Fraunhofer IESE, Germany
Ramin Tavakoli Kolagari	Nuremberg Institute of Technology, Germany
Elena Troubitsyna	KTH Royal Institute of Technology, Sweden
Marc Zeller	Siemens AG, Germany

Steering Committee

Yiannis Papadopoulos	University of Hull, UK
Panagiotis Katsaros	Aristotle University of Thessaloniki, Greece
Marco Bozzano	Fondazione Bruno Kessler, Italy
Leila Kloul	Université de Versailles Saint-Quentin-en-Yvelines, France
Frank Ortmeier	Otto von Guericke University Magdeburg, Germany
Antoine Rauzy	Norwegian University of Science and Technology, Norway
Christel Seguin	ONERA, France
Marc Zeller	Siemens AG, Germany

Organizing Committee

Kai Höfig (General Chair)	Technische Hochschule Rosenheim

Program Committee Chair

Panagiotis Katsaros	Aristotle University of Thessaloniki

Additional Reviewers

Bieber, Pierre
Corradini, Franca
Geleta, Getachew Hagos
Gioulekas, Fotios
Mokos, Konstantinos
Qosja, Mario
Reichmann, Eik

Keynote

Scaling Law Challenges for Digital Twins

Rajiv Ranjan

Newcastle University, UK
Raj.Ranjan@ncl.ac.uk

Abstract. Digital twins are revolutionizing industries by providing real-time computing, monitoring, and predictive analytics capabilities. However, their success hinges on overcoming significant data and resource management challenges. This keynote will explore four key issues critical to the advancement and scalability of digital twins. First, we will discuss the complexities of real-time data processing within the modern computing continuum, emphasizing the need for seamless integration and efficient resource allocation across distributed systems. Second, we will explore the use of Large Language Models (LLMs) for dynamic verification of the resilience of digital twins, highlighting their potential to enhance adaptability and real-time decision-making. Third, we will examine end-to-end monitoring strategies to ensure data integrity, transparency, and reliability, enabling trust in automated decision processes. Finally, we will address the integration of emerging computational technologies, such as quantum accelerators (e.g., Quantum Brilliance) and neuromorphic chips (such as Intel Loihi and BrainChip Akida), at the edge network to accelerate data processing and improve the responsiveness of digital twins. This talk will provide insights into how these advancements can be leveraged to develop robust, scalable, and intelligent digital twin ecosystems, driving innovation and efficiency in real-world applications.

Contents

Safe Machine Learning

Probabilistic Analysis

Model-Based Design and Safety Assessment

Machine Learning and Automata Learning for System Safety

Failure Detection Isolation and Recovery Analysis

System Safety Assessment

AI-Driven Data Management Framework for Quality Assurance in Additive Manufacturing: A Case Study on the TRUMPF TruPrint 1000

Faiza Waheed$^{(\boxtimes)}$ ⓘ, Kai Höfig ⓘ, and Fabian Riß ⓘ

Technische Hochschule Rosenheim, Rosenheim, Germany
{faiza.waheed,kai.hoefig,fabian.riss}@th-rosenheim.de

Abstract. Our work demonstrates an innovative AI-driven approach to Quality Assurance (QA) in metal additive manufacturing (AM). We focus on real-time defect detection in 3D metal printing, which is increasingly used to manufacture small parts for applications in safety-critical devices, including parts for the aerospace, automotive, and medical industries. We propose a model-based failure and defect detection system that combines visual monitoring and input from various sensors to control the AM process. By using a deep learning model and incorporating live monitoring of data points, we enable early anomaly detection and thus ensure immediate operator intervention to stop and prevent defective prints to be used in safety-critical applications. These techniques help prevent energy waste, conserve material costs, resources, time, and increase the safety and reliability of the system. Our prototype framework automates the classification of multiple defects, improving both the reliability of printed components and the efficiency of the manufacturing process by suggesting in-situ improvement techniques. We also highlight the technical challenges associated with data synchronisation and acquisition, as well as multiple sensor integration. Data collection is used not only for QA but also as valuable documentation for process validation and to maintaining an in-house learning center. Overall, our AI-driven approach improves the accuracy of non-destructive testing (NDT) over traditional post-production inspection methods. We propose a framework for the integration of AI to improve process control, making it more reliable for safety-critical industries and providing strong guidance for future model-based QA applications in AM processes. This framework can be applied for QA on TRUMPF TruPrint L-PBF 3D printing machines.

Keywords: Additive Manufacturing · Quality Assurance · Deep Learning · Defect Detection · Non-Destructive Testing

1 Introduction

Additive Manufacturing (AM) presents challenges in quality assurance due to process variability and material stresses that cause defects [18]. When used in

P. Katsaros (Ed.): IMBSA 2025, LNCS 15755, pp. 3–17, 2026.
https://doi.org/10.1007/978-3-032-05073-1_1

safety or reliability critical applications, additive manufacturing on the one hand provides great opportunities for producing spare parts across industries including aerospace, automotive and healthcare, along with individual systems and special parts that cannot be produced with other technologies [7,8]. On the other hand, defects can be obscured during the printing process, affecting the safety and reliability of the broader system. An efficient defect detection system is therefore crucial for such applications. The AI4Green project at Technische Hochschule Rosenheim addresses these issues for the TRUMPF TruPrint 1000 machine [13], which is available at the Additive Manufacturing Lab. Having ecological factors in mind as one of the central goals for this research project, we also want to improve AI-based defect detection for additive manufacturing as a resilient safety and reliability measure for critical applications by integrating multiple sensors to make the system more robust and defect-free. The project focuses on integrating AI for defect detection with live process monitoring. This paper explores data management by focussing on:

- Scalable data architecture for heterogeneous AM data.
- Image-based defect detection using deep learning.
- Integration of sensors for real-time data and more comprehensive in-situ monitoring (Eddy Current, Acceleration and Thermography).
- Quality assurance and management of the defect detection model.

In Sect. 2, we first describe the overall data management architecture that is being used to capture data from the TRUMPF TruPrint 1000 machine, along with image data for AI training. Section 3 introduces the development of the application which includes the dashboard to visualise live and historical sensor data. The application also provides defect tracking during the printing process and operator validated data management. Section 4 shows how labels are generated and combined with the data for supervised machine learning (ML). Since it is possible to detect the defects not only visually, but also with other sensors, Sect. 5 demonstrates how we are exploring methods to incorporate multi-sensor data in the in-situ NDT process. Sections 6 and 7 summarise our work and provide an outlook on future developments.

2   Data Management Architecture

This section outlines the system architecture for comprehensive data collection, transformation, and storage from the TRUMPF TruPrint 1000 machine. An overview of the data architecture is shown in Fig. 1 [12].

2.1   Data Ingestion Workflow

The various sensor data points are available from the TRUMPF TruPrint 1000 machine via Open Platform Communications Unified Architecture (OPC UA) protocol as nodes. Image and machine parameter data (such as part geometry, laser scan speed, laser power, etc.) are stored in a folder on a dedicated server for the TRUMPF machine, which is then accessed using server message block (SMB). The data from accelerometer and thermal camera is also stored in the databases via SMB. Additionally, the Amiquam dedicated server provides data readings from the Eddy Current Sensor, which are then also available via OPC UA as nodes.

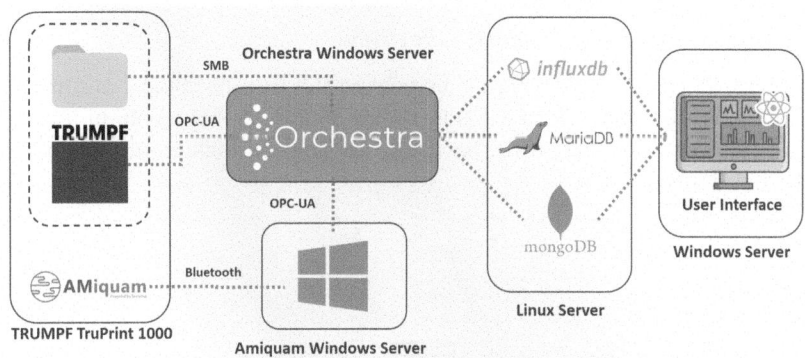

Fig. 1. Data Management Architecture

With complex workflows and management processes in Orchestra [14], we obtain and store these data points in the respective databases. The complex architecture for obtaining and storing data points from the TRUMPF TruPrint 1000 machine to the databases is discussed in more detail by the authors in [12].

2.2   Database Systems

We have implemented three specialised databases based on the requirement of specific data points:

– **MariaDB**: Stores image metadata and also layer-wise greyscale images from the Basler acA3800-14um camera. This database handles ~2000+ images per print job with ~1 s query latency.
– **InfluxDB**: Handles storage of high-frequency time-series data such as temperature, oxygen levels, and gas flow rates. InfluxDB can handle high data insertion rates and batch writes, so that multiple sensor readings can be stored with the same timestamp. This makes it ideal for real-time, large-scale data storage.
– **MongoDB**: Captures loosely structured data such as print job metadata, part geometries and dynamic machine parameters (laser power, scan speed).

3   Application Development

Having explained the data ingestion architecture, we will now focus on visualising the data. To provide the operator with real time data and tracking of defects in the printing process, a dashboard has been developed using React.js for the frontend visualisation and FastAPI for the backend, including interaction with the databases and execution of the AI Model for Anomaly detection [4].

3.1   Application Architecture Overview

The application-level architecture that powers the live dashboard and real-time defect detection is shown in Fig. 2. The system consists of three main layers: the frontend (interactive dashboard), backend (application logic + model inference) and the database layer.

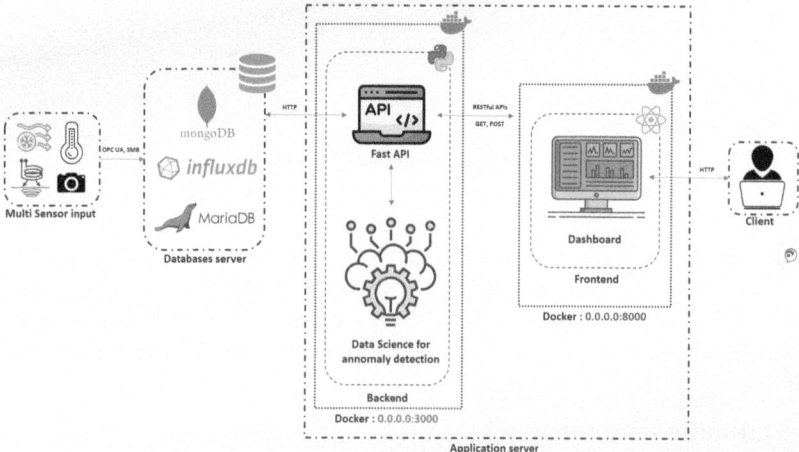

Fig. 2. Application architecture

- **Database layer** provides access to databases.
- **Backend**, implemented in FastAPI, extracts data from databases and exposes RESTful APIs for the frontend to retrieve machine parameters and sensor data. It also handles the operation of the anomaly detection model for real-time image analysis and provides inferences.
- **Frontend** is built with React.js and presents machine status, visual and historical data trends, along with notification & alerts.

3.2   Database Layer

The database layer provides structured access to persistent data storage and securely stores machine parameters, sensor data, images, and other relevant information that serves as the foundation for the application.

3.3   Backend and Data Pipeline

Once the data is safely stored in the databases, it can be accessed for processing and visualisation in the dashboard application. Our Python-based framework ensures seamless data flow between the databases and data forwarding in a structured format, to the dashboard for visualisation, while also addressing latency, schema flexibility and batch data handling challenges. In addition to data retrieval, the backend also manages inference tasks and supports various application services. The backend communicates with the frontend through RESTful APIs, serving as the bridge between the user interface and the underlying data systems. Backend APIs are designed for extensibility, making future integration of additional sensors or AI models straightforward.

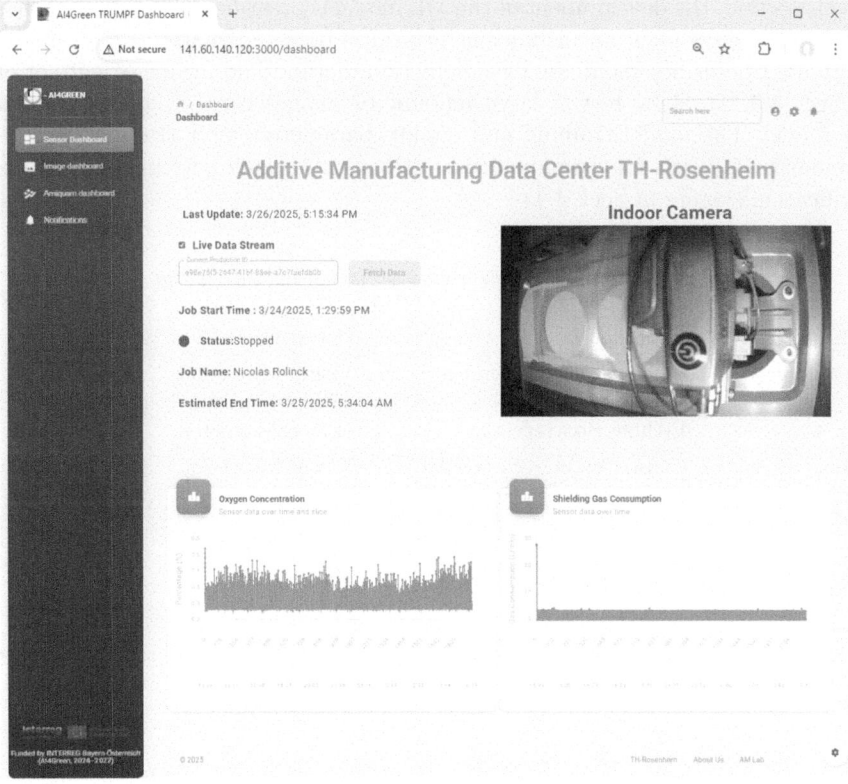

Fig. 3. Live quality assurance dashboard with defect alerts

3.4   Frontend Dashboard Functionality

The dashboard (Fig. 3) enables intuitive interaction for the operator, where they may observe and infer the printing process. It also enables traceability of sensor data and parameters for individual printed layers. The dashboard offers the following key insights:

- Machine status and live camera-feed
- Live and Historical process trends
- Real-time defect alerts/notifications

Enhancements to the dashboard, including ensuring scalability and modularity for future extensions such as role-based access control and operator instruction integrations are discussed in Sect. 6.

4   Image Processing and Defect Detection

In this section, the development of the ML model is described. The cause of those defects is the result of an insufficient printing process or material distribution. Section 4.1 describes the anomalies, detection method and means of mitigation. In Sect. 4.2, we show how a large amount of images can be labeled to train our model. The model training and quality parameters after training are then summarized in Sect. 4.3. To implement mitigation strategies, we present a simple notification system in Sect. 4.4.

Table 1. Distinct Defect Classes Based on Visual Data

Defect	Root Cause	Detection Method	Mitigation
Protruding Defect	Often resulting from overheated zones, prolonged laser focus or Etching Spatter	Visual Inspection or Thermography or Accelerometer	Adjust laser parameters
Groove Defect	Caused by uneven powder distribution or prior layer distortion	Visual Inspection or Eddy Current	Increase powder volume
Recoating Defect	Indicating a malfunction or obstruction in the recoater blade movement	Visual Inspection	Adjust recoater mechanism
Cavity Defect	Sub-surface or visible voids due to insufficient sifting of powder material	Visual Inspection + Eddy Current + Thermography	Increase powder volume

4.1   Defect Classification

Defects in Laser Powder Bed Fusion (L-PBF) arise from complex printing process phenomena such as insufficient fusion, recoating anomalies, powder spatter, and overheating [6,19]. We identified and focused on the following four defect classes based on visual distinctiveness and impact on the integrity of the part (see

Table 1). Defects can change the reliability and durability of the produced part and are thereby potentially points of failure for safety-critical parts. During actual production, it is crucial to know the exact operating parameters (geometry of the part, etc.) to decide if a defect is harming these requirements.

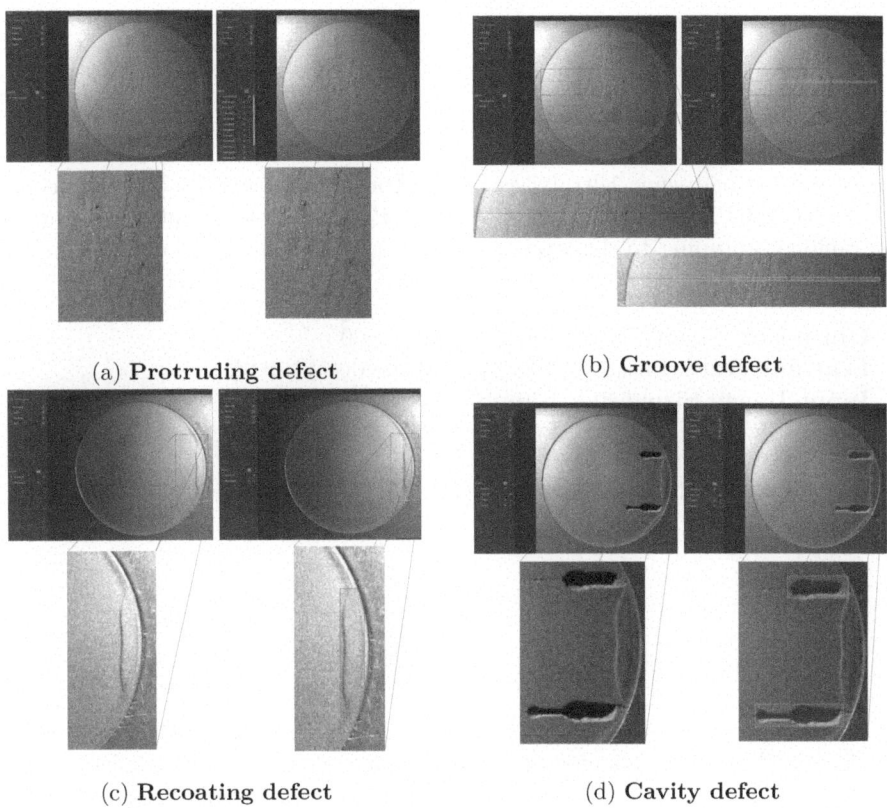

(a) **Protruding defect**   (b) **Groove defect**

(c) **Recoating defect**   (d) **Cavity defect**

Fig. 4. Various defects in additive manufacturing

Defects can be classified according to their severity and location. Minor defects, such as isolated powder spatter in non-print area, may not require operator intervention and hence can be ignored in terms of anomaly detection. Additionally, non-severe defects can be in non-load-bearing regions, such as support structures that are not the final part. These support structures are removed by cutting and sanding after the part printing has been completed. Defects in these regions pose minimal risk. These non-severe defects eventually heal during subsequent layers of powder deposition. The defects which are considered major or critical, require operator intervention. The course of action depends on the type, size and location of the defect.

4.2 Data Labelling

Using Labelbox [9], we annotated ∼600 images with four classes of defects. Image data augmentations, including rotation, flipping, shearing and noise injection, increased the the dataset size by a factor of four. The four types of defect from in-situ monitoring of layer wise greyscale image data using a Basler acA3800-14um camera can be seen in Fig. 4.

4.3 Model Training

Building upon the previous study carried out by Wang et al. [17], a YOLOv9m model was trained using Ultralytics [16] PyTorch framework for 500 epochs on an NVIDIA RTX A4000 16 GB GDDR6 GPU. This configuration was used for rapid prototyping to deploy and observe the system in action. The model configuration included:

- **Optimiser**: AdamW with weight decay (0.0005)
- **Learning Rate**: Initial: 0.001, final (cosine decay): 0.01
- **Input Image Size**: 640 × 640 pixels
- **Batch Size**: 16

Final model performance for all classes:

- **Precision**: 84%
- **Recall**: 80%
- **mAP@0.5**: 84%
- **F1 Score**: 0.814
- **Inference latency**: ∼9 ms/image

These metrics indicate that the model is achieving a good balance between precision and recall, which allows for reliable defect alerts under controlled experimental conditions. However, ongoing work focuses on retraining with further annotated production data and incorporating expert feedback to refine annotations to improve recall >90%.

To gain in-depth insight into the model's performance, we can look at the results across different defect categories. The individual class specific metrics are listed in Table 2):

As the results indicate in Fig. 5, the model performs better for large defects (recoating and cavity), decently for protruding defects but struggles with groove defects, which are harder to infer (∼50% of groove defects are false negatives). Currently, operator validation is required for classification of defects, especially groove defects. Furthermore, a pipeline is under development to iteratively refine annotations through expert review and retrain the model to improve metrics. Our primary focus is to achieve >90% recall, via active learning and multi-sensor features. These goals are part of future work with the aim of ensuring that the system delivers results which meet the standards required for safety-critical applications.

Table 2. Normalised Defect Class Data with Evaluation Metrics

Defect Class	Images	Instances	Precision	Recall	mAP50	mAP50-95
All	1.00	1.00	0.84	0.80	0.84	0.56
Groove	0.65	0.26	0.62	0.45	0.54	0.22
Protruding	0.71	0.31	0.84	0.76	0.84	0.31
Recoating	0.46	0.12	1.00	1.00	0.99	0.89
Cavity	0.38	0.31	0.90	1.00	0.99	0.82

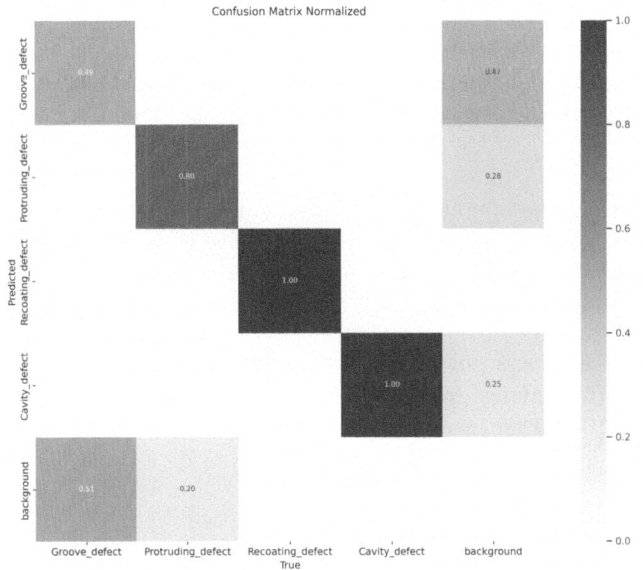

Fig. 5. Model YOLOv9m confusion matrix

4.4   Notification and Alert System

Implementing a robust and reliable warning and alert system within the live monitoring environment requires achieving higher levels of model performance, particularly the recall score. We must ensure false positives are minimised and enhance confidence in model inference. We have incorporated specific operator roles/actions for each defect category and severity in the system. To enable real-time quality assurance and operator intervention, model feedback is integrated into the dashboard as a live alerting system. Alerts are configured based on confidence thresholds and mapped to specific operator actions via a decision matrix. This matrix is designed to include:

– **Defect Severity Grading**:
  • *Minor*: Logged for operator review.

- *Major*: Notify operator with course of action (e.g. increase powder volume or pause printing).
- *Critical*: Notify operator via dashboard and escalate via email (e.g. halt production).
- **Operator Actions**:
  - *Pause/Stop*: Triggered for major/critical defects.
  - *Resume*: Requires manual override after inspection.
  - *Clean Recoater*: Requires manual cleaning after groove/recoating defects.
  - *Increase/decrease Powder Volume*: Requires operator to increase or decrease powder volume to alleviate cavity or groove defects.
- **Notification Pathways**:
  - *Dashboard*: Real-time alerts with defect visuals and suggested actions.
  - *Email*: Critical alerts include timestamps, layer number and data snapshots.

Feedback from the operator for data labelling is also logged from the dashboard. We are currently conducting comprehensive tests to validate the response of the system before deploying with full confidence of the operator. Our results demonstrate great potential for waste reduction, with estimated savings in:

- **Material**: ~30% less powder waste through early defect detection
- **Energy**: ~15% savings from aborted defective builds
- **Labour**: ~10% fewer inspection hours for verified parts

5   Multi-sensor Integration

Although image-based detection provides a robust visual picture of defects, NDT of AM parts requires a multimodal sensor strategy to capture subsurface and print process-related anomalies.

The extended framework integrates the following additional sensors:

- **Eddy Current Sensor**: to detect subsurface flaws, such as porosity and cracks, by electromagnetic induction [5].
- **Thermal Camera**: for monitoring real-time heat signatures to identify thermal inconsistencies that produce defects such as overheating or inadequate melting [11].
- **Accelerometer**: to capturing mechanical vibrations of the moving part to diagnose protruding defects or recoater failure.

The proposed integration of a multi-sensor architecture is illustrated in Fig. 6.

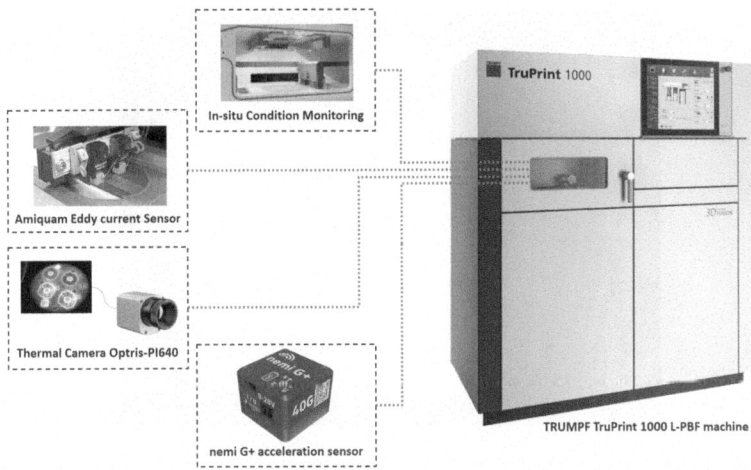

Fig. 6. Multi-sensor data fusion architecture

5.1   Eddy Current Sensor

We have implemented the Amiquam Eddy current sensor W1 TRUMPF TruPrint 1000/2000/3000/5000 [2]. It is calibrated to read stainless steel alloys (SS-316L) for our research. We can detect sub-surface anomalies from the Eddy current readings. We are currently in the phase of analysing the readings from the sensor and aligning it with image data to detect porosity and crack defects, which present as protruding or cavity defects in visual data. Key challenges include [5]:

– **EMI shielding**: These have to be mitigated via grounded enclosures and correct sensor placement
– **Probe lift-off calculation**: The calibration has to be accurate to maintain a consistent lift-off distance.
– **Calibration drift**: The sensor probes must be routinely recalibrated to ensure correct reference point.

5.2   Thermal Camera

We have installed the Optris PI640i thermal camera [10] to observe anomalies during the printing process. An image showcasing spatter/debris from laser etching is shown in Fig. 7:

  Thermal data specifically helps identify overheating zones [3, 11] that present as protruding defects visually. The reading from this sensor will be integrated into our defect detection model in the next phase of research.

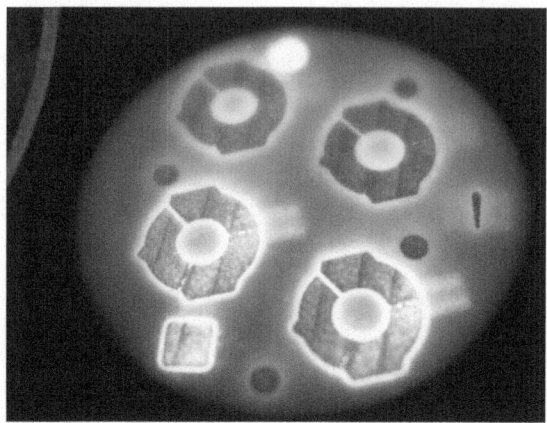

Fig. 7. Spatter from laser etching via Thermal imaging

5.3 Accelerometer/Vibration Sensor

Data from the nemi G+ wireless acceleration sensor [15] with a sampling rate of 4 kHz is implemented to detect failures associated with protruding or recoating defects. The vibration signal is passed through a low-pass filter with a cut-off to suppress high frequency noise [1]. Distinct peaks corresponding to recoater collisions become clearly visible in the filtered signal. By combining these vibration features with camera-based visual inputs, the model can accurately locate and assess the severity of defects. The vibration data is segmented layer-wise and mapped to the base plate to identify the precise layer and location of anomalies (see Fig. 8). Initial accelerometer data is being evaluated to define operational mechanisms/opportunities for integration into the anomaly detection framework. The resulting insights will be used to enhance model performance in future development.

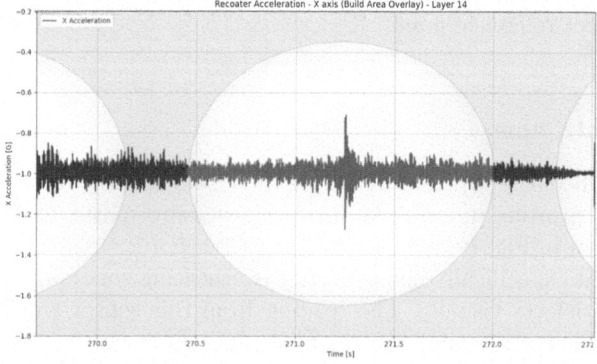

Fig. 8. Data from Accelerometer indicating potential Protruding defect

6   Challenges and Future Work

There are several practical challenges that have been presented during our research to date. Few of the challenges are listed below:

– **Data Volume and Prioritisation**: With the increase in sensor data input, it is key to prioritise critical sensor inputs to avoid computational bottlenecks.
– **System Security & User Authentication**: Implementing role-based access control and authentication systems is planned to ensure the integrity of the project.
– **Model Robustness**: The current dataset must be expanded to include edge cases and rare defects. We are investigating active learning to select samples for annotation dynamically.
– **Explainable AI (XAI)**: Implement XAI techniques to provide reasoning for anomaly detections and to increase operator trust

   Furthermore, it is important for safety-critical applications if defects decrease the level of robustness or reliability below an unacceptable threshold. Since minor defects can emerge during a printing process and are also very likely, our idea is to further improve the data collection in a way that it can be used for simulation using a digital twin of the part that contains such defects. That allows us to analyse the reliability of a produced part by simulating its performance under expected operating conditions, helping to determine whether it meets the safety and robustness requirements.

7   Conclusion

Our research proposes a comprehensive framework for AI-driven QA in AM, specifically applied to the TRUMPF TruPrint machine. The designed application architecture ensures efficient data ingestion and storage across databases for seamless access and processing. By integrating ML with real-time visual data, we demonstrate a system capable of identifying four distinct defects during the manufacturing process. Our framework not only enables defect detection, but also facilitates immediate operator intervention with the help of alerts and notifications with the help of a dedicated dashboard, thereby reducing material waste, energy consumption and man-hours. Additionally, maintaining a centralized data repository supports the establishment of a comprehensive learning center for operator training and continuous model improvement. While our framework shows promising results, ongoing efforts focus on improving model robustness via active learning, multi-sensor fusion and operator validation to meet the stringent requirements for critical and safety critical industry standards. Future work includes integration of multiple sensors and the implementation of analytics on the defects which have been identified from these data sources. We conclude that this work lays a strong foundation for scalable and intelligent QA solutions in AM, advancing the reliability and safety of safety critical parts for industrial sectors.

Acknowledgments. This work was funded by INTERREG Bayern-Österreich (AI4Green, 01.05.2024-30.04.2027).

Disclosure of Interests. The authors have no competing interests to declare which are relevant to the content of this article.

References

1. Python scipy butterworth filter tutorial. PythonGuides.com (2024), https:// pythonguides.com/python-scipy-butterworth-filter, demonstrates low-pass filtering
2. Amiquam, Inc.: Eddy current testing for additive manufacturing. https:// amiquam.net/product-category/w1/, Accessed 30 Apr 2025
3. Baumgartl, H., Tomas, J., Buettner, R., Merkel, M.: A deep learning-based model for defect detection in laser-powder bed fusion using in-situ thermographic monitoring. Prog. Addit. Manuf. **5**(3), 277–285 (2020). https://doi.org/10.1007/s40964-019-00108-3
4. Cardoso, A., Teixeira, C.J.V., Pinto, J.S.: Architecture for highly configurable dashboards for operations monitoring and support. Stud. Inf. Control **27**(3), 319–330 (2018). https://doi.org/10.24846/v27i3y201807
5. Ehlers, H., Pelkner, M., Thewes, R.: Online process monitoring for additive manufacturing using eddy current testing with magnetoresistive sensor arrays. IEEE Sens. J. **PP**(99), 1 (2022). https://doi.org/10.1109/JSEN.2022.3205177, license: CC BY 4.0
6. Fischer, F.G., Zimmermann, M.G., Praetzsch, N., Knaak, C.: Monitoring of the powder bed quality in metal additive manufacturing using deep transfer learning. Mater. Des. **221**, 111029 (2022)
7. Additive Manufacturing Technologies. Springer, New York (2015). https://doi.org/10.1007/978-1-4939-2113-3
8. Grasso, M., Colosimo, B.: Process defects and in-situ monitoring methods in metal powder-based additive manufacturing. J. Manuf. Sci. Eng. **139**(5), 1–11 (2017). https://doi.org/10.1115/1.4036641
9. Labelbox, Inc.: Image labeling and annotation for machine learning. https://docs.labelbox.com/docs/overview, Accessed 31 Mar 2025
10. Optris: Optrispi640 thermal camera. https://optris.com/products/infrared-cameras/precision-line/pi-640i/, Accessed 30 Apr 2025
11. Oster, S., Breese, P.P., Ulbricht, A., et al.: A deep learning framework for defect prediction based on thermographic in-situ monitoring in laser powder bed fusion. J. Intell. Manuf. **35**(4), 1687–1706 (2024). https://doi.org/10.1007/s10845-023-02117-0
12. Riß, F., Kraus, R.: Additive manufacturing – new possibilities for quality assurance and process understanding through intelligent data handling. Presented at the Orchestra Symposium 2024, November 2024, Accessed 12 Mar 2025
13. Rosenheim, T.H.: Labor additive fertigung. https://www.th-rosenheim.de/die-hochschule/labore/additive-fertigung, Accessed 12 May 2025
14. Soffico: Soffico - software solutions. https://soffico.de/, Accessed 12 May 2025
15. i4M Technologies GmbH: Nemig+ wireless accelerometer. https://nemi.one/products/nemi-g-plus.html (2025), Accessed 30 Apr 2025

16. Ultralytics: Ultralytics yolov9. https://docs.ultralytics.com/models/yolov9/ (2023), Accessed 12 May 2025
17. Wang, W., et al.: A real-time defect detection strategy for additive manufacturing processes based on deep learning and machine vision technologies. Micromachines **15**(1), 28 (2024)
18. Zhao, Y., Ren, H., Zhang, Y., Wang, C., Long, Y.: Layer-wise multi-defect detection for laser powder bed fusion using deep learning algorithm with visual explanation. Opt. Laser Technol. **174**, 110648 (2024)
19. Zitelli, C., Folgarait, P., Schino, A.: Laser powder bed fusion of stainless steel grades: a review. Metals **9**(7), 731 (2019)

Model-Based Safety Assessment for Flight Control Systems: Methodology and Case Study

Isabella Lanzani[1(✉)], Luca Perfetti[2], and Luca Uliano[2]

[1] Dipartimento di Elettronica, Informazione e Bioingegneria, Politecnico di Milano,
Milan, Italy
isabella.lanzani@polimi.it
[2] Leonardo Helicopter Division, Samarate, Italy
{luca.perfetti,luca.uliano}@leonardo.com

Abstract. Technological advances have increased complexity of avionics systems, requiring methods to efficiently and accurately derive both quantitative and qualitative safety assessments for certification. To address this challenge, Model-Based Safety Assessment techniques have emerged as promising solutions over the years. In December 2023, the new version of ARP4761A integrates MBSA formalism into the recommended practices for safety processes, as an alternative to classical safety assessment techniques (e.g. Fault Tree Analysis). The main contribution of the paper is to provide a case study demonstrating a successful application of an MBSA technique, to support the aforementioned safety process required by the certification authority. Accordingly, the generated outputs include probability of occurrence, DAL allocation, the elicitation of independence principles and requirements traceability. The example reported is a comprehensive MBSA process of an industrial rotorcraft Flight Control System: the article follows the architecture description, explains the safety model creation and comments on the derived results. In the final part of the article, lessons learned from the implementation of MBSA technology in an industrial environment are reported.

Keywords: Safety · MBSA · Cecilia Workshop · Aerospace

1 Introduction

Rotorcraft Flight Control Systems (FCSs) incorporate a diverse array of complex hardware and software components while frequently adopting innovative technologies and novel architectural designs. Although these advancements may present potential new failure scenarios, numerous methodologies have been developed to effectively address and mitigate the associated risks. ARP4761A [1], released in December 2023, presents recommended guidelines for performing safety assessment of civil aircraft, systems, and equipment. It has proposed

P. Katsaros (Ed.): IMBSA 2025, LNCS 15755, pp. 18–32, 2026.
https://doi.org/10.1007/978-3-032-05073-1_2

Model-Based Safety Assessments (MBSAs) methodologies as alternative methods for classical safety processes.

Even though the inclusion in the recommended practice is recent, the MBSA's academic and industrial activities span a long period of time. From an industrial perspective, the most relevant discoveries are listed below. MBSA is a popular safety discipline whose application in the avionics field has been observed on various occasions. In 2007, during the certification of the Falcon 7X Flight Control System, Dassault Aviation included an MBSA model as supporting material, demonstrating its relevance and alignment with standard assessments and analyses [2]. In the same year, a study over the Rudder Control System was conducted by Airbus and ONERA, that successfully convinced the former to launch internal research projects to investigate the viability and industrialization of model based safety analysis [3].

In 2022 a function from a Wheel Braking System (WBS) has been carefully created in Cecilia Workshop, showing, among the correctness of the overall analysis, that building a MBSA raised several questions that lead to a safer analysis and greater awareness from the engineers involved, compared with classical assessment like Fault Tree Analysis (FTA) [4]. In contrast to this research, the current analysis uses a more structured modeling methodology better suited to the hardware and software complexity of the FCS.

FTA has been expanded in the framework of MBSA, for instance, Component Fault Tree (CFT) [5] implements modularization in the FTA structure. It consists of FTA branches with a input and output failure ports. Indeed, among their benefits, they allow for the construction of libraries of specific components, to be reused when necessary.

In 2023 Cecilia Workshop was used to show the efficacy of MBSA for the development of Unmanned Aerial Vehicles (UAV) in the scope of SORA certification [6,7]. This sample of past achievement testify how MBSA techniques are industrially interesting in the scope of safety assessment for avionic certification.

Indeed, the identified advantages of MBSA are numerous, and the findings of this article further reinforce its effectiveness. The safety model created can be simulated, bringing a more intuitive mean to address and explain safety features to safety and not-safety experts. Indeed, this modeling approach provides a better understanding of the system safety assumptions and improves communication between different disciplines. This reduces the possibility of errors during the progress of both development and safety processes. The model itself acts as a database for all relevant safety aspect. From the user's point of view, safety models are modular and specific domain libraries can be shared between many different programs: in an industrial practice, this eases the creation of an internal dialect that increases the general awareness of security risks. Finally, it is possible (and recommended) to keep the safety model up to date with new information, which is particularly useful in the context of PSSA, where the design of the architecture is subject to constant changes until it is finalized.

The objective of this work is to support the Preliminary System Safety Assessment (PSSA) of a representative Flight Control System (FCS) using

Model-Based Safety Analysis (MBSA) techniques. Failure Propagation Models (FPMs) are developed within the Cecilia Workshop graphical tool, implementing the AltaRica DataFlow language.

Although the case study does not stem from a really existing industrial system, it is representative enough to effectively demonstrates the potentiality of the MBSA approach. The proposed modeling methodology is organized around three complementary views: system architecture, failure propagation rules, and safety observers. Through the case study, the authors illustrate how this structure can serve as a central artifact in the overall safety process—either as a repository of traceable safety requirements or as a source of safety analysis results.

To keep the case study realistic and in alignment with industrial safety processes [1], the functional failures considered are derived from a System Functional Hazard Assessment (SFHA) and the resulting safety assessments are evaluated against specific safety targets based on industry certification standards.

The methodology presented demonstrates how MBSA can be coherently integrated into the development lifecycle and effectively used to identify potential system safety issues.

The structure of this article is organized as follows. Section 2 describes the case study. Section 3 starts by explaining the basic features of Cecilia Workshop. It then continues from Sect. 3.2 with the MBSA model of the FCS: here the proposed methodology implemented is thoroughly examined. In Sect. 4, the safety results obtained are analysed and commented on. Section 5 expands over conclusions and future works.

2   FCS Architecture

For years, concerns have been raised about the efficiency and coverage of safety assessment techniques for highly integrated systems that perform complex, interrelated functions [8]. The FCS, as illustrated in Fig. 1, serves as a prime example for examining this issue.

The Flight Control Computer (FCC) is the central computing unit responsible for executing control laws and generating the corresponding actuator commands. It is composed of multiple sub-components whose behavior critically affects the overall system safety, thereby necessitating extensive internal redundancies and fault-tolerant mechanisms. Specifically, each FCC integrates a command (COM) lane and a monitor (MON) lane, both comprising a Field-Programmable Gate Array (FPGA) interface and a Central Processing Unit (CPU) (Fig. 2). FPGA MON is only receiving, while FPGA COM is receiving and transmitting. Both CPUs perform identical computations and generate the same outputs, which are then cross-checked for consistency. Additionally, an independent sub-component, known as the Passivation System (PS), is tasked with shutting down the FCC in the event of an internal failure or an inability to perform critical flight operations (e.g., due to a loss of input data). A final safety mechanism is given by Link Integrity eXaminer (LINX), reading via MON lane the output exiting from COM lane and assessing its correctness.

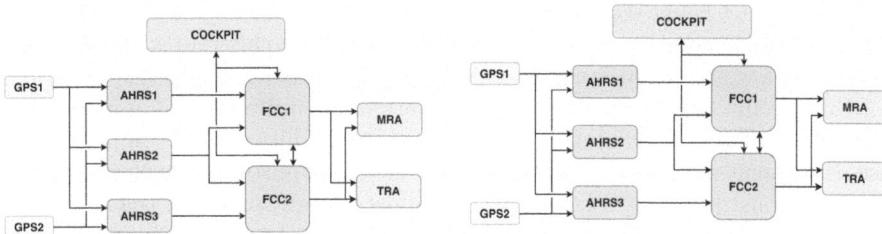

Fig. 1. Flight Control System

Fig. 2. Flight Control Computer

Among the various functions performed by the FCS, this article focuses on
the heading control function (HDG). Following functional decomposition from
[9], it is defined as an "aviate" function, a term for high priority functions managing core operations like stability. HDG is responsible for core stabilization and
tracking of the heading reference.

HDG relies on redundant external sensors, including inertial data from Attitude and Heading Reference Systems (AHRSs) and positioning data from Global
Positioning Systems (GPSs). The CPU performs calculation utilizing various
hybridized data (data originating from AHRSs corrected by GPSs data) for
heading tracking, while relying solely on inertial data for rotorcraft stabilization. This is achieved through a dual control loop: the heading control operates
as the outer loop, while the stabilization function serves as the inner loop.

Communication with the pilot happens via COCKPIT, both sending references via Mode Control Panel (MCP) and receiving the heading loss function
alert, via appropriate CAS (Crew Alerting System) light.

The Flight Control Computer (FCC) plays a critical role in managing the
rotorcraft's flight capabilities, requiring a Dual COM-MON configuration [10]
that follows the common Master-Standby scheme. To enable reconfiguration,
the two FCCs units share a signal (in Fig. 2 called FCC.request), allowing the
standby unit to detect when the master has been passivated and seamlessly take
its place. In this, only the designated Master FCC is responsible for transmitting output signals, to the cockpit and to the four electromechanical actuators
(EMA). There are three actuators for main rotor actuation (MRA) and one for
tail rotor actuation (TRA). Each actuator consists of an electrical board, which
acts as an internal controller, and the shaft. Given the focus on the heading
control function, only the TRA will be considered in the safety model.

The power distribution system has been omitted from the model for simplicity
and all components are assumed to be correctly powered.

3   MBSA Methodology

Cecilia Workshop, developed by Dassault Aviation and distributed by
SATODEV, is a graphical computational environment specifically designed to
perform MBSA [11].

At its core, Cecilia Workshop—hereafter referred to as Cecilia—enables engineers to model, simulate, and analyze complex safety architectures using AltaRica Data-Flow, a formal language specifically designed for safety applications [12,13]. Cecilia allows step-by-step simulation, identification of minimal cut sets, and evaluation of failure sequences and probabilities - key components in risk assessment methodologies. Moreover, Cecilia supports the development and reuse of robust libraries, a key aspect of industrial best practices that improves efficiency, scalability, and maintainability.

The proposed modeling methodology is described below. It consists of three separate views, each responsible for a specific task. Although this methodology is better suited for the FCS description (Sect. 2), it is general in nature and could be used to describe any kind of component or system interconnections.

1. **Architecture View** - Contains the model of the hardware architecture of the system. Defined components are extended with modes of failures.
2. **Failure Propagation View** - Contains the model for the functional logic of complex processing equipments. It must be consistent with the assigned functional design requirements.
3. **Safety View** - Contains the observers for the considered malfunction.

In a more complete system's functional safety evaluation, only the second view is supposed to be changed accordingly to the requirements of the new function considered. Meanwhile, the hardware interconnections shall remain the same (with the inclusion of components not modelled in this analysis, like MRA). Safety view remains the same if all functions share the same set of functional failure conditions (e.g. loss, erroneous, degradation...).

3.1   Overview of Cecilia's Capabilities

In this Section, a brief explanatory presentation of the Cecilia capabilities, explicative of the FCS safety model (described from Sect. 3.2 onwards), is reported. The aim is to give the reader an idea of the proposed approach, without delving too deeply into the specifics of the language [14].

All signals are defined as a specific "enumeration type" called "OLE" [15]. An "OLE" signal can take either the value "ok", "lost" or "err" and is representative of the lack of availability or integrity due to a failure event. Other types can be created to enhance the representativeness of the safety model; however, for PSSA purpose, OLE signals have been deemed sufficient.

Figure 3 represents a dummy application of the three views: basic events in the architecture view, logical flows in the failure propagation view, and observers in the safety view. In particular, this model shows the common "two-out-of-three" voting between three AHRS signals. Observers from the third layer are signals that are used to monitor specific system conditions that contribute to the identification of failure events. By defining relevant observers, analysts can systematically automate the extraction of critical failure scenarios. In this case, they assess the event of a loss and an erroneous signal from the consolidation.

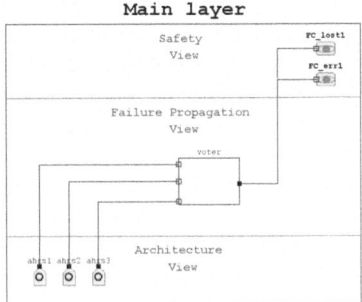

Fig. 3. Illustration of a dummy safety model in Cecilia Workshop

3.2   Safety Model

This Section aims to offer valuable guidance to streamline the MBSA process, explaining the methodology used for the FCS safety model. The complete FCS model and derived results can be found in the GitHub repository [16]. In Fig. 4 a schematic of the safety model for the FCS function provide heading control is provided. The flow direction is from bottom to top when crossing views, and from left to right within a specific view.

3.3   First Layer Architectural View

The architectural view (bottom part of Fig. 4) encompasses all hardware components of the FCS, along with their associated failure modes.

The objective of this view is to generate resources, which are defined as signals that convey the safety state—specifically integrity and availability—of a hardware component to another layer that models the system's logic. In Fig. 4, resources are all the signals generated from the architectural view, and are encapsulated depicted using circular colored icons. As it is shown by the sample of coloured arrows, resources are transmitted to the "next" failure propagation view, where they override all signals affected when the resource is either lost or erroneous.

Nominally, each component's output signals could be used to extract resources. However, a different approach was adopted, involving a classification of components, to avoid overly complicating the readability of the model. Many components are referred to as Safety-Embedded Elements (SEE), representing those whose safety behavior is straightforward (e.g., failure generators or fallible propagators) and can be directly represented and propagated in the architectural view. On the other hand, Safety-Critical Processing Elements (SCPE) are components that function as central processing units with advanced software logic. These components are difficult to model solely as hardware elements, so they require a separate representation (explained in Sect. 3.4) for their internal processes.

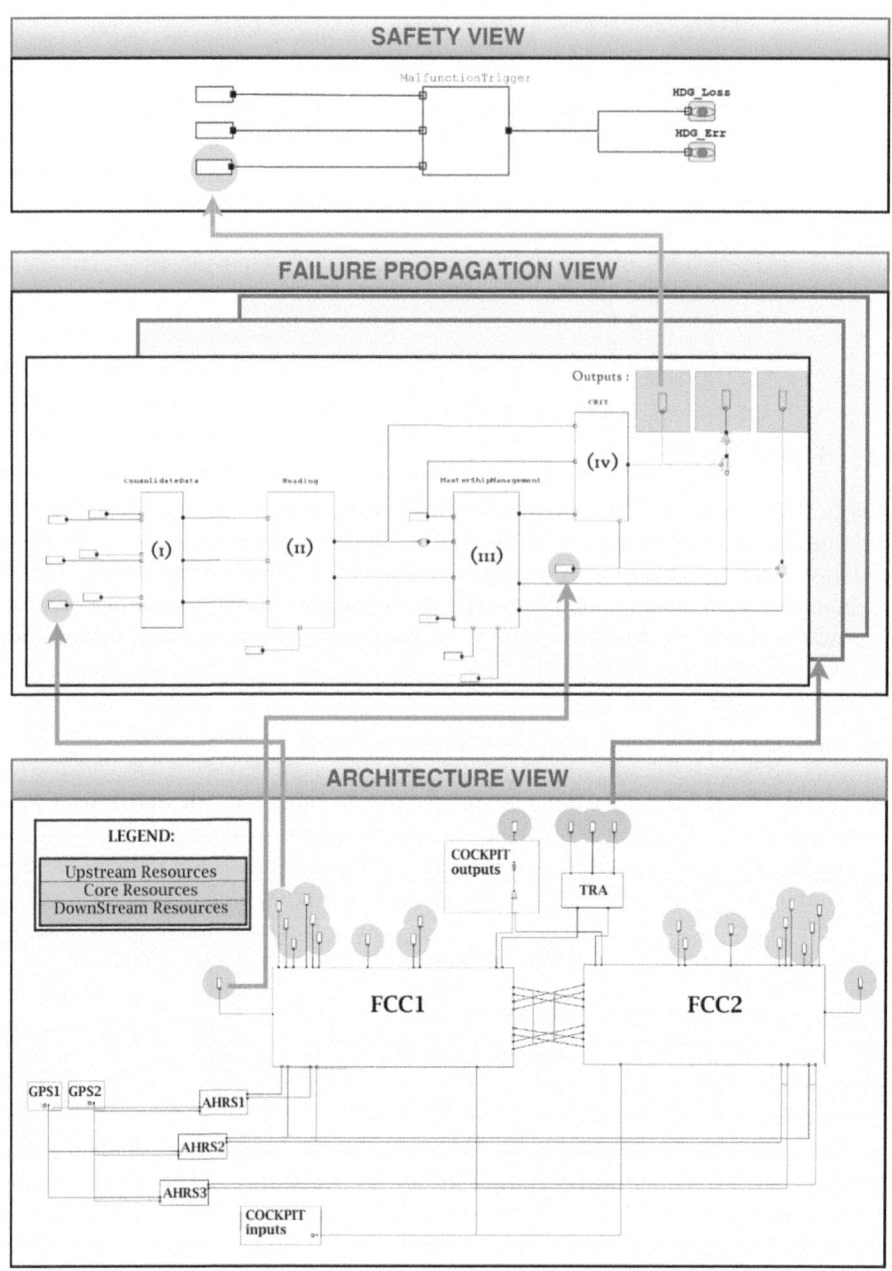

Fig. 4. Schematic of Safety Model for Provide Heading Control Function (Color figure online) .

In order to keep the architectural view as intuitive and simple as possible, the strategy adopted focus on the SCPEs.

This strategy led to the identification of three types of resources, which are coloured orange, green and blue respectively in Fig. 4):

- **UPSTREAM** : representative of the integrity and availability of the input signals acquired by a specific SCPE; this signals can be originated by (and can pass through) components and ports, before being processed by the specific SCPE.
- **CORE** : representative of the integrity and availability of the SCPEs themself
- **DOWNSTREAM** : representative of the integrity and availability of signals from downstream chain of components with respect to SCPEs; this signals can be originated by (and can pass throught) components, before being processed by the specific component .

Inside each FCC, the two CPU are demanded to perform the same operations and, in a "COM-MON" fashion, they monitor the capabilities of the FCC itself, requesting its turning off via PS (Fig. 5).

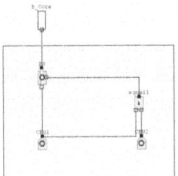

Fig. 5. Core resource generation

Observing again the bottom part of Fig. 4, upstream resources are represented in orange circular patterns and are generated from the top edge of the FCCs. The only two core resources, shown in green, originate from the sides of the FCCs. Downstream resources, depicted in blue, are instead generated by the "COCKPIT output" and "TRA."

3.4   Second Layer - Failure Propagation View

The most intricate and advanced part of the safety model is the failure propagation view (middle part of Fig. 4). In particular, this view is made by many sub-views whose outputs are then combined and propagated to the safety view. Of these sub-views, the more interesting ones are the instances for the two SCPEs, which represents the functional flow executed by the CPUs.

The term functionality in this Section is used to cover the execution of a specific task, but without demanding any correlation with the actual software partitions.

The failure propagation view bridges this gap by representing the nominal behavior as described in the functional design requirements. Whereas those are not yet present, the model will provide insight for the developing of Proposed

Safety Requirements (PSR), contributing and aiding the overall development process.

This Section describes the failure propagation between the 5 interconnected functionalities of the considered heading function (Represented explicitly in the middle diagram of 4):

- **Consolidate Data (I)**
  This module is responsible for executing consolidation procedures on inertial data received from external sensors. Its primary objective is to enhance safety margins against potential sensor failures.
- **Heading (II)**
  This module generates the heading control signal through a dual-loop control structure. The outer loop is designed around the heading control law, while the inner loop is centered on yaw rate stabilization. This architecture ensures system stability even in cases where heading control is no longer viable.
- **Mastership Management (III)**
  This functionality manages the transition between master and standby states of the FCC. It ensures a rapid response to failures by switching into master control when a malfunction is detected.
- **Continuous Built-In Test (CBIT) (IV)**
  CBIT is responsible for the system's self-diagnosis and failure detection. It generates failure signals that can deactivate a faulty FCC. The embedded monitoring mechanisms triggers the failure response when any of the following conditions are met:
  - *Control Monitor*: verifies availability of the control signal generated by the heading functionality.
  - *Cross-Wrap Monitor*: ensures availability and integrity of the transmitted control signal by comparing its readings (via MON FPGA after transmission through COM FPGA) with the computed value.
  - *Cross Lane Monitor*: assesses the operational status of the physical processors responsible for lane data processing, detecting potential failures through COM-MON detection logic.

As highlighted in the previous description, many functionalities actively mitigate specific hardware failures. Therefore, incorporating Failure Detection, Isolation, and Recovery (FDIR) within the scope of a PSSA is crucial. Is it the case for the MASTER-STANDBY reconfiguration, that happens whereas a CBIT monitor detects either an internal failure or the impossibility to successfully carry out its fundamental actions (e.g. stabilization). With Cecilia it is possible to simulate this scenario.

3.5   Third Layer - Safety View

Selected outputs of the failure propagation view are then collected inside the safety view (top part of Fig. 4) and combined accordingly to the specifics of the malfunctions (via the suitable block **Malfunction Trigger**). In the case at hand, safety results are centered around two functional failures: loss of heading control function (referred to as *HDG_LOSS*) and erroneous heading control function (referred to as *HDG_ERR*). An observer for each functional failure was defined easily by testing the availability and integrity of the TRA output signal, resulting from the failure propagation view. Although outside the scope of this article, it is worth mentioning that any combination of signals can be utilized to describe more complex functional failures (including function degradations, combinations of malfunctions, and detectability aspects).

4   Results

In this section, a comprehensive evaluation of the results obtained from the analyzed safety model is presented. The results are assessed against safety targets, derived from industrial certification specifications, considering that all FCS components have already been associated with known failure rates and DAL.

The following results have been structured into paragraphs: addressing quantitative results, DAL (Design Assurance Level) analyses, independence principles and safety requirements traceability.

Quantitative Results. Failure rates assigned to the failure modes of the component (located on the architecture view) are summarized in Table 1.

Table 1. Equipment basic events and associated failure rates [1/FH]

Sensors				FCC					
AHRS.lost	1E-5	GPS.lost	1E-5	FPGA.lost	1E-4	CPU.lost	1E-5	PS.lost	1E-4
AHRS.err	1E-6	GPS.err	1E-6	FPGA.err	1E-5	CPU.err	1E-6	PS:err	1E-5

Cockpipt				TRA			
MCP.lost	1E-5	CAS_light.lost	1E-6	elect_board.lost	1E-6	shaft.lost	1E-6
MCP.err	1E-6	CAS_light.err	1E-7	elect_board.err	1E-7	shaft.err	1E-7

Quantitative results in Table 2 are automatically obtained from the safety model in the form of MCS [17]. Here an example of three minimal cut sets taken from HDG_LOSS:

Order 1 : AV.TRA.Shaft.loss
Order 2 : AV.FCC1.FPGA1.loss , AV.CCU2.CPU2.err
Order 3 : AV.AHRS1.loss , AV.AHRS2.LOSS , AV.AHRS3.loss

"AV" stands for Architecture View and indicates the originating view of the failure events. The first minimal cut set is a single point of failure involving the tail actuator shaft alone, which is sufficient to cause the loss of the heading function. The second minimal cut set consists of a combination of two failure events: the loss of the first FPGA in the first FCC, which prevents proper signal transmission to the actuator, and an erroneous behavior of the second CPU in the second FCC, which, due to PS logic, triggers a complete shutdown of the FCC. Finally, the third-order minimal cut set involves the loss of all inertial sensors that, following the chosen consolidation logic, will cause HDG_LOSS.

Table 2. Quantitative results

	Loss of Heading Control		Erroneous Heading Control	
	Quantity of MCS	Probability per flight hour [1/FH]	Quantity of MCS	Probability per flight hour [1/FH]
Order 1	2	2.00E-6	3	1.20E-6
Order 2	87	1.17E-7	10	1.22E-9
Order 3	1	1.00E-15	57	4.12E-13
Order 4	0	0	36	7.33E-20
Order 5	0	0	6	1.12E-24
Total	90	2.12E-6	112	1.20E-6

Assuming compliance with the type-certification requirements for civil rotorcraft systems, specifically referring to CS29.1309 [18], the delineated FCS architecture conforms to MAJ severity (a failure condition that remotely occurs, i.e., quantitative probability of occurrence less than or equal to 10^{-5} per flight hour) for both HDG_LOSS and HDG_ERR. Looking at the "Order 1" MCS, HDG_LOSS presents Single Point of Failures (SPFs) only due to the single TRA (namely basic events from shaft and electronic board). SPFs for HDG_ERR include the TRA shaft, the electronic board, and the MCP. Clearly, if the objective is to eliminate SPFs (a common goal in civil avionics systems, albeit for CAT severity), both the TRA and the MCP must be replaced with alternatives that incorporate a certain level of internal redundancy.

Correctness of DAL Allocation. To minimize the likelihood of design errors in a stringent development process, Design Assurance Levels (DAL) are assigned to critical items, as defined by aerospace standards such as ARP4761A [1]. The following assessment focuses on key aspects related to check the correctness of the allocation of a specific DAL. Cecilia supports DAL verification by Common Attribute Analysis (CAA) [11]: it associates attributes to failure modes and analyses the resulting attribute combinations within the MCS.

For the scope of the current analysis, consider the proposed DAL allocation:

- **DAL-A** : TRA.elect_board, TRA.shaft
- **DAL-B** : AHRS, GPS, FCC.FPGA, FCC.CPU, FCC.PS
- **DAL-C** : MCP, CAS_light

Table 3. DAL allocation correctness for HDG_LOSS

MCS	Quantity	DAL-A	DAL-B
A	2	yes	yes
B B	87	yes	yes
B B B	1	yes	yes

Table 4. DAL allocation correctness for HDG_ERR

MCS	Quantity	DAL-A	DAL-B
A	2	yes	yes
C	1	no	no
B B	10	yes	yes
B B B	57	yes	yes
B B B B	36	yes	yes
B B B B B	6	yes	yes

Table 3 and Table 4 represent the DAL allocation correctness analysis performed, where DAL compliancy has been tested against DAL-A and DAL-B targets.

In Tables 3 and 4, the column titled "Combination" lists all minimal cut sets generated by the MBSA procedure, sorted according to their respective DAL attribute combinations.

According to ARP4761A [1], the DAL allocation process requires verification that all minimum cut sets combinations are acceptable.

For example, a DAL-A requirement can be satisfied with two independent DAL-B allocations, but not with multiple DAL-C allocations.

Acceptance rules require that when a higher target level is achieved using multiple instances of the next lower target level, these instances must be independent. For simplicity, we assume that all independence requirements elicited in this manner are verified.

HDG_LOSS DAL allocation is compliant with DAL-A (from Table 3).

However, HDG_ERR does not meet the conditions for either DAL-A or DAL-B. Indeed, MCP appears in a minimal cut set of order 1 (third row of Table 4) with a DAL-C allocation. An erroneous failure from the MCP would not be detected and would blindly led to an erroneous heading control, jeopardizing rotorcraft stability. Hence, changing MCP component may be necessary in order to raise the HDG_ERR to DAL-B.

Independence Principles. The proposed MBSA safety process can elicit independence principles. The procedure is performed via 'cut set analysis', as opposed to the 'AND-gate analysis' of FTA (ARP4761A). The principles consist of a list of pairs of components contained in at least one minimal cut set.

In addition, independence assertions are exploited to generate independence principles. These assertions can be seen as early insights into the robustness of the system under analysis [19]. This objective was achieved by developing an external algorithm that took advantage of the modularity of the automatically generated Cecilia MCS.

There are two independence assertions:

- The first looks at functional redundancies between components, ensured by the semantics of generated MCS; it applies to component combinations with different behaviors and functionalities, relying on the assumption that a common cause of failure affecting both is preliminarily not considered. Whereas more than one component is considered, they are collected in a unique assertion.

– The second checks failure modes between components inside generated MCS, assuming that different failure modes (Loss and Erroneous) of the same component cannot be generated by a common cause (e.g. AHRS1.err and AHRS2.loss).

Partial results, coming from the application of independence assertions, are shown in Table 5 and Table 6.

Table 5. Independence Principles - Functional redundancies

ID	Independence Principles
1	FCC1.FPGA1 AND FCC1.FPGA2 AND FCC2.FPGA1 AND FCC2.FPGA2
	Are functionally redundant components considered in the independent principles
2	FCC1.PS AND FCC2.PS
	are functionally redundant components considered in the independent principles
3	FCC1.CPU1 AND FCC1.CPU2 AND FCC2.CPU1 AND FCC2.CPU2
	are functionally redundant components considered in the independent principles
4	AHRS1 AND AHRS2 AND AHRS3
	are functionally redundant components considered in the independent principles

Table 6. Independence Principles - Similar mode of failure

ID	Independence Principles
...	...
10	FCC1.FPGA1 AND FCC1.FPGA2
	share an identical failure mode in at least one minimal cut set and are considered in the independent principles
...	...
22	FCC1.PS AND FCC1.CPU2
	do not share an identical failure mode in any minimal cut set and are not considered in the independent principles
...	...

Requirement Traceability. Cecilia models do not currently incorporate any synchronization procedures with other tools (e.g. requirement managers such as DOORS [20], or MBSE tools like CAPELLA [21]), which are heavily relied upon in industrial practice. A basic method has been implemented to trace requirements related to Cecilia safety models. The approach leverages the ability to add comments to specific class instantiations (e.g., CBIT from the failure propagation view). The generated report will include all comments from every instance within the safety model. With a synchronization procedure, it would be possible to extract and store these comments into the requirement manager used for the industrial application at hand.

This procedure could serve multiple purposes:

– ensure the integration of safety-relevant design requirements into the model, offering support material on the overall correctness of the results;
– facilitate the extraction of PSR into the central requirement manager, written with a unique identifier;
– allow internal comments to be imported in the model, enhancing readability for all domain-experts participating in the process.

5   Conclusion and Future Works

This work demonstrates a successful application of MBSA techniques in the field of aerospace and safety-critical systems. Specifically, it focuses on the impact of FCS failures, which, due to the criticality of the system, could pose a significant risk to human life. The article is centered on the FCS development phase, for production of the safety material for PSSA.

In an industrial application, safety models would significantly assist and support the overall development process by producing clear and intuitive results, even for complex systems. They would likely limit the risk of modeling errors compared to more indirect system representations (e.g. FTAs), also by implementing the traceability of design requirements.

Moreover, MBSA enhances communication between departments, as failure effects are often overlooked by non-safety experts. It enables the expertise from various fields to be captured within the safety model, creating a single, unified source of system safety information.

MBSA introduction on a realistic industrial workflow has been considered to develop straightforward solutions that facilitate the integration of model-based safety artifacts.

Future works aim to continue with this practical analysis over the advantages and disadvantages of a MBSA industrial introduction. The creation of an equipment general library for avionic considerations is currently under development. A comparison against other MBSA tools is envisioned (e.g. HiP-HOPS [22]). Moreover, even though the authors do not anticipate divergent conclusions compared to manually derived results, validating MBSA results against other probabilistic techniques remains a key objective for further studies. Scalability issues for more complex systems shall be investigated.

The safety analysis and modeling of the Flight Control System (FCS) will be further developed, as it offers an ideal case study for exploring safety in critical avionics scenarios. The model will be extended to incorporate more complex and interconnected functions. The ultimate objective is to scale the Model-Based Safety Assessment (MBSA) approach to support the complete Preliminary System Safety Assessment (PSSA) of the FCS.

Disclosure of Interests. Author Isabella Lanzani has received research grants from Leonardo S.P.A. Company.

References

1. SAE, ARP 4761A: Guidelines and Methods for Conducting the Safety Assessment Process on Civil Airborne Systems and Equipment, Annex N, ARP 4761A (2023)
2. FALCON 7X Certification Collection 27_1-300, Primary Flight Control System Safety Analysis, Dassault Aviation reference DGT91338
3. Bernard, R., Aubert, J.-.J., Bieber, P., Merlini, C., Metge, S.: Experiments in model based safety analysis: flight controls (2007)
4. Frazza, C., Darfeuil, P., Gauthier, J.: MBSA in aeronautics: a way to support safety activities. IMBSA (2022)
5. Kaiser, B., et al.: Advances in Component Fault Trees. CRC Press (2018)
6. Mathou, C., Delmas, K., De Saqui-Sannes, P., Chaudemar, J.-C.: Safety-oriented dynamic procedure modeling. SysCon (2024)
7. Mathou, C., Delmas, K., Chaudemar, J. -C., de Saqui-Sannes, P.: Modeling UAS flight procedures for SORA safety objectives. SysCon (2023)
8. SAE, ARP 4754: Guidelines for Development of Civil Aircraft and Systems, ARP 4754 (2010)
9. K. Wasson, N. Neogi, M. Graydon, J. Maddalon, P. Miner, and G. F. McCormick. Functional Hazard Assessment for the eVTOL Aircraft Supporting Urban Air Mobility Applications: Exploratory Demonstrations. 2022
10. Moir, I., Seabridge, A., Jukes, M.: Civil Avionis Systems - Ch 4. System Safety. 2nd edn. Wiley, United Kingdom (2013)
11. Dassault Aviation. Cecilia Worskhop User's Manual version 6.0. (2019)
12. Prosvirnova, T.: AltaRica 3.0: a model-based approach for safety analyses (2014)
13. Prosvirnova, T., et al.: The AltaRica 3.0 project for model-based safety assessment (2013)
14. Prosvirnova, T., Batteux, M., Rauzy, A.: AltaRica 3.0 language specification (2020)
15. Prosvirnova, T., et al.: Strategies for modelling failure propagation in dynamic systems with AltaRica. IMBSA (2022)
16. https://github.com/Sabeast-4/FCS-SafetyModel
17. Prosvirnova, T., Rauzy, A.: Automated generation of minimal cut sets from AltaRica 3.0 models. IJCCBS (2015)
18. EASA. Certification specification for large rotorcraft (2023)
19. Lanzani, I., Uliano, L., Scattolini, R.: Integration of commonalities in the paradigm of model-based safety analysis in aerospace (2024)
20. https://www.ibm.com/docs/en/engineering-lifecycle-management-suite/doors/
21. https://mbse-capella.org/
22. Papadopoulos, Y., et al.: Engineering failure analysis and design optimisation with HiP-HOPS (2011)

Multi-approach Based Safety Analysis of a Wastewater Treatment System

Anne Fernet[(✉)] and Leïla Kloul

DAVID Laboratory, University of Paris-Saclay (UVSQ), Versailles, France
{anne.fernet,leila.kloul}@uvsq.fr

Abstract. Wastewater treatment systems are critical for protecting eco-systems and public health, yet the prediction of untreated effluent dis-charges from wastewater treatment plants (WWTPs) and their impact on plant performance remain largely underexplored. In this work, we examine the safety and reliability of a wastewater treatment system serv-ing one of the largest agglomerations in Paris, France. We are interested in predicting failures that lead to untreated effluent discharges into the Seine River. The system comprises two WWTPs connected by a bypass channel designed to mitigate untreated discharges from the plant with lower capacity. Despite flow management efforts, both plants frequently face overloading. This is particularly true during heavy rainfall, which significantly increases the likelihood of untreated discharges. To address this issue, we combine fault tree analysis and machine learning tech-niques to evaluate vulnerabilities and predict discharges. The approach is based on real-world data and demonstrates promising predictive capa-bilities despite the challenges of a small dataset. The findings support decision-making efforts to mitigate untreated wastewater discharges and enhance system reliability.

Keywords: Wastewater treatment plants · System of systems · System reliability · Fault tree analysis · Neural networks

1 Introduction

Wastewater treatment plants (WWTPs) play a critical role in protecting public health and ecosystems by treating wastewater before its release into the environ-ment. However, these systems face significant challenges during heavy rainfall, which can overwhelm their capacity and lead to untreated effluent discharges into natural waterways. While WWTPs are designed to handle average daily flows with allowances for stormwater, extreme weather events increasingly sur-pass these limits. Climate change, with its associated rise in intense and frequent rainfall, exacerbates this issue, even for well-dimensioned systems. During such surges, facilities may activate spillways to divert excess water, thereby preventing infrastructure damage but releasing untreated or partially treated wastewater–a serious environmental and public health hazard.

© The Author(s), under exclusive license to Springer Nature Switzerland AG 2026
P. Katsaros (Ed.): IMBSA 2025, LNCS 15755, pp. 33–47, 2026.
https://doi.org/10.1007/978-3-032-05073-1_3

The Grand Paris Sud (GPS) region [4], the second-largest urban community in France by population, faces these challenges through its two interconnected WWTPs: Evry and Exona. These plants are connected via a bypass channel intended to mitigate overloads at the smaller Exona plant by transferring excess flow to the larger Evry plant. While effective in reducing discharges at Exona, the bypass channel increases Evry's load, particularly during heavy rainfall, raising the overall risk of untreated discharges into the Seine river. Accurately predicting the conditions leading to effluent discharges is critical for improving the system's resilience.

This study seeks to improve the safety and operational reliability of the GPS wastewater treatment system by addressing two key objectives: identifying critical vulnerabilities within the system and developing predictive tools to forecast effluent discharges. To achieve these aims, we use a dual approach that integrates fault tree analysis (FTA) and machine learning techniques. FTA offers a systematic framework for analyzing system failures, providing both qualitative and quantitative insights into the pathways leading to untreated discharges. This method enables a comprehensive understanding of how physical components, such as bypass channels and treatment basins, interact with external factors like weather events. Simultaneously, multilayer perceptron (MLP) models, a class of artificial neural networks, are used to predict discharge events and bypass volumes. MLP models excel in capturing complex, nonlinear relationships between variables such as rainfall intensity and plant loads, making them particularly well-suited for this application. Combining these two methods allows us to identify critical system components, evaluate their impact on discharge likelihood, and develop predictive models to support data-driven decision-making. The findings contribute to improving wastewater management strategies and mitigating the risks of untreated discharges, especially in the context of increasing rainfall variability and extreme weather events.

The remainder of this paper is structured as follows: Sect. 2 reviews related work on WWTP safety analysis and prediction. Section 3 describes the treatment plant system under study. Section 4 outlines the methods applied. Section 5 details the dataset and preprocessing steps. Section 6 presents the results, and Sect. 7 concludes with perspectives for future work.

2   Related Work

WWTPs have been studied from multiple perspectives, including effluent quality prediction, system reliability assessment, inflow forecasting, and overflow or discharge detection. Traditional approaches to modeling WWTP behavior fall into two broad categories: mechanistic (deterministic) models and data-driven models. Mechanistic models integrate physical and empirical knowledge and remain widely used for their interpretability, but they are often complex and difficult to calibrate. In contrast, data-driven models have gained popularity due to the increasing availability of monitoring data and their ability to handle complex, nonlinear relationships [3].

Newhart et al. [11] provide a comprehensive review of fault detection and variable prediction in WWTPs, targeting key outputs such as pollutant concentrations, effluent flow, and sludge sedimentation levels. They note the limitations of linear statistical models (e.g., multiple regression, principal component analysis), especially given the non-linear, interdependent, and non-stationary nature of WWTP data. More advanced methods, such as neural networks, have shown greater robustness in this context.

A large body of research evaluates WWTP performance through effluent quality metrics, such as pollutant concentration. For instance, Taheriyoun and Moradinejad [16] use FTA to estimate failure probabilities when concentration thresholds are exceeded. Kristjanpoller et al. [7] apply a reliability, availability, maintainability (RAM) framework and conclude that human factors are the most critical risk for WWTP failure.

Research has also focused on forecasting influent and effluent flow. Duarte et al. [3] review various machine learning techniques for predicting effluent flow, including K-nearest neighbors, random forests, and neural networks. They argue for hybrid approaches combining data-driven and mechanistic models to improve interpretability. Similarly, Wei and Kusiak [17] apply deep neural networks to predict short-term wastewater flow using rainfall and historical flow data, showing improved long-term forecasting performance.

Storm overflow (SO) prediction, particularly from sewer systems, has also been explored. Meyers et al. [10] use multivariate logistic regression to predict annual SO occurrences and show that such statistical models can rival hydraulic simulations while being less computationally demanding. Ma et al. [9] provide a broad overview of SO prediction methods, noting a trend toward AI-based approaches. Most methods focus on short-term forecasts and often omit contextual socio-economic variables such as day of the week or time of day, which may affect inflow volumes.

While extensive work has focused on effluent quality and influent flow prediction, relatively few studies have addressed the forecasting of untreated effluent discharges from WWTPs. This gap motivates the present study, which aims to contribute a complementary approach combining safety analysis and machine learning for discharge prediction. A notable exception is Hammond et al. [12], who used machine learning to detect unreported sewage spills from two UK WWTPs. By analyzing daily effluent flow patterns, they trained binary classifiers including logistic regression, random forests, and gradient boosting classifiers, with event duration monitoring (EDM) data as ground truth. Their models achieved over 96% accuracy in distinguishing spill from non-spill days. However, their approach depends on high-resolution data (over 800,000 flow measurements) and detailed spill annotations, which are not available in our context. Furthermore, differences in infrastructure and operational conditions limit the direct transferability of their approach.

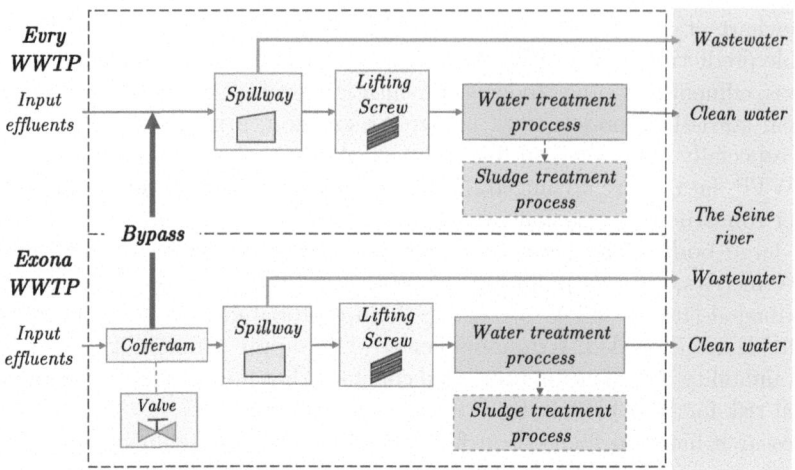

Fig. 1. Flow diagram of the wastewater treatment system

3   The Treatment Plant System

The GPS region manages drinking water distribution and wastewater treatment for 19 of its 23 towns. To optimize wastewater management, the operations of two neighboring WWTPs – Evry and Exona – have been combined. The Evry plant, with a treatment capacity of 48,000 m³/day, is the largest of the two and serves as the primary facility for the region. It treats a mixture of domestic and industrial wastewater, as well as stormwater collected from the sewage network. The Exona plant, with a nominal capacity of 15,620 m³/day, is smaller and more vulnerable to flow fluctuations, especially during heavy rainfall. Both plants are equipped with spillways that discharge excess untreated effluent into the Seine when the facilities are overloaded. To further mitigate overloads, a bypass channel connects the two plants. Positioned upstream of the Exona plant, the bypass transfers excess raw water to the Evry plant, helping to balance the flow between the facilities. The bypass system is also used during maintenance or in the event of a failure at Exona, ensuring continued wastewater treatment with minimal disruption. The bypass inlet features a cofferdam, which determines the flow rate of the bypass channel by setting the minimum effluent level required for the bypass to activate. The cofferdam height is currently adjusted manually using a valve. Figure 1 presents a simplified flow diagram of the system.

4   Modeling the GPS System

This section outlines the analytical approach and machine learning techniques used to model the system, assess its vulnerabilities and predict untreated effluent discharges.

4.1   The Fault Tree Model

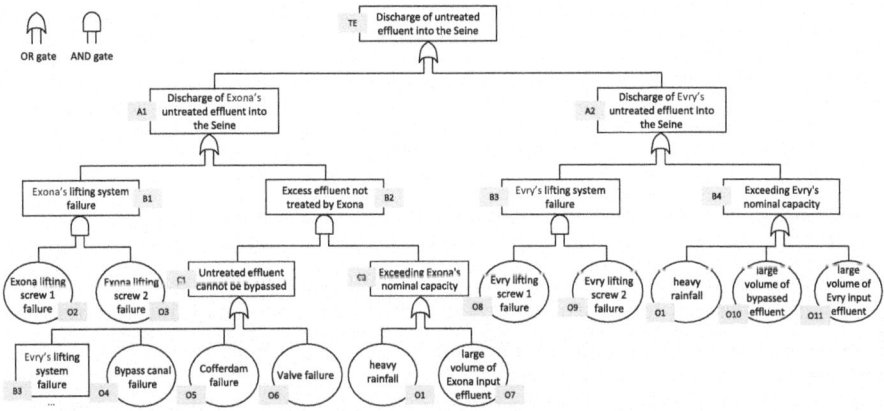

Fig. 2. Fault tree of the GPS wastewater treatment system

FTA models the combinations of elementary events (failure causes) that can lead to critical system failures, using a tree-like structure with logic gates to represent their interdependencies. This approach systematically identifies how various factors contribute to system failure and quantifies the probability of such occurrences. FTA also highlights critical paths – minimal combinations of events leading to failure.

Once the fault tree is constructed, qualitative analysis identifies the Minimum Cut Sets (MCSs), while quantitative analysis evaluates the system's reliability directly from the fault tree or the MCSs [8].

The system's reliability is determined using the equation:

$$R_{sys} = 1 - P(TE) \qquad (1)$$

where $P(TE)$ represents the probability of the top event.

Figure 2 presents the fault tree developed for the wastewater treatment system, in which the top event corresponds to the discharge of untreated effluent into the Seine River. This top event results from either a discharge at the Exona plant or at the Evry plant – two dependent sub-events that may occur independently or simultaneously under stress conditions.

At Exona, a discharge may occur under two conditions:

– Failure of the lifting system, which prevents the plant from processing incoming wastewater.
– Excess effluent beyond treatment capacity, which can arise during heavy rainfall or increased inflows. In this case, the plant relies on the bypass system to divert excess water to the Evry plant. However, this mitigation can fail if the

bypass channel itself malfunctions (e.g., due to valve or cofferdam failure), or the lifting system at Evry is already inoperative, preventing it from receiving additional flow from Exona.

At Evry, a discharge may also occur under two main conditions:

- Failure of the local lifting system, similar to Exona.
- Inflows exceeding the plant's nominal capacity, especially during heavy rainfall events, leading to an overflow even if the system is functioning.

Overall, discharges may be triggered by external factors, such as extreme rainfall and unusually high wastewater inflows, or by internal component failures, including breakdowns of lifting screws, bypass channel, valves, or cofferdams. The fault tree structure captures these interdependencies, enabling the analysis of how combinations of failures and stress conditions contribute to untreated discharges.

In this study, MCSs are used for both qualitative and quantitative evaluations of system reliability.

4.2   Neural Network Model

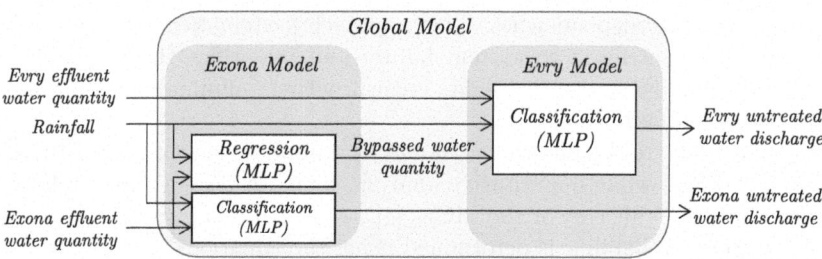

Fig. 3. MLP models of the GPS wastewater treatment system

We aim to predict a specific system failure: the discharge of untreated effluent into the Seine river. Given that our dataset includes known occurrences of these discharge events, we can apply supervised learning methods to address the problem. Supervised learning can be divided into two main types: regression and classification. Regression is used for predicting continuous outputs, which can take on an infinite number of possible values within a range, making them quantitative variables. Classification, on the other hand, deals with categorical outputs, referred to as qualitative variables, where the result belongs to distinct categories [5].

The MLP, a type of artificial neural network, is widely used for both regression and classification tasks. It consists of multiple layers of interconnected neurons, where each connection is weighted. In each neuron, an activation function processes the input received from the previous layer and produces an output for the next layer.

In our wastewater treatment system, effluent discharges can occur from either the Exona or Evry plant, with a bypass channel allowing for the partial or complete diversion of Exona's inflow to Evry. Key variables in the analysis include rainfall, the volume of effluent bypassed and the amount of wastewater discharged from each plant. Rather than predicting exact discharge volumes, we focus on identifying whether discharge events occur. We model the two plants separately: first, using a regression model to estimate the volume of effluent bypassed from Exona to Evry, followed by a classification model to predict discharge occurrences at Exona. Next, we develop a classification model to forecast the likelihood of a discharge event at the Evry plant. Finally, these models are integrated to form a comprehensive representation of the entire system model, as illustrated in Fig. 3.

Table 1. Performance metrics

Metrics	Regression	Classification
Error	MAE	BCE
Accuracy	$\dfrac{\hat{y} - y < p_{diff} \times y}{\text{Total predictions}}$	$\dfrac{TP}{TP + FP}$
Recall	-	$\dfrac{TP}{TP + FN}$

TP: True Positive, FP: False Positive, TN: True Negative, $\hat{y}$: prediction, y: target, p_{diff}: error percentage

Training Process and Performance Metrics. The models are trained using the stochastic gradient descent algorithm [5]. The learning process relies on backpropagation, where the gradient of the loss function with respect to each weight is computed and used to adjust the weights of the neural network in a way that reduces the error. Hyperparameters, such as the number of hidden layers, number of neurons in each layer, learning rate, and activation functions, are fine-tuned using a random search approach [14]. Each combination of hyperparameters is evaluated through a k-fold cross-validation process, where the dataset is divided into k subsets (folds). The model is trained on $k - 1$ folds and tested on the remaining fold, and this process is repeated k times, with each fold serving as the test set once. The average performance across all folds is used as the evaluation metric.

To assess the MLP's performance, different metrics are applied to regression and classification tasks. They are summarized in Table 1. For regression tasks, mean absolute error (MAE) is used to measure the average magnitude of the prediction error. For classification tasks, binary cross entropy (BCE) serves as the loss function [13]. Additionally, accuracy and recall are used as evaluation metrics for classification. Accuracy measures the proportion of correct predictions, while recall focuses on the model's ability to correctly identify positive cases (discharge events).

5   Dataset

The dataset used for training and evaluating the models consists of 365 daily records from the year 2023, provided by the GPS region's delegate [15]. It includes daily inflows at the Exona and Evry WWTPs, daily rainfall, and bypass volumes from Exona to Evry. This dataset is used to train MLP models for both regression (bypassed volume prediction) and classification (discharge event prediction).

5.1   Data Description

The dataset contains the following variables:

- Effluent inflow to the Exona plant (m^3/day)
- Effluent inflow to the Evry plant (m^3/day)
- Volume of effluent bypassed from Exona to Evry (m^3/day)
- Daily rainfall (mm/day)

In 2023, four untreated discharge events were recorded at each plant. However, three of these occurred on the same days for both plants, resulting in only five distinct discharge days across the entire year. This strong class imbalance poses a challenge for training robust classifiers and motivates the use of data augmentation techniques.

5.2   Data Processing Steps

To ensure the dataset was suitable for model training, the following steps were applied:

1. *Feature selection.* We retained only variables relevant to the forecasting tasks, focusing on those known to influence WWTP discharge events – namely rainfall, effluent loads, and bypass volumes.
2. *Data cleaning.* Records corresponding to known anomalies, such as maintenance periods and mechanical failures, were manually removed. This step was necessary to avoid biasing the models with values that do not reflect normal operational behavior.
3. *Data augmentation.* Given the small number of discharge events, the dataset is highly imbalanced. To train classification models effectively, we applied the synthetic minority over-sampling technique (SMOTE) [2] to increase the representation of rare events. For regression, where standard SMOTE is not directly applicable, we used a variant adapted for continuous output values [1].

70% of the dataset is used for training and model selection via k-fold cross-validation, while the remaining 30% is held out as an independent test set for final evaluation.

5.3 Dataset Variants for Model Training

Different versions of the dataset were constructed depending on the task (regression or classification) and the specific target plant. Table 2 summarizes the main characteristics of each dataset.

Table 2. Summary of datasets used for MLP training

Name	Total size	Exona discharges	Evry discharges
original	365	4	4
cleaned	304	3	2
RG-Exona	1065	7	4
CL-Exona	602	301	200
CL-Evry	604	302	200

RG: regression dataset, CL: classification dataset

5.4 Preparation by Task

Regression MLP - Bypassed Volume Prediction. Exona underwent significant maintenance during March, May, June, and December, leading to atypical bypass behavior. Since precise maintenance dates were not available, we manually excluded records from these periods to avoid contaminating the model with outliers unrelated to system load or rainfall. Additionally, bypass volumes were capped at $5000\,\mathrm{m}^3$ to remove extreme values that could skew the regression model. A regression-adapted version of SMOTE [1] was applied to smooth the distribution and support generalization.

Classification MLP - Exona Discharge Prediction. Among the four discharge events at Exona, one showed inconsistencies in accompanying variables (e.g., rainfall and inflows) and was excluded. The remaining three events were used as positive samples.

Classification MLP - Evry Discharge Prediction. Two of the four recorded discharges at Evry were linked to mechanical failures (lifting screw malfunctions). Because the objective is to predict discharges due to external conditions (e.g., rainfall and load), these cases were excluded. Including mechanical breakdowns would introduce noise and require separate failure models not addressed in this work.

6 Experimental Results

This section presents the qualitative and quantitative analysis using the fault tree model, along with the numerical results of the forecasting MLP models.

6.1   FTA Results

Table 3 presents the basic events included in the fault tree, along with their estimated failure probabilities. These values were derived either from manufacturer
data (for mechanical components) or from threshold exceedance frequencies (for
external factors such as rainfall or flow volumes).

Table 3. Failure probability of basic events

Component	Symbol	Probability of failure	Component	Symbol	Probability of failure
Rainfall	O_1	0.01	Exona effluent	O_7	0.04
Exona lifting screw 1	O_2	0.0009	Evry lifting screw 1	O_8	0.0009
Exona lifting screw 2	O_3	0.0009	Evry lifting screw 2	O_9	0.0009
Bypass channel	O_4	0.0007	Bypassed effluent	O_{10}	0.03
Cofferdam	O_5	0.001	Evry effluent	O_{11}	0.02
Valve	O_6	0.0009			

Qualitative Analysis. The fault tree yields five two-element MCSs: (O_4, O_7),
(O_5, O_7), (O_6, O_7), (O_2, O_3), and (O_8, O_9). Additionally, three single-element
MCSs – rainfall (O_1), inflow at Evry (O_{11}), and bypassed volume (O_{10}) – are
identified as critical. Although not associated with physical components, these
variables strongly influence system performance, particularly the sizing of pipes
and treatment basins.

This sensitivity is illustrated by the fact that the Exona plant exceeded its
nominal capacity on 56% of the days in 2023 [15], underscoring the need for
reliable bypass operation. Among the physical MCSs, the lifting screw failures at
Evry (O_8, O_9) are especially relevant: two discharge events in 2023 were directly
attributed to their malfunction. This highlights the importance of redundancy
and regular maintenance to prevent such failures.

Quantitative Analysis. Failure probabilities for components O_2 to O_6, O_8,
and O_9 are estimated from mean time to failure (MTTF) data and specifications
of comparable systems. For rainfall and plant inflows, we use empirical frequencies of threshold exceedance: 19.9 mm/day for rainfall, 20,000 m^3/day at Exona
and 55,000 m^3/day at Evry. Using the failure probabilities in Table 3, the probability of the top event (untreated discharge into the Seine river) is computed
as:

$$P(TE) = P(O_2 \cdot O_3) + P(O_4 \cdot O_7) + P(O_5 \cdot O_7)+$$
$$P(O_6 \cdot O_7) + P(O_1) + P(O_8 \cdot O_9)+$$
$$P(O_{10}) + P(O_{11}) = 0.06$$

According to Equation (1), the system reliability with respect to untreated effluent discharges is:

$$R_{sys} = 1 - 0.06 = 0.94 = 94\%$$

This result is consistent with observed data – 8 discharge events out of 365
days – and confirms the model's ability to reflect operational risks. The FTA
helps identify system vulnerabilities and informs decisions regarding maintenance prioritization and infrastructure upgrades to reduce the risk of untreated
effluent discharges.

6.2   MLP Results

Model Configuration. The MLP models use a multi-layer architecture optimized with the Adam algorithm [6]. ReLU activation functions are applied in
hidden layers, with a linear output activation for regression and a sigmoid activation for classification tasks.

Hyperparameters were optimized via random search over the following
ranges: learning rate (10^{-2}–10^{-4}), batch size (10–80), number of layers (2–3),
neurons per layer (25–100), and dropout rate (0.4–0.6). The best hyperparameter configuration was chosen based on cross-validation results on the training
set.

Performance Evaluation. Table 4 summarizes the performance of each model
on the test set, averaged over 15 independent runs. Figures 4, 5 and 6 illustrate
test set predictions from the best-performing models.

Regression Model (RG-Exona). The regression model achieved a MAE of 357
on the test set. Using a tolerance threshold of 25% relative error, the model
reached 71% accuracy. As shown in Fig. 4, the learned mapping between input
load and bypass volume approximates a quasi-linear function, indicating effective
generalization.

Table 4. Performance of MLP models (averaged over 15 runs)

Metric	RG-Exona	CL-Exona	CL-Evry	Combined system
Error (MAE/BCE)	357	0.5	0.3	0.3
Accuracy (%)	71	98	99	99
Recall (discharge, %)	–	100	100	100

RG: regression model, CL: classification model

Classification Model (CL-Exona). The binary classifier for Exona, trained with BCE, achieved 98% accuracy and 100% recall. The confusion matrix reports 91 true positives, 3 false positives, 87 true negatives, and 0 false negatives – demonstrating that SMOTE-based augmentation effectively addressed class imbalance. False positives mostly occurred during periods of high rainfall or input load (Fig. 5).

Classification Model (CL-Evry). The Evry model performed similarly, with 99% accuracy and 100% recall. This consistency indicates strong robustness in detecting discharge events and handling class imbalance. The prediction patterns are comparable to those observed for Exona (Fig. 6).

Combined Prediction: Bypass and Dicharge. Integrating the bypass regression model (RG-Exona) with the Evry discharge classifier (CL-Evry) did not affect classification performance, confirming that the combination preserves accuracy and recall. This hybrid setup supports predictive monitoring of bypass-related discharge risks under varying flow conditions.

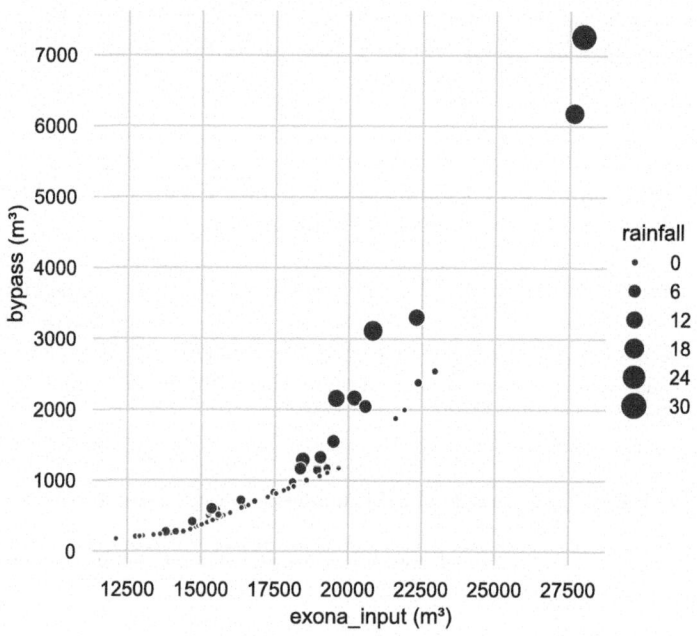

Fig. 4. Evaluation of RG-Exona model on test set

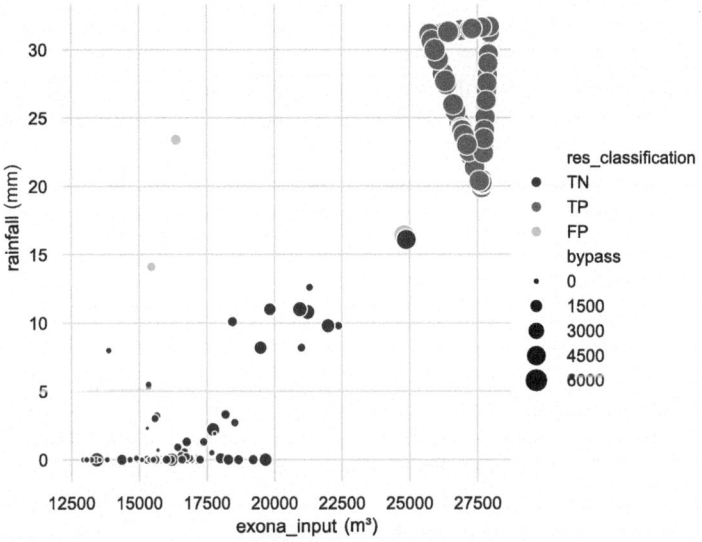

Fig. 5. Scatter plot of test set features colored by predicted class (CL-Exona model)

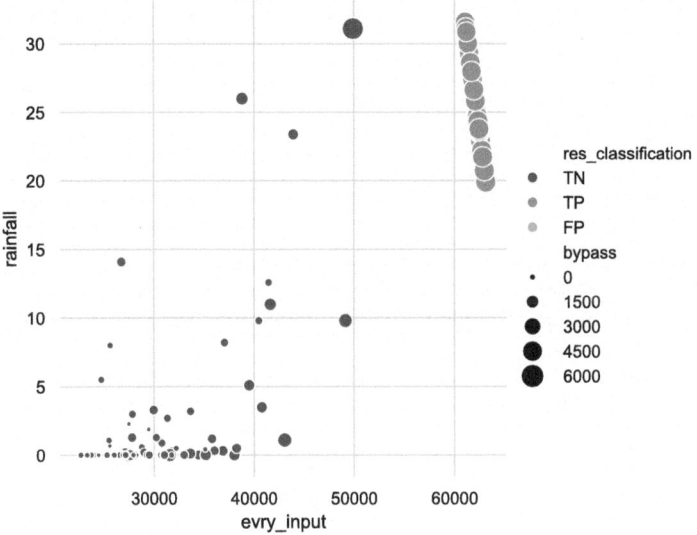

Fig. 6. Scatter plot of test set features colored by predicted class (CL-Evry model)

7 Conclusion

In this study, we addressed the challenge of predicting untreated effluent discharges from WWTPs by integrating FTA with machine learning techniques. Applied to a real-world system in the GPS region, this combined approach enabled both structural vulnerability assessment and the development of data-driven predictors for discharge events.

The FTA identified critical failure paths and quantified overall system reliability, revealing the significant influence of external stressors such as rainfall and hydraulic load. Despite being trained on a small and imbalanced dataset, the MLP models demonstrated strong predictive performance, particularly in detecting rare discharge events. Data augmentation using SMOTE was effective in mitigating class imbalance, although the scarcity of failure events remains a modeling challenge.

These results provide practical tools for operators and decision-makers seeking to anticipate and mitigate untreated discharges in the context of increasing climate variability. Future work will focus on hyperparameter tuning, incorporating additional features, and exploring deeper neural network architectures. In particular, integrating user behavior data – such as temporal patterns in water consumption – and employing advanced augmentation techniques tailored to rare events may further enhance predictive accuracy and support the development of more resilient wastewater management strategies.

Acknowledgments. This work is supported by the Grand Paris-Sud territorial collectivity and the french LabCom HYPHES (ANR-21-LCV1-0002).

Disclosure of Interests. The authors have no competing interests to declare that are relevant to the content of this article.

References

1. Atif Hassan, V.S.K.: reg-resampler 2.1.1, python library (2020)
2. Chawla, N.V., Bowyer, K.W., Hall, L.O., Kegelmeyer, W.P.: Smote: synthetic minority over-sampling technique. J. Artif. Intell. Res. **16**, 321–357 (2002). https://doi.org/10.1613/jair.953
3. Duarte, M.S., et al.: A review of computational modeling in wastewater treatment processes. ACS ES&T Water **4**, 784–804 (2024). https://doi.org/10.1021/acsestwater.3c00117
4. Grand paris sud: web site of the grand paris sud agglomeration. https://www.grandparissud.fr/ (2024), Accessed August 2024
5. James, G., Witten, D., Hastie, T., Tibshirani, R.: An introduction to statistical learning: with application in python. Springer (2013). https://doi.org/10.1007/978-3-031-38747-0
6. Kingma, D.P., Ba, J.: Adam: a method for stochastic optimization. arxiv preprint arXiv:1412.6980 (2014). https://doi.org/10.48550/arXiv.1412.6980
7. Kristjanpoller, F., Cárdenas Pantoja, N., Viveros, P., Mena, R.: Criticality analysis based on reliability and failure propagation effect for a complex wastewater treatment plant. Appl. Sci. **11**, 10836 (2021). https://doi.org/10.3390/app112210836
8. Lee, W.S., Grosh, D.L., Tillman, F.A., Lie, C.H.: Fault tree analysis, methods, and applications & a review. IEEE Trans. Reliabil. **R-34**, 194–203 (1985). https://doi.org/10.1109/TR.1985.5222114

9. Ma, S., Zayed, T., Xing, J., Shao, Y.: A state-of-the-art review for the prediction of overflow in urban sewer systems. J. Clean. Prod. **434**, 139923 (2024). https://doi.org/10.1016/j.jclepro.2023.139923

10. Meyers, S.D., Landry, S., Beck, M.W., Luther, M.E.: Using logistic regression to model the risk of sewer overflows triggered by compound flooding with application to sea level rise. Urban Climate **35**, 100752 (2021). https://doi.org/10.1016/j.uclim.2020.100752

11. Newhart, K., Holloway, R., Hering, A., Cath, T.: Data-driven performance analyses of wastewater treatment plants: a review. Water Res. **157** (2019). https://doi.org/10.1016/j.watres.2019.03.030

12. Peter, Hammond, A.C., Singer, M., Suttie, V.T., Lewis, A.P., Smith: detection of untreated sewage discharges to watercourses using machine learning. Clean Water **18**, Pagestart–pageend (2021). https://doi.org/10.1038/s41545-021-00108-3

13. Wang, Q., Ma, Y., Zhao, K., Tian, Y.: A Comprehensive Survey of Loss functions in machine learning. Ann. Data Sci. 1–26 (2020). https://doi.org/10.1007/s40745-020-00253-5

14. Ramadhan, M., Sitanggang, I., Nasution, F., Ghifari, A.: Parameter tuning in random forest based on grid search method for gender classification based on voice frequency. DEStech Trans. Comput. Sci. Eng. (2017). https://doi.org/10.12783/dtcse/cece2017/14611

15. Saur: 2023 annual report of the delegatee (2023)

16. Taheriyoun, M., Moradinejad, S.: Reliability analysis of a wastewater treatment plant using fault tree analysis and Monte Carlo simulation. Environ. Monit. Assess. **187**(1), 1–13 (2014). https://doi.org/10.1007/s10661-014-4186-7

17. Wei, X., Kusiak, A.: Short-term prediction of influent flow in wastewater treatment plant. Stoch. Env. Res. Risk Assess. **29**(1), 241–249 (2014). https://doi.org/10.1007/s00477-014-0889-0

Application of a MBSA Approach on a Representative Subsystem of EGNOS (European Geostationary Navigation Overlay Service)

Franck Jonon[1], Emmanuelle Bialet-Carbonne[1(✉)], and Lorenzo Bitetti[2]

[1] Thales Alenia Space, 26 Avenue Jean-Francois Champollion, BP 33787 Toulouse Cedex 1, France
`franck.jonon@thalesgroup.com,`
`emmanuelle.bialet-carbonne@thalesaleniaspace.com`
[2] Thales Alenia Space, 5 Allée Gabians Cannes La Bocca, 06150 Cannes, France
`lorenzo.bitetti@thalesaleniaspace.com`

Abstract. RAMS (Reliability, Availability, Maintainability, and Safety) are crucial disciplines in the space industry. As in other fields (e.g. air traffic management, aeronautics, rail, etc.), space systems or systems-of-systems are becoming increasingly complex, leading to increasingly complex safety assessments, with the growing difficulty of ensuring the completeness and integrity of analyses. Faced with this increasing complexity, a more sophisticated safety approach is required, which has led to the need to experiment Model-Based Safety Analysis (MBSA) at Thales Alenia Space. In the aim of evaluating the interest and added value of a MBSA approach, a benchmark, on the static aspects, of two commercially available MBSA tools, Cecilia Workshop (Satodev) and System Analyst (Thales), has been performed on a representative subsystem of EGNOS (European Geostationary Navigation Overlay Service), the European SBAS (Satellite-Based Augmentation Systems). This article briefly introduces the scope and objectives of the activities performed by Thales Alenia Space. Then, it focuses on the methodology used: the case study, the two MBSA tools, the subsystem modeling principles for both tools, and the evaluation strategy. Furthermore, it presents the results: (i) a comparison of Cecilia Workshop outputs versus System Analyst outputs (ii) tool evaluation matrix synthesis. Finally, we conclude with the next steps identified to ultimately implement a MBSA approach on SBAS-type projects.

Keywords: RAMS · Model-Based Safety Analysis (MBSA) · benchmark · Cecilia Workshop (Satodev) · System analyst (THALES) · EGNOS

1 Introduction

RAMS (Reliability, Availability, Maintainability, and Safety) are crucial disciplines in the space industry. As in other fields (e.g. air traffic management, aeronautics, rail, etc.), space systems or systems-of-systems are becoming increasingly complex, leading

P. Katsaros (Ed.): IMBSA 2025, LNCS 15755, pp. 48–59, 2026.
https://doi.org/10.1007/978-3-032-05073-1_4

to increasingly complex safety assessments, with the growing difficulty of ensuring the completeness and integrity of analyses. Faced with this increasing complexity, a more sophisticated safety approach is required, which has led to the need to experiment Model-Based Safety Analysis (MBSA) at Thales Alenia Space [1].

This study falls within the field of navigation usage and more particularly concerns European Geostationary Navigation Overlay Service (EGNOS). EGNOS is the European Satellite-Based Augmentation Systems (SBAS) designed to improve the performance of existing positioning, navigation, and timing services over Europe, by providing an augmentation, with correction data and integrity information, to Global Navigation Satellite Systems (GNSS) signals (GPS, GLONASS, and Galileo in the future) [2–5]. GNSS signals can encounter various types of errors in the travel from satellites to user receivers, affecting positioning accuracy that EGNOS can correct either directly or indirectly by reducing their impact. While many users may not be significantly affected by this lack of precision, certain applications (such as aviation, maritime, rail, road, agriculture, etc.) require this precision and hence need to correct these errors or alert the user promptly when such errors occur and cannot be corrected. The EGNOS system comprises a Space Segment and a Ground Segment. The Space Segment consists of three GEO satellites that broadcast integrity messages and corrections to EGNOS users equipped with EGNOS-compatible receivers. The Ground Segment includes forty geographically distributed Ranging and Integrity Monitoring Stations (RIMS) across Europe for collecting GNSS data, two Mission Control Centers (MCCs), and six Navigation Land Earth Stations (NLES) transmitting the correction and integrity signals to the GEO satellites. Each MCC contains two modules: a Central Processing Facility (CPF) using RIMS data to compute estimations of GNSS errors applicable to users and generate the integrity message, and a Central Control Facility (CCF) for overall EGNOS system monitoring and control [3–5].

The main objective of this study is to initiate an MBSA strategy within the RAMS department for Domain Navigation France (DNF) – Business Line Observation, Exploration & Navigation (BLOEN) at Thales Alenia Space. To achieve this goal, a benchmark, of two commercially available MBSA tools, Cecilia Workshop (Satodev) and System Analyst (Thales), has been performed on CCF, selected as a representative subsystem of EGNOS.

Some functions associated to EGNOS are "EU restricted". This marking applies to information and material the unauthorized disclosure of which could be detrimental to the interests of the European Union or of one or more of the Member States. In this publication, information cannot be disclosed in order to preserve this confidentiality.

2   Methodology

2.1   Case Study

The goal of this study is to experiment Model-Based Safety Assessment strategy and focusing on the modeling of a specific EGNOS subsystem. The Central Control Facility (CCF) has been selected for the several reasons developed below:

– The CCF complexity level makes it a representative example of a complex sub-system and an ideal test case for evaluating MBSA strategies in SBAS applications. The complexity is mainly driven by the complexity of the architecture. The overall CCF subsystem consists of four identical CCF chains in redundancy based on master/slave mechanism with hot or cold redundancies, with seamless or delayed transitions. These CCF chains are housed within the two EGNOS Mission Control Center (MCC) sites, with each MCC housing two CCF chains.
– CCF is also an interesting candidate because, in operation, this is the only EGNOS's subsystem involving, via actions on a Human Manual Interface (HMI), an operator.
– The diversity in HardWare (HW) components hosting respectively FirmWare (FW) or SoftWare (SW) components was also a criterion for selection.

2.2 Selected Tools: Cecilia Workshop and System Analyst

The two selected tools are:

Cecilia-Workshop, is a commercial on the shelf, developed by Satodev, a Dassault Aviation subsidiary specialized in safety tools [6].

System Analyst, is free to use and community driven, with contributions from Thales engineers [7, 12].

The choice of tools, in this study, was decided within the framework of Thales MBSA Safety Working Group (SWG). MBSA SWG, at Thales group level, is constituted by several RAMS Manager, or RAMS Head of Discipline, from different Group Business Units (GBU) and different Business Lines (BL). The MBSA Safety Working Group aims to pool and share practices, processes and tools. Among the various MBSA tools available on the market, for this study, these two tools were selected after presentations and training sessions due to their user-friendliness and the potential insights that could be derived from the analysis conducted using these tools.

Although there are similarities in the overall modeling approach for applying MBSA in both software programs, each solution follows its own modeling philosophy, offers specific tools to assist with modeling, automates certain tasks, and provides various output generation options. As a result, the process of creating models of the same system in these two software programs differs significantly at each working step.

2.3 MBSA Implementation and Consistency Checks Between Models

To effectively perform MBSA, a structured methodology, derived from the V-cycle methodology common in systems engineering, should be followed. The process begins with creating a system model using MBSE principles, representing the system's functional and physical architectures. At this stage, RAMS engineers identify hazards and define the safety requirements to be integrated into the system model. Safety engineers then extend the system model by incorporating failure modes, fault behaviors, and other safety-related aspects. This integration ensures that safety considerations are embedded within the system design. With the safety-extended model in place, various safety analysis techniques, such as FTA or FMECA can be applied. In MBSA, these analyses are often automated, using the system model as a direct input, significantly reducing the time and effort required compared to traditional methods [8] and improving communication and co-engineering among stakeholders.

The MBSA process includes regular reviews and iterations to accommodate design changes, ensuring that the safety model remains aligned with the system model. This iterative approach is vital in complex systems, where changes can have significant safety implications [9, 10].

In this study CCF subsystem modeling is implemented with the two selected tools, and both models are peer reviewed by external peers to ensure the correctness of the CCF behavior implementation. After that, the significant outputs models, like minimal cut sets are analyzed and compared, to ensure that the result of the implementation is consistent between the two models.

2.4 MBSA Tool Evaluation Strategy

To carry out the evaluation we used a strategy known as Alternative Scaling, a method commonly used within the Thales Group to evaluate tools, equipment, or COTS software alternatives. The evaluation process integrates technical decision-making criteria with an assigned weight (an integer between 2 and 3) to each criterion, reflecting its importance relative to the others. These criteria were drawn from a checklist based on our needs, which can be grouped as follows:

EGNOS project specific needs: In EGNOS project context, tools ability to generate safety outputs (such as FTA, FMECA, minimal cut sets) is mandatory, as these outputs are required by the project. Thus, this criterion has been rated as a priority of 3. Moreover, due to EGNOS system size and complexity, scalability is required; a hierarchical modeling approach is required to effectively manage multiple components and interactions while ensuring the tool can adapt to evolving project requirements. Since multiple RAMS engineers possibly work simultaneously on this project, multi-user access is also essential. These last two criteria have been assigned a rating of 2.

Company Rules and Practices Compliance: According to Thales practices, two criteria are particularly emphasized and weighted at 3. First, tools must be adaptable for use across all domain application systems. Second, tools shall ensure strong consistency with existing Model Based System Engineering (MBSE) baseline, by permitting MBSE project import. This promotes the integration and harmonization of data throughout the project and minimizes the risks of incompatibility between functional and dysfunctional models. Other important criteria for selecting a tool at Thales group in general and Thales Alenia Space, in particular, include potential dependency on the tool supplier, the tool's capability for configuration management of models at different stages of a dynamic project, and the challenges associated with certifying the tool for safety.

Costs: Financial criteria must be taken into account during the evaluation of a tool. This includes the acquisition costs, such as the product price, licenses, additional equipment, and training costs if necessary, as well as ongoing usage charges for maintenance and potential enhancements of the tool. Acquisition costs are well established, so this criterion has been assigned a weight of 2. In contrast, usage charges may be less familiar yet hold greater significance, thus receiving a weight of 3.

Ease of Use and Performance: The intrinsic performance of the tool, including its reliability in producing correct results and the simulation time for complex and large models, is crucial. Additionally, the tool's ability to verify locally model consistency is a key criterion. This warrants a weight of 3 for these two aspects. The ease of use should also be assessed, considering factors such as ergonomics, the complexity of the software, training requirements, and the availability of a component library. This evaluation is important since MBSA introduces new practices for RAMS engineers. Furthermore, the availability and quality of support and documentation for users are critical components of the assessment, along with the time spent on modeling, particularly where automatic task capabilities are concerned. While these latter criteria hold significance, they are considered to be of somewhat lesser importance, which justifies the assignment of a weight of 2 to them.

For each criterion, we identified the grades that could be given, based on different scales: 0 to 2, 1 to 2, or 1 to 3. Each value was accompanied with a description that the evaluated tools needed to meet to be assigned that value. To account for the use of different scales and to prevent bias between criteria, a scaling factor was applied to each criterion. A scaling factor of 3 was used for criteria with a maximum value of 2, and a scaling factor of 2 was used for those with a maximum value of 3. Figure below (Fig. 1) shows the evaluation matrix, which was applied to compare Cecilia Workshop and System Analyst.

	Criteria	Scaling factor	Weight	Criteria possible Values
1	Future dependance to the supplier	3	2	0: blocking 1: Dependence from supplier 2: Independence from supplier
2	Acquisition cost (product price, licenses, necessary equipment, team formation cost)	2	2	1: Acquisition engenders high costs (>5000 €) 2: Acquisition engenders reasonable costs (between 2000 € and 5000 €) 3: Acquisition engenders small costs (<2000 €)
3	Scalability	3	2	1: Difficulty to adapt 2: Easily adaptable
4	Availability and Quality of support and documentation	3	2	0: No support and poor documentation 1: Difficult to request and obtain support, bad documentation 2: Easy to request and obtain support, good documentation
5	Usage charge (Maintaining costs, Improvement cost)	3	2	1: High usage charge 2: Reasonable usage charge
6	Flexibility of use for every space application systems	3	3	0: Not adapted for any space systems 1: Not particularly adapted for all space systems (complex systems, dynamic systems) 2: Adaptable for all space systems (complex systems, dynamic systems)
7	Easiness to handle (ergonomics, complexity of the software program, needed formation, available examples)	2	2	1: Difficult to handle (complex tool, consequent needed formation, not many examples) 2: Moderately difficult to handle (low needed formation, few training examples) 3: Easy to handle (almost no needed formation, plenty of examples)
8	Consistency with System Engineering baseline (architectural model import possibilities, continual coherence between functional and dysfunctional models in case of modifications)	2	3	1: No import possibilities and no continual coherence between models 2: Import possibilities, but no continual coherence between models 3: Import possibilities and continual coherence between models
9	Generate Safety outputs (FTA, FMEA/FMECA, min cut sets)	3	3	1: Cannot provide all desired outputs for RAMS needs 2: Can provide all desired outputs for RAMS needs
10	Rapidity of use (time spent for modeling, available library, possible automatic tasks)	2	2	1: Long modeling time, no library avaible and automated tasks to save time 2: Correct modeling time, library avaible and few automated tasks to save time 3: Modeling time shorten thanks to a rich library and time-saving automated tasks
11	Model verification	3	3	0: No local tool to verify model consistency 1: Tool to verify the model available 2: The tool to verify the model is available and permits a good model behavior comprehension for the modeler
12	Performance (reliability on results, simulation time)	2	3	1: Provides bad performance 2: Provides good performance
13	Track change/configuration management	3	2	1: No track change/configuration management tool integrated 2: Track change/configuration can be managed internally
14	Multi user utilization	3	2	1: No possibility to have access to a same model on different machines at the same time 2: Possibility to have access to a same model on different machines at the same time
15	Tool certification for safety	3	2	1: Difficult to certify 2: Easy to certify

Fig. 1. Evaluation Matrix Criteria

3 Results

3.1 MBSA Implementation

This part describes the implementation of MBSA methodologies (static model) in Cecilia Workshop and System Analyst.

With Cecilia Workshop

Since there is no possibility to import a functional model file (e.g., a Capella file), the model has to be created from scratch, directly in Cecilia Workshop.

Specification: To ensure efficiency in modeling, a specification file was created using Excel. This specification file firstly describes the functions the CCF should perform and the failure conditions. It also reports on different versions of the model, including remarks and changes. It finally enables to find all the modeled items (components, equipment, modeling tools, flux, state …).

Modeling: The modeling process should then proceed systematically through structured steps.

1. The first step involves creating the needed **Parameters** (λ, μ) and assigning values to each. Once these parameters established, they can be associated with failure or repair events in the component definitions, rather than using single fixed values. The advantage of this approach is that if multiple components share the same parameter, any changes to the parameter's value during the design process can be updated across the entire model in one action, with no need to manually adjust each instance individually.

2. The second step involves creating **Types**. There are two categories of Types that are useful in the CCF model: **States** and **Flows**.

   State Types are registers that list possible states (e.g., Nominal, Loss) or statuses (e.g., Master, slave, hot/cold back up …) of components or equipment. These registers are then used to define components or equipment, specifying the various states/statuses they can assume. For example, the State Type *ComponentState_NL*, used for repairable hardware items, includes two possible states: *Nominal* and *Loss*. In the event of a failure, the state changes from *Nominal* to *Loss*, and if the component is repaired, it changes back from *Loss* to *Nominal*.

   Flow Types, on the other hand, are registers that represent flows (e.g., data flow, electrical power flow, zonal failure flow, or common cause failure flow) and list the states these flows can take, each with an associated color. These flows are also used in the definition of components or equipment. During simulation, the link representing the flow will adopt the color corresponding to the current state of the flow. For example, the Flow Type Command_DataFlow_Nominal_Loss_Working represents the data sent by the CCF to EGNOS Ground subsystems for control missions. This data can be Nominal if there is no failure in the CCF chain components it passes through and the CCF is in Master status. It can be Loss if there is a failure in the CCF chain components it passes through. Or it can be Working if there is no failure in the CCF chain components it passes through, but the CCF is not in Master status.

3. In the third step, **Operators** are created. These are useful for defining functions in AltaRica language that will be used multiple times throughout the model. For instance, an operator can calculate the state of a component or equipment based on

its inputs or assign the appropriate icon to an item according to its current state. An operator has one output and a specific number of inputs, and the code written in AltaRica determines the output based on these inputs. Once defined, an operator can be referenced in the code when defining the behavior of components or equipment, helping to simplify and streamline the code.

4. Once Parameters, Types, and Operators have been established, the next step is to model **Components**. These Components can either represent actual system behavior units or serve as modeling tools that do not exist in the real system but help ensure the global model closely mirrors reality. In the case of the CCF model in Cecilia-Workshop, specific modeling tools were created to, for example, compute equipment states based on their constituent parts, initialize information data, or create observers. A Component acts as a flow processor with an internal state, reacting to events and interacting with other components through flow propagation. When an event occurs, the Component determines the internal state change and updates the flow values emitted by its interfaces.

   The Component definition window consists of several tabs, including:

   - An *I/O* Tab, to define the flow variables transmitted or received by the component or states variables, categorized as input, output, or local (e.g., for internal state). Clear naming conventions are used for easy identification, and predefined Types can be utilized for automatic updates
   - A *States* Tab, to specify the state variables of the component, including their types and initial values.
   - An *Events* Tab, in which the events the component responds to are listed, along with associated parameters and laws (e.g., Dirac, exponential).
   - An *Icons* Tab, to associate graphic representations with the various states of the component. The icons are important to make the global model comprehensive during simulation: the icon of a component or equipment changes when its state changes.
   - An *AltaRica Code* Tab, containing the code that dictates how the component's state changes in response to events and how information flow is managed in each state.

   Once each component created, its code syntax and consistency are verified to ensure not having inputted errors.

5. The fifth step concerns the creation of **Equipment**, which are assemblies of components and/or other equipment. The Equipment definition interface is similar to that of a component, with a few key differences. While the *States* and *Events* tabs are specific to Components, two new tabs appear in the Equipment definition box:

   - A *Content* Tab, where the internal architecture of the equipment is built. Components or other equipment can be linked together, as well as with the equipment's input/output points. It is important to note that Cecilia Workshop does not validate links between inputs and outputs if the flow nature does not match at connection points.

– A *Synchronizations* Tab, enabling to synchronize events across the components within the equipment. During simulation, these synchronizations ensure that specific events occur simultaneously or under certain conditions.

6. In the final step, once all components and equipment have been created, the **Global Model** can be assembled by dragging and dropping items from the Cecilia Workshop tree and linking them. The simulation mode, which allows events to be triggered in the desired sequence, helps verify the overall model behavior. By testing various hazardous scenarios. It permits to identify some modeling errors and confirm the accuracy of the overall model.

The final model includes around fifty components, implemented thanks to real subsystem information.

The switching process from a CCF chain to another in case of failure in the master chain, is managed thanks to a modeling tool, and statuses transitions delays have been handled with synchronizations. This was the most challenging part of that modeling work in Cecilia workshop.

With System Analyst

Unlike Cecilia-Workshop, System Analyst allows for the import of a Capella model. However, in the case of the CCF system, the model from the System Engineering team was not available. Although it would have been possible to model both architecture and behavior aspects directly in System Analyst, as done in Cecilia Workshop, we opted to first create the architecture model in Capella and then import it in System Analyst to input the behavior aspect. The following sections outline the work carried out in both Capella and System Analyst.

Architecture Modeling in Capella and Import in System Analyst

Capella is a modeling tool designed for complex systems. Based on the **Arcadia** method, **Capella** guides users through various stages, including **Operational Analysis** to define system needs from the end-user perspective, **System Analysis** to translate these needs into functional requirements, **Logical Architecture** to design an abstract, technology-independent architecture, **Physical Architecture** to specify the concrete implementation of logical blocks into physical components, and **EPBS** (**Engineering Product Breakdown Structure**) to detail the final product's structure, components, interfaces, and interactions.

In the Physical Architecture model of Capella, the palette offers a set of tools to define the physical implementation of a system. It includes **Node Physical Components** which represent physical entities like hardware or software parts. **Behavioral Physical Components** are used to model components that exhibit behaviors, such as control systems. **Physical Functions** describe the specific actions performed by these physical components, connecting the physical architecture to the logical functions defined in the Logical Architecture earlier. The palette also includes tools for defining interfaces, physical links, and exchanges, allowing the modeler to detail how components interact and communicate together.

There are some import limitations:

– Only the Physical Architecture model from Capella can be imported into System Analyst.

– Only Physical Functions and their functional exchange links are transferred correctly, with the function/sub-function hierarchy preserved. Unfortunately, Node and Behavior Physical Components, along with their links, are not imported.
– There are issues with the import of Physical Function names; in Capella, the function names are imported as descriptions in System Analyst.

To mitigate these limitations and avoid errors during modeling in the MBSA tool, adjustments to the Capella model are necessary before import into System Analyst. This involves structuring Physical Functions into a function/sub-function hierarchy based on the desired level of detail and renaming them as physical components or equipment, where parent functions represent equipment and child functions represent their constituent components. Functional exchange links should also be added between sub-functions. Once imported into System Analyst, the CCF system's equipment, sub-equipment, and components are all correctly linked, requiring only a simple reorganization. The naming issue can be easily resolved using System Analyst's Excel spreadsheet editing mode, which provides access to all component names and descriptions. To address this, we proceed to the creation of Visual Basic for Application (VBA) macro that automatically transfers the name of each component from its description box to its name box.

Dysfunctional Behavior Modeling in System Analyst
After import, the next step was to incorporate the component's behavioral aspects. Unlike Cecilia-Workshop, System Analyst does not rely on AltaRica code to define the dysfunctional behavior of each component, except for the dynamics box, which will be discussed later. Instead, it relies on logical tools (e.g., AND, OR gates) and event gates to construct logical diagrams. The software then utilizes its own simulation engine, "Agate" [11], for simulation and analysis.

In System Analyst, the inputs and outputs of the components are integer-valued flow variables. The software also associates the different types of failure modes (e.g., Loss, Nominal) with the integer values of these inputs and outputs. The goal of modeling the behavioral logic of the functions is to account for all possible scenario combinations and configure the output based on these combinations. To establish this behavioral logic between the various inputs and outputs, System Analyst offers several tools, including:

– The logical operator AND functions, taking multiple input flows and returning the maximum value among them.
– On the contrary, the logical door OR, returning the minimum value of all incoming flows.

A combination of logical operators, events with associated parameters and laws, and input/output ports is used to represent the component behavior. A stepwise simulation mode permits to verify the logical diagram accurately reflected the intended behavior.

After the implementation of these logical diagrams for each components, observers should be placed to generate RAMS results (minimal cut sets, FTA, FMEA/FMECA).

In a final step specific to the CCF system, creation of dynamic blocks to implement the switching procedure from a Master CCF chain to a Slave one, with potentially non-instantaneous transition delay. System Analyst recently added the possibility to create dynamic blocks.

Once all these steps done, the final model of the CCF system in System Analyst was completed.

Additionally, another similar model was created without the dynamic blocks to generate a graphical FTA. This was necessary because System Analyst does not allow graphical static fault trees generation from a model that includes dynamics but allows static evaluation of dynamic model such as Min Cut Set generation and quantification, FMECA generation. Both models, with and without dynamic blocks, yielded the same minimal cut sets.

3.2   Consistency Checks Between Cecilia Workshop and System Analyst Modeling

Cecilia-Workshop and System Analyst both provides essential outputs for the Safety Analysis of the system once the static model is finalized. Three files can be generated and exported from Cecilia-Workshop, once the modeling done: a Failure Mode Effect Analysis (FMEA), minimal sequences and minimal cut sets. For System Analyst, it is also possible to generate and export minimal sequences, minimal cut sets, FMEA and Fault-tree Analysis (FTA).

To validate the models, a reliable approach is to compare the minimal cut sets generated by both MBSA tool solutions. Ideally, identical lists of combinations should be obtained. Although consistent spellings were used for modeling items and events in both software programs, the minimal cut sets produced were automatically formatted differently, necessitating data processing to make the two lists comparable.

To address this, a VBA macro was created. This macro adjusts the format of the minimal cut sets from System Analyst to match the format used in Cecilia-Workshop. It then compares the two lists and identifies any combinations of failure events that appear in one list but not the other.

After a few adjustments in the models, the two lists were found to be perfectly aligned: both contained no first-order cut sets, 72 s-order cut sets, and 4 608 third-order cut sets. This confirmed the consistency and coherence of the two models.

3.3   MBSA Tool Evaluation Matrix

The figure below (Fig. 2) presents the completed evaluation matrix detailing the grades assigned to Cecilia-Workshop and System Analyst for each criterion. These grades are supported by justifications based on observations made during the implementation of the CCF system in both tools. A final score was calculated for each tool by summing the products of the alternative grades, the criteria weights, and the corresponding scale factors for each criterion. The tool with the highest final score is selected as the preferred alternative. System Analyst achieved a score of 163, while Cecilia-Workshop scored 118.

	Criteria	Grade Cecilia-W.	Grade System A.	Grade Justification for each criteria Cecilia-W.	Grade Justification for each criteria System A.
1	Future dependance to the supplier	1	2	Developped by Satodev.	Community driven solution, with Thales engineers involment and contributions.
2	Acquisition cost (product price, licenses, necessary equipment, team formation cost)	1	3	Costly product and licence, expensive team formation, but can be install on every computer.	Community driven solution, with contributions from Thales engineers, no licence needed, can be installed on every computer.
3	Scalability	1	2	External supplier and final product.	Community driven solution, with contributions from Thales engineers, ease scalability. Tool still in development.
4	Availability and Quality of support and documentation	1	2	Accessible external supplier that can provide support with additional fees, documentation not up to date.	Support is important and it is easy to request thanks to Thales engineers involved in tool development. High quality level documentation.
5	Usage charge (Maintaining costs, Improvement cost)	1	2	Annual licence, improvements would cost.	No planned usage charge: tool is free of charge.
6	Flexibility of use for every space application systems	1	2	Modeling through AltaRica scripts offers the liberty to analyze complex and dynamic systems, but a "too complex system" warning message rises quickly and engenders limits in the use of the tools.	No restriction in the use of the tool for a complex/dynamic model.
7	Easiness to handle (ergonomics, complexity of the software program, needed formation, available examples)	1	2	Ergonic tool but AltaRica language needed to be integrated, formations can be provided with charge, few example are available.	Ergonomic, moderately complicated to use (no coding knowledge required, except temporally for dynamics), a detailed and complete example is available.
8	Consistency with System Engineering baseline (architectural model import possibilities, continual coherence between functional and dysfunctional models in case of modifications)	1	2	The model has to be started from scratch in the tool (no import possible from Capella), Model consistency cannot be stated.	Import from Capella possible, enabling to initial consistence between functional and dysfunctional models. However, if a change occurs in the SE models, consistency will be broken.
9	Generate Safety outputs (FTA, FMEA, FMECA, min cut sets)	1	2	2 out of 3 outputs can be exported : minimal cut sets, FMEA/FMECA.	3 out of 3 outputs can be exported : FTA, minimal cut sets, FMEA/FMECA.
10	Rapidity of use (time spent for modeling, available library, possible automatic tasks)	2	2	Costly in time when modeling new component (for the code). But library is rich. Time saved with all instances of a component automatically updated when this component is modified.	Modeling time shorther than with AltaRica code. Initial library is poor, but component can be added to library from other projects. Take much time to model the dysfunctional part complex and redundant model.
11	Model verification	2	1	Efficient tool verifies AltaRica script syntaxt and model consistency. The graphical approach with icon enables a good comprehension of the model, and can facilitate errors identification.	No automatic verification tool available. Nevertheless, it is possible to verify manually the model behavior, thanks to a stepwise simulation tool.
12	Performance (reliability on results, simulation time)	2	2	One identified error on results, but globally reliable. No significant time to generate results.	Good reliability. No significant time to generate results.
13	Track change/configuration management	2	1	Several versions can be easily stored and locked.	No integrated track change/configuration managing tool, but external mitigation solution can be organized (e.g. PALMA).
14	Multi user utilization	1	1	Multi-user utilization impossible.	Multi-user utilization impossible.
15	Tool certification for safety	1	1	Will have to be certified as a tool not already used for space navigation programs. Nevertheless, it is still possible to use the alternative without any certification, under the following conditions: all the outputs of the tool shall be challenged and reviewed by a peer committee.	Will have to be certified as a new tool. Nevertheless, it is still possible to use the alternative without any certification, under the following conditions: all the outputs of the tool shall be challenged and reviewed by a peer comittee.
	TOTAL	118	163		
		2	1		

Fig. 2. Evaluation Matrix and Scores for Cecilia-Workshop and System analyst.

Overall, both tools perform their intended functions reliably and robustly. Cecilia Workshop gives a clear comprehension of the model behavior in simulation thanks to the graphical approach of failure propagation. Moreover, model checks and verification embedded in the tool, as well as configuration management, are the others strengths that distinguish Cecilia from System Analyst. On the other hand, one of the main advantages of System Analyst is that it offers the ability to import a Capella model, thus facilitating consistency between systems engineering modeling and RAMS modeling. The ability to generate fault trees is also a major criterion, at least during methodological transition phases, both to validate these methodological changes and to ensure continuity in the nature of the RAMS documentation we are committed to deliver. Finally, less critical but nevertheless important, System Analyst has the advantage of being free of charge and community-driven. Because, contributions of Thales engineers are involved and contribute in tool development, support and training is easily available and free. Furthermore, it offers us a greater scalability than a commercial product.

4 Conclusion

This study succeeds in initiating a MBSA strategy within the RAMS department for Domain Navigation France (DNF). The benchmark of two commercially available MBSA tools, Cecilia Workshop and System Analyst, to perform MBSA of CCF, selected as a representative subsystem of EGNOS, give an advantage to System Analyst. The next phase of evaluations will focus on another critical need in the frame of EGNOS project: the use of MBSA for availability analysis. Availability computation is essential to ensure that the system remains operational and accessible at specific times and under certain conditions. The CCF model will need to be adapted to compute availability, allowing for a comparison with the results obtained in a classic way by RAMS team. The ultimate goal would be to model the entire EGNOS system in order to validate the MBSA approach on an entire SBAS project.

Acknowledgments. Thanks to the Cecilia-Workshop team (SATODEV), who, as part of this final-year internship at the Ecole Polytechnique de Montréal (Canada), provided us their tool free of charge and responded to our requests for support. We would also like to thank the System Analyst team, in Thales for the significant support provided, as well as the quality of the discussions, throughout this study.

References

1. Lisagor, O., Kelly, T., Niu, R.: Model-based safety assessment: review of the discipline and its challenges. In: The Proceedings of 2011 9th International Conference on Reliability, Maintainability and Safety, IEEE, pp. 625–632. Guiyang, China (2011)
2. EUSPA Europa "EGNOS -What is SBAS". https://www.euspa.europa.eu/eu-space-progra mme/egnos. Accessed 15 Apr 2025
3. ESA "ESA Navipedia - EGNOS General Introduction". https://gssc.esa.int/navipedia/index. php/EGNOS_General_Introduction. Accessed 15 Apr 2025
4. EGNOS GSC "About EGNOS". https://egnos.gsc-europa.eu/egnos-system/about-egnos. Accessed 15 Apr 2025
5. ESA "How does EGNOS work". https://www.esa.int/Applications/Satellite_navigation/ EGNOS/How_does_EGNOS_work. Accessed 15 Apr 2025
6. CECILIA SATODEV. https://satodev.com/en/rams-software/cecilia/. Accessed 15 Apr 2025
7. SYSTEM ANALYST. https://www.system-analyst.fr/. Accessed 15 Apr 2025
8. Frédéric, M., Michel, B., Prosvirnova, T., d. Bossoreille, X. : Model-based safety assessment: comment renforcer la confiance dans les modèles?. In : Congrès Lambda Mu 23, Paris Saclay - France (2023)
9. Joshi, M.P., Heimdahl, S.P.M., Whalen, M.W.: Model-based safety analysis. NASA (2013)
10. Abdellatif, A.A., Holzapfel, F.: New methodology for model-based safety analysis. In: 2019 IEEE Aerospace Conference. Big Sky, MT, USA (2019)
11. Clement, E., Le Berre, N., Milcent, F. : Nouveau moteur pour l'évaluation de modèles dynamiques de grandes tailles . In Congrès Lambda Mu 24, Bourges – France (2024)
12. Breton, S., Thomas, T., Le Com, P., Clement, E. : SYSTEM-ANALYST – un outil MBSA pour l'analyse des risques, libre de diffusion et compatible avec ARBRE-ANALYSTE ET OPEN- ALTARICA . In Congrès Lambda Mu 21, Reims – France (2018)

Safety Analysis Methods in Aerospace: A Case-Based Comparison of FTA and MBSA

Isabella Lanzani[1]([⊠]), Luca Perfetti[2], and Luca Uliano[2]

[1] Dipartimento di Elettronica, Informazione e Bioingegneria, Milan, Politecnico di Milano, Italy
isabella.lanzani@polimi.it
[2] Leonardo Helicopter Division, Samarate, Italy
{luca.perfetti,luca.uliano}@leonardo.com

Abstract. Safety-critical areas, such as aerospace, require in-depth and rigorous analysis of the systems under failures. In accordance with industry standards, complex assessments are created to describe how failures can lead to specific functional failures and to verify compliance with specific certification targets. This article reports on a comparison between two independent methods on which the assessments are based. The first is the well-known Fault Tree Analysis (FTA), the *de facto* industrial standard. While the second is the analysis of the system Failure Propagation Model (FPM) included within the newest paradigm of Model-Based Safety Assessment (MBSA). The objective of this work is to evaluate key parameters to highlight the characteristics of both techniques while integrating them into an industrial process for civil aviation development, in particular during the Preliminary System Safety Assessment (PSSA). A benchmark is provided by analysing a realistic rotorcraft flight control system on which both methods are developed.

Keywords: Model-Based Safety Assessment · MBSA · Fault Tree Analysis · FTA

1 Introduction

In safety-critical domains, such as aerospace, ensuring system dependability is of utmost importance. In this context, safety assessment processes aim to identify, evaluate, and mitigate risks stemming from potential system failures.

During these safety evaluations, the extracted likelihood of risks is tested against the target probability thresholds established in coordination with various certification authorities. Indeed, safety assessments are extremely crucial for product development: they may highlight non-compliance issues against these targets in the early phases of the development process. This enables for safety-driven updates to the system under consideration that reduce time and costs.

P. Katsaros (Ed.): IMBSA 2025, LNCS 15755, pp. 60–74, 2026.
https://doi.org/10.1007/978-3-032-05073-1_5

To do so, different engineering fields, such as aeronautical, automotive, and others involving complex systems, adopt the Preliminary System Safety Assessment (PSSA) as one of the main artifacts during the system development process. To finalize the PSSA, analytical methods are required to systematically define and evaluate undesirable scenarios that affect complex systems. Among the most popular methodologies, Fault Tree Analysis (FTA) has long been used for its structured, deductive approach to hazard analysis.

Accordingly, Model-Based Safety Analysis (MBSA) may be used as an alternative to FTA. It consists of Failure Propagation Models (FPM), written using specific modeling languages, to represent and assess the model of the complex system, extracting its relevant safety-features.

This paper presents a comparative analysis of FTA and FPM, focusing on their practical application within the aerospace industry. The goal is to provide insight into their effectiveness, usability, and scalability in real-world industrial settings, highlighting trade-offs and considerations for safety engineers and system architects.

The experimental set-up for this comparison is the early phases of the development of a Flight Control System (FCS) for a civil rotorcraft, following the guidance of aerospace recommended practices [1,2]. By performing both analyses using the same input set, we ensure result consistency and assess the respective advantages and disadvantages of the two methodologies.

The structure of the article is devised as follow. In Sect. 2 the case study is presented, with the unified set of inputs necessary for the evaluation of either assessment. Section 3 contains both a high-level description of the aerospace safety process and a more in-depth explanation of the two quoted assessments, FTA and FPM. In Sect. 4, the lessons learned are discussed. Lastly, Sect. 5 presents conclusions and future works.

2   Case Study: A Rotorcraft Flight Control System

The proposed case study concentrates on one of the main functionalities of a rotorcraft FCS: to provide heading control. The function is responsible for the generation and execution of the correct actuation movements for tracking a certain heading reference. This is crucial to perform rotorcraft attitude control and coordinated flight. For both the mentioned analyses, a common set of inputs is required: the preliminary selected structural architecture of the FCS, and a subset of system-level assumptions (identified as meaningful for safety considerations). These are behavioral constraints which influence the failure propagation rules within the heading control function.

In this way, we identify the necessary input as the synchronization between structural information, defining components and connections, and behavioral implications, describing how the system is expected to react in nominal or faulty conditions. According to that, in the next sections, the system under analysis is described.

2.1   FCS Structure

The Flight Control Computer (FCC) is the computing system responsible for executing control laws and generating control signals. It consists of several sub-components, the behavior of which has a significant impact on the safety of the overall system, requiring extensive internal redundancies. Specifically, each FCC integrates a command (COM) lane and a monitor (MON) lane, both comprising a Field-Programmable Gate Array (FPGA) interface and a Central Processing Unit (CPU) (Fig. 2). FPGA MON is only receiving, while FPGA COM is receiving and transmitting. Both CPUs perform identical computations and generate the same outputs, which are then cross-checked for consistency. Additionally, an independent sub-component, known as the Passivation System (PS), is tasked with shutting down the FCC in the event of an internal failure or an inability to perform critical flight operations (e.g., due to a loss of input data). A final safety mechanism is given by Link Integrity eXaminer (LINX), reading via MON lane the output exiting from COM lane and assessing its correctness (Fig. 1).

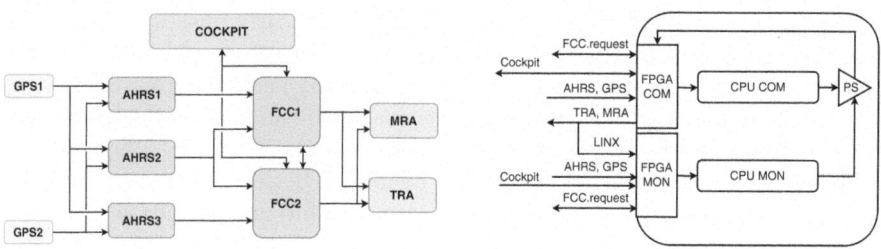

Fig. 1. Flight Control System   **Fig. 2.** Computer Control Unit

Among the various functions performed by the FCS, this article focuses on the heading control function (HDG). Following functional decomposition from [3], it is defined as an "aviate" function, a term for high priority functions managing core operations like stability. HDG is responsible for core stabilisation and tracking of the heading reference.

HDG relies on redundant external sensors, including inertial data from Attitude and Heading Reference Systems (AHRSs) and positioning data from Global Positioning Systems (GPSs).

Communication with the pilot happens via COCKPIT, both sending references via Mode Control Panel (MCP) and receiving the heading loss function alert, via appropriate CAS (Crew Alerting System) light.

The Control Unit (FCC) plays a critical role in managing the rotorcraft's flight capabilities, requiring a Dual COM-MON configuration [4] that follows the common Master-Standby scheme. To enable reconfiguration, the two FCS units share a signal (in Fig. 2 called FCC.request), allowing the standby unit to detect when the master has been passivated and seamlessly take its place. In this, only the designated Master FCC is responsible for transmitting output signals, to the cockpit and to the four electromechanical actuators (EMA). There are three actuators for main rotor actuation (MRA) and one for tail rotor actuation (TRA). Each actuator consists of an electrical board, which acts as an internal controller and a shaft. Given the focus on the heading control function, only the TRA is considered in the safety model.

The power distribution system has been omitted from the model for simplicity and all components are assumed to be correctly powered.

2.2 FCS Behaviour

We identify a sample of system-level assumptions to provide insights into the desired functional behavior and the expected effects of failures. Selected assumptions are listed in Table 1 and they are divided into the following clusters:

- **Sensor acquisition**: description of measurements acquisition from the sensors
- **Control law computations**: description of the heading mode engagement and control laws behaviors
- **Pilot involvement**: description of pilot involvement in the function
- **Reconfiguration procedures**: description of the conditions for reconfiguration procedures, enabling the standby FCC to enter as master
- **Equipment behavior**: describes the expected equipment behavior under specific conditions

It is necessary in the prospect of a complete safety process - but outside the scope of this work - to verify these assumptions.

3 Safety Assessment Process in Civil Aviation Industry

Safety assessments in the field of aviation have become increasingly important in ensuring airworthiness and safety. Over the years, the development of structured regulations and guidelines has formed the basis of an industrial process definition.

The SAE ARP4754B [1] and its EUROCAE counterpart ED-79A, collectively known as the 'Guidelines for the Development of Civil Aircraft and Systems', are considered the primary source of guidance on processes in the civil aviation industry. They emphasize the integration of systems engineering and safety processes throughout the product life-cycle. These practices incorporate requirement validation and design verification involving safety objectives. To comply with certification requirements, safety assessments are produced during development: PSSA is one of them. PSSA includes quantitative and qualitative methodologies to assess the safety design, among them FTA and MBSA are included.

In the following sections, an exhaustive explanation of the structure of the assessments is provided for both methodologies. To provide an example of both assertions, a small example involving sensor consolidation logic is discussed.

3.1 Fault Tree Analysis

Fault Tree Analysis (FTA) is a widely used technique in industrial practice for assessing system, reliability and safety. It involves constructing Boolean logic-based trees which map out all possible combinations of failures–ranging from

Table 1. System-level assumptions

ID	Description
Sensor acquisition	
S1	Inertial data originates by AHRS. For the availability of this generated signal, AHRS needs to be available. For the integrity of this generated signal, AHRS needs to generate a correct output
S2	FCC receives three redundant inertial data: two from AHRS components and one via other FCC. From them, a consolidated inertial signal is produced by the two-out-of-three logic or from the only available signal in the case both the others have been lost
S3	Hybridized data originates by the hybridization between measures from an AHRS and two redundant GPS. For the availability of this generated signal, AHRS needs to be available and both GPSs needs to be coherent and available. For the integrity of this generated signal, AHRS needs to generate a correct output and both GPSs needs to generate a correct output
S4	Both FCCs receive three hybridized data: two from AHRSs components and one via other FCC. From them a hybridized consolidated data is produced by two-out-of-three coherent source signals
Control law computation	
C1	Heading function is implemented with an outer loop for heading reference tracking and an inner loop for stabilization
C2	Outer loop for heading reference tracking is requested by the pilot. It uses the hybridized data to feed the control law
C3	Inner control loop for stabilization is always active and uses the output of heading control loop or a safe preselected values as the reference. It uses the inertial data to feed the control law. Safe preselected values enter if the heading mode has not been requested by the pilot or if the output of the heading control law has been found unavailable
Pilot involvement	
P1	The pilot from cockpit is able to engage heading mode by requesting a heading reference to track
P2	Loss of outer loop for heading reference tracking must be communicated to pilot via CAS-light on cockpit
Reconfiguration procedure	
R1	The initialized master FCC computer activates the PS when one of the following conditions occurs: 1. a major internal failure is detected; 2. the FCC does not have enough data to perform stabilization; 3. the FCC receives an incoherent signal from LINX.
R2	A major internal failure - sufficient to trigger PS activation - consists of one of the following scenarios: 1. The COM lane and the MON lane are in mismatch 2. PS itself fails with an improper activation
R3	Standby FCC continuously monitors the availability of the master FCC, hence it is immediately aware of its passivation, either due to PS activation or due to an internal failure
Equipment behavior	
E1	(FPGA) FPGA fails only as a unique block hence if it occurs all FPGA output signals have failed
E2	(FPGA) A failure of a single FPGA is always detected by the COM-MON logic
E3	(PS) The PS, if activated, would cut all outputs from the FPGA-COM (this safety mechanism is not influenced by an erroneous failure of the FPGA-COM)

systems and equipment to individual components–that could lead to a specific undesired event, known as the Top-Level Event (TLE) [5]. The Basic Events (BEs), which represent the root causes of failure, are at the lowest level of the tree. Failure rates are assigned to each BE and then propagated through the tree using logical gates (such as AND and OR) to calculate the overall probability of the TLE. This approach enables engineers to evaluate how likely a critical system failure is, based on the likelihood of individual component failures.

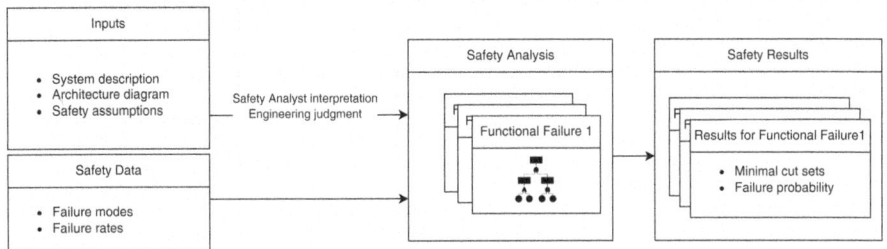

Fig. 3. FTA approach

In this approach (Fig. 3), the safety analyst uses the acquired understanding to manually construct fault trees to calculate Minimal Cut Sets (MCSs) (defined as all the unique combinations of component failures that lead to TLE) and failure probabilities [2].

Figure 4 shows an example of an FTA, with a branch generated by the Isograph Fault Tree Analysis Software [6]. This logic explains the eventuality of the loss of consolidated inertial sensor signal for the system in Sect. 2. Those data are crucial for the operational capability of the FCS and for the accomplishment of the heading control function. This happens either when a loss is generated from all three sensors (right side), or when two of them show a discrepancy while the third has lost its availability (left side).

3.2 Model-Based Safety Assessment

The term MBSA is broadly used, in particular it refers to two main research and applicative branches. The first consists in extending design models to incorporate safety data; notable results uses Scade Design Verifier [7], Matlab&Simulink [8], SysML applied to safety [9,10] etc.

The second and more promising branch consists of the use of a suitable language, separated from design description but created to specifically address system safety aspects. This FPM, that became the primary source of the system safety information, contains the architecture, failure mode models, safety-relevant functional behavior (e.g., reconfigurations, monitoring, etc.), failure conditions, and possibly additional data depending on the analysis objective. Indeed, this "safety model" represents both the system architecture and its normal and dysfunctional behaviors. The model itself is then analyzed using a suitable computational tool set to generate outputs such as failure sequences, MCS, or other results (see Fig. 5).

Several different languages were developed for this later purpose, such as AltaRica [11], AADL [12], nuXmv [13]. For this paper, FPM are built in AltaRica DataFlow language [14], compiled in Cecilia Workshop tool from Dassault

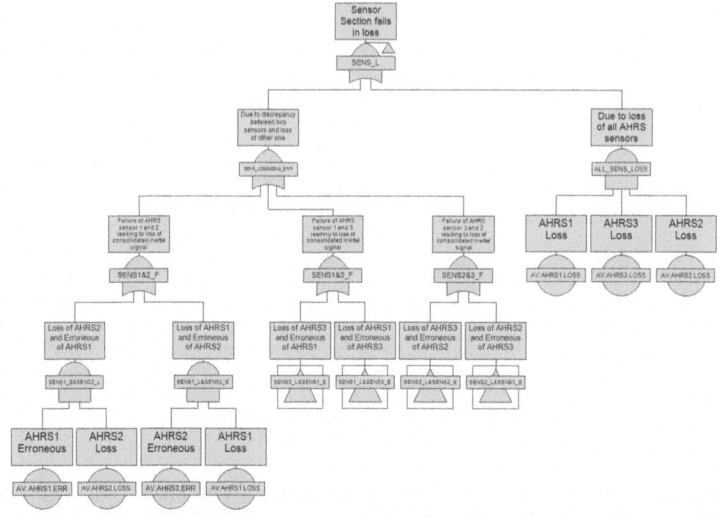

Fig. 4. FTA consolidation logic

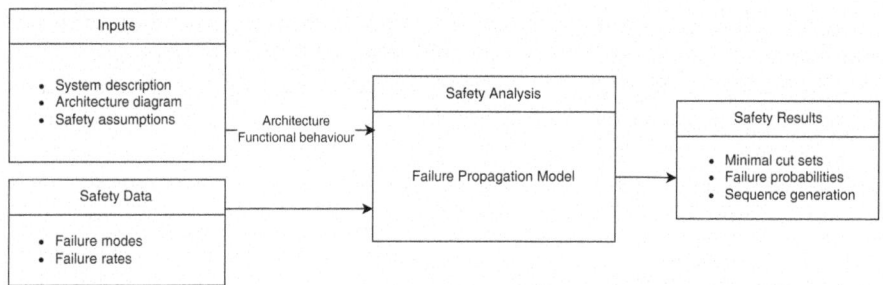

Fig. 5. MBSA approach

Aviation [15]. AltaRica DataFlow language enables the flexible textual construction of basic elements, while Cecilia graphical interface allows these elements to be graphically connected and composed in suitable libraries and projects. Results from FPM are extracted from observers, defined as the combination of signals that represents the failure scenario, equivalently to TLE in FTA.

Models in AltaRica define a specific state automaton, called Guarded Transition System [16], which formalizes the system both in nominal and in degraded conditions. In it, events force a change of the internal states, used to specify how the input and internal state of the object would combine to produce an output. The majority of the signals (in this article) are defined in a OLE triplet, whose values are "ok", "loss" and "erroneous": this definition models the integrity and availability of a specific signal or of a specific component [17]. In general, more modes could be defined here. For the purposes of the PSSA, however, OLEs are considered significant enough for analysis.

The same consolidation logic of Sect. 3.1 is expressed in this methodology in Fig. 6.

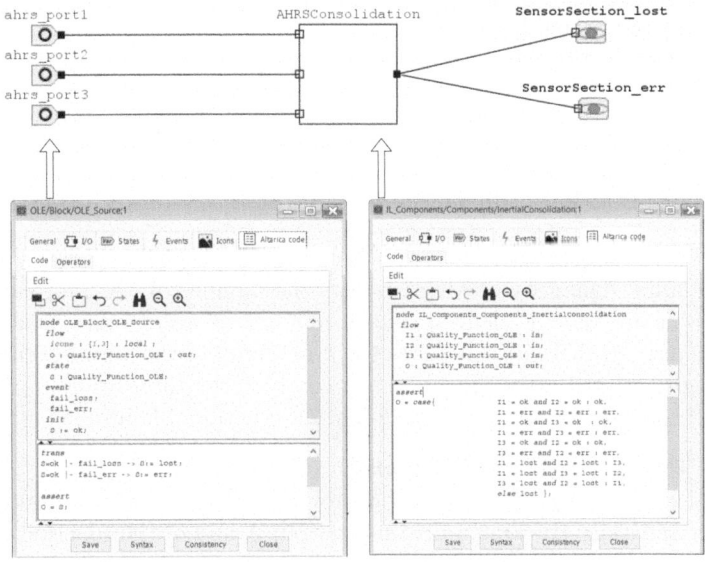

Fig. 6. Cecilia consolidation logic

The three AHRS are instances of *OLE_Source class*, eligible to fail as loss (due to the event "fail_loss") or as erroenous (due to the event "fail_err"). The three signals are then propagated into the *AHRSConsolidation* block that implements in a textual and univocal form the consolidation logic previously described. Finally, the highlighted observer captures the consolidated signal in case of loss.

A user can define this kind of elements and assemble them in more complex structures that, thanks to Cecilia graphical interface, can be assessed and simulated efficiently.

It could be worth mentioning that safety models are intrinsically able to contain more information on the system than FTA or other static assessments; nevertheless here dynamic results are not addressed, since the objective is to cover the same analysis with both methods. The interested reader could find information in other related works [18].

4   Results

Hereafter, results arising from the application of both methodologies to the described FCS architecture are compared.

Results from both methodologies are translated into the form of MCSs, summary of which is reported in Table 2.

Table 2. Quantitative probabilistic results

	Loss of Heading Control		Erroneous Heading Control	
	Quantity MCS	Probability [1/FH]	Quantity of MCS	Probability [1/FH]
Order 1	2	2.00E-6	3	1.20E-6
Order 2	87	1.17E-7	10	1.22E-9
Order 3	1	1.00E-15	57	4.12E-13
Order 4	0	0	36	7.33E-20
Order 5	0	0	6	1.12E-24
Total	90	2.12E-6	112	1.20E-6

The column "Quantity of MCS" counts the number of MCS for each order. The order of an MCS is defined as the number of events that make up the MCS. Column "Probability" observes the probability of the failure scenario with respect of the related order. The last row contains the total results.

Table 2 contains results from the following functional failure:

- Loss of Heading Control (HDG_LOSS)
  Defined as the loss of Heading Control function, which is responsible for heading reference tracking and stabilization. A loss of the function happens, while in heading mode, when the execution of tail actuator fails silently due to the presence of one or more components failures
- Erroneous Heading Control (HDG_ERR)
  Defined as an erroneous behavior of Heading Control function. This occurs, while in heading mode, when the movement of tail actuator fails erroneously and unpredictably due to the presence of one or more components failures.

This Section analyzes in detail HDG_ERR. Nevertheless, a more broad and complete database of the results, containing information over both functional failures, can be found in a GitHub repository [19].

Broadly speaking, there is a typical trade-off between integrity and availability: the system architecture is designed to prioritize integrity, frequently opting to 'fail silently' whenever internal faults are detected.

Internal failure detection algorithms often respond by rendering the faulty signal inactive, which prevents its propagation but increases signal loss. This behavior reduces the likelihood of erroneous signals affecting critical functionalities, but it implies that erroneous failure scenarios occur only under specific and rare combinations of failure modes, where the fault manages to penetrate the built-in safety barriers.

Erroneous scenarios are typically triggered by improper signal generation that bypasses single-source monitoring. This happens because the faulty signal appears realistic from a integrity perspective (e.g., it passes checksum and bit count checks). After, it propagates further into the system when independent sources are either non-redundant or degraded in specific ways that prevent multi-source monitoring from being activated.

particular, this latter represents the event in which an erroneous reference signal is received by the FCC. Order 2 presents 10 minimal cut sets:

- 6 from certain combination of the first FCC internal failures (e.g. the erroneous COM Lane is not isolated because of the loss of PS, that prevents the reconfiguration).
- 3 are from all combinations of inertial sensors where two have failed erroneously
- 1 is from the two GPSs that have failed erroneously

Order 3 presents 57 MCS:

- 54 minimal cut sets where a reconfiguration occurred and the new master FCC generates an erroneous
- 3 minimal cuts are from a undetectable combinations of AHRS failures (namely, two fails as loss and one as erroneous)

Similarly, minimal cut sets of order 4 and 5 contain the combination between events that trigger the passivation of the first FCC (caused by erroneous AHRS) with those that generate an erroneous from the second FCC.

We now examine how each methodology produced this same result presented in Table 2.

For the FTA, developed within Isopgrah's Reliability Workbench (see Fig. 7), the assessment was created by 4 "OR-branches" structure, containing the relevant sections: communication, sensor, computation and actuation.

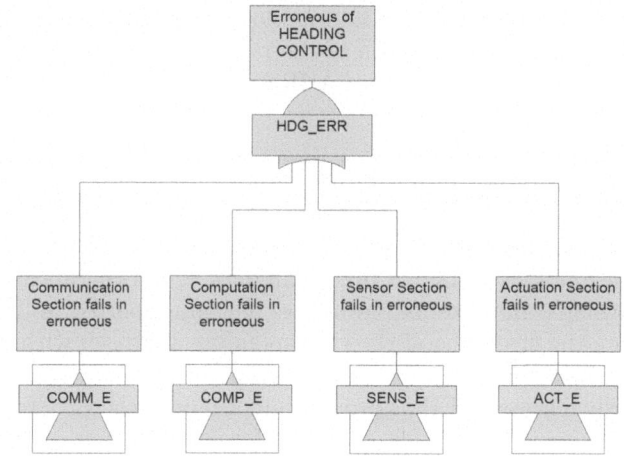

Fig. 7. Fault Tree Analysis for the Erroneous Heading Control

The MBSA model was written in Cecilia Workshop. In Fig. 8 it is possible to identify three main views, instantiated in the Main view:

inside this view failure rates are defined

- **Internal logics for FCCs**: containing an abstract representation on the functional partitions of each FCC (e.g. consolidate data, compute control law...); it models the effect of (internal and external) failures on the FCC itself, the foreseen mitigations and the overall effect at rotorcraft level
- **Safety**: defines the safety observers; those are boolean triggers that activates when the system appears in a specific configuration (e.g. the failure scenario)

It is clear from Fig. 8, how FPMs are built to represent the system in various levels of granularity and abstraction, and requires the consistency between these levels to be maintained. The observer for the HDG_ERR is defined as a combination of the signal exiting from this logic views (e.g., the control signal generated and the Master/Standby status of each FCC) and from the architecture view (e.g., the capability of the actuator to receive and move accordingly).

The observer for other functional failure (e.g. HDG_LOSS) are defined equivalently in the same Safety view of the FPM.

Observing the complexity of the internal logic of the FCC, as reported in Fig. 8, it becomes evident that FPM can encapsulate a significant amount of system-level information, greater than what can be extracted from FTA. At the same time, it offers a more intuitive and structured representation of the system's behavior. Accordingly, a practical example is reported in Table 3, representative of the simulation in Fig. 9.

Indeed, it is possible to inject in simulation a defined failure (or combination of failures) to assess its (or their) effect at rotorcraft level. In the failure scenario of Fig. 9, purple color represents the loss failure of the FPGA of the FCC1 (1), that is then transmitted (2) to the internal logics for FCC1 view (3), resulting in its passivation and the generation of the request to engage FCC2 as master (4). Blue and orange colors (erroneous AHRS2 and AHRS3) can be equivalently contextualized.

4.1 Comparison Evaluation

Conducting this analysis provided a deeper understanding of the respective advantages and limitations of the two techniques. The experimental outcomes have been translated into evaluation indices and are reported in Table 4. Each index highlights the strengths of the corresponding approach with respect to a specific safety objective.

As previously discussed, FPMs provide a more comprehensive representation of the system compared to standard FTAs. However, this increased expressiveness comes at the cost of greater modeling effort. We notice that a single FTA is generally quicker to develop, as it focus solely on a specific malfunction scenarios and do not require consideration of the interactions between unrelated malfunctions or system components. For this same reason, addressing a small number of functional failures would be more time-convenient using FTA.

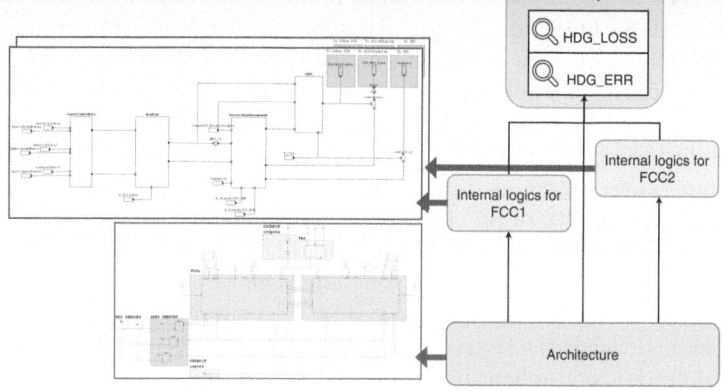

Fig. 8. FPM for the Heading Control (schematic)

Table 3. Sample of failure events and effects - Practical Example

Failure event	Requirements involved	Effect on the Rotorcraft	Color
FCC1.FPGA1.loss	E1, E2	Detection and passivation of FCC1, FCC2 enters as Master	Purple
AHRS2.err	S1, S2	FCC2 suffers a reduction in safety margins for the generation of the inertial consolidated signal	Blue
AHRS3.err	S1, S2	FCC2 propagates an erroneous inertial consolidated signal resulting in erroneous heading control function	Orange

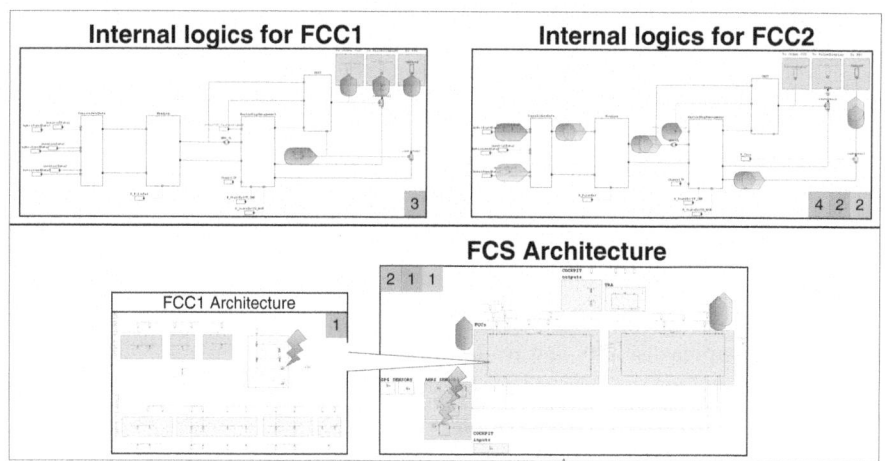

Fig. 9. FPM - Practical Example

contain observers for multiple functional failures. Indeed, in the case at hand, observers for HDG_LOSS and HDG_ERR share the same project and only differs in the observers definition. In theory, a single FPM could contain all program functions and functional failures, but this would incur a higher modeling cost: we discourage this practice, proposing a function-to-function approach. Moreover, the possibility to build specific libraries allows for the reuse of many artifacts in different functions or, even, in different programs. One key advantage of MBSA is the enhanced reusability of previously developed models, in contrast to conventional FTA, where the tree for each functional failure scenario must be individually constructed. Consequently, we conclude that FPM is indeed better suited to covering multifunctional, complex systems, recouping the modeling costs in the long term through the expressiveness and reusability of past knowledge.

Regarding the comprehensibility and the readability of the assessment, non-safety experts have found the capabilities of MBSA more intuitive. In particular, consulted system engineers considered the ability to simulate fault injection to assess its effect a valuable contribution to the development process.

One of the key strengths of MBSA techniques is their ability to efficiently update the safety assessment following design changes. We test this capability in our case study, by introducing new requirements–either not initially considered or intentionally modified–and observing the impact on both artifacts. While the update effort in FTA varies significantly, in FPM it remains consistently low. Indeed, the object-oriented nature of the AltaRica language allows for immediate propagation of changes across all models that instantiate the modified class. In contrast, FTA lacks such modularity: in the worst-case scenario, a single modification may affect all FTAs, requiring manual updates across each of them. For this same reason, during the early design phases (PSSA), where frequent and rapid system modifications are expected, FPM is better suited to produce timely results and to promptly address potential safety concerns.

Table 4. Comparison evaluation

Performance Index	FTA	MBSA
Representativeness of the real system		✓
Modeling cost	✓	
Expressiveness of the assessment		✓
Rapidity for the single assessment	✓	
Reusability of past knowledge		✓
Comprehensibility and readability of the artifact	✓	✓
Ability to update with new information		✓
Flexibility for early design phases		✓

5   Conclusions and Future Work

From an industrial point of view, the decision between FTA and FPM is highly context-dependent. In the case of complex systems or organizations with multiple concurrent development programs, FPM offers clear advantages in terms of reusability, maintainability, and overall process optimization. Future work aims to improve requirement traceability, considered as a fundamental asset in Model-based paradigms. Currently, the requirements traced textually in the Cecilia model are collected through generated reports, and then uploaded in the shared requirement repository. Automatizing this process would surely benefit the overall program management.

The simulative capabilities of FPM facilitate communication among experts from different domains, as the models offer a more faithful representation of the actual system. We argue that developing a dedicated safety model significantly enhances the shared understanding of safety implications across engineering teams, thereby contributing to the overall reliability of the system. In the proposed case study, we focus on a single function–the heading control–but a broader safety assessment could be carried out more rapidly and consistently. This is because, when following good modeling practices, each functional safety model would inherit common architectural patterns and logic from a centralized library. Such standardization reduces both the likelihood of human error and the effort required to update the safety assessment after design changes. Indeed, the possibility to create specific libraries is an appealing attribute of this methodology and their effectiveness will be tested in the mentioned more complex analysis. Although building these comprehensive models is typically more time-consuming than constructing fault trees, they offer clear advantages in terms of simulation capabilities, model coherence, and overall comprehensibility.

As intended by the authors, the structure of the utilized safety model will be explained and treated in more details in a separate article.

References

1. SAE, ARP 4754: Guidelines for Development of Civil Aircraft and Systems, ARP 4754 (2010)
2. SAE, ARP 4761A: Guidelines and Methods for Conducting the Safety Assessment Process on Civil Airborne Systems and Equipment, ARP 4761A (2023)
3. Wasson, K., Neogi, N., Graydon, M., Maddalon, J., Miner, P., McCormick, G.F.: Functional hazard assessment for the evtol aircraft supporting urban air mobility applications: exploratory demonstrations (2022)
4. Moir, I., Seabridge, A., Jukes, M.: Civil Avionis Systems - Ch4. System Safety, 2nd edn. Wiley, Hoboken (2013)
5. Ruijters, E., Stoelinga, M.: Fault tree analysis: a survey of the state-of-the-art in modeling, analysis and tools (2015)
6. https://www.isograph.com/software/reliability-workbench/fault-tree-analysis-software/fault-tree-analysis/

7. Ansys. Scade suite: Model-based development environment for critical embedded software (2022b). https://www.ansys.com/products/ embedded-software/ansys-scade-suite

8. Lisagor, O., Kelly, T., Niu, R.: Model-based safety assessment: review of the discipline and its challenges (2011)

9. Helle, P.: Automatic SysML-based safety analysis (2012)

10. Mhenni, F., et al.: Flight control system modeling with sysml to support validation, qualification and certification (2016)

11. Batteux, M., Prosvirnova, T., Rauzy, A.: AltaRica 3.0 assertions: the whys and wherefores (2017)

12. Delange, J., et al.: Validate, simulate, and implement ARINC653 systems using the AADL (2009)

13. Bittner, B., et al.: The xSAP safety analysis platform (2016)

14. Prosvirnova, T., Batteux, M., Rauzy, A.: AltaRica 3.0 Language Specification (2020)

15. Dassault Aviation. Cecilia Worskshop User's Manual version 6.0 (2019)

16. Rauzy, A.B.: Guarded transition systems: a new states/events formalism for reliability studies (2008)

17. Prosvirnova, T., et al.: Strategies for Modelling Failure Propagation in Dynamic Systems with AltaRica (2022)

18. Albore, A., Dal Zilio, S., Infantes, G., Seguin, C., Virelizier, P.: A ModelChecking approach to analyse temporal failure propagation with altaRica (2017)

19. https://github.com/Sabeast-4/SafetyAnalysisMethods

Cybersecurity Analysis

MBCA: A Model-Based Approach for Cybersecurity Analysis of Cyber-Physical Systems

Antoine Sfeir[✉], Macaire Medenou, and Raoul Guiazon

Airbus Protect, 31700 Blagnac, France
{antoine.sfeir,macaire.medenou,raoul.guiazon}@airbus.com

Abstract. Cyber-physical systems are increasing in complexity and interconnectivity. Performing cybersecurity risk analysis and identifying all possible attack scenarios manually have become challenging and time consuming. This is similar to the problem being tackled for the studies of Reliability, Availability, Maintainability and Safety (RAMS) of complex systems where Model-Based Safety Analysis (MBSA) is proposed as a solution.

As a continuation of the research conducted in this PhD thesis [1] we introduce, in this paper, the methodology Model-Based Cybersecurity Analysis (MBCA). This novel methodology is inspired by MBSA and provides a practical and interactive approach to representing and automatically computing cyber Threat paths (attack sequences) via a model. To illustrate this technique, we model the cybersecurity attributes of a drone and part of its ground control infrastructure using the software SimfiaNeo, which supports the MBSA methodology. The cybersecurity attributes selected for our modeling approach correspond to security measures, vulnerabilities, attacker's actions, and safety feared situations.

We apply MBCA using SimfiaNeo to compute the different Threat paths of the considered system architecture. Each sequence consists of the attack source, the target, and the attack path that leads to the feared situation; these elements constitute a threat scenario. We also illustrate the integration of the MBCA approach in Security Risk Assessment (SRA) methodologies and throughout a product development cycle.

Keywords: Model-Based · Cybersecurity · Cyber-Physical Systems · Security Risk Assessment · Cyberattack

1 Introduction

Cyber-Physical Systems (CPS) are increasingly prevalent across critical infrastructure, manufacturing, and transportation. CPS are progressively more complex and highly connected which expands the potential surface of attack available for cyber threats. Model-Based System Engineering allows the handling of complex systems by managing multiple requirements from different disciplines while allowing easier communication across engineering teams. For Reliability, Availability, Maintainability and Safety

© The Author(s), under exclusive license to Springer Nature Switzerland AG 2026
P. Katsaros (Ed.): IMBSA 2025, LNCS 15755, pp. 77–91, 2026.
https://doi.org/10.1007/978-3-032-05073-1_6

(RAMS) studies, Model-Based Safety Analysis (MBSA) is proposed as a solution capable of handling the complexity of systems. In Cybersecurity, Security Risk Assessments (SRA) and attack scenarios identification are still performed manually and thus have become challenging and time consuming.

As a continuation of the research conducted in this PhD thesis [1] we introduce, in this paper, the methodology Model-Based Cybersecurity Analysis (MBCA). It offers a practical and interactive way to represent and automatically compute cyber attack paths (attack sequences) in a model. We also illustrate the integration of this MBCA approach in SRA methodologies and throughout a product development cycle.

The framework defined in this paper consists of an MBCA technique used within a SRA methodology and with potential application throughout a product development cycle. The attack paths computed will trigger Safety feared situations. To perform our studies we use the tool SimfiaNeo[1] which already supports the MBSA methodology and is adapted to our purpose.

To present our work, this article is structured in the following manner. First, we start by reviewing the relevant related works. Second, we describe the MBCA methodology. Third, we proceed to illustrate the proposed technique by modeling the cybersecurity attributes of a drone and part of its ground control infrastructure using the software SimfiaNeo. Finally, we conclude by discussing open points and potential next steps.

2 Related Works

2.1 Publications

Model-Based for cybersecurity is explored in multiple works.

The inclusion of cybersecurity in the design operations, specifically with the emergence of Model-Based System Engineering (MBSE) tools, is examined in [4]. They define the relation between cybersecurity and model-based with the use of Ebios RM[2] and UML[3]. They highlight the fact that the combination of MBSE and cybersecurity is a winning strategy if used in anticipation [3].

[2] introduces an aspect-oriented modeling approach for attacks in automotive CPS, which adds a security layer into model-driven design methods. They model an autonomous vehicle and introduce potential attack scenarios using the Ptolemy II[4] model-based tool. However, since this methodology only illustrates the impact of attacks on system functionality, additional advancements are required to represent security properties and mitigation strategies.

[14] describes that a model-based approach can support an effective co-engineering between cybersecurity and systems engineering in the process of defining system architecture. In fact, SysML-Sec introduced in [14] and detailed in [15], is based on the System Modeling Language (SysML) and facilitates the representation of security-related

---

[1] SimfiaNeo software - Airbus Protect.

[2] https://cyber.gouv.fr/la-methode-ebios-risk-manager.

[3] https://www.uml.org/what-is-uml.htm.

[4] https://ptolemy.berkeley.edu/ptolemyII/index.htm.

components within a system. It provides a methodology for development, incorporating formal security analysis and model validation. This approach integrates safety and functional properties [6].

The related works listed above do not explore automatic computations of attack paths. In the scope of this paper, we focus on the approaches where a tool is used to analyze complex and interconnected models. This topic is explored in works such as a PhD thesis [1] which is the foundation of our work. To address the risks raised by the presence of CPS, they propose a model-based process which enables them to assess the impact of cyberattacks on the safety of CPS. The approach is based on the formal modeling language AltaRica and the tool SimfiaNeo. They also introduce a new heuristic called 'footprint' that can be used to prioritize the analysis of the most relevant sequences of attacks. It reduces the state-space explosion with sequences of cyberattacks by computing only prioritised attack sequences as explained in detail in [12]. The footprint accelerates massively the generation of sequences. Their approach can significantly reduce the time needed to compute outputs, making it more accessible for industry adoption.

In article [5], the authors conduct an experiment to analyze the effects of multi-step cyber attacks on the safety of CPS. The model is represented with the formal language AltaRica which allows the automatic calculation of sequences of attacks leading to feared safety situations.

2.2 Methodologies

SRA and MBSA constitute two essential pillars of the work done in this paper. Thus, before diving into the explanation of MBCA we will introduce these methodologies.

Security Risk Assessment for Cyber-Physical Systems

A SRA for CPS aligning with established guidelines such as the DO-356A / ED-203A [7], can be systematically conducted through four key steps:

Step 1: **Threat condition identification and evaluation** involves systematically cataloguing potential vulnerabilities and assets, assessing their intrinsic weaknesses, and considering the operational context. This step builds upon methodologies outlined in attack tree analysis and common vulnerability scoring systems (CVSS), as demonstrated by [8, 9], their work on vulnerability assessment in Supervisory Control And Data Acquisition (SCADA) systems.

Step 2: **Threat scenario identification** (i.e. attack paths) constructs realistic attack vectors by combining identified threats with potential system weaknesses, often employing techniques like attack tree modeling [10].

Step 3: **Security measure characterization** involves evaluating the effectiveness of existing or proposed security controls in mitigating identified threats, often utilizing metrics such as attack surface reduction, residual risk, and security posture analysis.

Step 4: **Level of threat evaluation** involves quantifying the residual risk by combining the likelihood of attack paths with their potential impact, often using risk matrices or probabilistic risk assessment techniques.

The execution of the SRA facilitates informed decision-making regarding security investments and risk mitigation strategies, ensuring the CPS's resilience against evolving cyber threats.

Model-Based Safety Analysis (MBSA)

To conduct studies on Reliability, Availability, Maintainability & Safety (RAMS), traditional approaches are faced with the challenge of increasing complexity of systems. MBSA is a methodology proposed as a solution to perform these studies on complex systems [16].

The ARP4761A / ED-135 [17] is an Aerospace Recommended Practice giving guidelines to conduct safety assessment on civil aircraft, systems and equipment. In its revision A, the appendix N mentions that "The term Model-Based Safety Analysis (MBSA) is a generic term for a family of techniques and methods based on a Failure Propagation Model". The MBSA method consists of building a model focused on dysfunctions where the structuring is aligned with the system architecture. In general, commercial MBSA tools offer a graphical interface where all the data is stored in one place. Therefore, communication is accelerated and traceability is facilitated. These tools also embed powerful engines that produce RAMS outputs including the computation of scenarios leading to feared situations. Some MBSA tools integrate a bridge with the MBSE tool Capella which allows the user to import the system architecture facilitating the modelisation [18]. Furthermore, they allow the creation of libraries which allows the re-use of elements [13].

We chose the tool SimfiaNeo which is a RAMS tool developed by Airbus Protect that allows the use of MBSA. It is based on the AltaRica DataFlow language incorporating Guarded Transition Systems (GTS). Bricks representing functional and dysfunctional behavior of system units are modelled locally. The MBSA model assembles multiple bricks using flows that propagate data between bricks Fig. 1.

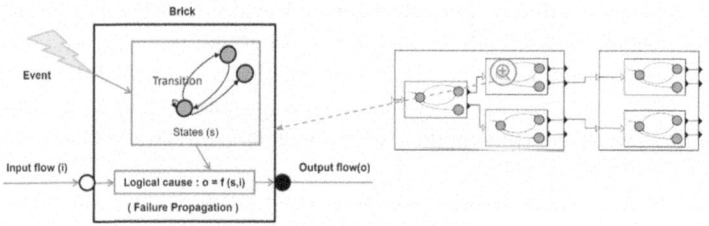

Fig. 1. Overall MBSA model [11]

The MBSA model in SimfiaNeo in AltaRica DataFlow is a translation of a Discrete Events System (DES). The representation of DES is described in [1, 5]. A DES is a five-tuple $< V, E, T, s0, CS >$:

- V is a finite set of variables;
- E is a set of events (attacks);
- T is a set of transitions, i.e., of triples $< e, g, i >$, where:

- e is an event from E;
- g is a Boolean condition on variables of V, called the guard of the transition;
- i is an instruction, i.e., a mechanism that modifies the current values of variables.

- s0 is the initial state of the system, where a state is a valuation of all variables of V. Thus, s0 is the initial valuation of all variables of V;
- CS is a set of critical states cs characterized by a Boolean condition on the values of the variables of V.

3   Model-Based Cybersecurity Analysis (MBCA)

This section introduces the methodology Model-Based Cybersecurity Analysis (MBCA) and its integration into a SRA process. The aim is to automate the second step of the SRA (Threat scenario identification). This manual identification has become challenging and time consuming with the increasing complexity of cyber-physical systems. It might be worth noting that a standard IT risk assessment based on EBIOS RM assesses typically less than 20 threat scenarios, while an aircraft assessment assesses typically hundreds around 500 for an Airbus A350.

Therefore, MBCA is proposed here as a solution that can drastically reduce the time needed and the complexity of this activity of the SRA. The cybersecurity attributes selected for our modeling approach correspond to security measures, vulnerabilities, attacker's actions, and safety feared situations. Before diving into the description of the MBCA methodology, we first need to define some terms:

- Safety feared situations: A configuration of the system being studied that is unwanted from a safety point of view. In the scope of this paper, Safety feared situations are the consequence of a successful cyberattack.
- Attacks: Exploitation of functionalities and/or vulnerabilities of a system for triggering a safety feared situation.
- Attack path: The route an attacker may follow from its entry point into the system towards its target.
- Security Measure: Any physical or behavioral component which helps in the protection of a cybersecurity attribute such as Confidentiality Integrity Availability (CIA) of an asset.
- Vulnerability: A flaw or weakness in system security procedures, design, implementation, or internal controls that could be exercised (unintentionally triggered or intentionally exploited) and result in a security breach or a violation of the system's security policy. (ED202B)

Moreover, MBCA is based on MBSA and the representation of attack propagations on CPS uses also DES with its five-tuple $< V, E, T, s0 >$ described above. But in the case of MBCA, E is a set of attacks.

3.1   Definition of MBCA

Model-Based Cybersecurity Analysis (MBCA) is based on the MBSA method. This novel methodology offers a practical and interactive way to represent and automatically compute cyber attack paths in a model. The system architecture, the vulnerabilities, the attacker's actions, and the feared situations are included in the model. MBCA assists in the identification and modeling of attack paths as shown in Fig. 2.

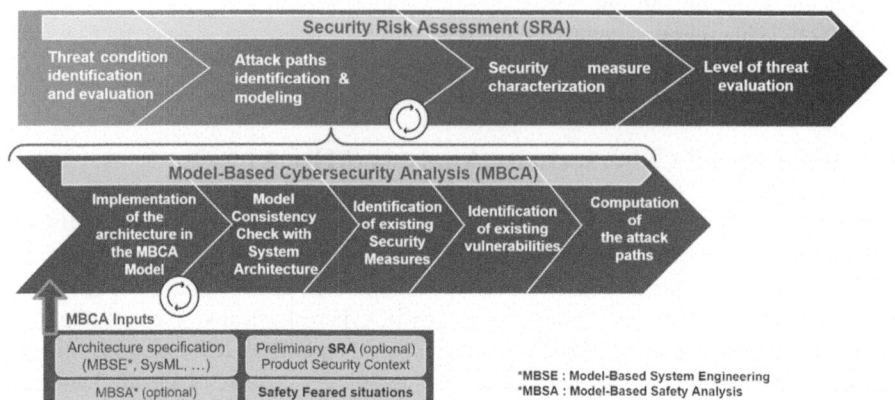

Fig. 2. MBCA within an SRA

Firstly, the system architecture is modeled. Secondly, a model consistency check with the system architecture is performed. Thirdly, security measures and vulnerabilities are integrated into the model along with the system's feared situations. Finally, an automatic calculation of attack paths is performed. The results allow the identification of attack paths in the modeling step of the SRA including ones not yet discovered manually. Consequently, new vulnerabilities are discovered which require new security measures. An update of the MBCA model is then possible leading to a recalculation of the attack paths. In the overall process presented in Fig. 2, iterations between the different steps are encouraged.

The conception of an MBCA model requires inputs such as an architecture specification model (MBSE, SysML, etc....). Another essential input is a list of Safety feared situations to be included and computed in the model. Additional optional inputs such as a preliminary SRA or an MBSA model would accelerate the overall process. The modeling of the system architecture in the cybersecurity model could be derived from the initial system architecture filtered to highlight cybersecurity relevant components.

3.2 Interaction Between the V-model and MBCA with SimfiaNeo Activities

In this section, we present our vision for the interaction between the V-model and MBCA with SimfiaNeo activities as illustrated in Fig. 3.

In the top-down part of the V-model, the computation and the visualization of the attack paths with SimfiaNeo resulting from the preliminary analysis assists the analyst in the phases of identifying attack paths and defining attack paths for the assessed asset. Similarly, these phases allow the SimfiaNeo model to be fed with new attack paths, new security measures and new vulnerabilities discovered during these phases.

In the upper part of the V-model, the calculation of the various attack paths, highlighting each attack vector associated with its vulnerability, and the step-by-step simulation of these in the SimfiaNeo model help the analyst in the security assessment and evaluation phases of the object analyzed.

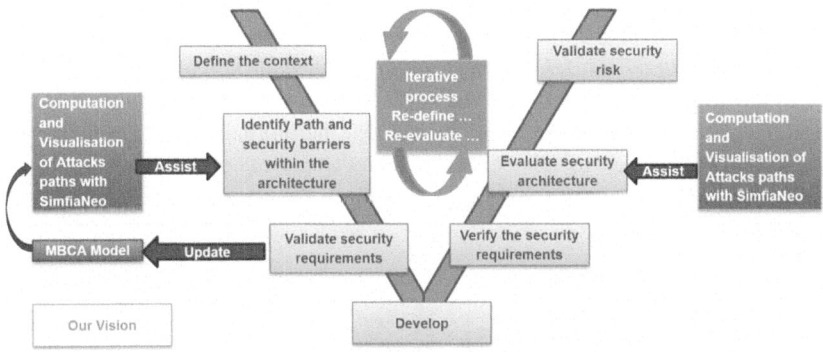

Fig. 3. Interactions overview of V-Model and MBCA SimfiaNeo activities

3.3 Decomposition of the MBCA Model

The MBCA model contains different subsystems of the system architecture. Bricks represent these subsystems and can be defined as atomic or hierarchical. A hierarchical brick is a brick that contains sub-bricks. An atomic brick represents the behavior of a subsystem and does not contain any brick inside of it. We made the choice to represent vulnerable components containing vulnerabilities/security measures with hierarchical bricks Fig. 4. Inside these cybersecurity hierarchical bricks, atomic bricks represent each vulnerability associated with the vulnerable component. Different ways of modeling exist, this way of modeling is chosen to improve the visualization of the vulnerabilities/security measures in the diagrams.

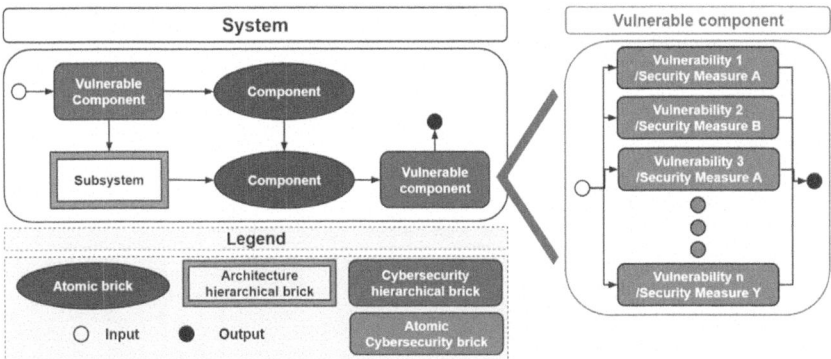

Fig. 4. Decomposition of an MBCA model

The next step is the exploitation of the vulnerabilities. An *attacker brick* is added to the existing model. It represents the attacker's behavior and triggers unwanted behavior in the system. Following that, the different attacks exploiting the vulnerabilities are implemented.

The exploitation of the vulnerabilities can be represented in 2 approaches: a decentralized approach and a centralized one. To explain the different approaches, we consider a model where the attacker exploits vulnerabilities in subsystems 1 and 4. In the centralized approach the *attacker brick* triggers each step of the attack. It resembles a command centre of the whole system. As seen in Fig. 5, the attacker is then connected to all the subsystems with vulnerabilities to be exploited. Furthermore, links are created between the bricks and the attacker to deliver feedback on the success of the attacks.

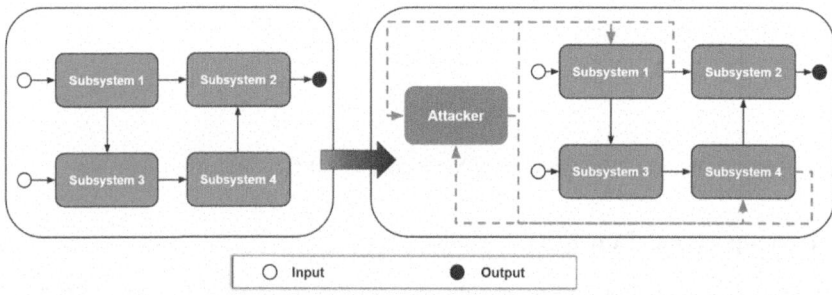

Fig. 5. MBCA model in centralized approach

In the decentralized approach, the *attacker brick* triggers exclusively the initial exploitation of the attack. The exploitation of each brick affects the linked bricks by enabling the trigger of their associated vulnerabilities. Practically, as seen in Fig. 6 each brick has a compromise status. If a brick is compromised, a flag is raised to account for it. The flag is a necessary guard to allow the trigger of the vulnerabilities downstream corresponding to the connected bricks. The expert's work is to select which following bricks will be affected by the exploitation of a given brick. In the case where the exploit of a vulnerability in a brick should have an effect on another brick to which it is not physically connected - for example a VPN -, a new link called virtual link is created. Otherwise, the existing physical link is used.

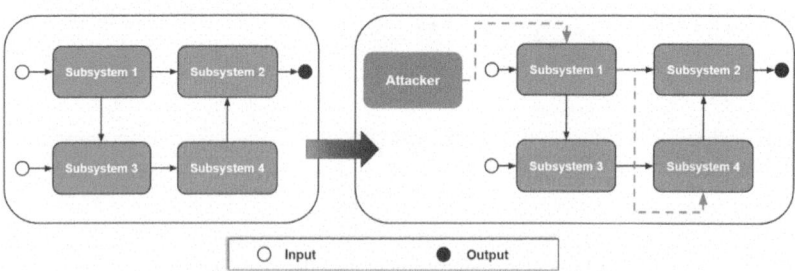

Fig. 6. MBCA model in decentralized approach

The 2 approaches allow the identification of the same attack paths. However, moving forward we chose to adapt the decentralized approach. We found it easier to propagate in this approach the exploitation of vulnerabilities because it allows us to focus on a single brick at a time during the model construction. The vulnerabilities of each subsystem are modelled independently allowing their reusability. On the contrary, in the centralized approach the overall modeling takes into account the *attacker brick*, thus reducing the reusability of the bricks in other architectures. Additionally, the decentralized approach delivers a simpler visual representation involving less links between different bricks.

3.4 Application on a Drone Use Case

We model the cybersecurity attributes of a drone and part of its ground control infrastructure using the software SimfiaNeo. At our disposal, we have the system architecture where the drone interfaces with 2 laptops, Air Traffic Control (ATC), a GNSS satellite and an external aircraft. We also have a preliminary SRA that requires the implementation of security measures in 3 components of the architecture: the Ground Server, the Telemetry Receiver and the Multi-Band Transceiver (MBT). A list of security measures provided by the preliminary SRA is summarized in Table 1.

Table 1. Identified Security Measures

Security Measures: Multi-Band Transceiver	
Security Measure 1.1	Access Control
Security Measure 1.2	Access Control VPN
Security Measure 1.3	Firewall: Limits access with respect to a saved list of external addresses
Security Measure 1.4	GNSS jamming detection: Detects interference in satellite signals
Security Measures: Ground Server	
Security Measure 2.1	Access Control
Security measures: Telemetry Receiver	
Security Measure 3.1	Access Control

The MBCA Drone Model

In SimfiaNeo, we implemented the drone model, represented feared situations, and computed attack paths using the footprint [12].

The model in Fig. 7 represents the MBCA model in SimfiaNeo including the system architecture. The Ground Server, Telemetry Receiver and Multi-Mode Transceiver

(MBT) are represented by hierarchical bricks. All three of them contain an access control as mentioned in Table 1. Therefore, we constructed an access control brick and put it in the library, in order to re-use it in the 3 concerned hierarchical bricks. Furthermore, we added 2 vulnerabilities in the MBT hierarchical brick which are the Firewall corruption and the deactivation of the GNSS jamming detection.

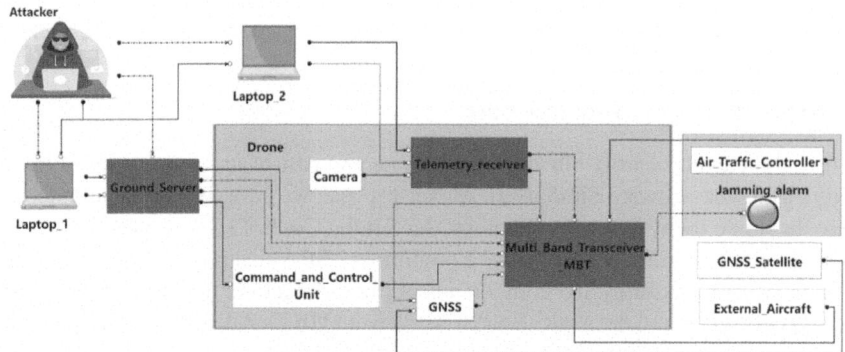

Fig. 7. MBCA Drone model in SimfiaNeo

The MBCA model will be uploaded on the Airbus Protect SimfiaNeo github[5]. Table 2 shows an example, where we apply the definition of a DES given above in the article on a part of the model containing the *Attacker* and the *Telemetry_receiver_access_control* (inside the *Telemetry_receiver*) with the links between them. In the example below, we consider that the *Attacker* has already compromised *Laptop_2*. The MBCA drone model in SimfiaNeo represents an AltaRica DataFlow translation of the DES definition used in Table 2.

Table 2. Application of a DES

Set V of variables	*Bypass_triggered_status:* {**true, false**} in the brick *Attacker* *Access_control_status:* {**Nominal, Compromised**} in the brick *Telemetry_receiver_access_control* *link_Attacker_Telemetry_receiver:* {**Nominal, Compromised**} which is the link between bricks
Set of events E is composed of attack techniques	Trigger_bypass from the brick *Attacker* Bypass_Telemetry_receiver from the brick *Telemetry_receiver_access_control*

(continued)

Table 2. (*continued*)

Set of transitions T	**t1** e: Trigger_bypass g: (*Bypass_triggered_status* $==$ false) i: *Bypass_triggered_status* $\leftarrow$ **true** and *link_Attacker_Telemetry_receiver* $\leftarrow$ **Compromised** **t2** e: Bypass_Telemetry_receiver g: (*Access_control_status* $==$ **Nominal**) and (*link_Attacker_Telemetry_receiver* $==$ **Compromised**) i: *Access_control_status* $\leftarrow$ **Compromised**
Initial states	*Bypass_triggered_status* $=$ **false** *Access_control_status* $=$ **Nominal** *link_Attacker_Telemetry_receiver* $=$ **Nominal**
Set of Critical Situations CS	*Access_control_status* $==$ **Compromised**

Results.

By applying the footprint feature of SimfiaNeo, we compute the sequences Table 3 that lead to the corruption of the Firewall list embedded in the MBT with the requirement [Number of events in a sequence < 6 i.e. order < 6]. We consider that in this critical situation, the attacker has elevated permissions, leading to multiple Safety feared situations including the corruption of the Firewall list. The results show that there are multiple attack paths available. For instance, the attacker can bypass the access control of the Telemetry receiver as done in Seq_1 or steal the credentials and then login, gaining access to previously forbidden actions (Seq_2, Seq_3 or Seq_4).

Table 3. Attack paths leading to the corruption of the Firewall list

Code	Attack sequences/ Attack paths	Order
Seq_1	Attacker.Compromise_Laptop_2 & Laptop_2.attacked & Telemetry_Receiver_Access_Control.bypass & MBT_Access_Control.bypass & Firewall.corrupt_list	4
Seq_2	Attacker.Steal_credentials & Attacker.Log_in_using_stolen_credentials & Laptop_1.log_in & Laptop_2.log_in & MBT_Access_Control_VPN.log_in & Telemetry_Receiver_Access_Control.bypass & Firewall.corrupt_list	5
Seq_3	Attacker.Steal_credentials & Attacker.Log_in_using_stolen_credentials & Laptop_1.log_in & Laptop_2.log_in & MBT_Access_Control.log_in & Telemetry_Receiver_Access_Control.bypass & Firewall.corrupt_list	5
Seq_4	Attacker.Steal_credentials & Attacker.Log_in_using_stolen_credentials & Laptop_1.log_in & Laptop_2.log_in & Telemetry_Receiver_Access_Control.bypass & MBT_Access_Control.bypass & Firewall.corrupt_list	5

SimfiaNeo offers the possibility to visualise each sequence generated. For example, Fig. 8 visualizes the sequence Seq_1 from Table 3.

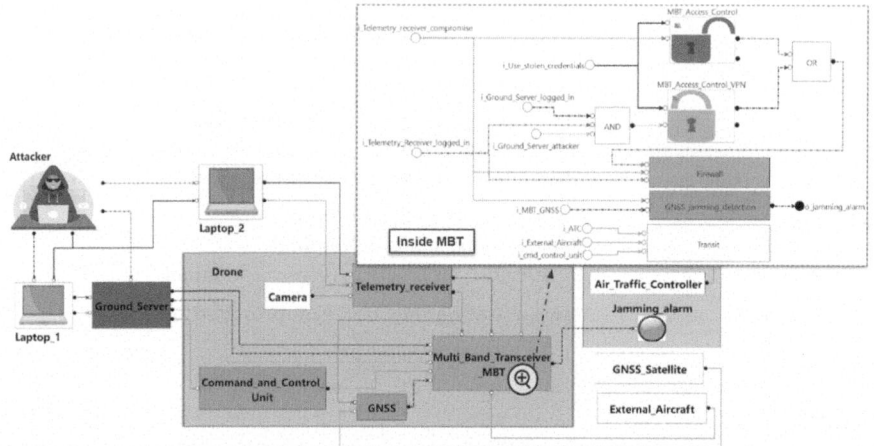

Fig. 8. Seq_1 leading to the corruption of the Firewall list.

In this section, we will show an example of addition of a security measure to the system architecture.

The action of bypassing the Telemetry receiver's access control is present in each sequence of Table 4. In order to enhance the security of the system and increase the difficulty of the attack, we chose to add to the Telemetry receiver a security measure. Therefore, we have extended its processing and communication capabilities to include the functionality of IP filtering with the addition of a firewall in the Telemetry receiver. We recomputed the attack paths. The results show that the IP filtering is present in each sequence increasing the order of all the sequences by 1.

Table 4. Attack paths recomputed after the addition of new security measures

Code	Attack sequences / Attack paths	Order
Seq_1	Attacker.Compromise_Laptop_2 & Laptop_2.attacked & IP_filtering.Corrupt_IP_filtering & Telemetry_Receiver_Access_Control.bypass & MBT_Access_Control.bypass & Firewall.corrupt_list	5
Seq_2	Attacker.Steal_credentials & Attacker.Log_in_using_stolen_credentials & Laptop_1.log_in & Laptop_2.log_in & MBT_Access_Control_VPN.log_in & IP_filtering.Corrupt_IP_filtering & Telemetry_Receiver_Access_Control.bypass & Firewall.corrupt_list	6

(*continued*)

Table 4. (*continued*)

Code	Attack sequences / Attack paths	Order
Seq_3	Attacker.Steal_credentials & Attacker.Log_in_using_stolen_credentials & Laptop_1.log_in & Laptop_2.log_in & MBT_Access_Control.log_in & IP_filtering.Corrupt_IP_filtering & Telemetry_Receiver_Access_Control.bypass & Firewall.corrupt_list	6
Seq_4	Attacker.Steal_credentials & Attacker.Log_in_using_stolen_credentials & Laptop_1.log_in & Laptop_2.log_in & IP_filtering.Corrupt_IP_filtering & Telemetry_Receiver_Access_Control.bypass & MBT_Access_Control.bypass & Firewall.corrupt_list	6

4 Conclusion and Perspectives

In conclusion, we introduced Model-Based Cybersecurity Analysis (MBCA) and inte-grated it into the product development cycle. We used our internal tool SimfiaNeo in order to support the construction of an MBCA model of a drone which allowed us to generate attack sequences automatically. This novel methodology is introduced in order to assist the manual identification of attack paths in SRA.

MBCA applied in SimfiaNeo allows the visualisation of the attack paths. It is a great asset as it would help security analysts to exchange more efficiently with systems engineers and illustrate the impact of the vulnerabilities in the systems. Moreover, the digitalization and automation would enable security analysts to quickly test the effect of adding or removing security measures over the security level of the overall system, enabling faster iterations than what is possible today. Currently, SRAs are done manually which makes it more difficult to achieve full traceability between different architecture updates. MBCA applied in SimfiaNeo enhances traceability throughout the product's design with the creation of multiple versions of the project. Therefore, the security measures implemented at each step of the product development are saved.

The most suitable level of abstraction of the model is still under investigation. A higher system level representation, where multiple subsystems interact with one another, might be the level of abstraction where MBCA is most useful. That's because, at this level, manual tasks are difficult to perform.

A future direction could be to study the impact of cyberattacks on safety and of safety issues on cybersecurity, however we suspect that it would require a different modeling approach in order to account for the specific emergent behaviour that arises when Safety and Cybersecurity views are combined.

As next steps, we foresee the creation of a SimfiaNeo library of exploita-tion/vulnerabilities, that allows re-usability across different MBCA models and facili-tates the creation of models. We could also optimize the cybersecurity architecture of a system by automatically identifying the paths with respect to the cheapest attack cost (energy, level of experience, means of attacks, execution time …) or the severity of the attack scenarios. This a limitation of our current approach as the most relevant attack paths are not necessarily the ones generated, especially as the models get more complex. This would also enable the optimisation of a system's architecture to maximize the minimal attack cost [18].

Additionally, there could be a generation of automatic recommendations to help with the identification of relevant Security Measures. And in the validation part of the development cycle, SimfiaNeo could be used to generate verification and validation tests to be performed on the system.

The aeronautical scope used in this article could be modified to include multiple feared situations and the integration of MBCA to non aeronautical SRA.

References

1. Serru, T.: Model-Based Security Assessment of Cyber-Physical Systems: Analyzing The impact of cyberattacks on safety using Altarica. PhD Thesis, CERGY PARIS UNIVERSITÉ (2023). https://hal.science/hal-04191802v1/document
2. Wasicek, A., Derler, P., Lee, E.: Aspect-oriented modeling of attacks in automotive cyber-physical systems. In: 51 St Annual Design Automation Conference, San Francisco, CA USA (2014)
3. Navas, J., Vorin, J., Stephane, P., Bonnet, S.: Towards a model-based approach to systems and cyber security co-engineering. In: 29th Annual Incose international symposium, vol. 29, no. 1. Wiley Online Library, pp. 850–865 (2019)
4. Martin, P., Flaus, J.: Study on the mutual contribution of model-based concepts and cybersecurity. In : Proceedings of the Congrès Lambda Mu 24 –24e Congrès de Maîtrise des Risques et de Sûreté de Fonctionnement, Institut Pour la Maîtrise des Risques, Bourges, France (2024)
5. Serru, T., Nguyen, N., Batteux, M., Rauzy, A.: Modeling cyberattack propagation and impacts on cyber-physical system safety: an experiment. Electronics 12, 77 (2022)
6. Paul, S., et al.: Recommendations for Security and Safety Co-engineering (Release n°3) - Part a, Technical report (2016). https://doi.org/10.13140/RG.2.1.3124.9044
7. EUROCAE. AIRWORTHINESS SECURITY METHODS AND CONSIDERATIONS. Technical Report ED-203A The European Organisation for Civil Aviation Equipment (2018). Cited on page/s ix, 3, 11, 16, 17, 28
8. Ten, C.W., Liu, C.C., Manimaran, G.: Vulnerability assessment of cybersecurity for SCADA systems. IEEE Trans. Power Syst. 23(4), 1836–1846 (2008)
9. Ten, C.W., Liu, C.C., Manimaran, G.: Cybersecurity for critical infrastructures: attack and defense modeling. IEEE Transactions on Systems, Man, and Cybernetics-Part A: Systems and Humans 40(4), 853–865 (2010)
10. Roy, A., Kim, D., Trivedi, K.: Attack countermeasure trees (ACT): towards unifying the constructs of attack and defense trees. Security and Communication Networks 5(8), 929–943 (2012)
11. Niol, J., Méric, N., Tlig, M.: Behavior and semantic modeling for the safety of critical autonomous systems. Lambda Mu 22 (2020)
12. Serru, T., et al.: Generation of cyberattacks leading to safety top event using altarica: an automotive case study. In Proceedings of the Congrès Lambda Mu 23 " Innovations et Maîtrise des Risques Pour un Avenir Durable "–23e Congrès de Maîtrise des Risques et de Sûreté de Fonctionnement, Institut Pour la Maîtrise des Risques, Angers, France (2022)
13. Monteil, L., Aulnette, R., de Bossoreille, X., Sagaspe, L.: Définition d'une synergie entre une méthode et un outil pour une étude MBSA. In : Proceedings of the Congrès Lambda Mu 24 –24e Congrès de Maîtrise des Risques et de Sûreté de Fonctionnement, Institut Pour la Maîtrise des Risques, Bourges, France (2024) https://hal.science/hal-04963728v1

14. Apvrille, L., Roudier, Y.: SysML-Sec: a sysml environment for the design and development of secure embedded systems. In: Annual International Conference of the Asia-Pacific Council on Systems Engineering 2013. Yokohama, Japan (2013). https://hal.telecom-paris.fr/hal-022 88385
15. Li, L.: Safe and Secure Model-Driven Design for Embedded Systems. Ph.D. thesis, Telecom Paris (2018)
16. Papadopoulos, Y., McDermid, J.: Hierarchically Performed Hazard Origin and Propagation Studies, Computer Safety, Reliability and Security, 1698 of LNCS, pp. 688–688 (1999)
17. ARP4761A: Guidelines for conducting the safety assessment process on civil aircraft, systems, and equipment. Technical report, SAE International (2023)
18. Da Silva M., Nguyen, N.: Quantitative Security Metrics: Assessment of Cyberattack Scenarios for Cyber-Physical Systems (2025)

Cybersecurity Threat Detection Through Business Process Log Analysis

Barbara Pernici[1] , Fotios Gioulekas[2], Athanasios Tzikas[2],
Konstantinos Gounaris[2], Evangelos Stamatiadis[2], Thomas Schaberreiter[3],
and Cinzia Cappiello[1(✉)]

[1] Politecnico di Milano, Milan, Italy
{barbara.pernici,cinzia.cappiello}@polimi.it
[2] 5th Regional Health Authority of Thessaly and Sterea, Larissa, Greece
{fogi,vstam}@dypethessaly.gr, atzi@uhl.gr, kgounaris@ghv.gr@polimi.it
[3] CS-AWARE Corporation, Tallinn, Estonia
thomas.schaberreiter@cs-aware.com

Abstract. Cybersecurity management and orchestration are critical concerns in modern digital environments. Detecting anomalies effectively can mitigate risks and prevent breaches. This paper explores the application of methods and techniques from business process log analysis to detect cybersecurity threats, starting from system-level logs generated while using organizational information systems. Until now, cybersecurity threat detection has predominantly relied on identifying anomalies at the technical level. However, an organization's business and operational levels contain rich information relevant to uncovering cybersecurity issues that cannot be detected through technical analysis alone. Business process log analysis provides a data-driven approach to comprehending the actual behavior of systems, enabling the identification of deviations from normal process execution that may indicate potential security threats. We propose a framework integrating process discovery and conformance checking to identify anomalous behavior patterns from system-level logs. A key aspect of our approach is its adaptability to user-defined policies and requirements, which guide the anomaly detection process. In this way, we guarantee that identified anomalies are relevant and actionable within the given context of an organization. The framework has been applied to real-world scenarios, and we demonstrate its effectiveness in identifying irregular activities.

1 Introduction

Organizations typically engage in two main cybersecurity management activities: risk management and incident management. Risk management, which includes Business Continuity and Disaster Recovery measures, is generally more structured and executed on a regular basis. However, in practice, many organizations only implement formal procedures after a significant security event [21]. Incident management focuses on identifying, diagnosing, and resolving IT anoma-

P. Katsaros (Ed.): IMBSA 2025, LNCS 15755, pp. 92–107, 2026.
https://doi.org/10.1007/978-3-032-05073-1_7

lies, whether accidental or malicious. This task largely falls to IT personnel and is often manual and resource-intensive.

Cybersecurity management is, to a large extent, a knowledge management problem. From the relevant knowledge domains, both risk and incident management demand up-to-date insights into industry best practices, emerging threats, and the ability to adapt solutions to an organization's unique circumstances [17]. While information from external sources (e.g., best practice documents, threat intelligence feeds, and even social media) is readily available, internal organizational knowledge—such as how systems and services interact in daily operations and how issues are addressed—is rarely documented [10]. Increasing regulatory requirements, like GDPR [6] and the more recent Network and Information Security Directive 2 (NIS 2 [23]), now push many organizations to formalize their previously ad hoc or implicit risk management processes.

Cybersecurity management can benefit from making tacit knowledge in an organisation explicit and digitally available [5]. Artificial Intelligence and Machine Learning (AI/ML) can actively support knowledge extraction efforts by continuously analyzing organizational data and operations. Through this continuous monitoring, AI/ML tools help organizations detect system- and process-specific anomalies that might otherwise remain undetected, enhancing situational awareness and improving overall security and resilience. It can ensure the right information is available to the right person to address or mitigate cybersecurity issues. This paper presents an approach for cybersecurity threat detection based on the business process log analysis and driven by user-defined policies and requirements. Such an approach is enabled by the information and data available through the CS-AWARE/CS-AWARE-NEXT cybersecurity management platform.

CS-AWARE/CS-AWARE-NEXT [3,15] are two European projects that aim to introduce an innovative socio-technical approach for cybersecurity management [12]. By identifying and visualizing the organization's social and technical assets, dependencies, and the information flows generated by daily human and technological activities, this approach enables a clear understanding of the organization's security position. Moreover, the approach is designed to apply not only to large organisations, but also to smaller organisations, such as municipal utility providers or SMEs covered by the NIS2 directive. The platform supports applications that detect and report attacks, anomalies, and incidents using a Human-in-the-loop (HITL) approach. Its development follows a five-step iterative process (see Fig. 1 [4]):

- *Step 1 - Requirements Collection*: Periodic workshops and focus groups gather organizational needs and constraints.
- *Step 2 - Application Design*: Leveraging internal and shared ecosystem knowledge—including public data repositories, cybersecurity news, and threat intelligence—the system selects, adapts, and customizes algorithms to organizational contexts.
- *Step 3 - Implementation*: The designed applications are developed and prepared for deployment.

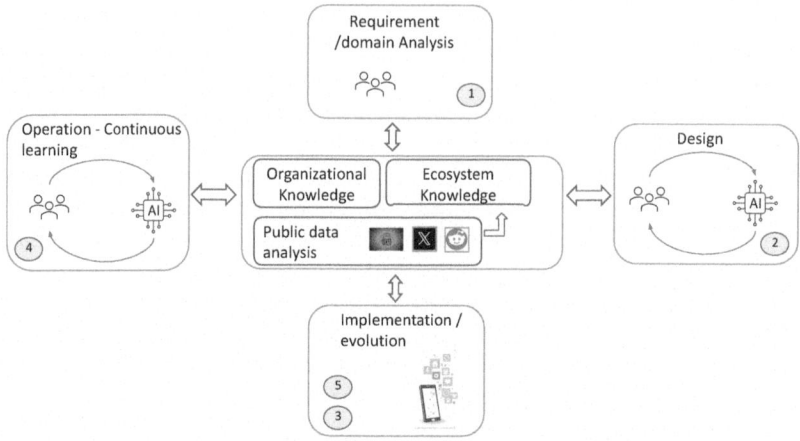

Fig. 1. Application Development lifecycle.

- *Step 4 - Operation*: Once launched, the applications monitor and alert on security issues in real time.
- *Step 5 - Continuous Improvement*: User feedback on the alerts and reports is used to refine and evolve the applications, ensuring they remain effective and context-aware over time.

The remainder of the paper is organised as follows: Sect. 2 presents related work. Section 3 details how knowledge is managed by CS-AWARE/CS-AWARE-NEXT platform. Section 4 presents the business process log analysis and describes how contextualisation can increase awareness and decision support. Sections 5 and 6 present a realistic use-case in the healthcare sector and illustrate how process mining can support organisations in cybersecurity management tasks. Finally, Sect. 7 concludes the paper and provides an outlook for future work.

2   Related Work

In Europe, cybersecurity management within organizations is increasingly regulated by legal mandates. Since introducing the European cybersecurity strategy in 2013—later updated in 2020 [7]—the European Union has devoted substantial effort to establishing a legal framework that encourages a more secure digital environment. Among these regulations, the GDPR and NIS/NIS2 are particularly influential, requiring a wide range of European businesses and organizations to adopt formal, legally compliant cybersecurity practices.

Various formal organizational risk management approaches exist, with the NIST cybersecurity framework [18] and the ISO/IEC 27000 family of standards [9] among the most widely recognized. While these are considered well-suited for larger organizations with the necessary resources, it remains uncertain whether smaller entities—now required to implement formal cybersecurity measures for the first time under NIS 2—will be able to adopt these frameworks on a broad scale.

Security Information and Event Management (SIEM) systems are widely used, advanced tools for incident management, offering real-time anomaly detection [8]. However, they are typically tailored to the needs of large organizations and often prove too costly for smaller entities. Moreover, current SIEM solutions generally concentrate on network and infrastructure-level anomalies from technological factors. They do not extend to deeper, context-sensitive monitoring that accounts for an organization's social dynamics and the complex behaviors arising from its unique business processes.

The complexity and rapid evolution of modern cyber threats have outpaced the capabilities of traditional data analysis techniques, justifying the growing use of AI/ML in cybersecurity management [22]. By leveraging Artificial Intelligence (AI) systems, particularly those based on Machine Learning (ML) and big data architectures, organizations can more effectively detect and mitigate these sophisticated threats. Intelligent cybersecurity management utilizes a variety of AI-driven methods with the ultimate goal of enabling informed, automated decision-making in cyber applications and services [20]. For decades, ML has played a prominent role in cybersecurity, supporting widely recognized tasks such as malware detection, intrusion detection, and spam filtering. Typically, these ML algorithms are trained on security-related data collected from diverse sources, including network behavior, database activity, application logs, and user interactions. An extensive survey of ML techniques for cybersecurity can be found in [20]. In supervised learning scenarios, ML techniques are often employed for anomaly detection, enabling the classification and prediction of malware attacks or other cyber anomalies. Common approaches include decision trees [24], logistic regression, and random forests [14]. Unsupervised learning methods, on the other hand, uncover latent patterns and structures in unlabeled data [20], with clustering techniques commonly used to group similar data points [13]. Additionally, association learning facilitates the development of recommendations and guidelines for adopting rule-based ML models in incident response and risk management, as demonstrated in [19].

However, over the past decade, researchers have increasingly explored how process mining, originally developed to discover, analyze, and enhance business processes, can also be leveraged to strengthen cybersecurity. Process mining methods work by extracting insights from event logs and audit trails, which are also abundant in IT infrastructures and security-related systems. Considering business processes allows organizations to build context-aware security policies and protection systems. Early applications of process mining to security focused on Compliance and Conformance Checking, i.e., ensuring that processes adhered to regulatory and organizational security constraints. For example, in [2], authors analyze and classify deviations with respect to the intended purpose of data and the context in which data are used, and provide a novel algorithm to identify non-conforming user behavior. In particular, they consider both data and process perspectives for conformance analysis. Also [1] uses process mining to detect anomalous process executions and check process conformance.

In addition to the presented approaches, we aim to propose an approach to link technical logs to business processes and besides, to check for deviations related to process execution we allow users to add their own rules, policies, and constraints to improve the cybersecurity threat detection further.

In the CS-AWARE-NEXT project, we are exploiting such algorithms, adding a context-aware perspective. The organisational knowledge and context will be considered to operationalise threat intelligence in organisational risk and incident management.

3   The CS-AWARE-NEXT Approach in Anomaly Detection

Currently, the CS-AWARE-NEXT platform relies on log files from multiple organizations to detect anomalies and attacks. Data collection is handled by installing log agents on various network devices, such as routers and firewalls, to monitor network traffic, as well as on pilot servers that capture a broad range of logs. These include Windows Event Logs (e.g., security, application, and system channels) and syslog entries from Linux and other systems. To store all these data, CS-AWARE-NEXT employs a data lake architecture that contains and manages large volumes of raw data. Each source in the data lake is described by a data catalog, which includes various metadata types. These metadata help data scientists understand the data values, their characteristics, and their suitability for the task at hand.

To identify common attack types, such as denial-of-service or brute-force attempts, we employ machine learning methods (e.g., k-Nearest Neighbors and Random Forest) trained on both network-level and operating systemlevel logs. In this respect, the training phase was conducted using public datasets (e.g., CSE-CIC-IDS2018[1]), which contain both normal and malicious traffic. Because the behavior of these threats is well understood, we achieved strong performance in anomaly detection, with F1 scores ranging from 0.88 to 0.97. We also developed additional methods to detect irregularities in log entry counts by analyzing patterns over time, including trends, seasonal fluctuations, and sudden spikes.

However, it is necessary to highlight that this task is still complex due to the dynamic nature of cyber threats and the complexity of modern IT environments. For example, the most common problems are high false positive rates and data quality issues. Anomaly detection systems can sometimes misclassify normal activities as anomalies, causing alert overload and reducing trust in their outcomes. Additionally, poor data quality—characterized by missing values, incorrect formats, redundancy, and flawed database design—can limit the effectiveness of such algorithms. To address these issues, the approach focuses on creating a robust data preparation pipeline. Through data cleaning techniques

---

[1] https://www.unb.ca/cic/datasets/ids-2018.html.

such as standard imputation, removing irrelevant or redundant columns, and eliminating duplicate rows, the goal is to ensure higher-quality input data and, in turn, more reliable and informative analytical results.

Handling large, continuous data streams in real time can be computationally demanding. To manage this complexity, a Lambda architecture is employed. It uses a "speed layer" for immediate anomaly detection and classification of incoming data, as well as a batch layer" to store and analyze historical data over time [11]. Note that all these methods are contained in what we call the AI-NEXT module, which is dedicated to data analysis.

The main problem is that cyber threats are constantly evolving to evade detection. Anomaly detection systems must adapt to these changes and continuously update their models to detect new types of anomalies. Moreover, as described in the previous sections, organisations have their process models and policies. Therefore, additional context-aware anomalies need to be considered.

For this reason, we propose the human-in-the-loop anomaly detection support. In fact, one of the core aspects provided by the CS-AWARE methodology is the ability to achieve and model a holistic understanding of how business processes of an organisation work, how they map to infrastructure, and how their behaviour can be monitored in day-to-day operation. This allows the monitoring of behaviour patterns of particular interest to the organisation and is based on realistic baselines provided by the employees/users of the organisation.

The CS-AWARE platform is able to gather the following data in machine-readable form:

- The asset(s) a monitoring pattern is related to.
- The log files and individual log file parameters that allow monitoring for specific behaviour.
- The baseline/range that defines normal behaviour.
- Users' requirements in terms of security constraints to ensure that their data, systems, and applications are protected against unauthorized access, misuse, or threats.

The users accessing and defining this information have full control over the process and can change/adapt the monitoring patterns to implement the user-in-the-loop anomaly detection (steps 3 and 4 in Fig. 1).

4   Context-Aware Cybersecurity Threat Detection

We aim to enhance the accuracy and effectiveness of our existing anomaly detection tools. In this approach, we aim to leverage the rich context and information about normal and abnormal behavior that can be found at the application level of organizational systems. This approach, in fact, leverages the strengths of machines and humans, addressing the limitations of purely automated or manual approaches. We aim to incorporate rules-based methods and process mining techniques. The former are based on rules defined by analysts using organisational and ecosystem knowledge. Rules-based systems can tailor the anomaly detection procedure to the organisation's requirements. Process mining techniques can analyse event logs to identify patterns and deviations from expected workflows, aiding anomaly detection. In this way, they can identify hidden patterns and anomalies in organisational processes that may not be apparent through manual inspection. Compared to the more traditional anomaly detection approach presented in the previous section, context-aware anomaly detection can rely on application-level logs because context is provided by the humans working with the services and applications.

Log sources that this approach can leverage are application/service logs and audit logs, as well as database logs and audit logs. Network logs to understand the information flows and user interactions between services/components involved in a business process are a very useful source of information as well.

Logs on this level are less standardized than the log sources used for more traditional anomaly detection, since services and applications are often unique and in the professional context often custom-made and tailored to a specific business process of an organisation. Therefore, they also require more context-specific analysis and an increased effort from the employees of an organization to provide this context. Our experiments with real-world organisations show, however that legal and regulatory requirements (especially for organisations in Europe that need to follow NIS and GDPR), a more thorough analysis of business processes is required anyways to understand the dependencies and information flows of activities and business processes performed within their organisation, therefore a defined approach to achieve this including the ability to do real-time monitoring of threats is a welcome addition for those organisations rather than an additional burden.

In detail, our approach integrates three key elements (i) business processes models (e.g., Business Process Model and Notation (BPMN) representations of the process), (ii) low-level system-generated logs, (iii) security business rules and constraints. By combining these elements, we establish a process baseline that describes the expected process execution. Leveraging process mining and log analysis, we can identify deviations that may indicate potential cybersecurity threats. However, aligning BPMN diagrams with low-level logs is a significant challenge due to the intrinsic differences between high-level process models and the granular, technical nature of system logs. Common issues are related to granularity mismatch, semantic misalignments, and event correlation. BPMN models represent high-level, human-understandable process steps (e.g., "Receive Order"), while logs contain fine-grained, system-level events (e.g., API calls, database queries, system actions). As a result, a single BPMN activity may correspond to multiple log events, or some log events might not map directly to any BPMN activity. Correlating events is not a trivial task since, for example, logs might lack unique identifiers (like case IDs) to tie them to a specific process instance. To this purpose, it is not possible to rely solely on similarity or automated matching techniques, as BPMN models and logs frequently use different terminologies. In fact, while BPMN employs descriptive, business-oriented terms (e.g., "Verify Customer Identity"), logs typically use technical identifiers or codes (e.g., "Auth API call" or "Query Database X"), which may not explicitly reference the broader business context. To address these challenges, an initial, thorough analysis is required. This involves studying and aligning BPMN models and logs to establish a reliable mapping between them. As demonstrated in Sect. 6, this alignment process is crucial for ensuring accurate integration and analysis.

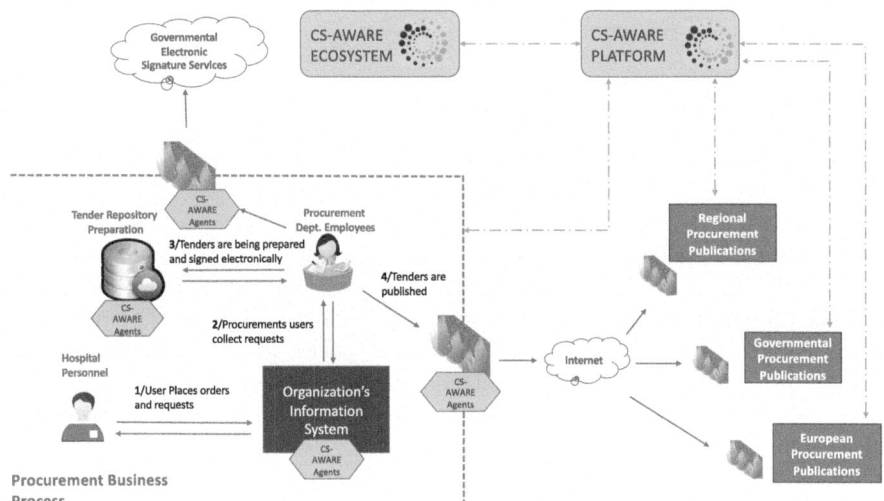

Fig. 2. Monitoring of Procurement Business Process.

5   An Example Use-Case The Procurement Process

The relevance and the potential impact of our approach are demonstrated with a realistic scenario within the context of healthcare ecosystems. Several cyber-incidents have been reported lately in the health sector [16]. The healthcare ecosystem comprises a plethora of components, such as all of its departments and clinics that provide services to patients, and all operational flows require dedicated access policies. Patient medical data (personally identifiable information) are stored and updated according to local, regional, national, and European regulations. We focus our analysis on the case of the procurement department flow of a Public Sector organization.

Figure 2 delineates a typical deployment of the business process of procurement flows within an EU's public sector institution. The procurement process itself constitutes a complex process since not only does it include the organization's infrastructure tangible and intangible good purchases but also specific procurements for citizens' services (i.e., healthcare facilities, municipalities, nursing homes, social care, and schools). It should be noted that in the case of healthcare and social care sectors, several interdisciplinary personnel and specialties collaborate apart from the common administrative staff within the operational flow of procurements. Furthermore, in various surgical operations that take place in healthcare institutions, the purchase of specific medical products is highly critical for the outcome because they should be specified and conducted according to the physical conditions of the individual patients. Moreover, hospital infrastructure procurements involve the participation of technical staff and biomedical engineers due to the complex nature of the facilities (e.g., power supply, O_2 and water supply, MRI scanners, etc.).

5.1 Organizational Requirements

The procurement process is supported by dedicated Information Systems. Authorized users verify the availability of a product or service and, if necessary, submit a procurement request. These requests are systematically classified and reviewed by specialized personnel of the procurement department. Preparing a tender is a time-consuming process, as it requires the cooperation of staff from the procurement, legal, and financial departments, specialized in every procurement case, apart from the definition of the specifications. Procurement staff manages this collaboration by centralizing tender preparation materials in a designated repository, enabling the content to be developed, refined, and finalized efficiently.

Once the tender is finalized, the designated procurement officer electronically signs it. Depending on the budget and relevant legal requirements, the signed tender is then uploaded to the appropriate regional, national, or European procurement platforms in compliance with National and EU regulations. After publication, suppliers can access the digital tender and submit their bids accordingly.

Figure 2 illustrates how the CS-AWARE platform monitors the procurement business process. The CS-AWARE agents gather organizational system and business process descriptions and low-level logs. These data are then stored in the platform's data lake, where they are analyzed to identify potential cybersecurity threats. Once threats or anomalies are detected, the findings can be shared within the CS-AWARE ecosystem.

The CS-AWARE ecosystem consists of organizations that adopt the platform's approach, enabling collaborative information sharing to enhance awareness of current and emerging threats or attacks. For instance, an organization can share analysis insights to alert others, particularly those in the same geographical area or with similar operational characteristics, about potential risks. This approach builds a shared defense mechanism, improving cybersecurity across the ecosystem.

6 Process Mining Analysis

The procurement process was thoroughly analyzed to identify and depict its transactions and actors. Moreover, the duration of every transaction was identified to produce the relevant timestamps. Internal and external actors were acknowledged as long as possible transactions are executed among them.

6.1 Available Logs

The analysis of the procurement process was conducted by examining and correlating logs collected from firewalls, access logs from data repositories, and database infrastructures. This approach also considered user behavior and their access patterns to these systems. Login and logout user logs were also analyzed. Full network traffic based on SPAN (Switched Port Analyzer) ports was not considered an option because it would lead to significant network traffic overhead, deteriorating the available throughput for the institution's daily operations while also demanding higher processing power. Within this context, analyzing syslog events and access logs required significantly less computational power and introduced negligible traffic overhead to the network infrastructure. Thus, it has been chosen as the prominent solution for an organization with a complex infrastructure and many employees who access it.

User access logs, shared data repository logs, and database access logs were designated to be used for the internal procurement transactions. In contrast, firewall syslogs were designated to be used for external procurement transactions. Events are logged in three separate file types, one per source.

Finally, all the logs were anonymized before the execution of any analysis due to GDPR compliance regulations and restrictions.

6.2 Experiments

Experiments have been performed to test the possibility of generating potential alerts when a business-level constraint is violated.

From Event Logs to Organizational Requirements. Integrating the three logs posed some specific challenges, as log data are not all relevant to the process, the number of significant events is a subset of the events, and users' data are anonymized. In addition, the logs are provided in plain text, and each requires a separate parsing function.

In the case study, specific users are controlled by the Domain Controller. Data from Active Directory (AD) include a security ID (SID) and users are to be anonymized (user1, user2, ...).

Specific PCs with the associated users communicate with the organization file server and have full access rights to the shared folder. Access data are derived from the fileserver log. Users SIDs are provided, file server IP, Computer-Names, Computers' IPs and domain names are anonymized.

Procurement users access certain external IPs. Data are derived from Firewall logs contain anonymized IPs for the internal network as they are related to users (networkxx). The external public websites involved in the process are available from the organization (although in the case study discussion, they are also anonymized to avoid leaking organization information - webserver1, webserver2, ...).

Data Preparation. An integrated log is created, joining the AD and fileserver logs over Security IDs and the resulting table with the firewall log using the anonymized version of the internal network address. This choice might create some spurious traces when the Security ID is renewed for a user and if the user connects from a different network address. In the specific case study, typical of administrative processes, users always connect from the same device with the same network address. Only one case of SID renewal has been recorded; therefore, the resulting integrated event log is suitable for the analysis.

The organization has provided anonymized user IDs of interest for the process, which can be used to analyze anomalies of the users involved in the process.

Log Analysis. In Table 1, we present the organizational constraints that have been specified, subdividing them into the following categories: Time constraints on users' activity, Potentially damaging actions, Linking activities to user sessions, Precedence constraints, Path condition.

Table 1. Process Constraints and Relevant Events

Process Constraints	Relevant Events
Time constraints on users activity: during the working hours 7-16pm from Monday to Friday access or activity outside this time-frame is considered malicious and should be tracked	Timestamps from syslogs
Potentially damaging actions: users can perform actions (maybe accidentally) where files or folders are deleted or moved This should be tracked	Access data from fileserver — syslogs Capture move & delete actions
Linking activities to user sessions: Activities should be performed during login sessions	Relevant logged events (according to given list)
Precedence constraint: Documents must be signed before uploading them to external web servers	External IP access and Delete event proxy for signature
Path condition: Only a given subset of the users are enabled to upload to webserver1	External IP access

A mapping from logs containing fine-grained events to business events needs to be performed, to be able to reconstruct activities at the business level. The choice has been to select some significant events for the process, called sentinel events, to recognize the start or termination of a given activity (see Table 1). In particular, from the fileserver logs, events accessing data objects are tracked, deletion requests are considered as proxies for the signature of files, as signed files are moved to a different folder. From the firewall logs, events accessing external web servers are considered. The relevant events are filtered from the integrated table to preserve information useful to join the files possibly provided by other events.

6.3   Results

The original log files for October 21–25 have been extracted from the datalake. They have a total size of 34,56 GB for 627 items, as the size of each single log file type has a maximum allowed size in the datalake.

The integrated event log contains 321,726 relevant events for 13 users.

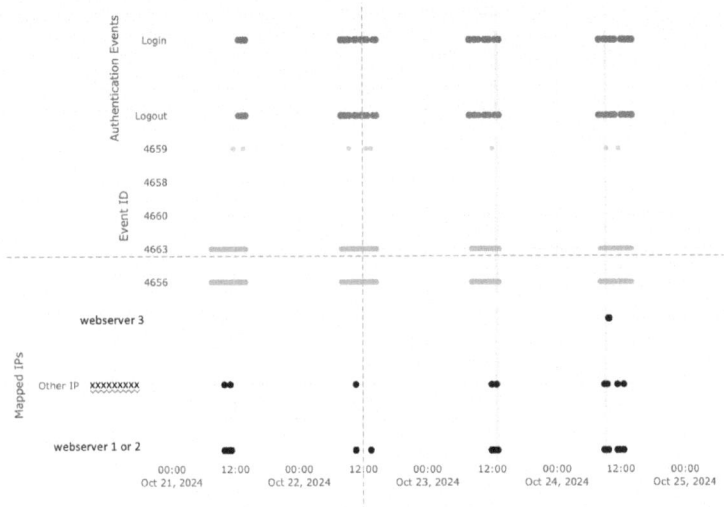

Fig. 3. Log analysis for a user

As a first point, we start the discussion of the results by identifying a session. As it can be seen from the log representation in Fig. 3, which represents a typical log for a user, it is clear that login and logout events are not only associated with the user sessions but are also associated with access requests to files, which require authentication. As a result, most of the "sessions", i.e., intervals between a login and a logout event, are very short (under 1 min) and the longest session identified in a week was 40 min long. As it was not possible to distinguish those different types of accesses, we decided that sequences of login/logout events are a manifestation of user activity, therefore we identify a session as a sequence of login/logout events with small time differences. Once this assumption is made, the following main anomalies can occur:

– login/logout activities outside working hours. After investigation, this problem can also be related to users not logging out from the system and continuing to work from home. This anomaly can occur either with other types of events being performed or without any event occurring
– activities outside sessions
– accesses to anomalous webservers: while a list of allowed webservers was provided, other accesses were also identified and considered anomalous.

A summary of the results of the analysis is presented in Table 2. For each performed analysis, whenever possible, we propose one or two rules that can be checked on the integrated log to send alerts on possible anomalies.

Table 2. Analysis and Proposed Rules

Performed Analysis	Results	Proposed Rules
Activity profiling by user	Anomalies: - sessions left open - AD w and w/o filesrv activities in the night	Rule 1: Time constraint for login/logouts outside 7-16 with other activities Rule 2: Time constraint for login/logouts outside 7-16 without other activities
Analysis of delete and prepare to delete events	Rare events, also at night Link to doc signature seems weak	Rule 3: Time constraint for delete events outside 7-16
Sessions identification	Sessions cannot be identified, mostly clusters of login/logout events. In many cases, activities do not correspond to login/logouts.	Rule 4: Session identification: start end of groups of events. Signal activities outside sessions.
Precedence constraint	Delete events rarely precede the upload of documents to an external website.	Rule 5: Missing delete event(s) within 24 hrs before external upload.
Access to external IPs depending on user	webserver1 cannot be distinguished from webserver2 (same IP).	No rule.

The integrated log was also analyzed with Apromore[2], a state-of-the-art process mining tool, which can provide a reconstruction of the business process, as shown in Fig. 4. The process diagram helps identify, beyond the above-mentioned anomalies, other possible critical issues in the process. In particular, the main problem in this case is the access to a web server that was not indicated for the

---

[2] https://academic-cloud.apromore.org/.

process. In addition, the number of instances of the event "Handle to an object requested" is greater than Logons and Logoffs, and could be an anomaly if the user was not already logged on just before the start of the log.

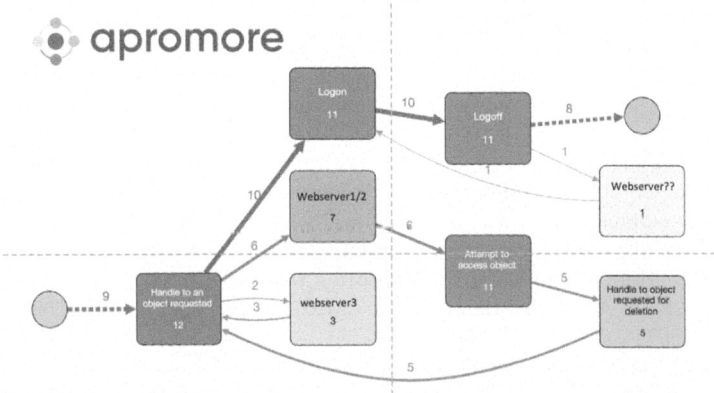

Fig. 4. Business process analysis with Apromore for one user

7   Concluding Remarks and Outlook

In this paper, we presented an approach to cybersecurity threat detection conducted from a business process perspective. In fact, unlike traditional methods that focus exclusively on technical-level anomaly detection, our framework integrates insights from the business and operational levels of an organization. A key strength of our approach lies in its adaptability to user-defined policies and requirements, ensuring that detected anomalies are both relevant and actionable within the organizational context.

Through application to a real-world business process in the healthcare context, we demonstrated the framework's effectiveness in detecting irregular activities that could compromise system integrity.

Future work will focus on expanding the framework's capabilities, scaling to handle large and diverse log datasets, and integrating advanced process mining techniques to improve detection accuracy.

Acknowledgments. Funded by the European Union (Grant Agreement No 101069543). Views and opinions expressed are however those of the author(s) only and do not necessarily reflect those of the European Union or the European Commission. Neither the European Union nor the granting authority can be held responsible for them. The authors thank Claudio Di Salvo for his support in the experimental part.

References

1. Aalst, W.M., Medeiros, A.K.A.: Process mining and security: detecting anomalous process executions and checking process conformance. Electron. Notes Theor. Comput. Sci. **121**, 3–21 (2005)
2. Alizadeh, M., Lu, X., Fahland, D., Zannone, N., Aalst, W.M.: Linking data and process perspectives for conformance analysis. Comput. Secur. **73**, 172–193 (2018)
3. Andriessen, J., Schaberreiter, T., Papanikolaou, A., Röning, J. (eds.): Cybersecurity Awareness, Advances in Information Security, vol. 88. Springer, Cham (2022). https://doi.org/10.1007/978-3-031-04227-0, https://link.springer.com/10.1007/978-3-031-04227-0
4. Cappiello, C., et al.: Human-in-the-loop anomaly detection and contextual intelligence for enhancing cybersecurity management. In: Natural Language Processing and Artificial Intelligence for Cyber Security (NLPAICS 2024) (2024)
5. Cho, S.Y., Happa, J., Creese, S.: Capturing tacit knowledge in security operation centers. IEEE Access **8**, 42021–42041 (2020). https://doi.org/10.1109/ACCESS.2020.2976076
6. European Commission: Regulation of the European Parliament and of the Council of 27 April 2016 on the protection of natural persons with regard to the processing of personal data and on the free movement of such data, and repealing Directive 95/46/EC (General Data Protection Regulation). Regulation (EU) 2016/679, April 2016
7. European Commission: The EU's Cybersecurity Strategy for the Digital Decade. Joint Communication to the European Parliament and the Council - JOIN(2020) 18 final (2020)
8. Granadillo, G., González-Zarzosa, S., Diaz, R.: Security information and event management (SIEM): analysis, trends, and usage in critical infrastructures. Sensors **21**, 4759 (2021). https://doi.org/10.3390/s21144759
9. ISO/IEC 27000:2016: Information technology – security techniques — information security management systems – overview and vocabulary. Tech. rep., ISO/IEC (2016)
10. Jasimuddin, S.M., Saci, F.: Creating a culture to avoid knowledge hiding within an organization: The role of management support. Front. Psychol. **13** (2022). https://doi.org/10.3389/fpsyg.2022.850989, https://www.frontiersin.org/journals/psychology/articles/10.3389/fpsyg.2022.850989
11. Kiran, M., Murphy, P., Monga, I., Dugan, J., Baveja, S.S.: Lambda architecture for cost-effective batch and speed big data processing. In: 2015 IEEE International Conference on Big Data (Big Data), pp. 2785–2792 (2015). https://doi.org/10.1109/BigData.2015.7364082
12. Kupfersberger, V., Schaberreiter, T., Wills, C., Quirchmayr, G., Röning, J.: Applying soft systems methodology to complex problem situations in critical infrastructures: the cs-aware case study. Int. J. Adv. Secur. **11**, 191–200 (2018), http://eprints.cs.univie.ac.at/5904/
13. Landauer, M., Skopik, F., Wurzenberger, M., Rauber, A.: System log clustering approaches for cyber security applications: a survey. Comput. Secur. **92**, 101739 (2020)
14. Leevy, J.L., Hancock, J.T., Zuech, R., Khoshgoftaar, T.M.: Detecting cybersecurity attacks across different network features and learners. J. Big Data **8**(1), 1–29 (2021)

15. Luidold, C., et al.: Increasing cybersecurity awareness and collaboration in organisations and local/regional networks: The CS-AWARE-NEXT project. In: Sustainable, Secure, and Smart Collaboration (S3C) Workshop 2023 (2023), http://CEUR-WS.org/Vol-3574/paper_5.pdf

16. McGlave, C., Neprash, H., Nikpay, S.: Hacked to pieces? the effects of ransomware attacks on hospitals and patients (2024), http://dx.doi.org/10.2139/ssrn.4579292

17. Melaku, H.M.: A dynamic and adaptive cybersecurity governance framework. J. Cybersecur. Priv. 3(3), 327–350 (2023)

18. National institute of standards and technology: the NIST cybersecurity framework (CSF) 2.0. cybersecurity white paper (CSWP) 29, February 2024, https://doi.org/10.6028/NIST.CSWP.29

19. Ozawa, S., Ban, T., Hashimoto, N., Nakazato, J., Shimamura, J.: A study of iot malware activities using association rule learning for darknet sensor data. Int. J. Inf Sec. 10(1), 83–92 (2020)

20. Sarker, I.H.: Cyberlearning: effectiveness analysis of machine learning security modeling to detect cyber-anomalies and multi-attacks. Internet Things 14, 100393 (2021)

21. Securities, A., Comission, I.: Spotlight on cyber: Findings and insights from the cyber pulse survey 2023. Report 776, November 2023

22. Shukla, S., Parada, J.I., Pearlson, K.: Trusting the needle in the haystack: cybersecurity management of ai/ml systems. In: Arai, K. (ed.) Advances in Information and Communication, pp. 441–455. Springer (2022)

23. The European Parliament and the Council of the European Union: Directive (EU) 2022/2555 of the European Parliament and of the Council of 14 December 2022. Official Journal of the European Union L333/80 (2022)

24. Vu, Q.H., Ruta, D., Cen, L.: Gradient boosting decision trees for cyber security threats detection based on network events logs. In: Baru, C.K., et al. (eds.) 2019 IEEE International Conference on Big Data (IEEE BigData), Los Angeles, CA, USA, 9–12 December 2019, pp. 5921–5928. IEEE (2019). https://doi.org/10.1109/BIGDATA47090.2019.9006061

Interpretable and Trustworthy Attack Diagnosis for UAVs Using SafeML

Isadora G. Ferrão[1]([✉])(iD), David Espes[1], Catherine Dezan[1],
Roberto G. Pacheco[2], André Luiz de Oliveira[3], Ana Quaresma[4],
and Kalinka Castelo Branco[4]

[1] Université de Bretagne Occidentale, Brest, France
isadoraferrao@usp.br
[2] Universidade Federal Fluminense, Rio de Janeiro, Brazil
[3] Universidade Federal de Juiz de Fora, Juiz de Fora, Minas Gerais, Brazil
[4] University of São Paulo, São Carlos, Brazil

Abstract. Unmanned Aerial Vehicles (UAVs) are increasingly employed in critical applications such as public safety, logistics, and infrastructure monitoring. As their autonomy grows through Machine Learning (ML) model integration, new challenges emerge related to security, reliability, and model interpretability. Cyberattacks such as GPS spoofing and jamming can compromise UAV navigation systems, while ML models often operate as opaque black boxes, limiting operator trust in high-stakes environments. This paper proposes a diagnostic framework based on the SafeML technique to enhance the trustworthiness of ML-driven UAVs. SafeML applies statistical monitoring using the Empirical Cumulative Distribution Function (ECDF) and Wasserstein Distance to detect Out-Of-Distribution (OOD) data and quantify prediction reliability at runtime. The study evaluates multiple ML models, including Random Forest (RF), LightGBM, and XGBoost, on a UAV dataset featuring real-world GPS spoofing and jamming scenarios. Experimental results show that the best models achieve accuracies above 98%, with SafeML effectively identifying low-confidence predictions that correlate with classification errors.

Keywords: UAV Security · SafeML · Runtime Monitoring · GPS Spoofing · Jamming · Trustworthy AI

1 Introduction

Unmanned Aerial Vehicles (UAVs), also known as drones, have been widely used in critical applications such as public safety, environmental monitoring, supply delivery, and infrastructure inspections [1]. Their ability to operate autonomously in dynamic environments makes them sophisticated tools in potentially dangerous scenarios. However, this increasing autonomy introduces new operational and cyber risks that directly challenge these systems' safety, reliability, and acceptability in real environments [2]

P. Katsaros (Ed.): IMBSA 2025, LNCS 15755, pp. 108–123, 2026.
https://doi.org/10.1007/978-3-032-05073-1_8

With the advancement of Artificial Intelligence (AI) techniques, particularly ML models, UAVs have gained greater capability in navigation, obstacle detection, risk analysis, and real-time decision-making. However, despite their benefits, ML-based systems face important structural challenges, where highly accurate models often lack interpretability and are perceived as black boxes, limiting human operators' trust, especially in critical contexts where quick decisions are required [3]. In addition, these systems are sensitive to changes in the data domain. Concept drift situations or changes in input data distribution (out-of-distribution) can induce unexpected failures in classifiers, seriously compromising mission safety.

Targeted cyberattacks, such as GPS spoofing, denial of service (DoS), or manipulation of planned trajectories, further aggravate this vulnerability [5]. Although classical security techniques (encryption, authentication, IDS) offer point defenses, they do not guarantee continuous assessment of the reliability of ML algorithms during runtime. It is in this context that the emerging field of SafeAI, and more specifically, the SafeML technique [4], is situated, a statistical approach that monitors the distance between data distributions using measures based on the ECDF, to diagnose potential logical failures in ML models during runtime.

Given the gaps identified in the literature, such as the absence of solutions that combine safety, statistical confidence monitoring, and interpretability in UAVs, this study proposes developing and validating an embedded diagnostic system based on SafeML [4]. The system aims to provide an additional layer of security, continuously monitoring the AI classifiers used in UAVs under adverse operational scenarios, emphasizing detecting anomalous behaviors induced by cyberattacks.

Thus, the central objective of this study is to systematically and empirically evaluate SafeML's effectiveness in improving the reliability and interpretability of autonomous security systems in UAVs.

This paper is organized as follows. Section 2 presents a discussion on related works. Section 3 introduces the proposed methodology, built upon SafeML, to support safety and security evaluation of unmanned aerial vehicles. Section 4 illustrates the results of applying our methodology for evaluating the effectiveness of machine learning classifiers in supporting attack detection. Section 5 presents a discussion on the results and sketches future work.

2 Related Works

Studies indicate that UAVs are vulnerable targets for cyberattacks that exploit these vehicles' dependence on wireless communications and embedded sensors [5]. Attacks such as GPS spoofing [6], which deceive the UAV's navigation receivers by simulating legitimate signals, have been documented as the cause of critical trajectory deviations. Although ML-based approaches have been proposed to detect these anomalous patterns, such as pseudo-range and SNR analysis, these solutions generally lack validation in realistic and robust operational scenarios.

Furthermore, denial-of-service (DoS) attacks and the injection of malicious commands into the planned trajectory represent substantial risks [5]. Although some studies report detection rates above 99% using supervised models, these numbers often result from testing on simulated and highly controlled datasets, compromising their generalization. There is also a recurring challenge in differentiating between legitimate technical failures and deliberate attacks, especially in contexts where action must be immediate.

Approaches based on deep reinforcement learning (DRL) have gained attention for their adaptability in dynamic environments. However, the use of DRL in security contexts still presents serious obstacles [7]. The main limitation lies in the difficulty of interpreting the learned policies, a particularly critical problem when the UAV operates in urban environments, where mistaken decisions can cause material damage and loss of human life. In addition, DRL still faces risks associated with adversariality, data privacy, and overfitting to specific training scenarios.

The lack of explainability in AI models embedded in UAVs is also widely recognized as a barrier to operational adoption [8]. Although accurate, models such as deep neural networks are often treated as "black boxes," which compromises the trust of human operators. These models' performance heavily depends on the representativeness of the training data. When confronted with unseen or out-of-distribution data, the risk of failure increases.

In response to these limitations, recent research has explored approaches combining security and interpretability [9]. Models that integrate federated learning, secure computation, and differential privacy have shown promising results in intrusion detection. Methods based on autoencoders and unknown input observers (UIOs) have effectively detected anomalies and trajectory attacks. However, such approaches still lack mechanisms that quantify the confidence in the model's decisions and communicate uncertainties in a way that is understandable to the operator.

In this context, the SafeML technique stands out as an alternative [4]. Based on statistical distance measures, primarily through the ECDF, SafeML can detect variations in the input data distribution during system execution. This capability allows continuous monitoring of ML classifiers' performance and the generation of early warnings about possible logical failures. Despite its proven results in areas such as autonomous vehicles and robotics, the application of SafeML in UAVs, especially in attack scenarios, remains little explored.

This chapter thus presents gaps in: (i) the scarcity of security approaches that integrate attack detection with statistical reliability analysis; (ii) the absence of interpretable real-time mechanisms applicable to UAVs operating under processing constraints; and (iii) the lack of empirical studies that evaluate the impact of different statistical thresholds on the performance of embedded detection systems. In this sense, this study seeks to fill these gaps by systematically investigating the use of SafeML to reinforce the reliability and explainability of AI systems embedded in UAVs under attack conditions.

3   Methodology

Ensuring security in UAVs is a crucial concern, especially with the advancement of sophisticated cyberattacks targeting navigation and control systems. This study proposes a methodological framework for the development and validation of a diagnostic system capable of detecting cyberattacks, specifically GPS spoofing and jamming. It uses ML models combined with the SafeML technique to assess the reliability of real-time predictions.

3.1   Definition of Attack Scenarios

In this work, GPS spoofing and jamming attacks were selected due to their prevalence in the literature and their direct impact on UAV navigation and control systems [5]. In particular, GPS spoofing consists of transmitting falsified GNSS signals to deceive the receiver, causing it to compute incorrect positions, velocities, and times. This attack can divert UAVs from their planned routes, lead them into restricted areas, or cause collisions, especially in formation operations or dense urban environments. Studies have shown that spoofing attacks can increase positioning errors by up to 20 m, drastically compromising navigation accuracy.

Similarly, GPS jamming involves emission interference signals that overwhelm the receiver, preventing it from capturing legitimate satellite signals. This results in the total or partial loss of GPS-based navigation capability, which can lead to mission interruption. Research indicates that jamming can reduce UAV mission completion rates by up to 40%, highlighting its severity.

The choice of these attack scenarios is justified by the need to develop and test more effective detection and mitigation mechanisms. Despite advances in techniques such as ML to identify interference, challenges remain, such as real-time detection and adaptation to different operational environments. Additionally, the integration of alternative navigation systems, such as inertial navigation units (INS) and visual odometry, has shown promise in reducing the impacts of these attacks, but further research is needed for optimization and practical implementation.

Therefore, by simulating and analyzing GPS spoofing and jamming attacks, we aim to contribute to the development of more resilient and secure UAVs, capable of operating reliably even in hostile environments or under deliberate interference attempts.

3.2   Description and Justification of the Data

In this study, we employed a dataset specialized in cyberattacks on UAVs [10], collected under controlled experimental conditions, to realistically represent the threat vectors that these systems face in operation. The dataset includes three main classes: benign flight conditions, GPS spoofing attacks, and jamming/interference attacks. The dataset's structure was designed to capture representative communication signals, control parameters, and system states.

The dataset includes detailed attributes such as:

- RF signals between the UAV and the control station (frequency, bandwidth, amplitude, modulation);
- Control and command data (speed, altitude, direction);
- Embedded sensor data (IMU, raw GPS, barometer);
- Onboard images and timestamp metadata.

This richness of information is essential to capture the subtleties between normal and anomalous operations. The presence of different domains of information (spatial, temporal, spectral) makes the dataset particularly suitable for training classification models sensitive to non-trivial behaviors.

The data was generated using specific instrumentation: for spoofing, the Keysight EXG N5172B signal generator was used in combination with a HackRF transmitter from Great Scott Gadgets, programmed via the GPS-SDR-SIM tool, injecting falsified GNSS signals with coordinates of a point in Shanghai (30.286502, 120.032669). The jamming attack was simulated by transmitting white Gaussian noise using the same HackRF, with an amplitude of 0.3 and gain of −48 dB.

The dataset comprises 6,078 samples of benign flights, 498 samples of GPS spoofing, and 1,460 samples of active interference, representing a balanced spectrum between safe and malicious operations.

3.3 Data Preprocessing and Balancing

Data preprocessing consisted of a sequence of essential steps to ensure the dataset's integrity, quality, and representativeness. Initially, raw data underwent exploratory inspection to identify and remove duplicate, inconsistent records or entries with missing values in critical attributes such as GPS signal, frequency, control commands, and inertial measurements. Missing values were handled using linear interpolation for continuous temporal data or class-based statistical imputation for categorical attributes.

Next, normalization was applied to continuous data using Min-Max scaling [0, 1]. This step is particularly relevant for distance-based algorithms and improves convergence in gradient-based models. Normalization also ensures that attributes with naturally distinct magnitudes, such as signal amplitude and altitude, do not dominate the learning process.

A strong imbalance was observed regarding class distribution, with most samples corresponding to benign flights (6,078), while spoofing and jamming were underrepresented (498 and 1,460 samples, respectively). Such imbalance could compromise the models' ability to correctly identify malicious events, leading to predictive bias toward the majority class and high false negative rates, which are unacceptable in security contexts.

To mitigate this problem, the SMOTE (Synthetic Minority Over-sampling Technique) [11] method was used, which synthesizes new minority instances by interpolating feature vectors between nearest neighbors. Unlike simple oversampling techniques, SMOTE reduces the risk of overfitting by creating varied synthetic examples rather than replicating existing samples. This technique was applied separately to the spoofing and jamming classes to balance the proportions among the three classes and ensure the model learns discriminative representations for each one.

After cross-validation, this balancing was validated through confusion matrix analysis, ensuring the trained model maintained adequate sensitivity to the minority classes. As a result, the balanced dataset became more appropriate for classifier development.

3.4   Choice of ML Models

We selected five models due to their distinct characteristics:

- **SVM:** effective in nonlinear decision boundaries and resistant to overfitting;
- **Random Forest:** versatile, interpretable, and noise-resistant;
- **Gradient Boosting:** excellent at capturing complex relationships;
- **XGBoost and LightGBM:** optimized boosting techniques with high performance and efficiency;

The selection was guided by experiences reported in the cyber-physical systems security literature [4].

3.5   Evaluation Metrics

We selected metrics that cover not only accuracy but also operational utility:

- **Precision and Recall:** indicate sensitivity and selectivity.
- **F1-score:** balances precision and recall, which is crucial in imbalanced classes.
- **Execution Time:** essential for embedded applications.
- **Confusion Matrix:** evaluates performance by class.

3.6   Training and Validation

A rigorous approach was adopted for the training stage to ensure model generalization and avoid partitioning bias. The initial dataset split was done in a stratified manner, maintaining class proportions in both training and testing partitions. A 70% split was chosen for training and 30% for testing, allowing the model to learn patterns with a sufficient amount of data while reserving a representative sample for final performance evaluation.

During the modeling process, 10-fold cross-validation was applied, a well-established practice in the literature to reduce variance and ensure that the model is evaluated across different subsets of the data. This method divides the training set into 10 subsets (folds), using nine to train the model and the tenth for validation. The process is repeated until each fold has been used as the validation set exactly once, and the results are aggregated to obtain more reliable performance estimates.

The grid search algorithm was used to find optimal hyperparameters, exploring combinations of parameters such as maximum tree depth, learning rate, number of estimators, splitting criteria for tree-based algorithms, and penalties and kernels for SVM. Given the imbalanced nature of the classes and the importance of balancing precision and recall, the objective function for the search was the maximization of the F1 Score.

Training and validation were performed on the Google Colab platform, which provides GPU-based computational infrastructure (NVIDIA Tesla T4). This enabled experiment parallelization and reduced training time, which is especially relevant for more complex models such as XGBoost and LightGBM. Furthermore, integration with libraries such as Scikit-learn, XGBoost, and Light-GBM enabled consistent reproduction of experiments with complete control over parameters.

This stage provided tuned and validated models ready for integration with the SafeML-based reliability monitoring mechanism.

3.7   Implementation of SafeML

The SafeML technique was implemented to monitor the reliability of classifier predictions during the operational phase by measuring statistical distances between the data used in training and the data observed during runtime. This approach is especially useful for identifying OOD scenarios where model accuracy may degrade.

The SafeML implementation process was divided into two main phases: *offline training* and *online application*.

Training Phase. During the training phase, the model was trained using 70% of the dataset, as previously described. After training, statistical parameters of the empirical distributions of the input variables were extracted by class, including the mean (μ_i), variance (σ_i^2), and the ECDF, denoted by $F_1(x)$. These elements are fundamental for calculating statistical distance during application.

Additionally, probability density functions (PDFs) were constructed per class based on the input data sampling. These parameters serve as a reference baseline for detecting significant deviations at runtime.

Application Phase. In the application phase, the system receives unlabeled data in real time. Input variables are collected in a sliding window (*sample buffer*). From these samples, operational ECDFs $F_2(x)$ are estimated and statistical parameters equivalent to those obtained in the training phase.

Prediction reliability is then estimated using the Wasserstein Distance (WD), which quantifies the difference between $F_1(x)$ and $F_2(x)$, as defined by the equation:

$$WD = \int_{-\infty}^{+\infty} |F_1(x) - F_2(x)| dx \tag{1}$$

If the observed distance is below a predefined threshold (in this study, values ≤ 0.5 were considered acceptable), the system assumes a high degree of reliability in the predictions. Higher distances are interpreted as indicators of OOD scenarios and potential classification errors.

Additionally, the Chernoff Error Bound was applied to estimate the probability of error under the operational distributions, given by:

$$P(error) = P(C_1)^\lambda P(C_2)^{1-\lambda} \cdot \int_{-\infty}^{+\infty} \left[P(x|C_1)^\lambda P(x|C_2)^{1-\lambda} \right] dx \tag{2}$$

where:

- $P(C_1)$, $P(C_2)$: prior probabilities of the classes;
- $P(x|C_i)$: conditional probability distribution for class C_i;
- $\lambda \in [0, 1]$: weighting parameter between the distributions.

The Chernoff Bound provides a theoretical upper limit for the probability of error, serving as an indicator of the risk of incorrect decisions. Low values of WD and error probability indicate high prediction reliability; higher values suggest a need for intervention or model revalidation.

Thus, the integration of SafeML enables monitoring the model's behavior and quantifying the confidence level associated with each prediction, contributing to the operational safety of UAVs in adverse environments.

3.8   SafeML Threshold Evaluation

The proper selection of the threshold for interpreting the statistical distances calculated by SafeML is critical to the approach's success. Low values may lead to excessive false positives, frequently flagging benign scenarios as suspicious, compromising system usability. On the other hand, very high thresholds reduce sensitivity, hindering the early detection of anomalous behaviors that subtly diverge from training data.

In this study, we conducted a systematic analysis of three distinct thresholds applied to the WD value: 0.3 (high sensitivity), 0.5 (moderate), and 0.7 (tolerant). Each threshold was evaluated in terms of its ability to correctly identify OOD data and maintain the false alarm rate within acceptable operational limits. For this, we observed the proportion of samples flagged as "low reliability" versus the actual accuracy of the classifier on those samples.

3.9   Ensemble Learning

As a complementary test, we conducted an evaluation based on ensemble learning techniques to verify whether the combination of distinct classifiers could increase the robustness and reliability of the attack detection system. This approach is particularly relevant in critical domains such as UAV security, where incorrect decisions can compromise mission integrity.

The best-performing individual models were selected, and their predictions were combined using the majority voting technique. In this scheme, the class predicted by at least two models is taken as the final prediction. This strategy seeks to reduce variance between models and compensate for potential individual errors through consensus among the algorithms.

3.10   Integrated Analysis of Results

The predictions were analyzed with an overlay of SafeML indices. Cases with low reliability were correlated with classification errors, allowing for an interpretable diagnosis of model limitations. Such integration is essential for real-time security applications.

4   Results

The diagnostic system for attack detection in this study achieved the following accuracies: GB with 78.14%, DT with 92.52%, MLP with 92.57%, SVM with 95.72%, XGBoost with 97.91%, Logistic Regression (LR) and LightGBM with 98.08%, and RF with the highest accuracy of 98.15%.

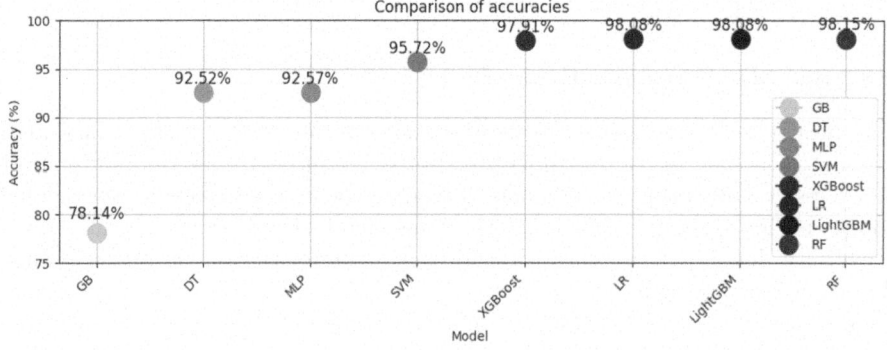

Fig. 1. Comparison of accuracies - attacks

As observed, models like GB, DT, and MLP achieved lower accuracies ranging from 78.14% to 92.57%, indicating inferior capabilities in capturing attack patterns in the data compared to more modern models such as XGBoost, LR, Light-GBM, and RF, which demonstrated superior accuracies ranging from 97.91% to

98.15%. These results can be justified by their inherent ways of handling data, for instance, tree-based models like XGBoost, LR, LightGBM, and RF are known for their ability to model non-linear relationships. These models mitigate overfitting and enhance performance on new datasets by utilizing ensemble learning methods, as seen in XGBoost and RF, which aggregate predictions from multiple decision trees. Meanwhile, LR benefits from regularization techniques to control model complexity, maintain generalization capability, and avoid overfitting (Fig. 1).

When comparing accuracy performance with processing time, it can be observed that models like MLP and SVM, despite achieving quick classification times of 0.96 s and 0.97 s, respectively, showed more moderate accuracies ranging from 78.14% to 92.57%. These results may be attributed to how they handle data complexity. For instance, MLP, a feedforward neural network with hidden layers, may not efficiently capture non-linear relationships in flight data.

Models like LR and LightGBM, which demonstrated high accuracies between 97.91% and 98.15%, had longer classification times of 3.13 s and 3.42 s, respectively. These models employ more sophisticated approaches to modeling, such as the case of LR, which controls overfitting and allows for greater generalization, and GB with fast decision trees, in the case of LightGBM, enabling adaptation to non-linear patterns in the data. However, this results in increased classification time, possibly due to the need for additional processing to compute predictions weighted across multiple boosting iterations.

Table 1 presents the results obtained from performance metrics, where each model was evaluated based on precision, F1-score, and recall. As observed, models such as SVM, MLP, DT, RF, XGBoost, and LightGBM demonstrated high precision values, with SVM achieving 0.94, MLP 0.91, LR and RF 0.98, and XGBoost and LightGBM 0.98. Models like LR, RF, XGBoost, and LightGBM achieved the highest precision and, consequently, a greater ability to minimize false positives.

Table 1. Comparison of performance metrics - attacks

Model	Precision	F1-score	Recall
SVM	0.94	0.95	0.95
MLP	0.91	0.91	0.94
LR	0.98	0.98	0.99
DT	0.93	0.97	0.97
RF	0.98	0.98	0.98
GB	0.78	0.81	0.79
XGBoost	0.98	0.98	0.99
LightGBM	0.98	0.98	0.99

Regarding the F1-score, LR, RF, XGBoost, and LightGBM also showed superior results above 0.98. On the other hand, GB exhibited lower performance with an F1-score of 0.81. Regarding recall, LR, RF, XGBoost, and LightGBM again stood out with values of 0.99, indicating that these models could capture the majority of attack instances, thereby minimizing false negatives.

4.1   SafeML

Table 2 presents the results of applying SafeML to the models, underlining their accuracies across different phases: normal training, SafeML-influenced training, SafeML application, and the final confidence level assigned by SafeML. Initially, we observe that the classifiers' accuracy during normal training varies considerably, ranging from 78.14% to 98.15%. In the SafeML application phase, where models are tested with unlabeled data, a slight decrease in accuracy compared to normal training is noted, as expected. However, it is important to note that the accuracy values remain acceptable, ranging between 77.15% and 98.02%.

Table 2. SafeML - Security

Classifier	Normal Train (%)	SafeML Application (%)	Trusted Level (%)
SVM	95.72	94.32%	91.72%
MLP	92.57	91.49%	89.97%
LR	98.08	98.02%	97.10%
DT	92.52	90.52%	87.04%
RF	98.15	98.10%	97.32%
GB	78.14	77.15%	74.30%
XG	97.91	96.78%	95.53%
L. GBM	98.08	97.25%	96.80%

In the Trusted Level assigned by SafeML, the models have Trusted Levels assigned by SafeML ranging from 74.30% to 96.80%. Models like GB and DT exhibit the lowest Trusted Levels, with 74.30% and 87.04%, respectively. This suggests that, despite achieving reasonable accuracies during training and application with SafeML, these models may present more significant uncertainty in their reliability. On the other hand, models such as LR, RF, XGBoost, and LightGBM achieved higher Trusted Levels, ranging from 94.09% to 96.80%.

Comparison of SafeML Thresholds. Table 3 presents a comparative analysis of the sensitivity of the confidence thresholds used in the application of SafeML. We evaluated the impact of choosing thresholds 0.3, 0.5, and 0.7 on

Table 3. Impact of thresholds on SafeML performance

Threshold	OOD Detection	False Positives	Average F1-score
0.3	95.4%	21.6%	0.88
0.5	90.1%	8.2%	0.95
0.7	71.5%	3.4%	0.89

three metrics: OOD scenario detection rate, false positive rate, and the system's average F1-score. As observed, the threshold of 0.5 offers the best balance between performance and operational reliability.

This result reinforces the choice of threshold 0.5 as the most stable default value for critical environments such as UAVs, where it is necessary to balance anomaly sensitivity and confidence in normal operations.

4.2 Ensemble Learning

As previously discussed, our system did not achieve maximum accuracy with any single model. Therefore, we focused on individually analyzing the diagnostic results of the three top-performing models: RF, LR, and LightGBM. These models were selected based on their superior individual performance metrics, including accuracy, precision, recall, and F1-score. Specifically, RF and Light-GBM exhibited excellent capabilities in capturing complex non-linear relationships in the data through ensemble and boosting techniques. Meanwhile, LR was chosen due to its simplicity, computational efficiency, and strong performance, providing a complementary linear perspective that enhances overall diagnostic robustness when combined with other models.

Unlike the safety system, where more accurate models showed a clear trend of better diagnosis among different failures, we did not observe a distinct accuracy differentiation among these models in detecting attacks, as seen in Fig. 2. The lack of differentiation may be justified by the fact that we are considering only

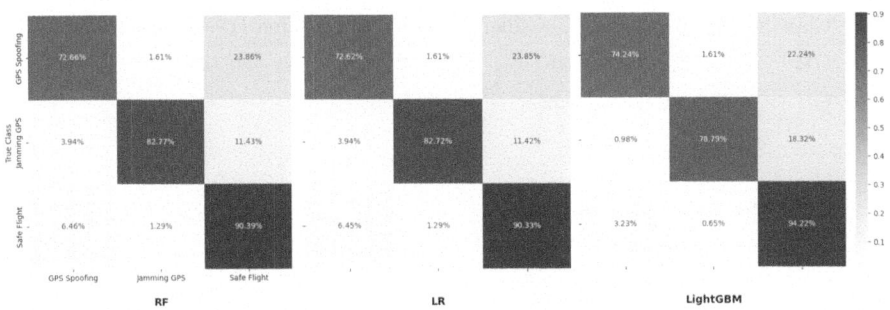

Fig. 2. Confusion matrices for UAV attack detection using RF, LR, and LightGBM models

three classes of attacks (GPS spoofing, jamming, and safe flights) compared to the fault system, which covers eight distinct classes. The analysis revealed that, although subtle, there are differences between the RF and LR models compared to LightGBM, particularly in the GPS Spoofing and safe flight classes.

Table 4 presents the ensemble learning results of the classifiers with the highest accuracy. The combination of LR and RF achieved an accuracy of 98.08% in both training and application, resulting in a Final Trusted Level of 97.28%. Furthermore, the combination of LightGBM and RF demonstrated a training accuracy of 98.08%, with an application of 97.70% and a Final Trusted Level of 97.03%.

Table 4. Security Ensemble with RF - High Accuracy

Classifier	Accuracy train	Classifier	Accuracy application	Trusted level final
LR	98.08%	RF	98.08%	97.28%
L.GBM	98.08%	RF	97.70%	97.03%

To explore the potential for improvement even in classifiers with lower accuracy, we also performed a combination involving the GB classifier, presenting the weakest results, as it's possible to see in Table VIII. The combination of GB and RF resulted in a training accuracy of 78.14% and an application accuracy of 87.58%, raising the Final Trusted Level to 85.14%. Similarly, by combining GB with LR, we achieved an application accuracy of 88.08% and a Final Trusted Level of 86.84%. These results demonstrate that ensemble learning can improve confidence and accuracy in fault detection in critical systems, even for classifiers with lower performance (Table 5).Please check and confirm if the inserted citations of Fig. 1 and Table 5 are correct. If not, please suggest an alternate citations.

Table 5. Security Ensemble with GB - Low Accuracy

Classifier	Accuracy train	Classifier	Accuracy application	Trusted level final
GB	78.14%	RF	87.58%	85.14%
GB	78.14%	LR	88.08%	86.84%

During the tests with SafeML, we observed that samples with higher WD (WD > 0.5) frequently coincided with classification errors, especially in spoofing cases with smooth transitions or hybrid signals. In one of the analyzed examples, the RF classifier incorrectly classified a spoofing case as benign. SafeML, however, indicated a confidence level of only 62%, correctly signaling the risk of error.

5   Discussions and Future Works

This section addresses the research questions that guided the development of this study.

RQ1: How well do ML models classify spoofing and jamming attacks in UAVs? The experimental results demonstrate that ML classifiers can effectively distinguish between benign UAV operations and malicious events such as GPS spoofing and jamming. Among the models tested, RF, LR, XGBoost, and LightGBM achieved accuracies above 97.9%, with RF reaching the highest accuracy at 98.15%. Precision, recall, and F1-score metrics confirmed these results, indicating high sensitivity and low false positive rates. These findings validate the suitability of tree-based and boosting models for handling the nonlinearities and noise typical in UAV telemetry and sensor data under attack conditions.

RQ2: How does the SafeML reliability index correlate with classification errors in adversarial scenarios? SafeML demonstrated strong potential as a real-time reliability estimator. When applied during inference, it successfully identified low-confidence predictions in scenarios involving data drift or attack-induced anomalies. Notably, instances with high Wasserstein Distance (WD ¿ 0.5) were frequently associated with classification errors, especially in borderline or ambiguous spoofing cases. This correlation highlights the effectiveness of SafeML in providing an interpretable confidence layer that enhances trust in ML-based decisions, particularly in UAV missions.

RQ3: What is the optimal SafeML threshold to balance false alarms and undetected attacks? The evaluation of different WD thresholds (0.3, 0.5, 0.7) revealed that a threshold of 0.5 offers the best balance between sensitivity and specificity. At this value, the system achieved a 90.1% detection rate for OOD samples, while maintaining a manageable false positive rate of 8.2% and a high average F1-score of 0.95. Thresholds below 0.3 increased sensitivity but led to excessive false positives, while thresholds above 0.7 reduced false alarms at the expense of early anomaly detection. Therefore, 0.5 is recommended for UAV operations requiring real-time decisions with interpretable confidence margins.

RQ4: Does using ensembles improve prediction accuracy and reliability in attack scenarios? The ensemble learning approach, particularly the combination of RF with LR and LightGBM through majority voting, proved to be beneficial. It preserved or even improved accuracy (up to 98.08%) while increasing the final SafeML Trusted Level, indicating greater prediction stability. Moreover, ensemble strategies improved accuracy and confidence metrics by combining weaker classifiers, such as GB, with stronger ones. These results suggest that model diversity positively contributes to robustness, making ensemble techniques especially promising in UAV systems operating in highly variable or adversarial environments.

Despite the promising results, some limitations remain. The experimental setup was based on pre-collected datasets under controlled conditions. Future work should include real-time deployment on UAV hardware to validate performance under operational constraints (e.g., limited computational and energy resources). Furthermore, integrating SafeML with explainable AI (XAI) techniques could further enhance operator trust and interpretability of the system's decisions.

Acknowledgments. We thank Coordenação de Aperfeiçoamento de Pessoal de Nível Superior Brasil (CAPES) Finance Code 001, CEPID/CEMEAI (FAPESP grant 2013/07375-0), and CAPES Pro-Defesa (V3084362P) for their valuable support.

References

1. Mohsan, S.A.H., Rehmani, M.H., Wang, W., Luan, T.H.: Unmanned aerial vehicles (UAVs): practical aspects, applications, open challenges, security issues, and future trends. Intel. Serv. Robot. **16**(1), 109–137 (2023). https://doi.org/10.1007/s11370-022-00437-6
2. He, H., et al.: The challenges and opportunities of human-centered AI for trustworthy robots and autonomous systems. IEEE Trans. Cogn. Dev. Syst. **14**(4), 1398–1412 (2021). https://doi.org/10.1109/TCDS.2021.3085601
3. Antoniadi, A.M., Ducournau, A., Mouchet, E., Hebbalaguppe, R., Vie, K., Bousquet, G.: Current challenges and future opportunities for XAI in machine learning-based clinical decision support systems: a systematic review. Appl. Sci. **11**(11), 5088 (2021). https://doi.org/10.3390/app11115088
4. Aslansefat, K., Sorokos, I., Whiting, D., Tavakoli Kolagari, R., Papadopoulos, Y.: SafeML: safety monitoring of machine learning classifiers through statistical difference measures. In: Bozzano, M., Bittner, E. (eds.) Model-Based Safety and Assessment (IMBSA 2020), LNCS, vol. 12299, pp. 197–211. Springer, Lisbon, Portugal (2020). https://doi.org/10.1007/978-3-030-61470-6_13
5. Krishna, C.G.L., Murphy, R.R.: A review on cybersecurity vulnerabilities for unmanned aerial vehicles. In: *Proceedings of the 2017 IEEE International Symposium on Safety, Security and Rescue Robotics (SSRR)*, pp. 194–199. IEEE (2017). https://doi.org/10.1109/SSRR.2017.8088161
6. Altaweel, A., Mukkath, H., Kamel, I.: GPS spoofing attacks in FANETs: a systematic literature review. IEEE Access **11**, 55233–55280 (2023). https://doi.org/10.1109/ACCESS.2023.3275480
7. Bai, Y., Liu, Y., Zhang, Y., Zhang, H., Liu, Z.: Toward autonomous multi-UAV wireless network: a survey of reinforcement learning-based approaches. IEEE Commun. Surv. Tutorials **25**(4), 3038–3067 (2023). https://doi.org/10.1109/COMST.2023.3295065
8. Javaid, S., Khan, A., Ullah, F., Rehman, A., Almogren, A., Ghaleb, F.A.: Explainable AI and monocular vision for enhanced UAV navigation in smart cities: prospects and challenges. Front. Sustain. Cities **7**, 1561404 (2025). https://doi.org/10.3389/frsc.2025.1561404
9. Mohale, V.Z., Obagbuwa, I.C.: A systematic review on the integration of explainable AI in intrusion detection systems to enhancing transparency and interpretability in cybersecurity. Front. Artif. Intell. **8**, 1526221 (2025). https://doi.org/10.3389/frai.2025.1526221

10. Whelan, J., Sangarapillai, T., Minawi, O., Almehmadi, A., El-Khatib, K.: UAV attack dataset. IEEE Dataport (2020). https://doi.org/10.21227/00dg-0d12
11. Chawla, N.V., Bowyer, K.W., Hall, L.O., Kegelmeyer, W.P.: SMOTE: synthetic minority over-sampling technique. J. Artif. Intell. Res. **16**, 321–357 (2002)

Safe Machine Learning

Incorporating Failure of Machine Learning in Dynamic Probabilistic Safety Assurance

Razieh Arshadizadeh[✉], Mahmoud Asgari, Zeinab Khosravi,
Yiannis Papadopoulos, and Koorosh Aslansefat

School of Computer Science, University of Hull, Hull HU6 7RX, UK
R.Arshadizadeh-2021@hull.ac.uk

Abstract. Machine Learning (ML) models are increasingly integrated into safety-critical systems, such as autonomous vehicle platooning, to enable real-time decision-making. However, their inherent imperfection introduces a new class of failure: reasoning failures often triggered by distributional shifts between operational and training data. Traditional safety assessment methods, which rely on design artefacts or code, are ill-suited for ML components that learn behaviour from data. SafeML was recently proposed to dynamically detect such shifts and assign confidence levels to the reasoning of ML-based components. Building on this, we introduce a probabilistic safety assurance framework that integrates SafeML with Bayesian Networks (BNs) to model ML failures as part of a broader causal safety analysis. This allows for dynamic safety evaluation and system adaptation under uncertainty. We demonstrate the approach on an simulated automotive platooning system with traffic sign recognition. The findings highlight the potential broader benefits of explicitly modelling ML failures in safety assessment.

Keywords: Machine Learning Failure · Probabilistic Safety Assessment · Bayesian Networks · SafeML · Autonomous Systems · Runtime Safety Assurance

1   Introduction

The growing demand for safe and efficient Autonomous Vehicle (AV) systems has spurred interest in platooning, where multiple AVs follow a lead vehicle at a defined inter-vehicle distance. Platooning aims to improve traffic flow, reduce fuel consumption, and enhance road safety by minimizing human errors [8,11,19,22]. Typically, a human-driven lead vehicle is followed by one or more autonomous vehicles that adjust their speeds to maintain safe gaps. This coordination enhances both safety and operational efficiency by reducing reaction times and synchronized movements [13,18,20]. However, the safety and effectiveness of platooning systems depend on their ability to adapt to changing road and environmental conditions. Traditional frameworks often rely on static parameters, e.g.,

P. Katsaros (Ed.): IMBSA 2025, LNCS 15755, pp. 127–143, 2026.
https://doi.org/10.1007/978-3-032-05073-1_9

fixed speed limits, that may be insufficient in dynamic road contexts. Unpredictable weather changes or new traffic signs can render such static speed limits inadequate, highlighting the need for real-time adaptation [11].

Recent studies address this through Dynamic Safety Contracts (DSCs) and Conditional Safety Certificates (ConSerts) [20]. Despite proving effectiveness by enabling AVs to adapt their behaviours, e.g., to dynamically maintain safety, a significant limitation of DSCs and ConSerts lies in their reliance on binary conditional variables, which may not fully capture the probabilistic nature of real-world traffic scenarios [11,13,18,19]. To improve reasoning under uncertainty, BNs have been introduced as a flexible framework for safety assessment in AVs [13]. BNs support probabilistic reasoning, integrating diverse factors into cohesive safety evaluation. The use of BNs has demonstrated effectiveness in managing uncertainty in AV systems, particularly for vehicle platooning applications where real-time decision-making is required to ensure safe inter-vehicle distances. Yet, the framework developed in [13] employs a fixed speed limit, which limits its applicability to dynamically changing traffic scenarios [11,13,19].

Meanwhile, ML models, particularly Convolutional Neural Networks (CNNs), enable AVs to interpret road scenes, including traffic signs, for adaptive decision making. CNNs excel at identifying visual patterns, making them well-suited for traffic sign recognition. However, they are sensitive to uncertainties, such as sensor noise, lighting variations, and distributional shifts between training and operational data. These factors can undermine prediction reliability, posing safety risks if left unmanaged [17]. To mitigate this, techniques like as Probabilistic CNNs (PCNNs) have been developed that can provide uncertainty in their predictions, providing a measure of confidence [17]. Another approach, SafeML, evaluates prediction reliability by measuring distributional shifts of incoming operational data from the training data. When a shift is detected, predictions can be flagged as unreliable, prompting safety-preserving responses like speed reductions [3].

In this work, we propose a novel framework that integrates BNs with SafeML to potentially enhance the safety of platooning by dynamically adapting speed limits in response to real-time road signs and environmental conditions. By fusing information from both the ML model and SafeML, the BN enables AVs to maintain safety under uncertainty. The core innovation lies in the explicit modeling of ML failures within a dynamic runtime safety assurance framework. This approach is evaluated in a simulated platooning environment, focusing on its potential to improve safety rather than on real-time performance. While the framework is demonstrated in the context of AV platooning, it is broadly applicable to intelligent systems requiring dynamic, uncertainty-aware safety assessment, offering a flexible and extensible solution for runtime assurance across domains.

2   Related Works

2.1   SafeML

SafeML employs statistical tools, such as Empirical Cumulative Distribution Function (ECDF)-based statistical distance measures, to monitor classifier performance at runtime. The method quantifies distributional shifts in upcoming data and estimates potential performance degradation accordingly. It also incorporates a human-in-the-loop mechanism to improve safety under conditions such as concept drift. The concept was introduced by Aslansefat et al. [3]. The initial idea was extended for image classification in [2]. The study introduced bootstrapping-based p-value calculation to validate distances and increase accuracy. SafeML has also been extended for time-series prediction and regression tasks [1]. The issue of defining a well-tuned appropriate threshold of unacceptable drift was investigated in [9]. The study proposed a method for automatic tuning that optimises performance.

SafeML has shown promising results in numerous applications such as security intrusion detection [3], autonomous driving system [2], safety zone estimation and object detection in robotics [4,6], and offshore wind turbine blade inspection using UAVs [15]. H. Farhad et al. [10] proposed a model-specific version of SafeML in which the last layer of a deep neural network and the latent features of the networks have been used to drive statistical distance measures. The approach has also been extended for Machine Learning explainability. A method called SMILE (Statistical Model-agnostic Interpretability with Local Explanations) [5] uses SafeML statistical distance measures to provide explanations for specific classification in relevant tasks. SafeML has recently been cited in the German Industry Standard for Machine Learning Uncertainty Quantification (DIN SPEC 92005) [7] .

2.2   Runtime BN and Safety Models

Bayesian networks (BNs) are probabilistic graphical models with a flexible architecture, capable of reasoning under uncertainty. They provide a global assessment of various dependability properties, such as reliability and availability, by aggregating local information from different sources. Structurally, BNs represent relationships among random variables using a directed acyclic graph (DAG), where nodes represent variables and edges represent conditional dependencies. If an arc points from node X to node Y, then X is the parent of Y and exerts a direct (deterministic or probabilistic) influence on it [14]. This structure enables both causal reasoning and probabilistic inference.

In recent years, BNs have gained widespread adoption in dependability engineering, particularly for safety and reliability assessments [12]. Their utility in aggregating and propagating uncertain information makes them well-suited for complex dynamic systems such as AVs. Several studies have explored runtime assurance and adaptability in AV platooning. Early projects such as PATH and SARTRE pioneered adaptive cruise control, and intervehicle communication with a focus on efficiency and safety of platoons [13]. Müller et al. [18]

proposed an application of Dynamic Safety Contracts (DSC) to platooning. In this approach, they provided modular runtime checks for qualitative and quantitative safety conditions and highlighted the need for adaptive and situation-aware decision-making in dynamic situations. Schneider and Trapp [20] proposed conditional safety certificates (ConSerts) for open adaptive systems, delivering runtime safety guarantees via condition-based contracts.

Among more recent advancements, Kabir *et al.* employed BNs to manage uncertainty in AV systems, notably demonstrating their value in safe and adaptive AV platooning [13]. However, their framework assumes a fixed speed limit and does not support complex perceptual tasks such as traffic sign recognition. Moreover, it does not address the uncertainty introduced by ML models. In response, Gautam et al. proposed a hybrid decision-making framework combining probabilistic CNNs (PCNN) and BNs. Their approach supports real-time decision-making under uncertainty, particularly for traffic sign recognition in platooning scenarios [11]. Nonetheless, their proposal neither explicitly accounts for the imperfect reliability of ML models nor does it address out-of-distribution (OOD) data.

In our work, we present a new framework that incorporates SafeML as a real-time evaluator within a BN framework. SafeML quantitatively assesses ML uncertainty through statistical measures and feeds this information into the BN to support dynamic reliability modeling. This integration enables the system to adapt to changing data distributions, improving real-time safety assurance. By treating ML model reliability as a first-class input to decision making, we bridge the gap between probabilistic reasoning and dynamic learning-based perception in AV platooning.

3   Method

3.1   Bayesian Risk Assessment Loop

The central mechanism of our approach to dynamic risk assessment is a BN that is continuously updated with information about the system's state. To incorporate assessments of ML reasoning failures, we propose a mechanism for connecting SafeML monitors to the BN as illustrated in (see Fig. 1).

The process begins with the acquisition of ML-generated data and reasoning outcomes, including classification results and contextual input signals. These outputs are passed into the SafeML module, which performs two key functions:

(i) estimating confidence by measuring the similarity between distributions of operational inputs and training data, and
(ii) deriving prior probabilities that reflect the likelihood of reasoning failure, encapsulating the statistical trustworthiness of the ML model's predictions.

These prior probabilities are then fed to the BN module, which carries out two main inference tasks:

(a) updating the probabilistic graphical model with real-time evidence, and

(b) computing posterior distributions over safety-relevant system states.

The final output of this pipeline is a quantified risk outcome that reflects the system's operational safety status. This output can be used not only for decision support but also as feedback input for the next processing cycle that uses fresh ML and other system data. The result is a closed-loop safety monitoring mechanism that adapts continuously to evolving operational conditions, providing robustness against both distributional shifts and reasoning anomalies.

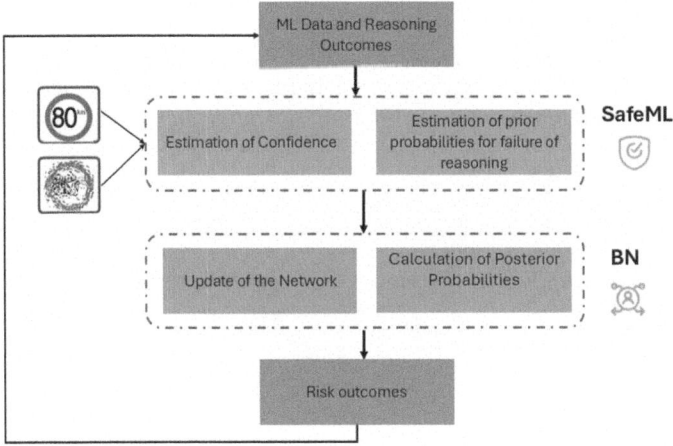

Fig. 1. A cyclic integration of SafeML with a Bayesian Network for confidence estimation, risk assessment, and proactive mitigation.

3.2 SafeML-Augmented CNN for Traffic Sign Recognition

Figure 2 provides a detailed view of the proposed dynamic safety assurance framework in the context of an AV platooning scenario, illustrating the integration of ML, statistical validation, and probabilistic reasoning with the BN providing dynamic risk estimation. Our ML component for traffic sign recognition employs a CNN architecture trained on the German Traffic Sign Recognition Benchmark (GTSRB) dataset. The model's architecture involves sequential convolutional layers, max-pooling, dropout regularization for generalization, and fully connected layers to classify traffic signs effectively.

The process begins with raw visual inputs from vehicle-mounted cameras, which are processed by a trained ML classifier to generate traffic sign predictions. These predictions are simultaneously passed to a SafeML module, which evaluates whether the input sample lies within the training distribution (in-distribution, ID) or deviates from it (out-of-distribution, OOD). This evaluation uses the Wasserstein distance between input and training data, followed by a bootstrap-based p-value calculation. SafeML outputs a binary reliability signal (ID or OOD), indicating the trustworthiness of the ML decision. Both the predicted class and the SafeML reliability signal are provided as evidence to the BN, alongside contextual variables such as inter-vehicle distance, speed compliance, sensor accuracy, and system-specific thresholds. The BN captures semantic relationships between these variables, allowing the inference engine to compute posterior distributions over key safety-relevant states (e.g., SystemState, SystemStateBQC, DetectionQuality). Decision nodes such as 'SpeedWithinLimit', 'IsItSafe', and 'DistanceComparison' evaluate operational conditions in real time.

The BN output allows the system to assess the overall safety status under uncertainty, differentiate between root causes of potential failure (e.g., ML misclassification vs. sensor error), and issue targeted mitigation actions. Thus, safety-critical decisions are not made solely on raw ML predictions but are contextually informed, statistically validated, and probabilistically reasoned.

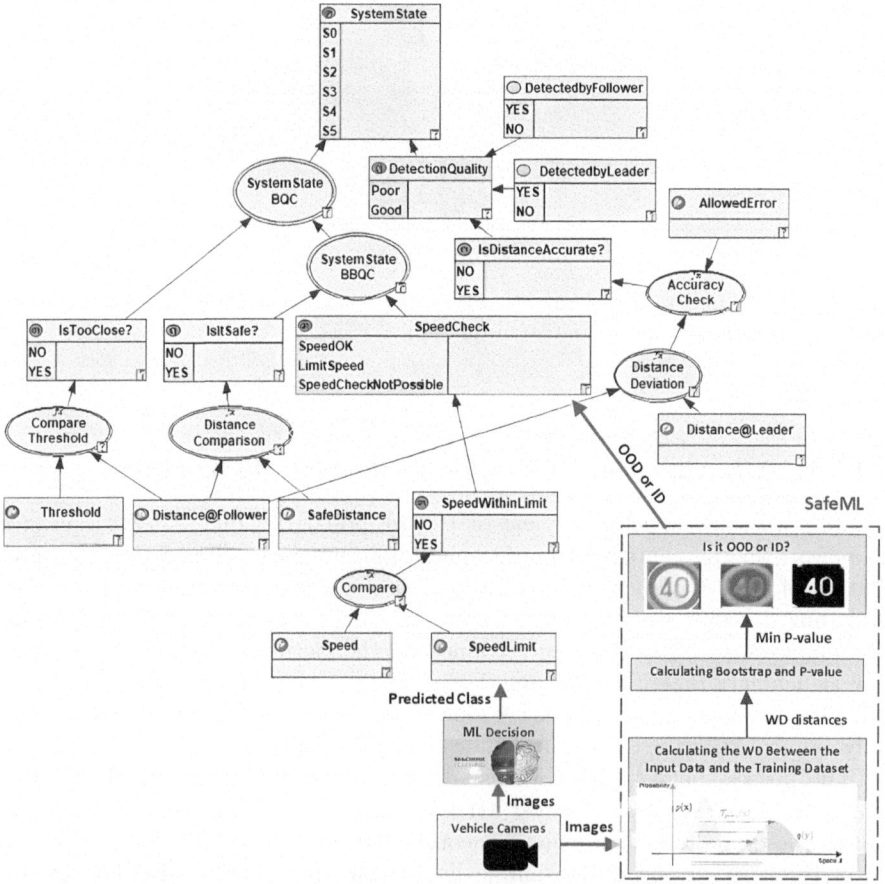

Fig. 2. Bayesian network integrating ML and SafeML for runtime safety assurance.

3.3   Mathematical Formulation

This subsection presents the mathematical background supporting our proposed SafeML-enhanced runtime assurance framework.

Wasserstein Distance. The Wasserstein distance between two probability distributions P and Q is defined as [23]:

$$W(P,Q) = \inf_{\gamma \in \Gamma(P,Q)} \int_{\mathbb{R}^n \times \mathbb{R}^n} \|x - y\| \, d\gamma(x,y) \tag{1}$$

where $\Gamma(P,Q)$ denotes the set of all joint distributions with marginals P and Q, and $x, y \in \mathbb{R}^n$ represent samples drawn from these distributions.

Bootstrapped P-Value. To statistically assess whether a test input belongs to the same distribution as the training set, we compute a p-value using bootstrap resampling:

$$\text{p-value} = \frac{1}{B} \sum_{b=1}^{B} \mathbf{1} \left(W(X_b^*, X_{\text{train}}) \geq W(\hat{X}, X_{\text{train}}) \right) \tag{2}$$

Safety Check. The final decision about the reliability of ML classification is based on the minimum p-value across the three RGB channels:

$$\text{Unreliable} = \begin{cases} 0 & \text{if } \min(\text{pval}_R, \text{pval}_G, \text{pval}_B) > 0.01 \\ 1 & [[\text{otherwise}]] \end{cases} \tag{3}$$

In other words, the input is flagged as *unreliable* if any of the three colour channels yields a statistically significant deviation (p-value ≤ 0.01). This conservative criterion ensures that a significant deviation in even a single channel is sufficient to reject the in-distribution assumption.

Bayesian Integration of ML and SafeML Outputs. Each system component, ML predictions, SafeML outputs, and contextual signals, is encoded as a node in the main decision-making model, i.e., the BN. These nodes, modeled as random variables, are interconnected in the BN with edges showing interdependencies. The ML classifier outputs a predicted label `MLDecision`, while SafeML generates a reliability indicator (`SafeML_Status`, i.e., ID or OOD). These two variables condition downstream nodes representing safety-relevant aspects such as the speed compliance, intervehicle distance, and ultimately the system's operational state.

The conditional probability distribution of a node V_i given its parent nodes is denoted as [23]:

$$\Pr\{V_i \mid \text{Parents}(V_i)\}. \tag{4}$$

Using the chain rule of Bayesian Networks, the joint probability distribution over all nodes $V_1, V_2, \ldots, V_n$ is given by [23]:

$$\Pr\{V_1, V_2, \ldots, V_n\} = \prod_{i=1}^{n} \Pr\{V_i \mid \text{Parents}(V_i)\} \tag{5}$$

This formulation enables the BN to infer the most probable system state by combining the semantic output of the ML model with the statistical reliability estimates from SafeML. Notably, even when contextual values (e.g., speed and distance) alone may not indicate a high-risk condition, the presence of an OOD SafeML flag increases the posterior probability of a fallback safety mode or alert state. In our implementation, `MLDecision` and `SafeML_Status` are treated as observed evidence nodes. Their values condition the posterior inference in the BN, allowing for soft fusion of semantic correctness and statistical trustworthiness.

4   Experimental Setup

4.1   Platooning Scenario

The experimental scenario builds upon a platooning system proposed in [13] and extended in [10], with key enhancements that integrate ML-based perception and statistical runtime validation. Modern platooning systems allow multiple AVs to follow a human-operated lead vehicle while maintaining a defined inter-vehicle distance. This cooperative formation, commonly referred to as Cooperative Adaptive Cruise Control (CACC), improves fuel efficiency, reduces traffic congestion, and increases overall road throughput. Each follower vehicle dynamically adjusts its speed in real time to ensure safe spacing. Despite its operational benefits, platooning introduces safety challenges due to the close proximity between vehicles. Sudden changes in speed or unexpected environmental conditions can lead to increased collision risk. Traditional systems rely on speed limits and static parameters, which may be insufficient under real-world, dynamic conditions. A key goal is therefore to maintain safe vehicle spacing while complying with traffic regulations. While static verification methods are commonly applied during design time, they lack adaptability at runtime. When encountering inputs that deviate from the trained distribution, the system must be able to detect such anomalies and respond accordingly. Runtime anomaly detection is thus essential for triggering safety-preserving actions in unfamiliar conditions.

4.2   Node Design and Safety Integration

The BN that dynamically controls safety in our platform integrates contextual and system-level indicators to infer the current safety state. Each node represents either a measurable input, a logical condition, or a latent assessment. Key nodes and their interactions are described below:

ML Decision (Classifier Output): Encodes the predicted traffic sign class (e.g., speed limits) from a CNN trained on the GTSRB dataset. The predicted class is used as a semantic input to inform downstream nodes about the expected driving behaviour.

SafeML Status: Receives the statistical decision from SafeML, which estimates whether an input sample is within the training ID or OOD.

Speed Limit: Converts the predicted traffic sign class to a numeric speed value (e.g., "30 km/h sign" class 30 km/h).

Speed Within Limit: Evaluates whether the vehicle's current speed (measured via onboard sensors) is within ML-inferred legal limit.

Speed Check: Combines *SafeML Status* and *Speed Within Limit* to assess whether the traffic sign is both reliable and obeyed. It acts as a gatekeeper that links model validity and behavioral compliance.

Safe Distance: Determines whether the inter-vehicle distance is safe, using LIDAR and telemetry data. The outcome is binary (safe/unsafe).

Detection Quality: Evaluates sensor reliability, including agreement between leader and follower vehicles, and the accuracy of distance measurements. High-quality detection improves confidence in distance-based decisions.

Is It Safe?: A fused node that integrates outputs of *Speed Check*, *Safe Distance*, and *Detection Quality* to determine immediate operational risk.

System States (S_0 to S_5): This final system state node aggregates multi-source observationsincluding model confidence, speed compliance, inter-vehicle distance, and sensor reliabilityinto a discrete system state that gives the current safety level. Table 1 presents the semantics of each state based on MAP (Maximum a Posteriori).

Other Supporting Nodes: Several auxiliary nodes (e.g., *Compare*, *CompareThreshold*, and *DistanceDeviation*) are used to enable logical reasoning such

Table 1. System states with corresponding safety conditions and recommended actions inspired by [13].

State	Name	Description and Recommended Action
S_0	Fully Safe	All safety conditions satisfied (speed, distance, SafeML, perception); proceed with normal operation.
S_1	Safe with Uncertainty	System largely safe, but one component uncertain (e.g., speed or detection); continue with caution and monitor.
S_2	Warning	Minor safety deviation detected (e.g., slight distance or sensor issue); drive cautiously.
S_3	Elevated Risk	Major safety violations (e.g., unsafe distance or speed); immediate actions like deceleration required.
S_4	High Risk	Multiple critical issues (e.g., close proximity, unreliable detection); emergency actions (e.g., hard braking) and fallback mode activation needed.
S_5	Critical ML Failure	ML perception deemed unreliable (due to OOD or adversarial input); activate fallback safety mode (e.g., degraded ACC).

as threshold checks and distance consistency, but do not directly appear in the final safety decision node.

4.3 Implementation

The dynamic safety monitoring system was implemented in Python using standard deep learning and scientific libraries. A custom Sequential CNN was trained on the German Traffic Sign Recognition. The architecture includes three convolutional layers with ReLU activation, two max-pooling layers, three dropout layers for regularization, a dense layer with 256 units (ReLU), and a final softmax layer for classification across 43 classes. Runtime reliability is assessed via a SafeML-inspired approach that uses distribution-based distance metrics to identify OOD inputs. Safety reasoning is performed with a BN implemented in Python using the pyAgrum library for probabilistic inference.

ML-based predictions and SafeML's validation are automatically integrated into the BN safety model as follows: the CNN prediction of the traffic sign (Speed Limit) is passed to the Speed Limit node. The SafeML node receives the p-value resulting from the bootstrap-based statistical test. If this p-value falls below a predefined threshold (e.g., 0.01), the system considers the input as OOD and degrades safely by transitioning into ACC mode. This hybrid BN-based structure enables the system to manage ML uncertainty in a principled way and dynamically select the safest action under varying degrees of input quality.

Experiments were conducted using the GTSRB dataset, a widely adopted benchmark for traffic sign classification. It includes over 50,000 color images across 43 categories of regulatory, warning, and speed signs. Images vary significantly in resolution, illumination, angle, and environmental background, making it a suitable benchmark for testing the real-world ML testing [16,21]. For this study, 80% of the data was used for training the CNN, and the remaining 20% was used for validation. The training set was typically used to learn traffic signs, while the validation and test set was utilized to assess the model's performance and reliability during deployment. We focused on misclassified samples from the test set. These samples were treated as potential OOD instances for the purposes of SafeML evaluation. During runtime, each test image was compared against the training samples of the predicted class rather than the ground truth class. This approach reflects a realistic deployment scenario in which only the model's prediction is available at the time of decision-making. By using this strategy, we assessed whether SafeML can detect internal failures of the ML model, particularly those arising from distributional shifts that may not be apparent under conventional accuracy-based metrics.

5   Results

5.1   SafeML Analysis of a Misclassified Sample

To assess the robustness of the classifier, we applied *SafeML* to the images that were misclassified by the CNN. This experiment investigated whether the misclassifications stemmed out of OOD inputs rather than general prediction confidence. Following SafeML, we computed the Wasserstein distance and bootstrap-based p-values between each misclassified and the ID training samples of the predicted class across the RGB channels. The results are shown in Table 2. As shown, the model misclassified test samples by confusing class 4 with class 3, or class 5 with class 8. Nevertheless, SafeML successfully flagged these cases as OOD. Specifically, p-values for all three RGB channels were below 0.01, strongly rejecting the null hypothesis of distributional similarity with over 99% confidence. These findings demonstrate that SafeML of detecting even subtle statistical deviations and can effectively identify unreliable predictions.

Table 2. SafeML results for misclassified test samples.

OOD Detection	p-value	Wasserstein Distance	Channel	Predicted Class	True Class
OOD	0.0000	0.0005	0	3	4
OOD	0.0000	0.0005	1	3	4
OOD	0.0000	0.0006	2	3	4
OOD	0.0000	0.0004	0	8	5
OOD	0.0000	0.0004	1	8	5
OOD	0.0000	0.0004	2	8	5

Visual inspection further supports the statistical evidence. As shown in Fig. 3, the pixel intensity histograms for each RGB channel reveal distinct deviations between the misclassified test image (orange) and the in-distribution for the predicted class (blue). The test image —originally from class 4 but predicted as class 3— shows a narrow, high-peaked distribution in contrast with the broader distribution of training samples. Additionally, Fig. 4 compares a typical class 3 training sample (left) with the misclassified test image (right). The test image exhibits strong darkness and occlusion, confirming its deviation from the expected class distribution.

5.2   Bayesian Inference Results and System State Evaluation

Figure 5 presents the output of the BN, executed in real-time upon detection of an *OOD* input by the SafeML module. The BN integrates inputs from speed compliance, inter-vehicle distance, ML predictions, SafeML reliability checks, and sensor-level accuracy to estimate the system's most probable state.

System Interpretation Based on Posterior Distribution. The most likely system state is S_5 with a posterior probability of 54.08%, indicating a high level of uncertainty due to unreliable sensor input or statistical anomalies. Crucially, this result demonstrates the significant influence of the SafeML node on downstream reasoning. Although speed and distance readings could not on their own justify

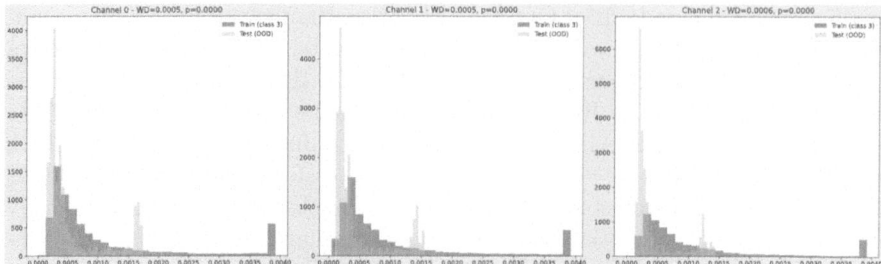

Fig. 3. Histogram of pixel values per RGB channel comparing the misclassified test image (orange) and the class 3 training distribution (blue). (Color figure online)

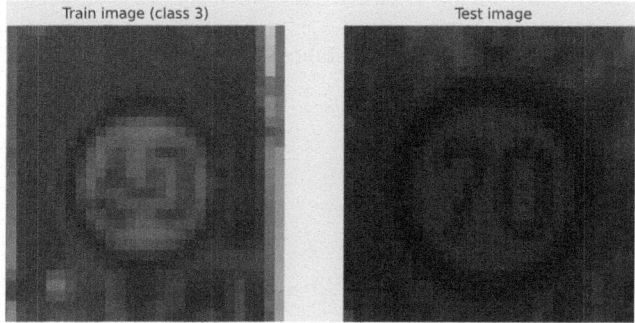

Fig. 4. Visual comparison between a training sample from class 3 and a misclassified test image. The latter shows clear signs of darkness and low contrast.

entering a critical state, the OOD flag raised by SafeML prompts the system to transition to fallback control (ACC mode) as a precaution.

Contextual Interpretation. Interestingly, in the evaluated scenario, contextual nodes such as `SpeedWithinLimit`, `SafeDistance`, and `DetectionQuality` remained within acceptable ranges, contributing little risk to the overall system state. Despite their nominal status, the BN still assigned the highest probability to the critical fallback state (S5). This highlights the dominance of the `SafeML_Status` node, whose OOD flag alone was sufficient to override otherwise normal sensor inputs. This underscores the value of explicitly treating reasoning failure in safety assessment.

5.3 Discussion

To evaluate the benefit of explicit representation of ML reasoning failure in a dynamic probabilistic safety assessment, we compared the system behaviors in scenarios with and without the SafeML component. This evaluation focused specifically on the system's ability to handle ML misclassifications and distributional shifts. The experiments were conducted under stable environmental

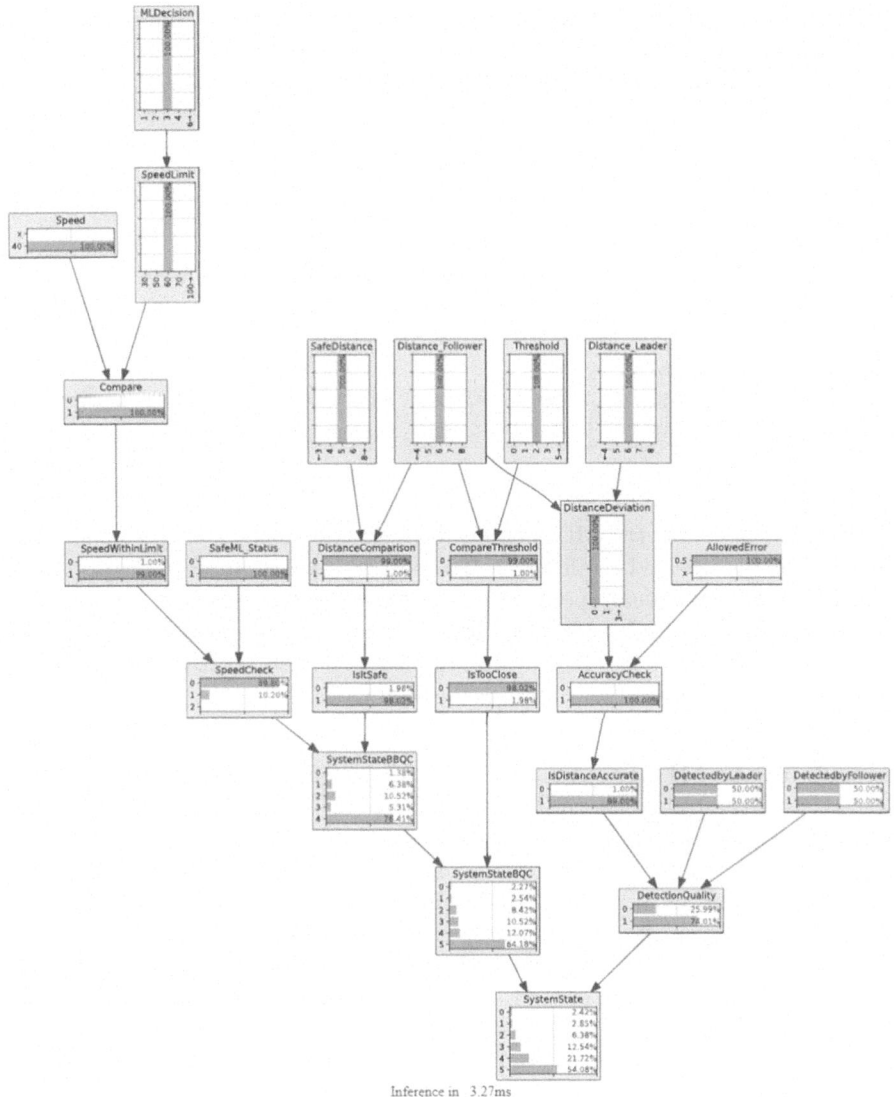

Fig. 5. Posterior probabilities of system states under combined SafeML and MLDecision evidence.

parameters (Safe Distance = 5, Distance Follower = 6, Threshold = 2, Distance Leader = 6, Allowed Error = 0.5). Detailed numerical results are presented in Tables 3 and 4.

System Performance Without SafeML. System performance was first assessed without SafeML, relying solely on ML-based traffic sign classification outputs. Table 3 summarizes the results under different scenarios.

Table 3. System performance without SafeML under various ML misclassification conditions.

No.	MLDecision	True Class	Speed Limit	Speed	S0	S1	S2	S3	S4	S5
1	Speed limit > Speed	5	80	60	**0.4247**	0.1372	0.1169	0.1513	0.1293	0.0407
2	Speed limit < Speed	3	60	70	0.1019	0.0900	0.2049	**0.3179**	0.2456	0.0397
3	Speed limit = Speed	5	80	80	**0.4247**	0.1372	0.1169	0.1513	0.1293	0.0407
4	Speed limit > Speed	5	100	80	**0.4247**	0.1372	0.1169	0.1513	0.1293	0.0407
5	Speed limit < Speed	2	30	60	0.1019	0.0900	0.2049	**0.3179**	0.2456	0.0397
6	Speed limit = Speed	2	60	60	**0.4247**	0.1372	0.1169	0.1513	0.1293	0.0407

In scenarios where the ML classifier correctly identified the traffic sign, the systems reliably inferred a safe state. However, in cases of misclassification, particularly when the actual speed exceeded the correct speed limit, the system continued to report a fully safe state. This outcome reveals overreliance on potentially dangerous incorrect ML outputs. Rows 1 to 3 show correct classifications, whereas rows 4 to 6 represent misclassification cases.

Impact of SafeML Integration. In a second set of experiments, we used SafeML to distinguish between ID and OOD inputs. This integration allowed the system to dynamically adjust its behavior based on information about whether to trust or not traffic sign recognition and informed more nuanced transitions between safety states in the BN. Table 4 illustrates the impact of SafeML intervention on these transitions under various contextual conditions.

The impact of SafeML is evident in rows 1–8 where `SafeML_Status = 1`. In each of these cases, the system assigns the highest probability to state **S5**, signaling a shift to the most conservative safety response. Notably, this includes instances like rows 5 and 6, where the ML prediction was correct, but SafeML incorrectly flagged the input as OOD. Despite the false alarm, the system's fallback to a safe state is non-disruptive and aligns with safety-first design priorities. In contrast, rows 9 and 10 illustrate the system's behavior when SafeML did not intervene (`SafeML_Status = 0`). Here, the safety outcome is dictated solely by the ML prediction and contextual parameters such as speed. In row 9, the speed exceeds the (misclassified) speed limit, causing the system to activate state **S3**, indicating elevated risk. In row 10, the speed is below the predicted limit, resulting in assignment to state **S0**—considered fully safe. These outcomes highlight the limitations of relying on ML outputs alone: erroneous inferences can propagate unchecked in the absence of runtime validation.

Table 4. System state probabilities for misclassified samples under low statistical distance.

No.	SafeML_Status	MLDecision	True Class	Speed Limit	Speed	S0	S1	S2	S3	S4	S5
1	1	3	1	60	40	0.0242	0.0285	0.0638	0.1254	0.2172	**0.5408**
2	1	3	8	60	90	0.0302	0.0410	0.0997	0.1761	0.2281	**0.4249**
3	1	3	7	60	40	0.0242	0.0285	0.0638	0.1254	0.2172	**0.5408**
4	1	5	1	80	40	0.0242	0.0285	0.0638	0.1254	0.2172	**0.5408**
5	1	5	5	80	90	0.0302	0.0410	0.0997	0.1761	0.2281	**0.4249**
6	1	5	5	80	40	0.0242	0.0285	0.0638	0.1254	0.2172	**0.5408**
7	1	8	5	120	40	0.0242	0.0285	0.0638	0.1254	0.2172	**0.5408**
8	1	3	4	60	40	0.0242	0.0285	0.0638	0.1254	0.2172	**0.5408**
9	0	3	3	60	90	0.1019	0.0900	0.2049	**0.3179**	0.2456	0.0397
10	0	4	4	70	40	**0.4247**	0.1372	0.1169	0.1513	0.1293	0.0407

6   Conclusion

This paper introduced a probabilistic runtime safety assurance framework that combines statistical reliability assessment using SafeML with semantic decision-making via Bayesian Networks. The approach explicitly models ML failures, particularly those arising from OOD inputs, and integrates them into system-level reasoning for adaptive control in autonomous vehicle platooning. Experimental results demonstrated that SafeML significantly improves the system's ability to detect and mitigate high-risk scenarios, especially when ML predictions are unreliable. Crucially, the integration allowed the system to transition into conservative fallback states in response to statistical deviations, even in cases where conventional indicators (e.g., speed or distance compliance) suggested no apparent risk. This underscores the importance of incorporating distributional awareness into safety-critical ML applications.

While the framework exhibits strong performance in capturing latent hazards, occasional false negatives from SafeML indicate the need for enhancement. Nevertheless, the system maintained a robust and conservative response profile, consistent with safety-by-design principles. Future work will extend the framework to support temporal reasoning and dynamic sensitivity adjustment of SafeML under varying uncertainty levels. Additionally, we plan to integrate dynamic context-aware fallback strategies and countermeasure selection into the BN to support proactive safety management. Finally, validation in more complex, multi-agent scenarios and real hardware will be pursued to evaluate real-time performance and real-world applicability.

References

1. Akram, M.N., et al.: Stadre and stadro: Reliability and robustness of ml forecasting using s-d measures. In: SAFECOMP 2022 Wkps. pp. 289–301. Springer (2022)
2. Aslansefat, K., Kabir, S., Abdullatif, A., Vasudevan, V., Papadopoulos, Y.: Toward improving confidence in autonomous vehicle software: a study on traffic sign recognition systems. Computer **54**(8), 66–76 (2021)
3. Aslansefat, K., Sorokos, I., Whiting, D., Tavakoli Kolagari, R., Papadopoulos, Y.: SafeML: safety monitoring of machine learning classifiers through statistical difference measures. In: Zeller, M., Höfig, K. (eds.) IMBSA 2020. LNCS, vol. 12297, pp. 197–211. Springer, Cham (2020). https://doi.org/10.1007/978-3-030-58920-2_13
4. Aslansefat, K., et al.: Safedrones: Real-time reliability evaluation of UAVs using EDDIS. In: IMBSA 2022, Munich. pp. 252–266. Springer (2022)
5. Aslansefat, K., et al.: Explaining black boxes with a smile: Statistical model-agnostic interpretability with local explanations. IEEE Software (2023)
6. Cho, H., Lee, K., Choi, N.: Kim: online safety zone estimation and violation detection for nonstationary objects in workplaces. IEEE Access **10**, 39769–39781 (2022)
7. DIN SPEC 92005: Machine Learning – Uncertainty Quantification. Technical report, Berlin, Germany (2022). https://www.din.de/en/wdc-beuth:din21:343195966
8. Fagnant, D.J., Kockelman, K.: Preparing a nation for autonomous vehicles. Transp. Res. Part A: Pol. Pract. **77**, 167–181 (2015)
9. Farhad, A.H., et al.: Keep your distance: determining sampling and distance thresholds in ml monitoring. In: Seguin, C., Zeller, M., Prosvirnova, T. (eds.) IMBSA 2022. LNCS, vol. 13525, pp. 219–234. Springer, Cham (2022). https://doi.org/10.1007/978-3-031-15842-1_16
10. Farhad, A.H., Sorokos, I., Akram, M.N., Aslansefat, K., Schneider, D.: Scope compliance uncertainty estimate. arXiv preprint arXiv:2312.10801 (2023)
11. Gautam, V., Gheraibia, Y., Alexander, R., Hawkins, R.D.: Runtime decision making under uncertainty in autonomous vehicles. In: Proceedings of the Workshop on Artificial Intelligence Safety (SafeAI 2021). CEUR Workshop Proceedings (2021)
12. Kabir, S., Papadopoulos, Y.: Applications of BNS and petri nets in safety, reliability, and risk assessments: a review. Saf. Sci. **115**, 154–175 (2019)
13. Kabir, S., et al.: A runtime safety analysis concept for open adaptive systems. In: Papadopoulos, Y., Aslansefat, K., Katsaros, P., Bozzano, M. (eds.) IMBSA 2019. LNCS, vol. 11842, pp. 332–346. Springer, Cham (2019). https://doi.org/10.1007/978-3-030-32872-6_22
14. Kabir, S., Walker, M., Papadopoulos, Y.: Dynamic system safety analysis in hiphops with petri nets and Bayesian networks. Saf. Sci. **105**, 55–70 (2018)
15. Kabir, S., et al.: Combining drone-based monitoring and machine learning for online reliability evaluation of wind turbines. In: International Conference on Computing, Electronics & Communications Engineering (iCCECE), pp. 53–58. IEEE (2022)
16. Kaggle Contributor: GTSRB - German Traffic Sign Recognition Benchmark (2021). https://www.kaggle.com/datasets/meowmeowmeowmeowmeow/gtsrb-german-traffic-sign
17. McAllister, R.T., et al.: Concrete problems for autonomous vehicle safety: advantages of Bayesian deep learning. International Joint Conferences on AI, Inc. (2017)
18. Müller, S., Liggesmeyer, P.: Safety assurance for emergent collaboration of open distributed systems. In: ISSREW, pp. 249–256. IEEE (2016)

19. Reich, J.: Systematic engineering of safe open adaptive systems shown for truck platooning. Ph.D. thesis, TU Kaiserslautern (2016)
20. Schneider, D., Trapp, M.: Conditional safety certification of open adaptive systems. ACM Trans Autonom. Adapt. Syst. (TAAS) 8(2), 1–20 (2013)
21. Stallkamp, J., et al.: The German traffic sign recognition benchmark: a multi-class classification competition. In: IJCNN. pp. 1453–1460. IEEE (2011)
22. Tsugawa, S., Jeschke, S., Shladover, S.E.: A review of truck platooning projects for energy savings. IEEE Trans. Intell. Veh. 1(1), 68–77 (2016)
23. Villani, C.: Optimal Transport: Old and New, Grundlehren der Mathematischen Wissenschaften, vol. 338. Springer, Berlin (2008)

Safer Skin Lesion Classification with Global Class Activation Probability Map Evaluation and SafeML

Kuniko Paxton[1]([✉])(iD), Koorosh Aslansefat[1](iD), Amila Akagić[2](iD),
Dhavalkumar Thakker[1](iD), and Yiannis Papadopoulos[1](iD)

[1] School of Computer Science, University of Hull, Cottingham Road,
Hull HU6 7RX, UK
k.azuma-2021@hull.ac.uk
[2] Faculty of Electrical Engineering, University of Sarajevo, Zmaja od Bosne bb,
Sarajevo 71000, Bosnia and Herzegovina

Abstract. Recent advancements in skin lesion classification models have significantly improved accuracy, with some models even surpassing dermatologists' diagnostic performance. However, in medical practice, distrust in AI models remains a challenge. Beyond high accuracy, trustworthy, explainable diagnoses are essential. Existing explainability methods have reliability issues, with LIME-based methods suffering from inconsistency, while CAM-based methods failing to consider all classes. To address these limitations, we propose Global Class Activation Probabilistic Map Evaluation, a method that analyses all classes' activation probability maps probabilistically and at a pixel level. By visualizing the diagnostic process in a unified manner, it helps reduce the risk of misdiagnosis. Furthermore, the application of SafeML enhances the detection of false diagnoses and issues warnings to doctors and patients as needed, improving diagnostic reliability and ultimately patient safety. We evaluated our method using the ISIC datasets with MobileNetV2 and Vision Transformers. Our code for the experiment is available on GitHub (https://github.com/Kuniko925/ExplainForSafe).

Keywords: SafeML · Class Activation Map · Explainability · Skin lesion classification · Medical image classification

1 Introduction

In recent years, skin lesion classification models have achieved remarkable improvements in diagnostic accuracy, with some surpassing the performance of dermatologists [18]. These high-performance models have the potential to support clinical decision-making and alleviate physicians' workload. However, despite their effectiveness, studies have consistently reported a lack of trust in such models among medical professionals [29]. To foster wider clinical adoption, it is essential not only to achieve high predictive accuracy but also to enhance model transparency by clearly explaining the basis of predictions [12, 22].

To this end, various explainability techniques have been proposed, such as Class Activation Mapping (CAM) [44] and local interpretable model-agnostic explanations (LIME) [33], to visualize the model's reasoning process. These visualizations have been shown to improve clinicians' trust. However, the reliability of these explanations remains uncertain. While they can expose instances of shortcut learning, the quantitative relationship between the quality of explanations and model performance is still unclear.

LIME, for example, offers local explanations, but suffers from inconsistency due to sensitivity to kernel size and local perturbations [34, 42]. Some efforts have been made to address these issues, but a definite solution remains elusive. CAM-based techniques such as Gradient-weighted Class Activation Mapping (Grad-CAM) [36] attempt to highlight visually salient image regions by computing gradients for filters or vectors in the target layer. Variants such as Integrated Gradients [37], seCAM [9] and Score-CAM [41] also emphasize class-relevant features. However, in most studies, the results yielded by application of these CAM tools are used merely as supplementary diagnostics [23].

We argue that explainability can and should play a more central role, especially in mitigating misdiagnoses and alerting users to anomalous predictions. Most explainability tools only highlight the saliency of the input image with respect to the predicted class [36, 37, 41], overlooking insights from all potential classes. This narrow focus can result in misleading visualizations. For example, even when a model misclassifies a lesion, as shown in Fig. 2, if the highlighted region aligns with the lesion area and attention to other classes is absent, the prediction may falsely appear reliable. Such cases present serious risks of misdiagnosis.

To address this, we propose Global Class Activation Probabilistic Mapping (GCAPM), an evaluation method that analyzes activation regions across all classes for a given input. By normalizing and probabilistically aggregating class activation maps on a pixel level, we can more comprehensively assess the model's diagnostic behaviors. Additionally, class output weights are integrated into visualisation, offering a unified view of attention distribution across all classes, regardless of whether the final prediction is correct. GCAPM produces a segmented output of the model's regions of interest, which can be quantitatively compared to the ground truth lesion annotations using metrics such as sensitivity and false positive rates.

Beyond clinical settings, skin lesion models are increasingly being deployed in mobile applications and web-based self-diagnosis tools, especially in areas with limited access to medical care and long waiting times. These tools, while valuable, may cause potential patients to neglect their illness or place too much trust in the application. To improve the safety of such applications, we incorporate the principles of safeML as proposed in [7]. SafeML monitors data drift of operational data from training data using Empirical Cumulative Distribution Functions (ECDF). Since models cannot identify unknown data during deployment without labels, drift detection is critical for identifying potential model degradation. We adapt this concept by establishing thresholds during offline model development based on GCAPM metrics and using these to flag abnormal predictions at runtime, even in the absence of ground truth labels.

While explainability helps identify regions that influenced prediction, it does not inherently eliminate prediction uncertainty. As illustrated in Fig. 2, both high-confidence predictions and consistent attention maps can still lead to incorrect classification. Explainability, thus, is a lens into model attention, not a validation of correctness. Therefore, rather than relying solely on visual explanations, our approach introduces explainability-guided statistical reliability checks. When predictions are statistically flagged as uncertain, the system prompts human intervention instead of issuing an unchecked result. Traditional CAM approaches are insufficient for ensuring diagnostic safety based on visual explanation alone. Our GCAPM-based safety mechanism introduces a principled framework for evaluating and trusting model outputs, improving diagnostic reliability and accountability. This is especially important for reducing risks associated with self-diagnosis and for supporting clinicians in real-world practice.

We validate our approach using ISIC 2017 [16] and 2019 [16, 24, 39], two of the most widely adopted benchmarks for skin lesion diagnosis, alongside modern deep learning architectures such as CNN-based MobileNet2 [35] and Vision Transformer [17], which have increasingly replaced traditional CNNs since 2020.

2   Related Work

2.1   Visualizing the Skin Lesion Classifier's Diagnostic Behavior

In the study by [30], LIME was used to visualize model classification results which reportedly enhanced doctors' trust in the system. Similarly, [25] visualised model outputs via output channels to explain predictions. However, their studies did not evaluate the quality of the explanations provided by LIME, leaving it unclear whether such visualisations improved diagnostic safety.

In [18], saliency maps were used to visually confirm that the model focused appropriately on the lesion areas. Yet, these explanations were limited to the predicted class, and there was no analysis of how the focus point differed across other potential classes. To improve interoperability, [26] proposed an ensemble of explainability techniques, which is useful for analyzing consistency and variation, but it lacks support for simultaneous multi-class analysis.

A hierarchical tree-based approach in [32] utilized segmentation and clustering to extract texture features, aiming to present results in a human-friendly format. However, it did not evaluate how much the extracted features contributed to the model's decision. Concept Relevance Propagation [2] attempts to identify not only which areas the model attends to, but also the underlying concepts those areas represent. Still, verifying the correctness of these learned concepts remains challenging and often requires expert labeling which is an inherently difficult task in medical contexts.

Some studies used Grad-CAM saliency maps with lesion segmentation [31] which resembles our approach. However, these methods typically threshold the saliency map at 0.5 for a single class, disregarding attention to alternative classes. Moreover, it is also uncertain whether this threshold is appropriate.

Overall, previous research has mainly focused on *post hoc* explanations for the predicted class and passively communicating them to clinicians. In contrast, our approach actively communicates potential model failures by visualizing attention across all relevant classes, thereby supporting both explainability and diagnostic safety.

2.2   Safer ML Using Statistical Data Drift Detection

Runtime model monitoring and human-in-the-loop mechanisms are foundational pillars of AI safety. SafeML is a technique that uses statistical tools to monitor machine learning model performance during deployment. A key component of SafeML is the detection of data drifts, i.e., measuring the divergence between distributions of incoming data and relevant training data using statistical metrics such as ECDF-based distance measures. This allows SafeML to estimate potential performance degradation when the model encounters significantly different data from those seen during training. SafeML also brings a human into the loop, particularly when significant drifts are detected to help make safer decisions. The concept of SafeML was first introduced in [7], and it has since evolved and been cited in the German Industry Standard for Machine Learning Uncertainty Quantification (DIN SPEC 92005) [28].

The method was adapted for image classification tasks [5] by incorporating a bootstrapping-based approach to improve the validation of distributional changes. A follow-up study applied SafeML to time-series and regression problems [3], where additional metrics were introduced to assess model robustness. However, a notable challenge remains in determining appropriate thresholds for drift detection. To address this, [21] proposed an adaptive mechanism for automatic threshold selection.

SafeML has demonstrated applicability across diverse domains, including intrusion detection [7], autonomous driving [5,8], robotic safety systems [6,15], and UAV-based wind turbine inspection [27]. A more recent study [20] presented a tailored version of SafeML that examines internal layers and features of neural networks to improve drift detection accuracy. This approach was further extended for Large Language Model safety under the name SafeLLM [40].

In this paper, our distinct contribution in SafeML is an extension of the concept that integrates explainability and coverage factors to evaluate its application on skin cancer detection tasks.

2.3   Research Questions

Our study addresses the following research questions:

- **RQ1:** Does the application of the GCAPM method improve the reliability of explainability in skin lesion classification models compared to conventional CAM-based methods?
- **RQ2:** How can we quantitatively evaluate the risk by comparing the quality of explainability with diagnostic performance, and what insights can be drawn from the results?
- **RQ3:** How can the integration of SafeML improve the detection of abnormal diagnoses in skin lesion classification models, particularly in clinical and mobile health settings?

2.4   Contributions

This study makes the following key contributions to enhance the performance, interpretability, and ultimately provides active safety monitoring, of skin lesion classification models: (1) GCAPM evaluation allows for more intuitive, reliable, and quantitative explanations of model predictions across all potential classes, improving on previous approaches. (2) By comparing the quality of explainability with the model's diagnostic performance, it becomes possible to establish the risk of misdiagnosis and prediction errors. (3) The integration of SafeML in this context enables proactive detection of abnormal diagnostic results and uncertainties in model predictions.

3   Methodology

We adopt a two-stage structure comprising an offline and a runtime process shown in Fig. 1. In the offline stage, the relationship between segmentation outputs and the qualitative metrics of explainability is analyzed. The runtime stage builds on this knowledge to detect anomalies and ensure reliable predictions.

3.1   Global Class Activation Probabilistic Mapping (GCAPM)

The central idea in our proposal is to explain which class each pixel is associated with, rather than simply visualising pixel-level attention. While various CAM-based methods can be used for this, Grad-CAM is adopted as the base method. In Grad-CAM, the importance α_k^c of a target layer A^k corresponding to the target class c is computed using global average pooling of gradients as shown in Eq. 1. A weighted linear combination is performed by summation and then ReLU (Rectified Linear Unit) is applied to obtain a Grad-CAM that extracts only the scores that contribute positively to the target class.

$$\alpha_k^c = \frac{1}{Z} \sum_i \sum_j \frac{\partial y^c}{\partial A_{ij}^k}, \quad \text{Grad-CAM} = \text{ReLU}\left(\sum_k \alpha_k^c A^k \right) \tag{1}$$

Then, the class c that shows the highest attention at a pixel position (h,w) is selected, and its class index is stored as $C_{h,w}$ as shown in Eq. 1. This makes it possible to visualize which class each pixel is most strongly associated with. The GCAPM calculation process is performed according to the steps shown in Algorithm 1.

$$C_{h,w} = \text{argmax}_c P(c|\text{cam}(h, w)) \tag{2}$$

Algorithm 1. GCAPM Visualization

Input: input image x, trained classifier f, **Output**: GCAPM I
Initialize Grad-CAM array M
for Each class c in all classes of f **do**
    Get prediction class score y^c by $f_c(x)$
    Calculate the gradient of the activation map A^k to y^c using Eq. (1)
    Calculate Grad-CAM m of c by Eq. (1)
    Apply Eq. (2) to m.
    Append m to M
end for
for pixel(i,j) i and j are index of location of M **do**
    Assign the class with the highest activation at (i, j) to I
end for
return I

3.2   SafeML Evaluation

While Mean Intersection over Union (Mean IoU) is a standard metric for segmentation [43], it is not sufficient to capture the underestimation of attention to lesion areas. Instead we use Attribute Sensitivity (Att Sensitivity) (Eq. 3) and Attribute False Positive Rate (Att FPR) (Eq. 4). Att Sensitivity is a metric of how well the model focused on the lesion areas. Att FPR is a metric of how much the model focused on non-lesion areas by mistake. Note that in this study, we use metrics such as sensitivity and FPR, but these differ from the definitions typically used in classification tasks and measure the spatial overlap between model GCAPM and lesion regions. Therefore, the prefix 'Att' is used to indicate that these metrics do not explicitly indicate classification performance.

$$\text{Att Sensitivity} = \frac{\text{True Positive}}{(\text{True Positive} + \text{False Negative})} \tag{3}$$

$$\text{Att FPR} = \frac{\text{False Positive}}{(\text{False Positive} + \text{True Negative})} \tag{4}$$

3.3   Selective Prediction

In practical deployments, prediction labels are unavailable making it challenging to detect misclassifications. To mitigate this, we propose a selective prediction framework using a meta-classifier (see Eq. 5).

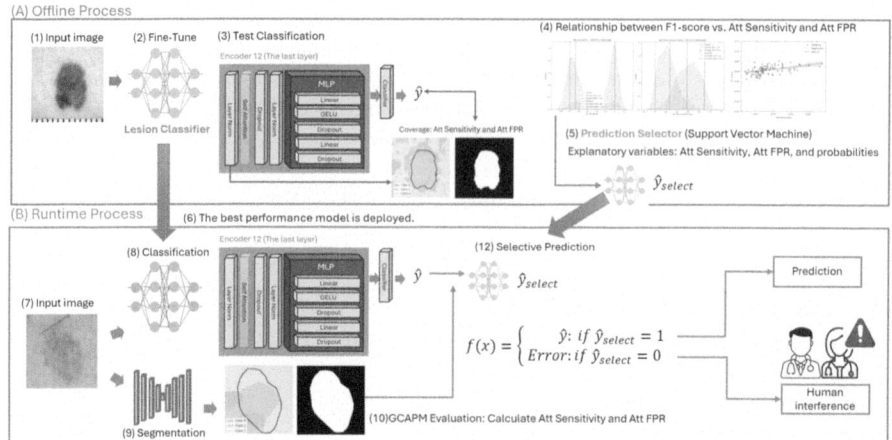

Fig. 1. Safety Skin Lesion Detection Procedure: Using the knowledge gained from offline collection and accumulation of coverage estimation rates of GCAPM and segmentation, anomaly detection is performed during runtime diagnosis. When an anomaly is detected, we alter human intervention to ensure model reliability.

$$f(x) = \begin{cases} \hat{y} : \hat{y}_{select} = 1 \\ \varepsilon : \hat{y}_{select} = 0 \end{cases} \tag{5}$$

This meta-classifier takes as input the model's prediction probabilities, along with Att sensitivity, Att FPR, and performs binary classification to determine whether the prediction of the original lesion diagnosis model is accurate or not. If the meta-classifier predicts the original diagnosis correctly, the prediction is accepted. Otherwise, human intervention is triggered. This selective prediction framework helps reduce the risk of providing users with potentially incorrect diagnoses by enabling timely human oversight.

4   Experimental Setup

4.1   Dataset

Offline Dataset: We used the ISIC 2017 (3 classes) and the ISIC 2019 (3 classes) for training and validation. While, ISIC2019 originally contains eight classes, we selected three to simplify the validation process. These datasets are the most widely used publicly resources for skin lesion classification. To avoid duplication, we excluded overlapping samples between ISIC2017 and ISIC2019, following the method described in [10]. While ISIC2017 provides segmentation annotations, ISIC2019 does not. To address this, we generated segmentation masks for ISIC2019 using DeepLabV3 with a ResNet backbone, fine-tuned on the HAM10000 [38,39] dataset, achieving a Mean IoU of 88% and Pixel Accuracy of 97%. **Runtime Dataset:** To simulate data shift conditions, we created five versions of the original dataset by applying Gaussian blur at five intensity levels, ranging from 10% to 50%. As shown by the F1 scores shown in Fig. 4, the performance of the model declined progressively as the level of blurring increased.

4.2   Models

Lesion Classifier: We evaluated our approach on two model architectures: the CNN-based pre-trained MobileNetV2 [35] and transformer-based Vision Transformer [17]. These models were trained with an initial learning rate of 1e-5. After a five-epoch warm-up phase, the learning rate was gradually decreased until the final epoch. Training was run for up to 50 epochs, and the model with the lowest validation loss was selected as the best performing version. **Selective Predictor:** For the selective prediction task, we used a Support Vector Machine [11,13,19] as the metalearning model. SVM was chosen for its strong generalization performance despite being a relatively simple, yet effective, weak learner.

5   Results

5.1   Risk Mitigation by Improvement of Explainability

Results in Fig. 2 demonstrate that our proposed GCAPM method effectively highlights instances where the model attends to different classes within the lesion during prediction. These nuanced patterns are often overlooked by conventional approaches that only visualise the predicted class. By enabling a deeper understanding of the model's focusing mechanisms, GCAPM enhances explainability and contributes to reducing diagnostic risk.

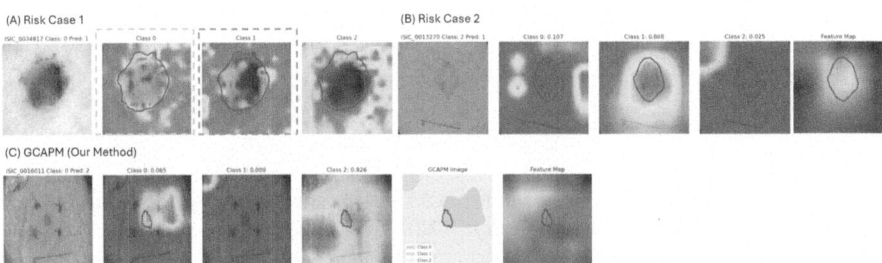

Fig. 2. Risk Case 1 is Grad-CAM in classes of ISIC 2019. The red line shows the boundary of the lesion. The yellow-framed image is the actual class, and the green is the predicted class. Risk Case 2: The original image, Grad-CAM for each class, and the feature map are shown. Despite the incorrect prediction, the focus area was intensive on the lesion site. On the surface, the explanation seems reasonable. GCAPM is our method. This clearly displays potential other predictions. (Color figure online)

5.2   Risk Assessment by Correlation of Coverage and Performance

Figure 3 shows the distribution of data density for Att sensitivity and Att FPR. These results show clear trends in prediction behaviour. In particular, for MobileNet, inaccurate predictions tend to cluster in areas with low attribute sensitivity, while accurate predictions are more prevalent in areas of high sensitivity. In contrast, the distribution of FPR remains relatively uniform distribution for accurate predictions, indicating that as the GCAPM prediction progresses, the model's overemphasis on specific attributes decreases, leading to more stable predictions. These findings suggest a strong connection between attribute metrics and prediction accuracy. Specifically, Att sensitivity and Att FPR can serve as supplementary indicators of trust in the model's predictions.

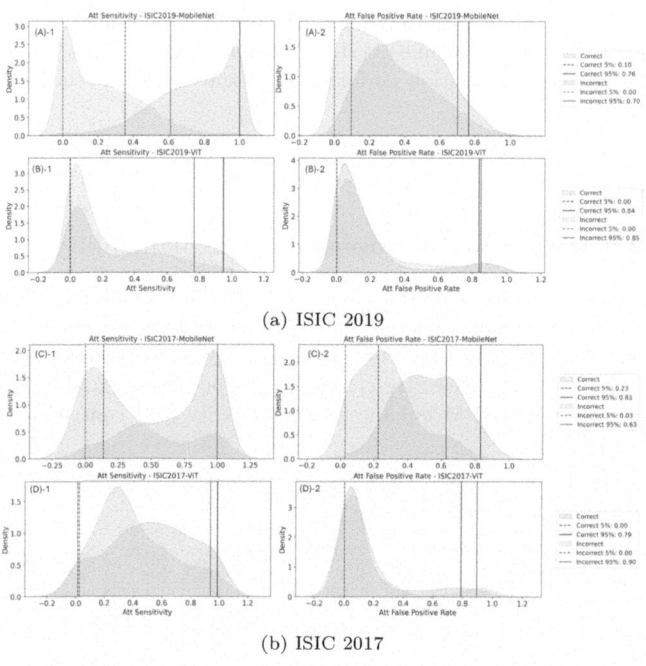

Fig. 3. Density of Attributes performance: (A) to (D) correspond to the combinations of MobileNet and Vision Transformer in ISIC2017 and ISIC2019, respectively, and show the data density of the attributes performance in each model.

Table 1 shows the correlation between attribute metrics and prediction performance. For the MobileNet trained on ISIC 2017, moderate positive correlations were observed between attribute metrics and prediction performance metrics, including F1 score and accuracy. A similar pattern was observed in the MobileNet-ISIC 2019 combination. On the other hand, the lesion ratio, defined as the proportion of lesion pixels in the full image, showed no significant correlation with predictive performance. This suggests that the lesion size has limited impact on model accuracy, reinforcing our hypothesis that attribute-based metrics can be reliable indicators for evaluating model trustworthiness and guiding risk mitigation.

Table 1. Correlation Between Attribute Metrics and Predictive Performance

Dataset	Model	Coverage	F1 Score	Accuracy	Lesion ratio
(A) ISIC2017	MobileNet	Att Sensitivity	**0.48**	**0.48**	−0.11
		Att FPR	**0.48**	**0.50**	0.06
(B) ISIC2017	ViT	Att Sensitivity	0.28	**0.35**	−0.05
		Att FPR	0.11	0.08	0.05
(C) ISIC2019	MobileNet	Att Sensitivity	**0.66**	**0.69**	0.08
		Att FPR	0.15	0.22	0.18
(D) ISIC2019	ViT	Att Sensitivity	−0.14	−0.12	0.07
		Att FPR	0.00	0.03	0.04

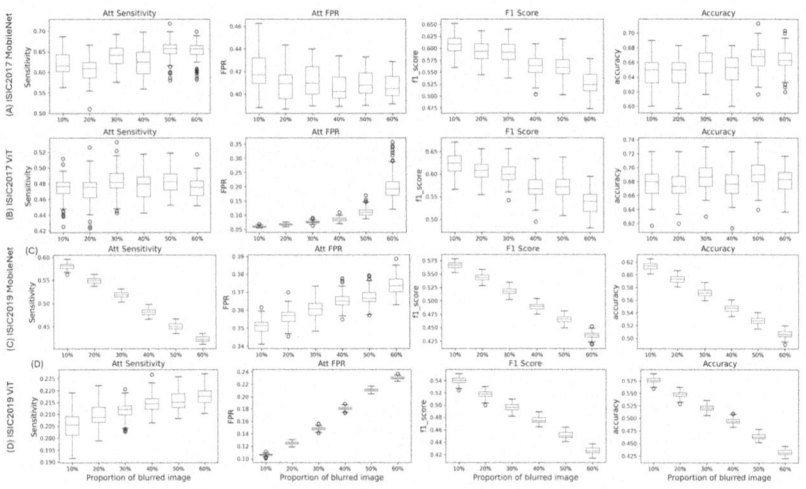

Fig. 4. Attributes and Predictive Performance each Data: (A) shows the MobileNet model from ISIC 2017, (B) shows the Vision Transformer from ISIC 2017, (C) shows the MobileNet from ISIC 2019, and (D) shows the changes in attribute and prediction performance when using the Vision Transformer from ISIC 2019.

5.3 Improvement Abnormal Diagnosis Detection in Runtime

Figure 5 presents the results of evaluating prediction accuracy both within and outside the confidence interval (CI) (Fig. 3) of the attribute metrics and for data with a prediction probability of 50% or more presented in Fig. 5. The experimental findings show that the lesion classifier achieves high diagnostic accuracy within the CI. Specifically, MobileNet yielded accurate predictions for around 80% of the data within the CI, while the Vision Transformer (ViT) on the ISIC 2017 achieved correct predictions for approximately 70% of the data. In contrast, prediction accuracy outside the CI dropped to around 30%, indicating a substantial decline in reliability.

Furthermore, the prediction accuracy within the CI was consistently higher than that of data with prediction probabilities exceeding 50%. This suggests that CI that is

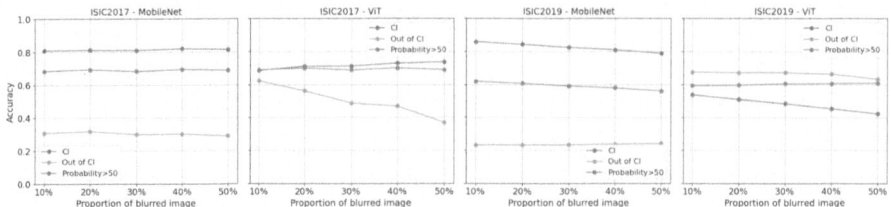

Fig. 5. Prediction Accuracy in CI, Out of CI, and Probability

derived from attribute metrics offers a more precise and reliable indication of prediction certainty than probability scores alone.

Table 2. Improvement of Accuracy by Runtime Selective Prediction

Dataset	*Model	10% Acc	Inacc	20% Acc	Inacc	30% Acc	Inacc	40% Acc	Inacc	50% Acc	Inacc
(A) ISIC2017	MobileNet	0.91	0.80	0.91	0.77	0.89	0.77	0.88	0.76	0.86	0.74
(B) ISIC2017	ViT	0.90	0.68	0.87	0.66	0.82	0.66	0.82	0.68	0.84	0.75
(C) ISIC2019	MobileNet	0.94	0.85	0.93	0.85	0.92	0.85	0.90	0.84	0.88	0.83
(D) ISIC2019	ViT	0.96	0.89	0.96	0.87	0.96	0.85	0.96	0.84	0.95	0.83

Table 2 shows the results of applying a runtime selective prediction strategy. This experiment tested whether a selective predictor could reliably determine the accuracy of the lesion classifier's predictions under increasingly challenging conditions, including 10% to 50% artificially produced contamination to the data, as shown in Fig. 4.

Even under these challenging conditions, the selective predictor idenitifed correct predictions with approximately 90% accuracy across most settings. Moreover, it successfully flagged inaccurate predictions with over 75% accuracy in all cases except Pattern (B). These results confirm the effectiveness of the proposed framework in proactively detecting and avoiding high risk misdiagnoses. They show a potential for this method to significantly improve diagnostic safety by enabling the system to prevent predictions likely ot be incorrect, reducing the risk of misdiagnosis by a very large margin in most of our experiments.

6   Discussion and Future Work

6.1   Discussion

The experimental findings demonstrate that GCAPM significantly contributed to explainability, i.e. clarifying the reason for diagnosis, and reducing the risk of misdiagnosis. By visualizing class-wise attention lesion areas, even in challenging or ambiguous cases that are often overlooked with conventional methods, GCAPM helped clarify the reasoning behind predictions.

Moreover, accurate predictions tended to concentrate in areas with high Att Sensitivity, while incorrect predictions tended to occur in regions with low Att Sensitivity. Att FPR remained relatively uniform reflecting the model's ability to converge towards the correct class while reducing excessive dependence on any particular class. These results suggest that Att sensitivity and Att FPR, as measured in GCAPM, are effective indicators of prediction reliability.

Furthermore, data within the confidence interval CI derived from attribute metrics consistently showed higher diagnostic accuracy than data selected based solely on prediction probability. Additionally, under simulated conditions of degraded model performance (with 10–50% data contamination), the selective predictor maintained approximately 90% accuracy in distinguishing correct from incorrect predictions. In misdiagnosed cases, risk was successfully detected with 75% accuracy, excluding pattern (B) in Table 2.

Collectively, these findings indicate that our safety monitoring framework, introducing GCAPM and selective predictors inspired by SafeML, has the potential to significantly improve the performance of diagnostic support by proactively avoiding predictions with a high risk of misdiagnosis.

6.2   Future Work

In this study, we simulated data drift by adding random noise. Future work will focus on evaluating fairness and generaliztion by analysing the impact of skin tone variations on diagnoses. While public datasets used in this study contain mainly light skin tones, realistic environments are likely to encounter more diverse skin tone populations. Assessing the framework's adaptability and fairness under these conditions is a key next step. Moreover, we plan to explore applicability in broader AI domains, including Generative AI models like Large Language Models and Large Vision Models.

6.3   Research Limitations

This study utilised a CAM method compatible with both ViT and MobileNet. GCAPM was computed probabilistically across all classes. While ViT has the potential to extract richer and more meaningful features through its self-attention mechanism, the explainability of attention layers is not always intuitive or interpretable. Although advanced methods such as Attention Rollout [1], Attention Flow [1], and Deep Taylor Decomposition [14] have been proposed, explanability research specific to ViT remains at early stages. Further work is needed to develop methods that offer transparent and reliable interpretation of ViT structures. Additionally, the proposed method assumes access to the internal structure of the model, potentially limiting applicability to commercial and proprietary systems. In such cases, model-agnostic approaches like SMILE [4] can be considered.

7   Conclusion

This study addressed two issues associated with deploying DL in medical diagnosis: (1) the risk that a false prediction may appear trustworthy due to misleading single-class explanability visualization, and (2) the risk related to the inherent uncertainty in deployment scenarios where ground-truth labels are unavailable. The former risk was avoided using GCAPM, while the latter uncertainty was reduced by combining GCAPM with a selective predictor. Our results demonstrate that the proposed system contributes to enabling safer and more reliable use of DL in medical settings, with limitations noted and further work outlined.

Acknowledgments. The authors would like to thank the Data Science, Artificial Intelligence, and Modelling (DAIM) Institute at the University of Hull for their support. Furthermore, the authors extend their heartfelt gratitude to Dr. Jun-ya Norimatsu at ALINEAR Corp. for technical advice with the experiments.

References

1. Abnar, S., Zuidema, W.: Quantifying attention flow in transformers. arXiv preprint arXiv:2005.00928 (2020)
2. Achtibat, R., et al.: From attribution maps to human-understandable explanations through concept relevance propagation. Nat. Mach. Intell. **5**(9), 1006–1019 (2023)
3. Akram, M.N., Ambekar, A., Sorokos, I., Aslansefat, K., Schneider, D.: StaDRe and staDRo: reliability and robustness estimation of ml-based forecasting using statistical distance measures. In: Trapp, M., Schoitsch, E., Guiochet, J., Bitsch, F. (eds.) SAFECOMP 2022. LNCS, vol. 13415, pp. 289–301. Springer, Cham (2022)
4. Aslansefat, K., Hashemian, M., Walker, M., Akram, M.N., Sorokos, I., Papadopoulos, Y.: Explaining black boxes with a smile: statistical model-agnostic interpretability with local explanations. IEEE Software (2023)
5. Aslansefat, K., Kabir, S., Abdullatif, A., Vasudevan, V., Papadopoulos, Y.: Toward improving confidence in autonomous vehicle software: a study on traffic sign recognition systems. Computer **54**(8), 66–76 (2021)
6. Aslansefat, K., et al.: SafeDrones: real-time reliability evaluation of UAVs using executable digital dependable identities. In: Seguin, C., Zeller, M., Prosvirnova, T. (eds.) IMBSA 2022. LNCS, vol. 13525, pp. 252–266. Springer, Cham (2022). https://doi.org/10.1007/978-3-031-15842-1_18
7. Aslansefat, K., Sorokos, I., Whiting, D., Tavakoli Kolagari, R., Papadopoulos, Y.: SafeML: safety monitoring of machine learning classifiers through statistical difference measures. In: Zeller, M., Höfig, K. (eds.) IMBSA 2020. LNCS, vol. 12297, pp. 197–211. Springer, Cham (2020). https://doi.org/10.1007/978-3-030-58920-2_13
8. Bergler, M., Kolagari, R.T., Lundqvist, K.: Case study on the use of the SafeML approach in training autonomous driving vehicles. In: Sclaroff, S., Distante, C., Leo, M., Farinella, G.M., Tombari, F. (eds.) ICIAP 2022, Part III. LNCS, vol. 13233, pp. 87–97. Springer, Cham (2022)
9. Cao, Q.H., Nguyen, T.T.H., Nguyen, V.T.K., Nguyen, X.P.: A novel explainable artificial intelligence model in image classification problem. arXiv preprint arXiv:2307.04137 (2023)
10. Cassidy, B., Kendrick, C., Brodzicki, A., Jaworek-Korjakowska, J., Yap, M.H.: Analysis of the ISIC image datasets: usage, benchmarks and recommendations. Med. Image Anal. (2021)
11. Cervantes, J., Garcia-Lamont, F., Rodríguez-Mazahua, L., Lopez, A.: A comprehensive survey on support vector machine classification: applications, challenges and trends. Neurocomputing **408**, 189–215 (2020)
12. Chanda, T., et al.: Dermatologist-like explainable AI enhances trust and confidence in diagnosing melanoma. Nat. Commun. **15**(1), 524 (2024)

13. Chang, C.C., Lin, C.J.: LibSVM: a library for support vector machines. ACM Trans. Intell. Syst. Technol. (TIST) **2**(3), 1–27 (2011)
14. Chefer, H., Gur, S., Wolf, L.: Transformer interpretability beyond attention visualization. In: Proceedings of the IEEE/CVF Conference on Computer Vision and Pattern Recognition, pp. 782–791 (2021)
15. Cho, H., Lee, K., Choi, N., Kim, S., Lee, J., Yang, S.: Online safety zone estimation and violation detection for nonstationary objects in workplaces. IEEE Access **10**, 39769–39781 (2022)
16. Codella, N.C., et al.: Skin lesion analysis toward melanoma detection: a challenge at the 2017 international symposium on biomedical imaging (ISBI), hosted by the international skin imaging collaboration (ISIC). In: 2018 IEEE 15th International Symposium on Biomedical Imaging (ISBI 2018), pp. 168–172. IEEE (2018)
17. Dosovitskiy, A., et al.: An image is worth 16x16 words: transformers for image recognition at scale. arXiv preprint arXiv:2010.11929 (2020)
18. Esteva, A., et al.: Dermatologist-level classification of skin cancer with deep neural networks. Nature **542**(7639), 115–118 (2017)
19. Fan, R.E., Chang, K.W., Hsieh, C.J., Wang, X.R., Lin, C.J.: Liblinear: a library for large linear classification. Mach. Learn. Res. **9**, 1871–1874 (2008)
20. Farhad, A.H., Sorokos, I., Akram, M.N., Aslansefat, K., Schneider, D.: Scope compliance uncertainty estimate. arXiv preprint arXiv:2312.10801 (2023)
21. Farhad, A.H., Sorokos, I., Schmidt, A., Akram, M.N., Aslansefat, K., Schneider, D.: Keep your distance: determining sampling and distance thresholds in machine learning monitoring. In: Seguin, C., Zeller, M., Prosvirnova, T. (eds.) IMBSA 2022. LNCS, vol. 13525, pp. 219–234. Springer, Cham (2022)
22. Gertych, A., Faust, O.: AI explainability and bias propagation in medical decision support (2024)
23. Hauser, K., et al.: Explainable artificial intelligence in skin cancer recognition: a systematic review. Eur. J. Cancer **167**, 54–69 (2022)
24. Hernández-Pérez, C., et al.: BCN20000: dermoscopic lesions in the wild. Sci. Data **11**(1), 641 (2024)
25. Hosny, K.M., Said, W., Elmezain, M., Kassem, M.A.: Explainable deep inherent learning for multi-classes skin lesion classification. Appl. Soft Comput. **159**, 111624 (2024)
26. Hryniewska-Guzik, W., Longo, L., Biecek, P.: CNN-based explanation ensembling for dataset, representation and explanations evaluation. In: Longo, L., Lapuschkin, S., Seifert, C. (eds.) xAI 2024. CCIS, vol. 2154, pp. 346–368. Springer, Cham (2024). https://doi.org/10.1007/978-3-031-63797-1_18
27. Kabir, S., Aslansefat, K., Gope, P., Campean, F., Papadopoulos, Y.: Combining drone-based monitoring and machine learning for online reliability evaluation of wind turbines. In: 2022 International Conference on Computing, Electronics & Communications Engineering (iCCECE), pp. 53–58. IEEE (2022)
28. Kläs, M.: DIN SPEC 92005: Machine Learning – Uncertainty Quantification. DIN SPEC 92005, Beuth Verlag GmbH (DIN - Deutsches Institut für Normung), Berlin, Germany (2022). https://www.din.de/en/wdc-beuth:din21:343195966, standard for methods and measures for quantifying uncertainty in machine learning models
29. Metta, C., et al.: Explainable deep image classifiers for skin lesion diagnosis. arXiv preprint arXiv:2111.11863 (2021)
30. Nigar, N., Umar, M., Shahzad, M.K., Islam, S., Abalo, D.: A deep learning approach based on explainable artificial intelligence for skin lesion classification. IEEE Access **10**, 113715–113725 (2022)

31. Nunnari, F., Kadir, M.A., Sonntag, D.: On the overlap between grad-cam saliency maps and explainable visual features in skin cancer images. In: Holzinger, A., Kieseberg, P., Tjoa, A.M., Weippl, E. (eds.) CD-MAKE 2021. LNCS, vol. 12844, pp. 241–253. Springer, Cham (2021). https://doi.org/10.1007/978-3-030-84060-0_16

32. Pintelas, E., Liaskos, M., Livieris, I.E., Kotsiantis, S., Pintelas, P.: A novel explainable image classification framework: case study on skin cancer and plant disease prediction. Neural Comput. Appl. **33**(22), 15171–15189 (2021). https://doi.org/10.1007/s00521-021-06141-0

33. Ribeiro, M.T., Singh, S., Guestrin, C.: "why should i trust you?" explaining the predictions of any classifier. In: Proceedings of the 22nd ACM SIGKDD, pp. 1135–1144 (2016)

34. Saadatfar, H., Kiani-Zadegan, Z., Ghahremani-Nezhad, B.: Us-lime: increasing fidelity in lime using uncertainty sampling on tabular data. Neurocomputing **597**, 127969 (2024)

35. Sandler, M., Howard, A., Zhu, M., Zhmoginov, A., Chen, L.C.: Mobilenetv2: inverted residuals and linear bottlenecks. In: Proceedings of the IEEE Conference on Computer Vision and Pattern Recognition, pp. 4510–4520 (2018)

36. Selvaraju, R.R., Cogswell, M., Das, A., Vedantam, R., Parikh, D., Batra, D.: Grad-cam: visual explanations from deep networks via gradient-based localization. In: Proceedings of the IEEE International Conference on Computer Vision, pp. 618–626 (2017)

37. Sundararajan, M., Taly, A., Yan, Q.: Axiomatic attribution for deep networks. In: International Conference on Machine Learning, pp. 3319–3328. PMLR (2017)

38. Tschandl, P., et al.: Human-computer collaboration for skin cancer recognition. Nat. Med. **26**(8), 1229–1234 (2020)

39. Tschandl, P., Rosendahl, C., Kittler, H.: The ham10000 dataset, a large collection of multi-source dermatoscopic images of common pigmented skin lesions. Sci. Data **5**(1), 1–9 (2018)

40. Walker, C., Rothon, C., Aslansefat, K., Papadopoulos, Y., Dethlefs, N.: Using large language models to recommend repair actions for offshore wind maintenance. In: Journal of Physics: Conference Series, vol. 2875, p. 012025. IOP Publishing (2024)

41. Wang, H., et al.: Score-cam: score-weighted visual explanations for convolutional neural networks. In: Proceedings of the IEEE/CVF Conference on Computer Vision and Pattern Recognition Workshops, pp. 24–25 (2020)

42. Xiang, X., Yu, H., Wang, Y., Wang, G.: Stable local interpretable model-agnostic explanations based on a variational autoencoder. Appl. Intell. **53**(23), 28226–28240 (2023)

43. Zhang, Y., Mehta, S., Caspi, A.: Rethinking semantic segmentation evaluation for explainability and model selection. arXiv preprint arXiv:2101.08418 (2021)

44. Zhou, B., Khosla, A., Lapedriza, A., Oliva, A., Torralba, A.: Learning deep features for discriminative localization. In: Proceedings of the IEEE Conference on Computer Vision and Pattern Recognition, pp. 2921–2929 (2016)

CODIF: Counterfactual Data-Augmentations for Estimating Perception Influencing Factors

Christopher Meszaros[1]([✉]) [ID], Roman Gansch[1] [ID], and Peter Liggesmeyer[2] [ID]

[1] Corporate Research, Robert Bosch GmbH, Renningen, Germany
{christopher.meszaros,roman.gansch}@de.bosch.com
[2] Software Engineering Institute University of Kaiserslautern,
Kaiserslautern, Germany
peter.liggesmeyer@iese.fraunhofer.de

Abstract. Deep neural networks (DNNs) have become the state of the art for object detection tasks in autonomous driving systems (ADS). These models often perform safety-critical tasks, such as pedestrian detection and collision avoidance. Therefore, these models must demonstrate an elevated level of dependability within the operational design domain (ODD). Safety analysis requires a causal perspective to understand the effects of perception influencing factors within an ODD. However, the ODD contains complex causal relations that introduce several sources of confounding bias. This makes it difficult to estimate the causal effect of influencing factors within the ODD using associational metrics. Our framework eliminates confounding bias by taking a counterfactual data-augmentation (CDA) approach to estimate the causal effect of perception influencing factors. Our running example of an influencing factor is "half-occlusions" (visibility range of 40%–60%). Our framework describes a process of identifying relevant half-occlusion characteristics and assigning appropriate augmentations. Finally, a comparative analysis is presented between our causal metric and the associational metric, which is based on conditional probability.

Keywords: Safe AI · Causal inference · Explainability

1 Introduction

Deep neural networks (DNNs) have achieved significant practical success in the field of computer vision. Two technological trends have drastically increased the predictive power of DNN models: larger datasets and increased computational power [1]. These trends have established DNN models as the state of the art for all prediction problems involving high-dimensional inputs, such as images. Consequently, the industry is focusing on using DNN models to solve perception tasks, such as object detection or semantic segmentation, for autonomous driving systems (ADS).

P. Katsaros (Ed.): IMBSA 2025, LNCS 15755, pp. 159–174, 2026.
https://doi.org/10.1007/978-3-032-05073-1_11

The success of DNNs has come at the cost of decreased interpretability. Powerful computers enable the training of models with millions of parameters [2]. This enormous number of parameters has contributed to the black-box behavior of DNN models. Therefore, the validation strategies for these models are primarily based on an associational perspective (e.g., accuracy of the test set). These metrics are based on the i.i.d. assumption [3] (i.e., all samples are independent from each other and drawn from same distribution). Unfortunately, these associational metrics are not sufficient for validating safety-critical systems, such as object detection for ADSs.

Safety-critical systems require a high level of dependability that can be demonstrated through failure-modeling approaches. The key concept in failure modeling is to assess the effects of a fault on a system failure (e.g., false negatives in object detection) based on principles of cause and effect. This causal principle is lacking in associational-based metrics due to *spurious associations*. These types of associations are not necessarily derived from a causal mechanism between two variables but may be induced by confounding variable(s) (i.e., this phenomenon is known as confounding bias). Understanding the causal influence of faults within a safety-critical system is crucial for developing strategies to mitigate the probability of hazardous outcomes. Traditional fault modeling techniques rely on modeling assumptions that rarely hold in the operational design domain (ODD) of ADS [4].[1] These limitations have opened a line of research into using causal inference as a safety framework for AD/ADAS components; we will visit this line of research in Sect. 2.1.

Confounding bias arises when confounders have a causal influence on both the *exposure variable* and the *outcome* variable. The field of causal inference includes several methods for removing confounding bias. These methods can be performed through *observational studies* (e.g., IP weighting, matching) or through *interventional studies* (e.g., controlled experiments) [5,6]. The main concept behind all these techniques is to eliminate the causal influence of the confounders on the exposure variable. An interventional study is often an infeasible approach of testing ADSs due to excessive costs, exposure to hazardous outcomes, and a lack of controllability (e.g., weather). Current testing of ADSs focuses instead on observational approaches, simulation, and synthetic data.

ISO 21448 identifies several safety-relevant factors affecting perception including weather conditions, distance, occlusion, brightness, and others (we will refer to these as *influencing factors*) [7,8]. The ODD contains many complex causal relations that introduce several sources of confounding bias [4,9]. For example, there are at least two confounding variables when estimating the causal effect of occlusion on the false negative (FN) rate in a pedestrian detection model: Time of day and adversarial weather conditions (e.g., rain). Both influencing factors have a causal effect on the probability of occlusion (i.e., affecting

---

[1] e.g. Fault tree analysis (FTA) assumes independence between basic events while failure mode and effects analysis (FMEA) reasons from a single point of failure. These modeling assumptions allow the probability of failure to propagate through principles of cause and effect.

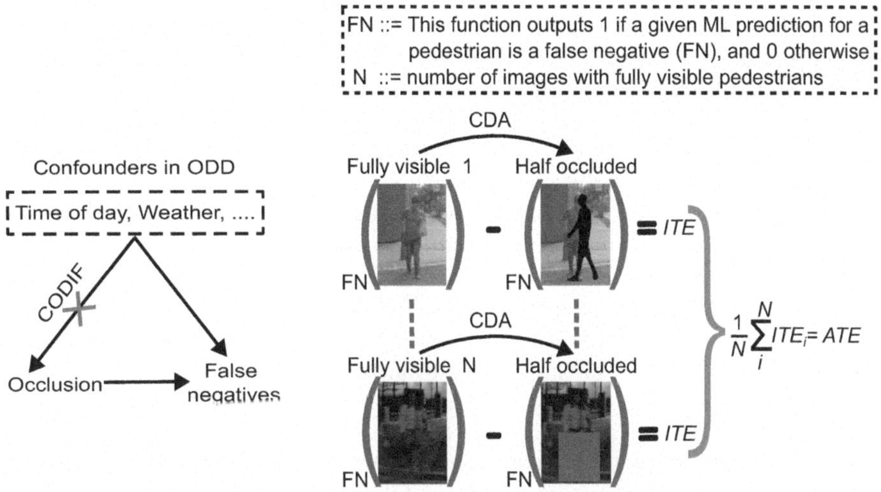

FN ::= This function outputs 1 if a given ML prediction for a pedestrian is a false negative (FN), and 0 otherwise
N ::= number of images with fully visible pedestrians
Confounders in ODD
Time of day, Weather, ...
CODIF
Occlusion
False negatives
CDA
Fully visible 1
Half occluded
FN
FN
= ITE
CDA
Fully visible N
Half occluded
FN
FN
= ITE
$\frac{1}{N}\sum_{i}^{N} ITE_i = ATE$

(a) Causal structure (b) CODIF implementation

Fig. 1. The objective of our framework is to remove the causal influence from confounders, thereby computing the effects of occlusion (i.e. exposure variable) from a causal perspective (Fig 1a). The framework estimates the *average treatment effect* (ATE) using *counterfactual data-argumentation* (CDA) (Fig 1b)

the presence of dynamic actors within a scene, such as cars and other pedestrians). Furthermore, these factors also affect the image quality and consequently perception performance. Nighttime affects image quality by reducing brightness. Rainy conditions affect image quality by introducing blur to image (e.g., water droplets on the camera lens).

Our approach to eliminating confounding bias is based upon ideas of *Counterfactual data-augmentation* (CDA). A counterfactual is a hypothetical scenario with conditions that were not observed (i.e., contrary to fact). For example, *what if* a pedestrian was occluded by another walking pedestrian (Pedestrian *1* in Fig. 1b)? *What if* the bottom part of a pedestrian was occluded (Pedestrian N in Fig. 1b)? The key concept in counterfactual analysis is to hold all other relevant variables constant while manipulating the influencing factor of interest. Pixel-level augmentations can effectively maintain relevant conditions (e.g., image brightness, blur, distance) in the image while modifying the influencing factor of interest. The outcome variable (e.g., FN rate) will have different effects between an observed/original image and a counterfactual/augmented image. Measuring this difference allows us to analyze the causal effect at an individual level, which is known as *individual treatment effect* (ITE). Samples typically affected by confounding (e.g., nighttime images such as pedestrian N in Fig. 1b) can equally be exposed to the influencing factor. Consequently, this helps eliminate the confounding bias within the ODD. Computing the average for all ITEs results in the *average treatment effect* (ATE), as illustrated in Fig. 1b.

Therefore, to address confounding bias, we propose **CO**unterfactual **D**ata-augmentations for evaluating **I**nfluencing **F**actors (**CODIF**). Our contributions can be summarized as:

1. We formalize a CDA framework for estimating the causal effects of perception-influencing factors.
2. We present experimental results demonstrating the impact of occlusion characteristics (shape, size, and color) on perception performance.
3. We provide descriptive statistics on occlusion shapes and blocking objects for half-occluded pedestrians in the ODD of nuScenes [10].
4. Lastly, we make a comparative analysis between an associational metric and a causal metric based on the CODIF framework.

Our running example of an influencing factor is half-occlusions (visibility range of 40% to 60%) recurring within an ODD, while the outcome variable is false negative (FN) rate in a pedestrian detection model. While this paper focuses on occlusion as a perception-influencing factor, the CODIF framework can be applied to estimate other influencing factors. For example, simple augmentations such as blur and brightness adjustments can be used with the CODIF framework to estimate the effects of motion blur and difficult lighting conditions in night scenes, among others.

2   Related Work

2.1   Causal Inference for AD/ADAS Verification

The authors of [11] used a causal approach, specifically Causal Bayesian Networks (CBN), to model the effects of influencing factors on an Advanced Emergency Braking System (AEBS). Their causal model included several variables and causal relations in the ODD, such as time of day, fog, rain, and more. One of the interesting "safety queries" the authors investigated was the causal effect that an object detector model has on the number of collisions performed by the AEBS. The objective was to investigate whether improving the accuracy of an object detection model improves the avoidance of collisions within the AEBS. The authors modeled rainy weather condition as a confounder within this investigation because rain affects the object detection (adding image blur) while also affecting the brake systems (because rain causes wet ground resulting in less friction). The improvement to the AEBS performance by improving object detection alone was negligible. These types of safety queries provided a proof of concept for identifying the effects of faults using causal inference and for determining appropriate fault mitigation measures.

The authors of [4,12,13] also utilized CBNs for modeling the effects of influencing factors within the ODD. These studies specifically focused on the FN rate for a LIDAR-based perception system. The influencing factors considered by these authors are occlusion, illumination, weather conditions, and more. The authors assumed the causal relations between the influencing factors based on expert knowledge. The assumed causal structure is key to removing confounding bias and estimating the causal effect of influencing factors. The authors found that occlusion has a larger causal impact on FN than does illumination. The authors of [13] extended the framework from [12] to include a methodology for updating the CBN with new influencing factors and causal relations using independence testing. Traffic density was discovered to be a confounder for occlusion, as a dependency was demonstrated using independence testing.

The authors of [14] also targeted their modeling towards perception, although using cameras as the sensors. The authors estimated ATEs for several safety-relevant factors such as rain, fog, and traffic density. The authors used the ATEs as a metric for inferring the generation of risky scenarios for ADSs. Unlike [12, 13], who assumed a causal structure based on expert knowledge, the authors of [14] used causal discovery methods, combined with domain knowledge, to construct their causal structure. The causal discovery algorithm is based on a greedy algorithm that optimizes for Bayesian Information Criterion (BIC).

The previous studies can be categorized as using an *observational study* approach within causal inference. The data is observed and then reweighted based on an assumed (or, as in [14], discovered) causal structure. Our CDAs can be best described as an intervention-augmentation approach, where the augmentation is equivalent to interventions as described in [15]. Although our method addresses potential confounding bias by exposing every sample to the treatment/augmentation, it is still susceptible to systematic bias introduced by the augmentations themselves. However, the augmentations can be assessed qualitatively (through visualization) and quantitatively (sensitivity analysis in Sect. 3.2). While the previous studies in [11–14] rely on the assumption of the causal structure, as typical in observational studies.

2.2   Counterfactual Data-Augmentation

Several studies are utilizing augmentations from a causal perspective to reduce bias from the domain [15–21]. This approach trains the models on augmented images to reduce the bias and improve domain generalization. These augmentations can include brightness, rotation, scale, translation, and more. The idea is to create counterfactual samples in which the relevant predictive features are isolated from spurious associations arising within a domain. The augmentations in these papers typically employ a wide variety of augmentations to extend the dataset as much as possible. Ideally, retraining the data on the augmented samples compels the ML model to learn the relevant features.

Our augmentations are more restricted and systematic, specifically designed to approximate half-occlusions within the ODD. The other studies employ wider augmentations to specifically target bias from the ODD as a whole. Although we argue that the CODIF framework can be extended to use other augmentations (e.g., blur, brightness) for estimating other influencing factors of perception performance for a given ODD. To our knowledge, using a CDA to approximate typical influencing factors within an ODD is a novel approach.

3   Methodology

Our CODIF framework consists of **three steps**.

1. Identify relevant characteristics within the ODD
2. Performing sensitivity analysis for each characteristic.
3. Computing ATE using approximated counterfactuals.

Steps One through Three will be covered in the following subsections. We use the nuScenes dataset [10] for testing the ML models. Data preprocessing of nuScenes and the ML setup are detailed in Appendix A.1 and Appendix A.2, respectively.

3.1   Identify Relevant Characteristics within the ODD

Since images are high-dimensional, it is infeasible to consider the effects of an influencing factor at a pixel level. Therefore, this step collects information about recurring characteristics within the ODD and makes modeling assumptions through discretizing the characteristics. The identified characteristics will later correspond to specific augmentations performed in Steps 2 and 3.

One of the identified characteristics for occlusion is *shape*. We investigated and annotated a sample of 1000 half-occluded pedestrian. For reference, there is 20504 half-occluded pedestrians (after pre-processing in Appendix A.1) in which 1000 and were drawn at random. The annotation included categorizing the type of shape of the half-occlusion and labeling the type of blocking object that causes the occlusion. The following is a description of each shape, corresponding blocking object, and its augmentations implementation:

- **Horizontal bottom**: This occlusion shape occlude the bottom part of a pedestrian. These occlusions are typically caused by objects such as cars, fences, and construction barriers. The bottom part of the ground truth bounding box (GT bbox) will be augmented. The extraction of GT bboxes are described in Appendix A.1
- **Vertical right/left**: These shapes occlude the vertical side (either left or ride). These types of shapes consists mainly of buildings, lamp poles. The augmentations will be performed vertically on either the left or right side of the GT bbox.
- **Human standing/walking**: These shapes result when a pedestrian stands or walks in front of another. To perform this augmentation, a semantic mask of a standing/walking human from the nuImages dataset was taken. This semantic mask was pasted onto the pedestrian GT bbox with slight offset to resemble the occluding pedestrian.
- **Vertical middle**: These occlusion shapes are mainly captured by trees, poles, and traffic signs. Augmentations will be performed on a vertical slice in the middle of GT bbox of a pedestrian.

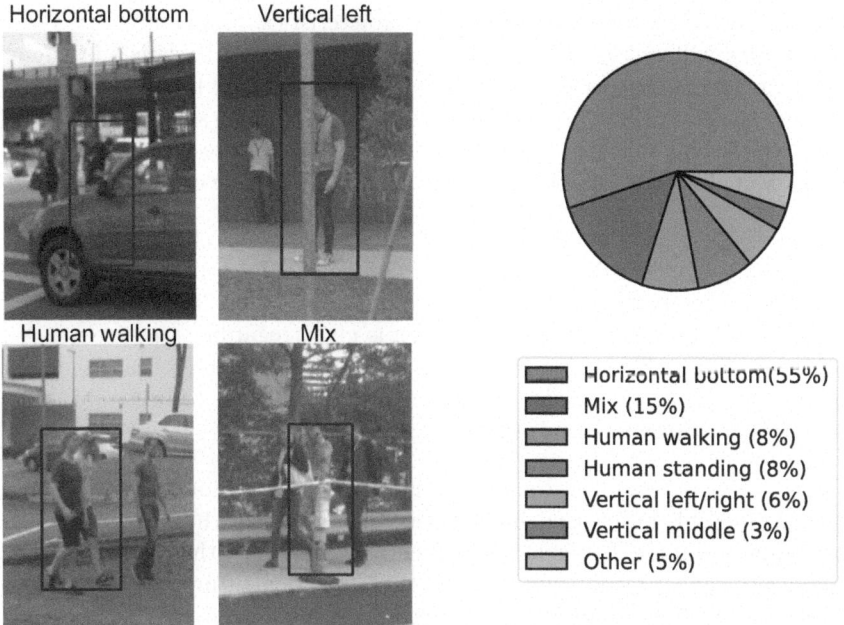

(a) Visual examples of half-occlusions.   (b) Marginal distribution of the half-occlusion shapes.

Fig. 2. Half-occlusion shapes typically recurring within the ODD. These occlusions are all in the visibility category of 40–60% for the nuScenes dataset [10]. Figure 2b shows the manual annotation of occlusion shapes for 1000 pedestrians within the visibility category of 40–60% (we will refer to these as half-occlusions).

The manual annotation of 1000 half-occluded pedestrians from nuScenes resulted in the distribution of occlusion shapes shown in Fig. 2b. We decided to exclusively focus on simple half-occluding shapes that were above 1%. This filtering removes the rare "simple shapes" grouped in the category described as "*other*" in Fig. 2b. In this category were simple shapes such as "horizontal top" (2 out of 1000), where only the top part of a pedestrian is occluded. Another rare simple shape in this category is "two-vertical." This simple shape occludes both sides of the pedestrian, leaving the middle part visible. Although these simple shapes most likely result in a FN, their low-occurrence rate will not significantly affect the average within the ATE metric.

Our annotations also included another category labeled as *mix*. An example of these half-occlusions can be seen in bottom right within Fig. 2a. These types of half-occlusions are performed by several objects at once. These occlusions typically occur when groups of people are clustered together. Although this type of occlusion shape occurs an estimated 15% of the time, modeling this type of shape is outside the scope of this paper due to the complexity of the shapes.

Our methodology considers two more characteristics: *color* and *size*.[2] These characteristics will not be investigated empirically (as with *shapes in Figure 2b*) due the vast color spectrum of blocking object and due to the difficulty in annotating the size of half-occlusions at pixel level. Instead, some rationale will be given for the chosen categorizations and further investigated in the sensitivity analysis (Sect. 3.2). The following size distributions were selected:

- **Static**: The size parameter has static value of 50% (occluding half of the pedestrian). This distribution is mainly chosen as a reference.
- **Uniform**: Size parameter is randomly assigned between 40 % and 60%. This is a natural assumption if no information is given regarding the size.
- *left* and *right*: These distributions have a size parameter that is denser around 40% (less occluded), and 60% (more occluded) respectively. More information can be found in Appendix A.3

For color, we categorized the augmentations into black or gray. Gray augmentations may blend into the environment more readily, while black augmentations stand out more. Uni-colored augmentations simplify the implementation and reduce the experimental run time. Section 4 explores future potential extensions of the CODIF framework with more complex augmentations (e.g. diffusion models).

3.2 Performing Sensitivity Analysis for Each Characteristic

The second part of the framework analyzes the effects of the identified characteristics. Significant effects will be used to justify relevant augmentations for the counterfactuals in the last step of the CODIF framework. We will use notion of probability and *do*-calculus to formalizes this step.

- Let *FN* be a variable denoting either True (T) or False (F) for a false negative
- Let *v* denote the *visibility category* according to nuScenes.[3]
- Let *A* denote the exposure variable, in our case the "exposure" is the type of augmentation (examples in Fig. 3). $A = 0$ indicates no augmentation.

$$ATE = \underbrace{P(FN = T|do(A = a), v = 4)}_{\text{Augmented images}} - \underbrace{P(FN = T|do(A = 0), v = 4)}_{\text{Original images}} \quad (1)$$

The "*do*" operator in Eq. 1 signifies the intervention of a variable, resulting in independence from other variables. The augmented pixels for each image receive a fixed pixel value, and therefore considered independently occluded without

---

[2] We define the size parameter as occluding a pedestrian between 40%–60%.

[3] There are four visibility categories within nuScenes: Category 1(0%–40%), Category 2(40%–60%), Category 3(60%–80%), Category 4(80%–100%). We will refer to category 2 as half-occlusion, and category 4 and as "fully visible.".

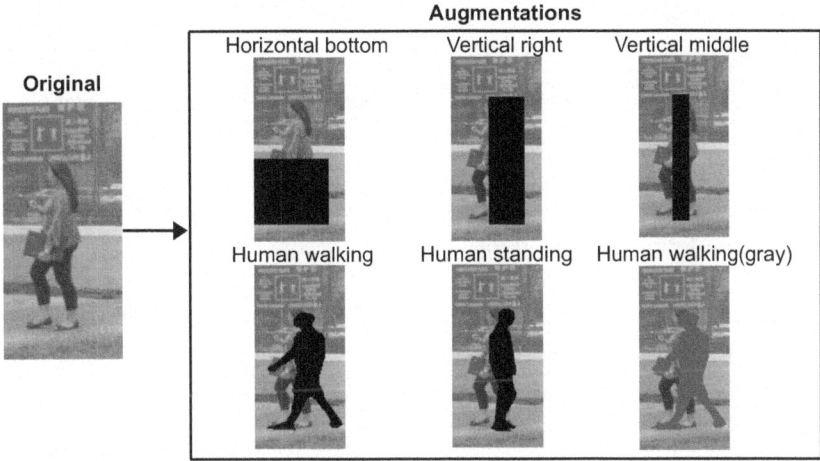

Fig. 3. Examples of CDAs corresponding to half-occlusions within the ODD

any influence from other variable (e.g., confounders within the ODD). The difference between the two *do* operations in Eq. 1 describes the ATE for a specific augmentation a.[4]

ML models might be affected differently depending on factors such as model complexity, training data, and various other factors. Therefore, our work will investigate the effects on two ML models: RetinaNet and YoloV3. The results can be observed in Table 1 and Table 2. A high positive number is interpreted as a significant increase in the probability of outputting an FN. A negative number means that the specific augmentation reduces the probability of outputting a FN. The results will be utilized in next section to justify appropriate counterfactuals.

3.3   Computing ATE Using Approximated Counterfactuals

Section 3.2 computed the ATE for a specific set of occlusion characteristics. In contrast, this section uses counterfactual notation to computes the ATE for half-occlusions as they typically occur within the ODD

- Let i represent a specific sample (i.e., instance of a fully visible pedestrian)
- Let V be the set of samples representing fully visible pedestrians
- Let $FN_i^{A=a} \in \{0, 1\}$ be the *counterfactual outcome* of a FN. The variable outputs 1 if sample i returns a FN from an ML model under augmentation a. The variable outputs 0 if no FN is returned from the ML model

---

[4] This metric is the *conditional average treatment effect* (CATE), since the analysis conditions on fully visible pedestrians. This conditioning might introduce additional bias; for example, fully visible pedestrians are more likely to be closer, leading to easier detection. Our methodology does not conditions on half-occluded pedestrians, since that requires a complex augmentation of "un-occluding" an object. Our conditioning on fully visible pedestrian allows for easier augmentations.

Table 1. ATE for a given occlusion characteristic on FN rate - RetinaNet

Shapes	size distributions + color							
	Static		*uniform*		*left*		*right*	
	black	gray	black	gray	black	gray	black	gray
horizontal bottom	0.393	0.404	0.398	0.403	0.310	0.307	0.77	0.496
Vertical right	0.461	0.353	0.458	0.378	0.369	0.237	0.547	0.489
Vertical left	0.471	0.366	0.466	0.372	0.377	0.256	0.557	0.495
Human standing	−0.178	−0.068	−0.179	0.070	−0.178	−0.078	−0.1789	−0.054
Human walking	−0.179	−0.098	−0.179	−0.099	−0.179	0.101	−0.180	−0.092
Vertical middle	0.239	0.126	0.240	0.127	0.244	0.106	0.247	0.160

Each cell corresponds to augmentation a in equation equation 1

Table 2. ATE for a given occlusion characteristic on FN rate - Yolov3

Shapes	size distributions + color							
	Static		*uniform*		*left*		*right*	
	black	gray	black	gray	black	gray	black	gray
horizontal bottom	0.393	0.404	0.398	0.403	0.310	0.307	0.77	0.496
Vertical right	0.461	0.353	0.458	0.378	0.369	0.237	0.547	0.489
Vertical left	0.471	0.366	0.466	0.372	0.377	0.256	0.557	0.495
Human standing	−0.178	−0.068	−0.179	0.070	−0.178	−0.078	−0.1789	−0.054
Human walking	−0.179	−0.098	−0.179	−0.099	−0.179	0.101	−0.180	−0.092
Vertical middle	0.239	0.126	0.240	0.127	0.244	0.106	0.247	0.160

Each cell corresponds to augmentation a in equation equation 1

The following is a formalization of the procedure illustrated in Fig. 1b where the counterfactuals are equivalent to the half-occluded augmented images.

$$ATE = \frac{1}{|V|} \sum_{i \in V} \underbrace{FN_i^{A=0}}_{\text{original image}} - \underbrace{FN_i^{A=a}}_{\text{Counter factual}} \qquad (2)$$

Each augmentation a in Eq. 2 is assigned to replicate the context around sample i. This step is known as *abduction* in counterfactual analysis. An accurate abduction step is especially important if the characteristic produces a significant difference in Table 1 and Table 2 obtained from the sensitivity analysis in previous section (Sect. 3.2). For example, the color characteristic has a significant effect on the FN rate for the two ML models. The effect of the color can be observed by comparing two neighboring cells for the same row (i.e., holds the shape and size distribution constant). The significant difference is particularly evident for human shapes. The reasoning is that human shapes "blend in" more in the environment than black augmentations as seen in Fig. 3). The following

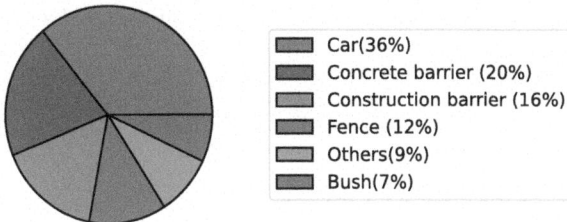

Fig. 4. The distribution of blocking objects within horizontal bottom.

abduction rule will be applied to each augmentation a in Eq. 2 to provide a more appropriate color.

$$a = \begin{cases} \textbf{Black,} & \text{if sample } i \text{ is a night scene} \\ \textbf{Gray or Black,} & \text{if sample } i \text{ is a daytime scene} \end{cases} \qquad (3)$$

Daytime samples will contain an equal distribution of black and gray augmentations to represent the range of colors in daytime scenes. Nighttime augmentations will be exclusively black to represent darker occlusions.

The abduction rule for the shape attribute will be based upon the marginal distribution obtained within the ODD (Fig. 2b). Each counterfactual sample i in Eq. 2, is assigned an shape based on following updated (removal of "mix" and "other") probabilities: horizontal bottom (70%), vertical left/right (8%), vertical middle (4%), human walking (9%), and human standing (9%). However, Table 1 and Table 2 shows only minor differences between vertical left and vertical right (similarly for human standing and walking). This can be observed by comparing two rows within a column (i.e., holding size distribution and color constant). Therefore, it can be argued that these shapes can be used interchangeable, since the minor differences wont significantly affect the ATE.

A significant difference can be observed between the left and right size distributions in Table 1 and Table 2. This indicates the importance of an appropriate abduction step that accurately estimates the size distribution for each counterfactual sample i. Since horizontal bottom is a larger part of the ODD (Fig. 2b), the focus will direct towards estimating a correct size distribution for this shape. Figure 4 shows that horizontal bottom occlusions are predominantly caused by cars. These occlusions are typically characterized by the front edge of a car (as seen in top left example in Fig. 2a). Given these observations, a portion of the horizontal bottom shapes will be characterized by two normal distributions (one for male and one for female). The parameters can be inferred by using the human height distributions (obtained from [22]) and assuming a car edge height of 79cm (resembling a small SUV according to [23]). The rest of the augmentations were assigned uniform or a *left-flatter* (see Appendix A.3).[5]

---

[5] Here we assume that distant pedestrians (15+ meters) result in noisy values of the size parameter, which is equivalent to a uniform distribution. We will also assume that closer pedestrians are more visible, resulting in a left-flatter distribution.

Table 3. Comparative analysis between an associational and a causal metric

Metric	ML models	
	RetinaNet	*Yolov3*
Associational (Eq. 4)	0.104	0.169
Causal/CODIF (Eq. 2)	−0.182	−0.061

The result from Eq. 2 will be compared to an associational metric. Following the same notation as Eq. 1, we define the following metric

$$Associational = P(FN = True|v = 4) - P(FN = True|v = 2) \qquad (4)$$

The above associational metric simply takes the difference between two conditional probabilities: probability of a FN conditioned on fully visible pedestrians and the probability of a FN conditioned on half-visible pedestrians.

4   Discussion and Conclusion

Table 3 indicates that the associational metric gives a lower probability of a false negative for half-occluded pedestrians compared to fully visible pedestrians. This is a counterintuitive metric from a safety-engineering perspective since it suggests that larger occlusions improve the perception performance. The confounders given in the introduction (Time of day and weather conditions) can be used to describe these results. These confounders cause a reduction in the number of occluded pedestrians in nighttime and adversarial weather scenes. Consequently, half-occluded pedestrians are positively associated with images of better quality, thus reducing the probability of an FN. Our causality-based framework removes the bias caused by the confounder by estimating counterfactual samples through the three steps of the CODIF framework. The causal metrics in Table 3 are more intuitive because they show that half-occlusions worsen the probability of a false negative. Safe AI engineering can benefit from using the causal metrics provided by CODIF to prioritize fault mitigation efforts targeting perception-influencing factors with the largest causal impact.

The abduction steps in Sect. 3.3 can be extended for each characteristic. More statistical properties of the ODD or increased meta-data around a sample can be collected within the first part of the framework (Sect. 3.1). The information collected at this step can be used to increase the accuracy in representative counterfactuals in Sect. 3.3. For example, a pedestrian captured by the front camera within a close range is most likely occluded by another walking pedestrian (e.g., in a crosswalk scenario). Hence an augmentation with a human walking shape would be assigned for these fully visible pedestrians.

Simple augmentations (e.g., blur, masking, and brightness) provide a straightforward implementation of estimating causal effect of perception influencing factors corresponding to occlusion, motion blur, and nighttime scenes.

However, simple augmentations may not always accurately represent realistic scenes in the ODD. Future work could investigate a framework based on *causal abstraction*, to draw an equivalence between high-level augmentations (e.g., diffusion models) and simple uni-colored augmentations. Conceptually, high and low-level augmentations could be used interchangeably if they produce similar causal effects [24]. For example, horizontal bottom occlusions are caused by arguably uni-color objects (e.g., front edge of car, construction barrier). Small pixel differences between several similar objects (e.g., different red cars) should not have a large difference in causal effect and could hypothetically be abstracted away.

A   Appendix

A.1   Data pre-processing of nuScenes

The *visibility* attribute in the nuScenes dataset is defined as *"the percentage of object pixels visible in the panoramic view of all cameras."* This definition is different from classical definition of "occlusion" wherein the occlusion attribute is only captured from one camera. The following steps were done to filter out pedestrian annotations which does not fit the classical definition of occlusion.

1. Project pedestrian 3D box corners onto image coordinates
2. Filter out all annotations projected 3D box corners outside image coordinates
3. Filter out all pedestrian annotations which are captured by two cameras. For example, there is a small overlap between all adjacent cameras such as "CAM_FRONT" and CAM_FRONT_RIGHT

The filtering resulted 80k fully visible annotated pedestrians, and 26k of half-occluded pedestrians. Step 1 was also used to create Ground truth (GT) 2D-bounding boxes (bbox). The two 3D corners projected onto the image farthest from each other were used to create the 2D bbox. These GT bboxes were used to determine FN and as a reference to perform the augmentations. E.g., Horizontal bottom augments 50% of the bottom GT bbox.

A.2   Machine Learning Set Up

We used the *mmdetection* framework for running inference on Machine learning ML models [25]. The two models we used are RetinaNet [26] (I.e Retina-net: retinanet_x101-32x4d_fpn_2x_coco) and yolov3 [27] (yolov3_d53_fp16_mstrain-608_273e_coco).

Our code specified that all bounding box prediction with an IoU below 0.3 or a *classification score* below 0.1 will be considered an false negative. The PASCAL VOC baseline sets the threshold at 0.5 [28]. Our reasoning for a using a "softer" IoU threshold is that the created 2D GT boxes are slightly larger since they are recreated from 3D box coordinates.

A.3 Size Distributions

The **left** and **right** distributions can be argued for by plotting the histogram of the visibility categories in nuScenes and observing the neighboring bins for half occlusions. Assuming a *smoothness prior*, there will be denser regions around 40% and 60% occlusions, since the neighbor bins occur in much higher amount. The exponential function was utilized with parameters to scale and shift the distribution. The exponential distribution is

$$f(x, \frac{1}{\beta}) = \frac{1}{\beta} exp(-\frac{(x - \alpha)}{\beta}) \tag{5}$$

The scaling parameter for the *left* distribution is set to $\beta = 0.03$, while the shifting parameter is $\alpha = 0.03$. The parameters for the *right* distribution are set to $\beta = 0.03$ and $\alpha = 0.07$. The x-values are multiplied by -1 to flip the distribution across the x-axis. Lastly, the "left-flatter" distribution is set by $\alpha = 0.1$ and $\beta = 0.1$. The scaling parameters results in certain densities around the x-values of 0.4–0.6, that define how many augmentations are of a certain size (Fig. 5).

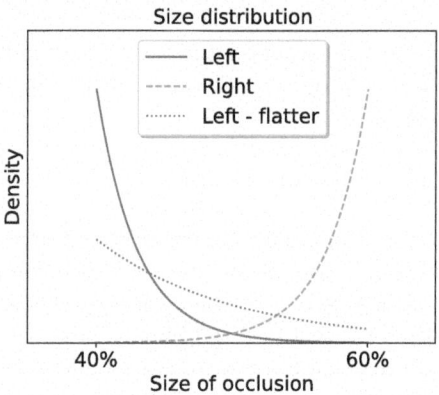

Fig. 5. Visualization for *left/right* size distributions used in Sect. 3.2

References

1. Goodfellow, I.J., Bengio, Y., Courville, A.: Deep Learning. MIT Press, Cambridge (2016). http://www.deeplearningbook.org
2. Villalobos, P., Sevilla, J., Besiroglu, T., Heim, L., Ho, A., Hobbhahn, M.: Machine learning model sizes and the parameter gap (2022)
3. Grünbaum, D., Stern, M.L., Lang, E.W.: Quantitative probing: validating causal models with quantitative domain knowledge. J. Causal Inference **11** (2023)

4. ADEE, M.S.A.: Model Based System Analysis Techniques to Determine Propagation Paths of Functional Insufficiencies in Software Intensive Systems. Ph.D. thesis, Technische Universität Kaiserslautern (2023)
5. Pearl, J., Glymour, M., Jewell, N.: Causal Inference in Statistics: A Primer. Wiley (2016)
6. Hernan, M., Robins, J.: Causal Inference: What If. CRC Press, Chapman & Hall/CRC Monographs on Statistics & Applied Probab (2024)
7. Xing, X., Jia, T., Chen, J., Xiong, L., Yu, Z.: An ontology-based method to identify triggering conditions for perception insufficiency of autonomous vehicles (2022)
8. Hoss, M., Scholtes, M., Eckstein, L.: A review of testing object-based environment perception for safe automated driving. Autom. Innov. **5**, 223–250 (2022)
9. Burton, S., Habli, I., Lawton, T., McDermid, J., Morgan, P., Porter, Z.: Mind the gaps: assuring the safety of autonomous systems from an engineering, ethical, and legal perspective. Artif. Intell. **279**, 103201 (2019)
10. Caesar, H., et al.: nuscenes: a multimodal dataset for autonomous driving (2020)
11. Maier, R., Grabinger, L., Urlhart, D., Mottok, J.: Causal models to support scenario-based testing of adas. IEEE Trans. Intell. Transp. Syst. **25**(2), 1815–1831 (2024)
12. Adee, A., Gansch, R., Liggesmeyer, P.: Systematic modeling approach for environmental perception limitations in automated driving. In: 2021 17th European Dependable Computing Conference (EDCC), pp. 103–110. IEEE (2021)
13. Adee, A., Gansch, R., Liggesmeyer, P., Glaeser, C., Drews, F.: Discovery of perception performance limiting triggering conditions in automated driving. In: 2021 5th International Conference on System Reliability and Safety (ICSRS), pp. 248–257. IEEE (2021)
14. Jiang, Z., Liu, J., Sun, P., Sang, M., Li, H., Pan, Y.: Generation of risky scenarios for testing automated driving visual perception based on causal analysis. In: IEEE Transactions on Intelligent Transportation Systems, pp. 1–14 (2024)
15. Ilse, M., Tomczak, J.M., Forré, P.: Selecting data augmentation for simulating interventions (2020)
16. Rahul, M., Chiddarwar, S.S.: A causality-inspired data augmentation approach to cross-domain burr detection using randomly weighted shallow networks. Int. J. Mach. Learn. Cybern. **14**(12), 4223–4236 (2023)
17. Reddy, A.G., Bachu, S., Dash, S., Sharma, C., Sharma, A., Balasubramanian, V.N.: On counterfactual data augmentation under confounding (2023)
18. Zhong, Z., Zheng, L., Kang, G., Li, S., Yang, Y.: Random erasing data augmentation (2017)
19. DeVries, T., Taylor, G.W.: Improved regularization of convolutional neural networks with cutout (2017)
20. Hsu, C.-Y., Lin, L.-E., Lin, C.H.: Age and gender recognition with random occluded data augmentation on facial images. Multimedia Tools Appl. **80**, 11631–11653 (2021)
21. Yun, S., Han, D., Oh, S.J., Chun, S., Choe, J., Yoo, Y.: CutMix: regularization strategy to train strong classifiers with localizable features (2019)
22. Roser, M., Appel, C., Ritchie, H.: Human height. Our World in Data (2021). https://ourworldindata.org/human-height
23. Crocetta, G., Piantini, S., Pierini, M., Simms, C.: The influence of vehicle front-end design on pedestrian ground impact. Accident Anal. Prevent. **79**, 56–69 (2015)
24. Beckers, S., Halpern, J.Y.: Abstracting causal models (2019)
25. Chen, K., et al.: MMDetection: open mmLab detection toolbox and benchmark. arXiv preprint arXiv:1906.07155 (2019)

26. Lin, T.-Y., Goyal, P., Girshick, R., He, K., Dollár, P.: Focal loss for dense object detection. In: Proceedings of the IEEE International Conference on Computer Vision (2017)
27. Redmon, J., Farhadi, A.: Yolov3: an incremental improvement (2018)
28. Everingham, M., Gool, L.V., Williams, C.K.I., Winn, J.M., Zisserman, A.: The pascal visual object classes (voc) challenge. Int. J. Comput. Vis. **88**(2), 303–338 (2010)

The Information Meta Model for Machine Learning IM^3L: A Structured Approach to ML Integration in Engineering Systems

Zhibao Mian[1]([⊠])(iD), Ramin Tavakoli Kolagari[2]([⊠])(iD), and Alexander Fischer[2](iD)

[1] School of Digital and Physical Sciences, FoSE, University of Hull, Hull, UK
`Z.Mian2@hull.ac.uk`
[2] Technische Hochschule Nürnberg Georg Simon Ohm, Nürnberg, Germany
`{ramin.tavakolikolagari,a.fischer}@th-nuernberg.de`

Abstract. Machine learning (ML) has become an essential technology in the development of modern software-intensive systems, particularly in safety-critical domains such as autonomous driving. However, despite the maturity of model-driven and software engineering practices in these domains, the integration of ML components often remains unsystematic and poorly aligned with established engineering workflows.

To address this challenge, this paper proposes the *Information Meta Model for Machine Learning (IM^3L)*, a conceptual modeling language that supports the structured design of ML components in complex system contexts. IM^3L enables engineers to systematically capture and reason about key characteristics of ML-based functionality—including data structure and semantics, class and feature relationships, learning method, and relevant quality metrics—in a way that aligns with established model-driven engineering (MDE) practices. This approach fosters interdisciplinary alignment and establishes a robust foundation for traceability, comparability, and quality assurance within existing model-driving engineering (MDE) practices.

To illustrate the practical application of the proposed approach, the paper presents a representative example utilizing the German Traffic Sign Recognition Benchmark (GTSRB) dataset within a prototypical object detection scenario. The example demonstrates how IM^3L can be used to systematically document and structure the critical properties and underlying assumptions of an ML-based system. This facilitates a well-grounded understanding of the system's intended functionality and its integration within the broader system context prior to implementation.

Keywords: Machine learning · Information meta model · Model-driving engineering · Safety-critical systems

1 Introduction

While machine learning (ML) has been extensively adopted to support intelligent decision-making in numerous critical application domains, there remains a

P. Katsaros (Ed.): IMBSA 2025, LNCS 15755, pp. 175–189, 2026.
https://doi.org/10.1007/978-3-032-05073-1_12

conspicuous lack of integration with the established principles of model-driven engineering (MDE) in the current scientific literature. This gap is especially pronounced among teams without prior ML expertise, impeding their capacity to develop solutions that fully leverage contemporary technological advances.

In this paper, we introduce a novel information meta model for machine learning (IM^3L), designed to bridge this gap by consolidating foundational concepts from both ML and MDE domains. IM^3L provides a structured representation of the key elements that govern ML behavior including dataset structure, classes and features, their interrelations, the applied learning method, and performance metrics, without prescribing any domain specific languages (DSL). Instead, IM^3L can be instantiated within existing frameworks such as EAST-ADL [8] or AADL [10] to enhance their support for ML components.

The synergy between MDE and ML promises to advance both the systematic understanding and the disciplined engineering of ML-based systems by enabling rigorous design, comprehensive documentation, and partial automation of downstream tasks such as configuration and code generation. Furthermore, by abstracting and formally modeling an ML solution's key properties, IM^3L can promote safer design practices, facilitate traceability, and lay the groundwork for more disciplined development processes. This approach not only lowers the barrier for non-specialists to participate in ML system development but also fosters collaboration between domain experts and data scientists.

2 Related Work

A recent survey by Naveed et al. [18] systematically reviews Model-Driven Engineering (MDE) for ML (MDE4ML), highlighting motivations such as effort reduction and quality improvement, and identifying key modeling features, tool support, and the limited attention given to non-functional aspects such as safety and trust. Similarly, Raedler et al. [20] emphasize that MDE for AI is still in its early stages and lacks comprehensive methods and broad industrial adoption. Safsar et al. [22] demonstrate the integration of deep convolutional neural networks into EAST-ADL for autonomous vehicle perception.

Conceptual frameworks/languages have been proposed for modeling ML processes [17], ML pipelines [26], and datasets [11,15,21], but they often lack the quantitative measures needed for analysis. For instance, dataset quality is usually represented generically using attributes like *name*, *type*, or *value*, as in [21] , [15]. Similarly, Hartsell et al. [14] present a model-driven methodology for safety assurance of Learning-Enabled Components (LECs), but the modeling of ML-specific assets remains at a high level, with quantitative measures deferred to future work.

Antony et al. [1,5] analyze how dataset characteristics such as noise, class imbalance, and outliers impact SafeML's performance. Their findings underline the importance of dataset modeling for ML. Related work in meta-learning [7] also suggests that dataset characteristics play a central role in algorithm selection and performance. Meta-feature extractor tools [2,3] support the automated characterization of datasets, but remain disconnected from MDE approaches.

Efforts such as Arbiter [27] aim to support ethical ML through DSL-based documentation of model training processes, while other work explores meta-modeling for meta-learning algorithms [13]. However, these remain at early conceptual stages and do not provide detailed modeling constructs for data or learning algorithms that meet the demands of ML-based system development.

3 Background

Originating from collaborative efforts among European automotive stakeholders, EAST-ADL emerged as a robust tool for depicting complex system architectures and designs, as described in Sect. 3. Its rich modeling capabilities encompass the representation of software and hardware components, along with their interactions and dependencies. Key attributes highlighted include EAST-ADL's handling of requirements, analytical tools, interoperability with other modeling languages, and extensive tooling support. As a pivotal asset in automotive system design, EAST-ADL empowers engineers to enhance system quality, safety, and efficiency throughout the development life cycle (Fig. 1).

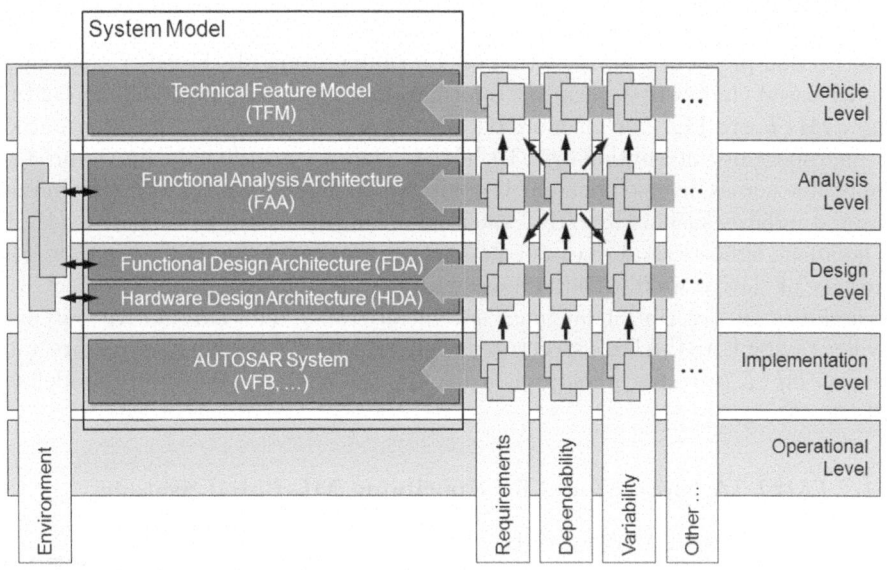

Fig. 1. *EAST – ADL* Structural Overview with Extensions, from [8].

The Electronics Architecture and Software Technology—Architecture Description Language (EAST-ADL) serves as a modeling language within the automotive and embedded systems sector, facilitating the depiction of intricate system architectures and designs. EAST-ADL offers a systematic approach to model both software and hardware components, delineating their interactions and dependencies within their operational context. This language empowers engineers to encapsulate architectural decisions, analyze system behaviors, and enhance the development process of automotive systems in terms of quality, safety, and efficiency [8].

Originally conceived through collaboration among European automotive manufacturers, suppliers, and research institutions, EAST-ADL emerged from the "Model-Based Analysis and Design of Novel Architectures for Dependable Electric Vehicles" (MAENAD) project (www.maenad.eu). This endeavor aimed to furnish a modeling language and accompanying analysis techniques tailored for advanced embedded control systems, with a primary focus on automotive applications.

EAST-ADL stands as a robust modeling language in the automotive and embedded systems realm, adept at delineating the architecture and design complexities of modern systems. With its comprehensive modeling capabilities, support for diverse requirements, analytical prowess, interoperability with other languages, and extensive tooling support, EAST-ADL emerges as an indispensable asset for engineers engaged in automotive system design [8].

4   The IM^3L Model

This section presents a novel meta model for integrating ML-based systems into model-based engineering, termed "Information Meta Model for Machine Learning" (IM^3L, see Fig. 2 or for more details please refer to https://git.informatik. fh-nuernberg.de/international/im3l). IM^3L offers a versatile modeling approach applicable across diverse domains. It combines terms and best practices from relevant standards such as ISO/IEC 23053 in a comprehensive meta model. IM^3L is language-agnostic and does not depend on any particular DSL; however, for the sake of clarity, we illustrate its use with EAST-ADL (please refer to Sect. 3), an architecture description language specifically tailored for automotive systems. By leveraging EAST-ADL's structured representation of system architecture and design, IM^3L provides a comprehensive approach for systematically modeling ML.

4.1 IM^3L: A Meta Model for Specifying ML-Based Systems

Figure 2 provides an overview of the IM^3L meta model. The remainder of this section delves into detailed explanations of selected meta entities within the broader context of an overall ML engineering approach.

MachineLearningFunctionType.   The `MachineLearningFunctionType` serving as the foundational entity that encapsulates both the dataset(s) and the ML model specification. This entity serves as a cohesive unit that encapsulates the essential components necessary for performing ML tasks. The concept of a "Type", as intended by the `MachineLearningFunctionType`, refers to the EAST-ADL [8] and AUTOSAR (www.autosar.org) Type–Prototype concept,

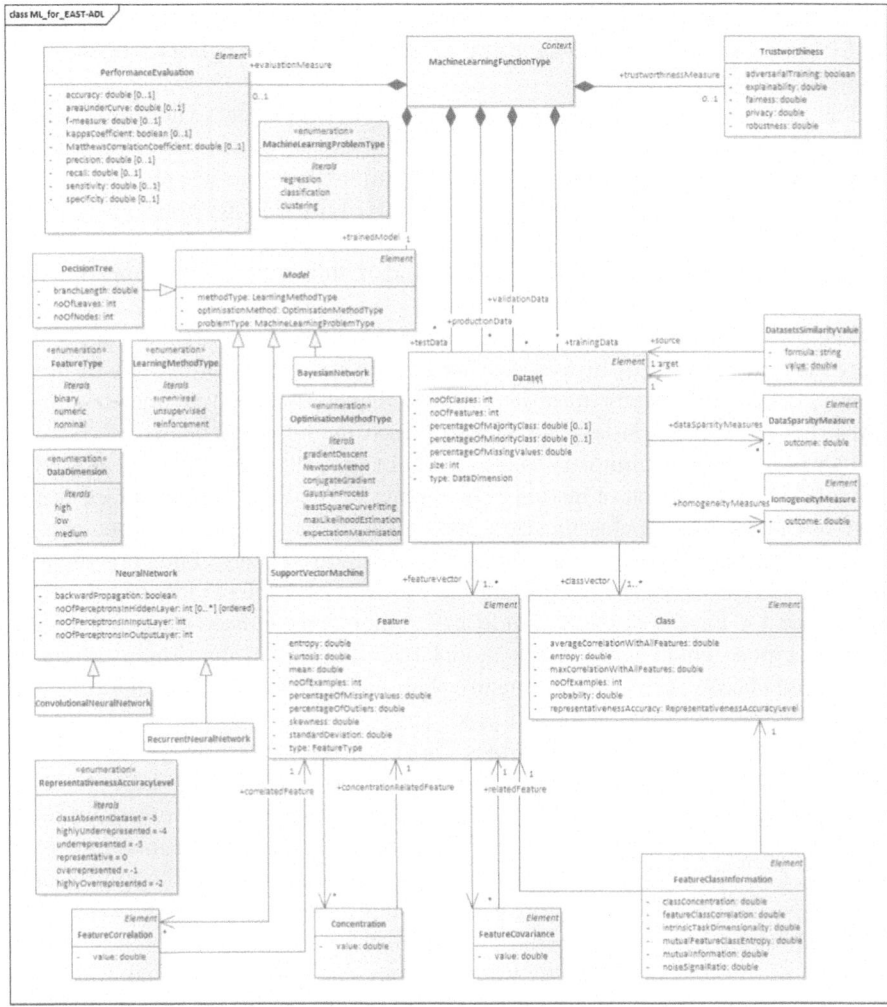

Fig. 2. IM^3L Meta Model.

which revolves around the idea of defining reusable templates or blueprints for components within a system.

The `MachineLearningFunctionType` encompasses commonly employed `Performance` and `Trustworthiness` metrics, which are not exhaustively delineated within this study. It produces a `predictedOutput`. Additionally, it comprises diverse datasets comprising `testData`, `validationData`, and `trainingData`, alongside the ML `Model`.

Dataset. The `Dataset` entity encapsulates several critical characteristics essential for modeling `testData`, `validationData`, and `trainingData`. These characteristics include:

The number of classes (`noOfClasses`) attribute represents the total number of distinct classes or categories present in the dataset. For classification tasks, a higher number of classes might pose greater complexity to the learning algorithm.

The number of features (`noOfFeatures`) attribute denotes the total number of input variables or features available in the dataset. The dimensionality of the dataset is determined by this count, and it influences the complexity and expressiveness of the model.

The percentage of majority class (`percentageOfMajorityClass`) metric calculates the proportion of instances belonging to the most frequent class in the dataset. It provides insight into the class imbalance issue, where one class dominates the dataset, potentially leading to biased model performance.

The percentage of minority class (`percentageOfMinorityClass`) attribute calculates the proportion of instances belonging to the least frequent class or category in the dataset. In classification tasks, class imbalance occurs when certain classes are significantly underrepresented compared to others. The percentage of minority class provides crucial insights into the distribution of class labels within the dataset. A lower percentage indicates a more pronounced class imbalance, which can pose challenges during model training and evaluation. Addressing imbalanced classes is essential to ensure that the model learns to generalize well across all classes and avoids biased predictions.

The percentage of missing values (`percentageOfMissingValues`) metric quantifies the extent of missing or incomplete data within the dataset. Missing values can arise due to various reasons such as data entry errors, equipment malfunction, or intentional omission. Assessing the percentage of missing values is crucial for understanding the data quality and determining the appropriate handling strategy. High percentages of missing values in certain features may necessitate data imputation techniques to fill in the gaps or might require the exclusion of affected instances or features from the analysis. Managing missing values effectively ensures the integrity and reliability of the dataset for machine learning tasks, preventing biased or erroneous model outcomes.

The size (`size`) of the dataset refers to the total number of instances or samples it contains. Larger datasets often provide more representative and diverse samples, facilitating robust model training and evaluation.

The `type` (`high, low, medium`) is a qualitative descriptor that categorizes the dataset based on its size relative to common benchmarks or thresholds. A `high` type indicates a large dataset with a substantial number of instances and features. Conversely, a `low` type denotes a dataset with relatively few instances or features. A `medium` type lies between these extremes, offering a moderate-sized dataset for analysis and learning.

Closely related to the `Dataset` are the following three measures.

Datasets Similarity Value. The `DatasetsSimilarityValue` quantifies the degree of similarity between datasets, facilitating comparative analysis. This similarity is computed by assessing the metafeature distance between two datasets.

Data Sparsity Measure. The `DataSparsityMeasure` refers to the sparsity in terms of instance count relative to feature dimensionality—i.e., a high-dimensional feature space with limited data points. Separately, the Data Sparsity Ratio (DSR) measures class imbalance by comparing the size of the smallest class to the total dataset size.

Homogeneity Measure. A metric known as the Homogeneity Measure `HomogeneityMeasure` gauges the uniformity of covariances within a dataset. This measure is calculated using the standard deviation ratio (SDR) [25].

The SDR reflects the geometric mean ratio of standard deviations across individual class populations to those of the dataset sample.

Various other metrics are also available. In [24], it's discussed that techniques like the Kolmogorov-Smirnov and X^2 tests can assess homogeneity for unbinned and binned data types respectively. Furthermore, questions of homogeneity extend to all facets of statistical distributions, encompassing parameters like location, marginal distributions, skewness (please refer to Sect. 4.1), and joint distributions. For a comprehensive analysis, examining alterations in the entire marginal distribution might be necessary. Alternatively, for a more focused study, investigating changes in skewness could suffice. This highlights the importance of selecting an appropriate measurement based on the dataset characteristics.

A complementary `HeterogeneityMeasure` can be derived by quantifying inter-class dissimilarity. One effective approach computes the mean pairwise distance between class-specific covariance matrices using a matrix norm (e.g., Frobenius norm). This allows for a fine-grained analysis of structural variation between class distributions and can inform both robustness assessments and preprocessing strategies in ML pipelines.

Feature. The `Feature` entity constitutes the elemental components of the `featureVector`, embodying several key properties essential for comprehensive analysis. These properties include:

The `entropy` property quantifies the inherent uncertainty or randomness within the distribution of values associated with a feature. Higher entropy indicates greater unpredictability, often implying lower information gain. This is formally captured by *Shannon entropy*, defined as:

$$H = -\sum_{i=1}^{n} p_i \log_2(p_i) \tag{1}$$

Here, n is the number of possible outcomes, and p_i is the probability of outcome i [23].

In the context of machine learning datasets, let x be a predictive attribute and y a target attribute. The entropy of x or y is computed as:

$$H(v) = - \sum_{val \in \phi_v} P(v = val) \log_2(P(v = val)) \tag{2}$$

where $v \in \{x, y\}$ and ϕ_v is the set of distinct values in vector v [9].

The joint entropy $H(x, y)$ measures the combined uncertainty of x and y:

$$H(x, y) = - \sum_{i \in \phi_x} \sum_{j \in \phi_y} P(x = i, y = j) \log_2(P(x = i, y = j)) \tag{3}$$

where ϕ_x and ϕ_y denote the distinct values of x and y respectively, and $P(x = i, y = j)$ is the joint probability of x and y assuming those values [9].

From this, the mutual information (MI) between x and y—quantifying the amount of information one variable contains about the other—is derived as:

$$MI(x, y) = H(x) + H(y) - H(x, y) \tag{4}$$

This metric is widely used in feature selection, as it highlights the strength of dependency between predictive features and class labels [2,12].

The kurtosis measures the peakedness or flatness of the distribution of values relative to a normal distribution. Positive kurtosis indicates a sharper peak (presence of outliers), while negative kurtosis signifies a flatter distribution (lack of outliers) [19]. Kurtosis (Ku) can be defined as shown in equation (5) [16].

$$Ku = \left[\frac{n(n+1)}{(n-1)(n-2)(n-3)} \sum \left(\frac{x_i - \bar{x}}{s} \right)^4 \right] - \tag{5}$$

$$\frac{3(n-1)^2}{(n-2)(n-3)}$$

Here, n represents the number of instances in N, s is the sample standard deviation, and $\bar{x}$ denotes the mean.

The mean represents the average value of the feature across all instances. It provides a measure of central tendency within the feature's distribution.

Number of Examples (noOfExamples) denotes the total number of instances or samples in the dataset that contain valid values for the feature. It indicates the feature's prevalence within the dataset.

Percentage of Missing Values (percentageOfMissingValues, please refer to page 180): This metric calculates the proportion of instances in the dataset where the feature's value is missing or undefined. It reflects the completeness of the feature's data.

Percentage of Outliers (`percentageOfOutliers`): Outliers are data points that deviate significantly from the rest of the dataset. This property measures the proportion of instances within the feature that are considered outliers.

`Skewness` (Sk) is a measure of asymmetry. It is a shape parameter that quantifies the degree of asymmetry in a distribution. A distribution, or dataset, is considered symmetric if it appears identical when mirrored around its central point. Positive skewness indicates a longer tail on the right side of the distribution, while negative skewness implies a longer tail on the left side. The degree of skewness (Sk) can be defined as shown in equation (6), see [19].

$$Sk = \frac{1}{(n-1)} \sum_{i=1}^{n} \frac{(x_i - \overline{x})^3}{s^3} \tag{6}$$

Here, $\overline{x}$ represents the mean, s denotes the standard deviation, and n signifies the number of data points.

It is important to note that alternative definitions of kurtosis and skewness exist in the literature for different contexts. Various measures of skewness and kurtosis can be found in [19].

The standard deviation (`standardDeviation`) measures the dispersion or spread of values around the mean. Higher standard deviation values signify greater variability within the feature's distribution.

The `type` attribute categorizes the feature based on its nature or characteristics, such as `binary`, `numerical`, or `nominal`, see the enumeration `FeatureType`.

Class. The `Class` meta entity embodies the categorical labels assigned to instances within datasets, functioning as unique identifiers for different categories present in the data. For instance, in a dataset containing various fruits, classes might include "apple" or "pear". This entity is characterized by several properties crucial for understanding and analyzing datasets comprehensively. `averageCorrelationWithAllFeatures` measures the average correlation between instances of the class and all features in the dataset. `entropy` indicates the uncertainty or randomness associated with the distribution of instances within the class. `maximalCorrelationWithAllFeatures` identifies the maximum correlation between instances of the class and any individual feature in the dataset. `noOfExamples` denotes the total count of instances belonging to the class within the dataset. `probability` represents the likelihood of encountering instances belonging to the class within the dataset. `representativenessAccuracy` assesses the degree to which the class represents the underlying distribution of instances within the dataset accurately.

FeatureClassInformation. The `FeatureClassInformation` meta entity captures metrics that describe the relationship between a specific feature and a target class. One such property is `classConcentration`, which provides insight into how instances are distributed across different classes with respect to a given feature. Although the term "concentration coefficient" is not standard in the machine learning literature, the idea relates to the degree of association or alignment between attribute values and class labels, as explored in [4]. It can be seen as a measure of how selectively a feature activates across class boundaries.

Both `classConcentration` and other related indicators—such as `Feature-ClassCorrelation`—fall under the broader category of information-theoretic measures, as discussed in [2]. While `FeatureClassCorrelation` quantifies how well a feature separates different classes, the `intrinsicTaskDimensionality` reflects the underlying complexity of the classification problem. This measure is defined as the minimum number of features required to account for 90% of the total mutual information between all features and class labels [25]. To compute it, a cumulative distribution of mutual information values—sorted from most to least informative features—is used. The resulting value, denoted as ID, provides an estimate of the effective feature space dimensionality. The ratio of ID to the original number of features yields the `Intrinsic Dimensionality Ratio` (IDR), indicating potential feature redundancy or sparsity.

The properties `mutualFeatureClassEntropy` and `mutualInformation` quantify the amount of information shared between features and classes, aiding in feature selection and model training.

`mutualInformation` (MI) between two random variables measures the reduction in uncertainty about one variable given knowledge of the other [12]. It is zero if and only if the variables are statistically independent; higher values indicate stronger dependency. For an independent attribute x and target attribute y, the mutual information is defined as in equation (7) [2]:

$$MI(x, y) = H(x) + H(y) - H(x, y) \tag{7}$$

Here, $H(x)$ and $H(y)$ denote the Shannon entropy of x and y respectively, and $H(x, y)$ is their joint entropy.

`mutualFeatureClassEntropy` refers to the joint entropy $H(x, y)$ itself—that is, the total amount of uncertainty in the combined distribution of a feature and its associated class label. While mutual information quantifies shared information, mutual feature-class entropy reflects the total variability in the feature-class pairing. Lower values can indicate more structured or class-specific feature behavior, whereas higher values suggest greater variability and potentially more overlap between class distributions.

Finally, `noiseSignalRatio` assesses the extent of noise present in the data relative to the underlying signal, which influences both the robustness and generalizability of classification models.

FeatureCorrelation. (`FeatureCorrelation`) quantifies the correlation among features, as defined in (8) [25]:

$$FC = \frac{1}{T} \sum_{i=1}^{C} \sum_{j=1}^{d-1} \sum_{k=j+1}^{d} |P_{jk}| \tag{8}$$

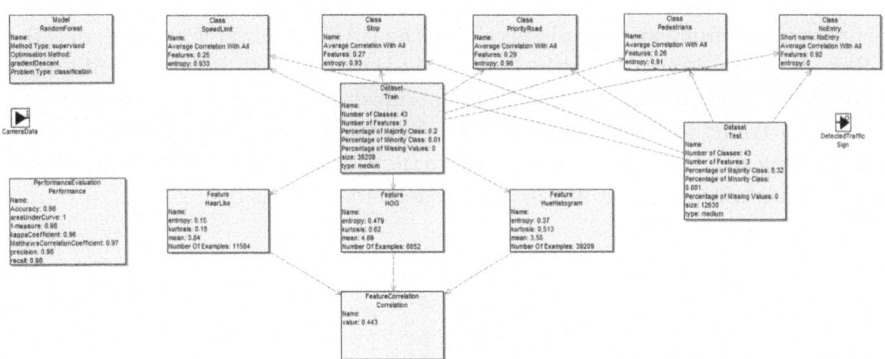

Fig. 3. IM^3L An example model for the `MachineLearningFunctionType` "TrafficSign-Recognition".

Here, $|P_{jk}|$ represents the absolute value of the Pearson correlation coefficient between features j and k, T denotes the total number of correlation coefficients aggregated, C signifies the number of classes, and d indicates the number of features.

NeuralNetwork. The `NeuralNetwork` meta entity serves as a representation of machine learning algorithms, particularly those based on neural networks. It encapsulates various properties essential for describing the architecture and behavior of such models. `backward Propagation` is a boolean attribute indicating whether the neural network employs backward propagation as part of its training process. `noOfPerceptronsInHiddenLayer` is an ordered list specifying the number of perceptrons in each hidden layer of the neural network. The ordering reflects the sequence of hidden layers from input to output. `noOfPerceptronsInInputLayer` indicates the number of perceptrons in the input layer of the neural network, representing the dimensions of the input data. `noOfPerceptronsInOutputLayer` specifies the number of perceptrons in the output layer of the neural network, determining the dimensionality of the network's output.

Subclasses of `NeuralNetwork` provide further refinement of semantics, tailoring the representation to specific machine learning approaches. For instance, subclasses may include Convolutional Neural Networks (CNNs), Recurrent Neural Networks (RNNs), or Deep Belief Networks (DBNs, not reflected in the meta model), each with its unique architectural characteristics and training methodologies. These subclasses enable more precise modeling and analysis of neural network-based algorithms.

5   Integrating the ML Model Into a System Model

In this section, we underscore the significance of establishing the relationship between ML entities and system modeling entities. To illustrate this integration, we present a minimalist example involving the EAST-ADL architecture, detailed in Sect. 3. Figure 3 introduces the `MachineLearningFunctionType` "TrafficSign-Recognition," encapsulating information about datasets and neural network processing for traffic sign recognition tasks. Leveraging the Type–Prototype concept introduced earlier, this `MachineLearningFunctionType` "TrafficSignRecognition" is instantiated as a prototype, as depicted in Fig. 4.

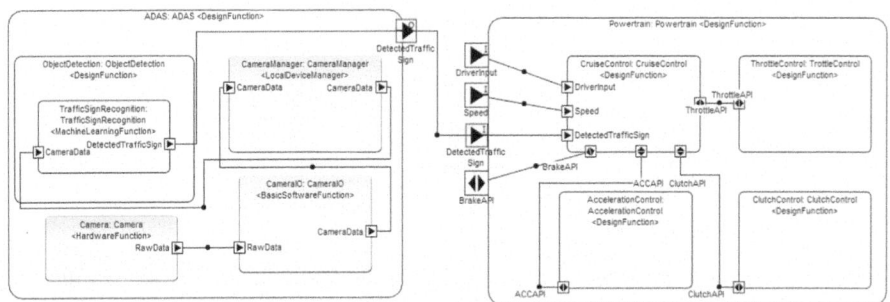

Fig. 4. $EAST - ADL$ model for the `MachineLearningFunctionType` "Vehicle", simplified excerpt.

Furthermore, we demonstrate the embedding of this instantiated prototype within the EAST-ADL model. Specifically, we illustrate the relationships among key components such as "Cruise Control", "Advanced Driver Assistance System (ADAS)" and the "Camera" within the context of the "Vehicle". The Camera-Data which is provided by a HardwareFunction "Camera" is further processed and then passed to a DesignFunction "ObjectDetection" which encapsulates the traffic sign recognition using machine learning. Recognized traffic signs are passed to the DesignFunction "CruiseControl", which can make the resulting driving decisions. By integrating the `MachineLearningFunctionType` prototype into the EAST-ADL model, we establish linkages between ML functionalities and system components showing how ML algorithms contribute to system behavior and functionality.

6   Conclusion and Future Work

In this paper, we address the integration of MDE into the development of ML systems. We propose the *Information Meta Model for Machine Learning* (IM^3L), a technology-agnostic modeling framework that enables precise definition and quantification of core ML system characteristics. (IM^3L) is technology-agnostic and can be easily integrated with established system modeling approaches such as EAST-ADL.

Through IM^3L, an ML-based system is not only characterized by metrics including dataset statistics, per-class and per-feature entropy, average inter-feature correlations, and performance evaluations (see Fig. 3), but is also formally represented and integrated into a system architecture, e.g., an EAST-ADL architecture (see Fig. 4). This unified modeling approach establishes a rigorous foundation for quality assurance activities, e.g., safety analysis and trustworthiness assessment in safety-critical domains like autonomous driving.

Future work will focus on extending IM^3L beyond its current limitations, particularly regarding the modeling of end-to-end learning-based agents. At present, IM^3L assumes modular, interpretable ML components (e.g., white-box object detection models) and does not yet support full sensor-to-control pipelines as used in autonomous agents. While these can be abstractly represented using the `MachineLearningFunctionType`, internal algorithmic dynamics remain opaque, and essential quality metrics (e.g., robustness, safety, or explainability) are not yet expressible. Beyond this, there are further open challenges from the model-driven engineering (MDE) perspective that warrant attention. First, the relationship between IM^3L models and concrete ML implementations (e.g., in Scikit-learn or PyTorch) remains unspecified. Given the overloading of the term"model" in ML and MDE, clarifying this link is crucial. One promising avenue could be the use of stepwise refinement: initially abstract IM^3L instances could be systematically refined toward implementation-level models, with verification or conformance checks between abstract and concrete stages. Alternatively, abstractions of trained ML models could be aligned post hoc with the original design models to support traceability and conformance. Moreover, recent developments in AutoML suggest a strong synergy: by linking IM^3L meta-entities (e.g., dataset characteristics, feature distributions) with automated algorithm configuration or selection strategies, it may become possible to close the loop from model specification to implementation. Finally, the development of reusable design knowledge could benefit from pattern-based modeling approaches. A particularly relevant contribution in this regard is the pattern language for hybrid learning and reasoning systems by van Bekkum et al. [6], which translates machine learning challenges into modular design patterns aligned with MDE thinking. Integrating such patterns into IM^3L could foster reuse and cross-disciplinary understanding.

References

1. Adegbola, A., Sharvia, S., Antony, J., Mian, Z., Aslansefat, K., Papadopoulos, Y.: Effects of dataset characteristics on the performance of safeml, unpublished
2. Alcobaça, E., Siqueira, F.: Meta-feature description table (2024). https://pymfe.readthedocs.io/en/latest/auto_pages/meta_features_description.html
3. Alcobaça, E., Siqueira, F., Rivolli, A., Garcia, L.P.F., Oliva, J.T., de Carvalho, A.C.P.L.F.: MFE: towards reproducible meta-feature extraction. J. Mach. Learn. Res. **21**(111), 1–5 (2020). http://jmlr.org/papers/v21/19-348.html
4. Alexandros, K., Melanie, H.: Model selection via meta learning: a comparative study. Int. J. Artif. Intell. Tools **10**(04), 525–554 (2001). https://doi.org/10.1142/S0218213001000647
5. Antony, J.: Effects of Dataset Characteristics on the Performance of SafeML. M.sc. thesis, The University of Hull (2022)

6. van Bekkum, M., de Boer, M., van Harmelen, F., Meyer-Vitali, A., Teije, A.: Modular design patterns for hybrid learning and reasoning systems. Appl. Intell. **51**(9), 6528–6546 (2021). https://doi.org/10.1007/s10489-021-02394-3

7. Brazdil, P., van Rijn, J., Soares, C., Vanschoren, J.: Metalearning: Applications to Automated Machine Learning and Data Mining. Springer, Cham (2022). https://doi.org/10.1007/978-3-030-67024-5

8. Cuenot, P., et al.: 11 the east-adl architecture description language for automotive embedded software. In: Giese, H., Karsai, G., Lee, E., Rumpe, B., Schätz, B. (eds.) MBEERTS 2007. LNCS, vol. 6100, pp. 297–307. Springer, Heidelberg (2010). https://doi.org/10.1007/978-3-642-16277-0_11

9. Edesio Alcobaça, F.S.: Api documentation -pymfe.info_theory.mfeinfotheory (2024). https://pymfe.readthedocs.io/en/latest/generated/pymfe.info_theory. MFEInfoTheory.html

10. Feiler, P.H., Lewis, B.A., Vestal, S.: The sae architecture analysis & design language (aadl) a standard for engineering performance critical systems. In: 2006 IEEE Conference on Computer Aided Control System Design, 2006 IEEE International Conference on Control Applications, 2006 IEEE International Symposium on Intelligent Control, pp. 1206–1211 (2006). https://doi.org/10.1109/CACSD-CCA-ISIC.2006.4776814

11. Giner-Miguelez, J., Gómez, A., Cabot, J.: A domain-specific language for describing machine learning datasets. J. Comput. Lang. **76**, 101209 (2023). https://doi.org/10.1016/j.cola.2023.101209

12. Guhanesvar: Feature selection based on mutual information gain for classification and regression (2021). https://guhanesvar.medium.com/feature-selection-based-on-mutual-information-gain-for-classification-and-regression-d0f86ea5262a

13. Hartmann, T., Moawad, A., Schockaert, C., Fouquet, F., Le Traon, Y.: Metamodelling meta-learning. In: 2019 ACM/IEEE 22nd International Conference on Model Driven Engineering Languages and Systems (MODELS), pp. 300–305 (2019). https://doi.org/10.1109/MODELS.2019.00014

14. Hartsell, C., et al.: Model-based design for cps with learning-enabled components. In: Proceedings of the Workshop on Design Automation for CPS and IoT, DESTION '19, pp. 1–9. Association for Computing Machinery, New York (2019). https://doi.org/10.1145/3313151.3313166

15. Idowu, S., Strüber, D., Berger, T.: Emmm: a unified meta-model for tracking machine learning experiments. In: 2022 48th Euromicro Conference on Software Engineering and Advanced Applications (SEAA), pp. 48–55 (2022). https://doi.org/10.1109/SEAA56994.2022.00016. https://www.danielstrueber.de/publications/ISB22-SEAA.pdf

16. Microsoft: Kurt function (2024). https://support.microsoft.com/en-us/office/kurt-function-bc3a265c-5da4-4dcb-b7fd-c237789095ab

17. Morales, S., Clarisó, R., Cabot, J.: A framework to model ml engineering processes (2024). https://arxiv.org/abs/2404.18531v1

18. Naveed, H., Arora, C., Khalajzadeh, H., Grundy, J., Haggag, O.: Model driven engineering for machine learning components: a systematic literature review. Inf. Softw. Technol. **169**, 107423 (2024)

19. NIST: Measures of skewness and kurtosis (2024). https://www.itl.nist.gov/div898/handbook/eda/section3/eda35b.htm

20. Raedler, S., Berardinelli, L., Winter, K., Rahimi, A., Rinderle-Ma, S.: Bridging mde and ai: a systematic review of domain-specific languages and model-driven practices in ai software systems engineering (2024). https://arxiv.org/pdf/2307.04599

21. Ries, B., Guelfi, N., Jahi, B.: An mde method for improving deep learning dataset requirements engineering using alloy and uml. In: Proceedings of the 9th International Conference on Model-Driven Engineering and Software Development, vol. 1: MODELSWARD, pp. 41–52. INSTICC, SciTePress (2021). https://doi.org/10.5220/0010216600410052

22. Safdar, A., Azam, F., Anwar, M.W., Akram, U., Rasheed, Y.: Modlf: a model-driven deep learning framework for autonomous vehicle perception (avp). In: Proceedings of the 25th International Conference on Model Driven Engineering Languages and Systems, MODELS '22, pp. 187–198. Association for Computing Machinery, New York (2022). https://doi.org/10.1145/3550355.3552453

23. Shah, C.: A Hands-On Introduction to Machine Learning. Cambridge University Press, Cambridge (2023)

24. Trusina, J., Franc, J., Ks, V.: Statistical homogeneity tests applied to large data sets from high energy physics experiments. J. Phys. Conf. Ser. **936**(1), 012046 (2017). https://doi.org/10.1088/1742-6596/936/1/012046. https://iopscience.iop.org/article/10.1088/1742-6596/936/1/012046/pdf

25. der Walt, V.: Data measures that characterise classification problems. Ph.D. thesis, University of Pretoria (2008). https://repository.up.ac.za/bitstream/handle/2263/27624/dissertation.pdf?sequence=1&isAllowed=y

26. Xiong, P., Buffett, S., Iqbal, S., Lamontagne, P., Mamun, M., Molyneaux, H.: Towards a robust and trustworthy machine learning system development: an engineering perspective. J. Inf. Secur. Appl. **65**, 103121 (2022)

27. Zucker, J., d'Leeuwen, M.: Arbiter: a domain-specific language for ethical machine learning. In: Proceedings of the AAAI/ACM Conference on AI, Ethics, and Society, AIES '20, pp. 421–425. Association for Computing Machinery, New York (2020). https://doi.org/10.1145/3375627.3375858

RAGuard: A Novel Approach for In-Context Safe Retrieval Augmented Generation for LLMs

Connor Walker[1,2(✉)] [iD], Koorosh Aslansefat[1,2] [iD],
Mohammad Naveed Akram[3] [iD], and Yiannis Papadopoulos[1,2] [iD]

[1] University of Hull, Cottingham Road, Hull HU6 7RX, UK
C.Walker-2018@hull.ac.uk
[2] AURA CDT, Hull, UK
https://www.deis-hull.com/connor-walker
[3] Fraunhofer IESE, Fraunhofer-Platz 1, 67663 Kaiserslautern, Germany

Abstract. Accuracy and safety are paramount in Offshore Wind (OSW) maintenance, yet conventional Large Language Models (LLMs) often fail when confronted with highly specialised or unexpected scenarios. We introduce RAGuard, an enhanced Retrieval-Augmented Generation (RAG) framework that explicitly integrates safety-critical documents alongside technical manuals. By issuing parallel queries to two indices and allocating separate retrieval budgets for knowledge and safety, RAGuard guarantees both technical depth and safety coverage. We further develop a SafetyClamp extension that fetches a larger candidate pool, "hard-clamping" exact slot guarantees to safety. We evaluate across sparse (BM25), dense (Dense Passage Retrieval) and hybrid retrieval paradigms, measuring Technical Recall@K and Safety Recall@K. Both proposed extensions of RAG show an increase in Safety Recall@K from almost 0% in RAG to more than 50% in RAGuard, while maintaining Technical Recall above 60%. These results demonstrate that RAGuard and SafetyClamp have the potential to establish a new standard for integrating safety assurance into LLM-powered decision support in critical maintenance contexts.

Keywords: Large Language Models · In-context Safety · AI Safety · RAGuard · Offshore Wind · Maintenance · Retrieval-Augmented Generation (RAG) · Decision Support · Safety-critical

1 Introduction

Accuracy and safety are paramount in Offshore Wind (OSW) maintenance, an industry characterised by challenging environmental conditions, remote operations, and highly complex technical tasks. Human error or inaccurate decisions during maintenance activities can lead to costly downtime, significant safety risks, and environmental hazards. As global reliance on OSW power grows, ensuring the reliability and safety of these operations becomes critically important.

© The Author(s), under exclusive license to Springer Nature Switzerland AG 2026
P. Katsaros (Ed.): IMBSA 2025, LNCS 15755, pp. 190–204, 2026.
https://doi.org/10.1007/978-3-032-05073-1_13

Recent advances in Artificial Intelligence (AI), particularly Large Language Models (LLMs), offer considerable promise as decision-support tools capable of assisting maintenance personnel by providing immediate access to relevant knowledge. LLMs have demonstrated powerful capabilities to generate context-aware recommendations, summarise complex documents, and support operational decision making. However, conventional LLM-based systems often falter when confronted with unexpected or highly specialised scenarios, primarily due to the limited availability of relevant, scenario-specific training data. This shortcoming is particularly problematic in OSW maintenance, where unexpected scenarios can significantly increase operational risks and decision complexity.

Addressing this challenge, we introduce RAGuard, an enhanced Retrieval-Augmented Generation (RAG) framework explicitly tailored for OSW maintenance contexts. RAGuard integrates in-context safety protocols directly into the retrieval and generation process, dynamically prioritising safety considerations based on real-time maintenance scenarios. Unlike traditional RAG systems, RAGuard leverages specialised technical documentation, such as maintenance manuals and technical data sheets, to retrieve highly relevant, context-specific information precisely when needed. This real-time retrieval process ensures that maintenance guidance remains accurate, current, and scenario-appropriate, significantly reducing the risks associated with unexpected situations.

To systematically assess the effectiveness of RAGuard, we propose an evaluation framework specifically designed to evaluate the safety and reliability of AI-based decision-support systems in OSW maintenance tasks. Preliminary evaluations suggest that RAGuard improves the quality and contextual relevance of maintenance guidance, indicating its potential to enhance operational safety. While further operational validation is required, initial results highlight RAGuard as a promising approach toward safer and more reliable decision-support systems in critical maintenance contexts.

The remainder of this paper is structured as follows: Sect. 2 reviews relevant literature on RAG methodologies and safety-focused AI. Section 3 provides an in-depth description of the RAGuard framework. Section 4 details our experimental methodology and newly proposed benchmark. Section 5 presents our empirical results and their implications, and Sect. 6 concludes with a discussion of contributions and future research directions.

2   Background

2.1   Retrieval-Augmented Generation

RAG is a paradigm that integrates information retrieval with generative models to improve knowledge-intensive Natural Language Processing (NLP) tasks. Foundational work by [7] introduces RAG models that combine a parametric neural generator with a non-parametric memory (e.g. a Wikipedia index), enabling the generator to retrieve relevant documents and produce more factual, specific answers. This approach achieved state-of-the-art performance on open-domain question answering tasks, outperforming purely parametric models. Recent advancements have further enhanced RAG. For example, [4] develops Atlas, a pre-trained RAG model that excels in few-shot learning settings. Atlas can attain over 42% accuracy on the Natural Questions benchmark using only 64 examples, surpassing a 540-billion-parameter closed-book model with far fewer parameters. Such progress demonstrates RAG's effectiveness in injecting up-to-date knowledge into LLMs while controlling model size and hallucinations.

2.2   Safety-Focused AI in Critical Domains

AI systems deployed in safety-critical industries (healthcare, aviation, energy, etc.) must be designed with rigorous safety and reliability considerations. In healthcare, for instance, the use of AI for clinical decision support raises concerns about accountability and patient harm. [3] argues that current safety assurance practices are not yet adjusted to AI-driven tools, which can make high-stakes decisions in ways that are opaque to clinicians. They emphasise the need for new frameworks of moral accountability and dynamic safety assurance throughout an AI system's lifecycle. In aviation, AI and Machine Learning (ML) are being applied to augment safety analysis and risk prediction. A recent systematic review by [2] shows that techniques like deep learning, time-series modelling, and optimisation algorithms are increasingly used to detect patterns in aviation data and enhance safety measures. These AI-driven methods support proactive safety management (e.g. predictive maintenance and improved air traffic control) to help prevent accidents before they occur. In the energy sector, especially nuclear power, AI offers potential to improve monitoring and emergency response in complex industrial systems. [5] surveys AI applications in nuclear power plants, noting that AI-based predictive analytics and real-time data processing could bolster reactor safety and decision-making. Their findings highlight early warning systems that use ML and Internet of Things (IoT) sensors to detect anomalies, coordinate with operators, and mitigate risks in critical scenarios. However, they also point out challenges such as the need for updated regulations and cybersecurity safeguards when integrating AI into safety-critical infrastructure.

2.3   Adaptive Retrieval Mechanisms

Adaptive retrieval mechanisms dynamically adjust how and when external information is fetched during generation, often making retrieval context-aware or safety-aware. Instead of a fixed one-pass retrieval, these approaches allow the AI to decide if additional knowledge is needed and to retrieve iteratively or on the fly. For example, recent RAG variants like Forward Looking Active REtrieval Augmented Generation (FLARE) and Self-RAG equip language models with the ability to trigger new retrievals based on the model's internal confidence or reflection tokens. This means the model can autonomously determine the optimal moments to query the knowledge base, stopping when enough information has been gathered. [1] proposes Self-RAG, where the model "self-reflects" on its draft answer and issues further queries if needed, which streamlines the retrieve-generate loop and improves answer accuracy. Similarly, [6] introduces an active retrieval strategy that monitors the generation process and fetches new evidence when the model's certainty falls below a threshold, thereby tailoring retrieval to the query's complexity. Beyond research prototypes, the concept of adaptive retrieval is evident in systems like OpenAI's WebGPT, which used reinforcement learning to train GPT-3 to invoke a search engine mid-generation. This allowed the model to decide when to look up information and even cite sources, behaving like an agent that can use tools. Equally important is making retrieval safety-aware, so that the information brought into the generation loop does not introduce harm or vulnerabilities. One line of work addresses filtering and control of retrieved content. For instance, security evaluations such as SafeRAG [8] show that without safeguards, adversarial or toxic documents can be injected into the retrieval corpus, leading to misleading or harmful outputs. This has underscored the need for robust retrieval filters and context validation. In practice, integrating content moderation–e.g. removing offensive or contradictory results before generation–is becoming a recommended step in RAG pipelines. By dynamically assessing the safety of retrieved passages (using allow-lists, block-lists, or classifier checks), an adaptive retrieval system can reject or down-weight unsafe context. Such context-aware and safety-conscious retrieval mechanisms are an active research area aimed at ensuring that AI systems remain reliable and aligned even as they pull in external information.

In summary, while existing approaches provide robust RAG methods and explore AI safety considerations in critical sectors, there is limited research on unifying these aspects for operational decision support. This paper addresses this gap by presenting RAGuard, a framework that integrates safety-aware retrieval filtering with context-specific generation to enhance reliability in OSW maintenance scenarios.

3   Methodology

3.1   Retrieval-Augmented Generation

RAG enhances LLMs by integrating external knowledge sources at inference time. Unlike traditional LLMs, which rely solely on their internal parameters–often outdated or insufficient for specialised domains, RAG enables access to up-to-date, domain-specific information through retrieval.

In a typical RAG pipeline, the user's query is embedded into a dense vector using an encoder (e.g., a bi-encoder like Dense Passage Retrieval (DPR)). Meanwhile, the external corpus is pre-encoded into the same vector space and stored in a similarity search index (e.g., Facebook AI Similarity Search (FAISS)). The retriever ranks passages based on similarity (cosine or inner product), and some systems apply additional filtering to discard irrelevant or low-confidence results.

The top-ranked passages are combined with the query to create an enriched prompt. In fusion-in-decoder architectures, passages are encoded separately, and the decoder attends to all inputs to extract relevant information. This retrieval-augmented setup enhances factual grounding and reduces hallucinations while keeping the model compact.

The generator integrates retrieved content into a coherent, informed response. Incorporating external evidence makes RAG outputs more accurate and context-aware than closed-book approaches. Figure 1 summarises each step of the RAG process below.

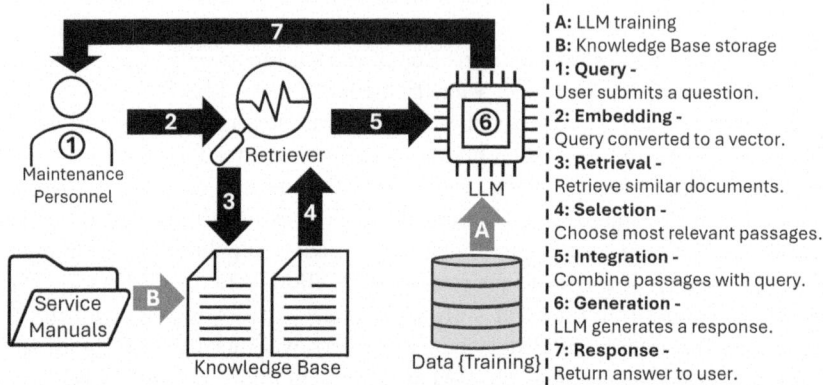

Fig. 1. Standard RAG Model Process

RAG Retrieval Parameters. As with LLMs, RAG systems include tunable hyperparameters that balance retrieval, latency, and noise robustness.

Before indexing, documents are divided into smaller chunks. *Chunk size* controls how much text is embedded at once. Smaller chunks improve retrieval granularity—helping to match precise content, but increase memory and latency. Larger chunks reduce total passages but may dilute relevance.

Chunk overlap determines how much text is shared between adjacent chunks (typically 25–50% of *chunk size*). It helps preserve context continuity—preventing important sentences from being split —at the cost of indexing more passages. Too little overlap risks breaking up meaningful context across chunk boundaries.

Top-k specifies how many chunks are returned to the LLM prompt. Higher values increase coverage but raise the chance of irrelevant content and computational load. Lower values reduce noise but may miss critical context. Standard RAG retrieves the K most relevant chunks by maximising the total score:

$$RAG(q; K) = \underset{D' \subseteq D, \ |D'|=K}{\arg\max} \sum_{d \in D'} s(q, d) \tag{1}$$

Here, q denotes the query, D is the full document corpus, D' is the selected subset of K passages, and $s(q, d)$ is the similarity score between the query and passage d. This optimisation ensures that the top-K passages with the highest aggregated relevance scores are retrieved.

Building on this, we introduce RAGuard which extends the pipeline with explicit safety mechanisms.

3.2 RAGuard

Although traditional RAG systems are effective in dynamically integrating external knowledge into generative processes, they do not explicitly prioritise safety considerations, potentially retrieving contextually relevant but operationally inappropriate or unsafe guidance. To address these limitations, we propose RAGuard, an enhanced RAG framework specifically developed to prioritise safety and contextual accuracy in OSW maintenance operations. The fundamental innovations of RAGuard compared to traditional RAG are safety cache integration, dynamic safety prioritisation, and safety-guided generation. We also propose an additional "SafetyClamp" layer on RAGuard to over-retrieve context passages, reserve predefined knowledge and safety slots, and dynamically fill any leftover slots to supply a full quota.

Safety Cache Integration. RAGuard utilises a dedicated cache that contains validated safety protocols and operational guidelines. Unlike a conventional RAG system that draws from a single monolithic document index, RAGuard maintains two parallel knowledge repositories: one containing general maintenance documentation and the other devoted exclusively to safety-critical content. This may include documents such as regulations, industry-specific protocols, and any other relevant information pertinent to the safe completion of all maintenance tasks within the given environment.

At retrieval time, the user's query is issued simultaneously against both corpora, ensuring that the model can draw on rich technical details, while also surfacing explicit hazard warnings, procedural safeguards, and regulatory guidelines. By isolating safety passages in their own index, we can apply dedicated filtering and scoring thresholds that reflect the gravity of risk management, without diluting the coverage or performance of the broader maintenance knowledge base.

The dual-stream retrieval process produces two ranked lists of passages; one optimised for technical relevance, and the other for safety assurance, which are then merged before context integration. This architecture therefore guarantees that every generated recommendation is grounded not only in accurate domain expertise but also in up-to-date, rigorously validated safety information. We propose two merging functions to this effect and evaluate the effectiveness of both.

RAGuard Retrieval Parameters. RAGuard introduces three new retrieval hyperparameters; *knowledge-k* (denoted k_{know}), *safety-k* (denoted k_{safe}), and *fetch-k* (denoted k_{fetch}). These control the balance between technical depth and safety oversight in the dual index setup. The aforementioned $top - k$ remains in use as the total number of passages passed to the prompt context.

3.3 RAGuard Retrieval

RAGuard modifies the standard RAG retrieval step by splitting the total K retrieved passages into two parts: k_{know} from a technical knowledge index, and k_{safe} passages from a safety-specific index. This ensures that the final context includes both technical and safety-relevant content, with $K = k_{know} + k_{safe}$.

At retrieval time, the user's query q is sent to both indices in parallel. Each index returns its top K passages according to a relevance score function (q, d). The two sets of results are then merged into a single list and passed into the LLM prompt. For instance, if $k_{know} = 2$ and $k_{safe} = 3$, the final prompt includes five passages: two from the knowledge index, and three from the safety index. The process can be formalised as follows:

Knowledge index retrieval:

$$M_{know} = \{d_1, d_2, \ldots, d_{k_{know}}\}, \quad d_i = \arg\max_{d \in D_{k_{know}}} s(q, d) \tag{2}$$

Safety index retrieval:

$$S_{safe} = \{d'_1, d'_2, \ldots, d'_{k_{safe}}\}, \quad d'_j = \arg\max_{d \in D_{k_{safe}}} s(q, d) \tag{3}$$

Combined prompt input:

$$RAGuard(q) = [d_1, \ldots, d_{k_{know}}, d'_1, \ldots, d'_{k_{safe}}] \tag{4}$$

In summary, RAGuard queries two indices simultaneously, retrieves fixed top results from each, and merges them into a structured LLM input. The next section introduces *SafetyClamp*, which extends this by enforcing safety quotas and over-retrieving to maximise coverage and control.

3.4 RAGuard with SafetyClamp

RAGuard with the additional SafetyClamp builds directly on the base framework by enforcing an absolute safety guarantee on every retrieved passage. Rather than simply interleaving k_{know} and k_{safe} candidates, SafetyClamp begins by over-retrieving a wider pool of contenders; for both the knowledge index and dedicated safety index, the system retrieves the top k_{fetch} passages by relevance. This over-retrieval ensures that, even under strict slot requirements or occasional index sparsity, there will always be enough qualified passages to fill every reserved slot.

Once both pools are retrieved, SafetyClamp assigns passages in a hard-guaranteed sequence. The first k_{know} slots are filled by the highest scoring passages from the knowledge index. Next, the pipeline selects exactly k_{safe} passages from the safety index. Unlike the base RAGuard, $K > k_{know} + k_{safe}$, meaning once this is complete, there are still empty slots for additional passages. These are filled by the combined retrieved pools from both indices, choosing the next highest scoring passages not yet selected, regardless of whether they come from the knowledge or safety index. Given that k_{fetch} exceeds the final K, this wildcard mechanism reliably completes the prompt without sacrificing safety guarantees or technical comprehensiveness.

We can formalise RAGuard with SafetyClamp in three steps, reusing M_{know} and S_{safe} defined by Eqs. 2 and 3. First, we over-retrieve a combined candidate list:

$$C = [c_1, c_2, \ldots, c_{k_{fetch}}] \tag{5}$$

where, $c_i = \underset{d \in D \setminus d \notin \{c_1, \ldots, c_{i-1}\}}{\arg\max} \quad s(q, d)$

Next, we remove any already selected passages from $M_{know} \cup S_{safe}$, preserving order to form the wildcard pool:

$$R = [r_1, r_2, \ldots] \tag{6}$$

where each $r_l = c_{i_l} \in C$ and $c_{i_l} \notin M_{know} \cup S_{safe}$, and, $i_1 < i_2 < \ldots$ are the indices of those survivors in C.

Finally, SafetyClamp guarantees exactly k_{know} knowledge passages, k_{safe} safety passages, and fills the remaining $(K - (k_{know} + k_{safe}))$ slots from R:

$$\text{SafetyClamp}(q; K; k_{know}; k_{safe}) =$$
$$[m_1, \ldots, m_{k_{know}}, s_{k_{safe}}, \ldots, r_1, \ldots, r_{K-(k_{know}+k_{safe})}] \tag{7}$$

Here $\{m_i\} = M_{know}$, $\{s'_j\} = S_{safe}$, and the rs are drawn from the filtered R. Because $k_{fetch} > K$, there are always enough wildcards to complete the list.

In essence, SafetyClamp ensures its dual objectives by allocating fixed slots for knowledge and safety passages, over-retrieving extra candidates as wildcards, and assembling the prompt to meet quota requirements and context size. This enforces a safety minimum while preserving technical depth, with over-retrieving preventing empty slots.

4   Evaluation

In this section, we describe how we measure each system's ability to deliver both accurate maintenance guidance and essential safety information under realistic OSW conditions. We first outline our curated evaluation dataset of domain-specific queries paired with "gold-standard" answers and regulatory excerpts. We then present the metrics used to quantify technical fidelity, safety compliance, and system efficiency. Finally, we report and analyse results for standard RAG, base RAGuard, and RAGuard with SafetyClamp, highlighting the trade-offs each design makes between precision, coverage, and latency.

4.1   Evaluation Dataset

The evaluation leverages a dataset of 100 maintenance-focused questions, each paired with a "gold-standard" technical answer and the corresponding safety context drawn from two key industry regulations: the Provision and Use of Work Equipment Regulations (PUWER) and the Work at Height Regulations (WAHR).

For every query, we manually curate the precise procedural steps that constitute the correct technical resolution, and annotated the relevant excerpts from PUWER and WAHR that articulate the required safety checks, hazard warnings, or permitted work practices. This structured format allows us to measure not only whether each system retrieves the passages necessary to reconstruct the technical solution, but also whether it surfaces the exact regulatory language needed to ensure compliance with both PUWER and WAHR.

By combining domain-specific questions with dual sources of ground-truth (technical and safety), our dataset provides a rigorous test bed for assessing how well RAG, RAGuard and RAGuard with SafetyClamp balance operational accuracy against mandatory safety requirements.

Crucially, we evaluate each of these three pipelines under all three retrieval paradigms: sparse (BM25), dense (DPR), and hybrid (a weighted fusion of BM25 and DPR scores), to isolate the effect of the underlying retriever on both technical fidelity and safety compliance.

4.2   LLM Prompt Structure

Each retrieval pipeline shares a common prompt template that clearly delineates technical guidance from safety considerations. At the top of the prompt, the model is instructed to use the provided context to answer the question and admit when it does not know an answer rather than hallucinating. The template then presents two labelled context sections: under "Maintenance Context", the passages retrieved from the technical knowledge index are inserted, and under "Safety Context", the passages from the safety index appear. As the standard RAG pipeline does not explicitly differentiate between general knowledge and safety, both sections are identical using the $top - k$ passages retrieved from one index. Following these sections, the user's query is posed with a "«QUESTION»" marker, ensuring that the LLM's attention remains focused on the specific maintenance task.

Below the question, the prompt ends with a structured "ANSWER" area containing two numbered slots. The first slot, labelled "1) Procedure:," is where the model should generate step-by-step maintenance instructions grounded in the technical context. The second slot, labelled "2) Safety Considerations:," allows explicit hazard checks, warnings, or regulatory requirements drawn from the safety context.

By splitting the expected output into these two clearly defined components, we can directly assess both the procedural accuracy of the generated guidance and the completeness of the safety advice during evaluation.

4.3   Evaluation Metrics

Hyperparameter Optimisation. To establish a fair basis for comparing all pipelines, we first perform a comprehensive hyperparameter selection step. In this, we sweep across the retrieval paradigms and a grid of quota settings (k_{know}, k_{safe}, k_{fetch}, and K).

For each combination, we measure *RetrievalRecall@K* on both technical and safety passages across 100 questions. This single metric allows identification of which retrieval regime and which hyperparameter values maximise the likelihood of fetching all required "gold-standard" passages.

Once we determine the best settings for each pipeline, we fix those values for the remaining evaluations. This two-stage approach ensures that all systems are compared under their strongest retrieval settings, yielding a more meaningful assessment of their safety-aware enhancements.

Retrieval Recall@K. We measure *RetrievalRecall@K* separately for technical and safety passages. For each query, we examine the set of passages provided to the LLM and record whether the "gold-standard" technical passage and the annotated safety excerpt appear among the $top - K$. Averaging over all 100 queries yields two recall scores; one reflecting the likelihood of finding the correct procedural context, and one capturing the chance of including at least one requisite safety clause in the prompt.

Safety Compliance Recall. This measures whether the retrieved safety passages collectively cover every regulatory requirement specified for a given question. We treat a query as compliant only if all PUWER and WAHR clauses annotated in the dataset appear somewhere in the safety-context feed. The resulting recall rate thus reflects each pipeline's ability to surface the full set of mandated safety checks.

Latency and Context Utilisation. To gauge the practicality of the real world, we measure the average end-to-end retrieval time over the full dataset, computing the ratio of occupied to available tokens in the LLM's context window ($K/max - content - size$). This reveals how each approach balances richer contextual grounding against system responsiveness and prompt-size constraints.

We ran all of our latency and context-utilisation measurements on a high-end workstation laptop to approximate a realistic "edge" deployment scenario. The machine is a Ubuntu 22.04.4 LTS system powered by a 13th-Generation Intel® i9-13980HX (24 threads @ up to 5.6 GHz), with 64 GB of DDR5-5600 RAM and an NVIDIA RTX 4090 GPU. Retrieval timings were recorded on the CPU only; the retriever indices live in memory and are served locally, while the context-window fractions assume a model with a 4,096 token window (4K model). We report both the mean and the standard deviation of 100 runs per pipeline, to display not only the "typical" latency but also its variability under this hardware configuration.

5   Results and Discussion

5.1   Hyperparameter Optimisation

We perform a full grid search over our four retrieval hyperparameters—K, k_{know}, k_{safe}, and k_{fetch}—subject to $1 \leq k_{know} < K$, $1 \leq k_{safe} \leq K - k_{know}$, and $K \in \{1, \cdots, 10\}$, $k_{fetch} \in \{25, 50, 75, 100, 125, 150, 175, 200\}$, plus the Base RAG cases ($k_{know} = k_{safe} = 0$, $k_{fetch} = \text{None}$).

If N is the number of distinct K values and F the number of k_{fetch} options, the total number of valid 4-tuples $(K, k_{know}, K_{safe}, k_{fetch})$ we test is:

$$|\text{settings}| = F \sum_{K=1}^{N} \frac{(K-1)K}{2} + N \qquad (8)$$

For $N = 10$ and $F = 8$, this yields 1,330 distinct configurations. For each we compute:

$$\text{Combined Recall} = \frac{1}{2}(\text{Knowledge Recall} + \text{Safety Recall}) \qquad (9)$$

and then select, for each of the nine pipelines, the configuration that maximises Combined Recall. The resulting optimal parameters and their achieved recall scores are reported in Table 1.

Table 1. Best Combined Recall for Each RAG Variant

RAG	Variant	K Values				Recall Metrics		
		top	know	safe	fetch	Knowledge	Safety	Combined
Dense	Base	10	–	–	–	0.925	0.09	0.508
	RG[a]	10	3	7	–	0.535	0.92	0.728
	RG-SC[b]	10	5	5	25	0.790	0.95	0.870
Hybrid	Base	4	–	–	–	0.595	0.01	0.303
	RG	5	1	4	–	0.380	0.74	0.560
	RG-SC	7	3	4	25	0.585	0.71	0.648
Sparse	Base	2	–	–	–	0.250	0.00	0.125
	RG	3	1	2	–	0.165	0.15	0.158
	RG-SC	4	2	2	25	0.250	0.15	0.200

[a]RG: RAGuard, [b]SC: SafetyClamp

The hyperparameter sweep clearly illustrates the trade-offs inherent in each pipeline. Base RAG maximises knowledge recall; Dense achieves nearly 93% correct technical retrieval when $K = 10$, but at the cost of almost zero safety coverage. Introducing RAGuard dramatically raises the safety recall to over 90%, yet reduces the knowledge recall by roughly half, since only three slots are reserved for technical content. RAGuard with SafetyClamp, by contrast, finds a middle ground: by over-retrieving and then guaranteeing both a proportional number of knowledge and safety passages (e.g. $k_{know} = 5, k_{safe} = 5$ for Dense + RAGuard and SafetyClamp), it retains high safety recall (95%) while still preserving a strong knowledge recall (79%), yielding the highest combined score (0.87).

Hybrid pipelines behave similarly but start from lower base knowledge recall, and sparse pipelines–inherently limited by BM25's coarse matching-cannot exceed 25% knowledge retrieval even when safety is ignored.

Overall, RAGuard with SafetyClamp consistently delivers the best balance, particularly under dense retrieval, by ensuring that neither technical accuracy nor mandated safety context are sacrificed.

5.2 Retrieval Recall@K

Figure 2 visualises each pipeline's performance in the technical-vs-safety recall@ K plane, using colour to denote the family (orange: Dense, red: Hybrid, green: Sparse) and distinct markers to indicate the retrieval method ('O': Base RAG, 'X': RAGuard, '■': RAGuard with SafetyClamp).

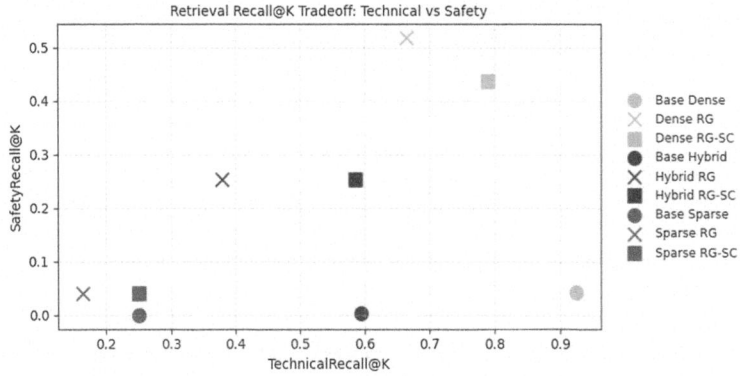

Fig. 2. Recall trade-off: Technical Recall@K vs Safety Recall@K

The plot reveals a clear three-way trade-off across methods and families. Within each colour band, the Base RAG point sits farthest to the right-maximising technical recall-but remains near the bottom with almost zero safety recall. RAGuard lifts each family sharply upward: for Dense, the jump from Base (0.925, 0.0425) to Dense+RAGuard (0.665, 0.5175) illustrates how interleaving yields large safety gains at the expense of roughly 26% points (pp) of technical recall. SafetyClamp occupies the middle ground, for example, Dense + RAGuard with SafetyClamp at (0.790, 0.4375) recovers most of the Base technical coverage while still boosting safety recall by 39 pp. Hybrid and Sparse variants follow the same pattern; SafetyClamp always improves safety over Base with only a modest drop in technical retrieval, and RAGuard pushes safety even further up.

Overall, SafetyClamp consistently dominates Base RAG in safety without sacrificing too much technical accuracy, and RAGuard sits at the front of the Pareto curve when safety is paramount.

5.3   Safety Compliance Recall

Figure 3 shows each pipeline's Safety Compliance Recall, that is, the fraction of queries for which *all* annotated PUWER and WAHR passages were successfully retrieved. The horizontal axis lists the nine methods, and the vertical axis gives the compliance rate from 0 to 1. Each bar's height corresponds exactly to the Safety Compliance Recall metric: for example, the "Dense + RAGuard" bar at 0.07 indicates that only 7% of queries retrieved every required safety excerpt under that configuration.

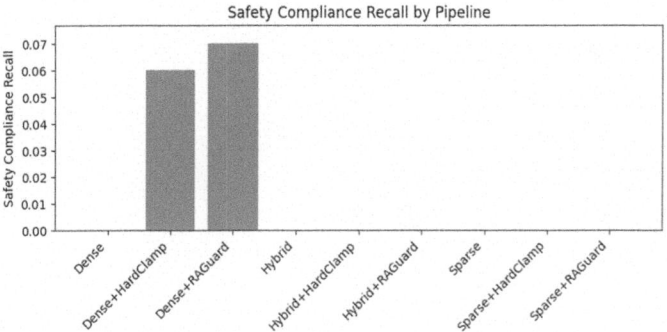

Fig. 3. Safety Compliance Recall by Pipeline

Despite improvements in the single-clause safety recall as presented earlier, full compliance rates remain very low for all pipelines. The best performer, Dense + RAGuard, achieves just 7% compliance, while its SafetyClamp counterpart achieves 6%. Hybrid and Sparse variants all fall at or near 0%, meaning they never retrieve *every* mandated safety clause in a single pass.

These results underscore a critical gap: even the most safety-focused retrieval strategies still omit at least one required regulation clause in over 90% of cases. To move toward reliable compliance in safety-critical contexts, future work must explore higher safety-slot budgets, multi-pass retrieval until exhaustively covered, or targeted post-retrieval verification steps.

Latency and Context Utilisation. Figure 4 illustrates the trade-off between retrieval latency and context utilisation across our three RAG families and retrieval methods. Each plot focuses on one family, and plots the average retrieval time on the vertical axis against the fraction of the LLM's context window occupied by retrieved passages on the horizontal axis. Within each plot, a circle denotes the Base RAG, an "X" denotes RAGuard, and a square marks Safe-tyClamp; all markers are outlined in black, with the error bars in the family's colour showing $\pm$ 1 standard deviation.

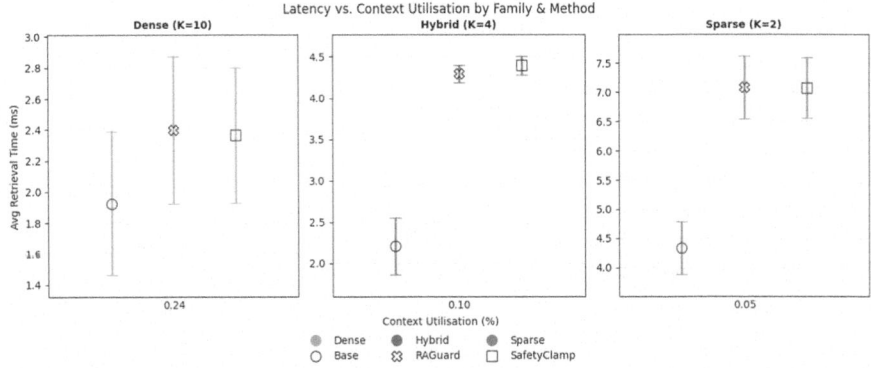

Fig. 4. Latency vs Context Utilisation for a 4K Model

Across all families, the Base RAG method sits at the leftmost (lowest context use) and lowest latency point. Introducing RAGuard shifts each marker slightly to the right—because it interleaves safety passages—at the cost of a modest increase in retrieval time (roughly 0.4–0.6 ms extra). SafetyClamp moves further right, due to its larger k_{fetch}, and imposes a further latency penalty; it still completes retrieval in under 3 ms for Dense, under 4.5 ms for Hybrid and under 7.5 ms for Sparse. Thus, the plot makes clear the Pareto front of methods: if the primary goal is minimal latency, and you can tolerate absence of safety guarantees, Base RAG is optimal; if you require safety integration, RAGuard and SafetyClamp offer progressively stronger safety coverage at predictable, bounded increases in retrieval time.

6 Conclusion

This work introduced RAGuard, an enhanced RAG framework for OSW maintenance that integrates safety-critical content with technical documentation. By using parallel indices and separate k_{know} and k_{safe} quotas, RAGuard ensures recommendations are grounded in domain expertise and validated safety protocols. We also proposed SafetyClamp, an over-retrieve and hard-clamp variant that guarantees slots for technical and safety passages even when an index is sparse.

Our evaluation, conducted on a curated dataset of 100 real-world OSW maintenance queries, showed that both RAGuard and SafetyClamp substantially outperform standard RAG in surfacing mandated safety clauses. Specifically, Safety Recall@K increased from near 0% (Base RAG) to over 50% (Dense RAGuard), with only modest reductions in Technical Recall@K. In hyperparameter sweeps, we found optimal configurations that balance technical fidelity and safety coverage. Latency measurements on a 13th-gen i9 laptop showed that these gains incur only a small retrieval overhead while offering very low context utilisation fractions, leaving ample room in LLM windows. Overall, RAGuard and its SafetyClamp extension provide a principled, lightweight mechanism for embedding safety guarantees directly into RAG pipelines, offering practical value in regulated high-stakes environments.

Future work includes several directions. First, we will carry out additional hyperparameter experiments, varying document chunk size and overlap to find the optimal indexing strategy. Second, we plan to integrate more regulatory and technical documents, reflecting the multiple standards and manuals used in real-world operations to ensure our system scales to complex scenarios. We will further investigate adaptive slot-sizing methods that adjust k_{know} and k_{safe} based on the complexity of each query. Finally, we will study how different retrieval configurations influence the quality and safety of the LLM's generated responses. Longer term, we aim to run live field trials to measure the end-to-end effects on maintenance decision accuracy, operational efficiency, and overall safety outcomes, gaining vital expert feedback.

Acknowledgments. This work was conducted under the Aura CDT program, funded by EPSRC and NERC, grant number EP/S023763/1 and project reference 2609857.

References

1. Asai, A., Wu, Z., Wang, Y., Sil, A., Hajishirzi, H.: Self-rag: learning to retrieve, generate, and critique through self-reflection (2023)
2. Demir, G., Moslem, S., Duleba, S.: Artificial intelligence in aviation safety: systematic review and biometric analysis. Int. J. Comput. Intell. Syst. **17**(1), 279 (2024)
3. Habli, I., Lawton, T., Porter, Z.: Artificial intelligence in health care: accountability and safety. Bull. World Health Organ. **98**(4), 251–256 (2020)
4. Izacard, G., et al.: Atlas: few-shot learning with retrieval augmented language models. J. Mach. Learn. Res. **24**(251), 1–43 (2023)
5. Jendoubi, C., Asad, A.: A survey of artificial intelligence applications in nuclear power plants. IoT **5**(4), 666–691 (2024)
6. Jiang, Z., et al.: Active retrieval augmented generation (2023)
7. Lewis, P., et al.: Retrieval-augmented generation for knowledge-intensive NLP tasks. In: Advances in Neural Information Processing Systems, vol. 33, pp. 9459–9474 (2020)
8. Liang, X., et al.: SafeRag: benchmarking security in retrieval-augmented generation of large language model (2025)

Probabilistic Analysis

Variance-Based Sensitivity Analysis for Probabilistic Risk Assessment

Jonathan Mboko[1,2](✉), Jérôme Morio[1,2](✉)(iD), Christel Seguin[1,2](✉),
Jean-Charles Chaudemar[1(✉)](iD), and Tatiana Prosvirnova[1,2(✉)]

[1] Fédération ENAC ISAE-SUPAERO ONERA, Université de Toulouse,
31000 Toulouse, France
jonathan.mboko@onera.fr
[2] ONERA/DTIS, Université de Toulouse, 31055 Toulouse, France

Abstract. In the safety assessment of critical systems, the probability of system failure over the mission duration constitutes a key reliability metric guiding design and certification decisions. Based on this indicator, safety-related design and certification decisions are made. Various types of models propose solutions to compute this probability of failure. However, there are always some epistemic uncertainties on the behavior of the system components, leading to some variance of the computed probability of failure regardless of the model. We assess the influence of epistemic uncertainties in the input parameters on the system failure probability through variance-based sensitivity indices. We then study the potential of importance sampling for the low-cost evaluation of sensitivity indices. We apply this methodology on different AltaRica 3.0 use cases and illustrate the efficiency and limits of sensitivity analysis in this safety context.

Keywords: Probabilistic Risk Assessment · Model-Based Safety Assessment · AltaRica · Sensitivity Analysis · Sobol' indices

1 Introduction

The probability of failure of a safety critical system is a key indicator to decide whether the frequency of a failure occurrence is acceptable or not. Events with severe consequences should be rare enough to be acceptable, e.g., the failure rate of catastrophic events shall be less than 10^{-9} per flight hour for large commercial aircraft. More often, such safety-critical top events result from combinations of failures in basic system components. Even minor epistemic uncertainties in the failure probabilities of basic components can result in substantial variability in the overall system failure probability.

Sensitivity analysis is the study of how uncertainty in the output of a code or system can be attributed to uncertainty in its inputs. It involves estimating sensitivity indices that quantify the influence of an input, or a group of inputs, on the output. Sensitivity analysis can be applied to traditional safety assessment

P. Katsaros (Ed.): IMBSA 2025, LNCS 15755, pp. 207–221, 2026.
https://doi.org/10.1007/978-3-032-05073-1_14

models like the fault trees to assess how the uncertainty of the probability of a top root event can be attributed to the uncertainty of the probability of the basic leaf failures.

Model-based safety analysis is an alternative to fault tree analysis that was introduced, among other things, to ease the modeling and analysis of failure propagation in complex systems. The goal of this paper is to assess experimentally the relevance and tractability of the sensitivity analysis of MBSA models.

For this purpose, we build AltaRica models of two variants of a typical system with a command-and-monitoring architecture. The failure propagation model of this system can be seen as a stochastic process and the example is small enough to support an exact analytic analysis of the probability of occurrence of some undesired events. The example helps us to highlight the effect of small epistemic uncertainties on the failure probability and provide two reference cases.

In order to assess the tractability of the sensitivity analysis in the general case, we consider some classical variance-based sensitivity indices. As their computation requires the estimation of many failure probabilities using Monte Carlo methods, we investigate the potential of importance sampling techniques to accelerate the estimation of sensitivity indices.

In the following, we first present the case studies. Then, we review the basics of the sensitivity analysis and we introduce different strategies to accelerate the computation of the sensitivity indices. Finally we present and discuss the experimental results.

2   Illustrative Case Study

We propose a simple concrete example to introduce concepts to safety specialists and then perform a sensitivity analysis on a comprehensive use case. We also introduce the AltaRica model for this example.

2.1   Command/Monitoring System

We choose a control system with the command/monitoring architecture shown in Fig. 1 below.

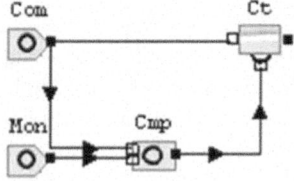

Fig. 1. Command/Monitoring pattern of safety architecture.

This architectural pattern is used, for instance, in fly-by-wire systems to reduce the risk of erroneous control occurrences (see, for instance, [4,6]). Indeed, the occurrence of an erroneous control may have a catastrophic effect on the flight, whereas the loss of control of some actuator can be recovered thanks to actuation redundancies. We propose to study two safety objectives:

- CAT_control_erroneous: the probability of occurrence of an erroneous control shall be less than 10^{-9} per flight hour.
- MINOR_control_lost: the probability of occurrence of a lost control shall be less than 10^{-3} per flight hour.

To achieve these objectives, the system contains four main components which are described below:

- *Com* and *Mon* are two numerical functions that compute the same control command using two different algorithms. They each have two failure modes. We assume that these components have specific failure modes with probabilities of occurrence that follow exponential distributions. They may produce an erroneous output with a rate $\theta_{err} = 10^{-5}$ or no output at all with a failure rate $\theta_{loss} = 10^{-3}$.
- The comparator *Cmp* checks the equality of the control commands issued by *Com* and *Mon*. A failure is detected when they disagree. We assume that *Cmp* cannot fail.
- The contactor *Ct* is closed or open. Initially it is closed and it transmits *Com* order. When the equality check becomes false, the contactor is latched open and it does not transmit anymore order. The *Ct* contactor is assumed to be failure-free and is the only mechanism available to safely reconfigure the architecture in operation when a failure is detected.

We also consider one component variant in our experiments: *CtReClosable* is a contactor that can be opened and then re-closed if the equality check becomes true again.

This command/monitoring system is considered in aircraft safety for missions of 1 h or more. For the sake of simplicity, we assume that the health of the system components is checked after each flight.

2.2 AltaRica Models of the Command/Monitoring System

The safety analysis of such systems can be based on advanced failure propagation models. For the practical model illustrations and experiments, we use the MBSA modeling language AltaRica 3.0 [18]. The AltaRica language enables to structure safety model as engineering models. It also provides assertions and transitions to specify the behaviour of the components in the structure. Then, the resulting overall model is a Guarded Transition System [19], which implicitly defines large general stochastic processes.

Our experiment considers two architectural variants of the Command/Monitoring system.

- Case 1 (Fig. 2): System with reclosable contactor and failures of Com and Mon only: *Com, Mon, Cmp, CtReClosable*

- Case 2 (Fig. 3): System with latchable contactor and failures of Com and Mon only: *Com, Mon, Cmp, Ct*

The figures below show the full reachability graphs for each case. The graphs highlight the states where the command *Ct.O* is either *ok* (normal command), *lost* (minor situation) or, *err* (catastrophic situation).

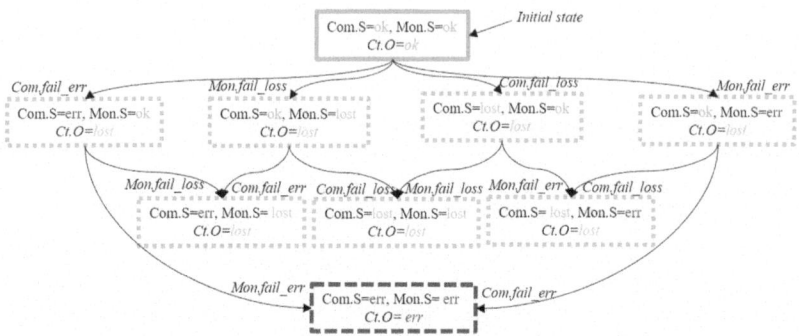

Fig. 2. Full reachability graph of the system with reclosable contactor and failures of Com and Mon.

In the first case, we can observe that the orders of occurrence of the failures of *Com* and *Mon* do not impact the reached states. Moreover, the contactor is reclosed after a simultaneous failure of *Com* and *Mon*, leading to a catastrophic state.

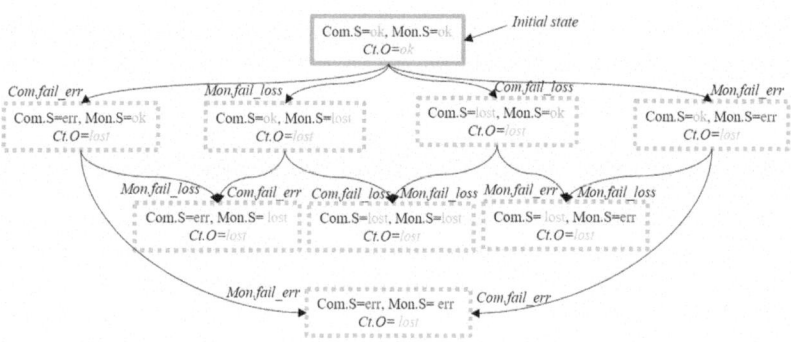

Fig. 3. Full reachability graph of the system with latchable contactor and failures of Com and Mon.

In the second case, the contactor is latch open after disagreement between *Com* and *Mon*. So the system cannot reach the catastrophic state.

We will in particular study the `CAT_control_erroneous` event associated with the Case 1 and the `MINOR_control_lost` event associated with Case 2, since the `CAT_control_erroneous` cannot be reached in Case 2, and `MINOR_control_lost` in Case 2 is equivalent to the union of the two failure events in Case 1.

2.3 Analytical Estimation of the Command/Monitoring System Safety Objective

These reachability graphs define a set of failure events that may occur during the system life. The firing dates of these events are random variables that follow exponential distributions parameterized by failure rate ϑ. We assume that the values of the failure rates are uncertain and may vary from one order as indicated in Table 1a). In the absence of further information on the failure rate uncertainties, we assume the failure rates to be uniformly distributed over their variation range. However, it should be noted that with additional dispersion information, other distributions (e.g., Gaussian) could be more appropriate, which would affect the resulting sensitivity analysis.

Table 1. Epistemic uncertainty propagation of the command/monitoring system failure probability.

Random variables	Failure rate	Failure rate range
X1: Com.fail loss	10^{-3}	$[5 \times 10^{-4} : 5 \times 10^{-3}]$
X2: Com.fail err	10^{-5}	$[5 \times 10^{-6} : 5 \times 10^{-5}]$
X3: Mon.fail loss	10^{-3}	$[5 \times 10^{-4} : 5 \times 10^{-3}]$
X4: Mon.fail err	10^{-5}	$[5 \times 10^{-6} : 5 \times 10^{-5}]$

a) Random variables associated to the failures of the case study.

	Event Probability
Lower bound CAT	2.49×10^{-11}
Higher bound CAT	2.50×10^{-9}
Lower bound MIN	1.01×10^{-3}
Higher bound MIN	1.00×10^{-2}

b) Extrema probabilities of considered failure events.

Using these values and the reachability graph, we can analytically compute the minimum and maximum values of the probabilities of occurrence of the undesired events `CAT_control_erroneous` (Case 1) and `MINOR_control_lost` (Case 2) as seen in Table 1b). The results show that the uncertainty of the failure rates may lead to the violation of the safety objectives. Consequently it is important to perform a sensitivity analysis to identify which variables have a significant impact on the failure probability and which uncertainties should be explored and reduced.

3   Sensitivity Analysis for Quantitative Risk Assessment

Unreliability. In order to more precisely define the probability of failure that we aim to study, we will use the frame of system reliability theory [2]. Given the system under study, we consider the random variable $\mathbf{t}_F$ of the system first time of failure. The reliability of the system at time t is then defined as $R(t) = P(t < \mathbf{t}_F)$, i.e. the probability that the system does not fail before t. The probability of failure before a given mission time T is then the unreliability defined by $F_T = F(T) = 1 - R(T) = P(\mathbf{t}_F \leq T)$.

In the simplest example of a system with no aging, $\mathbf{t}_F$ follows an exponential distribution characterized by the failure rate θ. The inverse of the failure rate is the average time of first failure and thus $F_T = 1 - e^{-\theta T}$.

Considered Safety Models. For more complex systems, F_T often does not have a simple analytical expression. To estimate F_T, we consider models that simulate the random variable $\mathbf{t}_F$. Assuming that we have such model, the unknown deterministic value F_T can be estimated through Monte Carlo as $\widehat{F}_n(T) = \frac{1}{n} \sum_{j=1}^{n} \mathbb{1}_{\mathbf{t}_F^j \leq T}$, where $(\mathbf{t}_F^j)_{j=1,...,n}$ are realizations of the model.

In the context of classic system safety assessment, we consider that the failure of the system is a function of the failure of independent basic components. For a given system modeled with d failure-prone independent components, we thus suppose that each individual component time of failure $\mathbf{t}_i$, $i = 1, ..., d$, can be fully characterized by a known probability density function (pdf) f_i. The system safety is then described as a deterministic input-output function $\mathcal{M} : \mathbb{R}^d \to \mathbb{R}$ with random input $\mathbf{X} = (\mathbf{t}_1, ..., \mathbf{t}_d)$, that is the vector of component time of failure, and with an output $\mathbf{Y} = \mathbf{t}_F = \mathcal{M}(\mathbf{X})$, the time of failure of the system. Sampling different realizations $\mathbf{t}_F^j$, $j = 1, ..., n$ for Monte Carlo estimation is then carried out using independent and identically distributed input samples $\mathbf{X}^j \sim f = \prod_{i=1}^{d} f_i$ and their evaluation through $\mathcal{M}$.

Uncertainty Modeling. Let us now consider the uncertainties in our model affecting the estimation of F_T. We assume that $\mathcal{M}$ adequately models the system for the purpose of the evaluation of F_T. The source of uncertainty is then reduced to its input $\mathbf{X}$. In probabilistic risk assessment, the uncertainties are divided into two types: aleatory uncertainties that stem from random phenomena, and epistemic uncertainties that arise from lack of knowledge of these phenomena [1]. The aleatory uncertainty is embedded in the modeling of the input variable $\mathbf{X}$ as a random variable and the epistemic uncertainty results from the uncertainty on the parametrization of the input pdf that best represents the random phenomena described.

When the input pdf f is fixed, then the value of F_T is also fixed and only its estimation $\widehat{F}_n(T)$ is subject to uncertainty. In practice, however, the input probabilistic model depends on multiple sources of information, each introducing its own uncertainties. In this article, we consider distribution parameter epistemic uncertainty for the densities f_i. This epistemic uncertainty is assumed to be a function of a parameter vector $\boldsymbol{\theta}$ and thus F_T also becomes a function of $\boldsymbol{\theta}$. In this context, knowing which vector component failure or group of vector component failure affects the most the variability of F_T can help to decide which epistemic uncertainty is significant or not, acceptable or not. We will for this task study the influence of the variability of the components of the parameter vector $\boldsymbol{\theta}$ on the variability of $F_T(\boldsymbol{\theta})$.

4   Sensitivity Analysis Problem

4.1   Expression of the Unreliability

For a given system, we consider a safety model defined as presented in Sect. 3. We first define the distribution of X_i as $X_i \sim f_{i,\theta_i}$, $i = 1, ..., d$ where f_i defines the parametric model of density (Gaussian, exponential,...) and θ_i is the corresponding parameter vector associated to f_i. In the following, we will consider for the sake of simplicity but without loss of generality $f_i = f$ and θ_i to be a scalar for each i. We thus denote the parameter vector $\boldsymbol{\theta} = (\theta_1, ..., \theta_d)$ and $\mathbf{X} \sim f_{\boldsymbol{\theta}}$ with $f_{\boldsymbol{\theta}} = \prod_{i=1}^{d} f_{\theta_i}$. The unreliability of the system at a given time T is then $F_T = P(\mathbf{Y} < T) = \mathbb{E}[\mathbb{1}_{\mathbf{Y}<T}] = \mathbb{E}_{f_{\boldsymbol{\theta}}}[\mathbb{1}_{\mathcal{M}(\mathbf{X})<T}]$.

We now connect this framework with the first ComMon example presented in Sect. 2. The failure model can be described as a function $\mathcal{M} : \mathbb{R}^4 \to \mathbb{R}$ with for input $\mathbf{X}$ a vector of dimension 4 having as pdf $f_{\boldsymbol{\theta}}(\boldsymbol{x}) = \prod_{i=1}^{4} \theta_i e^{-\theta_i x_i}$ with $\boldsymbol{\theta} = (\theta_1, ..., \theta_4)$ the vector of parameter characterizing the failure rates of the random variables described in Tab. 1a). The mission duration is fixed to $T = 1$ hour.

4.2   Sobol' Indices

The goal is to evaluate the effect of perturbations of $\boldsymbol{\theta}$ on F_T. To account for epistemic uncertainty in the input distribution, we consider now $\boldsymbol{\theta}$ as a random vector $\boldsymbol{\Theta}$ with density $h_{\boldsymbol{\Theta}}$ that has independent components. F_T then becomes a random variable $F_T(\boldsymbol{\Theta})$.

We will use a variance-based criterion to evaluate the influence of $\boldsymbol{\Theta}$ on $F_T(\boldsymbol{\Theta})$: the Sobol' indices [21]. It is a well-known sensitivity index in the framework of uncertainty quantification. Given a subset of variables $\boldsymbol{\Theta}_v$ from $\boldsymbol{\Theta}$, the Sobol' index $S_{\boldsymbol{\Theta}_v}^{F_T}$ quantifies the proportion of the variance of F_T explained by the variables $\boldsymbol{\Theta}_v$. These indices are positive, comprised between 0 and 1 and sum to 1. Thus, they are easily interpretable (0 meaning that $\boldsymbol{\Theta}_v$ has no influence on the variance of F_T and 1 that $\boldsymbol{\Theta}_v$ explains alone all the variance of F_T).

We will particularly focus on the first order Sobol' indices, i.e. the Sobol' indices for individual variables, and the total order Sobol' indices [11]; the total order Sobol' index associated with variable $\boldsymbol{\Theta}_i$ is defined as the sum of all the Sobol' indices of the subsets containing $\boldsymbol{\Theta}_i$. The first Sobol' index $S_i^{F_T}$ and total order Sobol' indice $S_{T_i}^{F_T}$ associated to the variable $\boldsymbol{\Theta}_i$ are respectively defined in the following way:

$$S_i^{F_T} = \frac{Var(\mathbb{E}[F_T|\boldsymbol{\Theta}_i])}{Var(F_T)}$$

$$S_{T_i}^{F_T} = 1 - \frac{Var(\mathbb{E}[F_T|\boldsymbol{\Theta}_{-i}])}{Var(F_T)}$$

with $\boldsymbol{\Theta}_{-i}$ being the vector $\boldsymbol{\Theta}$ with the i-th component removed.

For the ComMon case, we write the interval characterizing the uniform input distributions described in Table 1a) as interval centered around their mean $\theta_\mu = (\theta_{\mu,1}, ..., \theta_{\mu,4})$ with $\boldsymbol{\Theta}_i \sim \mathcal{U}[\theta_{\mu,i} - \alpha_i; \theta_{\mu,i} + \alpha_i]$, α_i constant, $i = 1, ..., 4$. Then, $S_1^{F_T}$ quantifies the proportion of the variance of F_T explained by the uncertainties on the parameter θ_1 characterizing the loss failure rate of Com event.

4.3   Estimation of the Sobol' Indices

A classical estimator for the Sobol' indices is the pick-freeze estimator [8].

In the model safety framework, estimating a Sobol' index $S_i^{F_T}$ consists of:

1. Generating $2m$ samples of $\boldsymbol{\Theta}$, $(\boldsymbol{\Theta}^{(k)})_{k=1,...2m}$ (see [8] for details)
2. Obtaining the quantities $(F_T(\boldsymbol{\Theta}^{(k)}))_{k=1,...2m}$ with calls to $\mathcal{M}$
3. Computing the estimator $\widehat{S}_{i,m}^{F_T} = PF_m(F_T(\boldsymbol{\Theta}^{(k)})_{k=1,...2m})$ with

$$PF_m : (Y_1, ..., Y_{2m}) \mapsto \frac{\frac{1}{m}\sum_{i=1}^m Y_i Y_{i+m} - (\frac{1}{m}Y_i)(\frac{1}{m}Y_{i+m})}{\frac{1}{m}Y_i^2 - (\frac{1}{m}Y_i)^2} \text{(see [8] for details)}$$

We recall hereafter two existing approaches for estimating Sobol indices, focusing on improving step 2 of the procedure to reduce the number of calls to $\mathcal{M}$.

Naive Estimation. If the probabilities $F_T(\boldsymbol{\Theta}^{(k)})$ are directly computable, the computation of this estimator requires the sampling of $2m$ vectors $\boldsymbol{\Theta}$ and the computation of the $2m$ probabilities $F_T(\boldsymbol{\Theta}^{(k)})$.

For a given $\boldsymbol{\theta}^{(i)}$, $F_T(\boldsymbol{\theta}^{(i)}) = \mathbb{E}_{f_{\boldsymbol{\theta}(i)}}[\mathbb{1}_{\mathbf{Y} < T}]$ is only available for simple and has to be estimated otherwise. This expectancy is estimated with the Monte Carlo method by sampling $\mathbf{X}^{(1)}, ..., \mathbf{X}^{(n)}$ according to $f_{\boldsymbol{\theta}(i)}$ and estimating $F_T(\boldsymbol{\theta}^{(i)})$ by the Monte Carlo estimator $\widehat{F_T^{MC}}(\boldsymbol{\theta}^{(i)}) = \frac{1}{n}\sum_{j=1}^n \mathbb{1}_{\mathcal{M}(\mathbf{X}^{(j)}) \leq T}$.

If these estimations are sufficiently accurate, performing the sensitivity analysis on $\widehat{F_T^{MC}}$ is equivalent to performing the sensitivity analysis on F_T. The Sobol' index estimate to compute would then be $\widehat{S}_{i,m}^{F_T^{MC}} = PF_m((\widehat{F_T^{MC}}(\boldsymbol{\Theta}^{(k)}))_{k=1,...,2m})$, requiring $2m \times n$ evaluations with the safety model $\mathcal{M}$.

The accuracy of the estimator $\widehat{F_T^{MC}}$ can be estimated using the same sample with the coefficient of variation (CV), i.e., $CV(\widehat{F_T^{MC}}) = \frac{\sqrt{Var(\widehat{F_T^{MC}})}}{\widehat{F_T^{MC}}} \approx \frac{\sqrt{1-\widehat{F_T^{MC}}}}{\sqrt{\widehat{F_T^{MC}}n}}$.

This typically means that to obtain a CV of 10% (which is considered reasonably accurate) for a probability of $10^{-\alpha}$, approximately $n = 10^{\alpha+2}$ samples are needed.

In the considered safety context, in particular for aeronautic applications, we are dealing with probabilities inferior to 10^{-4}, so we would need at least $n = 10^6$

outputs of the safety model to obtain probabilities estimated with CV of 10%, and thus in total more than $2m \times 10^6$ safety model evaluations for the estimation of one Sobol' index. Running the safety model is usually time consuming and thus a naive implementation would not be tractable. Moreover, if n is too low, most of the computed probabilities may be equal to zero, making the sensitivity analysis unreliable.

We will now analyze how to decrease the number of calls to the safety model while keeping a good estimation of the Sobol' indices.

Better Estimation with Importance Sampling. At equivalent simulation budget, the objective will be to have a better estimation than the naive method by improving the accuracy of the estimation of the probabilities $(F_T(\Theta^{(k)}))_{k=1,\ldots,m}$

A first solution is proposed in [13], using importance sampling (IS) [16]. Assuming that we have $(\mathbf{X}^{(i)})_{(i=1,\ldots,n)} \sim g$ independent and identically distributed with g an auxiliary pdf such that $g = 0 \implies \mathbb{1}_{\mathcal{M}(\cdot)\leq T} f_\theta(\cdot) = 0$, for a given $\boldsymbol{\theta}^{(i)}$, the IS estimate of $F_T(\boldsymbol{\theta}^{(i)})$ is given by

$$\widehat{F_T^{IS}}(\boldsymbol{\theta}^{(i)}) = \frac{1}{n} \sum_{j=1}^{n} \mathbb{1}_{\mathcal{M}(\mathbf{X}^{(j)})\leq T} \frac{f_{\boldsymbol{\theta}^{(i)}}(\mathbf{X}^{(j)})}{g(\mathbf{X}^{(j)})} \tag{1}$$

If we have already processed with the safety model $\mathcal{M}$ the output associated to the samples $(\mathbf{X}^{(j)})_{j=1,\ldots,n} \sim g$, we can thus estimate $F_T(\boldsymbol{\theta})$ for any value of $\boldsymbol{\theta}$ without additional calls to the safety model. Different techniques are available to find an efficient density g (e.g. Adaptive IS with Cross-Entropy [3], Improved Cross-entropy [17] or non parametric IS [14]) and thus to improve the precision of the estimator.

IS is then applied to determine a density g adapted for the estimation of $F_T(\boldsymbol{\theta}_\mu)$, with $\boldsymbol{\theta}_\mu$ being the mean of Θ [13], compute with $\mathcal{M}$ the n associated output, and use these results to evaluate all the probabilities $(F_T(\Theta^{(k)}))_{k=1,\ldots,m}$ using Eq. (1) The computation of the Sobol' index considered thus only requires n calls to the safety model. As the computation of different Sobol' indices only means evaluation of F_T with different $\boldsymbol{\theta}$, evaluation of other Sobol' indices is free in terms of number of calls to the safety model. For small variations of $\boldsymbol{\theta}$ around $\boldsymbol{\theta}_\mu$, the IS estimation of Eq.(1) without resampling will be accurate but it is no longer the case for bigger variations and thus it can bias the sensitivity analysis results.

To tackle this limitation, a possible alternative is to compute the different probabilities using multiple auxiliary pdfs that are adapted to different $\boldsymbol{\theta}$.

Proposed Method Using Multiple Importance Sampling. Multiple importance sampling (mIS) estimator [7] follows the same logic as the IS estimator, the difference being the use of samples coming from multiple auxiliary pdf instead of a single auxiliary distribution. Given l auxiliary pdfs $g_j, j = 1,\ldots,l$ and samples $(\mathbf{X}_{i,j}), i = 1,\ldots,n, =, j = 1,\ldots,l$ with $\mathbf{X}_{i,j} \sim$

g_j, the balanced heuristic mIS estimator of $F_T(\boldsymbol{\theta})$ is given by $\widehat{F_T^{mIS}}(\boldsymbol{\theta}) = \frac{1}{n} \sum_{j=1}^{l} \sum_{i=1}^{n} \mathbb{1}_{\mathcal{M}(\mathbf{X_{i,j}}) \leq T} \frac{f_{\boldsymbol{\theta}}(\mathbf{X}_{i,j})}{\sum_{k=1}^{l} g_k(\mathbf{X}_{i,j})}$ [16].

Instead of using one auxiliary pdf and corresponding samples adapted to a single point $\boldsymbol{\theta}_\mu$, Latin Hypercube Sampling (LHS) [12] is considered to propose a set of parameters $\boldsymbol{\theta}_j$ that well covers the support of Θ. The densities g_j are then determined with adaptive IS to be efficient for the estimations $\widehat{F_T^{IS}}(\boldsymbol{\theta}^{(i)})$. Finally, $F_T(\boldsymbol{\theta})$ is estimated with mIS by combining all the j estimations.

We will compare the efficiency of the 3 described approaches (naive, simple IS and mIS) on different test cases.

5   Practical Applications

5.1   Results with Exact Probabilities

In the proposed use cases, the unreliability F_T is available analytically. The estimation of the Sobol' indices can thus be done with the pick-freeze estimation procedure described in Sect. 4.3 precisely (no budget limitation due to calls to $\mathcal{M}$ of step 2.).

Table 2 summarizes the Sobol' indices obtained with regards to each individual uncertainty parameter (failure rate) of the model, for the two undesired events studied.

Table 2. First order Sobol' associated to the two failure case study

Component	Sobol' associated in Case 1	Sobol' associated in Case 2
X1: Com.fail loss	0	0.5
X2: Com.fail err	0.45	0
X3: Mon.fail loss	0	0.5
X4: Mon.fail err	0.45	0

In both studied cases, the Com and Mon components exhibit symmetrical behavior with respect to failure events (cf. Fig. 2, and Fig. 3); this symmetry is also reflected in the first-order Sobol' indices.

The influence of parametric uncertainties on the failure event differs significantly between the two use cases. For the `CAT_control_erroneous` event (Case 1), the majority of the variance of the unreliability is explained by the individual action of the parametric uncertainties linked to the erroneous events while the individual action of the parametric uncertainties linked to loss events has no influence on the variance of the unreliability. We obtain almost the opposite results for the `MINOR_control_lost` event (Case 2), with the individual action of the uncertainties linked to the loss events explaining all the variance of the unreliability. A notable difference between the two cases is also that in Case 2 the first order Sobol' indices sum to 1, meaning the interactions of the variables have no influence on the variance of the unreliability, while in Case 1, the first order Sobol' indices sum to 0.9, meaning that 10% of the variance of the unreliability is explained by interactions between the components in the model.

These results highlight that with the same system, depending on the safety objective, the most influential sources of uncertainty can be very different. For instance, in order to lower the uncertainty for the Case 2 unreliability, the parametric uncertainty on the loss events should be lowered, and in the same time lowering the uncertainty on the error events parameter would not have any effect on the unreliability variance.

5.2   Results with Probability Estimations

Without the unreliability function F_T directly available, the proposed solution consists in estimating F_T as accurately as possible in step 2 of the pick-freeze estimation of Sect. 4.3. The presented solutions with IS rely mainly on finding adequate auxiliary pdf g. However, this proves to be particularly difficult with AltaRica models. The behavior of unreliability function in the case of AltaRica models is indeed linked to the relative order of components failure, and the optimisation problem of finding the adequate parametric auxiliary pdf is difficult and not conclusive.

As seen in Fig. 4, Sobol' indices can be accurately estimated using the exact probabilities, but not using IS (and mIS). This is explained by the auxiliary sampling pdf function g not being adequate enough to estimate precisely the $F_T(\Theta)$.

To see the effect of the proposed Sobol' estimation techniques, we consider failure rate bounds leading to higher failure probabilities F_T and higher variations of its value, making the IS at equivalent budget more efficient and the difference between computed F_T values more apparent. We consider the bounds $[5 \times 10^{-3} : 5 \times 10^{-2}]$ for the erroneous event failure rate and $[5 \times 10^{-3} - 3 \times 10^{-3} : 5 \times 10^{-2} + 3 \times 10^{-3}]$ for the loss event failure rate. We used a LHS of size 3 for the mIS estimations, and compared with an equivalent budget (1500 calls to $\mathcal{M}$) to the simple IS solution.

As seen on Fig. 5, the estimation of the Sobol' indices, while still subject to large variance, is on average relatively well estimated. In particular, with these alternative bounds, the Sobol' indices linked to the erroneous and loss events are much closer to each other, and the relative order of the Sobol' indices is conserved with both IS and mIS (influence of the uncertainty linked to the loss events higher than the one linked to erroneous events), which is the most important factor for correct decision making, that is determining which epistemic uncertainty reduction must be prioritized.

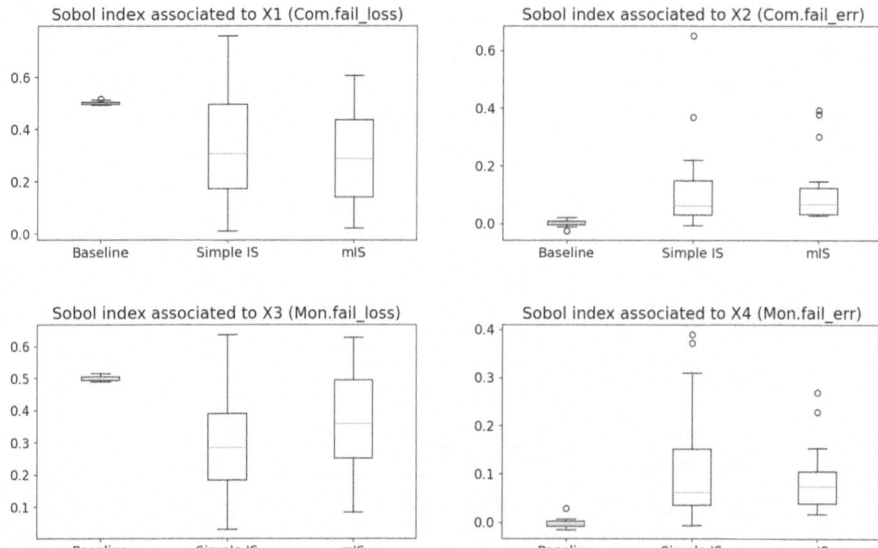

Fig. 4. First order Sobol' indices for MINOR failure event computed with exact probabilities and probabilities computed with IS and mIS (LHS of size 5) at equivalent budget (20 iterations with 2500 calls to $\mathcal{M}$).

Comparing IS and mIS methods, the estimation error at equivalent simulation budget is of the same order: due to the difficulty of finding adequate pdf function g, finding multiple not adequate enough g for different parameter points in the mIS method doesn't give for the test case a clear advantage compared to the simple IS method.

In a context where appropriate g can be found, the LHS size is an important hyperparameter to consider. A rule of thumb is to chose a LHS size of the order of the problem dimension (dimension of Θ).

6   Related Works

In this paper, we chose to study a classical global sensitivity indicator, but several other indicators can be considered, including local instead of global ones, or derivative-based instead of variance-based. [5] gives an overview of several of these indicators. [9] provides an overview of methods to derive input-output samples in a black-box context with epistemic uncertainty, and to analyze them.

In this work and in the mentioned papers, the epistemic uncertainties of the considered systems are modeled using probability theory: epistemic uncertainties are characterized by a pdf over the parameters of the pdf describing the aleatory uncertainties. This unified probabilistic framework facilitates the application of probabilistic tools and methods for sensitivity analysis.

However, other modeling propositions for epistemic uncertainties exist. The evidence theory [20] was specifically developed to model epistemic uncertainty.

Requiring weaker assumptions than probability theory, epistemic uncertainties are modeled using expert opinion and parameter ranges. [10] proposes a sensitivity analysis method similar to IS using evidence theory: the goal is to determine for a model which input variable contributes the most to the output with a sampling-based method. In the context of reliability with a drone application case, [15] proposes sensitivity analysis on fault tree using evidence theory.

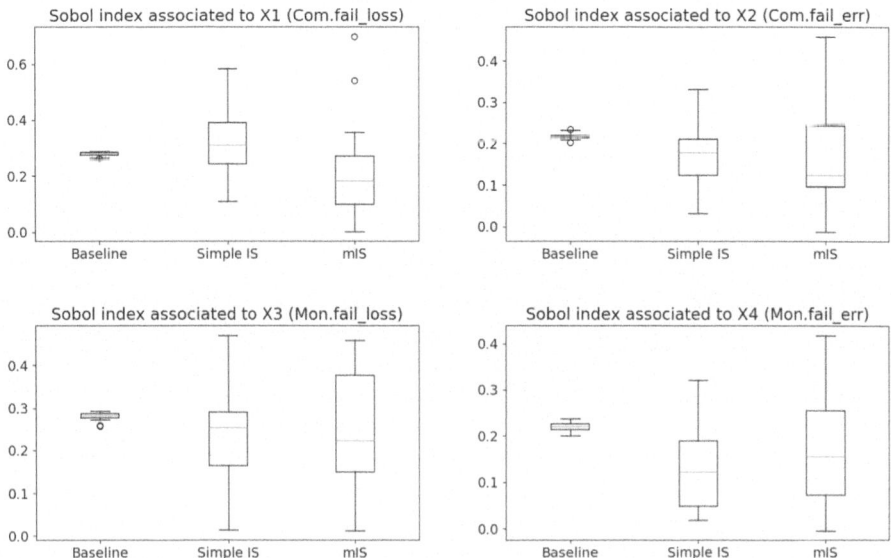

Fig. 5. First order Sobol' indices for MINOR failure event computed with true probabilities and probabilities computed with IS and mIS with alternative failure rate bounds.

7   Discussion

The presented sensitivity analysis method applies to any quantity that is estimated through Monte Carlo with a model reducible to the formalism introduced in Sect. 3. For models simulating a time of failure as presented, it can be interesting to perform sensitivity analysis on other reliability indicator function of t_f, such as the mean time to failure. The analysis we perform is indeed a reliability-oriented sensitivity analysis (ROSA [5]) specific to the considered quantity of interest (the unreliability at a given time T in this paper); the influential parameters for other quantities of interest may differ.

The proposed method is model-agnostic as the model is considered as a black-box although in the presented AltaRica context, more information about how the model works is available. The first improvement of the proposed method for AltaRica models would be to use this knowledge to derive an efficient IS density.

Adequate auxiliary pdfs to estimate F_T were indeed not consistently found for AltaRica models, which is crucial to effectively use the proposed mIS method. It is also to note that although theoretically applicable to any type of model (in particular, models with more complex logic in our safety context), IS can be particularly difficult to tune with high dimensional problems (systems with lots of failure events in our context).

It can also be noted that the core of the presented method (efficient estimation of multiple probabilities with varying input distribution parameter) can be used with the goal of estimating other sensitivity indicators that have sampling-based estimators.

8   Conclusion

We presented two variants of a simple typical failure-prone system with the MBSA modeling frame and the AltaRica 3.0 language. Leveraging the analytical expressions of failure probabilities, these simple cases allowed us to illustrate the value of performing sensitivity analysis with regard to the safety objectives and the epistemic input uncertainty of a model. A method to perform this analysis in general cases without analytical expression of the failure probability is presented, with the goal of obtaining good estimation of the considered sensitivity indicator with reasonable simulation budget. The applicability of this method to AltaRica models is currently constrained by the difficulty of finding suitable auxiliary pdf for AltaRica models. The findings and limitations of this project point to several clear directions for future research. As a prospect, a more complex case study is underway: the safety assessment of the midair collision avoidance system for an unmanned aerial vehicle (UAV).

References

1. Apostolakis, G.E.: A commentary on model uncertainty. In: Proc. Workshop I Adv. Topics Risk Reliab. Anal.–Model Uncertainty: Its Character Quantification, Annapolis, MD, pp. 973–980 (1994)
2. Bazovsky, I.: Reliability theory and practice. Courier Corporation (2004)
3. Boer, P., Kroese, D., Mannor, S., Rubinstein, R.: A tutorial on the cross-entropy method. Ann. Oper. Res. **134**, July 2002
4. Briere, D., Traverse, P.: Airbus a320/a330/a340 electrical flight controls - a family of fault-tolerant systems. In: Digest of Papers - International Symposium on Fault-Tolerant Computing, pp. 616 – 623 (07 1993)
5. Chabridon, V.: Reliability-oriented sensitivity analysis under probabilistic model uncertainty – Application to aerospace systems. Theses, Université Clermont Auvergne [2017-2020], November 2018. https://theses.hal.science/tel-02087860
6. Cieslak, J., Efimov, D., Zolghadri, A., Gheorghe, A., Goupil, P., Dayre, R.: A method for actuator lock-in-place failure detection in aircraft control surface servo-loops. In: IFAC Proceedings Volumes (IFAC-PapersOnline), vol. 19, August 2014
7. Elvira, V., Martino, L., Luengo, D., Bugallo, M.F.: Efficient multiple importance sampling estimators. IEEE Signal Process. Lett. **22**(10), 1757–1761 (2015)

8. Gamboa, F., Janon, A., Klein, T., Lagnoux, A., Prieur, C.: Statistical inference for Sobol pick freeze Monte Carlo method. Statistics **50**(4), 881–902 (2016)
9. Helton, J.C., Johnson, J.D., Sallaberry, C.J., Storlie, C.B.: Survey of sampling-based methods for uncertainty and sensitivity analysis. Reliability Eng. Syst. Saf. **91**(10–11), 1175–1209 (2006)
10. Helton, J.C., Johnson, J., Oberkampf, W.L., Storlie, C.B.: A sampling-based computational strategy for the representation of epistemic uncertainty in model predictions with evidence theory. Comput. Methods Appl. Mech. Eng. **196**(37–40), 3980–3998 (2007)
11. Homma, T., Saltelli, A.: Importance measures in global sensitivity analysis of nonlinear models. Reliability Eng. Syst. Saf. **52**(1), 1–17 (1996)
12. McKay, M.D., Beckman, R.J., Conover, W.J.: A comparison of three methods for selecting values of input variables in the analysis of output from a computer code. Technometrics **42**(1), 55–61 (2000)
13. Morio, J.: Influence of input PDF parameters of a model on a failure probability estimation. Simul. Model. Pract. Theory **19**(10), 2244–2255 (Nov 2011)
14. Morio, J.: Extreme quantile estimation with nonparametric adaptive importance sampling. Simul. Model. Pract. Theory **27**, 76–89 (2012)
15. Murtha, J.F.: An evidence theoretic approach to design of reliable low-cost UAVs. Ph.D. thesis, Virginia Tech (2009)
16. Owen, A.B.: Monte Carlo theory, methods and examples (2013). https://artowen.su.domains/mc/
17. Papaioannou, I., Geyer, S., Straub, D.: Improved cross entropy-based importance sampling with a flexible mixture model. Reliability Eng. Syst. Saf. **191**, 106564 (2019)
18. Prosvirnova, T.: AltaRica 3.0: a Model-Based approach for Safety Analyses. Theses, Ecole Polytechnique, November 2014. https://pastel.hal.science/tel-01119730
19. Rauzy, A.B.: Guarded transition systems: a new states/events formalism for reliability studies. Proceedings of the Institution of Mechanical Engineers, Part O: Journal of Risk and Reliability **222**(4), 495–505 (2008)
20. Shafer, G.: A mathematical theory of evidence, vol. 42. Princeton university press (1976)
21. Sobol, I.M.: Sensitivity estimates for nonlinear mathematical models. Math. Model. Comput. Exp. **1**(4), 407–414 (1993)

Causal Bayesian Networks for Data-Driven Safety Analysis of Complex Systems

Roman Gansch[1]([✉]), Lina Putze[2], Tjark Koopmann[2], Jan Reich[3], and Christian Neurohr[2]

[1] Robert Bosch GmbH, Corporate Research, Renningen, Germany
`roman.gansch@de.bosch.com`
[2] German Aerospace Center (DLR) e.V., Institute of Systems Engineering for Future Mobility, Oldenburg, Germany
`{lina.putze,tjark.koopmann,christian.neurohr}@dlr.de`
[3] Fraunhofer Institute for Experimental Software Engineering (IESE), Kaiserslautern, Germany
`jan.reich@iese.fraunhofer.de`

Abstract. Ensuring safe operation of safety-critical complex systems interacting with their environment poses significant challenges, particularly when the system's world model relies on machine learning algorithms to process the perception input. A comprehensive safety argumentation requires knowledge of how faults or functional insufficiencies propagate through the system and interact with external factors, to manage their safety impact. While statistical analysis approaches can support the safety assessment, associative reasoning alone is neither sufficient for the safety argumentation nor for the identification and investigation of safety measures. A causal understanding of the system and its interaction with the environment is crucial for safeguarding safety-critical complex systems. It allows to transfer and generalize knowledge, such as insights gained from testing, and facilitates the identification of potential improvements. This work explores using causal Bayesian networks to model the system's causalities for safety analysis, and proposes measures to assess causal influences based on Pearl's framework of causal inference. We compare the approach of causal Bayesian networks to the well-established fault tree analysis, outlining advantages and limitations. In particular, we examine importance metrics typically employed in fault tree analysis as foundation to discuss suitable causal metrics. An evaluation is performed on the example of a perception system for automated driving. Overall, this work presents an approach for causal reasoning in safety analysis that enables the integration of data-driven and expert-based knowledge to account for uncertainties arising from complex systems operating in open environments.

Keywords: Causal Inference · Safety Analysis · Fault Trees · Bayesian Networks · Automated Driving

---

R. Gansch and L. Putze—Contributed equally to this work.

© The Author(s), under exclusive license to Springer Nature Switzerland AG 2026
P. Katsaros (Ed.): IMBSA 2025, LNCS 15755, pp. 222–237, 2026.
https://doi.org/10.1007/978-3-032-05073-1_15

1   Introduction

Ensuring the safe operation of safety-critical complex systems that interact with their environment based on information obtained by perception components is a challenging endeavor. In particular, such perception components often rely on complex algorithms like machine learning to construct a world model out of sensory input. The verification and validation of these is notoriously difficult and reliance on statistical, non-causal metrics is unsatisfactory from a safety perspective [6]. Essentially, safety engineers are not interested in associations, but in causal explanations of how faults and failures are propagated within a system. An example for this is the well-known fault-error-failure model of Avizienis et al. [4]. Therefore, it is indispensable to integrate causal metrics for the safeguarding of safety-critical systems, especially regarding the perception components. In order to obtain causal information about complex systems and faults in their perception, Kramer et al. suggest to adapt fault tree analysis (FTA) for this task [16]. However, restricting the causal graph structure to trees drastically limits modeling possibilities. Moreover, the quantification of fault trees rests on the assumptions of stochastic independence of its base events which can conflict with handling of confounders. To overcome these inadequacies, we propose to use causal Bayesian networks (CBNs) to model and analyze the causalities behind fault propagation in complex systems, based on Pearl's causal theory [21].

The contributions of this work can be summarized as follows:

- a novel approach relying on CBNs combined with suitable causal metrics,
- a comparison between fault trees and CBNs, with a focus on quantification,
- evaluation of the approach for an automated driving perception system.

Following the introduction of Sect. 1, we cover the preliminaries and related work in Sect. 2, i.e. the role of causality in safeguarding complex systems. Section 3 covers in detail the example of an perception system for automated driving, before concluding with Sect. 4.

2   Causality in Safety Analysis

Safety of technical systems is achieved by applying multiple measures in combination during the complete system life-cycle. An integral part of safety engineering is the safety analysis. This analysis supplements the synthesis step during design and verifies that certain design criteria are fulfilled. Goals of the safety analysis are to identify faults and functional insufficiencies that propagate through the system and lead to hazards, as well as estimating the overall residual risk. A common approach is to model the fault propagation pathways (fault-error-failure chain) [4]. A wide range of methods have been adopted in industrial practice, each of which is useful within a certain context. Since the advent of highly automated systems adaption of established analysis methods have been done. For example, the ISO 21448 standard [11] recommends the application of *System-Theoric Process Analysis* (STPA) and *Cause Tree Analysis* (CTA) (an adaption of FTA) in combination with statistical analysis of the occurrence of triggering conditions (TCs). However, these simple methods often fail to include the complex relations or neglect the causal mechanisms. In particular, when artificial intelligence is utilized these practices are either too abstract or rely on unsatisfiable assumptions. In this paper we explore the use of CBNs focusing on a comparison with FTA. CBNs offer a quantitative approach to investigate causal influences on safety based on a data-driven approach. In contrast to FTA this approach does not require independence of specific factors and allows to model complex dependencies. Further it enables a shift from deterministic causation to probabilistic causation, i.e., a cause does not always lead to an effect, but rather might be suppressed due to factors not included in the model. In the next section we provide an overview of causal inference with examples illustrating its relevance for safety engineering.

2.1   Causal Inference

Causal theory formally describes the influence of a cause on an effect. It has been pioneered and frequently applied in the field of economics, sociology and medicine [21,22]. Recently, causal inference also has gained a lot of traction in the engineering domain [12,15,17,19,20]. Pearl characterizes causality with a 3-step ladder: The first level, *association*, involves predicting the outcome Y under observations of X which can be described by purely statistical quantities (observing). The second level, *intervention*, addresses the effect on Y given an intervention on X that sets X to a specific value while keeping the probabilities of the causes of X unchanged (doing). The third and highest level, *counterfactual*, examines what the value of Y would have been in a specific observation if X had been set to a different value through intervention under exactly the same conditions (imagining).

Causal intervention queries, and even some counterfactual queries, can be answered by means of intervention experiments or by estimation from observational data. In an intervention experiment the intervention is performed while collecting data, like e.g. in randomized control trials (RCTs). However, performing an intervention experiment is often not possible due to constraints in the experimental environment or ethical considerations.

The do-calculus introduced by J. Pearl enables the evaluation of interventional queries from observational data alone, without the need for additional experiments, a characteristic that is termed identifiability [21,22]. It relies on the do-operator $do(X = x)$ to formally expresses an intervention that sets the variable X to the value x. Using this operator, the do-calculus provides three inference rules that can be applied iteratively to transform an interventional query of the form $P(Y | do(X = x))$ into expressions involving only conditional probabilities obtainable from observational data. To apply the do-calculus, a causal model expressing the cause-effect relationships between variables is required. In this paper we use graphical causal models, which are directed acyclic graphs (DAG) to model these relationships. In this notation, an intervention $do(X = x)$ can be seen as removing all incoming edges to X, while setting X to the value x.

2.2   Causal Bayesian Networks

The advantage of using a graphical notation for the causal models is, that it integrates well with quantification of the variables as it is inherently similar to Bayesian networks (BN) [10] since both are built from DAGs. In a BN the direction of the arrows indicate the order of factorization of the joint probability distribution into conditional probability tables (CPT). The order of factorization can be freely chosen as it is only based on correlation which can be reformulated by the Bayes theorem. By selecting the arrow directions according to the causal relationships we obtain a causal Bayesian network (CBN).

In a CBN correlational as well as causal inferences can be performed. Previous work has explored the use of BN and CBN for safety, cf. Table 1. We distinguish between BNs that use only correlational structures and CBNs that use causal structures. A BN can only be used for correlational inference, while a CBN has the advantage of a causal structure interpretation for the modeler.

Building a CBN model can be separated into the task of structuring the DAG and quantifying the CPTs. For both either an expert-based or data-driven approach can be chosen. Learning the causal structure from data is referred to as *structure learning* or *causal discovery* [22]. Learning the conditional distribution from data is termed

Table 1. Related work on (causal) Bayesian network for safety analysis.

	Inference	
Structure	Correlation	Causation
Correlation	[10, 13, 23]	-
Causation	[1, 2, 27, 28]	[8, 14, 15, 17, 20]

parameter learning. The graph structure and the parameters can also be obtained through *expert knowledge* [18] or by combined approaches feeding expert-based constraints into learning algorithms. For our approach of using CBNs for safety analysis, we favor the expert-based approach to define the structure and parameter learning from data as it combines the best of both worlds. An expert-based structure is more appropriate to argue to capture the underlying causality, while expert judgment on quantifying probabilities is susceptible to bias [26].

The nodes in the CBN correspond to random variables whose value ranges can be dichotomous, categorical, ranked, or even continuous. Dichotomous variables only contain two states which have a binary true/false character. A FTA model only consists of these kind of variables. For a SOTIF oriented safety analysis the triggering conditions in the domain have to be included. These often require a continuous distribution or a mapping to categorical variables with multiple states (e.g., weather: sun, cloudy, rain, snow). While inference calculations can generally be performed on continuous multivariate distributions, it requires significant computational resources. Further, accurately quantifying continuous distributions demands a large amount of data. In practice, continuous distributions are either discretized to categorical nodes or described as parametric distributions that allow to analytically pre-solve the necessary integrals. The CBN examples in this paper only use categorical variables as these are similar to the dichotomous variables used in FTA. For implementation we use the python library pyAgrum [7].

2.3   From Correlation to Causation

To grasp the differences between association and causality and how it impacts safety engineering we examine some examples.

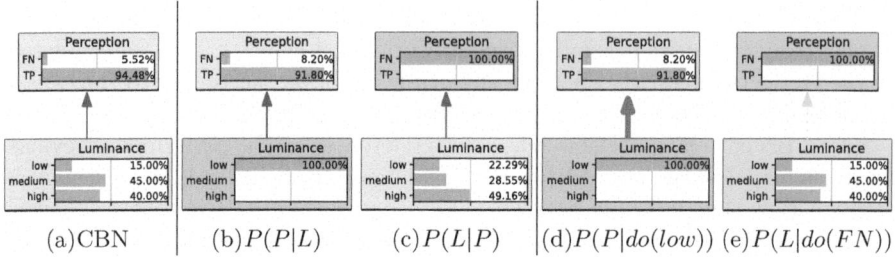

Fig. 1. Causal Bayesian network (CBN) consisting of two nodes: Perception (P) and Luminance (L) (left). Correlational inference is agnostic to the causal direction (center). Causal inference depends on the causal direction (right). Bold blue indicates a causal inference along a causal pathway, while a dashed gray indicates deletion due to intervention. (Color figure online)

First, consider a simple two node graph as shown in Fig. 1a. It represents the causal mechanism of a typical perception example for automated driving, where we are interested in the perception performance under the influence of a triggering condition. The upper node Perception (P) represents the performance of a camera-based object detection in terms of false negatives (FNs) and true positives (TPs). The lower node Luminance (L) corresponds to the light intensity of an object, ranked from low to high. To a human it is intuitively clear that luminance affects the performance of the camera-based object detection and not vice-versa. However, based on association alone we cannot distinguish both causal directions, cf. Fig. 1b and 1c. Conditioning on either of both variables leads to changes in the distribution of the outcome variable compared to the observed distribution of Fig. 1a. The correlation between the two variables is agnostic to the underlying cause-effect structure. In contrast, causal intervention queries can expose the cause-effect structure. Intervening on luminance has an effect on the perception, while changing the perception result does not affect the luminance, cf. Fig. 1d and 1e. Whether an intervention reveals some effect depends on the direction of the causal paths.

Another distinction between correlational and causal queries arises due to so-called confounding. The issue of confounding is encountered when there exists a common-cause, like Weather in Fig. 2. From the result of the correlational query $P(P|L)$ it seems that a high luminance improves the perception performance, cf. Fig. 2(b). But this result is affected by the change in the distribution of the weather conditions when conditioning on luminance. If we investigate the causal effect based on an intervention, i.e. if we keep the observed distribution of the

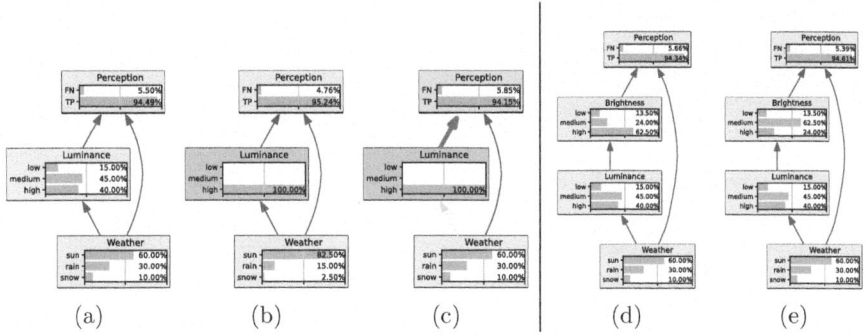

Fig. 2. (a) Causal Bayesian network for perception performance influenced by luminance and weather. Analysis results based on (b) correlation with $P(P|L = high)$ and (c) causation with $P(P|\,do(L = high))$. Safety measure design based on (d) correlation and (e) causation. Probabilities are given in Table 5.

weather conditions, we encounter indeed that high luminance on its own will decrease the performance of the perception, cf. Fig. 2(c).

The presented results have implications for the design of potential safety measures. In the given example, this can be a simple mechanism that modifies the brightness of the camera pictures in the pre-processing step of an AI-based object detection. Based on the result of the correlation analysis, a safety engineer will favor high brightness as a higher luminance correlates with better performance, leading e.g. to the CBN of Fig. 2(d). Compared to the marginal FN rate of the unmodified structure, the FN rate including the safety measure actually deteriorates from 5.5% to 5.66%. This demonstrates how interpreting correlation as causation can lead to a counterproductive system design. In contrast, applying the results of the intervention analysis to design safety measures, a shift of towards medium brightness seems most beneficial, resulting in the CBN of Fig. 2(e). Here, the marginal FN rate has actually improved from 5.5% to 5.39% providing an increased performance.

3   Use Case: Perception of Automated Driving Systems

To illustrate the application of CBNs and causal importance metrics for safety analysis of complex systems and to compare them to a classical FTA, we consider as example a perception subsystem commonly used for ADSs, cf. Fig. 3. Although the data is not from an actual implemented perception system, it closely reflects a potential real-world application. The perception subsystem consists of two redundant sensor modalities each with a software-based perception algorithm to classify objects from sensor data. Both modalities may employ different sensing principles and different perception algorithms each with specific functional insufficiencies and corresponding sensitivities to environmental TCs, e.g., Occlusion/ObjectSize for Sensor 1 and TrafficDensity/ObjectDistance for Sensor 2.

228   R. Gansch et al.

The performance reduction of each sensor as well as the perception subsystem can be captured using the FN rate as indicator.

3.1 Causal Modeling

A safety analysis seeks to identify the causal pathways of faults and functional insufficiencies emerging into system failures and pinpoint areas of improvement. A straightforward approach to model the perception system of Fig. 3 in a FTA as proposed for SOTIF oriented analysis [29] is shown in Fig. 4a. The TCs are included as base events that activate

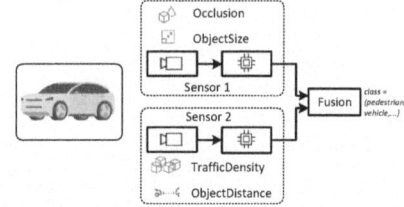

Fig. 3. Example architecture for an ADS perception use case.

a sensor insufficiency. As required by FTA, the base events are assumed to be independent.

Figure 4b models the same example as CBN. In contrast to FTA, CBNs are not restricted to a tree structure with independent base events. While such tree structure is usually adequate for modeling dependencies of a well-defined system architecture, domain-level nodes often exhibit complex interdependencies, necessitating a less restrictive framework. By modeling the example as CBN, dependencies of Occlusion on TrafficDensity and ObjectSize can be taken into account. Further, in the CBN the nodes representing active insufficiencies (Sen1Insuff, Sen2Insuff) are removed. These nodes do not represent actual causal artifacts but rather serve as subsidiary constructs to represent probabilistic relations in the FTA, which can be directly integrated into the CPTs of Sen1 and Sen2.

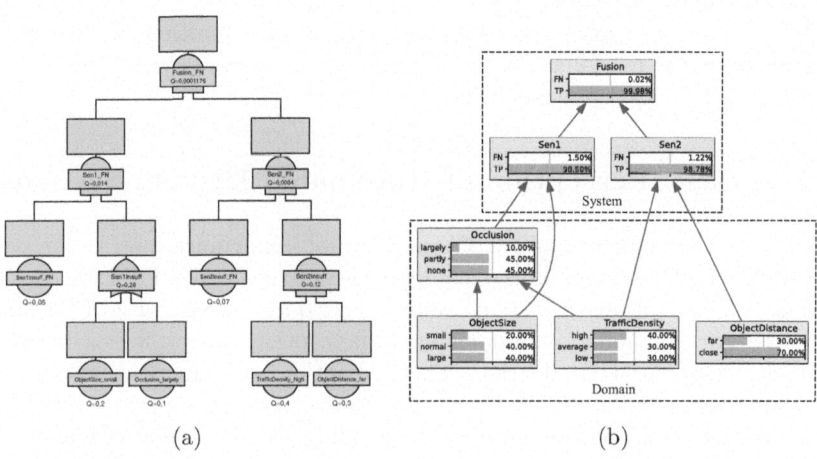

(a)   (b)

Fig. 4. Perception example modeled with (a) FTA and (b) CBN. The corresponding (conditional) probabilities are given in Table 6 and 7.

Without the restriction to dichotomous nodes imposed by FTA, the nodes of a CBN can be discretized into categorical variables. For example, Occlusion can be expanded into *largely, partly* and *none*. The refinement of node values is a valuable tool to approximate reality more closely. To enable a comparison, the CPTs assigned to the nodes in this example preserve the marginal rates of the FTA base events. However, in the domain part the additional relations between nodes are reflected in the CPTs, cf. Table 6, and in the system the AND/OR gates have been modified to a non-perfect relation, deviating a few percent, cf. Table 7. This reflects the semantic abstraction as we do not model on a detailed level of bits and pixels but rather on a higher abstraction level of objects in a camera picture. Therefore, we can not model fully deterministic fault propagation and have to account for some error terms due to the abstraction.

3.2   Causal Safety Metrics

CBNs as well as fault trees allow for quantitative evaluation of fault and failure propagation through the system. The state of the art in FTA are importance metrics that assess the impact of base events $(N_i)_{i \in I}$ on the top level event (T) to provide a ranking. Several importance metrics have been defined in literature, each providing a different ranking order [5,9,24]. For comparison with causal analysis we focus on the Birnbaum (BB) importance and the Risk Reduction Worth (RRW):

$$ \text{BB} = \frac{\partial P(T = fail)}{\partial P(N_i = fail)}, \qquad \text{RRW} = \frac{P(T = fail)}{P(T = fail | N_i = \neg fail)}. $$

The BB importance provides a sensitivity metric for a top event failure to a base event. For independent basic events it can also be written as $\text{BB} = P(T = fail | N_i = fail) - P(T = fail | N_i = \neg fail)$. It is also referred to as structural importance since it only responds to structural changes of the fault tree and not to the failure rates of the basic event. In contrast, the RRW measures the potential reduction in the probability of the top level event if the base event does not occur.

Table 2 provides the calculated importances for both, the fault tree as well as the CBN. The partial derivative of the BB importance is calculated by setting small soft evidences on the nodes (about 1%) and estimating the difference quotient. We observe slight deviations in the results of the FTA and the CBN, which can be explained by the couplings between the TCs and the

Table 2. BB and RRW importance for the TCs in the FTA and CBN model, respectively.

Triggering Condition	BB (1e−4)		RRW	
	FTA	CBN	FTA	CBN
ObjectSize	3.78	3.12	2.8	1.50
Occlusion	3.36	4.39	1.4	1.33
TrafficDensity	2.94	3.35	∞	3.59
ObjectDistance	3.92	3.52	∞	2.31

non-perfect OR/AND gates in the CBN. A significant difference occurs for the BB importance of Occlusion, due to the confounding effect of TrafficDensity.

While FTA importance metrics can be applied to CBNs, caution is required when interpreting the results. By restricting fault trees to a tree structure with

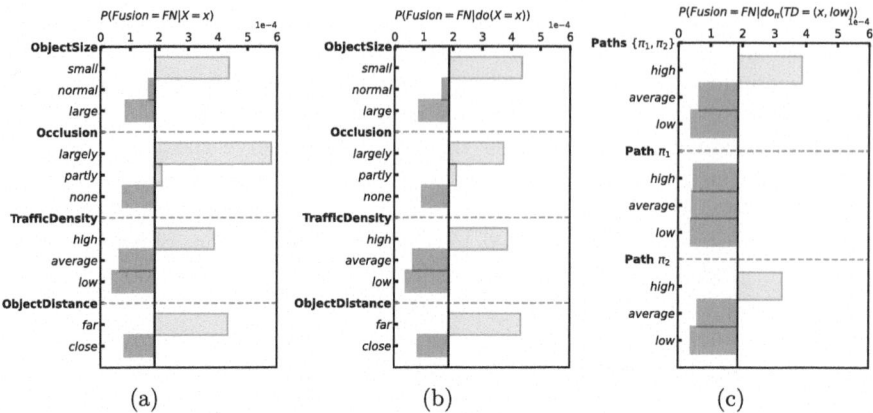

Fig. 5. Tornado charts for (a) correlational analysis, (b) causal intervention analysis for all TCs (X), and (c) for the categorical analysis of the path-specific effects of TrafficDensity (TD) on Fusion=FN via $\{\pi_1, \pi_2\}$, π_1 and π_2. The vertical line indicates the marginal probability $P(Fusion = FN)$.

independent base events, confounding effects are eliminated. This leads to equality of conditional probabilities $P(Y|X = x)$ and interventional probabilities $P(Y|\operatorname{do}(X = x))$ querying alongside the causal direction of the fault tree. Consequently, associative importance metrics can be interpreted causally in the FTA. However, for structures like the CBNs that cover more complex dependencies, this equality does not apply, as outlined in Subsect. 2.3. Figure 5 provides a visual comparison of the conditional and interventional probabilities resulting from the CBN in a tornado chart. For Occlusion, which has ObjectSize and TrafficDensity as confounding nodes, a significant deviation between correlation and causation can be observed. This illustrates, the importance of causal metrics for a comprehensive evaluation of CBNs.

In causal literature the average causal effect (ACE) and relative causal effect (RCE) are commonly used [15,22]. These metrics evaluate the structural importance of a node, similar to the BB importance. Both, the ACE and RCE are originally defined for dichotomic states as the absolute and relative difference of both possible interventions states. To apply both metrics for the SOTIF analysis, the metrics need to be generalized to categorical variables. For TCs it is usually possible to define a reference state x_{ref} representing the nominal conditions to which others are compared, like 'none' for Occlusion. Thus, we define

$$\text{ACE} = P(Y|\operatorname{do}(X = x)) - P(Y|\operatorname{do}(X = x_{ref})), \quad \text{RCE} = \frac{P(Y|\operatorname{do}(X = x))}{P(Y|\operatorname{do}(X = x_{ref}))} \tag{1}$$

where the comparative value x_{ref} can either be $\neg x$ for dichotomic analysis or a reference value for a categorical analysis. For further analysis we consider the RCE as relative metrics are easier to interpret. Safety measures to improve the system have to focus on mitigating the influence of TCs with a high RCE. However, similar to BB importance, the RCE does not consider the overall occurrence of a triggering condition and, hence, may not provide the best improvement of the system performance. It rather provides an argument to mitigate systematic issues leading to an increase of risk. To account for the occurrence of the TCs and evaluate how probability shifts affect the overall system performance, the RRW can be generalized to categorical variables and transferred to a causal metric, referred to as *Interventional Risk Reduction Worth* (IRRW):

$$\text{RRW} = \frac{P(Y)}{P(Y|X = x_{ref})}, \qquad \text{IRRW} = \frac{P(Y)}{P(Y|\,\text{do}(X = x_{ref}))}.$$

Table 3 shows the results of the categorical and dichotomic calculation of RCE, RRW and IRRW.

Table 3. Categorical and dichomotic evaluation of RCE, RRW and IRRW. Reference values are highlighted in gray.

Triggering Condition	State	Categorical			Dichotomic		
		RCE	RRW	IRRW	RCE	RRW	IRRW
Object Size	small	2.66			3.50	1.50	1.50
	normal	1.00			0.79	0.89	0.89
	large	0.51	1.14	1.14	0.33	0.73	0.73
Occlusion	largely	3.95			2.41	1.33	1.20
	partly	2.23			1.43	1.25	1.26
	none	1.00	2.49	1.97	0.40	0.69	0.79
Traffic Density	high	9.64			7.46	3.59	3.59
	average	1.6			0.29	0.83	0.83
	low	1.00	4.64	4.64	0.17	0.77	0.77
Object Distance	far	5.36			5.36	2.31	2.31
	close	1.00	2.31	2.31	0.19	0.43	0.43

Multiple Interventions. Besides single interventions, it is also possible to calculate multiple, combined interventions $P(Y|\,\text{do}(X_1 = x_1, X_2 = x_2, ...))$ [21]. This resembles the cut sets analysis in FTA, as it exposes cases where multiple TCs are necessary for a performance decrease of performance. Although an arbitrary number of interventions is possible, in the following we focus on pairwise interventions. Analogously to Eq. (1) we calculate the RCE^2 as:

$$\text{RCE}^2_C = \frac{P(Y|\,\text{do}(X_1 = x_1, X_2 = x_2))}{P(Y|\,\text{do}(X_1 = x_{1,ref}, X_2 = x_{2,ref}))}.$$

	ObjectSize			Occlusion			TrafficDensity			ObjectDistance	
	small	normal	large	largely	partly	none	high	average	low	far	close
ObjectSize – small				9.72	7.86	4.92	26.42	4.87	2.98	14.34	2.75
ObjectSize – normal				5.90	2.96	1.00	10.23	1.56	1.00	5.48	1.00
ObjectSize – large				4.92	1.98	0.51	5.24	0.77	0.48	2.80	0.50
Occlusion – largely	9.72	5.90	4.92				32.10	5.91	3.95	20.31	3.95
Occlusion – partly	7.86	2.96	1.98				18.16	3.34	2.23	11.49	2.23
Occlusion – none	4.92	1.00	0.51				8.13	1.50	1.00	5.14	1.00
TrafficDensity – high	26.42	10.23	5.24	32.10	18.16	8.13				23.02	2.91
TrafficDensity – average	4.87	1.56	0.77	5.91	3.34	1.50				1.85	1.33
TrafficDensity – low	2.98	1.00	0.48	3.95	2.23	1.00				0.76	1.00
ObjectDistance – far	14.34	5.48	2.80	20.31	11.49	5.14	23.02	1.85	0.76		
ObjectDistance – close	2.75	1.00	0.50	3.95	2.23	1.00	2.91	1.33	1.00		

Fig. 6. RCE_C^2 for pairwise interventions on TCs with the grayed states used as reference. Each intervention combination is given by a row and column pair.

Figure 6 shows the RCE^2 for all pairwise combinations of TCs in our perception example. Notably, TCs with a high impact from single intervention are also pronounced in the pairwise interventions. This is not true in general, as a positive and negative causal impact from two nodes may cancel each other. The pairwise intervention (Occlusion=largely, TrafficDensity=high) exhibits the highest $RCE^2 \approx 32.1$, primarily due to the Fusion node, whose CPT resembles that of an AND-gate. Interventions that influence both causal paths to an AND-gate typically result in a high causal impact – see also the combinations (TrafficDensity, ObjectSize) or (Occlusion, ObjectDistance). In contrast, pairwise combinations located in just a single incoming path to the Fusion node are ranked relatively low, as the AND-characteristic suppresses the causal impact. We conclude that regarding pairwise inventions on TCs, the Fusion node is the most critical component – as expected from a majority voting pattern. Therefore, improving on the Fusion node, e.g., the underlying algorithm, leads to a substantial FN rate reduction. Other safety measures should focus on individual contributors, i.e., (TrafficDensity=high, Occlusion=largely) and (TrafficDensity=high, ObjectSize=small), by fortifying perception algorithms against these.

Path-Specific Interventions. In the CBN approach, the graph is no longer restricted to a tree. Thus, there may be multiple paths linking a variable of interest to the outcome. E.g., the CBN of Fig. 4 contains two different paths connecting 'TrafficDensity' and 'Fusion', namely π_1 : TrafficDensity $\to$ Occlusion $\to$ Sen1 $\to$ Fusion and π_2 : TrafficDensity $\to$ Sen2 $\to$ Fusion. The contribution to the overall causal effects can differ along such paths. Therefore, to design precise safety mechanisms, an examination of the effects along individual paths is needed. To achieve this, we suggest *path-specific effects* that limit the scope of causal effects to individual paths [25].

The main idea is to model two interventions for a variable X at the same time. Set $X = x$ for the path(s) π under investigation and $X = x_{ref}$ for the remaining paths, denoted by $\mathrm{do}_\pi(X = (x, x_{ref}))$. For example, to investigate the path-specific effect of TrafficDensity=high on Fusion via the path π_1, the distribution of TrafficDensity is replaced by setting TrafficDensity=high as input for Occlusion and simultaneously to a comparative value, such as ¬high or low, as input for Sen2.

Table 4. Categorical evaluation of path-specific effects of TrafficDensity on Fusion = FN.

Path	State	APE ($\times 10^{-4}$)	RPE	$\frac{\text{APE}}{\text{ACE}}$
π_1	high	0.08	1.19	0.02
	average	0.03	1.07	0.12
	low	0.00	1.00	-
π_2	high	2.86	8.13	0.82
	average	0.20	1.50	0.82
	low	0.00	1.00	-

As in Subsect. 3.2, the comparative value can refer to the value's negation (dichotomic analysis) or to a reference value (categorical analysis).

Let us remark that the analysis of path-specific effects is a counterfactual query. In general, the path-specific effect $\mathrm{do}_\pi(X = (x, x_{ref}))$ on a variable Y via a set of paths π can be calculated form observational data if the causal effect $P(Y| \mathrm{do}(X = x))$ is identifiable and the value assignment of X is unambiguous. For DAGs without latent confounding the latter condition holds if π does not contain any causal paths from X to Y which start with the same arrow as a causal path from X to Y that is not in π, cf. [3, Theorem 5]. Figure 5c visualizes the path-specific effects of TrafficDensity on Fusion via different paths. The tornado chart shows the path-specific effects for $\pi = \{\pi_1, \pi_2\}$ – equivalent to the overall causal effect – and then for π_1 and π_2 on their own. The comparison of these path-specific effects indicates that almost the entire causal effect is transported via π_2. For a more detailed analysis of path specific effects we introduce the following metrics

$$\mathrm{APE} = P(Y| \mathrm{do}_\pi(X = (x, x_{ref}))) - P(Y| \mathrm{do}(X = x_{ref})),$$

$$\mathrm{RPE} = \frac{P(Y| \mathrm{do}_\pi(X = (x, x_{ref})))}{P(Y| \mathrm{do}(X = x_{ref}))},$$

$$\frac{\mathrm{APE}}{\mathrm{ACE}} = \frac{P(Y| \mathrm{do}_\pi(X = (x, x_{ref}))) - P(Y| \mathrm{do}(X = x_{ref}))}{P(Y| \mathrm{do}(X = x)) - P(Y| \mathrm{do}(X = x_{ref}))},$$

whose evaluation for π_1 and π_2 is given by Table 4. The average and relative path-specific effects APE and RPE are defined analogously to ACE and RCE, cf. Shpitser et al.[1], comparing an intervention to a comparative value for all

---

[1] The average path-specific causal effect is called 'effect along paths in π' [25].

paths. In addition, the ratio of APE by ACE provides a comparison of the impacts via the investigated paths against via the whole model. To interpret these metrics a comparison of the different paths is required. The values estimated for the example of Fig. 4 are given in Table 4.

4   Conclusion and Future Work

In this work, we considered CBNs for the safety analysis of safety-critical complex systems. CBNs provide a promising alternative to FTA, particularly when dealing with complex dependencies. FTA is not suited to grasp the fault and failure propagation in such systems. Hence, CBNs become necessary to model and analyze causal relations to ensure SOTIF. The key advantage is the combined approach of systematically addressing uncertainties using data as well as expert knowledge. To match FTA's quantification potential, we propose several causal importance metrics relying on causal inference. To account for the complexity of CBNs we considered path-specific causal effects. Finally, we evaluated the importance measures on an example perception system in the context of automated driving.

There are two main directions for future work. Firstly, the approach needs to be valida ted using real data coming from an actual complex system. As an intermediate step synthetic data from a simulation can be helpful. Secondly, when such data are available, causal learning (causal discovery) techniques can be integrated in the approach to obtain or verify parts of the causal graph.

A   Appendix Conditional Probability Tables

Table 5. Conditional probability tables for the confounding example of Fig. 2.

	Weather	Luminance low	medium	high
0.6	sun	0.05	0.4	0.55
0.3	rain	0.2	0.6	0.2
0.1	snow	0.6	0.3	0.1

Brightness (correlation) Luminance	low	medium	high
low	0.9	0.1	0
high	0	0	1

Brightness (causal) Luminance	low	medium	high
low	0.9	0.1	0
medium	0	1	0
high	0	0.4	0.6

Luminance (Brightness)	Weather	Perception FN	TP
low	sun	0.04	0.96
	rain	0.075	0.925
	snow	0.11	0.89
medium	sun	0.035	0.965
	rain	0.07	0.93
	snow	0.09	0.91
high	sun	0.04	0.0.96
	rain	0.08	0.92
	snow	0.105	0.895

Table 6. Conditional probability tables for the domain nodes in Sect. 3.

ObjectSize		TrafficDensity	
small	0.2	high	0.4
normal	0.4	average	0.3
large	0.4	low	0.3

ObjectDistance		Occlusion (FTA)	
far	0.3	largely	0.1
close	0.7	partly	0.45
		none	0.45

		Occlusion (CBN)		
ObjectSize	TrafficDensity	largely	partly	none
small	high	0.27	0.4	0.33
small	average	0.15	0.6	0.25
small	low	0.05	0.55	0.4
normal	high	0.2	0.45	0.35
normal	average	0.1	0.45	0.45
normal	low	0.1	0.4	0.5
large	high	0.05	0.5	0.45
large	average	0.01	0.42	0.57
large	low	0.01	0.3715	0.6185

Table 7. Conditional probability tables for the system nodes in Sect. 3.

		Sen1	
ObjectSize	Occlusion	FN	TP
small	largely	0.0495	0.9505
small	partly	0.04	0.96
small	none	0.025	0.975
normal	largely	0.03	0.97
normal	partly	0.015	0.985
normal	none	0.005	0.995
large	largely	0.025	0.975
large	partly	0.01	0.99
large	none	0.0025	0.9975

		Fusion	
Sen1	Sen2	FN	TP
FN	FN	0.95	0.05
FN	TP	0.0001	0.9999
TP	FN	0.0001	0.9999
TP	TP	0	1

		Sen2	
TrafficDensity	ObjectDistance	FN	TP
high	far	0.064	0.936
high	close	0.008	0.992
average	far	0.0056	0.9944
average	close	0.004	0.996
low	far	0.0024	0.9976
low	close	0.0032	0.9968

References

1. Adee, A., Gansch, R., Liggesmeyer, P.: Systematic modeling approach for environmental perception limitations in automated driving. In: 17th European Dependable Computing Conference, pp. 103–110 (2021)
2. Adee, A., Gansch, R., Liggesmeyer, P., Glaeser, C., Drews, F.: Discovery of perception performance limiting triggering conditions in automated driving. In: 5th International Conference on System Reliability and Safety, pp. 248–257 (2021)
3. Avin, C., Shpitser, I., Pearl, J.: Identifiability of path-specific effects. In: Proceedings of the 19th International Joint Conference on Artificial Intelligence, IJCAI'05, pp. 357–363, San Francisco, CA, USA (2005)
4. Avizienis, A., Laprie, J.C., Randell, B., Landwehr, C.: Basic concepts and taxonomy of dependable and secure computing. IEEE Trans. Dependable Secure Comput. 1(1), 11–33 (2004)
5. Birnbaum, Z.W.: On the importance of different components in a multicomponent system. University of Washington, Seattle, Tech. rep (1968)
6. Damm, W., Fränzle, M., Gerwinn, S., Kröger, P.: Perspectives on the validation and verification of machine learning systems in the context of highly automated vehicles. In: AAAI Spring Symposia (2018)
7. Ducamp, G., Gonzales, C., Wuillemin, P.H.: aGrUM/pyAgrum: a toolbox to build models and algorithms for Probabilistic Graphical Models in Python. In: Proceedings of the 10th International Conference on Probabilistic Graphical Models, vol. 138, pp. 609–612 (2020)
8. Déletang, G., et al.: Causal Analysis of Agent Behavior for AI Safety (2021)
9. Espiritu, J.F., Coit, D.W., Prakash, U.: Component criticality importance measures for the power industry. Electric Power Syst. Res. 77(5) (2007)
10. Fenton, N., Neil, M.: Risk Assessment and Decision Analysis with Bayesian Networks, 2 edn. CRC Press (2018)
11. International Organization for Standardization (ISO): ISO 21448: Road vehicles – Safety of the intended functionality (2022)
12. Issa Mattos, D., Liu, Y.: On the use of causal graphical models for designing experiments in the automotive domain. In: Proceedings of the International Conference on Evaluation and Assessment in Software Engineering 2022, pp. 264–265. EASE '22, New York, NY, USA (2022)
13. Jesenski, S., Stellet, J.E., Schiegg, F., Zöllner, J.M.: Generation of scenes in intersections for the validation of highly automated driving functions. In: 2019 IEEE Intelligent Vehicles Symposium (IV), pp. 502–509. IEEE (2019)
14. Jiang, Z., Liu, J., Sun, P., Sang, M., Li, H., Pan, Y.: Generation of risky scenarios for testing automated driving visual perception based on causal analysis. IEEE Trans. Intell. Transp, Syst (2024)
15. Koopmann, T., Putze, L., Westhofen, L., Gansch, R., Adee, A., Neurohr, C.: Grasping causality for the explanation of criticality for automated driving. IEEE Access 13, 54739–54756 (2025)
16. Kramer, B., Neurohr, C., Büker, M., Böde, E., Fränzle, M., Damm, W.: Identification and Quantification of Hazardous Scenarios for Automated Driving. In: Model-Based Safety and Assessment, pp. 163–178 (2020)
17. Maier, R., Grabinger, L., Urlhart, D., Mottok, J.: Causal models to support scenario-based testing of ADAS. IEEE Trans. Intell. Transp. Syst. 25(2), 1815–1831 (2024)

18. Neurohr, C., Westhofen, L., Butz, M., Bollmann, M.H., Eberle, U., Galbas, R.: Criticality analysis for the verification and validation of automated vehicles. IEEE Access **9**, 18016–18041 (2021)
19. Niu, Y., Fan, Y., Gao, Y., Li, Y.: A causal inference method for improving the design and interpretation of safety research. Saf. Sci. **161**, 106082 (2023)
20. Nyberg, M.: Failure propagation modeling for safety analysis using causal Bayesian networks. In: Conference on Control and Fault-Tolerant Systems, pp. 91–97 (2013)
21. Pearl, J.: Causality. Cambridge University Press, 2 edn. (2009)
22. Peters, J., Janzing, D., Schölkopf, B.: Elements of Causal Inference: Foundations and Learning Algorithms. The MIT Press (2017)
23. Qiu, M., Kryda, M., Bock, F., Antesberger, T., Straub, D., German, R.: Parameter tuning for a markov-based multi-sensor system. In: 47th Euromicro Conference on Software Engineering and Advanced Applications, pp. 351–356. IEEE (2021)
24. Ruijters, E., Stoelinga, M.: Fault tree analysis: a survey of the state-of-the-art in modeling, analysis and tools. Comput. Sci. Rev. **15–16**, 29–62 (2015)
25. Shpitser, I.: Counterfactual graphical models for longitudinal mediation analysis with unobserved confounding. Cogn. Sci. **37**(6), 1011–1035 (2013)
26. Skjong, R., Wentworth, B.H.: Expert judgment and risk perception. In: ISOPE International Ocean and Polar Engineering Conference, pp. ISOPE–I. ISOPE (2001)
27. Thomas, S., Groth, K.M.: Toward a hybrid causal framework for autonomous vehicle safety analysis. Proceedings of the Institution of Mechanical Engineers, Part O: Journal of Risk and Reliability **237**(2), 367–388 (2023)
28. Werling, M., Faller, R., Betz, W., Straub, D.: Safety integrity framework for automated driving. arXiv preprint arXiv:2503.20544 (2025)
29. Zeller, M.: Component Fault and Deficiency Tree (CFDT): combining functional safety and SOTIF analysis. In: Model-Based Safety and Assessment: 8th International Symposium, IMBSA, Munich, Germany, pp. 146–152. Springer (2022)

Model-Based Design and Safety Assessment

From Natural Language Requirement Specifications to Logic Properties

Theodoros Nestoridis, Konstantinos Mokos, and Panagiotis Katsaros[✉]

Aristotle University of Thessaloniki, Thessaloniki, Greece
{nestorid,kmokos,katsaros}@csd.auth.gr

Abstract. In a system under design, most functional errors encountered during the verification process are attributed to a misleading interpretation of system requirements. Therefore, the consistent reading of requirements, while mapping them to an unambiguous interpretation is of paramount importance. In requirements formalization, each natural language requirement is captured by one or more logical properties. In this process, we face the problem of consistently interpreting requirements, which stems from the varied use of natural language among engineers and the inherent ambiguities in the use of natural language. This paper introduces solutions that have been tested to demonstrate their effectiveness and utility. A set of templates - called boilerplates - for the specification of requirements in natural language is employed. Boilerplate-based requirements are then formalized into a logic language using an automated algorithm that eliminates ambiguity and ensures semantic consistency.

Keywords: requirements formalization · requirements engineering

1 Introduction

In requirements formalization, natural language requirements are consistently expressed in an unambiguous language that can be uniquely interpreted. By capturing the requirements as properties in a logic language we ensure that they are specified with sufficient precision, allowing effective verification and validation of the design. If the requirements are not formalized correctly, then the system product will likely contain functional errors, which can result in costly re-engineering efforts, delays or even potentially unsafe behavior.

Moreover, formalizing requirements in a logic language allows automating the verification process: logic properties can be derived directly from structured natural language. Typically, requirement formalization techniques cope exclusively with the logic structure associated with the syntax, while limiting the expressiveness and failing to address the inherent ambiguities of natural language.

A recurring challenge is the multiple different interpretations that might arise due to how the sentence structure (use of connectors and composition of simpler sentences) is perceived, the terminology and the style of expression used by the

© The Author(s), under exclusive license to Springer Nature Switzerland AG 2026
P. Katsaros (Ed.): IMBSA 2025, LNCS 15755, pp. 241–256, 2026.
https://doi.org/10.1007/978-3-032-05073-1_16

experts of different domains. In the Space Shuttle case study [2], requirements formalization revealed more errors than the subsequent formal analysis.

Our formalization approach for system requirements is based on a structured language [10,11] for specifying them (Boilerplate Language) and an ontology-based property derivation process. We bridge the gap between informal requirements and formal verification by eliminating both syntactic and semantic ambiguity through interpreting the Boilerplate Language with logic-based precision.

We demonstrate how this methodology enables the automated derivation of formal properties from boilerplate requirements and we validate the effectiveness of our approach by applying it on the design of a space system.

2   Related Work

Ambiguity and inconsistency in requirements are two critical challenges in their specification [4]. Ambiguities are introduced due to the use of natural language whereas inconsistencies during their interpretation and formalization into logic. Formalization should be applicable to a language with sufficient expressiveness to allow engineers to capture all necessary constraints and system behaviors.

FREPA [3] introduced an automated verification and validation pipeline. Natural language specifications are automatically translated into Linear Temporal Logic (LTL) properties. To achieve this, a Controlled Natural Language (CNL) is used, whose vocabulary and grammar are constrained to ensure clarity and consistency. Such constraints must not overly limit the expressiveness, as the language should still allow the specification of complex system behaviors.

Two well-known CNLs are EARS [9] and FRETish [5]. EARS uses sentence patterns that though they improve clarity, they limit expressiveness (no constructs for real-time or temporal constraints). An EARS extension [8] supports the direct translation of EARS requirements into LTL. However, the absence of timing constructs restricts its utility in specifying time-critical system behavior.

FRETish provides direct translation of requirements into temporal logic. It is more expressive than EARS, since it allows temporal constraints via a dedicated timing field. Nonetheless, there is no support for multiple triggering conditions, multi-actions, or compound timing constraints in a single requirement.

In [1,12], the authors address the problem of translating structured natural language into formal specifications using property patterns.

Rather than the translation of requirements, our approach lies in their formulation, which is an iterative process guided by boilerplates. This enables the interactive refinement of requirements and enhances traceability between the original natural language and the resulting logic specifications. Our boilerplate language [10,11] was developed using patterns from real industrial requirements. It is a semi-structured natural language designed to combine readability with expressiveness. Boilerplates allow for multiple conditions, various temporal constraints, and multi-actions (responses) within a single requirement. This improves the efficiency of the specification process and enhances its applicability in real-world, large-scale system development. Furthermore, boilerplates form the foundation for automated formalization pipelines that maintain consistency between domain ontologies and logic-based verification workflows.

3   Background

Ontology Architecture

A modular and extensible ontology architecture, the *Requirements Definition Ontology (RDO)* [10], is used that enables the semantic analysis of system requirements. It is structured around six interrelated ontologies (Fig. 1), designed to support the specification, organization, and reasoning for the requirements:

- **System and Attributes Ontology (SAO)**: A domain-independent upper ontology with core system concepts such as System, Function, Item, and Flow, used to express requirements. The SAO concepts and their relations are illustrated in black in Fig. 2.
- **Extended Attributes Ontology (EAO)**: A SAO extension with additional concepts such as Environment, Fault, Error, and Failure, for the specification of Fault Detection, Isolation, Recovery (FDIR) and interactions with the environment. The mapping of the EAO concepts onto the SAO is depicted (in red) in Fig. 2.
- **Requirement Boilerplate Ontology (RBO)**: Encodes the structural pattern of requirements using modular clause templates (Prefix, Main, Suffix), and defines placeholders mapped to SAO/EAO classes.
- **Domain-Specific Ontologies (DSOs)**: Extend EAO/SAO with domain-specific refinements, tailored to specific subsystems or applications.
- **Lexicographic Ontology (LO)**: Defines synonym/antonym relationships for placeholder terms, supporting paraphrasing and consistency checking.
- **RDO Instances**: Maintains a strict separation between ontology schemas and their instances, enabling the RDO ontology to remain reusable, context-independent, and maintainable across different system domains.

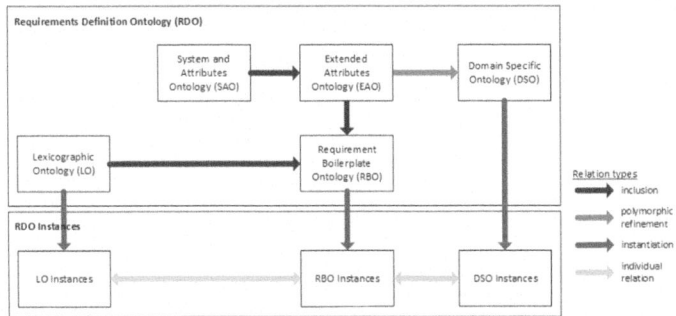

Fig. 1. Ontology architecture

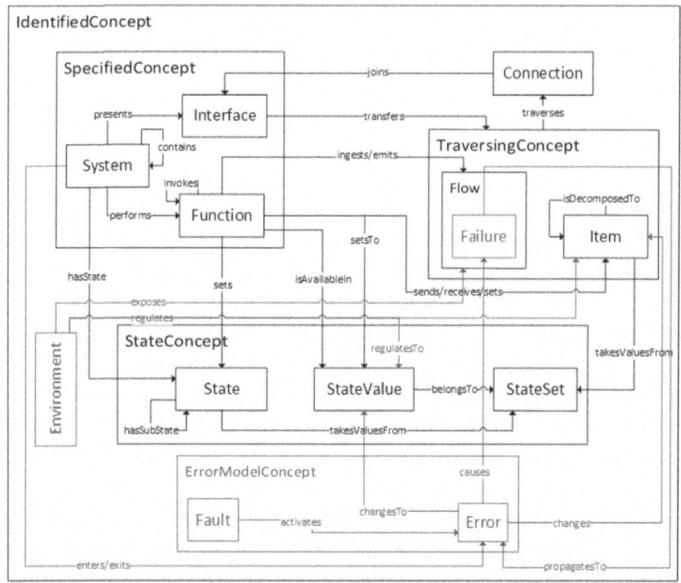

Fig. 2. Extended Attributes Ontology

These ontologies are connected through four types of relations: *inclusion, polymorphic refinement, instantiation,* and *individual relation.*

Boilerplate Language

Requirements are represented using a structured *boilerplate language* modeled within the RBO. A boilerplate requirement consists of one mandatory field and two optional. The mandatory field, called *Main*, describes the response (action) that a defined subject shall exhibit. The optional *Prefix* defines the scope and preconditions of the response, and the *Suffix* captures the related duration and timing constraints. The boilerplate language also supports specifying multiple Prefixes, Mains, and Suffixes using logical connectives. This feature enables the specification of multiple conditions and constraints within a single requirement.

Each clause contains `Placeholder`s, which refer to concepts from SAO, EAO, LO, or DSO. This semantic architecture enables unambiguous interpretation and automated reasoning using OWL and SHACL technologies. By mapping every requirement element to ontology classes and instances, we support semantic querying and semantic reasoning for the detection of incompleteness, inconsistencies, ambiguity, redundancy and for the inference of implicit assumptions. The full syntax of the boilerplate language is presented in [10] (c.f. Tables 3–7).

Example 1. (Example of a simple requirement).
Consider the case in which the software receives a reboot command, while already operating in Boot Mode, which causes the CPU to reset. The following requirement is specified in natural language:

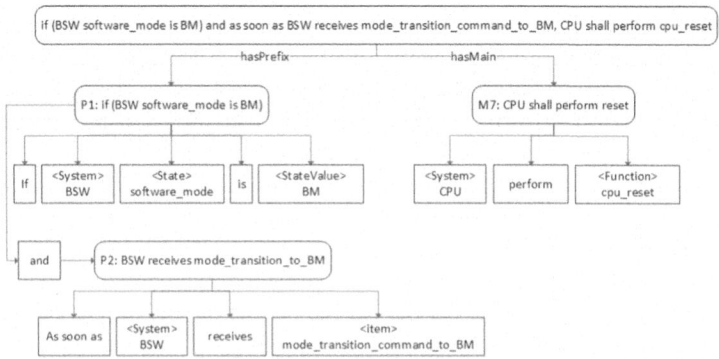

Fig. 3. Decomposition of the requirement in Example 1

"If the system is in Boot Mode and when Boot Software receives a command to transition to Boot Mode, then the CPU shall perform a reset."
Using the boilerplate language, the requirement is specified as follows:

P1: if <System:BSW> <State:software_mode> is <StateValue:BM> and
P2: as soon as <System:BSW> receives <Item: mode_transition_ command_to_BM>
M7:<System:CPU> shall perform <Function:cpu_reset>

Figure 3 shows how the example requirement is decomposed into the different parts of its boilerplate-based specification.

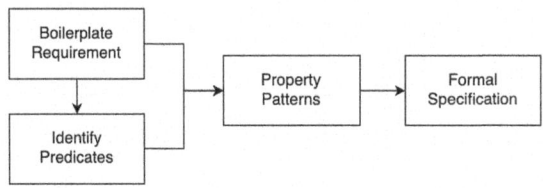

Fig. 4. Property derivation pipeline of a boilerplate requirement

4 Property Derivation

Semantically validated boilerplate requirements are transformed into formal specifications through deriving logic properties. Logic specifications need to capture the behavior expressed in boilerplate requirements and allow various analyses, including formal verification, simulation-based analysis and safety analysis.

Our property derivation approach builds on the modular structure of the boilerplate language and aims to the synthesis of *Past-time First-order LTL*

(PFLTL) formulas [6]. This is a logic language for safety properties that allows for both testing and runtime verification of traces of events with data [7]. We restrict property derivation exclusively to safety properties that in contrast to liveness are always monitorable (their violation can be detected within finite time).

The property derivation process consists of three main phases: identify predicates from the boilerplate clauses, select corresponding property patterns, and instantiate them to synthesize formal properties (Fig. 4).

Step 1: Predicate Extraction

The first step involves identifying logical predicates embedded in the boilerplate structure. These predicates serve as atomic relations in the temporal logic formula. Depending on the clause (prefix, main, suffix), predicates may express:

- State assertions, e.g., `"software_mode is BM"`
- Event triggers, e.g., `"send startup_housekeeping_report"`
- Temporal markers, e.g., `"within 0.2 s"` or `"after 200ms"`

Predicates reflect the domain semantics and system-specific behaviors, thus they are created from ontological bindings in DSOs and in the general RDO structure.

Example 2. Consider the requirement:
"If BSW software mode is BM, BSW shall send a Startup Housekeeping Report within 0.2 s."

P1: if <System:BSW> <State: software_mode> is <StateValue: BM>
M7:<System: BSW> shall perform <Function: send_startup_housekeeping_report>
S3: within 0.2 seconds

From this, we extract:

- Predicate $Q(le) =$ `is_software_mode(BM)`
- Predicate $M(r) =$ `perform(send_startup_housekeeping_report)`

These predicates will be next instantiated within property patterns.

Step 2: Pattern Identification and Matching. Property derivation is based on the grammar of the boilerplate requirement to identify the property pattern(s) that apply. Each clause corresponds to a syntactic rule with a semantic mapping.

Prefix Patterns: Prefix clauses define triggering conditions for the main clause. We express these clauses as logic implications, where the presence of a logical condition $Q(le)$ or the occurrence of some functionality $Q(oc)$ is followed by the main response $M(r)$. Table 1 presents mappings of the prefix templates to corresponding PFLTL property patterns.

Suffix Patterns: Suffix clauses express timing and ordering constraints on the main response. These may include constraints like deadlines ("within 1 s"), minimum duration ("for at least 0.5 s"), periodic triggers ("every 100ms"), or causal sequencing ("after access_NVM_signal"). Table 2 shows how the mentioned suffixes constrain the truth interval of the main predicate $M(r)$.

Table 1. Mapping of property patterns to the boilerplate syntax.

Prefix Boilerplate Syntax	Property pattern
P1: If/Unless <logical expression> where Q: Logical expression (le) and M: Main response (r)	$(M(r) \vee \neg@(\neg M(r) \, S \, Q(le)))$
P2: As soon as <occurring functionality> where Q: Occurring functionality (oc) and M: Main response (r)	$(M(r) \vee (\neg@(Q(oc)$ $\wedge@(\exists \, temp, \neg Q(oc) \, S \, (Q(temp) \wedge$ $\neg(temp = oc))))))$
P3: As long as <occurring functionality> where Q: Occurring functionality (oc) and M: Main response (r)	$(M(r) \vee (\neg@(Q(oc)))$

Main Clause: The main clause itself defines the system response to be verified. It can be abstracted to a propositional form (e.g., $M(r)$).

Step 3: Logical Translation. Using the identified predicates and corresponding property patterns, we instantiate a formal specification in temporal logic.

The property patterns in Tables 1 and 2 refer the following operators. **S** denotes operator Since, where $p \, S \, q$ indicates that q was true at some point in the past, and from that moment until now, p is continuously held. The bounded forms $p \, S[<= C] \, q$ and $p \, S[> C] \, q$ constrain occurrence of q within or beyond a time bound C, respectively. Negation is written as $\neg p$ and @ denotes that a predicate held in the immediately previous state. **P** expresses that a predicate held in some previous state, while $P[<= C] \, p$ and $P[> C] \, p$ restrict this within or beyond C time units. **H** indicates that p is held in all previous states, with $H[<= C] \, p$ and $H[> C] \, p$ providing bounded versions of this operator.

Example 3. From the previous example: "If BSW software mode is BM, BSW shall send a Startup Housekeeping Report within 0.2 s."

The aforementioned requirement is mapped as:

- Prefix: $Q(le) = $ `is_software_mode(BM)`
- Main: $M(r) = $ `perform(send_startup_housekeeping_report)`
- Suffix: $C = 0.2$

Combined into (FTP : First time in point):

$$((H(\neg M(r)) \rightarrow True \, \mathbf{S}[< C] \, FTP) \vee \neg@(\neg(H(\neg M(r)) \rightarrow$$
$$True \, \mathbf{S}[< C] FTP) \, \mathbf{S} \, Q(le)))$$

4.1   Template Composition and Advanced Cases

While individual boilerplate templates can be directly captured in logic through pattern-based translation, in reality requirements specification usually involves

Table 2. Mapping of suffix boilerplates to *Past-time First-order LTL* semantics

Boilerplate Syntax	Property pattern
S1: \<numerical affirmative\> | \<closed-interval\> [per \<time-unit\>]	cf. Sect. 4.2
S2: after/before **Flow**	
after **Flow**	$(M(r) \vee \neg @(\neg M(r)\, S\, F))$
before **Flow**	$F \to @(\neg F\, S\, M(r))$
where F: Flow and M: Main response (r)	
S3: [every / for a period of / within / for at least] \<number\> (\<time-unit\>) [from **Flow**]	
every ...	$\neg M(r) \to P[<= C]M(r)$
every ... from **Flow**	$(H(F) \wedge \neg M(r)) \to P[<= C]M(r)$
for a period of ...	$M(r) \to \text{True}\, S[<= C]FTP$
for a period of ... from **Flow**	$(\neg F \wedge M(r)) \to \text{True}\, S[<= C]F$
within ...	$H(\neg M(r)) \to \text{True}\, S[< C]FTP$
within ... from **Flow**	$\neg(\neg M(r)\, S[< C]\, F)$
for at least ...	$M(r)\, S[<= C]FTP$
for at least ... from **Flow**	$M(r)\, S[<= C]F$
for at most ...	$\neg(M(r)\, S[<= C]\neg FTP)$
for at most ... from **Flow**	$\neg(M(r)\, S[<= C]\neg F)$
where FTP: First timepoint, F: Flow, M: Main response (r)	
S4: at the beginning / at the end	cf. Sect. 4.2
S5: at even intervals	cf. Sect. 4.2
S6: concurrently with / sequentially to **Function**	
concurrently with **Function**	$M(r) \vee (\neg @F)$
sequentially to **Function**	$M(r) \vee (\neg @(F \wedge @(\neg F\, S\, \neg F)))$
where F: Function and M: Main response (r)	

combinations of multiple clauses. These combinations, especially those connected via logical operators such as AND, OR, and XOR, pose additional challenges for the derivation of formal properties.

To support such a composition, we introduce merging rules for property patterns derived from individual templates. A structured interpretation is applied based on the logical role and order of involved clauses. Table 3 shows how property fragments $g(S)$ and $h(S)$, for some response S, may be combined in PFLTL. We pay attention to exceptions where merging requires contextual adaptation.

Example 4. (Example of a compound requirement).
Consider the requirement:
"If the Boot Software (BSW) is in Boot Mode (BM) and no uncorrectable memory error is present, then BSW shall send housekeeping reports every 500 ms for at least 3 seconds after receiving the access NVM signal."

P1: if \<System:BSW\> \<State: software_mode\> is \<StateValue: BM\> and
P1: Unless \<Fault: uncorrectable_memory_error\> occurs
M7:\<System: BSW\> shall perform \<Function: generate_housekeeping_report
S3: every 0.5 seconds and for at least 3 seconds from \<Flow: access_NVM_signal\>

Table 3. Composition of property patterns from boilerplate-derived clauses.

Connective	Merged Property (PFLTL)	Explanation
AND	$g(S) \wedge h(S) ::= g(h(S))$ $h(S) \wedge g(S) ::= h(g(S))$	Left-hand property absorbs right-hand one as its response. Response S is replaced in outer context.
AND (Exception 1)	$g(S) = $ for at least C_1, $h(S) = $ for at most C_2 $g(S) \wedge h(S) ::= g(S) \wedge h(S)$	Bounds on the same response duration are logically conjuncted to enforce a closed interval.
AND (Exception 2)	$g(S) = P1$ $h(S) = P2$ $g(S) \wedge h(S) ::= Q(le) \rightarrow (h(S) \vee \mathbf{H}\,(\neg h(S)))$	Conditioned execution: if $Q(le)$ holds, then at the next occurrence of $Q(oc)$, the system must satisfy $M(r)$.
AND (Exception 3)	$Q(le) \rightarrow h(S)$	If $g(S)$ specifies if $Q(le)$ and $h(S)$ is a temporal constraint (e.g., from S3), the resulting formula is gated by $Q(le)$.
OR	$g(S) \vee h(S) ::= g(S)$ and $h(S)$ (as separate properties)	"OR" denotes two alternative requirement paths. Translated into distinct logical formulas to check each scenario independently.

This yields a more complex pattern, where we start by constructing the predicates of the requirement:

- Prefix P1_1: $Q(le_{p1_1}) = $ is_software_mode(BM)
- Prefix P1_2: $Q(le_{p1_2}) = $ occurs(uncorrectable_memory_error)
- Main: $M(r) = $ perform(generate_housekeeping_report)
- Suffix S3_1: $C_{s3\_1} = 0.5$
- Suffix S3_2: $F = $ access_NVM_signal, $C_{s3\_2} = 3$

First we formalize the prefixes:

- P1_1: If <System:BSW> <State: software_mode> is <StateValue: BM>
- P1_2: Unless <Fault: uncorrectable_memory_error> occurs

According to Table 3, these prefixes are combined using the AND rule

$$g(S) \wedge h(S) ::= g(h(S)).$$

as follows:

$$P1\_1 : \big(M(r_{p1\_1}) \vee \neg@\big(\neg M(r_{p1\_1})\, S\, Q(le_{p1\_1})\big)\big)$$

$$P1\_2 : \big(\neg M(r_{p1\_2}) \vee \neg@\big(M(r_{p1\_2})\, S\, Q(le_{p1\_2})\big)\big)$$

When both Prefixes are combined with the Main (excluding Suffix conditions for now) we obtain:

$$M(r_{PM}) : \Big(\big(\neg M(r) \vee \neg@\big(M(r)\, S\, Q(le_{p1\_2})\big)\big)$$
$$\vee \neg@\big(\neg\big(\neg M(r) \vee \neg@\big(M(r)\, S\, Q(le_{p1\_2})\big)\big)\, S\, Q(le_{p1\_1})\big)\Big)$$

Next, we introduce the suffixes:

- S3_1: every 0.5 s

– S3_2: for at least 3 s from <Flow: access_NVM_signal>

as follows:

$$S3\_1 : \neg M(r_{PM}) \to P[<= C_{s3\_1}]M(r_{PM})$$
$$S3\_2 : M(r_{PM})\, S[<= C_{s3\_2}]F$$

When both Suffixes are combined with $M(r_{PM})$ we obtain:

$$\neg(M(r_{PM})\, S[<= 3]F) \to P[<= 0.5](M(r_{PM})\, S[<= 3]F)$$

This compound formula expresses a nested periodic constraint for a continuous interval after the completion of a flow, conditioned by a composite prefix.

4.2 Limitations

Although a broad range of requirement patterns can be represented, several challenges and limitations still exist:

1. Some suffix templates (S1, S4, and S5) cannot be captured in temporal logic due to needs for statistical or semantic inference across sets of requirements. A series of consistency and synchronization checks will have to take place, which are beyond the scope of PFLTL.
2. Ambiguous timing references require disambiguation (cf. Sect. 6).

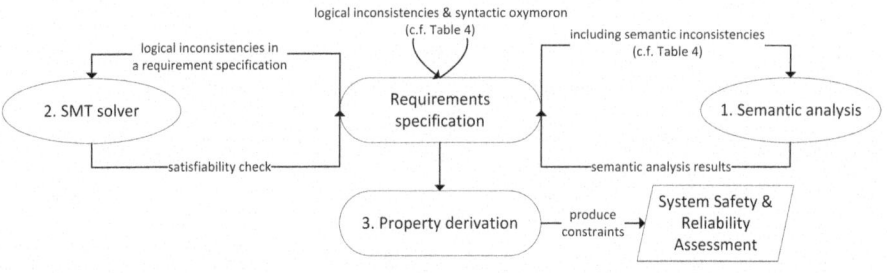

Fig. 5. Methodology for deriving formal properties from boilerplate requirements

5 Methodology for Property Derivation

Derivation of formal properties from boilerplate requirements follows a systematic pipeline involving semantic analysis, logical consistency checks, and property derivation (cf. Fig. 5). Throughout this process, logical contradictions and syntactic oxymorons are identified in individual boilerplate requirements (cf. Table 4), in order to prevent flawed specifications from propagating to subsequent analysis stages.

1. Semantic Analysis
   Initially, the boilerplate requirements are parsed and submitted to semantic analysis. This step identifies potential issues in clause combination, such as semantic inconsistency (cf. Sect. 6). Furthermore, this phase applies ontology-based reasoning [11] to detect deeper specification issues including incompleteness, inconsistency, ambiguity, and redundancy. The outcome of this step is a sanitized requirement specification, free from semantic contradictions that would undermine the subsequent formalization.
2. SMT-based Consistency Checking
   The requirement specification undergoes a logical consistency check using an SMT (Satisfiability Modulo Theory) solver. Satisfiability ensures that all clauses can coexist with no contradiction. If any inconsistency is found, it is fed back to the requirements engineer to revise the requirement specification.
3. Property Derivation
   Once the requirements are confirmed to be semantically and logically consistent, the property derivation phase takes place. Extracted constraints in PFLTL reflect the core behavioral expectations encoded in the requirements and are used for system safety verification.

This pipeline enables early detection of inconsistencies thus ensuring the validity of the requirements specification, which is eventually reflected in the formal properties used for the subsequent verification.

6 Challenges in Formalizing CNL Requirements

CNL serves as a bridge between natural language and formal logic, providing syntactic constraints to control ambiguity and increase clarity. However, even within a constrained grammar like the boilerplate language the task of formalization presents significant challenges that stem from syntax misuse, logical contradictions, semantic ambiguity, and missing contextual references.

The formalization process should therefore allow for validating logical coherence and semantic compatibility between boilerplate clauses. Table 4 summarizes inconsistency patterns, classified by their type and annotated with example template combinations and interpretation constraints. They reflect structural and semantic issues that arise when composing requirements using complex combinations of boilerplate clauses. These issues are complementary to those identified in [11]. They have not been addressed in earlier research, but they have been emerged through further semantic analysis and experimentation while trying to enforce logical constraints and align them with ontological semantics.

6.1 Types of Inconsistencies in Boilerplate Language

We classify formalization issues into tree major categories: logical, semantic and syntactic oxymorons. These categories reflect the sources of inconsistency that may arise when requirements are specified using the boilerplate language.

Table 4. Common inconsistency patterns in boilerplate-based requirements

Inconsistency type	Boilerplates/Properties	Explanation
Logical	Combination of "as soon as", "within", and "every" with AND **Constraint:** trigger and repetition must align	Immediate triggers (e.g., P2) cannot co-exist with periodic behaviors (S3: every)
Semantic	Prefix with logical expression: <item/system state is ON> AND <item/system state is OFF> **Constraint:** mutually exclusive conditions not allowed	Concepts referred in boilerplate clauses are not mutually exclusive in the ontology
Syntactic (oxymoron)	Mixing "for at least", "for at most" with "every" in wrong order **Constraint:** place duration last	When combined, duration constraints must follow the repetition keyword "every". Order affects interpretation

Logical Inconsistencies

Logical inconsistencies arise when boilerplate clauses introduce contradictions in time constraints, quantifiers, or conditional logic. These often involve improper combinations of suffix templates like S3 (duration), S1 (frequency), or temporal prefix templates like P2 (immediate trigger).

Example 5. (Incompatible trigger and repetition logic).
This example demonstrates a logical inconsistency caused by combining an immediate trigger clause with a periodic repetition constraint.
"As soon as stay_in_BM_flag is False, the BSW shall signal availability every 0.5 s."

```
P2: As soon as <Item: stay_in_BM_flag> is <StateValue: False>
M7:<System: BSW> shall perform <Function: signal_BSW_available_for_commanding>
S3: every 0.5 seconds
```

The prefix "as soon as" implies a one-time reaction, whereas the suffix "every" defines periodic behavior. Their combination is logically inconsistent.
Correct requirement specification:

```
P1: If <Item: stay_in_BM_flag> is <StateValue: False>
M7:<System: BSW> shall perform <Function: signal_BSW_available_for_commanding>
S3: every 0.5 seconds
```

Semantic Inconsistencies

Semantic inconsistencies occur when the logical content of a requirement contradicts itself at the semantic level even if the grammar is formally correct. This includes mutually exclusive conditions, according to the ontological relationships of the concepts referred in the boilerplate clauses.

Syntactic Oxymorons

Syntactic oxymorons result from technically valid grammar constructs that violate structural or interpretive constraints. They often stem from incorrect ordering of clause types, such as placing a duration after a condition that semantically implies periodicity. In the following example, while the syntax parses correctly, the semantics become ill-defined or misleading.

Example 6. (Incorrect ordering of suffix constraints).
This example demonstrates a syntactic inconsistency due to the ordering of suffix clauses of the boilerplate language. Suffixes with duration specifiers (e.g., "for at least...") must follow periodic constraints (e.g., "every...").
"The BSW shall periodically refresh the hardware watchdog for not less than 0.15 s and no more than 0.25 s, every 0.02 s."
Wrong boilerplate requirement:

```
M7:<System: BSW> shall perform <Function: refresh_hardware_watchdog>
S3: for at least 0.15 seconds and
S3: for at most 0.25 seconds and
S3: every 0.02 seconds
```

The order of suffixes affects the interpretation of time-bound constraints. In this case, the suffix expressing periodic execution must appear first to avoid a syntactic oxymoron.
Correct requirement specification:

```
M7:<System: BSW> shall perform <Function: refresh_hardware_watchdog>
S3: every 0.02 seconds and
S3: for at least 0.15 seconds and
S3: for at most 0.25 seconds
```

7   Case Study

The practical application of our methodology was validated using the Boot Software (BSW) requirements of the T1 Star Tracker system developed by Terma A/S [10]. In total 141 boilerplate requirements were formalized, e.g. for system initialization, memory access control, fault management, and command handling.

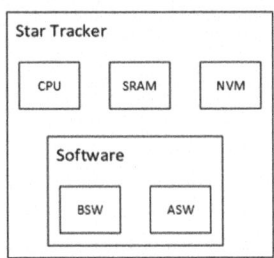

Fig. 6. Star Tracker system decomposition

The Star Tracker decomposition is shown in Fig. 6, where the BSW interacts with critical subsystems such as the CPU (Central Processing Unit), SRAM (Static Random-Access Memory), and NVM (Non-Volatile Memory). These components operate in coordination during boot, reconfiguration, and operational transitions, with the BSW ensuring a safe and reliable initialization sequence while managing commands, handling error events, and overseeing the transition to the execution of the Application Software (ASW). The complete system decomposition and further technical details are available in [10].

7.1   Satisfiability Results

According to the methodology described in Sect. 5, the verification process begins with checking the logical consistency of the requirements before any property derivation is performed.

To this end, we encoded the 141 boilerplate requirements into SMT formulas.

- 139 out of 141 requirements were found logically consistent and satisfiable.
- 2 requirements were flagged as unsatisfiable due to contradictions in their temporal constraints.

The following two requirements, related to the timing behavior of the BSW system, were found to be logically inconsistent:

STR_T1_SW_1584_1:

P2: As soon as <System: BSW> performs <Function: copy_ASW_image_in_NVM _to_RAM>
M7:<System: BSW> shall perform <Function: signal_BSW_available_for_commanding>
S4: at the end

STR_T1_SW_1585_2:

P3: As long as <Item: stay_in_BM_flag> is <StateValue: False>
M7:<System: BSW> shall perform <Function: autonomous_mode_transition_to _configuration_mode>
S3: for at most 5 seconds from <Flow: BSW_commanding_availability_signal>

A related requirement is the following:

STR_T1_SW_1584_2:

M6:<Function: signal_BSW_available_for_commanding> shall emit <Flow: BSW _commanding_availability_signal>

The contradiction arises because one requirement prescribes that the availability signal occurs only at the end, while the other requirement expects the system to react to that signal within a time-bounded window. The system cannot delay the signal until the end, while also assuming that actions happen immediately after it. This results in a conflict that renders the specification unsatisfiable.

To resolve the inconsistency, the temporal suffix at the end must be removed from **STR_T1_SW_1584_1**, allowing the signal to be emitted in time for the subsequent action.

STR_T1_SW_1584_1:

P2: As soon as <System: BSW> performs <Function: copy_ASW_image_in_NVM _to_RAM>

M7:<System: BSW> shall perform <Function: signal_BSW_available_for_commanding>

STR_T1_SW_1585_2:

P2: As long as <Item: stay_in_BM_flag> is <StateValue: False>

M7:<System: BSW> shall perform <Function: autonomous_mode_transition_to _configuration_mode>

S3: for at most 5 seconds from <Flow: BSW_commanding_availability_signal>

8 Conclusions

We proposed a methodology for transforming controlled natural language requirements into temporal logic specifications, using an ontology-driven boilerplate language and a structured property derivation process. Our approach ensures syntactic clarity and semantic precision by integrating semantic reasoning through domain ontologies and logical consistency checks based on an SMT solver.

The decomposition of requirements into modular clause structures enables systematic predicate extraction and the application of reusable property patterns. These are mapped to formal logic fragments, such PFLTL, facilitating automated property generation towards a verifiable specification.

The methodology was shown to effectively identify inconsistencies and generate valid properties for verification workflows on an industrial case study from the space domain. The results demonstrate its utility in eliminating ambiguity, and enabling early detection of specification errors.

Future work will focus on extending the expressiveness of the boilerplate language, refining logical translations to support richer compositions, and incorporating feedback mechanisms for iterative refinement. The framework aims to bridge the gap between informal requirements and formal verification, improving traceability and trust in safety-critical system development.

References

1. Autili, M., Grunske, L., Lumpe, M., Pelliccione, P., Tang, A.: Aligning qualitative, real-time, and probabilistic property specification patterns using a structured english grammar. IEEE Trans. Softw. Eng. **41**(7), 620–638 (2015)
2. Crow, J., Vito, B.: Formalizing space shuttle software requirements: four case studies. ACM Trans. Softw. Eng. Methodol. **7**(3), 296–332 (1998)
3. Feng, J., et al.: Frepa: an automated and formal approach to requirement modeling and analysis in aircraft control domain. In: ESEC/FSE 2020, pp. 1376–1386. ACM, New York (2020)
4. Franch, X., Palomares, C., Quer, C., Chatzipetrou, P., Gorschek, T.: The state-of-practice in requirements specification: an extended interview study at 12 companies. Requir. Eng. **28**(3), 377–409 (2023)

5. Giannakopoulou, D., Pressburger, T., Mavridou, A., Schumann, J.: Automated formalization of structured natural language requirements. Inf. Softw. Technol. **137**, 106590 (2021)
6. Havelund, K., Peled, D.: Runtime verification: from propositional to first-order temporal logic. In: Colombo, C., Leucker, M. (eds.) RV 2018. LNCS, vol. 11237, pp. 90–112. Springer, Cham (2018). https://doi.org/10.1007/978-3-030-03769-7_7
7. Havelund, K., Peled, D., Ulus, D.: First-order temporal logic monitoring with bdds. Form. Methods Syst. Des. **56**(1–3), 1–21 (2020)
8. Lúcio, L., Rahman, S., bin Abid, S., Mavin, A.: EARS-CTRL: generating controllers for dummies. In: Proceedings of Workshops co-located with ACM/IEEE 20th International Conference on Model Driven Engineering Languages and Systems (MODELS 2017). CEUR Workshop Proceedings, vol. 2019, pp. 566–570. CEUR-WS.org (2017)
9. Mavin, A., Wilkinson, P., Harwood, A., Novak, M.: Easy approach to requirements syntax (ears). In: 2009 17th IEEE International Requirements Engineering Conference, pp. 317–322 (2009)
10. Mokos, K., Katsaros, P., Bohn, P.: Model-based safety analysis of requirement specifications. J. Syst. Softw. **219**, 112231 (2025)
11. Mokos, K., Nestoridis, T., Katsaros, P., Bassiliades, N.: Semantic modeling and analysis of natural language system requirements. IEEE Access **10**, 84094–84119 (2022)
12. Vogel, T., Carwehl, M., Rodrigues, G.N., Grunske, L.: A property specification pattern catalog for real-time system verification with uppaal. Inf. Softw. Technol. **154**, 107100 (2023)

Model-Based Dependent Failure Analysis

Daniel Schneider[1] , Ioannis Sorokos[1(✉)] , Santiago Velasco[1] , Peter Munk[2] ,
and Markus Schweizer[2]

[1] Fraunhofer IESE, Fraunhofer-Platz 1, 67663 Kaiserslautern, Germany
{daniel.schneider,ioannis.sorokos,
santiago.velasco}@iese.fraunhofer.de
[2] Robert Bosch GmbH, 70465 Renningen, Stuttgart, Germany
{peter.munk,markus.schweizer}@de.bosch.com

Abstract. Dependent failures are a critical concern in safety engineering. If such dependencies remain undetected, crucial assumptions underlying safety concepts and safety argumentation may become invalid. **Dependent Failure Analysis (DFA)** is a method used to identify these dependencies. However, existing methods and techniques to perform DFA systematically and efficiently are lacking in modern model-based tool support. In this paper, we introduce a model-based DFA approach that comprises the associated process, modeling concepts, and interfaces with other model-based safety engineering techniques.

Keywords: Functional Safety · Dependent Failure Analysis · Model-Based

1 Introduction

Safety assurance is all about demonstrating that the risk associated with a system is acceptably low. To achieve this, safety engineering employs various methods, techniques, tools and specialized (typically domain-specific) standards. A common element across these safety assurance methods is understanding which fundamental events (i.e., component-level failures) within a system could lead to violations of system-level safety requirements. It is particularly crucial to verify that assumed statistical independence between these 'basic events' genuinely holds or that any statistical dependencies among basic events can be systematically and reliably detected.

Consequently, safety standards, such as ISO 26262 in the automotive domain [8], require a Dependent Failure Analysis (DFA). DFA systematically identifies issues that might undermine the necessary independence or freedom from interference among system components. Thus, DFA serves as a foundation for either preventing dependent failures or ensuring the system can tolerate them, thereby guaranteeing compliance with safety requirements at an adequate confidence level. DFA can be applied at various abstraction levels, including system, software, and hardware.

Currently, detailed guidance on conducting a DFA is absent from standards, and, to our knowledge, the state-of-practice lacks systematic, efficient, and effective DFA approaches. Typically, the industry employs tables combined with guidewords. However, this approach has several significant drawbacks:

© The Author(s), under exclusive license to Springer Nature Switzerland AG 2026
P. Katsaros (Ed.): IMBSA 2025, LNCS 15755, pp. 257–270, 2026.
https://doi.org/10.1007/978-3-032-05073-1_17

- Inefficiency due to manual and repetitive processes.
- Scalability issues, particularly when applied to complex systems.
- Lack of integration with other essential work products, such as system specifications and architecture documents.
- Prone to human errors due to its manual nature.
- Lack of systematic procedures and clear guidance, making it difficult to learn and consistently apply.
- Poor support for re-use across different projects or contexts.

This paper introduces a model-based approach to Dependent Failure Analysis (**DFA**), aimed at improving the effectiveness, efficiency, and quality of safety analyses in system development. By clearly identifying and documenting dependencies, cascading failures, and common cause failures, the presented methodology reduces the likelihood of overlooking critical safety issues. The approach primarily targets early phases of the development process and thus has been designed to operate based on system-level models. This should not fundamentally prevent its usage in other parts of the development process.

Section 2 introduces background, terminology, the most important requirements considered for the definition of the method, as well as related work. Section 3 provides descriptions of the DFA approach, the modeling concept and the tool support. Section 4 discusses the metamodel underpinning the information structure necessary to support the tooling approach. Section 5 concludes the paper with a summary and an outlook regarding future research.

2 Background, Requirements and Related Work

2.1 Background

The primary goal in safety engineering is to reduce the risks associated with a system to an acceptable level and, ideally, to provide a defensible argument with demonstrable evidence supporting this reduction. A crucial component in achieving this goal is the systematic development of a robust safety concept. This particularly involves conceptualizing and implementing measures designed to accomplish the necessary risk reduction.

A common methodology begins with conducting a hazard and risk analysis, identifying top-level safety requirements (denoted as 'safety goals' in the automotive domain), and subsequently decomposing these requirements onto specific finer grained system elements using methods such as Fault Tree Analysis (FTA) [3]. Qualitative FTA identifies minimal cut-sets (MCS), which are sets of basic system events whose occurrence leads to the violation of a top-level safety requirement. Additionally, quantitative FTA may estimate the probabilities of these events (or MCS) occurring. Safety mechanisms can then be designed and introduced to ensure each minimal cut-set has a sufficiently low probability of occurrence.

A fundamental assumption often made in this context is the statistical independence of events within each MCS. However, this assumption may not always hold true. Failures in one component could propagate to another component through unknown dependencies. Additionally, multiple component failures might result from a single external factor or unspecified interface, or faults within multiple components could stem from the same systematic error or inherent hardware characteristic. These scenarios represent dependent failures, defined as follows: *"failures that are not statistically independent, i.e., the probability of the combined occurrence of the failures is not equal to the product of the probabilities of occurrence of all considered independent failures"*- ISO26262:2018, Part 1, Definition 3.29.

Several types of dependent failures can be distinguished, based on the type of their causes. When two or more elements fail due to a single, specific root cause, the latter is called a **Common Cause Failure (CCF)**. In contrast, a **Cascading Failure (CF)** occurs in a sequence, propagating along a chain of dependencies - meaning one failure causes another, which may subsequently lead to further failures and so on.

The dependencies between elements arise due to **coupling factors**, which can also be categorized into different types. An example of a specific coupling factor type are shared resources, for instance, a shared power supply. A **Dependent Failure Initiator (DFI)** is an event or condition that triggers a dependent failure within the context of an existing coupling factor.

For instance, consider a scenario where a critical component of a commonly used power supply fails, resulting in the failure of the power supply itself. Consequently, multiple Electronic Control Units (ECUs), which rely on this power supply, also fail. Here, the ECUs experience a CCF due to their shared dependency on the power supply. The coupling factor is the jointly used power supply, and the DFI is the initial failure of the critical power supply component. Concurrently, there is also a CF from the critical power supply component, through the power supply, to the ECUs.

2.2 Related Work

In current industrial practice, DFA is typically conducted using Excel-based approaches. Practitioners follow general process guidelines and fill in structured Excel templates to document their analysis. Established safety analysis methods such as Failure Modes and Effects Analysis (FMEA), Fault Tree Analysis (FTA), Component Fault Trees (CFT) [3] or approaches based on HiP-HOPS [4] are widely applied. These analyses are supported by commercial tools such as FaultTree +, IQ-FMEA, Vector PREEvision, ANSYS medini analyze, ENCO SOX, LDRA tool suite, HiP-HOPS, and safeTbox [1, 5].

We note a clear trend toward the increased use of system modeling languages e.g., SysML, AADL (Architecture Analysis & Design Language), EAST-ADL (Electronics Architecture and Software Technology Architecture Description Language) with safety-specific extensions. Additionally, integrated toolchains connecting design, analysis and V&V, maybe even with safety engineering activities (e.g. safeTbox) have also been developed.

However, there is currently a noticeable lack of model-based approaches specifically tailored for DFA. To date, almost no recent solutions that we know of integrate DFA as a primary and explicitly supported concern into the model-driven engineering paradigm. We note that the overall DFA problem is not novel, as indicated by earlier work e.g. [6. 7] from 1987 and 1989. However, modern systems require technical support offered by corresponding tooling, and such DFA solutions will need to align with the modeling methods supported by the rest of the toolchain. Compliance of such an approach with modern industry standards, e.g. ISO 26262, is also relevant. Therefore, we find the relative lack of modern methods and tooling to be a gap.

One recent identified work addressing this gap is the paper by Bülent Sari and Hans-Christian Reuss [2] who propose a model-based DFA approach, addressing the specific decomposition and independence requirements of ISO 26262 for ASIL-D systems. Their method extends the EAST-ADL by enriching its hardware modeling, function modeling, and dependability packages. These extensions allow explicit modeling of multicore processor architectures, covering both hardware and software safety elements necessary to demonstrate independence between hardware and software components. Based on this modeling approach, they developed dedicated scripts that automatically analyze decomposition paths from system level down to software and hardware levels, generating detailed analysis outputs. In summary, Sari and Reuss' approach demonstrates the automated identification of potential coupling factors within multicore automotive systems and illustrates how dependent failure analysis can be embedded into a model-driven development process. It stands out as one of the few, if not the only, attempts so far to bring DFA into the realm of integrated, model-based safety engineering. In relation to our work, we propose a process that is not specific to EAST-ADL nor multicore processor architectures. Therefore, we view our approach as being more generalizable and transferable, as our coverage of DFA coupling factors is also broader.

Another recent approach relates to visualization techniques for simulation-based DFA [9]. The authors of the latter approach focus on supporting engineers in identifying the dependencies between events and observations collected during system simulation (specifically Discrete Event Simulation of digital twins). The authors further focus their attention on the problem of system maintenance. Therefore, the approach in [9] is focusing on later stages of the system's development lifecycle and specifically related to simulation. In contrast, our approach can be applied earlier in the system development lifecycle and instead focuses on supporting the initial and ongoing systems modeling of DFA-related elements, as will be discussed in later sections.

2.3 Research Questions

DFA is an analysis necessary for effective overall risk analysis and management and is explicitly needed to comply with the automotive industry standard ISO 26262.

Our research questions are as follows:

1. Can we specify a generic formal modeling and analysis process to help analysts perform DFA and identify relevant causes of dependent failures?
2. Can we provide model-based tool support that is compatible with existing state of practice in automotive (and possibly that of other domains) safety engineering?

3 DFA Process

It is assumed that the design process will follow an iterative approach, with designers and DFA analysts/safety engineers taking turns to analyze and add more details to the design as well as to the analysis models (Fig. 1). The following sections describe the process steps in conjunction with our proposed modeling concepts.

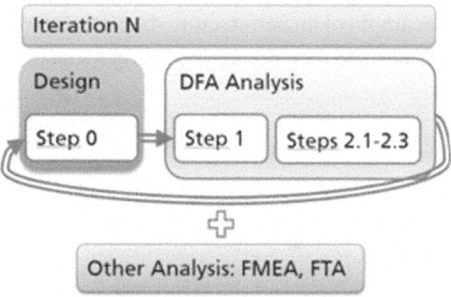

Fig. 1. DFA process overview

The DFA process is supported by a dedicated modeling approach designed to improve both the quality and efficiency of the analysis. This approach provides modeling constructs to facilitate the analysis, offers guidance for engineers, and lays the groundwork for implementing automation mechanisms. The modeling approach itself is based on a meta-model associated with the safeTbox tool, which is detailed in Sect. 4. Both the DFA process and the modeling approach are described in detail in the following sections.

3.1 Step 0: Architecture Modeling

This initial step lays the foundation for the DFA. Its goal is to create an architectural design that integrates functional and non-functional requirements, along with independence and freedom-from-interference requirements. During the first iteration, an initial architecture model is developed for the system under development that captures the system components ('items' as defined by ISO 26262). The model is subsequently updated and refined throughout later iterations, also incorporating measures identified through DFA and other safety analyses.

To support modeling DFA-specific concerns, the safeTbox modeling approach is extended with additional modeling elements, such as component types, component instances, several specialized flow types, and elements representing specific coupling factors like external influences or unintended impacts. **Component instances** depict concrete instances of a **component type**. Multiple instances of the same component type can be added to the same diagram (e.g., multiple sensors of the same type).

Flows have been further formalized, and specific flow types are represented by their own metamodel element type, including Data, Material, Electrical Energy LV (Low Voltage), Electrical Energy HV (High Voltage), Mechanical Energy and Thermal Energy. Flow types are assumed to be static to facilitate automation. Flexible alternatives, like dynamically adding or removing types, might adversely impact automation efficiency. Additionally, components include an explicit depiction of their assigned **ASIL level** (Automotive Safety Integrity Level), which roughly describes the degree of development integrity needed to address the associated risk. There are five ASIL levels, QM, A, B, C, D, in increasing order of integrity. It is assumed that the system design will be sufficiently detailed to assign dedicated ASIL levels to components. Flows from components with lower ASIL to those with higher ASIL are a possible source of DFs.

Figure 2 presents an example of an architecture diagram for an abstract system where the above elements have been used to annotate according to the proposed DFA extensions in safeTbox.

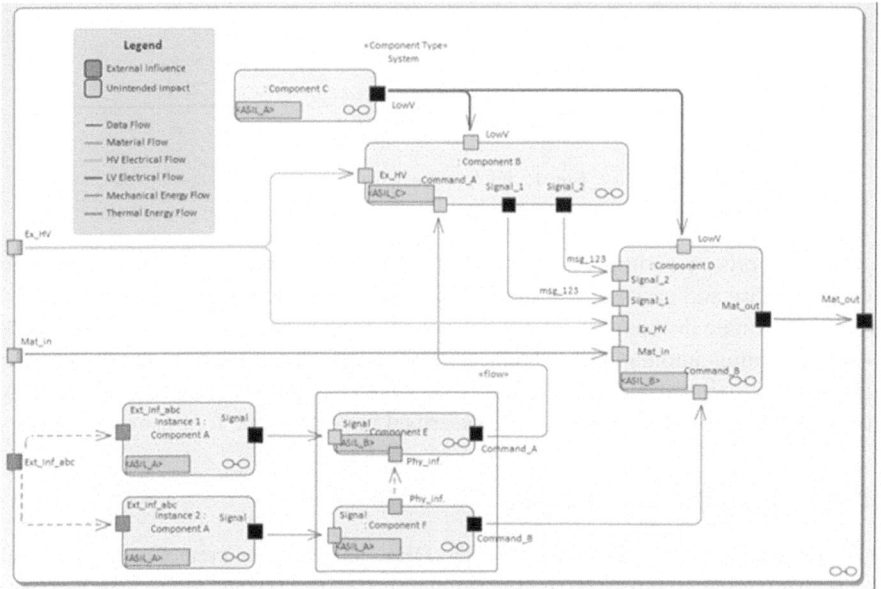

Fig. 2. Architecture diagram augmented with DFA concerns

In the following the modeling support for architecture-related coupling factors is briefly described:

- **Shared Resources:** Modeled explicitly as components. The abstraction level (system, hardware, software) significantly influences this modeling. Early development stages may omit certain shared resources that appear only later.
- **Components of Identical Type:** Supported by standard instantiation mechanisms.
- **Shared Information Inputs:** Represented by incoming ports at the system level. These inputs are not limited to data flows; other types of flows may also apply.
- **Communication:** Relevant because received information can, for example, be false/corrupted, lost, sent multiple times or in the wrong order. For the time being there is no dedicated element foreseen for the communication category as this can be supported by means of data flows and messages.
- **Environmental Influences:** Represented using dedicated "External Influence" ports, visually distinguished by a specific color (green color) from regular incoming flow ports.
- **Unintended Impacts:** Modeled similarly to environmental influences but within the system itself, utilizing a dedicated unintended impact port (blue color).
- **Systematic Coupling:** Not explicitly supported in the modeling approach. Systematic coupling factors come from aspects of the development that might affect the system,

but which are generally not tackled as part of functional requirements specifications. The modeling of such issues can be partially achieved by "misusing" existing constructs. For example, they could be integrated as part of the descriptions of DFIs of the type "Components of the same type" or through the external influence ports or unintended impact ports.

3.2   Step 1: Analysis Scoping

The first step of the actual DFA is the analysis scoping. The goal of this step is the identification and determination of components that shall be subject to the DFA by considering inter-component dependencies in the model. This step will be conducted mostly manually, i.e. the engineer selects a set of components after due consideration of the model as well as relevant context information. Table 1 presents an example of how this information can be documented.

Table 1. Analysis scoping example

Originator	Originator ASIL	Dependency Nature	Dependent Component	Dependent Component ASIL	DFA relevant (Yes / No)
Wheel sensor FL	ASIL A	Information flow	BCM	ASIL B	Yes
Wheel sensor	ASIL A	Instantiation	Wheel sensor FL	ASIL A	Yes
CAN	ASIL QM(B)	Coexistence	ADC	ASIL B	Yes

An algorithm analyzes the model and automatically obtains a list of dependent components on the basis of existing relationships. The following types of relationships are interpreted as dependencies and are documented in a table-like representation.

- **'Flow type':** Determined if there is a flow (data, material, ...), i.e. a dependency linking components which might have different ASIL levels.
- **Instantiation:** Determined if there is more than one instance of the same component type.
- **Coexistence:** Determined when a sub-component has a lower ASIL than another sub-component in the same aggregating component but is not connected through any flow.

Once a result table is filled automatically, the analyst shall decide whether the dependency needs to be investigated by the DFA or not. Moreover, the table could also be used as a list to check the completeness of the analysis.

3.3 Step 2: Dependent Failure Identification and Documentation

This is the main step of the DFA. It has the goal to identify and document CFs (step 2.1), DFIs (step 2.2), and CCFs (step 2.3).

Step 2.1: Cascading Failures Identification
For the identification of CFs, a path analysis is performed over the existing system model (i.e., the component architecture). The flows between the components are the drivers for the identification of pairs of dependent components and only such pairs of components will be investigated with respect to CFs at a time.

Given a pair of components, the failure modes at each of the components (originator and dependent component) are identified. Failure modes can further be associated with the outgoing interfaces of the components to indicate through which interfaces they are exposed. This implies modeling of the failure logic, which could be done by means of fault trees and ideally by component fault trees [3] to also capture the allocation to components and the propagation over ports. Table 2 presents an example of how this information can be documented.

Table 2. Examples of Cascading Failures

CF_ID	Origin	Failure Mode	Interface	Flow Type	Dependent Component	Failure Mode	Interface
CF_1	Wheel sensor FL	Speed too high		Data flow	BCM	Vehicle state cannot be determined	
CF_2	Wheel sensor FL	Speed too low	WS_FL	Data flow	CLU	Unlock Doors commission	Unlock_door_cmd

Cascading failures are represented by their own modeling element in the meta model. This element should be structured below the integrating component since it will relate failure modes of sub-components that interact with each other. The reuse of sub-components shall not lead to the reuse of the cascading failure, as they will be missing the dependent context. Joint re-use shall only occur when the integrating component is reused, as it will integrate the dependent components as well.

Before being able to model a cascading failure, the failure modes should be modeled in advance. As can be seen in the example below and from the metamodel, the failure mode might either be associated with a port or not. This depends on whether the failure effect can be exposed through one of the existing outgoing ports or not. The "DFA-FM Relation" connector should be used to establish the trace between the cascading failure and the failure mode. The "Originator Relation" is used to link the CF to the originator component instance. The "Dependent Component Relation" is used to link the CF to the dependent component instance. The trace between failure modes and ports shall be modeled with the help of the "FailureMode Port Relation" connection. Finally, the "Measure Relation" is used to connect the CF with a possibly existing measure. Measures can be created anew, or they can be reused when defining a CF. In the former case, the measure element should be added as child cascading failure when saving the changes to the model. In the latter case, the measure might already be part of another CF, DFI, or CCF, or may simply be located somewhere else (e.g., in a package).

The tool can support the user by suggesting potentially dependent components (also based on the table and model information established already in previous steps) as well as in the creation of failure modes and their association with ports. This can save a lot of modeling time as it will avoid many atomic modeling steps, and as there is no need to manually establish the traces between the elements.

Step 2.2. DFI Identification

A DFI is an event in relation to a generic coupling factor which might trigger a dependent failure for a given set of dependent components. Considering the coupling factor "shared resource power supply", an example for a DFI is a failure of the common power supply used by multiple components.

Similar to the preceding cascading failure identification, the analysis is based on the architecture model and the specified dependencies. This time, however, groups of dependent components are identified on the basis of potential coupling factors. These coupling factors serve as guidance and as a means for structuring (cf. Guidewords in e.g. a hazard and risk analysis) to support the engineers. The identification of DFIs and also of corresponding counter measures can further be supported by checklists and previously used (i.e. "proven") designs. In addition, the analysis can be informed by existing safety analyses. The minimal cut sets resulting from a fault tree analysis can be examined with respect to basic events that appear relatively often (e.g. power supply fails). This can hint at relevant dependent failures and corresponding DFI. Similar considerations are conceivable for other types of safety analyses, such as FMEA, as well.

Table 3. Examples of DFI failures

ID	Originator	Dependent Components	Coupling Factor	DFI	Measure
DFI_1	Battery	VCU, BCM, TCU	Shared resource power supply	Common power supply **failure**	Different power supplies
DFI_2	Sensor	Radar L, Radar R	Component of the same type (radar)	Same hardware parts failing in the same way	Diversity (diversity of components)

The identification of DFIs can be performed already in early design phases on a relatively high abstraction level and thus allows the early definition of independence measures such as, considering the example, introducing a secondary power supply. However, it needs to be checked if the measures address all relevant events (e.g. power supply failure modes). An overvoltage, for instance, would not be addressed by a secondary power supply. As hinted by Fig. 1, the DFA should further be revisited in case design iterations occur.

Similar to cascading failures, DFIs are modeled as children of the integrating component. The modeling of DFIs is slightly simpler than that of CFs because specific failure modes do not need to be specified. Nevertheless, the following relations "Originator Relation" and "Dependent Component Relation" still need to be modeled. Moreover, the information about the coupling factor and the DFI description need to be provided manually by the analyst for each DFI.

Tool support in this step can be the suggestion of dependent components from the list of combinations compiled for Step 1 as well as the existing model information. Based thereon the following information can be filled in automatically: Id, Originator, Dependent components, and Coupling Factor category. The DFI description is provided by the modeler, but the tool can provide suggestions for the coupling factor type (e.g. shared resource, component of the same type or shared information inputs).

In addition, a tool-supported complementary analysis is proposed. Suggestions for the different types of coupling factors are obtained from information explicitly available in the system model and obtained in the scoping step. However, there are some types of coupling factors where related information is typically not sufficiently covered by development specifications and models. In particular, environmental influences, unintended impact, and especially systematic couplings are factors that are likely to fall into this category. For this reason, it makes sense to have an additional dedicated analysis step for the identification of corresponding DFIs.

Our idea for this complementary analysis is to have an architecture view that is component-centered and shows the DFIs related to that component. A suitable abstraction level (considering the nature of the CF and DFI that are within the scope of this complementary analysis) is the system level, where the architectural elements are components consisting of hardware and software. The analysis approach itself can be a brute-force type of approach where guidewords or guide questions are used with respect to every architectural element. These guide questions are based on the coupling factors and their typical DFI. Consider, for instance, the environmental influence "Water Ingress". A question might be "Could there be water ingress affecting this component?". If yes, a follow-up question might be whether other components might be affected by the same instance of water ingress at the same time – e.g. because they are located in the same encasing. For any issue thus identified, a DFI element shall be added. We assume that the number of guide questions required (for a complete analysis) will be manageable, in particular if the analysis is conducted on the system level.

The DFIs added through this mechanism do not have a direct impact on the system model, as no new architectural elements are added to the diagram. Initially, the DFIs will be added to the model as children of the component in that context and will include a reference (i.e., a trace) to the component. It shall be noted that when the iterative approach is used over the set of relevant DFA components, it might be desirable to reuse existing DFIs. In other words, a DFI already defined in the context of one component will also, in the same manner, affect the component currently being analyzed. In this scenario, the DFI needs to be relocated to the component that is the parent of the affected components to ensure consistency of the reuse approach.

Step 2.3: CCF Identification

The CCF analysis can be viewed as a refinement of the (high-level) DFI identification, designed to show in more detail the initiating events or failure modes, the cause-effect relationships between the components, and particularly the actual common cause failure. In context of the example, for instance, overvoltage at the power source can lead to a failure mode of multiple components thus constituting a common cause failure. This is documented in Table 3 and Table 4 respectively.

Table 4. Examples of CCF failures

ID	Coupling Factor	DFI	Origin	Originator Failure Mode	Affected Components	CCF	Measure
CCF_1a	Shared resource power supply	Common power supply failure	Battery	No power supply	ECU1, ECU2, ECU3	ECUs shut down unintentionally	Different power supplies
CCF_1b	Shared resource power supply	Common power supply failure	Battery	Overvoltage	ECU1, ECU2	Multiple electronic components will be damaged at the ECU, causing complete failure	Overvoltage protection circuit

The refinement from DFI into CCF might for instance be desired if the goal is to better understand and decompose the different kinds of failures that can occur, if certain failures apply only to a subset of the dependent components, or if measures for these cause-effect failure relationships are defined separately. A comprehensive refinement from DFI to CCF might not be necessary if the DFI can be addressed on an abstract level by suitable measures and it can be clearly shown that these measures sufficiently address any conceivable CCF that could result from the DFI.

The procedure for identifying CCFs is similar to the one for the identification of the DFI. Ideally, the DFI have been already identified and the CCF are identified as part of a refinement. Same as for the cascading failure identification, failure logic models are very helpful for this step. It can be shown what base events a DFI implies in the failure logic and how these propagate through to trigger 2 or more top-level events (that are thus constituting a CCF).

Modeling support for CCFs can be seen as a combination of support for CFs and DFIs. Identification follows a similar approach as for the DFIs if done from scratch. Alternatively, the existing DFIs can be refined by adding information about the failure modes and/or split them into several ones in order to make a clearer distinction of the cause-effect relationship. The modeling elements and connectors are the same as for the modeling of CFs.

4 Metamodel

To implement the associated analysis, we extended the commercial model-based software tool safeTbox[1]. SafeTbox is implemented as an add-in to the modeling software tool Enterprise Architect[2] (EA). The safeTbox tool was previously implemented by extending EA's own metamodel, using its 'Model Driven Generation' profile mechanism[3]. The extensions discussed in this section build upon the safeTbox metamodel.

Figure 3 indicates the main extensions to the metamodel of the tool to support the DFA. As can be seen, the DFA subsection contains the new elements for CF, CCF, DFI, Coupling Factor Category and DFA (see definitions in Sect. 2.1). It should be noted that all the elements listed inherit ID and name properties by default.

- DFI (Dependent Failure Initiator): 'coupling Factor' documents which coupling factor is relevant
- CF (Cascading Failure): 'originator Failure Mode' traces the source failure mode that leads to the CF; 'dependent Component Failure Mode' traces the potential next failure mode triggered by the current CF
- CCFs (Common Cause Failures): properties are as per DFI and CF
- DFAComponentContext is used to trace between a DFA analysis and a specific system component.

These new elements are related to components (and their instances) on the right side of the figure. This allows the analysis of the graph of component relationships to check for specific flows which meet the conditions discussed in Step 2 (see Sect. 3.3).

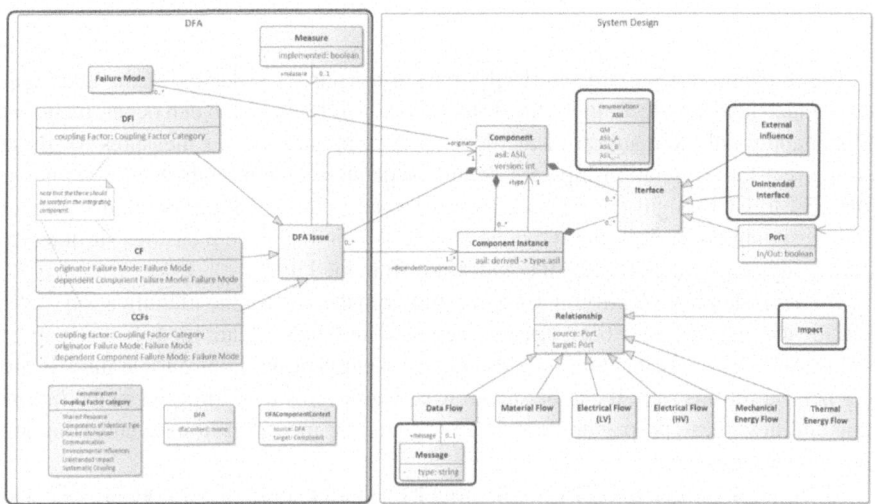

Fig. 3. Extensions to the safeTbox Metamodel (highlighted in red) (Color figure online)

---

[1] https://www.safetbox.de

[2] https://sparxsystems.com/

[3] https://sparxsystems.com/enterprise_architect_user_guide/17.1/modeling_frameworks/mdg_technologies.html.

5   Summary and Conclusion

In this paper we introduced a model-based DFA approach, aimed at improving the support and consistency of this important analysis. By systematically identifying and addressing dependent failures, this approach reduces the likelihood of overlooking critical dependencies.

The structured approach, together with a model-based design and corresponding tool support, supports effective handling of design changes and facilitates semi-automated change impact analyses. While initial modeling efforts may pose additional overhead, these are outweighed by automation-driven benefits.

In this regard, we answer both of our research questions in Sect. 2.3 affirmatively. However, we should note that our research questions, partially due to the scarcity of previous work, did not include detailed evaluation of benefits, limitations and performance assessment of the current solution. In relation to this point, the literature was also scarce in documenting how extensive and effort-intensive the challenge of performing DFA currently is in the industry. DFA has the potential for a wide range of applications, particularly as systems become more connected and external influences may have to be accounted. Therefore, we believe that further investigation regarding the need and value of such solutions is important.

Apart from evaluating our new tool features in further studies, we also identified the following points of future work. First, the safety and cybersecurity co-engineering topic is an important one given the increasing introduction of highly automated and autonomous systems. The approach we propose opens the possibility for modeling possibly hazardous communication channels, whose evaluation can then be managed by existing cybersecurity risk management processes. Secondly, the approach still relies on some manual input by the end user for the flow annotation. Recent advancements in Large Language Model (LLM) technology offer the potential for reducing the necessary manual input by e.g. offering smarter flow auto-completion or generating appropriate flows for typical systems faster for the end user. Naturally, given the risks involved in safety engineering, careful use and review of such results would have to be undertaken to avoid the introduction of additional errors due to LLM-related issues, such as hallucinations.

Disclosure of Interests. The authors have no competing interests to declare that are relevant to the content of this article.

References

1. Dropmann, C., Schneider, D.: SIAF: systematic interference analysis framework for household microprocessor services. 2024 IEEE 24th International Conference on Software Quality, Reliability and Security (QRS), Cambridge, United Kingdom, pp. 757–768 (2024). https://doi.org/10.1109/QRS62785.2024.00080
2. Sari, B., Reuss, H.: A model-driven approach for dependent failure analysis in consideration of multicore processors using modified EAST-ADL. SAE Technical Paper 2017–01–0065 (2017). https://doi.org/10.4271/2017-01-0065

3. Velasco Moncada, D.S.: Hazard-driven realization views for component fault trees. Softw. Syst. Model. **19**, 1465–1481 (2020). https://doi.org/10.1007/s10270-020-00792-8
4. Abdulhamid, A., Kabir, S., Ghafir, I., Lei, C.: An overview of safety and security analysis frameworks for the internet of things. Electronics **12**(14), 3086 (2023). https://doi.org/10.3390/electronics12143086
5. Cederbladh, J., Cicchetti, A., Suryadevara, J.: Early validation and verification of system behaviour in model-based systems engineering: a systematic literature review. ACM Trans. Softw. Eng. Methodol **33**(3, Article 81) (2024), https://doi.org/10.1145/3631976
6. Johnston, B.D.: A structured procedure for dependent failure analysis (DFA). Reliab. Eng. **19**(2), 125–136 (1987). https://doi.org/10.1016/0143-8174(87)90107-7
7. Hughes, R.P.: A framework for dependent failure analysis. Reliab. Eng. Syst. Saf. **24**(2), 139–149 (1989). https://doi.org/10.1016/0951-8320(89)90089-6
8. ISO: "ISO 26262–9:2018(en) Road vehicles — Functional safety – Part 9: Automotive safety integrity level (ASIL)-oriented and safety-oriented analyses," 2018, International Organization for Standardization (ISO)
9. Hilton, S.M., Langton, J., Conroy, P.: Visualization techniques for simulation-based dependent failure analysis. SAE Int. J. Advances & Curr. Prac. in Mobility **4**(4), 1057–1063 (2022). https://doi.org/10.4271/2022-01-0032

Comparative Analysis of Non-colored and Colored Petri Net Models for Availability Assessment of Safety-Critical Cloud Software in Railways

Martin Friebe[(✉)] and Florian Maassen

Siemens Mobility GmbH, 38126 Braunschweig, Germany
martin.friebe@siemens.com

Abstract. The integration of cloud software into safety-critical railway applications introduces new challenges in ensuring availability and reliability. Traditional modeling techniques may not adequately capture the distinction between safety-critical and non-safety-critical software components in cloud-based architectures.

This research explores the integration of safety criticality into Petri net modeling for availability analysis of cloud-based railway applications. Two Petri net models are developed and compared: a traditional non-colored model and an advanced colored model that explicitly represents the safety-critical aspects.

The comparative analysis quantifies the differences in availability and reliability metrics between the two modeling approaches. The findings demonstrate the importance of integrating safety criticality, as the colored Petri net model provides more accurate insights into the availability of safety-critical components.

The results contribute to the knowledge on availability modeling for cloud-based railway systems and provide practical implications for designing and maintaining these critical infrastructures to meet safety and reliability requirements.

Keywords: Cloud-based railway applications · Petri net modeling · Availability analysis

1 Introduction

Railway systems are among the most critical components of national infrastructure, serving as essential arteries for the movement of passengers and freight. In many countries, they form the backbone of the transportation network, linking urban centers, industrial hubs, and remote regions. The efficiency and reliability of railway operations are directly tied to economic productivity, environmental sustainability, and public safety. Consequently, ensuring the continuous, safe, and reliable operation of railway systems is a matter of national importance.

Given their role in transporting large numbers of people and high-value goods, railway systems are classified as safety-critical. Any malfunction or failure - whether due to technical faults, human error, or external disruptions- can have severe consequences,

P. Katsaros (Ed.): IMBSA 2025, LNCS 15755, pp. 271–284, 2026.
https://doi.org/10.1007/978-3-032-05073-1_18

including service delays, financial losses, environmental damage, and, in the worst cases, injury or loss of life. To mitigate these risks, railway systems must adhere to stringent safety and reliability standards, with availability and reliability being two of the most crucial performance indicators.

Availability refers to the proportion of time a system is operational and accessible when needed, while reliability measures the system's ability to perform its intended functions without failure over a specified period. In the railway domain, these attributes are not merely desirable - they are essential. High availability ensures that trains run on schedule, minimizing disruptions to passengers and logistics chains. High reliability reduces the likelihood of unexpected failures that could compromise safety or require costly maintenance interventions.

In recent years, the railway industry has been undergoing significant digital transformation, driven by the adoption of advanced information and communication technologies. Among these, cloud computing has emerged as a key enabler of innovation. Cloud-based solutions offer numerous advantages, including scalability, cost-efficiency, centralized data management, and the ability to deploy sophisticated analytics and decision-support tools. These capabilities are increasingly being leveraged to enhance operational efficiency, predictive maintenance, traffic management, and passenger services.

However, the integration of cloud technologies into safety-critical railway applications introduces a new set of challenges. Cloud environments are inherently dynamic and distributed, characterized by resource virtualization, multi-tenancy, and elastic scaling. These features, while beneficial, also introduce complexity and uncertainty in system behavior, particularly in terms of fault propagation, recovery mechanisms, and performance variability. Ensuring that cloud-based railway applications meet the same high standards of availability and reliability as traditional systems is therefore a non-trivial task.

Traditional modeling and analysis techniques, such as reliability block diagrams or fault tree analysis, often fall short in capturing the nuanced behavior of cloud-based architecture. These methods typically assume static system configurations and do not account for the concurrent, asynchronous, and stochastic nature of cloud operations. As a result, they may yield incomplete or misleading assessments of system dependability.

To address these limitations, researchers have increasingly turned to Petri nets - a formal modeling framework well-suited for representing concurrent, distributed, and event-driven systems. Petri nets provide a graphical and mathematical means of modeling system states, transitions, and interactions, making them particularly effective for analyzing complex behaviors such as failure propagation, redundancy, and recovery in cloud environments.

This research builds on this foundation by proposing an enhanced Petri net modeling approach that explicitly incorporates safety criticality into the analysis of cloud-based railway applications. Specifically, it compares a traditional non-colored Petri net model with a colored Petri net model that distinguishes between safety-critical and non-safety-critical components. By doing so, the study aims to provide more accurate and actionable insights into the availability and reliability of these systems.

The findings of this work have both theoretical and practical implications. They contribute to the growing body of knowledge on dependability modeling for cloud-based systems and offer guidance for railway operators and system designers seeking to ensure that digital innovations do not compromise the safety and reliability of critical infrastructure.

1.1 Literature Review

Petri nets have been extensively used in the literature for modeling and analyzing the availability and reliability of complex systems, including those in the railway domain. One of the early works in this area was by Schneeweiss [1], who proposed the use of Petri nets to model the availability of railway signaling systems, demonstrating how Petri net models could capture the dynamic behavior of the system and evaluate availability and reliability metrics.

Building on this foundation, several researchers have explored the application of Petri nets for availability and reliability analysis in various railway-related domains. For example, Zhang [2] and Di Febbraro [3] used Petri nets to model the availability of railway track circuits, considering factors such as component failures and maintenance activities.

In the context of cloud-based systems, Zhang et al. [2] presented a Petri net-based approach for modeling the availability of cloud computing infrastructures, capturing the dynamic behavior of cloud resources and evaluating the availability of cloud-based services. Similarly, Zimmermann et al. [4] analyzed the availability of a cloud architecture, primarily with the focus on disaster recovery and georedundancy, but ignored the importance of considering safety-critical architecture.

More recently, Zhou [5] proposed a colored Petri net model for availability analysis of cloud-based railway signaling systems, allowing for the representation of more detailed system characteristics, such as the different types of cloud resources and their interdependencies.

These studies have demonstrated the versatility and effectiveness of Petri net modeling for availability and reliability analysis in the railway domain, particularly in the context of cloud-based applications. The ability of Petri nets to capture the dynamic and concurrent nature of these systems, as well as their flexibility in representing various failure modes and recovery mechanisms, make them a valuable tool for researchers and practitioners.

1.2 Novelty

The research aims to close the gap in the existing literature by applying colored Petri net modeling techniques to specifically address the availability and reliability of the safety-critical components of cloud-based software in railway applications. This contrasts with previous studies that did not differentiate between safety-critical and non-safety-critical parts of the system.

By using colored Petri nets, it is possible to capture additional attributes and information related to the safety-critical nature of certain software components, allowing for a more detailed and accurate representation of the system's availability and reliability characteristics.

1.3 Objective

The primary objective of this research is to explore the possibility of integrating the safety criticality of software components into Petri net modeling for cloud-based railway applications. The aim is to quantify the differences in the availability and reliability analysis results between the traditional non-colored Petri net models and the more advanced colored Petri net models that can capture the safety-critical aspects of the system.

The objective of this research, then, is to explore how this additional level of detail and differentiation in the colored Petri net model affects the availability and reliability analysis results, compared to the non-colored Petri net model that does not make this distinction.

2 Petri Net Modeling Approach

2.1 Basic Modelling

Petri nets are a well-established modeling formalism that can be used to represent and analyze the availability and reliability of complex systems, including cloud-based railway applications. The basic Petri net model for availability modeling consists of the following key components as described in Table 1.

Places (P): The places in the Petri net represent the different states or conditions of the system. In the context of availability modeling, the places may represent the operational states of the system, such as "available," "unavailable," "under repair," and "in standby", which is depicted in Fig. 1 through an empty circle.

Transitions (T): The transitions in the Petri net represent the events or actions that cause the system to move from one state to another. These transitions may correspond to failures, repairs, switchovers, or other relevant system events, which is represented as either a black rectangle or an empty rectangle. Whereas the black rectangle indicates an immediate transition, and the empty rectangle operates with a delay.

Arcs (A): The arcs in the Petri net connect the places and transitions, indicating the flow of tokens (the dynamic elements in the net) and the dependencies between the different states and events.

Tokens (M): The tokens in the Petri net represent the current state of the system. The distribution of tokens across the places in the net reflects the system's status, such as the number of available components, the number of components under repair, or the number of standby components.

The basic Petri net model for availability modeling typically includes the following places:

- Available: Represents the state where the system or component is operational and available for use.
- Unavailable: Represents the state where the system or component is not operational and not available for use.

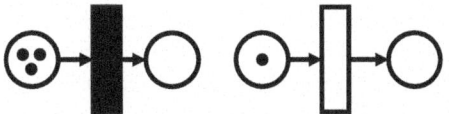

Fig. 1. Basic Petri Net Modelling symbols

- Under Repair: Represents the state where the system or component is undergoing repair or maintenance.
- Standby: Represents the state where the system or component is in a standby or backup mode, ready to be activated if needed.

The transitions in the basic Petri net model may include events such as:

- Failure: Transition from the "Available" state to the "Unavailable" state.
- Repair: Transition from the "Under Repair" state to the "Available" state.
- Switchover: Transition from the "Unavailable" state to the "Standby" state, or from the "Standby" state to the "Available" state.

By analyzing the behavior of the Petri net model, researchers can assess the availability and reliability characteristics of the cloud-based railway application, such as the steady-state availability, the mean time to failure, and the mean time to repair.

Modeling **Colored Petri Nets (CPNs)** involves extending traditional Petri nets by adding data, types, and more expressive capabilities to better represent complex systems - like cloud-based railway applications with safety-critical components.

Table 1. Core Components of a CPN

Component	Description
Places	Represent conditions or states. Each place can hold tokens of a specific data type (color set)
Transitions	Represent events or actions that may occur, changing the state of the system
Tokens	Carry data (colors). Unlike basic Petri nets, tokens are not indistinguishable
Arcs	Connect places and transitions, often with expressions that define how tokens are consumed or produced
Color Sets	Define the data types of tokens (e.g., INT, STRING, RECORD, PRODUCT)
Guards	Boolean expressions that must be true for a transition to fire

Modeling CPNs involves representing the dynamic behavior of a system through a structured network of places, transitions, and arcs, where tokens carry data values -referred to as "colors" - that encode relevant system attributes. Unlike traditional Petri nets, which treat all tokens as indistinguishable, CPNs allow tokens to represent complex data types, enabling a more expressive and compact model. The first step in constructing a CPN model is to define appropriate color sets, which specify the types of data that tokens can carry, such as component identifiers, operational states (e.g., UP, DOWN), or safety classifications (e.g., SAFETY_CRITICAL or NON_CRITICAL). These color sets form the foundation for modeling system heterogeneity and behavior.

This structure enables the modeling of concurrent processes, failure propagation, and recovery mechanisms in a way that is both rigorous and scalable. In the context of cloud-based railway applications, CPNs are particularly useful for distinguishing between safety-critical and non-safety-critical components, capturing their interactions, and analyzing their impact on overall system availability and reliability. Simulation tools such as CPN Tools can then be used to execute the model, collect performance metrics, and support decision-making in the design and maintenance of dependable systems.

2.2 Modelling Software TimeNet

A tool that has been utilized in several of the Petri net-based availability and reliability studies in the railway domain is the TimeNET modeling software. TimeNET is a powerful software package developed by the Center for Performance Evaluation and Design of Computer and Communication Systems (PEDC) at the Technische Universität Berlin [6].

TimeNET provides a comprehensive environment for the modeling, simulation, and analysis of stochastic Petri nets, including both non-colored and colored Petri net variants. The software supports a wide range of Petri net extensions, such as generalized stochastic Petri nets (GSPNs), deterministic and stochastic Petri nets (DSPNs), and fluid stochastic Petri nets (FSPNs), allowing researchers to select the most appropriate modeling formalism for their specific application.

One of the key features of TimeNET is its ability to perform transient and steady-state analysis of Petri net models, enabling the evaluation of availability, reliability, and other performance metrics. The software also offers advanced analysis techniques, such as sensitivity analysis and optimization, to help users gain deeper insights into the modeled systems.

Several of the studies referenced in the literature review, including the work by Schneeweiss [1] and Di Febbraro et al. [3], have utilized TimeNET as the modeling and analysis platform for their Petri net-based availability and reliability assessments in the railway domain. The versatility and robustness of the TimeNET software have made it a popular choice for researchers and practitioners working on complex, safety-critical systems like those found in the railway industry.

The availability of this specialized Petri net modeling tool has been instrumental in facilitating the adoption and application of Petri net-based techniques for availability and reliability analysis in the railway domain and beyond.

3   The Model

The proposed model in Fig. 2 represents a cloud computing architecture, focusing on the interaction between hardware layer, virtualization layer, and application layer. The model encompasses three distinct layers that capture the essential components of the cloud server infrastructure.

The foundational layer comprises physical machines (PM), representing the tangible computing infrastructure. Above this hardware layer, the architecture incorporates a virtualization layer, where software containers are implemented as virtual machines (VM), enabling efficient resource utilization and isolation. These containers serve as standardized, portable computing environments. The uppermost layer consists of service & safety applications, which can be dynamically loaded and executed within the virtual machines, representing the actual cloud services provided to end-users.

The Petri net formalization of this architecture defines places representing various resource states and availability across the three layers. Specifically, these include physical machine availability, VM states, and application deployment status. Transitions in the model capture the dynamic aspects of resource management, including allocation and deallocation processes, VM lifecycle management, and application deployment operations.

The token flow within this model represents the dynamic nature of cloud resource utilization, with tokens indicating available resources, active instances, and operational states across the architectural layers. This representation enables the analysis of resource utilization patterns, potential bottlenecks, and system performance characteristics.

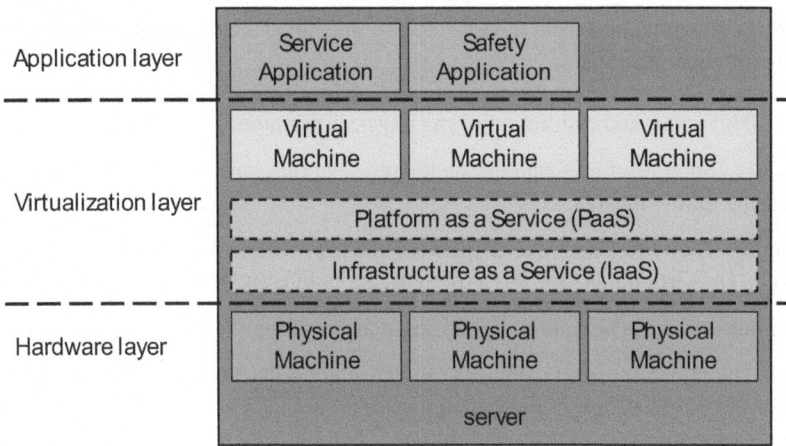

Fig. 2. The simplified model of cloud service hosting a Service Application and/or Safety Application

3.1 Modelling Input

Both the non-colored and colored Petri net models are built on the same underlying assumptions, such as:

- Same mean time to failure (MTTF) for the hardware components
- Same mean time to repair (MTTR) for the hardware components
- Same MTTF and MTTR for the software components

- Both models have 3 physical machines, with one machine serving as a backup for the software application
- The software application has a redundancy of 1, meaning there is one redundant instance running

With these common assumptions and parameters, the key difference between the two Petri net models is the explicit representation of the safety criticality of the software components in the colored Petri net model.

3.2 Traditional Non-colored Petri Net Model

The traditional non-colored Petri net model developed in this research, which is shown in Fig. 3, represents the availability and reliability of the physical machines that underpin the cloud-based railway application. This model captures the cycling of the physical machines through different states, including.

- idlePM: The physical machine is operational and available for use.
- failedPM: The physical machine has experienced a failure and is no longer available.

The transitions between these states are modeled using the following events:

- Failing: The transition from the Idle state to the Failed state, representing the failure of the physical machine.
- Repairing: The transition from the Failed state to the Idle state, representing the successful repair and restoration of the physical machine.

For the virtual machines running on the physical infrastructure, the Petri net model captures the following states:

- Running: The virtual machine is operational and providing its intended functionality.
- Failed: The virtual machine has experienced a failure and is no longer available.

The transitions between these states are modeled using the following events:

- Start: The transition from a non-operational state to the Running state, representing the successful initiation of the virtual machine.
- Failing (due to physical machine failure): The transition from the Running state to the Failed state, representing the failure of the virtual machine due to the failure of the underlying physical machine.
- Failing (standalone): The transition from the Running state to the Failed state, representing the standalone failure of the virtual machine, independent of the physical machine.

When a virtual machine fails, it releases the physical machine it was running on, which then transitions to the Repairing state to be restored to the Idle state.

3.3 Colored Petri Net Model

The key distinction in the colored Petri net model, which is shown in Fig. 4, is the representation of the virtual machines. Each token in the model contains additional information:

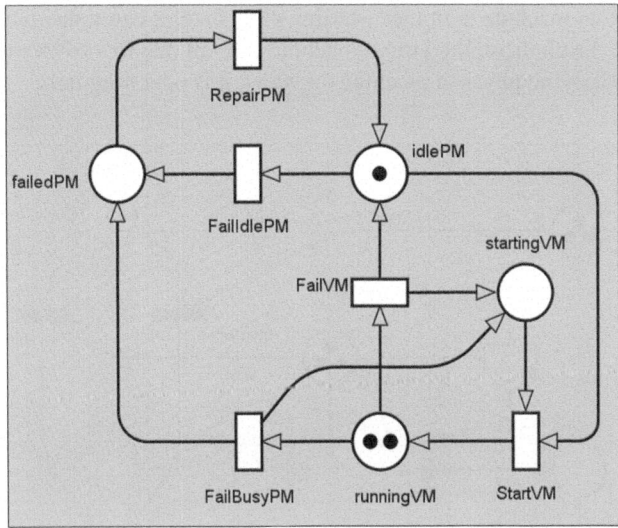

Fig. 3. The traditional non-colored Petri Net Model

- The physical machine on which the virtual machine is currently operating.
- Whether the virtual machine contains safety-related software or non-safety-related software.

Importantly, the colored Petri net model ensures that the two safety-critical software redundancies cannot be loaded onto the same physical machine. This is represented by the "Available PM without Safety VM" place, which gets flushed when a safety-related virtual machine is loaded.

Like the non-colored model, the colored Petri net model includes three physical machines, each with the following states:

RunningPM: The physical machine is operational and available for use.
FailedPM: The physical machine has experienced failure and is no longer available.

The transitions between these states are modeled using the following events:

- Failing: The transition from the "RunningPM" state to the "FailedPM" state, representing the failure of the physical machine.
- Repairing: The transition from the "FailedPM" state to the "RunningPM" state, representing the successful repair and restoration of the physical machine.

The virtual machines in the colored Petri net model start in the "UnassignedVM" state and can be loaded onto a physical machine if it is in the "RunningPM" state. The virtual machines represent either the safety-related or non-safety-related parts of the software application.

To capture the safety criticality, the model ensures that the two safety-related software redundancies cannot be loaded onto the same physical machine. This is represented by the "Available PM without Safety VM" place, which gets flushed when a safety-related virtual machine is loaded.

Once a virtual machine is in the "StartingVM" state, it can transition to the "Running VM" state. From there, the virtual machine can fail due to a software failure or be killed if the underlying physical machine on which it is operating fails.

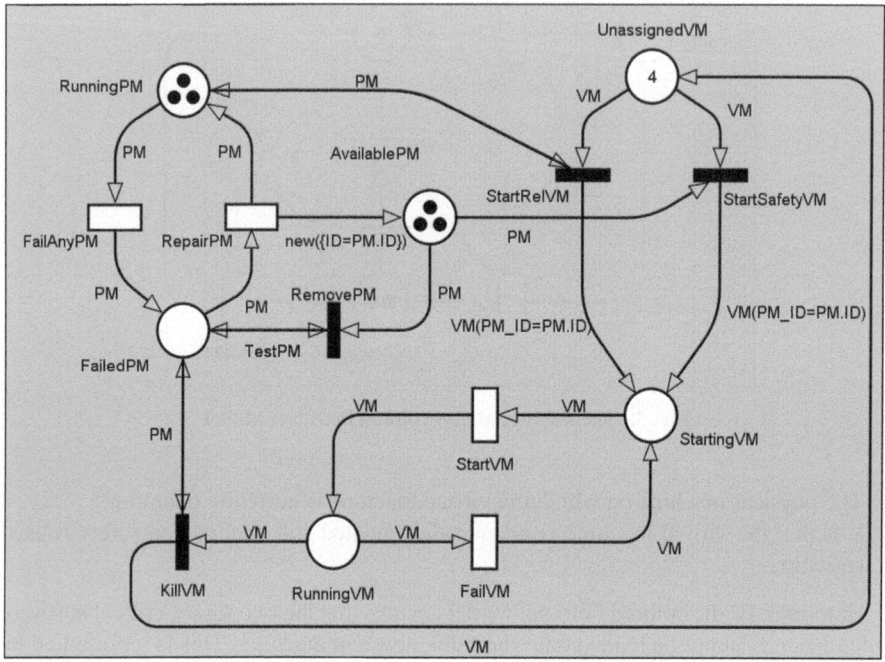

Fig. 4. The Colored Petri Net Model

3.4 Model Analysis and Evaluation

The results of the availability analysis using the two Petri net modeling approaches show that the availability metrics are in the same order of magnitude, around 10^{-6} (Table 2).

However, the non-colored Petri net model yields a slightly larger availability result, which can be considered a more optimistic assessment. In contrast, the colored Petri net model, which explicitly represents the safety criticality of the software components, shows a smaller availability metric. This difference can be attributed to the way the colored Petri net model enforces the separation of safety-critical software redundancies onto different physical machines. This prevents single points of failure for the safety-critical parts of the system. On the other hand, the non-colored Petri net model does not make this distinction, allowing non-safety-critical software components to potentially reside on the same physical hardware. This results in a more optimistic availability assessment.

The findings demonstrate that the colored Petri net model provides a more realistic and accurate representation of the availability characteristics of the cloud-based railway application, particularly for the safety-critical software components. This is a true

Table 2. Comparison of modelling results, between traditional non-colored Petri Net Model vs Colored Petri Net Model and the Colored Petri Net Model

Modelling Technique	Key Feature	Availability
Traditional non-colored Petri Net Model	No forced spread of VM with safety content, as it is not possible	0,99999979
Colored Petri Net Model	No forced spread of VM with safety content	0,99999979
Colored Petri Net Model	Forced spread of VM with safety content	0,99998799

reflection of the need to maintain strict separation and redundancy for safety-critical functions, which is not captured in the traditional non-colored Petri net approach. These results highlight the importance of integrating safety criticality into the modeling framework when assessing the availability and reliability of cloud-based railway applications, which is the key contribution of this research.

4   Conclusion

4.1   Limitations

The Petri net model presented in this paper provides valuable insights into cloud server behavior and resource management; however, it is essential to acknowledge its inherent limitations and underlying assumptions to ensure proper interpretation of the results.

The model operates under the assumption of homogeneous resources, where physical machines are considered to have uniform computing capabilities, and virtual machines maintain standardized resource configurations. This simplification, while necessary for model tractability, may not fully reflect the heterogeneous nature of real-world cloud infrastructures. Additionally, the model assumes perfect network connectivity between architectural layers and neglects communication delays, which could impact actual system performance.

Several architectural constraints limit the model's scope. First, complex load balancing mechanisms that are common in production environments are not explicitly represented. Second, while the model captures basic resource allocation patterns, dynamic scaling capabilities are represented in a simplified manner. Third, security considerations and their potential impact on resource availability and allocation strategies are not incorporated into the current model structure.

From a performance perspective, the model abstracts from certain real-world complexities. It does not account for gradual resource degradation over time or capture the granular performance variations that physical hardware might exhibit under different operational conditions. Furthermore, complex failure scenarios and their potential cascading effects across the system layers are not fully modeled.

These limitations affect the model's generalizability primarily in scenarios involving heterogeneous cloud environments, complex scaling requirements, or sophisticated failure recovery mechanisms. While the model provides valuable insights into fundamental system behaviors and resource utilization patterns, its applications to highly complex or specialized cloud deployments should consider these constraints during result interpretation.

4.2 Summary

The central insight of this study is the importance of integrating safety criticality into Petri net modeling for availability analysis of cloud-based railway applications. By comparing a traditional non-colored Petri net model with an advanced colored Petri net model, the results showed that while the availability metrics were in the same order of magnitude, around 10^{-6}, the non-colored model yielded slightly more optimistic availability results.

The key to this difference lies in the ability of the colored Petri net model to explicitly represent the safety criticality of the software components. This model enforces the separation of safety-critical software redundancies onto different physical machines, preventing single points of failure. In contrast, the non-colored model allows for the mixing of safety-critical and non-safety-critical components on the same hardware, leading to a more optimistic assessment of availability.

The comparative analysis of resource consumption between Colored Petri Nets (CPNs) and non-colored Petri Nets reveals significant differences in computational complexity and resource requirements. The fundamental distinction lies in the state space complexity, where CPNs exhibit exponentially larger state spaces due to their token differentiation through color attributes, whereas non-colored Petri Nets operate with indistinguishable tokens, resulting in a more manageable state space.

From a computational perspective, CPNs demand substantially higher resources for analysis and verification processes. This increased demand stems from the necessity to evaluate color functions, verify guard conditions, and calculate arc expressions – operations that are absent in non-colored Petri Nets. The state explosion problem, inherent in both types of nets, is particularly pronounced in CPNs due to the multiplicative effect of color combinations on the state space.

The enhanced modeling power and expressiveness of CPNs come at the cost of increased computational overhead in terms of both memory usage and processing requirements. While non-colored Petri Nets primarily store and process token counts, CPNs must maintain and manipulate complex data structures to handle color-related information, binding elements, and associated functions. This trade-off between modeling capability and computational efficiency represents a crucial consideration in the selection and application of Petri Net variants for specific modeling scenarios.

This research contribution represents an advancement in Petri net modeling, as it demonstrates the necessity of considering safety criticality for realistic and reliable availability analysis of cloud-based railway systems. The insights have important practical implications for the design, implementation, and maintenance of these critical infrastructures to meet stringent safety and reliability requirements.

By highlighting the differences between the non-colored and colored Petri net modeling approaches, the study underscores the value of integrating safety criticality into the assessment of cloud-based railway applications, which is a key contribution to the field.

Building upon the insights gained from the comparative analysis of non-colored and colored Petri net modeling approaches, there are several promising avenues for future research. One direction could involve expanding the colored Petri net model to incorporate additional details, such as the degradation of physical and virtual machines over time, different failure modes and their impacts, as well as maintenance strategies and their effects on reliability. Conducting sensitivity analyses to identify the most critical parameters influencing the availability of safety-critical components would also provide valuable guidance for system design and operation.

Validating the Petri net models against real-world data or simulation results and benchmarking the performance of the colored model against other techniques, would further strengthen the credibility and demonstrate the advantages of the proposed modeling approach. Exploring the applicability of the colored Petri net framework to other safety-critical domains beyond the railway industry could lead to cross-domain knowledge transfer and adaptability of the modeling methodology.

Finally, integrating the colored Petri net model into decision support systems for cloud-based railway applications could enable more informed design decisions, maintenance strategies, and resource allocation, leveraging the availability and reliability insights generated by the model. Pursuing these future research directions would build upon the foundational work presented in this study, further enhancing the understanding and practical applications of safety criticality in cloud-based railway systems.

4.3 Future Work

While the present study establishes a foundational understanding of cloud server behavior through Petri net modeling, several promising research directions warrant further investigation. This section outlines key areas for future research, focusing particularly on sensitivity analysis extensions and comprehensive dynamic behavior investigations.

The extension of sensitivity analysis presents significant research potential. Future work should investigate multi-parameter interactions and their combined effects on system performance, moving beyond single-parameter variations. The identification of critical threshold values that trigger significant behavioral changes could provide valuable insights for system design and optimization. Additionally, the application of advanced statistical sampling methods could enhance the robustness of sensitivity metrics, particularly in the context of cloud server architectures. Such analysis could reveal previously unidentified non-linear relationships between system parameters, contributing to a more nuanced understanding of system behavior.

Dynamic behavior analysis represents another crucial area for future research. The development of time-dependent workload profiles based on real-world cloud usage patterns would enhance the model's practical applicability. Investigation of complex failure scenarios and their propagation through system layers could improve understanding of system resilience. Furthermore, analyzing temporary resource bottlenecks and their impact on service delivery would provide valuable insights for operational optimization. The examination of system recovery mechanisms under various disturbance patterns, coupled with modeling of long-term resource degradation effects, could significantly contribute to the field's knowledge base.

The integration of these analytical approaches presents an opportunity for comprehensive system optimization. Future research should focus on developing adaptive parameter adjustment strategies based on sensitivity findings, potentially leading to more robust design guidelines for cloud server architectures. The development of predictive models for dynamic system behavior could enhance operational efficiency, while investigation of trade-offs between system stability and performance optimization could inform practical implementation strategies.

These research directions not only promise to advance theoretical understanding but also hold significant potential for practical applications in cloud computing infrastructure design and management. The proposed extensions would contribute to a more comprehensive framework for analyzing and optimizing cloud server architectures, ultimately leading to more reliable and efficient cloud computing systems.

Acknowledgments. We thank our colleagues from the RAMS Department for their valuable support and collaboration.

Disclosure of Interests. The authors declare that there are no financial or personal relationships that could be perceived to have influenced the work reported in this paper.

References

1. Schneeweiss, W.: Petri Nets for Reliability Modeling. LiLoLe Hagen (1999)
2. Zhang, D., Hu, H., Roberts, C.: Rail maintenance analysis using Petri nets. In: Structure and Infrastructure Engineering **13**(6), 783–793 (2016)
3. Di Febbraro, A., Giglio, D., Sacco, N.: On analyzing the vulnerabilities of a railway network with Petri nets. Transportation Research Procedia **27**, 553–560 (2017)
4. Zimmermann, A., Hotz, T., Hädicke, V., Friebe, M.: Analysis of Safety-Critical Cloud Architectures with Multi-Trajectory Simulation (2022)
5. Zhou, W., Dague, P., Liu, L., Ye, L., Zaidi, F.: A coloured petri nets based attack tolerance framework. In: 27th Asia-Pacific Software Engineering Conference (APSEC), Singapore, pp. 159–168 (2020)
6. Zimmermann, A.: TimeNET 4.4: a software toolkit for the performance evaluation of stochastic petri nets. In: Informatik-Berichte, Technical University of Ilmenau (2017)

MBSA Model-Exchange and Its Challenges

Tony Ghueldre[1]([⊠]) [iD], Wilkinson Joas[1,2] [iD], Julien Vidalie[1,3] [iD],
Xavier De Bossoreille[1,3] [iD], and Sébastien Duthoit[4] [iD]

[1] IRT Saint Exupéry, 31400 Toulouse, France
tony.ghueldre@irt-saintexupery.com,
wilkinson.joas2@safrangroup.com, {julien.vidalie,
xavier.de-bossoreille}@airbus.com
[2] Safran Aircraft Engines Villaroche, 77550 Moissy Cramayel, France
[3] Airbus Protect, 31700 Blagnac, France
[4] LGM, 100 Rue de Lannoy, 59650 Villeneuve d'Ascq, France
Sebastien.DUTHOIT@lgm.eu

Abstract. Safety studies are carried out on increasingly complex systems, pushing traditional methods like Fault Tree Analysis (FTA) to their limits. The Model-Based Safety Analysis (MBSA) is a method which brings a solution to those difficulties, also allowing a better representation of a complex system's dysfunctional behavior.

As of now, MBSA users embed a subsystem's behavior to a higher level system, enabling a more realistic model. However, sharing MBSA models in the extended enterprise context is not currently a widespread technique due to unsolved risks. This paper addresses four of these risks.

First, by sharing their model, a supplier risks to expose their architecture to a third party. A masking process shall be applied to a shared model, to protect the intellectual property.

Second, merging sub-models involves risks from a size point of view: if the model is too large it can be difficult to compute. Suppliers need to simplify large models without losing essential information.

Third, sharing a model without a proper documentation involves a risk of losing traceability. This can be addressed through effective communication throughout the V-cycle project lifecycle.

Finally, the usual MBSA tools are missing some aspects to mitigate the risks of model sharing and integration. Hence the need to update some of their functionalities.

By exploring solutions to these risks, this research aims to facilitate the exchange of MBSA models, ultimately enhancing collaboration and efficiency in the development of complex systems.

Keywords: MBSA · Model Exchange · Safety · RAMS · IP Protection · Simplification · Masking

P. Katsaros (Ed.): IMBSA 2025, LNCS 15755, pp. 285–298, 2026.
https://doi.org/10.1007/978-3-032-05073-1_19

1 Introduction

In complex systems development projects, multiple stakeholders, including suppliers and a final integrator, often collaborate to design, build, and deliver a system that meets stringent safety requirements. The collaboration among those stakeholders would benefit from efficient model-exchange to ensure consistent and accurate safety assessments, and ultimately, the overall safety of the system. Provided that intellectual property (IP) is protected, stakeholders would have a common reference—the model itself—to base their discussions upon. The final model could integrate all contributions to accurately simulate the dysfunctional system's behavior.

In a complex system, the final product can be based on several different units. Not all those units are meant to be produced by the final integrator, and it is common to have several different suppliers providing their units or subsystems, as represented in the figure Fig. 1. As a result, when building a MBSA model of the system, some models can be produced by other companies before being integrated in the final model. Note that it can be the same result in case suppliers are entities of the same company.

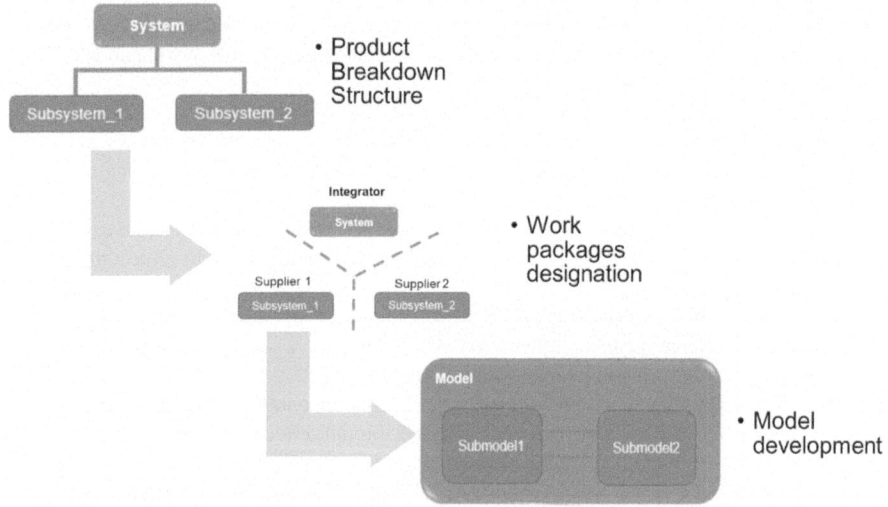

Fig. 1. Representation of the model development at system level

Due to the notable capability of MBSA to depict complexity in systems, we believe that it is a great candidate for safety assessment in the extended enterprise context. In particular, its native compatibility with libraries gives a straightforward path to exchange-models integration. Furthermore, with the addition of MBSA to the ARP4761 rev A [1], we firmly believe that the adoption of MBSA will rise steadily in the near future.

In this paper, we evaluate the challenges to MBSA model-exchange and how they could be tackled in the near future. We classify these challenges into three types:

- IP protection: As MBSA models contain an important amount of information about the system's architecture and its behavior, exchange models should provide ways to protect proprietary information.
- Traceability: As the MBSA models are to be used for certification, the exchange model has to be properly documented in order to allow for validation of the model. It means that the list of documents supplied to the integrator shall be enough to be compliant with the authorities, without compromising the supplier's IP.
- Readability/Computability: As the models carry the complexity of the systems, their combination can become overwhelming for the engineer or even for the tool, as computation times increase exponentially with the number of states in the system. A MBSA model-exchange methodology should ensure that the model is still readable for users and that the computation times do not explode to a point where the model is no longer usable.

We have proposed the concepts of masking and simplification in [6] as tools to address these challenges, in this paper we propose techniques to operate these concepts, as well as other approaches.

To present these challenges and potential answers, the remainder of this paper is organized as follows:

Section 2 presents related works, giving context for the challenges. Section 3 gives an overview of each challenge and the authors' contribution to addressing them. Section 4 discusses the explored methodologies, their results and the perspectives of this work.

2 Related Works

In recent years, the use of model-based methodologies to overcome the complications related to complexity has become more and more popular. As a safety pendant to Model-Based Systems Engineering (MBSE) [4], Model-Based Safety Analysis (MBSA) proposes to use formal languages dedicated to safety.

These models explicitly represent the architecture through components and the flows between them. They represent the dysfunctional behavior at the component level and compute the global behavior of the system through interactions between the components.

One of the most popular approaches to MBSA, the AltaRica language, was created by LaBRI in the nineties. AltaRica Data-flow, the second version of the language emerged with the development of MBSA tools[1]. However, implementing new aspects can be complex, so some projects were developed to demonstrate the real benefits of those methods[2].

2.1 Current Safety Practice

In the vast majority of safety analyses, the fault tree methodology is more commonly used than approaches like MBSA because of its well-established framework, fast implementation, and ability to systematically represent failures' logic, making it more practical for regulatory compliance and risk assessment across various industries.

---

[1] https://cordis.europa.eu/project/id/G4RD-CT-2000-00361.

[2] https://cordis.europa.eu/project/id/501848.

As part of the CoSMoS project, we developed a comprehensive questionnaire to gather insights into the main types of Reliability, Availability, Maintainability, and Safety (RAMS) models that are typically provided by suppliers and received by customers. This questionnaire was sent to the project members, but also to various companies in industries like aeronautics, space, etc. The results showed that the vast majority of FTA are read-only. Also, the exchange of FTA models between different software tools is highly limited due to the lack of a standardized format, proprietary data structures, and varying implementations of logical gates and failure modeling, making interoperability a significant challenge in safety analysis, even after the creation of OpenPSA [5].

2.2 Current Model-Exchange Practice

Model-exchange is a concern which is not restricted to the RAMS field. System Engineering has worked on data exchange, resulting in the ISO 10303[3] as well as on model-exchange. Different approaches were developed, linked to different contexts.

Co-simulation methods have emerged to address the need of coupling different models, potentially developed on different tools, with different languages. More precisely, the aim of co-simulation is to link the simulations of these models. This enables linking different engineering fields e.g. electrical, mechanical, thermic… Solutions like the FMI standard[4] inherently address the context of extended enterprise by allowing the concepts of black boxes and grey boxes, with grey boxes encompassing several different levels of readability. This approach addresses the topics of Intellectual Property and of Readability/Computability.

Model-to-model transformation consists in establishing dictionaries of correlations between types of objects in different languages/tools. One such example is the work from the Object Management Group. An application is the tool TeePee from IRT Saint Exupery. This approach addresses the topics of Traceability and Readability.

2.3 Model Exchange and IP Protection Practices in the Field of Model-Driven Engineering

Given its proximity to MBSA, it is pertinent to examine how the field of Model-Driven Engineering (MDE) has addressed the challenges associated with model sharing and intellectual property protection. MDE is a software development approach that focuses on creating and using models to simplify the design, development, and maintenance of complex systems software.

[7] reviews the state of the art in model composition within MDE, highlighting the importance of model composition for managing complexity and improving reusability in software development. Since its emergence, Software Engineering (SE) aims to alleviate complexity and improve reusability. Dijkstra [10] and Parnas [11] suggested the principle to reduce the ever-growing complexity of systems by dividing them into units of behavior or units of function.

---

[3] https://www.iso.org/standard/83105.html.

[4] https://fmi-standard.org/

Recent works in MDE have focused on IP protection. [9] proposes a comprehensive framework for protecting intellectual property (IP) in model-driven co-engineering processes by integrating advanced access-control, cryptography, and digital rights management (DRM) techniques. It aims to ensure that only necessary information is shared among collaborators while providing mechanisms to handle potential IP leaks. The Deltachain approach [8] introduces a method for securely sharing and collaboratively developing models by using encrypted deltas, ensuring intellectual property protection while allowing incremental updates. This system enables organizations to freely exchange model changes on untrusted hardware, maintaining a single source of truth without compromising sensitive information.

3 Considered Solution

3.1 IP Protection

To address the challenge of IP protection, we investigated the masking process on MBSA models. In the context of MBSA, masking refers to the practice of concealing certain details or aspects of a model to protect intellectual property, without affecting the properties of the model.

Masking Process
The masking process is designed to enable the sharing MBSA models between companies, without compromising the IP protection of the supplier. By applying masking to their model, the model developer could select which types of information they want to provide, and which types they would prefer to hide.

An example of information to remain hidden for IP reasons is the contingency plan for system malfunction: exposing this in a MBSA model, along with the "standard" documentation delivered, would cause a breach in the IP protection of the supplier. By masking a selection of events in their MBSA model, this challenge could be overcome. The model for exchange will be a grey box.

Another solution would be to use complete black boxes for MBSA models exchanged, meaning the customer would only receive a "brick" to integrate to their model, which would provide the necessary information for the customer to be able to run simulations and calculations.

Both methods can be developed, and our project is meant to implement those solutions in two MBSA tools. But before applying one masking method at the supplier level, it will be important to agree with the customer upon whether the model they will receive will match their requirements: it would be unfortunate to mask a mandatory aspect of a model.

The following figures represent examples of masking, based on [2]. The first figure represents the initial model (Fig. 2):

The second figure represent the initial model as a grey box (Fig. 3):

The last figure represents the initial model as a black box (Fig. 4):

Transition Towards Simplification
Currently, the closest implementation to masking is found in Cecilia Workshop version

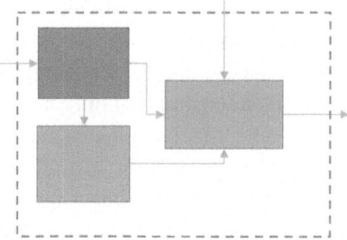

Fig. 2. A white box MBSA model

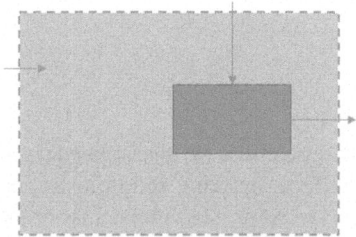

Fig. 3. A grey box MBSA model

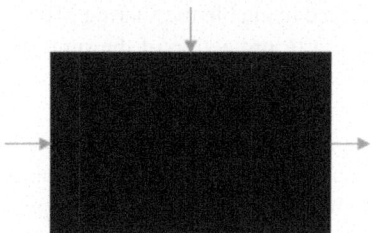

Fig. 4. A black box MBSA model

6.2.3, through the anonymization process, which randomizes the necessary model's features (events, names, etc.) and hides the rest (pictures, comments, etc.). For the most tenacious modelers it would also be possible to mask some model's features by hand in other tools, but automation of this process is not available.

Even though a model does not contain anything to be hidden for IP Protection, a customer could require it to be limited to a certain level of details while providing an exhaustive amount of information. In this case, a simplified model could address this need.

3.2 Traceability

In the scope of the CoSMoS project, traceability between customers and suppliers shall be managed within an extended enterprise context. The types of documentation identified to manage compliance and traceability can be classified into three categories:

Supplier-oriented documentation to define the requirements for the supplier from the customer's point of view. The internal documentation at supplier level to manage the correct description of the model-based approach. The customer-oriented documentation to describe the model and demonstrate the achievement of requirements.

Supplier-Oriented Documentation.
The supplier-oriented documentation describes all the requirements for which the supplier shall demonstrate compliance with RAMS performances requirements and model integration specifications. For RAMS performances, feared events, cut-set order requirement and common modes shall be integrated in the documentation. If specific observers are requested for simulation at integration level, they shall be specified and described. The customer shall describe all the interfaces and their types to easily allow the future integration. The customer shall also specify if there are special syntax needs and a level of abstraction to ensure the correct level of detail and optimize simulation.

Internal Documentation
The internal documentation shall describe the model from a supplier's perspective. Each block shall then have an overall description, the inputs and the outputs associated, the assumptions, the references to other documents used (e.g. Failure Modes and Effects Analysis), the different characteristics of the model, including flows, states, transitions and observers. All this information ensures that it is traced and up to date. The main goal of the documentation is to allow the correct understanding of the construction, the failure management and propagation, inputs/outputs and reconfigurations. An example approach is detailed in [3]. The generated documentation will be used to generate the customer-oriented documentation.

Customer-Oriented Documentation
The customer-oriented documentation describes the model but is tailored for an external use, ensuring that the customer receives all necessary information to understand and utilize the MBSA model effectively. It includes the presentation of the model built, its use, and perimeter. The documentation shall:

- Include a demonstration of compliance with the supplier-oriented documentation,
- Detail the results obtained, focusing on compliance with the requirements,
- Provide detailed explanations for cut sets and the critical sequences.

The model details are presented with adequate simplification and/or masking restrictions applied in order to easily allow for the integration use and the simulation of the sub-system model into the overall system. Assumptions that are dimensioning the results must be available to the customer, ensuring transparency and traceability. In the scope of the CoSMoS project, a compliance matrix has been defined to propose the compliancy checks of the document with regards to the supplier-oriented documentation requirements.

3.3 Simplification

In order to improve the integration operation in case of MBSA model-exchange, a well-defined simplification process has to be put in place, to enhance calculation while providing the necessary level of detail.

In MBSA, simplification refers to the process of reducing the complexity of a model to enhance its clarity. Information is usually lost during the process, so a conservative approach shall be applied to avoid any major alteration.

Model Merging
The easiest simplification process would be to gather several bricks into one. However, to keep the traceability, the probabilities of the final output states have to be identical and the cutsets or sequences leading to each final output state have to be kept, at least in a deliverable document for justification.

The following figure represents a simplification process merging three bricks into one (Fig. 5):

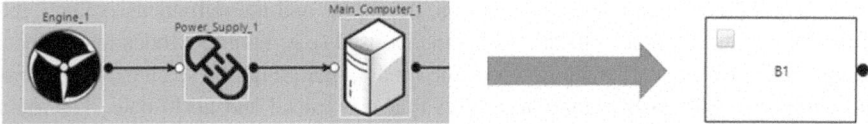

Fig. 5. A simplification of 3 bricks into only one

In order to apply the simplification process in a proper way, the probabilities associated to the state machine of the final brick were based on the truth table of each piece of equipment of the original model, as shown on Fig. 6 and Fig. 7:

Engine bloc		
State	**Output**	**Probability**
nominal	nominal	9,9988E-01
failed	failed	1,23E-04

Power supply bloc			
Input	**State**	**Output**	**Probability**
nominal	nominal	power	9,992E-01
failed	failed	noPower	7,943E-08
nominal	failed	noPower	6,458E-04
failed	nominal	noPower	1,230E-04

Fig. 6. Engine brick truth table (left) and power supply brick truth table (right)

The next figure represents the truth table of the simplified model, which can be retrieved by performing a summary of Fig. 7:

Hence the simplified model has 3 states, each one with its associated probability. As a conclusion, both models have the same quantitative results (Fig. 8).

However, the qualitative results are missing only with truth tables. The events leading to the transition from nominal state to lost state in the simplified brick will have to be listed, at least in a deliverable document for justification, as:

- Event 1: Engine bloc state = failed;

Main computer bloc			
Input	State	Output	Probability
power	nominal	nominal_data	9,988E-01
noPower	nominal	no_data	7,689E-04
power	lost	no_data	3,629E-04
noPower	lost	no_data	2,790E-07
power	erroneous	erroneous_data	4,270E-05
noPower	erroneous	no_data	3,283E-08

Fig. 7. Computer brick truth table

Main bloc simplified		
State	Output	Probability
nominal	nominal_data	9,988E-01
lost	no_data	1,132E-03
erroneous	erroneous_data	4,270E-05

Fig. 8. Simplified brick truth table

- Event 2: Power supply block state = failed;
- Event 3: main computer block state = lost.

The same list has to be performed for each transition of the simplified model. In the presented case, we treated the transition from nominal state to lost state, but the transition from nominal state to erroneous state has to be realized.

This list of events has to be performed in parallel to the truth tables. This way the traceability is maintained.

Model Flattening

The purpose of model flattening is to enhance the calculation time of the model, by reducing the number of calculations the tool has to perform. It can be performed by reducing the number of assertions and/or by reducing the number of events within the model.

The following figure presents an example of reduction of the number of assertions (Fig. 9):

On the left side, the original model contains at its top level an AND3 gate with 3 identical bricks as inputs, named "Assembly". "Assembly" contains 11 simple bricks named "SimpleBrick" with identical Boolean states. The output of each "SimpleBrick" sends the Boolean state of its parent. The "7oo11" brick is a voter sending False if at least 7 simple bricks have a False output. So, in the top level, the output "o1" is True if each "Assembly" brick contains a maximum of 6 "SimpleBrick" failed, otherwise it is False.

On the right side, the bricks called "Simplified Assembly" are simplified version of the former "Assembly" bricks, applying the reduction of number of assertions. "Simplified Assembly" brick contains 11 Boolean states, its output is False when at least 7 of

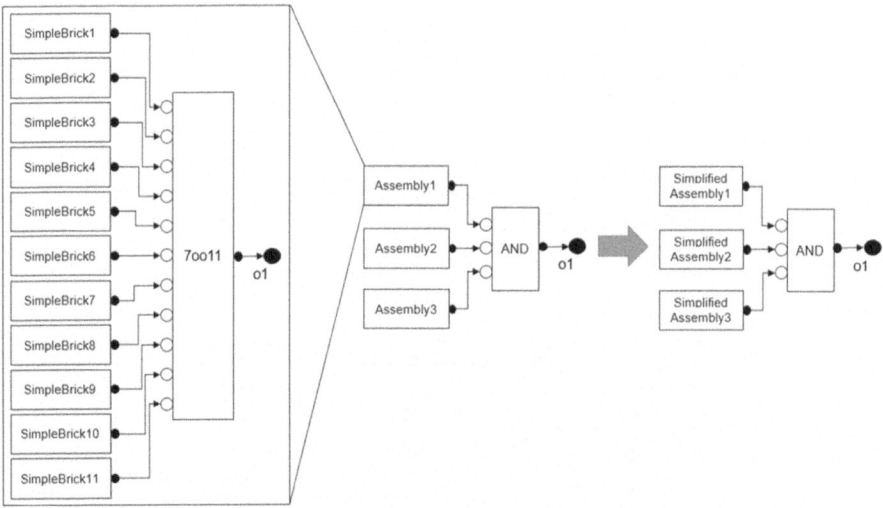

Fig. 9. Reduction of the number of assertions

those states are False. The AND3 gate and its "o1" output has the same behavior as the original model.

The following table presents the effect in terms of calculation time of the reduction of assertions with 2 to 5 "Assembly" / "Simplified Assembly" bricks:

Note: the number of redundancies is the number of "Assembly" / "Simplified Assembly" bricks. It also implies that the AND gate number of inputs is adapted to the number of redundancies (Table 1).

Table 1. Calculation improvements using simplification process

Redundancies	Calculation time on a complete model		Calculation time on a simplified model	
	Cecilia	SimfiaNeo	Cecilia	SimfiaNeo
2	-	3s	-	2s
3	2s	3min9s	2s	1min30s
4	22s	26min38s	17s	11min49s
5	1min52	2h16min	1min26	1h5min

The other type of simplification is performed by reducing the number of events in the model's state machine, as shown on the following figure (Fig. 10):

In the previous figure, the state machine from the left side represents a satellite payload made of 3 identical beams. Its state machine which goes from 0 beam failed (nominal) to 3 beams failed. The states "1 beam failed" can be reached from nominal

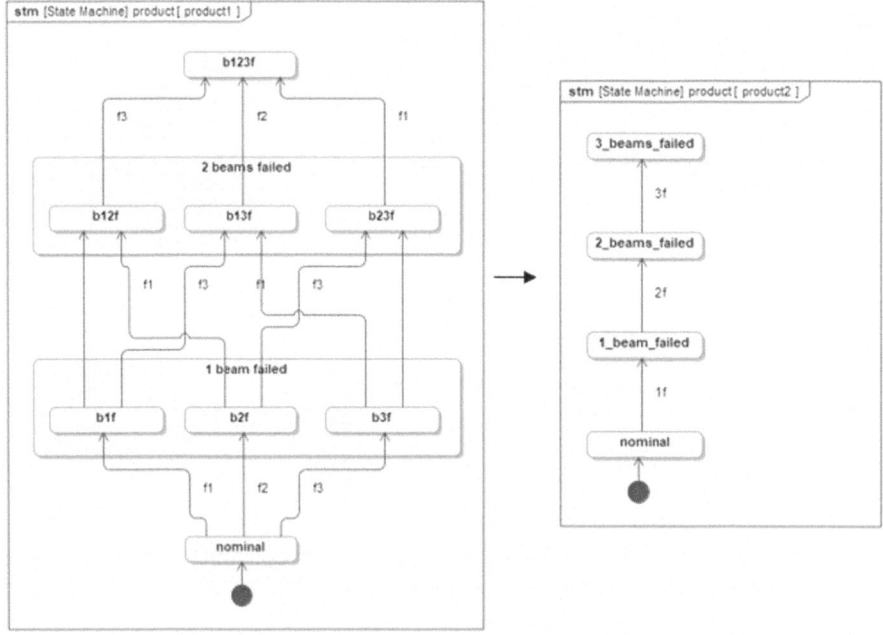

Fig. 10. Reduction of the number of events

state by one beam out of 3 being failed, and "2 beams failed" can be reached from "1 beam failed" by 1 beam out of the remaining 2 being failed.

In the end, the state machine can be simplified by gathering the identical events leading to one state, providing the state machine on the right side.

Once again, the model has to be built correctly in order to keep the traceability for both qualitative and quantitative aspects.

Cutsets Merging

This simplification process is based on the cutsets provided by a MBSA model. The simplified model is built by combining the cutsets of each failure scenario identified in the original model. Each failure scenario results in a state of the simplified model. The failures leading to each state are gathered by order.

The following example represents, as a simplified model, the failure scenario "State = failed" of the original model, merging all the failures based on their order. Note that the intermediate states are mandatory to keep the same order of failures between the two models (Fig. 11).

Without any complementary data, the model is a grey box. But the traceability can be required, leading to having the list of failures of the original model in the final model, along with their associated probabilities. It can be performed as detailed below:

- For the quantitative aspect: the cutsets' probabilities are summed into a single order N probability, which will be evenly distributed between all transitions.

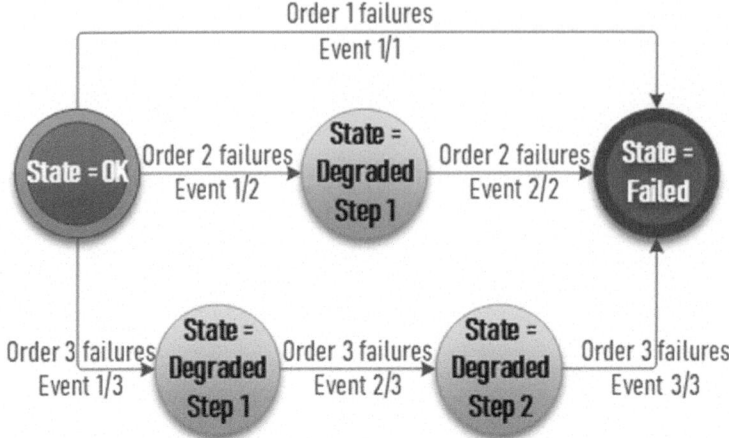

Fig. 11. Cutsets merging

- For the qualitative aspect: the list of failures from the original model is to be kept in the final model, at least in a deliverable document for justification.

Example from the previous figure:

Order 1 failures contains the following events: Engine_1.fail_stop, Engine_2.fail_stop, Power_supply_1.failure, Main_computer_1.failure, etc.

4 Conclusion

As the adoption of MBSA is acknowledged by the authorities through the revision A of the ARP 4761 [1], we aim to tackle the challenges of MBSA model sharing in an extended enterprise context.

We established three main challenges.

The first challenge is IP protection: Proprietary information from suppliers contained in the MBSA model shall be protected. In order to operate IP protection, we propose the concept of masking, which aims at hiding information from the user without modifying the model seen by the MBSA tool, i.e. with no impact on computations. In this paper we proposed some solutions for IP protection such as grey/black boxes, however a major challenge in the choice of the technological solution is interoperability. This is a key problematic of the CoSMoS project, which will be addressed in future work.

The second challenge is Traceability: Models need to be properly documented in order to make them simultaneously easy to understand and to justify their compliance with the system and authorities' requirements. We propose that there should be three levels of documentation for exchange models: supplier-oriented documentation, internal documentation, and customer-oriented documentation. Of course, this work now requires to further investigate the exact granularity that is required in this documentation. In parallel, we shall investigate how this documentation process could integrate seamlessly into the V-Cycle in order to allow proper validation and verification of both the models, and the system's conformity with safety requirements.

The third challenge is Readability/Computability: The integrator's model is a concatenation of multiple models. As this can result in a huge model composed of hundreds of blocks, it can make it difficult to understand. It can also make it nearly impossible to compute safety indicators, as the complexity of computations explodes with the number of states in the model. We believe that this challenge can be addressed through simplification, which encompasses techniques that reduce the complexity and size of the model, while maintaining a controlled impact on the results. In this paper, we presented the use of model merging, flattening, and cutsets merging for simplification. Note that we presently demonstrate the use of the latter technique with cutsets, i.e. in static models, however we believe that further work will show that it can be extended to sequences.

In future works the CoSMoS project will consider other scientific locks regarding the topic of MBSA model-exchange. In particular the synergy between FTA and MBSA will be addressed, in order to make it possible to import an artifact in a MBSA model that represents a FTA as part of the architecture. As MBSA and the CoSMoS project not only consider safety, but also availability, which means that in further work, the techniques we present in this paper will also have to be validated, and/or adapted, for a use in availability studies.

Acknowledgments. This work was conducted within the CoSMoS (Collaborative Safety (&RAMT) Modeling Studies) from IRT Saint Exupéry and would not have been possible without its funding. Therefore the authors would like to thank the project and its academic and industrial partners (ONERA, DGA TA, Airbus Protect, LGM, SATODEV, Naval Group, and Safran).

References

1. ARP4761A: Guidelines for Conducting the Safety Assessment Process on Civil Aircraft, Systems, and Equipment. SAE International (2023)
2. Amara, F., Agbossou, K., Cardenas, A., Dubé, Y., Kelouwani, S.: Comparison and simulation of building thermal models for effective energy management. In: Smart Grid and Renewable Energy, **06**, pp. 95–112 (2015). https://doi.org/10.4236/sgre.2015.64009
3. Berthier, S., Champion, S., Herpe, N., Lukas, T., Pelloquin, G.: Support methodology for the Model Based Safety Assessment (MBSA) realization (hal-05016294)
4. ISO/IEC/IEEE 24641:2023: Systems and Software engineering — Methods and tools for model-based systems and software engineering
5. Epstein, S., Rauzy, A.: Open-PSA Model Exchange Format. Version 2.0d (2008)
6. Ghueldre, T., Joas, W., Vidalie, J., De Bossoreille, X., ip protection using simplification and masking for model-based safety analysis (MBSA) model exchange. In ESREL-SRA-E (2025)
7. Abouzahra, A., Sabraoui, A., Afdel, K.: Model composition in model driven engineering: a systematic literature review. Inf. Softw. Technol. **125**, 106316 (2020)
8. Weber, T., Weber, S.: Model everything but with intellectual property protection-the deltachain approach. In Proceedings of the ACM/IEEE 27th International Conference on Model Driven Engineering Languages and Systems, pp. 49–56 (2024)
9. Martínez, S., Gerard, S., Cabot, J.: On the need for intellectual property protection in model-driven co-engineering processes. In Enterprise, Business-Process and Information Systems Modeling: 20th International Conference, BPMDS 2019, 24th International Conference, EMMSAD 2019, Held at CAiSE 2019, Rome, Italy, June 3–4, 2019, Proceedings 20, pp. 169–177 (2019). Springer International Publishing

10. Dijkstra, E.W.: A Discipline of Programming, Prentice Hall PTR, 1976 ISBN: 978–0132158718
11. Parnas, D.L.: On the criteria to be used in decomposing systems into modules. Commun. ACMmmun. ACM. **15**(12), 1053–1058 (1972). https://doi.org/10.1145/361598.361623

ACEditor: A Modeling Tool for Specifying and Synthesizing Executable Assurance Cases from Fault Trees

Luis Nascimento[1], André L. de Oliveira[1]([✉]) [iD], Regina Villela[1] [iD], Hiago Fonseca[1],
Kalinka Castelo Branco[2] [iD], Ran Wei[3] [iD], Richard Hawkins[4] [iD], and Tim Kelly[1,2,3,4] [iD]

[1] Universidade Federal de Juiz de Fora, Juiz de Fora, Brasil
{andre.oliveira,regina.braga}@ufjf.br
[2] University of São Paulo, São Carlos, Brasil
kalinka@icmc.usp.br
[3] University of Cambridge, Cambridge, UK
rw741@cam.ac.uk
[4] The University of York, York, UK
richard.hawkins@york.ac.uk

Abstract. Modern cyber-physical systems in the automotive and other critical domains demand the justification and demonstration they are safe and their components reliable. Assurance cases provide a means for justifying and assessing confidence in system dependability properties with references to design, safety, security, and reliability artifacts. Fault Tree Analysis (FTA) is one of the most popular safety analysis techniques, which is an integral part of Model-Based Safety Assessment.. However, the open and adaptive nature of autonomous systems, demands a paradigm shift from design-time to runtime system assurance. Although the Structured Assurance Case Metamodel (SACM) standard, its visual notation, and patterns extensions provide the foundations for runtime system assurance, enabling traceability between assurance cases and external artifacts, such as fault tree models, which are part of Executable Digital Dependability Identities (EDDIs) of cyber-physical system components, still remains a challenge. In this paper, we introduce ACEditor, a tool for specifying SACM assurance case patterns with traceability to external artifacts, which are part of a component EDDI, as a step towards runtime assurance demonstration.

Keywords: Cyber-physical systems · Model-based system assurance ·
Assurance cases · Fault tree analysis

1 Introduction

The presence of contemporary computer systems in domains such as healthcare, energy production, manufacturing, and transportation, e.g., autonomous railway, aerospace, and automotive systems equipped with sensors and mechanisms that control the vehicle's behavior, make them essential for the functioning and evolution of modern societies.

© The Author(s), under exclusive license to Springer Nature Switzerland AG 2026
P. Katsaros (Ed.): IMBSA 2025, LNCS 15755, pp. 299–317, 2026.
https://doi.org/10.1007/978-3-032-05073-1_20

Those systems interact with physical processes, modifying their behaviors in response to changes in their environment, becoming cyber-physical. For instance, autonomous automotive vehicles make their own decisions and take actions without or with minimum human intervention. To achieve this goal, an autonomous vehicle has to cooperate with other vehicles, traffic signs and light systems from the road infrastructure [1].

Cyber-physical systems in domains such as autonomous vehicles are often safety-critical since any malfunction might seriously harm their users, or the environment. For instance, a malfunction in an autonomous car may harm the driver or pedestrians. The vast economic potential and societal impact of CPSs with the raise of innovative applications in safety-critical domains such as autonomous cars and unmanned aerial vehicles demand justification and demonstration they are acceptably safe to operate in defined operational contexts [2, 3]. Such justifications are presented by listing all the identified safety goals (and their relationships), the contextual information on system configuration, operating environments, and the evidence that substantiates the safety goals are met, in a compelling argument typically organized in an assurance case [4]. Assurance cases provide an explicit means for arguing, justifying, and assessing confidence in safety, security, or other dependability properties of interest. An assurance case is a document that communicates a clear, comprehensive, and defensible argument (supported by evidence – e.g., design, analysis, process models) that a system is acceptably safe or secure to operate in a particular context [5].

In safety and security-critical CPS domains like autonomous vehicles, the development, review, and evaluation of an assurance case is a regulatory requirement, defined in assurance standards, e.g., ISO 26262 [6] for automotive functional safety, and ISO 21434 [7] for cyber-security, as part of the certification process. An assurance case is built upon references to a wide range of evidence items, and it demonstrates how different types of evidence (e.g., system design verification, and test case report) provide confidence in higher-level properties [8]. An assurance case supported by evidence is the key artefact for system safety and security acceptance and its release for operation.

The required evidence of system assurance can be provided by applying safety and reliability analysis techniques. Fault Tree Analysis (FTA) [9] and Failure Modes and Effects Analysis (FMEA) [10] are the most popular techniques. They support engineers in determining the ways a system can fail, and the likelihood of those failures. FTA and FMEA form the integral part of Model-Based Safety Analysis (MBSA). However, due to the highly open and adaptive nature of CPSs, i.e., systems can connect/disconnected to each other at runtime, and are capable of adapting their behaviors (by relying on Artificial Intelligence-AI) to changing contexts, the evidence and justification of system assurance need to change from design time to runtime. Since the most open and adaptive CPSs are safety-critical, it is imperative to ensure they remain safe and robust face to uncertainties introduced by AI. With this shift, we will have a transition from the current design time assurance cases produced from manually created artifacts to assurance case models that can be automatically synthesized and evaluated at runtime [11, 12]. To achieve this goal, we need to equip a CPS or a CPS component with all the information that uniquely describes its dependability characteristics (design, analysis, and process models) within a Digital Dependability Identity (DDI) [12].

DDIs produced at design time provide the basis for automated integration of components into systems at development-time, and dynamic integration of independent systems into systems of systems at runtime. As one step into this direction, the Structured Assurance Case Metamodel (SACM) [13] issued by the Object Management Group (OMG) provides the foundations for runtime model-based system assurance. SACM defines a standardized metamodel and a visual notation for representing structured assurance cases. SACM was developed to support interoperability between different assurance case approaches (e.g., GSN [8], CAE [14]). SACM was used in the DEIS project [2] as a backbone for its Open Dependability Exchange (ODE) [15] metamodel, which defines the appropriate format of a DDI, in a first step towards runtime assurance of open and adaptive CPSs. SACM enables the specification, traceability to evidence, and automated synthesis of executable SACM assurance case patterns (templates) from design and analysis (ODE) models. Assurance case patterns are useful in capturing good practice in system argumentation for re-use, by defining the required system information to instantiate abstract assurance claims and evidence to support those claims [16].

Although SACM and ODE metamodels provide the backbone for the assurance of CPSs at runtime, enabling the traceability between assurance case placeholders and fault tree models, which is part of a CPS/CPS component DDI, is still a barrier. To fill this gap, in this paper, we introduce ACEditor a model-driven tool for the specifying executable SACM assurance case patterns with traceability to DDI information. We applied ACEditor in the specification of an SACM assurance case pattern with traceability to FTA results, and later instantiate it with information from fault tree models from an automotive wheel braking system. In Sect. 2, we provide an overview of the concept of Digital Dependability Identity, SACM, and its pattern extensions needed for the reader to understand the contributions of this paper. In Sect. 3, we introduce the ACEditor. Section 4 presents the model-driven methodology to synthesize assurance cases from fault trees. In Sect. 5, we illustrate the evaluation in the automotive domain. In Sect. 6, we discuss the related work, and we present the conclusions and sketch future work in Sect. 7.

2   Background

In this section, we describe the concept of Digital Dependability Identity. We also provide an overview of the Structured Assurance Case Metamodel (SACM), and its extensions to support the specification of assurance case patterns with traceability to DDI information, needed for the reader to understand the contributions of this paper.

2.1   Digital Dependability Identity and the ODE Metamodel

A Digital Dependability Identity (DDI) comprises all the information that uniquely describes the dependability characteristics (e.g., design, analysis, and process models) of a CPS or a CPS component [2]. DDIs provide the basis for automated and dynamic integration of independent systems into systems of systems in the field at runtime. The Open Dependability Exchange (ODE) [15] metamodel defines the appropriate format of a DDI. Therefore, the ODE metamodel provides the basis for the representation and exchange of safety information (e.g., FME(D)A, FTA, and Markov Chains) between open-adaptive CPSs and CPS components. The SACM metamodel is the backbone of the ODE, providing the formal traceability between assurance cases and DDI information. Therefore, SACM assurance case patterns (templates) can be instantiated based on the information from CPS and CPS component DDIs.

2.2   The Structured Assurance Case Metamodel and Its Patterns Extensions

SACM [13] defines a metamodel and a visual notation for representing structured assurance cases. It was developed to support interoperability with well-established assurance case frameworks such as GSN [8] and CAE [14]. SACM metamodel comprises five packages. **Structured Assurance Case Base Classes** capture the foundational concepts and relationships of the base elements of the SACM metamodel used, through inheritance, by the rest of the metamodel. **Structured Assurance Case Terminology package** defines the concepts of Term, Expression, and external interface, which support the definition of a controlled and reusable vocabulary referred to in the argumentation of an assurance case. **Assurance Case Packages** define the concept of modularity in assurance cases. **Argumentation Metamodel** defines the abstractions for representing structured arguments. **Artefact Metamodel** specifies the concepts for structuring evidence in assurance cases.

   SACM Base Classes: **SACMElement** contains the basic properties shared among all elements of a structured assurance case. A SACMElement contains a + *isAbstract* Boolean flag to indicate whether or not it is considered abstract, and an + *isCitation* Boolean flag to denote whether or not an element is part of an assurance case pattern. A SACMElement may contain a reference to another SACMElement that the SACMElement cites (citedElement). It may also contain an abstractForm reference to another abstract SACMElement to which this concrete SACMElement conforms. ModelElement refines SACMElement with a + *name* (of a LangString type), and references to **Description**, **ImplementationConstraint**, and other **Utility Elements**. An *UtilityElement* is the base element for a number of auxiliary elements that can be added to **ModelElements**, and it may contain a **MultiLangString** to describe its content in multiple languages. **LangString** is the SACM format for Descriptions, with the same purpose of a String with additional specification of the language used for its + *content*. **ExpressionLangString** extends **LangString** to denote a structured expression, which can be (optionally) used to refer to an ExpressionElement (Term or Expression) in the TerminologyPackage. A ModelElement can contain a multi-language Description, which may contain **Terms** and **Expressions** that provide its content, i.e., a Description that provides the text of a Claim. ModelElement can also contain zero or more ImplementationConstraints, used for specifying instantiation rules for assurance case patterns/templates. An ImplementationConstraint specifies the details of a constraint that must be satisfied to convert a referencing ModelElement from isAbstract = true to isAbstract = false. The language used in the specification of an ImplementationConstraint is limited to computer languages. ImplementationConstraints described in natural language cannot be used in the automatic instantiation of assurance case patterns. Abstract **Terms** referenced in ModelElement's Descriptions have an + externalReference property with the *url* to external artifacts (files, models), which are part of a CPS/CPS component DDI.

In addition, ImplementationConstraints with queries, written using computer languages such as Object Constraint Language (OCL) and Epsilon Object Language (EOL) [17], to DDI models (e.g., fault trees) provide the traceability between the assurance case and the evidence (in this case, an ODE-compliant model). **SACM base** package provides concepts to express assurance cases in natural and computer languages, and describing ModelElements precisely.

SACM Argumentation Metamodel: A structured argument is expressed through Claims, citations of artifacts, or ArtifactReferences (e.g., Evidence or Context for Claims), and relationships between these elements, expressed via AssertedRelationships. Figure 1 illustrates the concrete syntax of the main SACM Argumentation elements in its visual notation. A Claim is represented by a rectangle, which the claim statement (description) is written within the rectangle, and a unique identifier is placed at the top left corner of the rectangle. An inferential relationship between Claims (AssertedInference) is represented by a line with a solid arrowhead, and a solid dot in the middle of the line that can be used as a connection point. An ArgumentReasoning, used to describe non-obvious relationships between Claims and ArtefactReferences, is expressed by an annotation symbol. This symbol can be attached to an AssertedInference, which connects Claims, or to an AssertedEvidence/AssertedContext that connects Claims to ArtefactReferences. ArtefactReference is represented by a document symbol, to provide a clue to its meaning (as an artefact), with an arrow placed on the top right of the symbol to denote a reference. A needsSupport Claim, i.e., a claim stated as requiring further evidence or argument is represented by a rectangle decorated with three dots at the bottom. Abstract claims and abstract AssertedRelationships, used in the specification of assurance case patterns, are expressed as doted rectangles and doted arrows, respectively. A detailed description of SACM metamodel and its visual notation is available in [13].

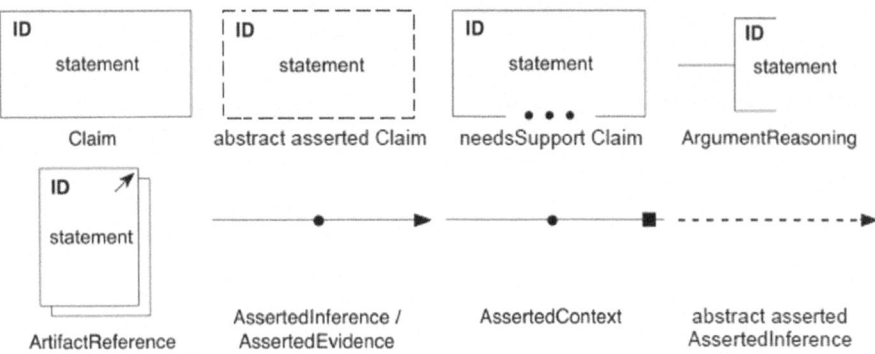

Fig. 1. Visual notation of SACM argumentation elements.

SACM patterns extensions [18, 19] support the specification of assurance case patterns with explicit traceability to design, safety and security analysis models, which are part of a CPS/CPS component EDDI. SACM pattern extensions added semantics to ImplementationConstraints to support the specification of structural relationships between argumentation elements. It also enabled traceability between terminology elements and external artifacts for specifying executable assurance case patterns. SACM

Multiplicity, **Optionality**, and **Choice** implementation constraint subtypes support the specification of structural relationships between argumentation elements. They have same semantics of their counterparts in the Goal Structuring Notation (GSN) patterns extensions [16]. **Mapping** constraint supports traceability between abstract terminology elements and information from external artifacts. A **Child** constraint defines hierarchical relationships between abstract SACM Terminology elements used during argument pattern instantiation. Child constraint enables the recursive instantiation of abstract terms based on the hierarchical structure of fault three models of a CPS/CPS component DDI. The specification of ImplementationConstraints to elements of an SACM argument pattern plays the role of a weaving model [20], enabling traceability between abstract Terms to information from external artifacts stored into DDIs. A detailed description of SACM patterns extensions are available elsewhere [18, 19].

3   Assurance Case Editor (ACEditor)

In this section, we introduce ACEditor, a modeling tool for the SACM visual and its patterns extensions to enable the specification of assurance case patterns with traceability to information from design and analysis (e.g., fault trees) artefacts, which are part of a component EDDI. ACEditor is built upon the Eclipse Modeling Framework (EMF) [21] platform using the Ecore language, and Graphical Modeling Framework (GMF) [22]. EMF was used for specifying the abstract syntax of the SACM assurance case modeling language and its patterns extensions in an Ecore model. We used GMF for developing the visual concrete syntax for the abstract syntax of the SACM assurance case modeling language [13].

ACEditor supports engineers at specifying and attaching implementation constraints to abstract terms, expressions, and argumentation elements of an SACM assurance case pattern. ImplementationConstraint is used to specify instantiation rules for SACM assurance case patterns. Those rules allow users to define queries to obtain information from design and safety models like fault trees, which are part of a CPS/CPS component EDDI, required for instantiating abstract SACM pattern elements. Model queries can be specified using a computer language such as Object Constraint Language (OCL), or EOL. In this paper, we considered EOL for specifying queries into fault trees and other component EDDI models. The tool allows users to specify Multiplicity (m), Optionality (o), and choice (c), Mapping (p), and Child (h) *implementation constraints* on elements of an SACM assurance case pattern.

Multiplicity, Optionality, and Choice patterns extensions are used for specifying structural relationships between SACM argumentation, artifact, and assurance case package elements. Mapping supports the specification of traceability between abstract SACM terminology elements and information from external artefacts. Child pattern extension defines hierarchical relationships between abstract terminology elements used during assurance case pattern instantiation. ACEditor supports the specification of user-defined implementation constraint subtypes by creating extension points to its pattern extensions module. Implementation constraints attached to abstract SACM argumentation and terminology pattern elements are further used to hold Epsilon programs for pattern instantiation. Figure 2 illustrates the SACM Assurance Case Editor (ACEditor) architecture.

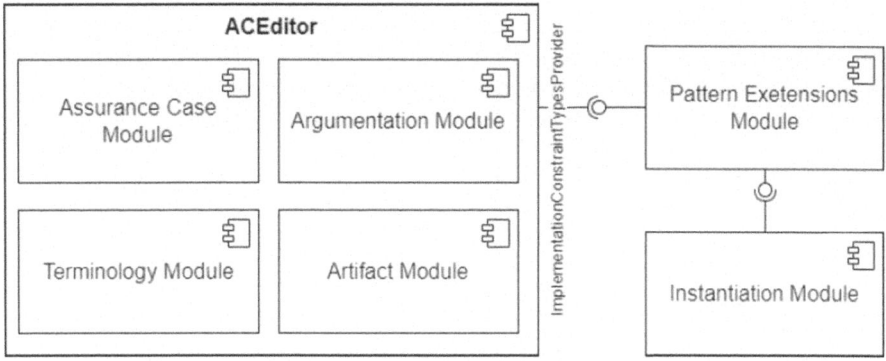

Fig. 2. SACM ACEditor architecture.

Assurance Case module supports **modularity** (**F1** feature stated in [11]) allowing system safety and security to be argued on a component basis as part of a CPS component EDDI that can be later integrated into a CPS assurance case model. In SACM, modularity is supported by **AssuranceCase**, **Argument**, **Artifact**, and **Terminology package**, **package interface**, and **package binding** elements illustrated in the assurance case modularity palettes from the editor shown in Fig. 3. Assurance Case Packages palette contains AssuranceCasePackage, AssuranceCasePackageInterface, and AssuranceCasePackage-Binding used to support modularity in assurance case modeling. AssuranceCasePackage package is the core element of an Assurance Case. An AssuranceCasePackage is the parent container element, i.e., it may contain other **assurance case**, **argument**, **artifact**, and/or **terminology package** elements.

An AssuranceCasePackage is an assurance case module. An AssuranceCasePackage consists of arguments (ArgumentPackages), evidence descriptions contained in ArtifactPackages, and terminology definitions stored into TerminologyPackages. Figure 3 illustrates the concrete syntax for AssuranceCasePackages and other SACM package elements. AssuranceCasePackage and other package elements are represented by a package figure with solid lines. Abstract package elements, used in the assurance case patterns, are represented by package figure with dashed line as illustrated in Fig. 3. Packages can contain other packages, including citations to other packages not contained within the same package. An AssuranceCasePackage can optionally have a separately declared interface (AssuranceCasePackageInterface), used to make part of the AssuranceCasePackage available externally so that it can be reused, which states selected packages contained by a package. Considering the scenario where components A and B are integrated into a system, assurance case packages ACP_a and ACP_b, which contain structured arguments concerning A and B system properties, are created. An assurance case package interface allows component developers to make part of the argumentation publicly available so that during system integration, ACP_a and ACP_b can also be integrated into a new assurance case package. An AssuranceCasePackageInterface and other package interface elements are represented by a package node decorated with a lollipop symbol. The premise of system integration in safety and security-related domains is integrating assurance cases of independent systems/components to form an overall assurance case

[11]. In SACM, this is handled by AssuranceCasePackageBinding, which binds two or more AssuranceCasePackageInterfaces to form an overall AssuranceCasePackage. An AssuranceCasePackageBinding is represented by a package node decorated with a two arch symbol, used to indicate the binding between package interfaces.

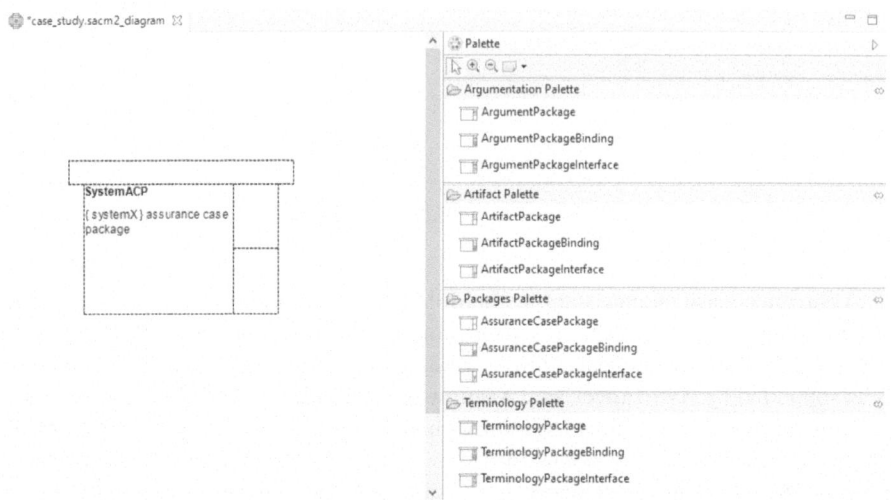

Fig. 3. Assurance case module view.

Argumentation module supports the specification of Claim (and its subtypes), ArgumentReasoning, ArtifactReference, AssertedInference, AssertedContext, AssertedArtifactInference, AssertedArtifactSupport, AssertedArtifactContext elements required for structuring the argumentation regarding system properties contained in an ArgumentPackage. A **needsSupport Claim** is represented by a rectangle decorated with three dots to indicate it requires further evidence or argumentation. An **axiomatic Claim**, decorated with a solid line, is used to indicate the truth of the assertion made in the argumentation. A **defeated Claim**, represented by a rectangle decorated with two diagonal lines, indicates a claim is defeated by evidence, supporting the specification of counter arguments in assurance cases (**F5 SACM feature**). An **asCited Claim**, represented by a rectangle decorated with square brackets, indicates a claim that cites another claim and it is supported by the cited claim. A dashed rectangle represents an **abstract Claim**, indicating a claim is part of an argument pattern or template. An ArgumentPackage may contain ArgumentPackageInterfaces, ArgumentPackageBindings, and other argument packages. Figure 4 illustrates the specification of Hazard Avoidance argument pattern in the SACM visual notation using the editor. Abstract claims are represented by dashed rectangles. Abstract AssertedInference and AssertedContext relationships are represented by dashed lines. Abstract terms, used in descriptions of Claims, ArgumentReasoning, ArtifactReference, are stated between brackets in Expressions that describe abstract argumentation elements. Abstract Terms are placeholders referencing information from external artifacts, e.g., design, safety/security analysis, or process models, required to instantiate them in a concrete assurance case model.

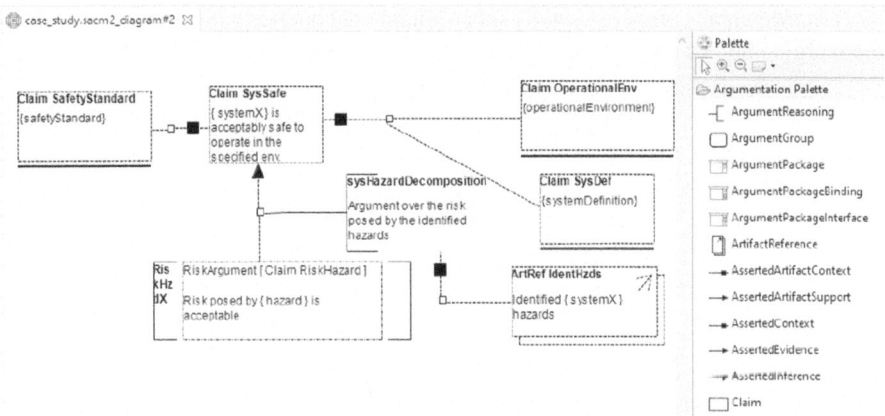

Fig. 4. Argumentation module view.

Terminology module provides elements that enable users to define controlled vocabularies (**F3** feature from SACM metamodel) to describe their argumentation with precision. TerminologyPackage is the container element for terminology assets (Term, Expression, Category, TerminologyGroup), and/or other TerminologyPackages. TerminologyPackage contains Term and Expression elements that can be used within the description of SACM argumentation and artifact elements. Figure 5 illustrates the table-based view of abstract and concrete Terms and Expression elements for the Hazard Avoidance argument pattern shown in Fig. 4. This view supports the specification and management of terminology elements of a TerminologyPackage. This view presents the type, unique identifier (gid), and the value of each terminology asset. It allows users to add and remove Term, Expression, Category, and TerminologyGroup elements. The terminology view also provides a user-interface for creating expressions by combining abstract and concrete terms (see Fig. 5a) used in the argumentation. The created expressions are presented in the expression visualization view (see Fig. 5b). The specification of an expression includes its gid, the language used (e.g., English), name, the separator used for creating multiple expressions, and text, which include references to abstract terms between brackets. ACEditor provides multi-language support (**F2** feature) for specifying expression elements, via SACM MultiLangString and LangString elements used to express the same semantics using different languages. For example, for expressing the term 'hazard' in both English and Portuguese, the user creates a MultiLangString with two LangString elements. SACM MultiLangString and LangString base elements provide multi-language to both natural and computer languages, i.e., languages like OCL and EOL used for specifying queries to obtain information from external artefacts (e.g., fault trees). Terminology module also provides a table-based user-interface to visualize the implementation constraints specified using the ACEditor Pattern Extension module, attached to abstract terminology elements (see Fig. 6). For instance, mapping and multiplicity implementtation constraints were attached to the hazard abstract Term used as description of a claim from Hazard Avoidance pattern. The traceability between abstract **Terms** and **information** from **external artifacts** (F6 feature) is achieved by setting their

+ *externalReference* property, and by specifying model queries within **implementation constraint** subtypes (SACM pattern extensions) attached to abstract Terms.

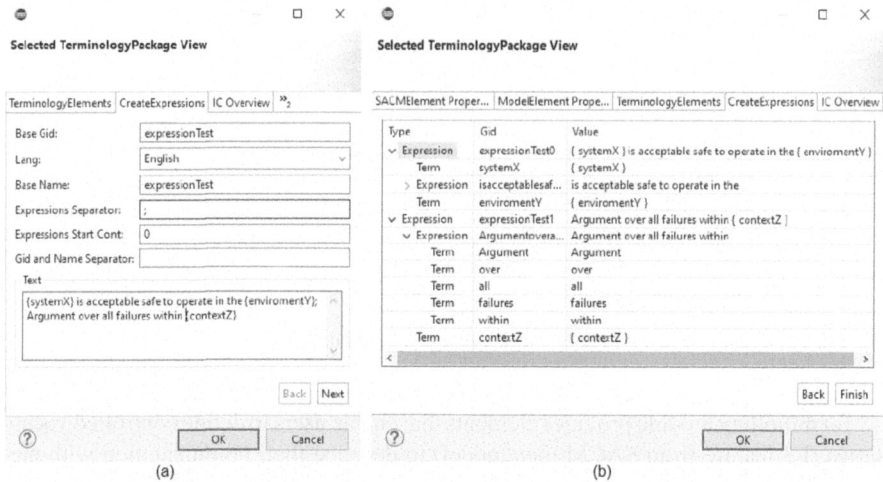

Fig. 5. Expression specification and visualization views.

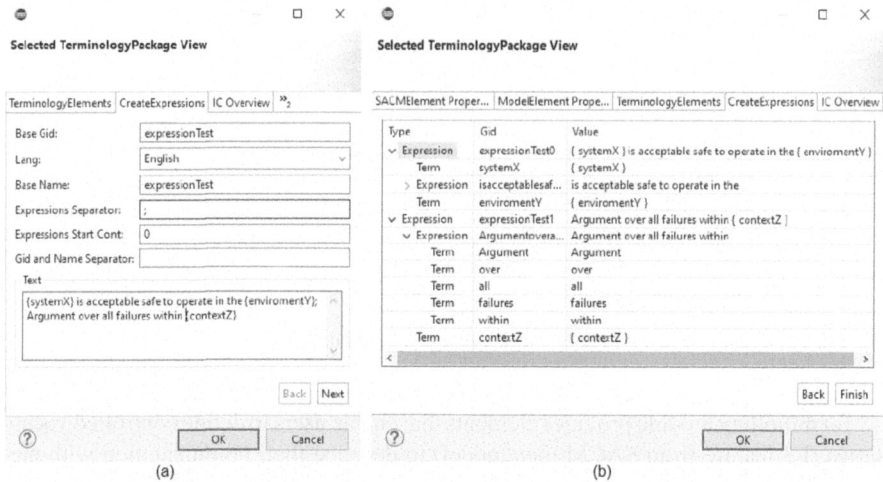

Fig. 6. Implementation constraints attached to terminology elements.

ACEditor supports the specification of user-defined implementation constraint subtypes. To achieve this goal it is needed to create an extension point to the editor by providing concrete implementations for ImplementationConstraintProvider extension point. **Pattern Extensions** module provides concrete implementations for ACEditor extension point to enable support for specifying **Mapping, Children, Multiplicity, Optionality**, and **Choice** SACM patterns extension constraint subtypes. Figure 7 illustrates the ACEditor user-interface for specifying implementation constraints to SACM ModelElements. It allows users to edit the name, description, to add and remove implementation constraints of a ModelElement. This user interface also supports users to assign **Notes** and **TaggedValues** that describe additional features of a ModelElement. For example, a mapping constraint with the model query External-Reference!t_system.all.collect(sls.a_name), is attached to {System} abstract Term. An assurance case pattern specification enriched with implementation constraints with traceability to external artifacts are inputs to the **Instantiation** module contains a certification algorithm that instantiates abstract elements from the pattern based on information obtained from external artifacts (**F7** feature). Due to space limitations, the artifact module is not detailed in this paper. The description of the Instantiation module is outside the scope of this paper.

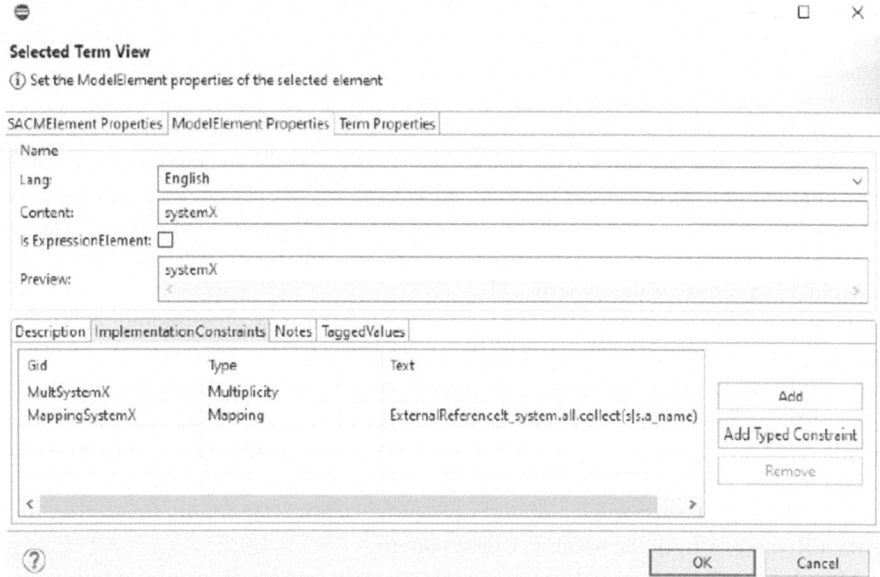

Fig. 7. Implementation constraint specification view.

4   Synthesizing Assurance Cases from Fault Trees

Here, we describe the steps for specifying (Sect. 4.1) and instantiating (Sect. 4.2) SACM argument patterns from fault tree models (i.e., EDDI information).

4.1   SACM Assurance Case Pattern Specification

Hazard avoidance [16] and Hazardous Software Failure Mode (HSFM) [17] assurance case pattern catalog are inputs to this phase. Here, engineers specify the structure of the assurance case pattern using the SACM visual notation. SACM assurance case modeling tools such as ACME [11] and ACEditor can be used to support the specification of assurance case patterns with explicit links to evidence. This phase encompasses the following steps:

Step 1: Specify the vocabulary. *Description:* In this step, we specify the placeholders using abstract SACM terminology elements (i.e., Terms and Expressions), and the textual information using concrete SACM Expression elements, which constitute the vocabulary of the targeted Hazard Avoidance and HSFM argumentation patterns used to build the assurance case pattern structure. Still in this step, we specify the relationships between abstract and concrete terminology elements to define expressions to be used as descriptions of SACM Claims, Reasoning, and Artifact Reference argumentation elements. Abstract SACM terms and expressions, via + *origin* and + *elements* properties respectively, provide the context to enable the automated instantiation of the pattern. SACM abstract Term and Expression elements enable an assurance case pattern specification to be machine-readable, i.e., it enables the specification of mappings between abstract terminology elements to the concrete information from design, safety assessment, and process models needed to instantiate abstract assurance case argumentation elements. *Output:* assurance case pattern vocabulary comprising concrete and abstract Term and Expression elements.

Step 2: Specify the argumentation elements. *Input*: the assurance case pattern vocabulary, i.e., abstract (non-instantiated) and concrete SACM terminology elements. *Description*: in this step, we specify the claims, artifact references, reasoning elements, and their relationships, using SACM AssertedRelationships, to define the hierarchical structure of the Hazard Avoidance and HSFM assurance case patterns. *Output*: the hierarchical structure of the pattern.

Step 3: Specify mappings between argumentation and terminology elements. *Input:* the assurance case pattern vocabulary and argumentation structure. *Description*: here, we define the description of each argumentation element (claim, reasoning, and artifact reference) specified in the pattern. A Description of an argumentation element includes explicit references to one or several SACM ExpressionElements. An expression element can be composed of both abstract and concrete SACM Term and Expression elements. *Output*: the assignment of descriptions to each SACM Claim, Reasoning, and Artifact Reference from the assurance case pattern.

Step 4: Specify implementation constraints associated with argumentation elements. *Inputs*: the assurance case pattern vocabulary, structure, and SACM argumentation elements (Claim, Reasoning, and Artifact Reference) enriched with SACM Description elements. *Description*: here, we assign Multiplicity and Optional SACM Implementation Constraint subtypes, defined into the SACM pattern extensions, to abstract Claims, Reasoning, and/or Artifact Reference assurance case pattern argumentation elements. In this step, we also assign SACM Choice implementation constraint to abstract SACM Asserted Relationship elements from the assurance case pattern. *Output:* assurance case pattern specification enriched with implementation constraints assigned to argumentation elements.

Step 5: Specify implementation constraints associated with terminology. *Inputs*: the assurance case pattern vocabulary, structure, and SACM argumentation elements (Claim, Reasoning, and Artifact Reference) enriched with SACM Description and implementation constraints elements. *Description*: here, we assign Multiplicity, Mapping, and

Children ImplementationConstraint subtypes, defined into the SACM pattern extensions, to abstract Terms. In this step, we also assign SACM Multiplicity implementation constraint to SACM Expression elements. *Output*: assurance case pattern specification enriched with implementation constraints assigned to terminology elements.

Step 6: Specify mappings between abstract Terms and FTA results. *Inputs*: the assurance case pattern vocabulary with implementation constraints, structure, and SACM argumentation elements (Claim, Reasoning, and Artifact Reference) enriched with SACM Description, implementation constraint elements, and the ODE metamodel. *Description*: in this step, we define model-based queries for the Mapping and *Children* implementation constraint subtypes assigned to abstract Terms. These queries provide traceability links between abstract terms of a pattern and ODE FTA package metamodel using a computer language such as EOL to map the values of these terms to FTA results. *Output*: an assurance case pattern specification enriched with traceability links to FTA results.

4.2 SACM Argument Pattern Instantiation

The instantiation of a SACM assurance case pattern for a target system based on information from FTA results demands:

Step 7: Performing system safety analysis. *Input*: system design. *Description*: in this step, the engineers must conduct safety analysis at both system, function, and component levels, e.g., using HAZOP at the system level to identify the potential hazards that malfunction the system, their safety risks, and safety goals; and fault tree analysis at function and component levels to identify how architectural subsystems and components may fail and contribute to the occurrence of hazards that may cause harm, and allocate functional and technical safety requirements to subsystems and components respectively. Model-Based Safety Assessment (MBSA) techniques such as HiP-HOPS [23], OSATE AADL [24], and Component Fault Trees [25] can be used to support this step. *Outputs*: fault tree models that describe the fault propagation paths for each identified system hazard.

Step 8: Integrating Fault Trees into the EDDI. *Inputs*: fault trees of each identified system hazard. *Description*: in this step, engineers execute a model transformation algorithm, produced by the authors, to convert the input fault tree models, e.g., specified using HiP-HOPs, into the Open Dependability Exchange (ODE) metamodel compliant fault tree format. For fault tree models produced using third-part MBSA tools other than HiP-HOPs, engineers need to specify a model transformation to map the tool metamodel elements to the ODE. *Output*: ODE fault tree compliant models.

Step 9: Execute the instantiation program. *Inputs*: an assurance case pattern, and the ODE fault tree compliant models. In this step, engineers provide the pattern and the fault tree models to the assurance case pattern instantiation program, developed by the authors in [18], to synthesize the system safety argument based on the FTA results. *Output*: a product safety argument for the targeted system with references to fault tree models.

5　Evaluation

We demonstrate the feasibility of ACEditor and our methodology in supporting the synthesis of a product assurance case from fault tree model information through executable SACM argument patterns for an automotive wheel braking system. HBS is a hybrid brake-by-wire system (Fig. 8) for electric vehicles propelled by four In-Wheel Motors (IWMs). The braking is achieved through the combined action of electrical IWMs, and frictional Electro-Mechanical Brakes (EMBs). While braking, IWMs transform the vehicle's kinetic energy into electricity, which charges the power train battery, increasing the vehicle's range. The system is activated when the driver presses the mechanical pedal. The Electronic Pedal component senses the driver's action, and it sends the braking forces, via a duplex bus system, to the WNC of each wheel brake module. Each WNC generates commands to the power converters to activate EMB and IWM braking actuators. While braking, the power flows from the auxiliary battery to the EMB and from IWM to the powertrain battery. Due to interactions between wheel-braking system components, different hazards with different causes and criticality (i.e., ISO 26262 Automotive Safety Integrity Level - ASILs) can arise.

In **step 1**, we built the pattern vocabulary by creating terms and expressions. The HSFMType abstract term is the abstraction for the top and intermediate events of a fault tree. The abstract term HSFMEvent represents the basic events of a fault tree, and it has a reference to the HSFMType term via its + *origin* property. Expressions are created referencing these terms through their + *element* property using the *$ < ExpressionElement.value > $* as the production rule for the expression value. In **step 2,** we created claims with no description. In **step 3**, the mappings between claims (7, 8) and the terminology elements were created by inserting a description within them. These descriptions contain ExpressionLangString elements referencing the abstract expressions 5 and 6 respectively. In **step 4**, multiplicity implementation constraint subtypes were attached to claims 7 and 8 due to the multiplicity of fault tree event types (i.e., top, intermediate, and basic events). In **step 5**, we added multiplicity implementation constraints to all terminology elements, also due to the multiplicity of fault tree events. A mapping constraint is assigned to both HSFMType and HSFMEvent abstract terms to map their values to fault tree events. Due to the hierarchical (parent and child) structure of FTA results, we added a ***Children(s)*** constraint to the HSFMType abstract term. Finally, in **step 6**, we specified queries (q1, q2, and q3) on the ODE-compliant fault tree model inside mapping and children implementation constraints subtypes. Query q1 was assigned to a mapping constraint to map the values of the abstract term HSFMType to the top- events of fault trees. The query q2 assigned to a children constraint maps the values of the abstract term HSFMType to intermediate events of a fault tree. The query q3 was assigned to a mapping constraint to map the values of the abstract term HSFMEvent to the basic events of a fault tree.

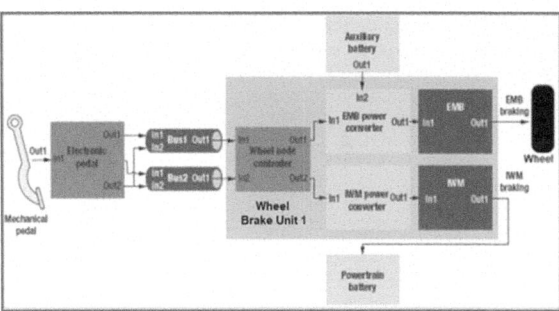

Fig. 8. Hybrid Braking System Architecture.

Figure 9 shows an excerpt of Hazardous Software Failure Mode (HSFM) argument pattern in the SACM visual notation using the ACEditor. The pattern decomposes the claim *ABSHSFMType* into the *AbsTypeSecondary* subclaim arguing the failure modes of other components that contribute to the current failure mode are acceptable. The *AbsType-Secondary* is further decomposed into *HSFMAccept* fault mitigation sub-claims arguing that all causes of each failure event specified in fault tree leaf nodes are acceptable, i.e., they do not lead the system to an unsafe state. For each fault tree non-leaf node, the *AbsHSFM* is decomposed into other "Absence Hazardous Software Failure Mode" (HSFM) fault mitigation citation claims referencing top-claims within other argument packages (i.e. recursive pattern instantiation) (Table 1).

Table 1. Abstract terms from the SACM assurance case pattern.

Step	Type	Gid	isAbstract	Value/Description	Constraints
1	Term	1	True	HSFMType	
1	Term	3	True	HSFMEvent	
1	Expression	5	True	{ HSFMType} is absent	
1	Expression	6	True	{ HSFMEvent} is acceptable	
2	Claim	7/8	True		
3	Claim	7	True	{ HSFMType} is absent	
3	Claim	8	True	{ HSFMEvent} is acceptable	
4	Claim	7	True	{ HSFMType} is absent	M
4	Claim	8	True	{ HSFMEvent} is acceptable	M
5	Term	1	True	HSFMType	m, p, s
5	Term	3	True	HSFMEvent	m, p
5	Expression	3	True	{ HSFMType} is absent	M
5	Expression	3	True	{ HSFMEvent} is acceptable	M
6	Term	1	True	HSFMType	m, p^{q1}, s^{q2}
6	Term	3	True	HSFMEvent	m, p^{q3}

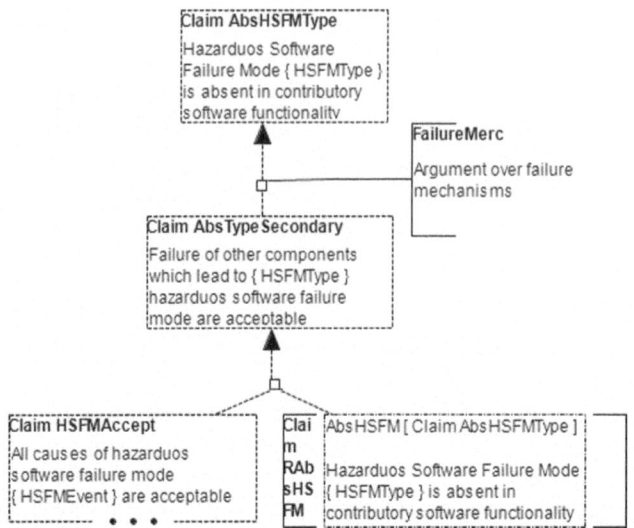

Fig. 9. Hazardous Software Failure Mode Assurance Case Pattern in SACM.

In the **step 7**, we conducted safety analysis using Fault Trees to identify and classifying the risk posed by hazards, and their failure propagation paths. We identified the following hazards for the wheel-braking system: No braking four wheels, and no braking three wheels, both classified as ASIL D. Figure 10 shows an excerpt of a fault tree for *no-braking four-wheel* hazard using HiP-HOPs. We converted the fault tree models into an Open Dependability Exchange (ODE) compliant fault tree model (**step 8**). Finally, the fault trees were synthesized into an assurance case for the wheel-braking system using the assurance case pattern instantiation program developed by the authors (**step 9**). Figure 11 illustrates the product safety argument resulting from **step 6** where the abstract claims have now been instantiated referencing FTA results. ODE Gates (i.e., top and intermediate events) are represented by claims A and C and ODE Output Events (i.e., basic events) are represented by claims within the B set.

6   Related Works

The AdvoCATE tool [26] supports the automatic assembly of safety arguments and the instantiation of argument patterns. However, it does not enable the creation of assurance arguments directly from models with traceability to one or more metamodels. It requires the creation of a table with data entries required to populate the assurance case pattern to instantiate it. Therefore, a data table needs to be created for each system to instantiate a specific pattern. The usage of data tables does not fully support interoperability and integration of assurance case patterns and evidence (i.e., design or analysis models). We address this issue by providing ACEditor that supports the concept of Executable Digital Dependability Identities (EDDI), enabling the specification of traceability between SACM pattern elements to fault tree models. [27] proposes an approach for automated model-based assurance case validation and management through a new concept called

Constrained Natural Language (CNL) using SACM implementation constraints. The approach aims to promote comprehensibility of the traceability from an assurance case to its supporting engineering model elements. However, this technique does not support yet the automatic instantiation of an assurance case pattern from evidence (e.g., fault trees).

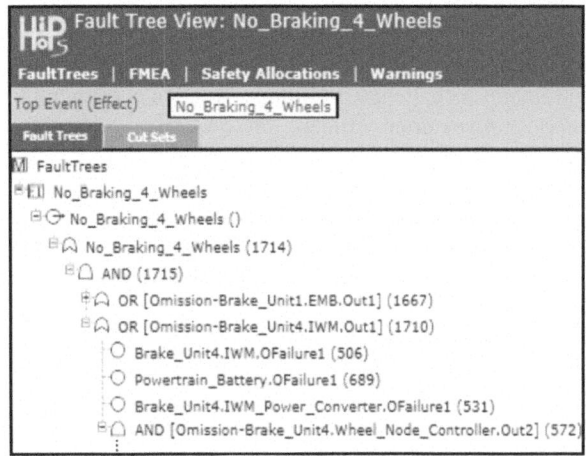

Fig. 10. Excerpt of no braking four wheels HiP-HOPs fault tree.

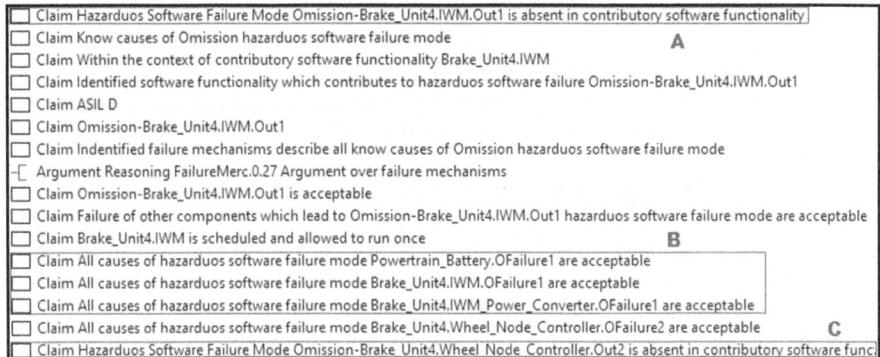

Fig. 11. HBS hazardous software failure mode assurance case.

7 Conclusion

In this paper, we introduced ACEditor, a model-driven tool support for specifying executable SACM argument patterns with traceability to component EDDI information. ACEditor supports the specification of executable implementation constraints into abstract SACM elements. We describe a process to support engineers during SACM assurance case patterns specification and instantiation with references to fault tree models. We evaluated the feasibility of ACEditor in a medium-sized illustrative automotive brake-by-wire system. ACEditor support safety engineers in specifying argument-evidence traceability in an assurance case, and it may reduce the complexity of maintaining SACM argument structures. The medium size and complexity of the models used in the evaluation are a threat to the validity. Case studies using cyber-physical systems from other safety and security-critical domains need to be conducted to properly evaluate usability aspects of ACEditor in industry settings. Although ODE model-based queries are simpler than metamodel-specific queries, simplifying the specification of those queries still remains a challenge. In future work, we also intend to use ontologies to simplify the queries into external artifacts.

Acknowledgements. This work was supported by CAPES, finance code 001, CAPES PRÓ-DEFESA under Grant V3084362P, FAPEMIG under Grant APQ-00743–22, and CNPq Brazilian research funding agencies, by the Secure and Safe Multi-Robot Systems (SESAME) H2020 Project under Grant 101017258, and by the Assuring Autonomy International Programme (https://www.york.ac.uk/assuring-autonomy).

References

1. Retouniotis, A., Papadopoulos, Y., Sorokos, I.: Andromeda: a model-connected framework for safety assessment and assurance. J. Syst. Softw. **220**(112256), 1–24 (2025)
2. Wei, R., Kelly, T.P., Hawkins, R., Armengaud, E.: DEIS: dependability engineering innovation for cyber-physical systems. In: Seidl, M., Zschaler, S. (eds.), Software Technologies: Applications and Foundations - STAF 2017 Workshops, Marburg, Germany, Lecture Notes in Comp. Science, vol. 10748, pp. 409–416, Springer (2017)
3. Trapp, M., Schneider, D., Liggesmeyer, P.: A safety roadmap to cyber-physical systems. Perspectives on the Future of Software Engineering, pp. 81–94, Springer (2013)
4. Wei, R., Jiang, Z., Guo, X., Yang, R.: DECISIVE: designing critical systems with iterative automated safety analysis. IEEE Transactions on Computer-Aided Design of Integrated Circuits and Systems **43**(5), 1346–1359. https://doi.org/10.1109/TCAD.2023.3340596
5. Kelly, T.P.: Arguing safety: a systematic approach to managing safety cases. Ph.D. dissertation, Department of Computer Science, Univ. York, York, U.K. (1999)
6. ISO 26262. Road Vehicles— Functional Safety, ISO/TC 22/SC 32 (2018)
7. ISO/SAE 21434: Road Vehicles – Cybersecurity Engineering, ISO/TC 22/SC 32 (2021)
8. Hawkins, R., Kelly, T.: A systematic approach for developing software safety arguments. In: 27th International System Safety Conference, pp. 25–33 (2010)
9. NASA.: Fault Tree Analysis Handbook for Aerospace Applications. WA, USA (2002)
10. NASA.: Failure Modes and Effects Analysis (FMEA) - A Bibliography. Technical Report. NASA Langley Technical Report Server (2000)
11. Wei, R., Kelly, T., Dai, X., Zhao, S., Hawkins, R.: Model based system assurance using the structured assurance case metamodel. J. Syst. Softw. **154**, 211–233 (2019)
12. Wei, R., Kelly, T., Reich, J., Gerasimou, S.: On the transition from design time to runtime model-based assurance cases. In: MoDELS (Workshops), pp. 56–61 (2018)
13. OMG.: Structured Assurance Case Metamodel (SACM) Version 2.2 (2025). https://www.omg.org/spec/SACM/2.2/About-SACM/

14. Bloomfield, R., Bishop, P.: Safety and assurance cases: past, present and possible future an adelard perspective. In: Dale, C., Anderson, T. (eds.) Making Systems Safer, (London), pp. 51–67, Springer London (2010)
15. Zeller, M., Sorokos, I., Reich, J., Adler, R., Schneider, D.: Open dependability exchange meta-model: a format to exchange safety information. In: Annual Reliability and Maintainability Symposium, Orlando, USA, pp. 1–7 (2023)
16. Kelly, T.P., McDermid, J.A.: Safety case construction and reuse using patterns. In: Safe Comp 97, pp. 55–69, Springer (1997)
17. Kolovos, D.S., Paige, R.F., Polack, F.A.C.: The epsilon object language (eol). In: Rensink, A., Warmer, J. (eds.) Model Driven Architecture – Foundations and Applications (Berlin, Heidelberg), pp. 128–142, Springer Berlin Heidelberg (2006)
18. Nascimento, L., de Oliveira, A.L., Villela, R., Wei, R., Hawkins, R., Kelly, T.: From fault tree analysis to runtime model-based assurance cases. In: Advanced Information Networking and Applications (AINA), 2024. Lecture Notes on Data Engineering and Comm. Technologies, vol 200. Springer, Cham
19. Nascimento, L., de Oliveira, A.L., Villela, R., Wei, R., Hawkins, R., Kelly, T.: Runtime model-based assurance of open and adaptive cyber-physical systems. In: International Conference on Advanced Information Networking and Applications. Cham: Springer International Publishing (2023)
20. Hawkins, R., Habli, I., Kolovos, D., Paige, R., Kelly, T.: Weaving an assurance case from design: a model-based approach. In: High Assurance Systems Engineering (HASE), 2015 IEEE 16th International Symposium on, pp. 110–117, IEEE (2015)
21. Eclipse. Eclipse modeling framework (emf) (2025). https://eclipse.dev/emf/
22. Eclipse. Graphical Modeling Project (2025). https://projects.eclipse.org/projects/modeling.gmf-runtime
23. Papadopoulos, Y., et al.: Engineering failure analysis and design optimisation with HiP-HOPS. Eng. Fail. Anal. 18(2), 590–608 (2011)
24. Delange, J., Feiler, P.H.: Supporting the ARP4761 safety assessment process with AADL. Embedded real time software and systems (ERTS2014) (2014)
25. Kaiser, B., Liggesmeyer, P., Mackel, O.: A new component concept for fault trees. In: Proc. of 8th Australian Workshop on Safety Critical Systems and Soft., pp. 37–46 (2003)
26. Denney, E., Pai, G., Pohl, J.: Advocate: an assurance case automation toolset. In: Inter. Conference on Computer Safety, Reliability, and Security, pp. 8–21, Springer (2012)
27. Wei, R., et al.: Automated model based assurance case management using constrained natural language. IEEE Transactions on CAD (2023)

Machine Learning and Automata Learning for System Safety

AI4Green: A Framework for AI-Based Resource Optimizations for Reliable Applications

Kai Höfig[1]([envelope]) [iD], Mario Döller[2] [iD], Faiza Waheed[1] [iD], Fabian Riß[1] [iD],
Michael Scholz[3] [iD], Joerg Bauer[3] [iD], Hannes Waclawek[4] [iD], Georg Schäfer[4] [iD],
Stefan Huber[4] [iD], Bernhard Heinzl[5] [iD], Michael Hellwig[6] [iD], and Steffen Finck[6] [iD]

[1] Technische Hochschule Rosenheim, Rosenheim, Germany
{kai.hoefig,faiza.waheed,fabian.riss}@th-rosenheim.de
[2] Kufstein University of Applied Sciences, Kufstein, Austria
mario.doeller@fh-kufstein.ac.at
[3] Technische Hochschule Deggendorf, Deggendorf, Germany
{michael.scholz,joerg.bauer}@th-deg.de
[4] Salzburg University of Applied Sciences, Salzburg, Austria
{hannes.waclawek,georg.schaefer,stefan.huber}@fh-salzburg.ac.at
[5] Software Competence Center Hagenberg GmbH, Hagenberg im Mühlkreis, Austria
bernhard.heinzl@scch.at
[6] Vorarlberg University of Applied Sciences, Kufstein, Austria
{michael.hellwig,steffen.finck}@fhv.at

Abstract. Climate change, increasing environmental pollution and rising resource consumption implicate sustainable and also reliable solutions to ensure a liveable and safe future for generations to come. Significant opportunities for savings lie in the field of business and industry, particularly by improving production processes. In this paper, we summarize our ongoing research from the *AI4Green* project funded by INTERREG Bayern-Österreich. We outline challenges and opportunities for reliable resource optimizations in challenging domains such as agriculture, robotics and production processes using artificial intelligence. We conclude that the optimization potential is high and provide an outlook of our future research activities to develop safe and reliable resource-optimal industrial AI-based solutions.

Keywords: CO2 footprint · Agriculture · Reinforcement Learning · Robotics · Additive Manufacturing · Quality Assurance · Multi-Sensor Fusion · Deep Learning · Defect Detection

1 Introduction

With of global challenges such as climate change, increasing environmental pollution and rising resource consumption, it is becoming increasingly important to find sustainable and also reliable solutions to ensure a liveable and safe future for

© The Author(s), under exclusive license to Springer Nature Switzerland AG 2026
P. Katsaros (Ed.): IMBSA 2025, LNCS 15755, pp. 321–332, 2026.
https://doi.org/10.1007/978-3-032-05073-1_21

generations to come. Significant opportunities for savings lie in the field of business and industry, particularly by improving production processes. With the growing digitization and automation, industrial systems (robotics, machinery, etc.) are operated through predefined, programmed processes, and a vast amount of runtime data is collected through sensors. Research has shown that significant optimization potential exists based on this runtime data using modern AI-based models and techniques. However, there are substantial barriers in transferring this knowledge from research to practical application in businesses, especially for safe and reliable applications, due to a lack of expertise, skilled professionals and lack of knowledge about the possibilities to ensure safety. Through three pilot initiatives in the fields of agriculture, robotics, and manufacturing, we aim to demonstrate existing optimization potential using modern AI-based methods. We seek to showcase potential savings in terms of CO_2 footprint, energy, and resources while meeting safety and reliability requirements through the development of reusable tools and demonstrating them in practical applications. In this article, we summarize our ongoing research from the *AI4Green* project funded by the INTERREG Bayern-Österreich program. Section 3 outlines challenges and opportunities for reliable resource optimizations in those challenging domains. In Sect. 4 we conclude that the optimization potential is high and provide an outlook of our future research activities to develop safe and reliable resource-optimal industrial solutions. The next section puts our work in perspective to European initiatives and legal obligations for systems from the industrial domain.

2   Related Work

The European Union has recognized the importance of sustainable industrial transformation through initiatives like the European Green Deal. This comprehensive strategy aims to make Europe the first climate-neutral continent by 2050, emphasizing the need for resource-efficient and competitive economies [6]. Complementing this, the Clean Industrial Deal outlines concrete actions to turn decarbonization into a driver of growth for European industries. It includes measures such as lowering energy prices, creating quality jobs, and fostering conditions for companies to thrive in a sustainable manner [7]. At the national level, Germany's Industry 4.0 strategy focuses on the digitalization of manufacturing industries to enhance competitiveness and resource efficiency. This strategy emphasizes the integration of information and communication technologies into traditional manufacturing processes to achieve smarter and more sustainable production [27].

Besides these political strategies for sustainability, all automated industrial applications need to comply with safety standards such as [10] and new standards are established to also integrate the use of artificial intelligence in such systems such as [11]. Furthermore, legal policies such as the EU AI Act [8] regulate the use of data and also pose requirements on rubustness/reliability on AI systems in applications classified as high-risk (e.g., industry).

3   AI4Green Pilot Initiatives

Here, we summarize the pilot initiatives of the *AI4Green* project[1]. Each initiative addresses a specific domain such as Agriculture (see Sect. 3.1), Robotics (see Sect. 3.2) and Production (see Sect. 3.3). All these domains have their own specific risks and safety requirements: in agriculture, the operation of the equipment involves risks for the environment. We focus here on data that is collected from swarm-based sensor platforms and the linked causes for risks as well as the potential for an resource optimal operation. In Robotics, we focus on industrial robots for production processes. The operation of such a machine itself is safety-critical as well as malfunctions could induce faults into the goods. Our goal here is to optimize the energy consumption by changing the path planning strategies. Therefore we focus mainly on the risks during operation. We show in the production domain how AI-based optimizations can be used to optimize the production of goods. In contrast to the robotic domain, we concentrate in this domain on the faults that are induced during production by AI-based optimizations and thereby increase safety of the goods and optimize the energy consumption of production machinery.

The main objective of the initiatives is to demonstrate the possibility of using AI-based optimization methods as well as optimization methods that are based on AI forecasts in different domains. Furthermore, the initiatives should demonstrate the extend of reducing the CO2 footprint with AI-based methods.

3.1   CO2 Reduction in Agriculture

The first pilot action focuses on CO2 reduction in agriculture, a sector that is increasingly adopting automation and digitalization to improve efficiency and reduce environmental impact. This is driven by the urgent need for sustainable practices to combat climate change, especially in resource-intensive sectors like agriculture. Mobile sensor platforms, such as drones, UAVs, etc. are being used for tasks like monitoring crop health, planning irrigation, and even automating afforestation or harvesting, allowing for more precise and efficient use of resources. This automation is crucial in improving efficiency and reducing energy consumption without compromising safety or reliability. Especially in the field of agriculture, this technology has a high potential as discussed and demonstrated in literature [21, 28].

The coordination of multiple mobile sensor platforms is a key factor in this automation, playing an increasingly crucial role in optimizing their performance. The goal of this pilot project is to develop and optimize mobile sensor platforms that operate in swarms for use across various application areas, including agriculture, forestry, and emergency response (search & rescue). Using automated coordination and information exchange between aerial and ground vehicles, drones could perform, e.g., aerial scanning and image data collection, which are then used by ground vehicles to carry out targeted actions like fertilization

---

[1] https://www.fh-kufstein.ac.at/en/research/research-projects/ai4green~w13307.

or harvesting. This cooperation ensures precise intervention, reduces overlaps and unnecessary operations, and ultimately saves resources.

Agricultural landscapes demand rapid, scalable, and intelligent monitoring systems for early detection of environmental stress, invasive species, and toxic flora. We extend a robust Multi-Agent Coverage Path Planning (MACPP) framework [2,3], initially designed for complex 3D environments, to the domain of precision agriculture. Leveraging Deep Reinforcement Learning (DRL), our decentralized UAV swarm system enables dynamic sensory monitoring of farmland, capable of adapting to changes mid-flight. The use of drones and other mobile sensor platforms has the potential to significantly reduce CO_2 emissions in agriculture, which is a major contributor to greenhouse gas emissions. According to a study, optimizing tractor routes can lead to significant reductions in diesel fuel consumption and other operating resources. However, despite the promising results of Deep Reinforcement Learning in industrial settings, their adoption in companies remains limited due to several challenges. These challenges include the lack of easily applicable tools, difficulties in transferring models trained in simulated environments to real-world settings, and the need for specialized expertise in reinforcement learning. The pilot action aims to address these challenges by developing and applying reinforcement learning methods to optimize mobile sensor platforms in agriculture. In doing so, we demonstrate how the automation and coordination of mobile sensor platforms can lead to sustainable transformation in agriculture, and lay the groundwork for applying similar swarm-based systems in other fields such as forestry and emergency response.

In particular, we demonstrate applicability to three critical agricultural use cases: detection of storm-induced crop damage, large-scale weed mapping, and identification of Jacobaea vulgaris (Jakobskreuzkraut), a toxic plant dangerous to livestock. Simulation and real-world experiments validate the frameworks robustness, scalability, and accuracy in complex outdoor environments.

Storm Damage Detection. After extreme weather events, UAV swarms are deployed to map structural and crop-level damage. By integrating LiDAR and camera data, damage zones are autonomously prioritized for inspection. It is planned that our model dynamically replans coverage when new damage areas are detected mid-flight.

Weed Detection. Weed mapping benefits from broad-scale multispectral coverage. Each UAV collects spectral data and performs on-board inference using lightweight CNNs. The swarming strategy ensures rapid and non-redundant field scanning, with higher resolution on areas flagged as weed-dense.

Jakobskreuzkraut Detection. Jacobaea vulgaris detection poses a specialized challenge due to its morphological similarity to non-toxic species. Using high-resolution RGB and multispectral cameras, combined with deep object detectors, our system identifies potential threats and marks them with GPS coordinates for follow-up action.

3.2   Energy Optimization in Robotics

In energy-intensive industries such as automotive manufacturing, industrial robots are major energy consumers. As such, optimizing their motion trajectories holds significant potential for reducing overall energy consumption [5,13]. Trajectory optimization focuses on generating energy-efficient motion plans while satisfying task-specific and operational constraints.

Classical control theory remains the de facto standard in industrial robotics in the context of trajectory planning. However, modern data-driven machine learning approaches – particularly Reinforcement Learning (RL) – have emerged as a promising alternative. RL has demonstrated superior adaptability and performance in complex, application-specific scenarios [15,17]. Despite its potential, concerns around safety, robustness, and reliability must be addressed. As outlined in [4], RL still faces substantial challenges before widespread deployment in real-world industrial settings is possible, among them:

- **Sample efficiency:** Learning directly on live systems often provides only limited interaction data.
- **Constraint handling:** Industrial systems impose safety and performance constraints that must never be violated.
- **Latency:** Highfrequency control loops require rapid policy inference with minimal delay.
- **Explainability:** Operators demand interpretable control policies to build trust and facilitate certification.

In the context of this research project, we introduce novel methods to enable RL in industrial environments for reliable and energy-efficient trajectory planning, addressing these challenges.

We have demonstrated – in both simulation and on a real-world robotic system – that careful problem formulation can dramatically increase sample efficiency [25]. Building on this result, our ongoing research seeks to establish a comprehensive *RL engineering pipeline*. Similar to established frameworks in data mining (e.g., CRISP-DM) and classical control, this pipeline will formalize the end-to-end processes needed for reliable, reproducible RL deployment in industrial contexts. We integrate Model Predictive Control (MPC) with RL by developing an *offline* MPC module that rapidly evaluates whether a candidate action will violate constraints at a given state. During online operation, the RL agent queries this module to filter or adjust actions in real time, ensuring both safety and low-latency policy execution.

In parallel, we investigate Physics-Informed Reinforcement Learning (PiRL) as a complementary approach that embeds domain knowledge – such as physical laws, system dynamics, or control constraints – directly into the learning process. Like MPC, PiRL leverages modeling principles, but does so within the RL framework to guide exploration, regularize learning, and improve policy robustness. This approach addresses core challenges in industrial RL deployment: physical priors can be used to constrain unsafe actions, shape more informative rewards, or reduce dimensionality through structured representations. As a result, PiRL has demonstrated improved sample efficiency, faster convergence, and safer policy execution, especially in simulation-to-reality transfer scenarios [1].

In robotics control, PiRL has shown promise across a range of applications, e.g., locomotion [22] or manipulation [16]. Here, physics-based surrogate models have been used to accelerate policy learning while ensuring stability and safe exploration in high-dimensional control spaces. Beyond robotics, PiRL is also gaining traction in other safety-critical domains, e.g., power systems, where grid stability constraints and physical flow models to are incorporated into RL-based controllers that adapt to load changes without compromising safety [20]. These applications illustrate how embedding physical understanding into data-driven learning not only improves performance but also brings us closer to reliable application of RL required in industry.

We aim to apply PiRL principles to industrial robotic systems by combining known dynamics with reinforcement learning policies. We see particular value in this hybridization for enabling energy-aware as well as constraint-compliant reliable control in manufacturing settings. Ultimately, PiRL offers a pathway toward more reliable, and physically grounded reinforcement learning to facilitate real-world adoption.

To enable explainability of learned policies and further improve sample efficiency, we investigate replacement of blackbox neural network approximators with polynomial models. We have already successfully applied machine learning optimized piecewise polynomials to energy minimization in cam profiles [29,30]. Our current work generalizes this method to RL agents, yielding both interpretable policies and reduced parameter dimensionality, thereby accelerating learning.

Additionally, we are investigating ways to integrate energyawareness into the RL workflow. We formulate policy search as a biobjective optimization, balancing task performance against energy consumption by combining these goals in the reward. By manually sweeping the relative weight between task and energy terms, we obtain a Pareto front of policies that trade off goal attainment and energy use. In future work, we will replace this manual tuning with an adaptive surrogatemodel approach: fitting a Gaussian process over the observed Pareto front to predict optimal weightings and guide exploration in a dataefficient, automated manner [26].

We plan to evaluate our methods on demonstrators of increasing complexity and apply them to real-world industrial scenarios in close cooperation with local company partners. Our position is that with a dedicated engineering pipeline, hybrid data-driven/model-based architectures, and explainable function approximators, RL is poised to improve standards of energyoptimal robotic control.

3.3   Resource Savings Through Product and Process Optimization

In this domain, we concentrate on the optimization of production by collecting data to predict the demand and the quality of products. We apply the collection of indicators for demand prediction to the domain of food production to reduce waste whilst maintaining food safety regulations. Secondly, we show how collected samples from rejected goods is used in 3D printing to increase safety of the product and also reduce waste during production.

Integrating circularity indicators into product configurations using detailed sustainability information provides advantages to both companies and customers. In addition to a transparent presentation of the product components, circularity indicators (e.g. recycling rate, material use efficiency, energy efficiency or LCA) are included in the product design process and a forward-looking assessment of the environmental impact of a product is carried out. The corresponding key figures are to be collected, compared with each other and integrated prototypically into the production processes. On the one hand, integration can take place via the development of sustainability scoring models, which evaluate products based on sustainability criteria. On the other hand, the concept of the Digital Product Passport (sustainable DPP) [23] offers an innovative, digital platform via which comprehensive sustainability information (origin, environmental impact, recyclability, etc.) of a product can be provided and transparently tracked. This helps to increase demand for environmentally friendly products and position the company as a pioneer in sustainability [14]. The concept of transparent, sustainable product configuration is illustrated in Fig. 1. A comparable demonstrator of this type will be developed together with the implementation partners throughout this project.

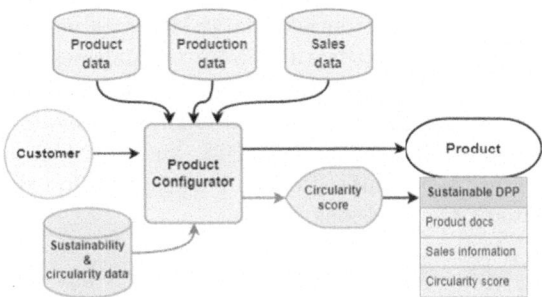

Fig. 1. Integration of circularity indicators into the product configurator and design of a sustainable digital product passport (sustainable DPP).

In addition to an application in the packaging sector, a greater use of recycled materials in injection molding [24] and the effects of production-relevant parameters on ESG-based indicators are to be investigated.

We implement this use case in the area of food production in catering companies. Providers of communal catering – such as corporate and university canteens, hospitals, and retirement homes – prepare meals for large groups of people on a daily basis. Due to the highly perishable nature of food, overproduction frequently results in significant resource waste. Conversely, underproduction must typically be avoided, as minimum quantity requirements imposed by clients or contractual obligations have to be met. This highlights the necessity for effective and data-driven strategies to optimize meal planning and align production more closely with actual demand.

A critical component of this process involves accurately forecasting both the number of guests and their meal choices. However, this task is complicated by a range of complex and interdependent factors, such as the influence of main dish offerings on dessert selection or the impact of weather conditions. Traditional machine learning methods that rely on mean-value estimations often deliver low predictive accuracy under such conditions. To address this, we propose the application and evaluation of advanced machine learning models, including NeuralProphet [32] and transformer-based approaches [18,33], to improve the forecasting of both guest numbers and main dish selections. Challenges such as overfitting and underfitting are taken into account by regularization terms, the usage of multiple models in an ensemble and cross-validation.

Furthermore, we aim to integrate meal participation forecasts into main dish prediction through the refinement of simulated extrapolation approaches [12,31]. These forecasting advancements will form the basis for developing meta-heuristic optimization methods tailored to meal production planning. The optimization objective here is to minimize the sum of the carbon footprint of all meals provided by a canteen within a given time frame. Constraints include, for example, the provision of a minimum number of different meals per day, the heterogeneity of the meals offered by day and per week and the provision of meals for different diets (e.g., vegetarian, vegan whilst maintaining food safety restrictions. Further research also investigates the potential of large language models (LLMs) [19] to automatically derive pre-defined features from textual meal descriptions, such as categorical classifications into vegan, vegetarian, or meat-containing dishes.

It is anticipated that the implementation of these methods will reduce overproduction in large-scale kitchens by up to 20%. Such a reduction would directly contribute to lowering food cultivation and transportation demands, thereby decreasing associated CO_2 emissions.

AI-Driven Quality Assurance in Additive Manufacturing: Complementary to the food production optimization project, we address AI-driven resource savings in Additive Manufacturing (AM), Specifically in the field of Laser Powder Bed Fusion (L-PBF) for 3D metal components. This process is also increasingly used for the manufacturing of critical safety parts in aerospace, automotive and healthcare applications, where defect-free production is essential [9,34]. We developed a multi-sensor quality assurance system for TRUMPF TruPrint 1000 enabling real-time anomaly detection by combining:

- Visual inspection (YOLOv9m, 83% precision)
- Eddy current sensing for sub-surface flaws
- Thermography for thermal anomaly detection
- Acceleration sensing for recoating failures

The system prevents the production of defective parts by early detection of failure points, thus reducing associated material waste by an estimated ~30% and energy consumption by $\sim$15% compared to post-build non-destructive inspection (NDT) methods. The integrated multi-sensor architecture is illustrated in Fig. 2.

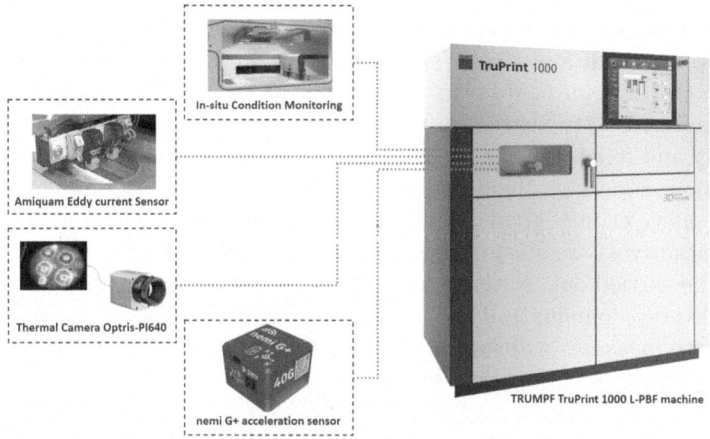

Fig. 2. Multi-sensor data fusion architecture

The system architecture in Fig. 2 ensures comprehensive data collection from multiple sensors, including:

– Machine parameters via OPC UA protocol
– Layer-wise images from ($\sim$2000+ images per print job)
– High frequency data ingestion to databases
– State-of-the-Art Dashboard for interactive operation along with anomaly detection

Our experimental results demonstrate resource savings, with estimated savings in:

– Material waste: $\sim$30%, by preventing unnecessary material usage in faulty builds.
– Energy: $\sim$15%, reducing energy consumption by aborting defective prints early.
– Man hours: $\sim$10%, reduction in post-processing hours by minimizing manual inspection of validated parts.

This approach demonstrates with great results how AI-driven quality assurance can simultaneously enhance the printed parts' reliability while reducing wastes in the production process.

4 Conclusion and Future Work

We addressed resource optimizations using AI-based algorithms in agriculture, robotics and production. Each domain has its own safety requirements and restrictions. AI-based algorithms need to provide a verifiable way of demonstrating safe operation. In the case of agriculture sensor networks, intense testing, large data collection and classic safety barriers during operation enable safety for AI. In the domain of robotics novel path planning using physics aware AI provides resource optimization potential, but safety is not the only issue. Also availability and reliability are very important since the stop of a production line is much more expensive than a safety stop in agriculture. In production, especially for safety critical goods, parts that erroneously judged to be good by an AI (false negatives) are most dangerous if no further non-destructive acceptance tests can be carried out. Nevertheless, the potential for resource optimization is high in all those domains and this potential is to be explored. A combination of classic safety measures will support the industrial usage of AI in the future and will be investigated throughout this project.

Acknowledgments. This work has been funded by the INTERREG Bayern-sterreich program 2021-2027 as part of the project AI4GREEN: Data Science for Sustainability (funding code BA0100172) with co-financing by the European Union.

Disclosure of Interests. The authors have no competing interests to declare which are relevant to the content of this article.

References

1. Banerjee, C., Nguyen, K., Fookes, C., Raissi, M.: A survey on physics informed reinforcement learning: Review and open problems. arXiv preprint arXiv:2309.01909 (2023). https://arxiv.org/abs/2309.01909
2. Bialas, J., Döller, M., Kathrein, R.: Robust Multi-Agent Coverage Path Planning for Unmanned Airial Vehicles (UAVs) in Complex 3D Environments with Deep Reinforcement Learning. In: Proceedings of the IEEE International Conference on Robotics and Biomimetics (IEEE ROBIO). IEEE, Samui, Thailand (2023)
3. Bialas, J., Döller, M., Walch, S., van Veelen, M., Mejia-Aguilar, A.: Optimizing multi-agent coverage path planning UAV search and rescue missions with prioritizing deep reinforcement learning. In: Proceedings of the IEEE International Conference on Robotics and Biomimetics (IEEE ROBIO). IEEE, Bangkok, Thailand (2024)
4. Dulac-Arnold, G., et al.: Challenges of real-world reinforcement learning: definitions, benchmarks and analysis. Mach. Learn. **110**(9), 2419–2468 (2021). https://doi.org/10.1007/s10994-021-05961-4
5. Eggers, K.B.: Energieeffizienter Betrieb von Industrierobotern. Dissertation, University of Hannover, Germany (2019). https://repo.uni-hannover.de/handle/123456789/5379

6. European Commission: The european green deal (2020). https://commission. europa.eu/strategy-and-policy/priorities-2019-2024/european-green-deal_en. Accessed 23 Apr 2025
7. European Commission: Clean industrial deal (2024). https://commission.europa. eu/topics/eu-competitiveness/clean-industrial-deal_en. Accessed 23 Apr 2025
8. European Union: Regulation (EU) 2024/1230 of the European Parliament and of the Council of 13 March 2024 laying down harmonised rules on artificial intelligence (Artificial Intelligence Act) and amending certain Union legislative acts, March 2024. https://eur-lex.europa.eu/legal-content/EN/TXT/? uri=CELEX:32024R1230, official Journal of the European Union, L 259, 12.4.2024, p. 1–172
9. Gibson, I., Rosen, D., Stucker, B.: Additive Manufacturing Technologies. Springer (2015). https://doi.org/10.1007/978-1-4939-2113-3
10. International Electrotechnical Commission (IEC): IEC 61508: Functional Safety of Electrical/Electronic/Programmable Electronic Safety-related Systems. IEC Standard, Parts 1–7 (2010)
11. International Electrotechnical Commission (IEC): ISO/IEC TR 5469:2024 Artificial intelligence - Functional safety and AI systems. IEC Technical Report (2024)
12. Keller, A., Scholz, M.: Trading on cryptocurrency markets: Analyzing the behavior of bitcoin. In: Proceedings of the International Conference on Information Systems (ICIS), p. 11. Association for Information Systems, Munich, Germany (2019)
13. Kemptner, P.: Energieeinsparung bei Industrierobotern. Automation (04/2013), 46–47 (2013). https://www.kemptner.com/files/fachartikel/x-Technik/xTechnik_ Siemens_RobotEfficiencyAT_1304.pdf
14. Kliestik, T., Zvarikova, K., Lăzăroiu, G.: Data-driven machine learning and neural network algorithms in the retailing environment: Consumer engagement, experience, and purchase behaviors. Econ. Manage. Financial Markets 17(1), 57–69 (2022)
15. Li, Y.: Deep Reinforcement Learning: An Overview, November 2018. https://doi. org/10.48550/arXiv.1701.07274, http://arxiv.org/abs/1701.07274
16. Liu, X.Y., Wang, J.X.: Physics-informed dyna-style model-based deep reinforcement learning for dynamic control. Proceedings of the Royal Society A: Mathematical, Physical and Engineering Sciences 477(2255), 20210618 (2021). https://doi. org/10.1098/rspa.2021.0618, http://arxiv.org/abs/2108.00128, arXiv:2108.00128 [cs]
17. Luo, J., Paduraru, C., Voicu, O., et al.: Controlling Commercial Cooling Systems Using Reinforcement Learning, December 2022. https://doi.org/10.48550/arXiv. 2211.07357, http://arxiv.org/abs/2211.07357
18. Nie, Y., Nguyen, N.H., Sinthong, P., Kalagnanam, J.: A time series is worth 64 words: Long-term forecasting with transformers (2023). https://arxiv.org/abs/ 2211.14730
19. Raiaan, M.A.K., et al.: A review on large language models: architectures, applications, taxonomies, open issues and challenges. IEEE Access 12, 26839–26874 (2024). https://doi.org/10.1109/ACCESS.2024.3365742
20. Raja Hossain, R., Huang, Q., Mahapatra, K., Huang, R.: Physics-Informed Deep Reinforcement Learning-Based Control in Power Systems. In: Smart Cyber-Physical Power Systems, pp. 67–77. John Wiley & Sons, Ltd. (2025). https://doi.org/10.1002/9781394334599.ch3, https://onlinelibrary.wiley.com/doi/ abs/10.1002/9781394334599.ch3

21. Rejeb, A., Abdollahi, A., Rejeb, K., Treiblmaier, H.: Drones in agriculture: A review and bibliometric analysis. Comput. Electron. Agriculture **198**(107017) (2022). https://doi.org/10.1016/j.compag.2022.107017

22. Rodwell, C., Tallapragada, P.: Physics-informed reinforcement learning for motion control of a fish-like swimming robot. Sci. Rep. **13**(1), 10754 (2023). https://doi.org/10.1038/s41598-023-36399-4, https://www.nature.com/articles/s41598-023-36399-4

23. Saari, L., Heilala, J., Heikkilä, T., Kääriäinen, J., Pulkkinen, A., Rantala, T.: Digital product passport promotes sustainable manufacturing: Whitepaper (2022). https://cris.vtt.fi/ws/portalfiles/portal/67162320/DPP_white_paper.pdf

24. Salcher, F., Finck, S., Hellwig, M.: Automated process capability analysis for product quality improvements. In: 2023 IEEE International Conference on Engineering, Technology and Innovation (ICE/ITMC), pp. 1–9 (2023). https://doi.org/10.1109/ICE/ITMC58018.2023.10332307

25. Schäfer, G., Krau, T., Rehrl, J., Huber, S., Hirlaender, S.: The crucial role of problem formulation in real-world reinforcement learning. arXiv preprint arXiv:2503.20442 (2025)

26. Schäfer, G., Seliger, R., Rehrl, J., Huber, S., Hirlaender, S.: Multi-objective reinforcement learning for energy-efficient industrial control. arXiv preprint arXiv:2505.07607 (2025)

27. Schroeder, W.: Germany's industry 4.0 strategy: Policy options for the future. https://uk.fes.de/fileadmin/user_upload/publications/files/FES-London_Schroeder_Germanys-Industrie-40-Strategy.pdf (2016). Accessed 23 April 2025

28. Upadhyaya, A., Jeet, P., Sundaram, P.K., Singh, A.K., Saurabh, K., Deo, M.: Efficacy of drone technology in agriculture: a review. J. AgriSearch **9**(3) (2022). https://doi.org/10.21921/jas.v9i03.11000

29. Waclawek, H., Huber, S.: Energy optimized piecewise polynomial approximation utilizing modern machine learning optimizers (2025). https://arxiv.org/abs/2503.09329

30. Waclawek, H., Huber, S.: machine learning optimized orthogonal basis piecewise polynomial approximation. In: Learning and Intelligent Optimization, pp. 427–441. Springer, Cham (2025). https://doi.org/10.1007/978-3-031-75623-8_33

31. Yang, M., Adomavicius, G., Burtch, G., Ren, Y.: Mind the gap: accounting for measurement error and misclassification in variables generated via data mining. Inf. Syst. Res. **29**(1), 4–24 (2018). https://doi.org/10.1287/isre.2017.0727

32. Yu, Z., Niu, K., Chen, X., Guo, Z., Li, D.: A hybrid model based on neural-prophet and long short-term memory for time series forecasting. In: Proceedings of the IEEE International Conference on Big Data, pp. 1182–1191. Osaka, Japan (2022https://doi.org/10.1109/BigData55660.2022.10020471

33. Zeng, A., Chen, M., Zhang, L., Xu, Q.: Are transformers effective for time series forecasting? Proceedings of the AAAI Conference on Artificial Intelligence **37**, 11121–11128 (2023). https://doi.org/10.1609/aaai.v37i9.26317, url-https://ojs.aaai.org/index.php/AAAI/article/view/26317

34. Zhao, Y., Ren, H., Zhang, Y., Wang, C., Long, Y.: Layer-wise multi-defect detection for laser powder bed fusion using deep learning algorithm with visual explanation. Optics Laser Technol. **174**, 110648 (2024). https://doi.org/10.1016/j.optlastec.2024.110648, https://doi.org/10.1016/j.optlastec.2024.110648

Analyzing Truck Platoons with Automata Learning and Model Checking

Jan Burkhardt and Florian Leitner-Fischer[✉]

DHBW Ravensburg, Fallenbrunnen 2, Friedrichshafen 88045, Germany
{burkhardt,leitner-fischer}@dhbw-ravensburg.de

Abstract. Ensuring the safety of systems like truck platoons remains a significant challenge, especially when formal models of system behavior are unavailable or difficult to construct. In this work-in-progress, we explore an approach that uses automata learning to infer models from observed system executions, which can then be analyzed through model checking. The goal of this approach is to enable safety analysis without relying on manually specified models. We are investigating the feasibility of this idea through a Truck Platooning case study-an increasingly relevant scenario in intelligent transportation systems where safety is critical. While this approach is still under development, early steps suggest potential for combining learning-based modeling with formal verification to support safety analysis in both simulated and physical settings.

Keywords: Automata Learning · Model Checking · Truck Platooning · Safety Analysis · Learning-Based Verification · Cyber-Physical Systems

1 Introduction

Safety-critical embedded systems are at the core of many aspects of modern life, whether in automotive applications, public transportation, medical devices, or other critical domains. The correct functioning of these systems is essential, and their complexity calls for rigorous validation and verification strategies to ensure safety and reliability.

A key challenge in validating embedded systems arises from their inherent nature: they are tightly integrated combinations of hardware and software, interacting continuously with their environment. Ideally, such systems would be verified holistically, under realistic operating conditions. However, practical and economic constraints often make full-system verification difficult or infeasible. As a result, a variety of approaches have been developed to address this challenge, including software simulation, formal verification of abstract models, hardware-in-the-loop, and software-in-the-loop testing.

Among these, Model Checking [5] stands out as a well-established technique for the automated analysis of system properties. Given a model of the system and

© The Author(s), under exclusive license to Springer Nature Switzerland AG 2026
P. Katsaros (Ed.): IMBSA 2025, LNCS 15755, pp. 333–347, 2026.
https://doi.org/10.1007/978-3-032-05073-1_22

a formal specification of the property of interest, a model checker can automatically verify whether the property holds or identify counterexamples-execution traces that violate the property. Crucially, however, this approach depends on the availability of a system model that accurately captures the behavior of the system under analysis.

In practice, constructing such models is often difficult, especially for complex embedded systems where the interaction between hardware, software, and environment plays a central role. Traditional modeling approaches rely on manual abstraction, which means they can only capture behaviors anticipated by the model designer. This raises the risk of overlooking unexpected or emergent behaviors that might lead to safety violations in the actual system.

In this work-in-progress, we explore an alternative approach: using automata learning [2] to automatically infer system models from observed execution traces. Specifically, we employ the AALpy tool [20] to learn automata representations of the systems behavior based on these observations. Our aim is to investigate whether such learned models can be effectively used for model checking-enabling safety analysis without relying on manually specified models.

We focus on embedded systems where hardware-software interactions and environmental influences are critical factors. These aspects are often abstracted away in traditional verification methods, which may limit the ability to detect certain classes of errors. By learning directly from the systems observable behavior-including the effects of environmental interactions-we hope to capture a richer, more realistic model of the systems dynamics.

To evaluate the feasibility of this approach, we are conducting a case study on truck platooning, an application domain where safety is paramount. Our setup involves scaled (1:8) truck models operating in a corresponding simulated and physical environment. While our research is ongoing, the initial goal is to assess whether learned models can support effective safety analysis in such settings.

The rest of this paper is organized as follows: Sect. 2 presents background information on model checking and automata learning, and introduces the truck platooning case study that serves as the basis for our approach. Section 3 details our analysis methodology applied to the case study. Section 4 provides an evaluation of our approach and discusses the key findings. Section 5 reviews related work, and Sect. 6 concludes with a summary and suggestions for future research directions.

2   Preliminaries

In this section, we briefly introduce the key concepts and tools used in our work: automata learning, Moore machines, the RPNI learning algorithm, model checking, and transition systems.

2.1   Automata Learning

Automata learning aims to infer formal models of system behavior from observed executions. In particular, learning algorithms based on Angluins classic L* algorithm [2] construct automata representations such as deterministic finite automata, labeled transition systems, probabilistic automata [28], or timed automata [14].

A distinction is commonly made between *active learning*, where the learner interacts directly with the system under learning (SUL) through queries, and *passive learning*, where the learner constructs a model from previously recorded execution traces. Several tools and frameworks support these learning approaches, including AALpy [20] and Jajapy [24].

In our work, we use AALpy to learn deterministic Moore machines from observed system executions, employing the RPNI algorithm [22] for passive learning.

2.2 Moore Machines

A *Moore machine* [19] is a type of finite-state machine where outputs are associated with states rather than transitions. Formally, a Moore machine is defined as the tuple:

$$M = (S, \Sigma, \Lambda, \delta, \lambda, s_0) \tag{1}$$

where:

- S: Finite set of states.
- Σ: Input alphabet.
- Λ: Output alphabet.
- $\delta : S \times \Sigma \rightarrow S$: Transition function.
- $\lambda : S \rightarrow \Lambda$: Output function.
- $s_0 \in S$: Initial state.

The key characteristic of a Moore machine is that the output depends solely on the current state, not on the incoming transitions.

2.3 RPNI Algorithm

The *Regular Positive and Negative Inference (RPNI)* algorithm [22] is a classic approach for learning deterministic finite automata (DFA) from labeled execution traces. Given a sufficient number of positive and negative examples (accepted and rejected traces), RPNI constructs the minimal DFA that recognizes the underlying regular language.

In our setting, RPNI is used within AALpy to learn Moore machines passively from observed executions of the system under analysis.

2.4 Model Checking

Model checking [5] is a formal verification technique used to automatically determine whether a system model satisfies a given property, often specified in a temporal logic such as Linear Temporal Logic (LTL). If the property is violated, the model checker produces a *counterexample*-a trace showing how the violation occurs.

In this work, we use the SpinJa model checker [9], a Java-based reimplementation of the explicit-state model checker Spin [8]. We choose SpinJa for its clean, object-oriented design and extensibility. Both Spin and SpinJa use Promela [8] as their modeling language.

2.5 Transition Systems

The system models analyzed in this work are formalized as *Labeled Transition Systems (LTS)*, following the standard definition for concurrent computing systems [4]:

$$L = (Q, A, \rightarrow) \tag{2}$$

where:

- Q: Set of states.
- A: Set of labels (actions or inputs).
- $\rightarrow \subseteq Q \times A \times Q$: Transition relation.

An LTS describes the possible execution sequences of a system. Each state $s \in Q$ can be associated with a set of atomic propositions that hold in that state, defining a *Kripke structure*.

For specifying system requirements, we use *Linear Temporal Logic (LTL)* [15], focusing on safety properties. In particular, we are concerned with the *reachability of unsafe (hazardous) states*, which can be specified as LTL formulas. Safety violations in this context correspond to finite execution fragments that lead to such states [4].

We write $T \models_l \varphi$ to denote that the transition system T satisfies the LTL formula φ, and $\sigma \models_l \varphi$ when an execution trace σ satisfies φ.

2.6 Platooning

Platooning refers to a cooperative driving scenario in which a manually driven lead vehicle is followed by one or more autonomously controlled vehicles. The primary objective is to reduce fuel consumption and increase traffic efficiency by allowing the follower vehicles to drive in the aerodynamic slipstream of the leader. Due to the reduced inter-vehicle distances, the followers operate below the typical assured clear distance required for safe braking. This makes platooning a safety-critical application, as maintaining a proper following distance is essential for both safety and efficiency. The system must ensure that the inter-vehicle distance remains within a defined range. A distance that is too short may result in a violation of safety requirements and increase the risk of collision, while a distance that is too large diminishes the aerodynamic benefits, reducing the fuel savings.

Fig. 1. 1:8-scale DHBW model truck

2.7 DHBW Model Truck Fleet

The Baden-Württemberg Cooperative State University (DHBW) maintains a fleet of 1:8-scale model trucks designed for research and education in autonomous driving and cyber-physical systems. Each model truck consists of a mechanical chassis and a modular electronic control unit referred to as the "electronic cube".

The chassis can be controlled via a standard RC transmitter. It features a rigid rear axle that serves as the drive axle and a front axle steered by a linear actuator. An Arduino microcontroller is responsible for interfacing with the drivetrain components, providing both control and measurement of the basic driving parameters.

The electronic cube includes various components such as control units, displays, lighting systems, sensors, and an Intel NUC (Next Unit of Computing) mini PC. The exact configuration of the electronic cube can be adapted depending on the specific use case.

For the experiments in this case study, the truck was equipped with a LIDAR sensor mounted at the front, which measures the distance to a preceding vehicle. The onboard Intel NUC runs Ubuntu 20.04 and manages all high-level tasks using the Robot Operating System (ROS). Communication between the sensors, actuators, and control logic is handled via ROS topics and services. Power is supplied by a 7V battery for the mechanical chassis and two 12V batteries for the electronic cube. Figure 1 shows one of the model trucks.

LIDAR. A LIDAR (Light Detection and Ranging) is a sensor that measures distances by emitting laser pulses and detecting their reflection from surrounding objects. The distance to an obstacle is calculated using the time-of-flight principle, which measures the time between emission and reception of the pulse. By rotating the laser beam, the LIDAR can scan its surroundings and generate a two-dimensional (2D) or three-dimensional (3D) point cloud, depending on the device type. The LIDAR used in our experiment operates in 2D and produces a planar point cloud. This point cloud enables the identification of the leading vehicle and the measurement of the inter-vehicle distance, which is crucial for the control of the follower truck.

2.8   Robot Operating System (ROS)

The Robot Operating System (ROS) is an open-source middleware framework widely used in robotics. [23] It provides hardware abstraction, device drivers, communication tools, and libraries for building robotic systems.

ROS-based applications are structured as nodes-independent processes that can represent hardware interfaces (e.g., a LIDAR driver or motor controller) or software components (e.g., autonomous behavior such as platooning). Nodes communicate via a publish-subscribe mechanism using topics.

A node can publish messages to a topic, while other nodes subscribe to it in order to receive and process those messages. In addition to topics, services offer peer-to-peer communication between two nodes, allowing for request-response interactions.

There are two major ROS versions: ROS 1 and ROS 2. They are not natively compatible but can be connected via a ROS 1bridge. Due to the use of legacy components on the model trucks, both ROS versions and the bridge are employed in our setup. ROS also includes a built-in 3D visualization tool called rviz, which can be used to display robot models, sensor data (such as point clouds), and various other aspects of the system state in real time.

3   Analyzing the Platoon Case Study

This section introduces the setup of the Truck Platoon case study, focusing on a one-dimensional scenario where vehicles follow a straight path without steering. We conduct experiments in two simulation environments and with 1:8-scale physical model trucks. Each setup is analyzed using the same data-driven modeling pipeline, which is visualized in Fig. 2.

The analysis pipeline proceeds as follows: First, event logs are recorded from the system execution. These logs are then processed into a sequenced input-output format suitable for automata learning. Based on this data, we infer a Moore machine using the Regular Positive and Negative Inference (RPNI) algorithm.

We deliberately choose Moore machines and the RPNI algorithm because they allow for efficient learning of deterministic state machines from observed system behavior, while preserving output determinism, which is particularly useful for reactive systems like platooning trucks. This approach is grounded in

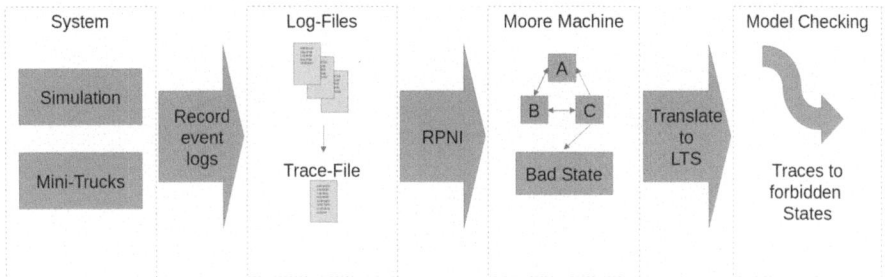

Fig. 2. Flow chart of the Platoon Case Study

established automata learning techniques and has been successfully applied in similar contexts for model inference and verification.

To enable formal model checking, the learned Moore machine is then transformed into a Labeled Transition System (LTS). This transformation is necessary because LTSs are the standard input formalism for most model checking tools. The conversion preserves the behavior of the original Moore machine while enabling compatibility with existing verification frameworks. While this step is not novel in itself, it is a pragmatic and commonly used method to bridge automata learning with formal verification.

3.1   Abstract Action-State Simulation

In this simulation, the leader truck randomly selects acceleration values from a predefined set. The follower reacts based on the observed distance to the leader. Since the simulation is not bound to real-time constraints, it enables rapid data generation for testing the entire analysis pipeline.

3.2   ROS-Based Dynamic Platoon Simulation

The second simulation mimics the behavior of a real cyber-physical system. As with the physical model trucks, communication is based on ROS. Both a leader and a follower vehicle are controlled by setting acceleration values. Using standard kinematic equations, each vehicle integrates acceleration into velocity and position at a specified update frequency. The leader can be controlled via a predefined command list or manually by adjusting acceleration. The follower has no access to the leaders intended actions. It receives the current inter-vehicle distance via a ROS topic and calculates its acceleration using a proportional controller (P-controller). The P-controller commands an acceleration proportional to the difference between the inter-vehicle distance and the desired distance. When the distance is farther than the desired distance, the Vehicle has to accelerate, when the distance is shorter it has to brake. A suitable proportional factor is determined by experiment. During the simulation, all relevant values are recorded in a logfile. Figure 3 shows a visualization of the simulation in RViz.

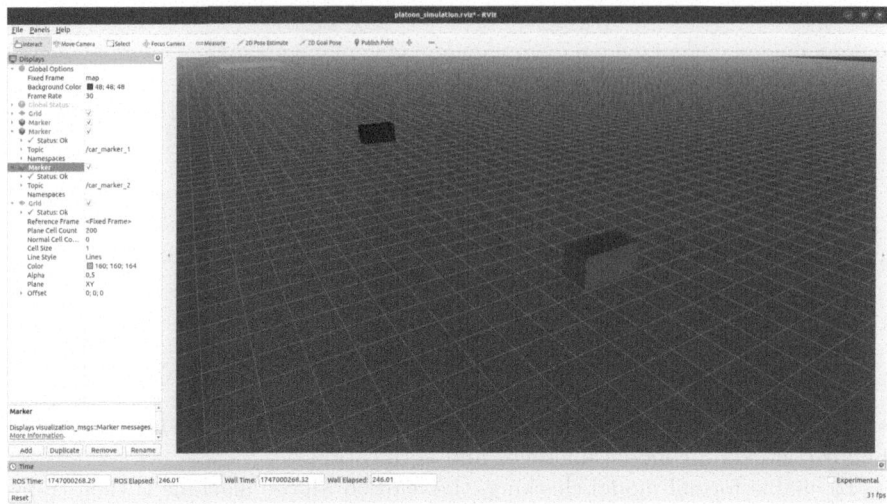

Fig. 3. A screenshot of the visualization of the simulation with RVIZ. The red box represents the Leader, the blue box the follower. (Color figure online)

3.3   Real World 1:8 Model Truck Experiment

In the real-world experiment, we use 1:8-scale model trucks. The leader is controlled manually via RC (radio control). The follower determines the distance to the leader using a LIDAR sensor and calculates its acceleration using the same P-controller as in the ROS-based simulation. This computation is triggered each time a new LIDAR message is received. Additionally, each event is logged. Since the leader's acceleration and velocity are not directly measured, they are estimated using kinematic equations based on previously logged distances and positions.

3.4   Processing the Logfiles

The logfiles generated by each system setup are aggregated and merged into a single file. This file contains execution traces from multiple runs, where each line represents a sequence of input events followed by the corresponding output or system state. Using these traces, the RPNI algorithm implemented in AALpy is applied to infer a corresponding Moore machine. Various combinations of input and output encodings are tested to analyze their influence on the size of the resulting automaton and to assess whether any combination leads to nondeterministic behavior.

3.5   Choice of Automaton Variables

The selection of input and output variables is crucial for successful automaton learning. On the one hand, the input representation should retain enough information to capture the systems essential behavior. On the other hand, overly detailed or redundant encodings may lead to unnecessarily large automata, splitting semantically equivalent states. Since the physical system is controlled by applying acceleration values to both the leader and the follower trucks, at least two input variables-one for each vehicle-are required. However, additional input variables (e.g., distance discretization, delay counters) can improve the learned model's precision, but they also increase the input space and, consequently, the size of the automaton. Careful trade-offs are therefore necessary when selecting which variables to include in the abstraction. Furthermore, all continuous values must be discretized before being used as automaton inputs or outputs. This can be achieved either by rounding values to a fixed precision or by mapping them into symbolic categories (e.g., too close, too far). These abstractions carry the risk of combining semantically different states into a single representation, potentially introducing non-deterministic behavior in the observed data. This can lead to nondeterministic behavior in the observed data, making it impossible to learn a valid automaton, as Moore machines are strictly deterministic.

3.6   Translating the Moore Machine to a LTS

To translate a Moore Machine to an LTS, we perform the following steps:

1. **States Mapping**: The states of the Moore Machine (S) become the states of the LTS (Q).
2. **Labels Mapping**: The input alphabet of the Moore Machine (Σ) becomes the set of labels (A) in the LTS.
3. **Transitions**: For each transition $\delta(s, a) = s'$, we define a transition $(s, a, s') \in \rightarrow$ in the LTS.
4. **Output Annotation**: Outputs from the Moore Machine ($\lambda(s)$) are associated with states in the LTS.
5. **Initial State**: The initial state of the Moore Machine (s_0) is the initial state of the LTS.

We then translate the corresponding LTS into promela code that we can use for model checking.

4   Evaluation

In this section, we present the results and interpretation of the Platoon case study. We specifically highlight the impact of variable selection on the learned automata and compare the results across both simulations and the real-world experiments.

4.1   Effect of Selected Variables on Analysis Results

As expected, using only a single input variable was insufficient to ensure determinism in the learned automata. It was necessary to include information from both vehicles to accurately capture the systems behavior. In particular, variables such as the inter-vehicle distance and the leaders current acceleration or velocity were essential. Without these information, only the followers states were used, while the output state is also determined by the leader.

The size of the automata depends strongly on the selected variables. Figure 4 shows an example where only the accelerations of the leader and the follower were used as input. The output consists of three abstract states: *Too Close*, *Too Far*, and *Good*. This configuration led to an automaton with only 4 states based on 2335 traces, learned in just 0.17 s. However, due to the abstraction, it was not possible to identify the reasons for entering an unsafe state. For other configurations with additional variables, it was possible to identify concrete causes for unsafe system states as we will show in Sect. 4.2. Examples of such learned automata are shown in Figs. 5 and 6.

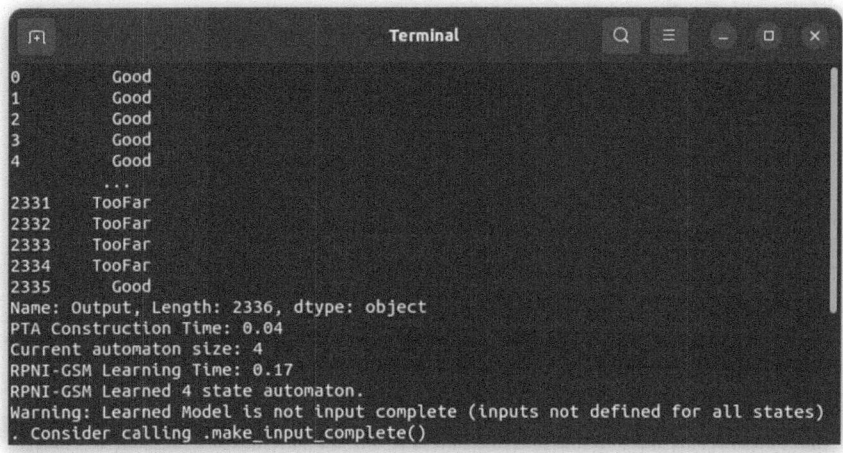

Fig. 4. Moore machine created from 2335 traces using acceleration values as input variables and three abstract states *Too Close*, *Too Far*, and *Good* as output variables. The resulting automaton has 4 states and was learned in 0.17 s.

4.2   Detection and Categorization of Safety Property Violations

As part of our current analysis pipeline, we applied model checking to the learned automata in order to identify violations of a safety property concerning the inter-vehicle distance within the truck platoon. Specifically, we verified whether the distance between the platoon leader and the following vehicle remained sufficient to ensure safe operation.

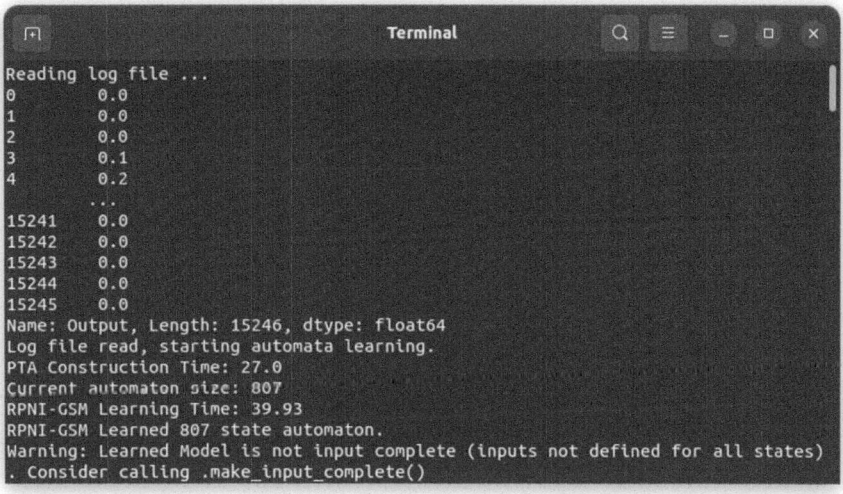

Fig. 5. Moore machine created from 15,246 traces. The resulting automaton has 807 states and was learned in 39.93 s.

In both simulation environments, model checking revealed safety property violations. For instance, in the abstract action-state simulation with a trace length of 1001 steps, the RPNI algorithm produced an automaton with 119 states. We applied the SpinJa model checker to this automaton, resulting in a full state-space exploration of 612 transitions and 788 paths. Among these, 52 paths were found to violate the safety property.

To gain further insight into the nature of these violations, we analyzed the corresponding counterexamples (an example is shown in Fig. 7) and manually categorized them into two recurring failure classes:

– **Late deceleration**: Cases in which the following vehicle initiated braking too late, leading to an unsafe reduction in distance to the lead vehicle.
– **Excessive acceleration**: Cases in which the following vehicle accelerated more aggressively than the lead vehicle, again resulting in an unsafe gap.

We observed the same failure classes in models derived from the ROS-based dynamic platoon simulation. This consistency across environments supports the validity of our approach and highlights how model checking of learned automata can reveal system-level safety risks.

The generated counterexamples not only validate the learned models but also guide future verification and system refinement. By linking learned behavior to formal safety analysis, this step demonstrates how automata learning can support interpretable and systematic reasoning about the correctness of cyber-physical systems.

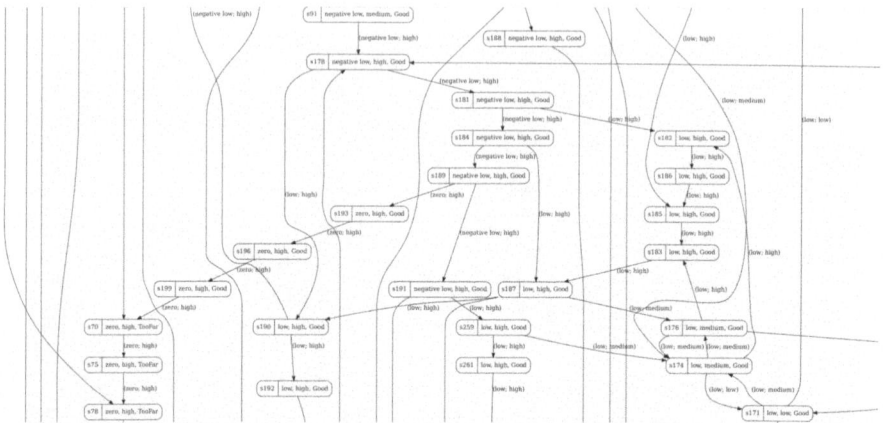

Fig. 6. Excerpt from a learned Moore machine using discretized input and output variables.

```
0:  3384 (proc 0 trans 3384): (loc == 0); loc=2; dist=0; a_lead=2; a_follow=0; sys_follow=0
1:  3402 (proc 0 trans 3402): (loc == 2); loc=12; dist=0; a_lead=1; a_follow=0; sys_follow=0
2:  3496 (proc 0 trans 3496): (loc == 12); loc=35; dist=0; a_lead=1; a_follow=1; sys_follow=0
3:  3698 (proc 0 trans 3698): (loc == 35); loc=70; dist=1; a_lead=0; a_follow=1; sys_follow=0
```

Fig. 7. Counterexample showing a too-late deceleration.

4.3   Evaluation of the Real-World Experiment

In contrast to the simulations, the real-world experiment represented the final stage of the pipeline, as the resulting automaton was too large to be translated into Promela and for the subsequent model checking. Using a trace of 33,689 entries, the smallest deterministic automaton that could be learned contained 33,251 states. The learning process took approximately 12 days (1,047,120.11 s) to complete, making it impractical for iterative experimentation. Manual selection and discretization of input and output variables proved unsuitable for handling the real-world data. Many configurations led to non-deterministic behavior, which violates the assumptions of the learning algorithm and caused failures during training. Even when determinism could be preserved, the resulting automata were extremely large and difficult to interpret. One possible reason for the low number of recurring states is the inherent noise and variability in real-world measurements. In contrast to the simulations, where initial positions and kinematic equations can be precisely controlled, real-world runs always begin with slightly different initial conditions and are affected by friction, uneven ground, and varying payloads. Additionally, the LIDAR sensor occasionally detected unintended objects instead of the leader truck, further introducing variability and error into the logged data.

5   Related Work

In past work automata learning has been used to learn models of communication protocols [1,6,25] while this work shows that automata learning can scale for realistic size use cases, the work primarily focuses on the protocol implementation. Automata learning was also applied to the validation and verification of autonomous systems [3,10,12,17,27], this work either focuses on software aspects of the systems only or on the general applicability of automata learning to the problem but does not focus on the interaction between system and environment and on the verification approach itself. Embedded and cyber-physical systems have been the subject of automata learning in the work of [11,14,16,21,26]. The combination of automata learning and model checking has been studied in [7,18].

In [16] learning-based testing was applied for software-in-the-loop (SIL) testing of a basic platoon simulator and demonstrated that both safety and performance properties can be analyzed when a model is directly learned from the simulation.

To the best of our knowledge, there is no work focusing on learning models from execution traces of a (scaled) physical truck platoon and providing a complete framework for verification and validation of the systems, including learning and verification of the model as discussed above.

6   Conclusion and Future Work

While the case study produced practical and interpretable results in both simulation environments, the same approach did not succeed in the real-world experiment. This outcome highlights a key insight: simulation alone is not sufficient when analyzing safety-critical systems. Real world experiments are essential to capture unpredictable behaviors and physical imperfections. A major challenge was the manual selection of discretization ranges, which often led to nondeterminism or excessively large automata. In future work we plan to address this by developing an iterative algorithm that dynamically refines the discretization based on observed nondeterministic transitions. An alternative direction is to shift from deterministic Moore machines to probabilistic state machines. This could better accommodate truly non-deterministic behaviors such as sensor noise or environment-induced disturbances, although it introduces new complexity in learning and verification. Furthermore, we plan to extend the approach by incorporating causality checking [13] into our framework to support the analysis of model-checking results.

References

1. Aichernig, B.K., Muškardin, E., Pferscher, A.: Active vs. passive: a comparison of automata learning paradigms for network protocols. Electronic Proceedings in Theoretical Computer Science **371**, 1–19, September 2022. https://doi.org/10.4204/EPTCS.371.1, http://arxiv.org/abs/2209.14031v1
2. Angluin, D.: Learning regular sets from queries and counterexamples. Inf. Comput. **75**(2), 87–106 (Nov 198). https://doi.org/10.1016/0890-5401(87)90052-6, https://linkinghub.elsevier.com/retrieve/pii/0890540187900526
3. Araujo, H., Mousavi, M.R., Varshosaz, M.: Testing, validation, and verification of robotic and autonomous systems: a systematic review. ACM Trans. Softw. Eng. Methodol. **32**(2), 1–61 (2023)
4. Baier, C., Katoen, J.P.: Principles of Model Checking. The MIT Press (2008)
5. Clarke, E.M., Grumberg, O., Peled, D.A.: Model Checking, 3rd ed. The MIT Press (2001)
6. Fiterău-Broştean, P., Janssen, R., Vaandrager, F.: Combining model learning and model checking to analyze tcp implementations. In: International Conference on Computer Aided Verification, pp. 454–471. Springer (2016)
7. Fogler, R., Cohen, I., Peled, D.: Accelerating black box testing with light-weight learning. In: International Symposium on Model Checking Software, pp. 103–120. Springer (2023)
8. Holzmann, G.J.: The SPIN Model Checker: Primer and Reference Manual. Addision–Wesley (2003)
9. de Jonge, M., Ruys, T.C.: The SPINJA model checker. In: van de Pol, J., Weber, M. (eds.) SPIN 2010. LNCS, vol. 6349, pp. 124–128. Springer, Heidelberg (2010). https://doi.org/10.1007/978-3-642-16164-3_9
10. Kamali, M., Dennis, L.A., McAree, O., Fisher, M., Veres, S.M.: Formal verification of autonomous vehicle platooning. Sci. Comput. Programm. **148**, 88–106 (2017). https://doi.org/10.1016/j.scico.2017.05.006, https://linkinghub.elsevier.com/retrieve/pii/S0167642317301168
11. Khosrowjerdi, H., Meinke, K., Rasmusson, A.: Virtualized-fault injection testing: a machine learning approach. In: 2018 IEEE 11th International Conference on Software Testing, Verification and Validation (ICST), pp. 297–308. IEEE, Vasteras, April 2018. https://doi.org/10.1109/ICST.2018.00037, https://ieeexplore.ieee.org/document/8367057/
12. Lee, J., Sedwards, S., Czarnecki, K.: Uniformly constrained reinforcement learning. Auton. Agent. Multi-Agent Syst. **38**(1), 1 (Jun 2024)
13. Leitner-Fischer, F., Leue, S.: Probabilistic fault tree synthesis using causality computation. Int. J. Crit. Comput.-Based Syst. (IJCCBS) **4**(2), 119–143 (2013)
14. Maier, A.: Online passive learning of timed automata for cyber-physical production systems. In: 2014 12th IEEE International Conference on Industrial Informatics (INDIN), pp. 60–66. IEEE, Porto Alegre RS, Brazil, July 2014. https://doi.org/10.1109/INDIN.2014.6945484, http://ieeexplore.ieee.org/document/6945484/
15. Manna, Z., Pnueli, A.: The temporal logic of reactive and concurrent systems: specifications, vol. 1. Springer Science & Business Media (1992)
16. Meinke, K.: Learning-based testing of cyber-physical systems-of-systems: a platooning study. In: Reinecke, P., Di Marco, A. (eds.) EPEW 2017. LNCS, vol. 10497, pp. 135–151. Springer, Cham (2017). https://doi.org/10.1007/978-3-319-66583-2_9

17. Meinke, K.: Active machine learning to test autonomous driving. In: 2021 IEEE International Conference on Software Testing, Verification and Validation Workshops (ICSTW), pp. 286–286. IEEE, Porto de Galinhas, Brazil, April 2021. https:// doi.org/10.1109/ICSTW52544.2021.00055, https://ieeexplore.ieee.org/document/ 9440164/

18. Mongelli, M., Muselli, M., Scorzoni, A., Ferrari, E.: Accellerating PRISM Validation of Vehicle Platooning through Machine Learning

19. Moore, E.F.: Gedanken-experiments on sequential machines. In: Automata Studies. Princeton University Press (1956)

20. Muškardin, E., Aichernig, B.K., Pill, I., Pferscher, A., Tappler, M.: AALpy: an active automata learning library. Innovations Syst. Softw. Eng. **18**(3), 417–426 (2022)

21. Niggemann, O., Biswas, G., Kinnebrew, J.S., Khorasgani, H., Volgmann, S., Bunte, A.: Data-Driven Monitoring of Cyber-Physical Systems Leveraging on Big Data and the Internet-of-Things for Diagnosis and Control

22. Oncina, J., Garcia, P., et al.: Inferring regular languages in polynomial update time. Pattern Recognit Image Anal. **1**(49–61), 10–1142 (1992)

23. Quigley, M., et al.: Ros: an open-source robot operating system, vol. 3, January 2009

24. Reynouard, R., Ingólfsdóttir, A., Bacci, G.: Jajapy: a learning library for stochastic models. In: International Conference on Quantitative Evaluation of Systems, pp. 30–46. Springer (2023)

25. Salva, S.: An Approach for Learning Behavioural Models of Communicating Systems (2022)

26. Schammer, L., Plambeck, S., Bahnsen, F.H., Fey, G.: Learning models of cyber-physical systems using automata learning. In: 2021 IEEE 45th Annual Computers, Software, and Applications Conference (COMPSAC), pp. 1224–1229. IEEE, Madrid, Spain, July 2021. https://doi.org/10.1109/COMPSAC51774.2021.00169, https://ieeexplore.ieee.org/document/9529368/

27. Selvaraj, Y., Farooqui, A., Panahandeh, G., Ahrendt, W., Fabian, M.: Automatically learning formal models from autonomous driving software. Electronics **11**(4), 643 (Feb2022)

28. Verwer, S., Hammerschmidt, C.: FlexFringe: Modeling Software Behavior by Learning Probabilistic Automata, August 2023. http://arxiv.org/abs/2203.16331, arXiv:2203.16331 [cs]

Q-SafeML: Safety Assessment of Quantum Machine Learning via Quantum Distance Metrics

Oliver Dunn$^{(\boxtimes)}$, Koorosh Aslansefat, and Yiannis Papadopoulos ⓘ

University of Hull, Hull East Yorkshire HU6 7RX, UK
o.dunn2-2021@hull.ac.uk
https://plennock.github.io/Honours-Stage-Project/

Abstract. The rise of machine learning in safety-critical systems has paralleled advancements in quantum computing, leading to the emerging field of Quantum Machine Learning (QML). While safety monitoring has progressed in classical ML, existing methods are not directly applicable to QML due to fundamental differences in quantum computation. Given the novelty of QML, dedicated safety mechanisms remain underdeveloped. This paper introduces Q-SafeML, a safety monitoring approach for QML. The method builds on SafeML, a recent method that utilizes statistical distance measures to assess model accuracy and provide confidence in the reasoning of an algorithm. An adapted version of Q-SafeML incorporates quantum-centric distance measures, aligning with the probabilistic nature of QML outputs. This shift to a model-dependent, post-classification evaluation represents a key departure from classical SafeML, which is dataset-driven and classifier-agnostic. The distinction is motivated by the unique representational constraints of quantum systems, requiring distance metrics defined over quantum state spaces. Q-SafeML detects distances between operational and training data addressing the concept drifts in the context of QML. Experiments on QCNN and VQC Models show that this enables informed human oversight, enhancing system transparency and safety.

Keywords: Machine learning · Quantum Computing · SafeML · Distance Measures · Quantum Machine Learning

1 Introduction

Safety monitoring in machine learning (ML) is crucial for safety-critical domains such as healthcare [2], transportation [3], and energy [9]. One such method, *SafeML*, uses parametric distance measures to assess how closely a model's predictions align with real-world data, helping detect weaknesses and uncertainty before or during deployment [24].

Originally developed to address out-of-distribution detection (OODD) in ML classifiers [19,21], SafeML now intersects with a growing field: quantum machine

P. Katsaros (Ed.): IMBSA 2025, LNCS 15755, pp. 348–364, 2026.
https://doi.org/10.1007/978-3-032-05073-1_23

learning (QML). QML leverages quantum computing principles such as super-position and entanglement to enhance ML tasks like classification and regression [15, 25].

As classical models transition to quantum environments, safety tools must also adapt. Yet, safety remains underexplored in QML, despite the well-known fragility of quantum systems and their sensitivity to noise [29]. This work introduces *Quantum SafeML*, an adaptation of SafeML that integrates quantum-specific statistical distance measures for safety monitoring in quantum settings [16, 22].

Here, "safety" refers to identifying unreliable or error-prone behavior in ML models–particularly incorrect or uncertain predictions. The goal is not formal correctness, but improved transparency and early risk detection during deployment.

1.1   Aims and Objectives

The goal is to develop a QML-compatible version of SafeML using quantum distance metrics to monitor prediction accuracy and model reliability. Key objectives:

- Identify suitable quantum distance measures.
- Evaluate their fit within the SafeML framework.
- Implement them on quantum datasets.
- Use them to assess QML model performance.
- Evaluate the overall effectiveness of Quantum SafeML.

1.2   Research Questions

- RQ1: How effective is SafeML at detecting labeling errors in QML?
- RQ2: Can it adapt across various QML implementations?
- RQ3: Which QML applications benefit most from such monitoring?

1.3   Scope and Limitations

QML is expected to impact future technologies, especially in safety-critical areas [27]. However, safety monitoring tools for QML remain immature. This work adapts SafeML to quantum contexts to provide a foundation for more robust safety practices and contributes to the validation of emerging quantum technologies [24, 29].

Due to limited access to quantum hardware, experiments used simulators such as Qiskit, PennyLane, and Cirq. This project used Qiskit for its built-in QML tools and extensive IBM documentation. While simulators don't fully replicate quantum noise, they are sufficient for proof-of-concept validation. The focus is on performance monitoring in classification tasks, not on outperforming classical models.

Unlike classical SafeML, this version is model-dependent and monitors classifier behavior post-decision, rather than input distribution drift. This shift accommodates quantum-specific outputs, such as density matrices, which are incompatible with classical SafeML's assumptions.

1.4   Paper Structure

Section 2 reviews related work in QML and SafeML. Section 3 outlines the research gap. Section 4 presents Quantum SafeML, followed by experiments in Sect. 5. Results and discussion appear in Sect. 6, with conclusions in Sect. 7.

2   Related Work

2.1   Quantum Computing and Machine Learning

Quantum computing introduces a new computational paradigm based on quantum mechanical principles like superposition and entanglement [20]. Although still in early development, recent research explores how quantum algorithms can support or enhance machine learning tasks [2,3,9]. Prominent approaches include quantum kernels, Boltzmann machines, and variational quantum circuits, which may offer expressivity or training benefits in specific contexts [15,25].

Quantum information theory contributes new tools to ML, such as density matrices and entropy measures, offering alternative ways to model uncertainty and correlations [3]. While widespread QML deployment is limited by hardware, its theoretical influence is shaping developments in model architecture and learning theory [16,22].

2.2   Out-of-Distribution Detection

Out-of-distribution detection (OODD) addresses the risk that models encounter test data different from their training distribution [24]. This issue is especially critical in domains like healthcare, autonomous driving, and security, where undetected distributional shifts can lead to serious failures [27,29].

Recent techniques include Bayesian uncertainty quantification, deep generative models for density estimation, and contrastive learning [19,21]. Many methods build on geometric properties of feature spaces or assume smoothness and separability in the learned representations [19]. There's also increasing focus on robustness guarantees and formal generalization metrics under shift, drawing on statistical learning and information theory [30].

Challenges remain, such as benchmark definition, calibration under shift, and understanding the links between OOD behavior and training-time regularization [24,29]. Ongoing research continues to explore the balance between novelty sensitivity and robustness to natural variation [21].

2.3   Runtime Safety Monitoring and SafeML

Runtime monitoring and human oversight are essential for safe ML deployment. SafeML supports this by applying statistical methods to assess model reliability during operation. It evaluates how much new input data deviates from the training distribution using empirical cumulative distribution function (ECDF)-based distance metrics. This helps estimate potential accuracy drops and prompts human intervention when data shifts are detected [8].

SafeML is one of few techniques cited in standards like Germany's DIN SPEC 92005 for ML uncertainty quantification [1]. It has been extended for image classification via bootstrapping methods [6], and to time-series and regression tasks using new robustness metrics [4]. Threshold tuning remains a challenge; automated threshold adjustment methods have been proposed [14].

Applications span fields such as intrusion detection [8], autonomous driving [6,10], robotics [7,12], and UAV inspection [18]. Recent work extends SafeML to analyze internal neural network layers for more precise distribution shift detection [13]. The SMILE extension builds on SafeML to offer model-agnostic explanations through empirical distance measures [5].

3   Research Gap and Problem Definition

While classical safety-monitoring techniques like SafeML have shown effectiveness in identifying classifier confusion through statistical distance metrics, their direct application to quantum systems remains unexplored. Key research gaps include:

– Absence of a quantum-adapted SafeML framework.
– Limited error estimation protocols for QML.
– No empirical method for analyzing false positives/negatives in QML using distribution-based techniques.
– Existing quantum distance metrics have not been integrated into safety monitoring.

Classical SafeML operates on deterministic predictions and employ metrics (e.g., Kolmogorov-Smirnov, Wasserstein) which are incompatible with quantum representations like density matrices. The difficulty is that quantum models de facto produce probabilistic outputs, requiring different representations and tools. As such, classical SafeML fails to account for:

1. Quantum data superposition and representation via density matrices.
2. Probabilistic outputs from quantum circuits.
3. Incompatibility of classical statistical distances with quantum data formats.

To address the above, we explore how SafeML can be meaningfully adapted to QML architectures using quantum-compatible statistical distance metrics. A core requirement is transforming predictions into density matrices:

$$\rho = \sum_i p_i |\psi_i\rangle\langle\psi_i| \tag{1}$$

where ρ encodes a quantum state as a probabilistic mixture of pure states $|\psi_i\rangle$. We propose, and evaluate a solution for meaningful safety monitoring of Quantum ML. Our study is limited to classification problems. Although such an approach may potentially generalize to other learning paradigms, regression and reinforcement learning are beyond the current scope.

4   The Quantum SafeML Method

The Quantum SafeML method extends the classical SafeML framework to accommodate the probabilistic nature of quantum computations. This is achieved by integrating quantum-specific distance metrics, namely trace distance, fidelity, Bures distance, and quantum relative entropy, to assess the similarity between quantum states and evaluate the reliability of QML models.

4.1   Trace Distance

Trace distance quantifies the distinguishability between two quantum states, providing a measure of how well one can differentiate between them. For density matrices ρ and σ, it is defined as:

$$D(\rho, \sigma) = \frac{1}{2} \operatorname{Tr} |\rho - \sigma| \tag{2}$$

Here, $|\rho - \sigma|$ denotes the trace norm of the matrix difference. A trace distance of 0 indicates identical states, while a value of 1 signifies completely distinguishable states [23].

4.2   Fidelity

Fidelity measures the similarity between two quantum states, reflecting the probability that one state will pass a test to identify as the other. For density matrices ρ and σ, fidelity is given by:

$$F(\rho, \sigma) = \left(\operatorname{Tr} \sqrt{\sqrt{\rho}\, \sigma \sqrt{\rho}} \right)^2 \tag{3}$$

A fidelity of 1 implies identical states, whereas 0 indicates orthogonal, i.e. completely distinct, states [17].

4.3   Bures Distance

Derived from fidelity, the Bures distance provides a metric for the geometric distance between quantum states:

$$D_B(\rho, \sigma) = \sqrt{2 \left(1 - \sqrt{F(\rho, \sigma)} \right)} \tag{4}$$

This metric is particularly useful in quantum information theory for comparing mixed quantum states [11, 26].

4.4   Quantum Relative Entropy

Quantum relative entropy measures the distinguishability between two quantum states, analogous to the classical Kullback-Leibler divergence. For density matrices ρ and σ, it is given by:

$$S(\rho\|\sigma) = \mathrm{Tr}\left(\rho \log \rho - \rho \log \sigma\right) \tag{5}$$

This quantity represents the information loss when approximating ρ with σ [28].

Quantum SafeML employs these distance metrics to compare two sets: one containing misclassified predictions for a specific label, and the other containing correctly classified ones. The computed distance metric can then be evaluated against the model's true accuracy, potentially within an optimization framework.

This process involves training models on a dataset as usual. During validation, classification outcomes are recorded and stored in a suitable format (e.g., density matrix or NumPy array). These sets are then analysed using the selected metrics and compared with the model's accuracy to yield a final assessment of classifier safety.

4.5   Differentiation from Classical SafeML

While Q-SafeML draws conceptual inspiration from the classical SafeML framework, it represents a significant methodological departure. Classical SafeML is fundamentally model-agnostic: it operates on data distributions alone, comparing statistical differences between the training set and new inputs to detect distributional shifts without direct reference to the classifier's internal behavior.

In contrast, Q-SafeML is inherently model-dependent. Rather than evaluating input drift, it assesses the reliability of a quantum classifier's outputs by comparing sets of correctly and incorrectly classified predictions using quantum distance metrics. This shift reflects the probabilistic and state-based nature of quantum machine learning, where outputs are quantum states (or statistical mixtures thereof), and the notion of "distance" must account for this complexity.

This adaptation is necessary because quantum systems encode both data and results in formats that are incompatible with classical statistical techniques. Therefore, while Q-SafeML preserves SafeML's core philosophy–detecting unsafe or unreliable model behavior using statistical comparisons–it operates at a fundamentally different layer of the machine learning pipeline: post-classification rather than pre-deployment (Figs. 1 and 2).

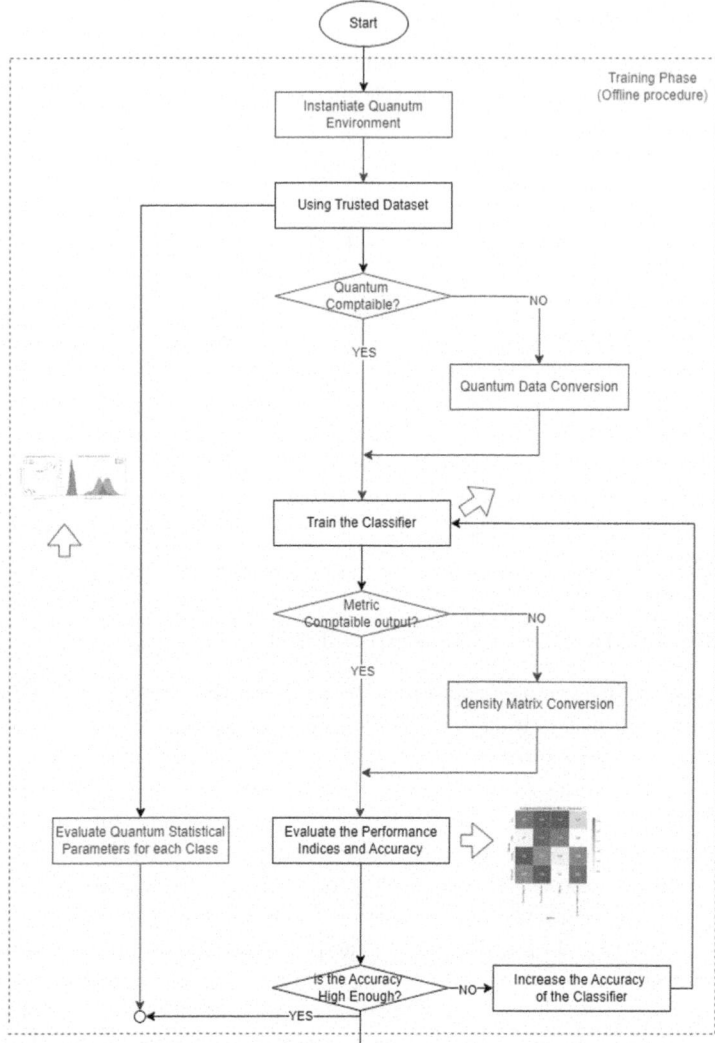

Fig. 1. Proposed Quantum SafeML method (training phase)

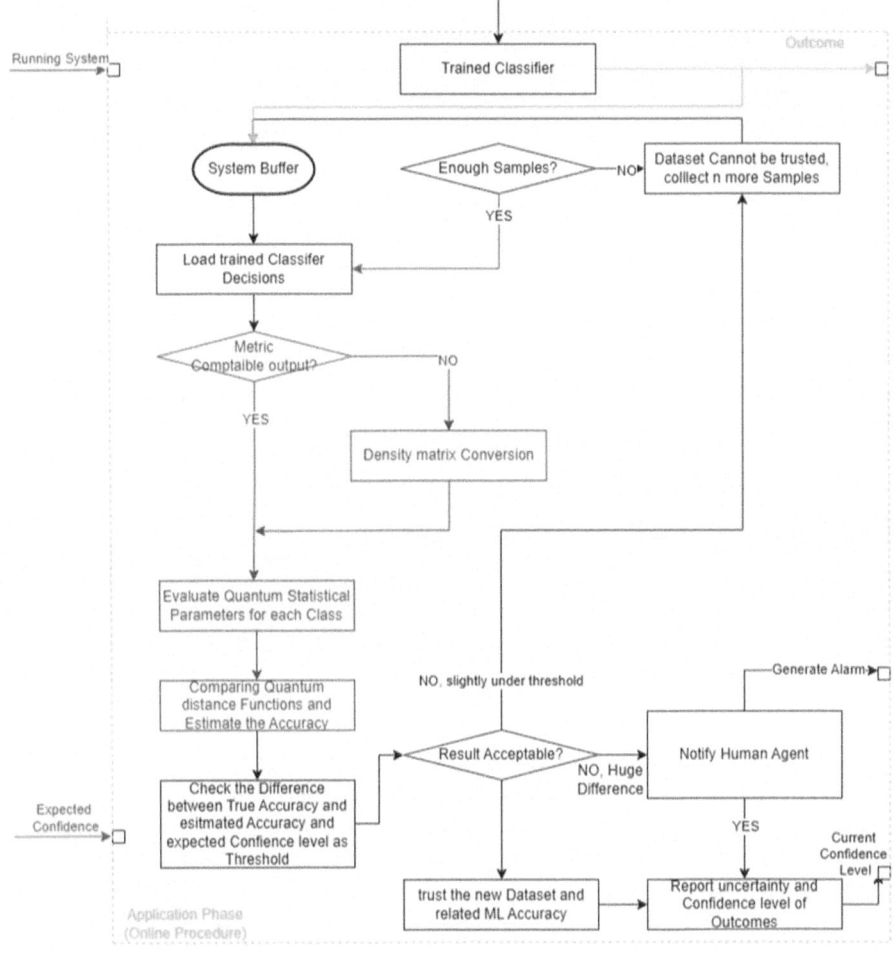

Fig. 2. Proposed Quantum SafeML method (online phase)

5   Case Studies

5.1   Quantum Environment Instantiation with Qiskit

Qiskit was chosen for quantum environment instantiation due to its robust simulation tools, active support community, and access to IBM quantum hardware. While alternatives like PennyLane focus on quantum machine learning, Qiskit offers a dedicated QML library, broader algorithmic support, and hybrid model compatibility. Recent updates, though introducing a steeper learning curve, have made Qiskit more future-proof and reliable for experimentation.

The simulated environment was built using Qiskit documentation and example notebooks, enabling accurate modeling of quantum behavior such as superposition and entanglement. Core components like quantum gates, circuit construction, and backend configuration were included to support scalable QML testing. This setup offers a controlled yet realistic platform for developing and evaluating the Quantum SafeML framework.

To assess the effectiveness of Quantum SafeML, we applied it to two quantum models: a Variational Quantum Classifier (VQC) evaluated on toy datasets and a Quantum Convolutional Neural Network (QCNN) applied to handwritten digit classification.

5.2   Quantum SafeML on a VQC with Toy Datasets

The VQC model, originally built for the Iris dataset, was extended to classify the Wine dataset (with 13 numerical features) as well as several synthetic datasets with randomised features. Quantum SafeML was then used to evaluate model performance using Bures distance, Trace distance, Fidelity, and Quantum relative entropy

Table 1. Quantum Metric Comparisons Across Datasets the VQC trained on.

Dataset	Bures Distance	Trace Distance	Fidelity	Quantum Relative Entropy	True Accuracy
Iris	0.7482	0.5000	0.4677	1.2396	0.5333
Wine	0.9036	0.3701	0.2517	1.0000	0.3056
Family	0.3352	0.0535	0.8893	0.2424	0.4250
Transport	0.3627	0.1299	0.8714	0.2823	0.1406

To assess how well quantum distance metrics reflect model reliability, we computed Pearson correlation coefficients between each metric and true classification accuracy. Quantum relative entropy showed the highest (moderate) correlation with accuracy ($r = 0.54$), followed by trace distance ($r = 0.48$). Fidelity and Bures distance showed weaker correlations. However, due to the limited number of datasets, these results are not statistically significant and should be interpreted cautiously.

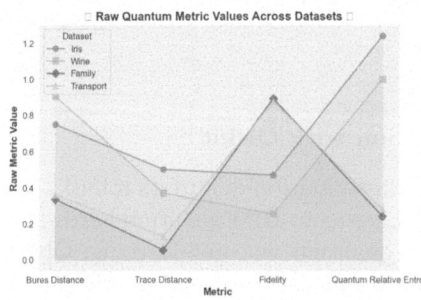 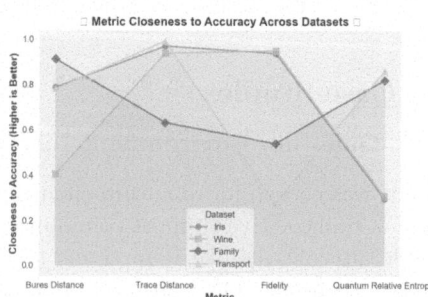

(a) Raw Quantum Metric Values Across Datasets

(b) Metric Closeness to Accuracy Across Datasets

Fig. 3. Comparison of Quantum Metric Values Across each of the Datasets the VQC trained on, and the overall model accuracy for each of these.

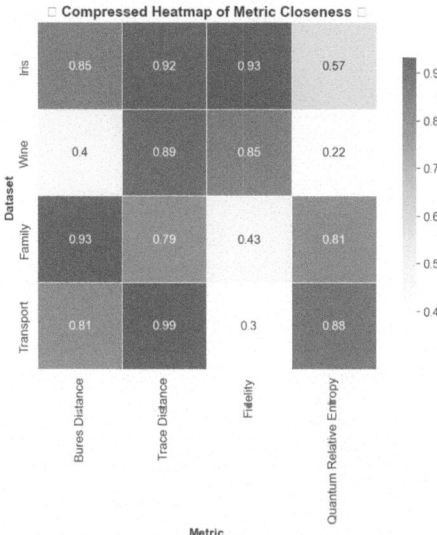

Fig. 4. Heatmap of Metric Values Across Different Datasets the VQC trained on.

Key findings from the analysis indicate:

- A quantum relative entropy value greater than 1 may indicate potential issues with matrix shape or structural integrity.
- The Wine dataset exhibits a notably lower accuracy of 30.6% and simultaneously higher metric distances, signaling a notable discrepancy in classification reliability.
- This discrepancy is visualised in Fig. 3, which shows the comparative metric values across datasets. Figure 4 further illustrates how these metric variations correlate with the classifier's predictive performance, reinforcing the observed performance degradation on the Wine dataset.

5.3   Quantum SafeML on a QCNN with Digit Dataset

The QCNN was applied to classify 8×8 handwritten digit images with dimensionality reduced via PCA to 6 principal features. Key findings include:

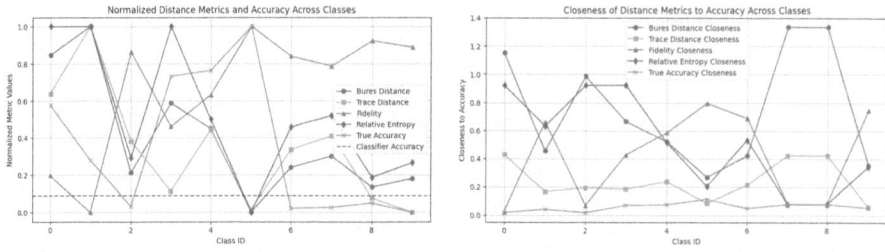

(a) Metric Values for QNN Classes   (b) Metric Accuracy Closeness in QNN

Fig. 5. Comparison of distance Metric Values through each of the different classes in the digits dataset, and the closeness to model accuracy for each of these.

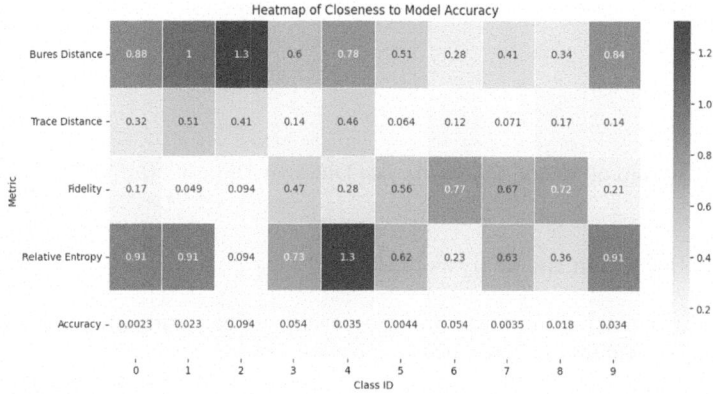

Fig. 6. Heatmap showing how each metrics closeness to model accuracy varies across the subsets derived from each class label.

– A high variance in the Bures distance was observed for classes 7 and 8, as illustrated in Fig. 5a. This suggests instability or heightened uncertainty in the model's internal representation of these classes.
– The heatmap presented in Fig. 6 reveals distinct class-specific patterns in quantum metric values, offering further insights into the model's interpretability and behaviour across the digit classes.

5.4   Exploring Threshold Values with Quantum Kernel Methods

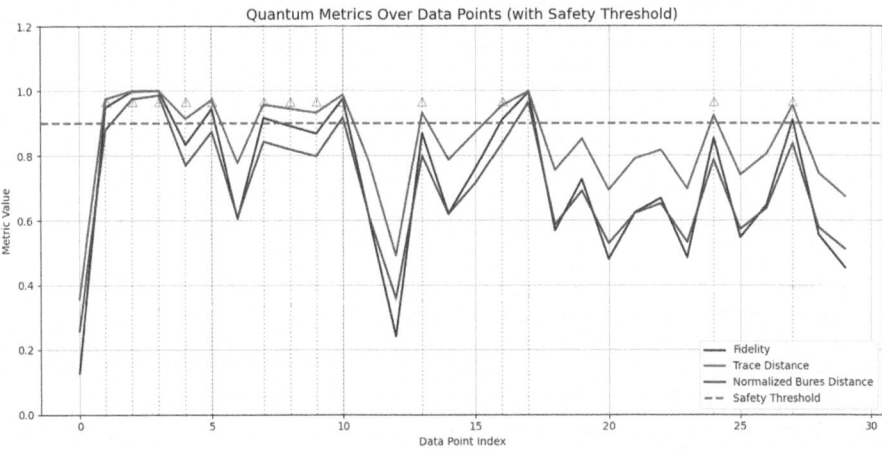

Fig. 7. Kernel-based metric values compared to threshold; exceeding the line suggests lower model confidence.

The thresholding framework operates by first normalizing the relevant safety metrics: the Bures distance is divided by $\sqrt{2}$ and the complement of fidelity (i.e., $1-$ fidelity) is computed. After normalisation, the system flags any samples whose metric values exceed predefined thresholds, marking them as potentially unsafe. This behaviour is illustrated in Fig. 7, which shows instances where the threshold has been breached.

6   Discussion

Quantum SafeML has demonstrated its ability to identify weaknesses in QML, particularly across both VQC and QCNN architectures, through application of quantum distance metrics. This section discusses the effectiveness, challenges, and implications of the approach.

6.1   Effectiveness of SafeML in Quantum Machine Learning

Quantum SafeML proved effective in delivering detailed performance assessments across multiple distance metrics, allowing for meaningful comparisons with classifier accuracy.

For VQC models, SafeML performed strongly across diverse datasets, despite tolerating some inconsistencies, e.g., from quantum relative entropy in sklearn toy datasets, where misclassified data could inflate results. Despite some shortcomings, the metrics provided valuable insight into model weaknesses nd uncertainty.

In the case of QCNNs, SafeML the method encountered greater complexity. The architectural intricacies of QCNNs made SafeML application more challenging, requiring careful configuration. However, it still remained capable of identifying prediction errors, offering insights into model behavior.

These findings suggest that among the evaluated metrics, quantum relative entropy and trace distance show the highest (moderate) correlation with model accuracy, indicating some potential as reliability indicators. In contrast, fidelity and Bures distance demonstrated weaker or inconsistent relationships. Given the small sample size and lack of statistical significance, these insights should be interpreted cautiously, and future work should explore combining metrics or integrating confidence thresholds for more robust monitoring.

6.2   Metric Selection and Application

Choosing the right metric for Quantum SafeML is heavily dependent on the specific goals of the safety validation process. The following insights were derived from the experiments:

- **Trace Distance** was the most consistent and interpretable metric, reliably capturing classifier confusion across various VQC tasks.
- **Bures Distance** performed well in noisy conditions and mixed quantum states, i.e. conditions expected in real quantum hardware, being more sensitive to noise.
- **Fidelity** excelled in generative tasks or for measuring state overlap. However, it was sensitive to encoding quirks and entanglement issues.
- **Quantum Relative Entropy** proved useful for asymmetric error evaluation and privacy-related divergence, though it required careful handling to avoid invalid or misleading results.

When used together, the metrics offered complementary insights. For instance, cases where fidelity and trace distance disagreed–such as in the Wine dataset–often corresponded to ambiguous classification boundaries or poorly separated feature spaces. This divergence can serve as a red flag, suggesting internal inconsistencies in the model's confidence. In contrast, convergence of all metrics typically aligned with high-accuracy predictions and more stable output states. This highlights the value of a multi-metric approach over relying on any single distance measure in isolation.

No single metric emerged as universally optimal. Instead, using multiple metrics in parallel, analyzing their convergence or divergence, provided a more holistic understanding of classifier performance.

6.3   Quantum Hardware Considerations

The study primarily relied on simulators, which assume idealized conditions unless explicitly configured otherwise. As such, they do not capture the full range of errors and noise present in current quantum hardware, such as gate infidelity, crosstalk, and decoherence. While Bures distance and quantum relative entropy are sensitive to such distortions and may behave differently under real hardware constraints, our simulation results likely present an optimistic view.

To mitigate this, future work will incorporate noise models available in Qiskit to simulate realistic hardware conditions more faithfully. Long-term, we aim to evaluate Q-SafeML on IBM Q and other public quantum backends. Additionally, reducing circuit depth and optimizing encodings may enhance the method's robustness on Noisy Intermediate-Scale Quantum (NISQ) devices.

6.4 Limitations and Challenges

A major challenge in applying SafeML lies in handling multiclass classification problems. Encoding valid quantum states across multiple output classes adds complexity, especially when mapping model predictions to quantum systems.

Additionally, SafeML was applied post-hoc, i.e. after model predictions were made. This may have limited its potential. A more integrated approach, potentially using continuous monitoring during training or metric-based loss functions, could offer more robust results.

Finally, practical issues inherent in live quantum environments, such as latency, calibration, and noise, were not fully accounted for in this study due to the reliance on simulators. These factors are likely to impact performance in real-world QML applications.

6.5 Evaluation of Initial Research Questions

RQ1: How Effective is SafeML in Detecting Labelling Errors in QML?
Quantum SafeML proved effective in identifying labelling errors in QML classification tasks. By applying distance metrics to density matrix representations, it reliably highlighted mislabelled instances and quantified their occurrence. For example, the Wine dataset exhibited lower accuracy and high divergence in metric values (see Table 1 and Fig. 3), indicating inconsistencies linked to potential labelling or model limitations.

RQ2: Is it Adaptable to Different QML Implementations? While this study focused solely on classification models, Quantum SafeML was tested across various architectures – specifically the VQC and QCNN (see Sects. 4.2 and 4.3). The flexibility of using multiple distance metrics enabled adaptation to datasets of varying dimensionality and structure. This adaptability is further supported by class-specific patterns observed in the QCNN analysis (Fig. 6), demonstrating its potential for generalisation to other QML contexts.

RQ3: Which QML Applications Benefit Most from Such Monitoring?
Among the tested models, the QCNN used for image classification exhibited the clearest benefit from Quantum SafeML. As highlighted in Figs. 5a and 6, distinct quantum metric behaviours across digit classes allowed targeted error

identification. This aligns with findings in Sect. 4.3, and mirrors the strengths of classical SafeML in computer vision applications.

7   Conclusion

This study evaluated the performance of different quantum distance metrics within the Quantum SafeML framework. The findings indicated that each metric has specific strengths and weaknesses depending on the classifier type and dataset. Trace distance emerged as the most stable, while Bures distance was most suited to noisy settings. Fidelity was well-suited for generative tasks, and Quantum Relative Entropy was most effective for evaluating asymmetric errors.

As quantum computing continues to develop, the safety and reliability of quantum machine learning models will remain a critical concern. Methods like Quantum SafeML, combined with careful metric selection, could play a vital role in making quantum models more transparent, trustworthy, and robust for real-world deployment.

8   Code Availability

Regarding the research reproducibility, codes and functions supporting this paper are published online at GitHub:
https://github.com/Plennock/Honours-Stage-Project.

References

1. DIN SPEC 92005: Machine Learning Uncertainty Quantification. DIN SPEC 92005, Beuth Verlag GmbH (DIN - Deutsches Institut für Normung), Berlin, Germany (2022). https://www.din.de/en/wdc-beuth:din21:343195966, standard for methods and measures for quantifying uncertainty in machine learning models
2. Adepoju, O., et al.: Quantum computing: a paradigm shift in computational technology. Int. J. Comput. (2019)
3. Ahmed, T., Kashif, M., Marchisio, A., Shafique, M.: Quantum neural networks: a comparative analysis and noise robustness evaluation. arXiv preprint arXiv:2501.14412 (2025)
4. Akram, M.N., Ambekar, A., Sorokos, I., Aslansefat, K., Schneider, D.: StaDRe and staDRo: reliability and robustness estimation of ml-based forecasting using statistical distance measures. In: Computer Safety, Reliability, and Security. SAFECOMP 2022 Workshops: DECSoS, DepDevOps, SASSUR, SENSEI, USDAI, and WAISE Munich, Germany, 6–9 September 2022, Proceedings, pp. 289–301. Springer (2022)
5. Aslansefat, K., Hashemian, M., Walker, M., Akram, M.N., Sorokos, I., Papadopoulos, Y.: Explaining black boxes with a smile: Statistical model-agnostic interpretability with local explanations. IEEE Softw. (2023)
6. Aslansefat, K., Kabir, S., Abdullatif, A., Vasudevan, V., Papadopoulos, Y.: Toward improving confidence in autonomous vehicle software: a study on traffic sign recognition systems. Computer **54**(8), 66–76 (2021)

7. Aslansefat, K., et al.: SafeDrones: real-time reliability evaluation of UAVs using executable digital dependable identities. In: Model-Based Safety and Assessment: 8th International Symposium, IMBSA 2022, Munich, Germany, 5–7 September 2022, Proceedings, pp. 252–266. Springer (2022)

8. Aslansefat, K., Sorokos, I., Whiting, D., Tavakoli Kolagari, R., Papadopoulos, Y.: Safeml: safety monitoring of machine learning classifiers through statistical difference measures. In: Zeller, M., Höfig, K. (eds.) IMBSA 2020. LNCS, vol. 12297, pp. 197–211. Springer, Cham (2020). https://doi.org/10.1007/978-3-030-58920-2_13

9. Benedetti, M., Lloyd, E., Sack, S., Fiorentini, M.: Parameterized quantum circuits as machine learning models. Quant. Sci. Technol. **4**(4), 043001 (2019). https://doi.org/10.1088/2058-9565/ab4eb5

10. Bergler, M., Kolagari, R.T., Lundqvist, K.: Case study on the use of the safeML approach in training autonomous driving vehicles. In: Image Analysis and Processing–ICIAP 2022: 21st International Conference, Lecce, Italy, 23–27 May 2022, Proceedings, Part III, pp. 87–97. Springer (2022)

11. Bures, D.: An extension of Kakutanis theorem on infinite product measures to the tensor product of semifinite w^*-algebras. Trans. Am. Math. Soc. **135**, 199–212 (1969)

12. Cho, H., Lee, K., Choi, N., Kim, S., Lee, J., Yang, S.: Online safety zone estimation and violation detection for nonstationary objects in workplaces. IEEE Access **10**, 39769–39781 (2022)

13. Farhad, A.H., Sorokos, I., Akram, M.N., Aslansefat, K., Schneider, D.: Scope compliance uncertainty estimate. arXiv preprint arXiv:2312.10801 (2023)

14. Farhad, A.H., Sorokos, I., Schmidt, A., Akram, M.N., Aslansefat, K., Schneider, D.: Keep your distance: determining sampling and distance thresholds in machine learning monitoring. In: Model-Based Safety and Assessment: 8th International Symposium, IMBSA 2022, Munich, Germany, 5–7 September 2022, Proceedings, pp. 219–234. Springer (2022)

15. Gil Fuster, E.M.: Variational quantum classifier. Bachelor's thesis, University of Barcelona (2018). https://diposit.ub.edu/dspace/bitstream/2445/140318/1/GIL%20FUSTER%20Elies%20Miquel.pdf

16. IBM: IBM roadmap to quantum-centric supercomputers (updated 2024). IBM Quantum Computing Blog (2024). https://www.ibm.com/quantum/blog/ibm-quantum-roadmap-2025?lnk=ushpv18r1

17. Jozsa, R.: Fidelity for mixed quantum states. J. Mod. Opt. **41**(12), 2315–2323 (1994)

18. Kabir, S., Aslansefat, K., Gope, P., Campean, F., Papadopoulos, Y.: Combining drone-based monitoring and machine learning for online reliability evaluation of wind turbines. In: 2022 International Conference on Computing, Electronics & Communications Engineering (iCCECE), pp. 53–58. IEEE (2022)

19. Kim, B., Kim, B., Hyun, Y.: Investigation of out-of-distribution detection across various models and training methodologies. Neural Netw. **175**, 106288 (2024). https://doi.org/10.1016/j.neunet.2024.106288

20. Ladd, T., Jelezko, F., Laflamme, R., Nakamura, Y., Monroe, C., OBrien, J.: Quantum computers. Nature **464**(7285), 45–53 (2010). https://doi.org/10.1038/nature08812

21. Liang, S., Li, Y., Srikant, R.: Enhancing the reliability of out-of-distribution image detection in neural networks. arXiv preprint arXiv:1706.02690 (2020)

22. Neven, H.: Meet willow, our state-of-the-art quantum chip. Google Blog (2024). https://blog.google/technology/research/google-willow-quantum-chip/

23. Nielsen, M.A., Chuang, I.L.: Quantum Computation and Quantum Information. Cambridge University Press (2002)
24. Paleyes, A., Urma, R.G., Lawrence, N.: Challenges in deploying machine learning: a survey of case studies. ACM Comput. Surv. **55**(6) (2022). https://doi.org/10.1145/3533378
25. Schuld, M., Sweke, R., Meyer, J.: The effect of data encoding on the expressive power of variational quantum machine learning models. Phys. Rev. A **102**(3), 032420 (2020). https://doi.org/10.1103/PhysRevA.102.032420
26. Uhlmann, A.: The transition probability in the state space of a *-algebra. Rep. Math. Phys. **9**(2), 273–279 (1976)
27. Union, E.: The EU artificial intelligence act: regulatory framework for trustworthy AI. https://artificialintelligenceact.eu (2024)
28. Vedral, V.: The role of relative entropy in quantum information theory. Rev. Mod. Phys. **74**(1), 197–234 (2002)
29. Xu, Z., Saleh, J.: Machine learning for reliability engineering and safety applications: review of current status and future opportunities. Reliab. Eng. Syst. Safety **211**, 107–530 (2021). https://doi.org/10.1016/j.ress.2021.107530
30. Zolfagharian, A., Abdellatif, M., Briand, L.C., Ramesh, S.: SMARLA: a safety monitoring approach for deep reinforcement learning agents. IEEE Trans. Softw. Eng. **51**(1), 82–105 (2025). https://doi.org/10.1109/tse.2024.3491496

Failure Detection Isolation
and Recovery Analysis

Towards a Unifying View of Fault Propagation Analyses and Notations

Marco Bozzano[✉] [ORCID], Alessandro Cimatti [ORCID], Alberto Griggio [ORCID],
and Fajar Haifani [ORCID]

Fondazione Bruno Kessler, 38123 Trento, Italy
bozzano@fbk.eu

Abstract. The design of complex systems requires a careful consideration of the possible hazards and failure conditions that may affect system functions, possibly compromising system reliability and safety. Complex systems must be able to detect components faults and isolate them before they can propagate and cause system failures. To this aim, Preliminary Safety Assessment analyzes failure conditions and allocate safety requirements to components and subsystems, based on a candidate system architecture. A modern way to conduct this analysis is via the use of fault propagation models, i.e. formal representations linking the occurrence of basic faults to their effects on other components and subsystems. Examples of such models include Timed Failure Propagation Graphs (TFPG), Finite Degradation Models (FDM) and Propagation Graphs over Finite Degradation Structures (PGFDS).

In this paper, we generalize previous models for fault propagation. We define a general formalism, called Unifying Propagation Graphs (UPG) which encompasses, and is strictly more expressive of, previous notations, and we formally define its syntax and semantics. We discuss the integration of UPG into the xSAP safety analysis platform, and the generalization of existing routines for fault propagation analysis to the complete fragment of UPG. Finally, as a first contribution, we extend the existing engine for computation of minimal cut sets of PGFDS to support interval timings, and we experimentally evaluate its performance.

Keywords: Failure Propagation Analysis · TFPG · FDM · PGFDS

This study was carried out within the Interconnected Nord-Est Innovation Ecosystem (iNEST) and received funding from the European Union Next-GenerationEU (PIANO NAZIONALE DI RIPRESA E RESILIENZA (PNRR) - MISSIONE 4 COMPONENTE 2, INVESTIMENTO 1.5 - D.D. 1058 23/06/2022, ECS00000043). This manuscript reflects only the authors' views and opinions, neither the European Union nor the European Commission can be considered responsible for them.
We acknowledge the support of the MUR PNRR project FAIR - Future AI Research (PE00000013), under the NRRP MUR program funded by the NextGenerationEU.

P. Katsaros (Ed.): IMBSA 2025, LNCS 15755, pp. 367–382, 2026.
https://doi.org/10.1007/978-3-032-05073-1_24

1   Introduction

The complexity of the functions carried out by modern engineering systems, in many domains such as avionics, railways and automotive, is continuously increasing, and demands a corresponding increase in the techniques to ensure the correctness and safety of their design. Complex systems must be able to detect and handle component faults, since their propagation may cause failures, i.e. conditions whereby larger parts of the system are no longer able to perform their intended function, possibly compromising system safety and creating risk of damage, harm to humans or the environment.

Domain-specific standards [1–3] describe structured techniques to assess the quality and robustness of system design. Typically, the design of complex systems follows a pattern whereby a system and its functions are hierarchically decomposed and allocated to subsystems and components. In particular, the goal of safety assessment is to assess and quantify the reliability and safety of a design architecture in presence of faults. In avionics, the process is initiated with a Functional Hazard Assessment (FHA) that aims to identify failure conditions and assess their severity and impact on system functions. Then, Preliminary System Safety Assessment (PSSA) consists in the systematic evaluation of a candidate system architecture, based on the results of FHA. PSSA links failure conditions and effects to appropriate safety requirements and allocates them to components. Finally, System Safety Assessment (SSA) validates the design by systematically demonstrating that the allocated safety requirements are met.

PSSA and SSA are supported by several safety assessment techniques. PSSA analyzes fault propagation paths. A formal approach to PSSA is based on abstract propagation models, e.g. graph models where nodes represent (failures of) system components or functions, and arcs represent propagation paths that specify how the degradation of one component may lead to the degraded or failed operation of another one. Recent models include formalisms such as Timed Failure Propagation Graphs (TFPG) [4–6], Finite Degradation Models (FDM) [7], Propagation Graphs over Finite Degradation Structures (PGFDS) [8,9] (compare Fig. 1). TFPG are a graph-based notation, whereby arcs may be decorated with propagation timings and system modes (enabling the propagation). Nodes without incoming edges are initial failures. Inner nodes extend Boolean conjunction and disjunction by considering system mode and timing constraints. FDM is an equational notation based on variable flows, modeling the effects of component degradation, based on Finite Degradation Structures (FDS) [10], modeling degradation level beyond the pure Boolean case (e.g. and $\parallel$ in Fig. 1). PGFDS is a hypergraph-based notation built on top of FDS and extending FDM by admitting cycle. PGFDS relaxes the notion of operators into relations between failure mode assignments.

SSA is based on classical techniques to identify links between faults and undesired (system-level) events, a.k.a. feared events or top-level events (TLE). Such techniques include Failure Mode and Effects Analysis (FMEA) and Fault Tree Analysis (FTA). The latter is carried out top-down, from the TLE to the basic faults, where former is done bottom-up. A notable problem for FTA is to

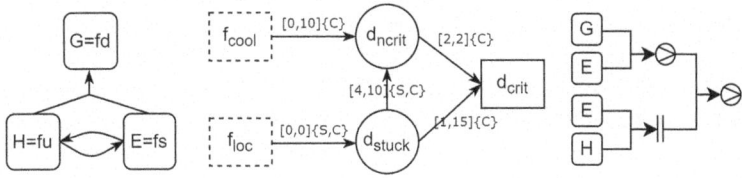

Fig. 1. Graphical representations: PGFDS (left), TFPG (center), FDM (right).

identify all the minimal combinations of faults that are possible explanation for a feared event, a.k.a. Minimal Cut Sets (MCS).

In this paper, we propose and design a novel and fully general formalism to model failure propagation, called Unifying Propagation Graphs (UPG). UPG provides a unifying view of failure propagation, in that it generalizes, and is more expressive of, existing notations such as TFPG, FDM, and PGFDS.

This paper gives the following contributions. First, we define UPG as an expressive and unifying formalism to model failure propagation. We formally define its syntax and semantics, and we show that it is strictly more expressive than TFPG, FDM and PGFDS.

Second, we design the integration of UPG into the xSAP [11,12], a state-of-the-art platform for model-based safety assessment, which provides library-based fault injection and automated model-based generation of safety artifacts such as FMEA tables and FTs. Moreover, it supports TFPGs analysis and synthesis, and TFPG validation w.r.t. to a behavioral (dynamical) model. We discuss the extension of xSAP to model UPG and the integration of the existing PGFDS engine of [8,9]. Together, the TFPG engine and the PGFDS engine enable solving problems such as TFPG analysis and synthesis, MCS computation, and validation w.r.t. a behavioral model. The integration is ongoing, our goal is to target the implementation of the existing routines for the complete fragment of UPG.

Third, as a first contribution, we solve a notable problem, namely we extend the existing engine for MCS computation of PGFDS to support interval timings. As in [8] we reduce the problem to symbolic search over a transition system, using efficient techniques for satisfiability modulo theories. We experimentally evaluate this extension on a set of benchmarks and show its effectiveness for the generation of MCS.

The rest of this paper is structured as follows. In Sect. 2 we present some preliminary notions. In Sect. 3 we present the syntax and semantics of UPG. In Sect. 4 we discuss how to embed UPG into xSAP as an extended version of TFPG. In Sect. 5 we discuss the extension of the [8] encoding with timings for MCS generation. In Sect. 6 we discuss the experimental evaluation. Finally, we draw some conclusions in Sect. 7.

Related Work. Traditional formalisms for failure propagation include Failure Propagation Transformation Notation (FPTN) [13] and Hip-HOps [14]. They focus on the description of common fault types and patterns, and on the analysis and synthesis of fault propagation through a system's architecture, however the specification of propagation relations is less expressive than in UPG.[1]

Timed Failure Propagation Graphs (TFPG) [4–6], constrain failure propagations using time bounds and system modes, however they do not consider levels of degradation, and they do not support cycles as in UPG. Moreover, UPG can constrain system modes in a more expressive way than TFPG.

Finite Degradation Models (FDM) [10] is an equational notation based on variable flows, modeling the effects of component degradation on top of Finite Degradation Structures (FDS) [10], which model levels of degradation as different values of faults organized into a semi-lattice. UPG generalize FDM by considering non-deterministic propagations, cycles and timings.

Propagation Graphs over FDS (PGFDS) [8,9] models failure propagation using a generic $canFail$ relationships, similarly to UPG, and are more expressive than FDM, since they enable non-deterministic propagations and cycles. UPG extend PGFDS by supporting timings and system modes, in a more expressive way than TFPG.

UPG notation also includes as a sub-case artifacts produced by FTA, i.e. Fault Trees, consisting in propagation trees rooted at a given TLE, and extensions such as Component Fault Trees (CFT) which admit multiple roots.

Finally, [15] presents a formalism for failure propagation which enables modeling sets of failure modes using a domain specific language. It is less expressive than FDM, in that sets of failure modes cannot be related by degradation order.

2   Preliminaries

An interval $\mathcal{I}$ is a subset of real numbers contained between two points. As in previous works on TFPG, in this paper, an interval is of the form (1) $[d_1, d_2]$ (closed interval), and (2) $[d_1, +\infty]$ s.t. $d_1, d_2 \in \mathbb{R}_{\geq 0}$ and $d_1 \leq d_2$. Note that in xSAP, TFPG can have *closed infinity interval* $[d_1, +\infty)$ and *open infinity interval* $[d_1, +\infty]$ but due to our focus on finite traces, we do not distinguish between them and simply use $[d_1, +\infty]$. We denote $INTV$ as the set of all such intervals. We define $min([d_1, d_2]) = d_1$ and $max([d_1, d_2]) = d_2$.

A finite degradation structure $(FM, \leq, \perp)$ is a finite partial order with domain FM and bottom $\perp \in FM$. Every element is called a *failure mode*.

TFPG. A TFPG [4–6,16], is a structure $G = \langle F, D, E, M, ET, EM, DC \rangle$ where (i) F is a non-empty finite set of initial components; (ii) D is a non-empty finite set of discrepancies s.t. $D \cap F = \emptyset$; (iii) $E \subseteq V \times D$ is a non-empty set of edges between the set of nodes $V = F \cup D$ and D; (iv) M is a non-empty set of system modes; (v) $ET : E \rightarrow INTV$ associates every edge in E with an interval; (vi) $EM : E \rightarrow 2^M$ associates every edge in E with some $M' \subseteq M$; (vii) $DC : D \rightarrow \{AND, OR\}$ defines a type for discrepancies. A node in F can become *active* at $t = 0$ by itself. An edge e is *active* at time t if and only if the

---

[1] An exception is given by propagation patterns such as $c \rightarrow d \vee e$, however note that for MCS computation this would generate the same results as $c \rightarrow d \wedge e$.

current (at ts) mode m satisfies $m \in EM(e)$. For an OR node w and an edge $e = (v, w) \in E$, once v and e become active at time t_v, w may become active at some time t_w, where $t_w - t_v \in ET(e)$, so long as e remains active from t_v to t_w (i.e. no mode switch into some $m' \notin EM(e)$). An AND node w may become active at t_w, when for all incoming edge (v, w), v may activate w at time t_w: for all (v, w), $t_w - t_v \geq min(ET((v, w)))$ and there is v s.t. $t_w - t_v \leq max(ET(v, w))$.

PGFDS. Given a *finite degradation structure* $D = (FM, \leq, \perp)$, a *PGFDS* [8,9] over D is a tuple $S = (J, C, canFail)$, where C is a finite set of *system components*, $J \subseteq C$ the components that can fail initially, $canFail: C \times FM \to \mathcal{F}$ is a map from $C \times FM$ to *can-fail formulas* ϕ of atoms $t_1 \leq t_2$ or $t_1 = t_2$ (with terms t_1 and t_2 built over variables C and constants from FM) or the usual compound Boolean sentence $\phi_1 \vee \phi_2$, $\phi_1 \wedge \phi_2$, or $\neg\phi$. For the semantics, a (PGFDS) *state* is a map $C \to FM$ and a *propagation* is a sequence of states $s_0 \ldots s_k$ s.t. $s_0(c) = fm$ implies $c \in J$; and $s_{i+1}(c) = fm$ implies either (i) $s_i(c) = fm$ or (ii) $s_i \models canFail(c, fm)$ (in which entailment for atoms are from the FDS D and entailment for Boolean formulas is the usual one). $\leq$ for FDS is generalized on states: $s \leq s'$ iff for all c it holds that $s(c) = fm$ and $s'(c) = fm'$ implies $fm \leq fm'$.

As we saw in the introduction, Fig. 1 shows alternative graphical representations used for differing formalisms. For PGFDS, it is possible to turn a can-fail formula, e.g. $canFail(G, fd)$, into DNF in which each disjunct is a source (a set of failure assignment to components) $\{H = fu, E = fs\}$, for one of the hyperedges leading to the head $G = fd$. TFPG representation is immediate from the definition. FDM [7] uses its flow variable definition where inner nodes are operators (where the domain is the failure modes of an FDS) generalizing Boolean operators[2]. Note that, as we will discuss in Sect. 4, our proposed formalism can be equivalently formulated as TFPG over FDS (at the price of introducing intermediate nodes for subformulas of $canFail$ formulas), therefore a TFPG-like graph representation is immediately possible.

3 Proposed Formalism: Unifying Propagation Graph

3.1 Syntax and Semantics

Our syntactic formulation is based on PGFDS, where each combination of a component and a failure mode is assigned a formula. A formula may represent different states in a more compact manner. For the purpose of integrating TFPG, we consider temporal and system mode restrictions as separate formula decorations. As we will see later (Example 2), dealing with system modes and intervals separately adds another dimension of expressivity.

Definition 1 (Unifying Propagation Graph). *Given a finite degradation structure $D = (FM, \leq, \perp)$ and a finite set of system modes M, a unifying*

---

[2] It is noteworthy to mention here that FDM is the first formalism involving FDS, but since we focus more on PGFDS and TFPG, interested reader may refer to [7,17].

propagation graph *(UPG) over D is a tuple* $S = (J, C, canFail)$, *where C is a finite set of* system components, $J \subseteq C$ *the components that can fail initially,*

$$canFail \colon C \times FM \to \mathcal{F}$$

is a map from $C \times FM$ to a can fail formula $canFail(c, fm)$ over C as variables with domain FM, where $\mathcal{F}$ is of the form

$$\phi \quad := \mid t_1 \leq t_2 | t_1 = t_2$$
$$\mid \phi_1 \vee \phi_2 \mid \phi_1 \wedge \phi_2 \mid \neg\phi$$
$$\mid \mathcal{I}\phi \mid M'\phi$$

with terms t_1 and t_2 built over variables C and constants from FM; $\mathcal{I}$ an interval; and $M' \subseteq M$. $\mathcal{I}\phi$ and $M'\phi$ are formulas with interval decoration and system mode respectively. A state formula is a formula without interval decoration and a path *formula is a formula with interval decoration.*[3]

The formalisms we unify use different notions of semantics such as activation time (TFPG), propagation graphs (PGFDS), formula evaluation (FDM). Here, we picked trace-based semantics and, to accommodate system mode and interval restriction, we bring the idea of super-dense semantics (in the context of hybrid system, see, e.g. [18]) where we combine index and timestamps. As we will see in Definition 2, we argue that this notion of semantics more closely describes the intuition of our intended operational semantics. Another alternative worth noting here is the transition system of timed automata from [19]. With this, it would be cumbersome to deal with subformulas that are *decorated* conjunction and disjunction with no explicit variables/states to be assigned.

A state is a tuple (i, μ, m, t) of an index in $\mathbb{N}$, a map $\mu : C \to FM$, a system mode $m \in M$ and a real number $t \geq 0$. A trace is a sequence of states $(0, \mu_0, m_0, t_0), \dots, (k, \mu_k, m_k, t_k)$ with $t_0 = 0$ and $t_i \leq t_{i+1}$. A sub-trace of τ is a contiguous subsequence of τ. τ^l represents the prefix of τ of length l and $\tau[l] = (l, \mu_l, m_l, t_l)$ is the state at index l. For a UPG where system mode is not relevant we may use the notation (μ, t). Two consecutive states corresponds to either discrete steps or propagation steps. A *discrete step*[4] is between two states $(i, \mu_i, m_i, t_i).(i + 1, \mu_{i+1}, m_{i+1}, t_{i+1})$ s.t. $t_i = t_{i+1}$ and either $m_i \neq m_{i+1}$ or $\mu_i \neq \mu_{i+1}$ (but not both) while a *propagation step* is when $t_i < t_{i+1}$ but $m_i = m_{i+1}$ and $\mu_i = \mu_{i+1}$. We assume *fault-persistence* for the failure modes, i.e. failure mode assignments persist: for any trace, if $\mu(c) = fm$ (noted $c \mapsto fm$ hereinafter) for $fm \neq \bot$ in some state, then it must hold in all later states.

Definition 2 (Semantics: state/path). *We define the semantics via state/path satisfaction for the can-fail formulas*[5].

---

[3] Note that, $t_1 \leq t_2$ (or $t_1 \geq t_3$) can be translated into $=$, but can be useful when we later talk about monotonic UPG.

[4] Following that system mode switches take no delay.

[5] Note that state satisfaction is also path satisfaction.

State formula (without interval):

$$
\begin{array}{llc}
(j,\mu,m,t) \models t_1 \le t_2 & \textit{iff} & \mu \models t_1 \le t_2 \\
(j,\mu,m,t) \models t_1 = t_2 & \textit{iff} & \mu \models t_1 = t_2 \\
(j,\mu,m,t) \models \phi \wedge \psi & \textit{iff} & (j,\mu,m,t) \models \phi \; \textit{and} \; (j,\mu,m,t) \models \psi \\
(j,\mu,m,t) \models \phi \vee \psi & \textit{iff} & (j,\mu,m,t) \models \phi \; \textit{or} \; (j,\mu,m,t) \models \psi \\
(j,\mu,m,t) \models \neg\phi & \textit{iff} & (j,\mu,m,t) \not\models \phi \\
(j,\mu,m,t) \models M'\phi & \textit{iff} & (j,\mu,m,t) \models \phi \; \textit{and} \; m \in M'
\end{array}
$$

Path formula (must fail)[6]:

$$
\begin{array}{ll}
\pi \models \phi \wedge \psi & \textit{iff } \pi \models \phi \textit{ and } \pi \models \psi \\
\pi \models \phi \vee \psi & \textit{iff } \pi \models \phi \textit{ or } \pi \models \psi \\
\pi \models M'\phi & \textit{iff there is } m \in M' \textit{ s.t.} \\
& \quad\quad \pi \models \phi \textit{ and } m \in M' \textit{ is the system mode} \\
& \quad\quad \textit{from the last state of } \pi \\
\pi \models \mathcal{I}\phi & \textit{iff there is } j_1, j_2, \textit{ s.t. } j_1 \le j_2 \le len(\pi) \textit{ and} \\
& \quad\quad t_{j_2} - t_{j_1} = max(\mathcal{I}) \textit{ and } \pi^{j'} \models \phi \textit{ for all } j_1 \le j' \le j_2
\end{array}
$$

path formula (can fail):

$$
\begin{array}{ll}
\pi \models_{cf} \mathcal{I}\phi & \textit{iff either } \pi \models \mathcal{I}\phi \textit{ or} \\
& \quad\quad \textit{there is } j_1, j_2, \textit{ s.t. } j_1 \le j_2 = len(\pi) \textit{ and} \\
& \quad\quad t_{j_2} - t_{j_1} \in \mathcal{I} \textit{ and } \pi^{j'} \models_{cf} \phi \textit{ for all } j_1 \le j' \le j_2 \\
\pi \models_{cf} \phi & \textit{iff } \pi \models \phi \textit{ for other } \phi \textit{ cases.}
\end{array}
$$

System mode restricts only the last state, due to it being able to arbitrarily change. Interval decoration $\pi \models \mathcal{I}\phi$ has the 'less than' restriction $j_2 \le len(\pi)$ to generalize fault persistence to formula. That is, once $\mathcal{I}\phi$ holds at some state, then it will hold at all later states. This makes it easier to relate to the original TFPG semantics for AND and OR discrepancies. Also, let us assume decorations bind the formulas stronger than the operators ($\{m_1\}c_1 = fm_1 \vee c_2 = fm_2$ is equivalent with $(\{m_1\}c_1 = fm_1) \vee (c_2 = fm_2)$)

Definition 3 (Semantics: UPG trace). $\pi = (0, \mu_0, m_0, t_0) \ldots (k, \mu_k, m_k, t_k)$ *is a trace of a UPG* $X = (J, C, canFail)$ *iff for all* $c \in C$ *and* $j \ge 0$

---

[6] For monotonic systems, negated state formula can be turned into a positive formula, but it may be used for a more concise formula (e.g. $\neg c = \bot$). We examined path formula and concluded that having negation means the introduction of a new kind of (modal) operator. For lack of space, we do not discuss this further, and assume that path formulas are without negation hereinafter.

(i) (can fail) if $\mu_j(c) = fm \neq \perp$ but $\mu_{j-1}(c) = \perp$ then either
  – $c \in J$,
  – $\pi^j \models_{cf} canFail(c, fm)$.
(ii) (must fail)

$$\pi_{j'} \models \bigvee_{fm \in FM \setminus \{\perp\}} canFail(c, fm) \rightarrow c = fm$$

for j' the maximum index $j \leq j'$ s.t. $t_{j'} = t_j$

In the rest of this paper, we consider traces where there is some failure in the first state $\pi[0]$, otherwise the prefix without failures can be removed. For $c \in J$ we additionally assume $j = 0$ in Definition 3.(i), which is w.l.o.g. for cut set enumeration purposes. Moreover, we rely on the notion of *FDS monotonicity* from PGFDS, i.e. $(i, \mu_i, m_i, t_i) \leq (i, \mu_i', m_i, t_i)$ iff $\mu \leq \mu_i'$, and in some examples we use an FDS called W2F $(\{\perp, fd, fu, fs\}, \leq, \perp)$ (from [20]) s.t. $\perp < fs, \perp < fd$, $fd < fu$ where fs, fd, fu maybe resp. called failed-safe, fail-detected, and failed-undetected. Finally, we say that a UPG is *cyclic* if there are two components and failure modes c, c' and fm, fm' s.t. $c = fm$ occurs (also transitively) in $canFail(c', fm')$ and vice versa.

Example 1 (Initial state, propagation step, and FDS-Monotonicity). With $J = \{d_1, d_2\}$, we define a UPG with the following can fail formulas and one if its traces.

$$canFail(c_1, fu) = [5, 5]\{m_2\}d_2 \geq fs$$
$$canFail(c_2, fu) = [5, 5]\{m_1\}d_1 \geq fd \wedge$$
$$c_1 \geq fd$$

$$\pi = (0, \{d_1 \mapsto fd, d_2 \mapsto fs\}, m_2, 0)$$
$$(1, \{d_1 \mapsto fd, d_2 \mapsto fs\}, m_2, 5)$$
$$(2, \{d_1 \mapsto fd, d_2 \mapsto fs, c_1 \mapsto fu\}, m_2, 5)$$
$$(3, \{d_1 \mapsto fd, d_2 \mapsto fs, c_1 \mapsto fu\}, m_1, 5)$$
$$(4, \{d_1 \mapsto fd, d_2 \mapsto fs, c_1 \mapsto fu\}, m_1, 10)$$
$$(5, \{d_1 \mapsto fd, d_2 \mapsto fs, c_1 \mapsto fu, c_2 \mapsto fu\}, m_1, 10)$$

This example illustrates some properties of the trace definition. First, the initial fail $d_1 \mapsto fd$ happens in $\pi[0]$ but started propagating in $\pi[3]$ when the system mode finally became m_1. Second, the super dense semantics divides the trace into three parts: $\pi[0].\pi[1]$ and $\pi[3].\pi[4]$ are propagation steps while the others are discrete steps. Last, one can see that the UPG is FDS-monotonic due to the use of $\geq$: once $c_1 \mapsto fu$ appears in some state (index 2), this state will also satisfy $c_1 \geq fd$ in $canFail(c_2, fu)$.

Interval. If $\phi = M'\phi$ then M' restricts the system mode only during propagation and can change afterwards. Moreover, during the propagation, e.g. for $[1, 2]c = f$, failure propagation from a state with $c \mapsto f$ from time 0 can only be completed at the earliest time 1 and have definitely completed at time 2. Mode switching within the allowed system mode decoration e.g. $[1, 2]\{m_1, m_2\}\phi'$ is possible. The state of index j_1 (compare Definition 2) represents the first state ϕ becomes true,

j' during a propagation, j_2 the first time $\mathcal{I}\phi$ becomes true, and $t > j_2$ the states where faults are persistent but there is no more restriction on the system mode. Notice that for $\mathcal{I} = \emptyset$, $\mathcal{I}\phi$ is simply **false** by definition ($\pi \not\models_{cf} \mathcal{I}\phi$).

Example 2 (Basic Example: TFPG with formulas). The following are various cases of decoration:

$$canFail^{(1)}(c', fm') = [1,2]\{m_1\}c = fm$$
$$canFail^{(2)}(c', fm') = [1,2][0,0]\{m_1\}c = fm$$
$$canFail^{(3)}(c', fm') = \{m_1\}[1,2]c = fm$$
$$canFail^{(4)}(c', fm') = [1,2]((\{m_1\}c_1 = fm_1) \vee (\{m_2\}c_2 = fm_2))$$
$$canFail^{(5)}(c', fm') = [1,1](\{m_1\}[1,1](\{m_2\}[1,1]\{m_1\}c_1 = fm_1))$$

Here, (1) is the usual edge in TFPG, (2) shows an instantaneous propagation in mode m_1, followed by another propagation in any mode, (3) is a propagation ending in system mode m_1, (4) enforces a similar propagation time for alternative TFPG edges, and (5) shows a sequence of system mode changes where the failure mode mapping in a state does not change.

Example 3 (Max delay). Given $canFail(d, g) = [0,5]\{m\}c = f$, the following are both accepted traces.

$$\pi = (0, \{c \mapsto f\}, m, 0).(1, \{c \mapsto f\}, m, 5).(2, c \mapsto f, d \mapsto g, m, 5).$$
$$(3, c \mapsto f, d \mapsto g, m', 5)$$
$$\pi' = (0, \{c \mapsto f\}, m, 0).(1, \{c \mapsto f\}, m, 5).(2, c \mapsto f, m', 5)$$

This example illustrates that at maximal delay, two cases can happen depending on which discrete step (failure mode assignment or system mode switch) happens first. In the first case, the propagation is finished then its system mode changes, while in the second one, mode changes before the propagation is completed.

Interval Decoration Sequence. An intermediate formula may have a satisfying trace where in some consecutive states time passes, without any change in the failure/system mode mapping, but they can be summed/partitioned.

Lemma 1 (Interval Sum/Partition). *Given $M'\phi$, it holds that*

$$[d_1, d_2]M'[d_1', d_2']M'\phi \quad iff \quad [d_1 + d_1', d_2 + d_2']M'\phi$$

Example 4 (Summing/partitioning of temporal decoration). For

$$\{m_3\}([1,1]c_1 = fm_1 \wedge [0.5, 0.5]\{m_2\}[0.5, 0.5]\{m_1\}c_2 = fm_2),$$

notice that the following is still a trace of $\{m_3\}[1,1]c_1 = fm_1$ despite there are states with timestamp 0.5 in between.

$$(0, \{c_1 \mapsto fm_1, c_2 \mapsto fm_2\}, m_1, \quad 0).(1, \{c_1 \mapsto fm_1, c_2 \mapsto fm_2\}, m_1, 0.5)$$
$$(2, \{c_1 \mapsto fm_1, c_2 \mapsto fm_2\}, m_2, 0.5).(3, \{c_1 \mapsto fm_1, c_2 \mapsto fm_2\}, m_2, \quad 1)$$
$$(4, \{c_1 \mapsto fm_1, c_2 \mapsto fm_2\}, m_3, \quad 1)$$

System Mode Sequence. For consecutive mode decoration, a satisfying trace must also obey the order of the modes in the decorations. This can more specifically expressed as the following lemma.

Lemma 2 (System Mode Sequence). $M_2M_1\phi$ *is equivalent to* $M_2 \cap M_1\phi$

System modes in different conjuncts do not have to obey any ordering restriction, but (in conjunction with temporal restrictions) may influence *when* a future failure can happen. An example is as follows.

Example 5 (Permutation by system mode). For the following

$$canFail(e_2, g_2) = [1, 1]e_1 = g_1 \qquad canFail(e_1, g_1) = [1, 1]\{m_2\}d_2 = f_2$$
$$canFail(tle, f) = e_2 = g_2 \wedge c = f \qquad canFail(c, f) = [1, 1]\{m_1\}d_1 = f_1 \wedge$$
$$[1, 1]\{m_2\}d_2 = f_2$$

with $J = \{d_1, d_2\}$, we have the following trace ($tle \mapsto \perp$ and $e_2 \mapsto \perp$ are omitted):

$(0, \{d_1 \mapsto f_1, d_2 \mapsto f_2, c \mapsto \perp, e_1 \mapsto \perp\}, m_1, 0)$

$(1, \{d_1 \mapsto f_1, d_2 \mapsto f_2, c \mapsto \perp, e_1 \mapsto \perp\}, m_1, 1).(2, \{d_1 \mapsto f_1, d_2 \mapsto f_2, c \mapsto \perp, e_1 \mapsto \perp\}, m_2, 1)$

$(3, \{d_1 \mapsto f_1, d_2 \mapsto f_2, c \mapsto \perp, e_1 \mapsto \perp\}, m_2, 2).(4, \{d_1 \mapsto f_1, d_2 \mapsto f_2, c \mapsto f, e_1 \mapsto \perp\}, m_2, 2)$

$(5, \{d_1 \mapsto f_1, d_2 \mapsto f_2, c \mapsto f, e_1 \mapsto g_1\}, m_2, 2)$

Here, $e_1 \mapsto g_1$ happens at timestamp 2. We can continue extending the trace, to reach TLE at timestamp 3. However, if m_2 holds between timestamp 0 and 1 and then m_1 afterwards, $e_1 \mapsto g_1$ can then happen earlier at timestamp 1 and thus also the TLE can be reached at timestamp 2.

UPG as a Unifying Formalism. The following shows how UPG relates to PGFDS and TFPG. Note that, if we also include other existing notions, UPG actually unifies other safety analysis formalisms such as FDM, static fault trees, and cyclic propagation graphs. We state the following relations (leaving the proofs to the reader, for space reasons) while the others can be checked in the literature.

Lemma 3 (From restrictive UPG to PGFDS and TFPG). *It holds that,*

(i) *there is a translation from a UPG X without interval decoration into a PGFDS X' s.t. a trace of X can be projected to a trace of X'; and*

(ii) *there is a translation from a negation-free Boolean UPG X into a TFPG X' s.t. for a trace of X, its activation time for every component corresponds to a possible sequence of activation times for F of X'.*

4   Implementation: UPG in xSAP

For the practical contribution, we would like xSAP to support UPG. To this aim, we extend TFPG with FDS, and show how to express UPG on top of this. A practical consideration for this is that xSAP already supports TFPG and that from theoretical side, by Lemma 3, Boolean UPG shares a close relationship with TFPG. So, we need to accommodate FDS into TFPG. First, we simply expand the definition of TFPG nodes to be some assignment of a failure mode to a component. So the set of nodes V become $F \times FM \uplus D \times FM$. Second, conjunctions and disjunctions in UPG amount to discrepancies with an explicit variable in D that will be assigned to true or false. We will now present its formalization.

TFPG over FDS as a Variant of UPG. A TFPG $G = \langle F, D, E, M, ET, EM, DC \rangle$ over FDS $S = \langle FM_S, \leq_S, \perp_S \rangle$ is a structure where[7]: (i) F is a non-empty finite set of initial components; (ii) D is a non-empty finite set of discrepancies s.t. $D \cap F = \emptyset$; (iii) $E \subseteq V \times (D \times FM)$ is a non-empty set of edges between the set of nodes $V = (F \times FM) \cup (D \times FM)$. For readability, we may write an edge as $\langle c, f \rangle \rightarrow_E \langle c', fm' \rangle$; (iv) M is a non-empty set of system modes (v) $ET : E \rightarrow INTV$ is a map that associates every edge in E with an interval; (vi) $EM : E \rightarrow 2^M$ is a map associating edges in E with a set of modes in M; (vii) $DC : D \rightarrow \{AND, OR\}$ is a map defining the discrepancy type.

For the semantics, we add the restriction that, for each component/discrepancy $d \in F \uplus D$, node (d, fm) can become active only for one $fm \in FM$.

We can translate a UPG into a TFPG over FDS by giving a unique label to all occurrences of subformulas in canFail and make them a unique discrepancy. For convenience we consider them without failure modes (and implicitly treat them as if they have Boolean failure modes (failing/not failing)). From this discrepancy and all of its subformulas, for intervals, if $\phi = \mathcal{I}\phi'$, then we make an edge from the discrepancy label of ϕ' into ϕ (the case for system mode is similar). Two syntactically similar subformulas, e.g. $canFail(c, f) = [0, 1]d = f$ and $canFail(c', f') = [0, 1]d = f$ need different discrepancies. This is because from state $(0, \{d \mapsto f\}, 0)$, we can have $(0, \{d \mapsto f\}, 0).(1, \{d \mapsto f, c' \mapsto f'\}, 0.5)(2, \{d \mapsto f, c' \mapsto f', c \mapsto f\}, 1)$ which is not possible if the subformula $[0, 1]d = f$ is given a single label used for both $c = f$ and $c' = f'$.

With this formalization, UPG can then alternatively take advantage of the visual format of TFPG (compare example in Fig. 2). Rounded boxes are atomic formulas, a circle is a disjunction, a box is a conjunction, a label on an edge is a decoration on a formula represented by its source node. The edge labeling, the potentially unlabeled discrepancies, and the nodes being from $C \times FM$ are the primary difference w.r.t. the original TFPG.

---

[7] The changes from the usual TFPG are in (iii) and its semantics that would have to accommodate FDS monotonicity.

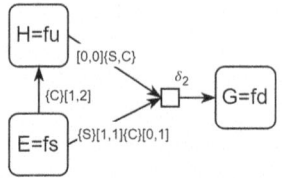

Fig. 2. UPG in TFPG-like graphical format

xSAP-Supported Format. We can easily extend the concrete syntax for TFPG in xSAP to handle FDS (and hence UPG). E.g., we extend the existing format by introducing the declaration of the list of failure modes of an FDS and their order, whereas edge definition declares components and failure modes. For backward compatibility, the declaration of a Boolean FDS may be omitted and in this case, node and edge declarations contain only component names.

5   SMT-Based Approach for Safety Analysis

As another further contribution on the practical side, we demonstrate cut set enumeration for UPG, by extending the SMT encoding from [8] with temporal constraints. A *cut set* for some decoration-free canfail formula TLE potentially with minimal-time *mintt* restriction and maximal-time restriction *maxtt* is an initial state (at timestamp 0) for which there is a trace to a state τ s.t. $\tau \models TLE$ at the earliest timestamp *mintt* and at the latest timestamp *maxtt*.

Definition 4 (SMT-Encoding of TFPG (With timing but no system mode)). *Given a TFPG X over an FDS S, its SMT encoding is defined as*

$$\varphi_{cs}^t = \varphi_{once} \wedge \varphi_{init} \wedge \varphi_{next}^t \wedge \varphi_{tle}$$

where $\varphi_{once} = \bigwedge_{c=fm, c=fm' \in D} \left(\neg F_{c,fm} \vee \neg F_{c,fm'} \right)$ is for unique mode assignment; $\varphi_{init} = \bigwedge_{(c,fm) \in F} (I_{c,fm} \rightarrow F_{c,fm})$ is for relating initial and propagation failure;

$$\varphi_{next}^t = (\bigwedge_{(c,fm) \in D \cap F} \left(F_{c,fm} \rightarrow \left(I_{c,fm} \vee canFail_{smt}^t(c, fm) \right) \right)) \wedge$$

$$(\bigwedge_{(c,fm) \in D \setminus F} \left(F_{c,fm} \rightarrow \left(canFail_{smt}^t(c, fm) \right) \right)))$$

for propagation relation; and

$$
canFail^t_{smt}(c, fm) = \begin{cases} \bigvee_{e=\langle d, fm' \rangle \to_E \langle c, fm \rangle} (F_{d,fm} \land o_d < o_c \land \quad //DC(c, fm) = OR \\ \quad t_d + ptime_{dc} = t_c \land \\ \quad min(ET(e)) \leq ptime_{dc} \leq max(ET(e))) \\ \\ \bigwedge_{e=\langle d, fm' \rangle \to_E \langle c, fm \rangle} (F_{d,fm} \land o_d < o_c) \land \quad //DC(c, fm) = AND \\ \quad t_d + ptime_{dc} = t_c \land min(ET(e)) \leq ptime_{dc} \land \\ \bigvee_{e=\langle d, fm' \rangle \to_E \langle c, fm \rangle} \quad ptime_{dc} \leq max(ET(e)) \end{cases}
$$

The formula ϕ_{tle} can be seen as a canfail formula $canFail^t_{smt}(tle) \land mintt \leq t_{tle} \land t_{tle} \leq maxtt$ for a decoration-free formula $canFail(tle)$.

FDS monotonicity is from [8]. We replace $F_{d,fm}$ in $canFail^t_{smt}(c, fm)$ with $\bigvee_{fm \leq \hat{fm}} F_{d,\hat{fm}}$. For the implementation generating only FDS-minimal cut-sets, we remove ϕ_{once} and replace $I_{c,fm}$ in φ^t_{next} with $\bigwedge_{fm' \leq fm} I_{c,fm} \land \bigwedge_{fm' \nleq fm} \neg I_{c,fm}$. Let us call the resulting encoding $\phi^{FM,t}_{cs}$. With this, we generate subset-minimal models w.r.t. I-vars $I_{c,fm}$ assigned to *true*. We get a cut set from such a model by collecting $c \mapsto fm$ s.t. fm is FDS-maximal among all fm' s.t. $I_{c,fm'} \mapsto true$ in the subset-minimal model (we call this extraction $modelToState^{FM}$ [8]). Its correctness builds upon the fact that the temporal restriction in the encoding already follows TFPG temporal restriction (see Sect. 2).

Theorem 1 (Cut set enumeration). *Given UPG X and a top level event TLE and its encoding $\phi^{FM,t}_{cs}$, we have*

$$
cutset(X, TLE) \subseteq \{modelToState^{FM}(\mu) | \mu \models \phi^{FM,t}_{cs}\}
$$

They coincide for FDS-monotone UPG.

6   Experimental Evaluation

We intend to have the full UPG formalism supported in xSAP. As an initial contribution, we extended the SMT-based encoding from [8] to accommodate temporal constraints, and we design an experiment to evaluate how temporal constraints affect performance.

Benchmarks and Experimental Setup. We use cyclic benchmarks *ladder* and *radiator* from [21]. The benchmarks have two types of components: modules and voters. In order to focus and accentuate the effect of temporal restrictions, we make the following simplification. We only use the ones with one voter, because it was shown [21] that the cyclicity for two and three voters rendered the problems much more difficult and cycle handling is not our focus here. For FDS, we add failure modes using the FDS with order $\bot < L < H$ without randomization and in such a way that the number of cut sets do not grow too large. We assign J

to only contain the modules and not voters. We randomize temporal decoration between $[0, 1]$ and $[1, 2]$ only for modules in the can-fail formulas. The number of components (representing the size of the benchmark instances) are multiple of three in $\{3, \ldots, 15\}$. For each instance, we try to generate cut sets that cause the top level event within 2 time-span up to 40 time-span (in multiples of two).

Experimental Results. Figure 3 shows the runtime and the number of cut sets w.r.t. the maximum TLE time. The main results are that (1) the runtime tends to be small for small and large maximum TLE time, (2) increases as the number of admissible cut sets (that can cause the given TLE within the time-bound) increase, (3) decreases when the admissible cut sets are the same as all cut sets (but may first have some increase when the max TLE time is tight). For each of the number-of-component parameter, the number of all minimal cut sets for *ladder* and *radiator* benchmarks are 12, 24 36, 48, and 60. For *ladder* benchmark, they are found for the maximum TLE times of 2, 2, 4, 6, and 10, while, for *radiator* benchmark, they are found for maximum TLE times of 2, 4, 6, 10, and 10.

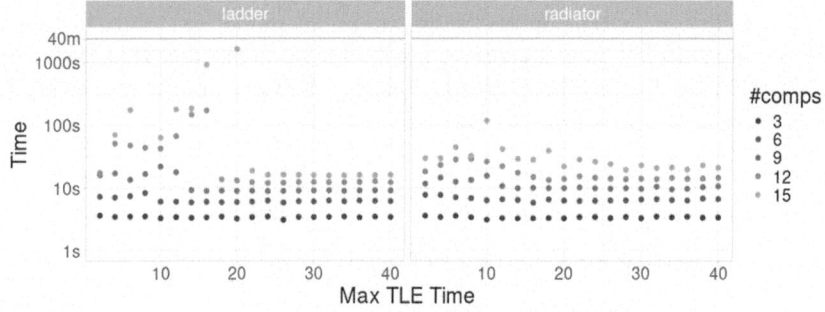

Fig. 3. Experimental Results

7   Conclusion and Future Work

In this work, we have proposed a new formalism for failure propagation called UPG, unifying and extending previous notations such as TFPG, FDM, PGFDS. We have designed the integration of UPG into the xSAP safety analysis platform, which will serve as an integrated platform for extended versions of the existing analysis and synthesis routines available for TFPG and PGFDS. As a first contribution in this direction, we have extended the encoding and the engine of [8,9] for MCS computation to support propagation timings, and demonstrated its performance on a set of benchmarks. We plan to make the integrated platform available in time for demonstration at the conference.

As part of our future work, we are considering further extensions of UPG. In particular, we want to investigate modeling aspects that are available in Dynamic Fault Trees, e.g. dynamic gates, spares and more complex forms of dependencies. Finally, we want to integrate probabilistic and observability aspects into UPG, with applications in monitoring and diagnosis.

References

1. IEC: Railway applications - Specification and demonstration of reliability, availability, maintainability and safety (RAMS) (2002)
2. ISO: Road vehicles - Functional safety (2011)
3. SAE: ARP4761A Guidelines and Methods for Conducting the Safety Assessment Process on Civil Airborne Systems and Equipment (2022)
4. Bozzano, M., Cimatti, A., Gario, M., Micheli, A.: SMT-based validation of timed failure propagation graphs. In: Proceedings of the AAAI, pp. 3724–3730. AAAI Press (2015)
5. Bittner, B., Bozzano, M., Cimatti, A., Zampedri, G.: Automated verification and tightening of failure propagation models. In: Proceedings of the 30th AAAI Conference on Artificial Intelligence (AAAI 2016), pp. 907–913 (2016)
6. Bittner, B., Bozzano, M., Cimatti, A.: Automated synthesis of timed failure propagation graphs. In: Proceedings of the IJCAI, pp. 972–978 (2016)
7. Yang, L., Rauzy, A.: FDS-ML: a new modeling formalism for probabilistic risk and safety analyses. In: Papadopoulos, Y., Aslansefat, K., Katsaros, P., Bozzano, M. (eds.) IMBSA 2019. LNCS, vol. 11842, pp. 78–92. Springer, Cham (2019). https://doi.org/10.1007/978-3-030-32872-6_6
8. Bozzano, M., Cimatti, A., Fernandes Pires, A., Griggio, A., Jonáš, M., Kimberly, G.: Efficient SMT-based analysis of failure propagation. In: Silva, A., Leino, K.R.M. (eds.) CAV 2021. LNCS, vol. 12760, pp. 209–230. Springer, Cham (2021). https://doi.org/10.1007/978-3-030-81688-9_10
9. Bozzano, M., Cimatti, A., Griggio, A., Jonás, M., Kimberly, G.: Analysis of cyclic fault propagation via ASP. In: Proceedings of the LPNMR, vol. 13416. LNCS, pp. 470–483. Springer (2022)
10. Rauzy, A., Yang, L.: Finite degradation structures. FLAP 6(6), 1447–1474 (2019)
11. Bittner, B., et al.: The xSAP safety analysis platform. In: Chechik, M., Raskin, J.-F. (eds.) TACAS 2016. LNCS, vol. 9636, pp. 533–539. Springer, Heidelberg (2016). https://doi.org/10.1007/978-3-662-49674-9_31
12. Bozzano, M., Cimatti, A., Gario, M., Jones, D., Mattarei, C.: Model-based safety assessment of a triple modular generator with xSAP. Formal Aspects Comput. 33(2), 251–295 (2021). https://doi.org/10.1007/s00165-021-00532-9
13. Fenelon, P., McDermid, J.A.: An integrated tool set for software safety analysis. J. Syst. Softw. 21(3), 279–290 (1993)
14. Papadopoulos, Y., McDermid, J.A.: Hierarchically performed hazard origin and propagation studies. In: Felici, M., Kanoun, K. (eds.) SAFECOMP 1999. LNCS, vol. 1698, pp. 139–152. Springer, Heidelberg (1999). https://doi.org/10.1007/3-540-48249-0_13
15. Delmas, K., Delmas, R., Pagetti, C.: SMT-based architecture modelling for safety assessment. In: 12th IEEE International Symposium on Industrial Embedded Systems, SIES 2017, pp. 1–8. IEEE (2017)

16. Abdelwahed, S., Karsai, G., Mahadevan, N., Ofsthun, S.C.: Practical implementation of diagnosis systems using timed failure propagation graph models. IEEE Trans. Instrum. Meas. **58**(2), 240–247 (2009)
17. Yang, L., Rauzy, A., Haskins, C.: Finite degradation structures: a formal framework to support the interface between MBSE and MBSA. In: Proceedings of the ISSE, Rome, Italy, pp. 1–6 (2018)
18. Manna, Z., Pnueli, A.: Verifying hybrid systems. In: Grossman, R.L., Nerode, A., Ravn, A.P., Rischel, H. (eds.) HS 1991-1992. LNCS, vol. 736, pp. 4–35. Springer, Heidelberg (1993). https://doi.org/10.1007/3-540-57318-6_22
19. Bengtsson, J., Yi, W.: Timed automata: semantics, algorithms and tools. In: Desel, J., Reisig, W., Rozenberg, G. (eds.) ACPN 2003. LNCS, vol. 3098, pp. 87–124. Springer, Heidelberg (2004). https://doi.org/10.1007/978-3-540-27755-2_3
20. Rauzy, A.: Mathematical foundations of minimal cutsets. IEEE Trans. Reliab. **50**(4), 389–396 (2001)
21. Bozzano, M., Cimatti, A., Griggio, A., Jonáš, M.: Efficient analysis of cyclic redundancy architectures via Boolean fault propagation. In: HS 1991-1992. LNCS, vol. 736, pp. 273–291. Springer, Cham (2022). https://doi.org/10.1007/978-3-030-99527-0_15

An ALTARICA-Based Modelling and Analysis Approach Enabling UAV Regulation Compliance

Pierre Bieber, Kevin Delmas$^{(\boxtimes)}$ (iD), Sergio Pizziol, Tatiana Prosvirnova, and Christel Seguin (iD)

ONERA Toulouse, 2 Avenue Marc Pelegrin, 31400 Toulouse, France
{pierre.bieber,kevin.delmas,sergio.pizziol,tatiana.prosvirnova,
christel.seguin}@onera.fr

Abstract. The increasing adoption of Unmanned Aerial Vehicles (UAVs) in various operations introduces new safety risks to people on ground and airspace users. As a result, EU regulations require the demonstration of safety for UAV-based operations, necessitating comprehensive hazard analyses that capture diverse event and failure contributions. This paper presents a generic, model-based approach for assessing UAV system safety, leveraging layered failure propagation models from [4]. Our twofold contribution includes: (1) a detailed exposition of each failure propagation layer's implementation in ALTARICA and their interconnections, and (2) the analysis of this layered model using associated ALTARICA tools to generate certification artefacts. A thorough case study on a rotary-wing UAV use-case illustrates our modelling methodology and its analysis capabilities.

Keywords: UAV Operations · ALTARICA · Regulatory Compliance · Failure Propagation Modeling

1 Introduction

Since 2019, Europe has established a comprehensive regulatory framework [14] for operations of Unmanned Aerial System (UAS), spanning several risk categories. Light UAS operations involving beyond visual line of sight (BVLOS) flights, over populated areas, or shared airspaces with manned aircraft often fall under the *Specific category*. To authorize such operations, a Specific Operation Risk Assessment (SORA) [15] is mandatory. The SORA identifies a comprehensive set of Operational Safety Objectives (OSOs) proportionate to the operation risk. Some OSOs request design analyses that are out of the paper scope *e.g.* the verification that an operative UAS behaves properly in foreseeable operational conditions or the analysis of performance of external services used during the operation (*e.g.* communication, GPS). The paper focusses on

P. Katsaros (Ed.): IMBSA 2025, LNCS 15755, pp. 383–397, 2026.
https://doi.org/10.1007/978-3-032-05073-1_25

the OSO that requests the analysis of the safety impact of UAS internal failure as defined by [11]. Two main safety assessments are recommended: Functional Hazard Assessment (FHA) and Probable Failure Qualitative Assessment (PFQA). The FHA identifies whether function degradation scenarios could lead to Loss of Control (LOC), such as unmitigated UAV crashes, and defines Failure Conditions with associated severity levels (ranging from Catastrophic to No Safety Effect). The PFQA must demonstrate that Failure Conditions leading to critical LOC situations are improbable (occurring less frequently than once in the drone's lifetime). Aviation authorities review these assessment results before granting operation authorization, recommending tabular formats for presenting both FHA and PFQA outcomes. While detailed guidance for conducting FHAs is available in [12], similar guidance for PFQAs was lacking.

This paper addresses this gap thanks to multi-layer synthetic models of failure propagation within the UAS and extended safety assessment tools. The synthetic modeling methodology follows the recommendations of the aeronautic standard [13]. and it relies on detailed design or failure knowledge provided *e.g.* by documents, experts, other models and tools used to assess specific physical effects of delays or degraded performances [6]. The novelty is to show how the multi-layer model of the UAS failure propagation ease the automation of the Probable Failure Qualitative Assessment. Moreover, the approach is applied to an ONERA drone such that safety models and analysis results are open to the scientific community.

Section 2 presents the *MediDelivery* use-case, providing technical insights into the operation's safety policy, emergency procedures for the UAV and its remote pilot, as well as the functional and hardware architectures of the UAV. Section 3 offers a brief overview of ALTARICA. Sections 4, 5, 6, and 7 present the four-layer model, which describes safety policy, procedures, functions, and hardware resources, respectively. Finally, Sect. 8 illustrates the Probable Failure Qualitative Assessment.

2   The *MediDelivery* Use-Case

In this article we will illustrate our work on a UAV-based medical good delivery operation between two hospitals in Toulouse (France). This operation fits into the Specific category because the remote pilot cannot directly observe the UAV, the UAV flies over either sparsely populated rural areas or populated suburban areas, and it flies below 120 m. The UAV should fly within a flight corridor (also called flight geography in the SORA) defined prior to the flight. If the UAV exits this corridor due to a technical failure or degraded conditions, some specific zones are identified during flight preparation to enable a controlled landing. Such zones called *Land As Soon As Practicable zones* are directly in the vicinity of the flight corridor and have been identified to minimize the presence of people during landing. Moreover, some forbidden zones are identified and should never be crossed due to an unacceptable hazard (*e.g.* assemblies of people).

2.1 Safety Strategy

The UAV in charge of performing the *MediDelivery* operation is a modified YAMAHA FAZER-R mono-rotor with a maximum take-off mass of approximately 100 kg and a span of 3.7 m. This UAV contains an ONERA developed avionics enabling autonomous navigation built on-top of the built-in piloting system of YAMAHA. To mitigate technical or adverse conditions that may arise during the operation, a set of control modes has been designed to prevent critical loss of control. Let us provide a non-exhaustive list of the possible control modes: 1. Hovering: the UAV hovers at the defined point. 2. Land As Soon As Practicable: the UAV lands in a *Land As Soon As Practicable zone*. If successful, the drone lands in the predefined zone; otherwise, a landing outside predefined zone is necessary. 3. Land As Soon As Possible: the UAV lands in an immediately adjacent area where the absence of third parties is not guaranteed. If applied, a controlled landing in a potentially occupied area is performed; otherwise, Land Immediately is necessary. 4. Land Immediately: The UAV flight is terminated through engine cutoff. If successful, the drone performs a ballistic descent; otherwise, an uncontrolled crash occurs.

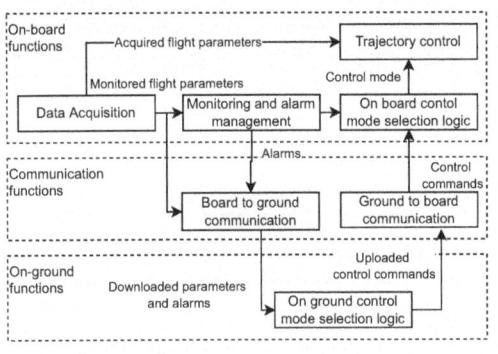

(a) Simplified functional architecture

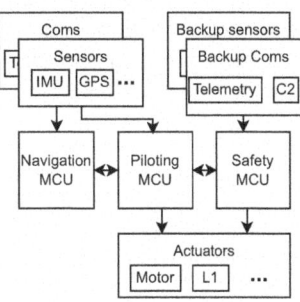

(b) Simplified physical architecture of the avionics of the FAZER

Fig. 1. Physical and functional architectures of *MediDelivery*

2.2 Emergency Procedures

Procedures precisely define the sequences of tasks to be performed by the actors of the systems when pre-defined emergency situations, called *initiators*, occur. An initiator examples, is external service (communication, localisation or UTM) transient or permanent loss Let us consider the procedure associated with the loss of the communication link between the UAV and the pilot. When a communication loss is detected by the UAV, it first hovers for a pre-defined time to wait for a recovery of the link. If the timeout is reached, then it will try to Land As Soon As Practicable. Note that other procedures may override the application of the Land As Soon As Practicable if the resource mandatory to its execution are not available or if a deviation from the intended trajectory is observed.

2.3   Functional Architecture

The technical tasks performed by the UAV are implemented thanks to on-board and on-ground functions. An overview of the functional architecture adapted from [4] is represented in Fig. 1a. The on-board UAV functions include: 1. Acquisition of data, which must capture available data for the considered UAV (e.g., airspeed or altitude). 2. Surveillance and alarm emission, which must capture the implementation of monitoring logic for sensor-transmitted data, such as *low battery level*, and emit treated alarms on-board and/or send them to the ground. 3. Mode selection logic, which must capture the selection of the control mode based on emitted alarms and ground commands. In our example the LandAS-APracticable can be selected if an order has been sent by either the on-board system or the ground while LandImmediately mode is considered a priority over the LandASAPracticable mode; if the conditions for both modes are met, the transition will be made to the LandImmediately mode. 4. Trajectory control, which must capture the control of the UAV's trajectory based on measured flight parameters and the selected piloting mode (includes control and actuation functions). Additional information concerning the dependencies between functions are provided to enable the failure propagation modelling. The dependencies are recorded as tables like Fig. 2b. In this case a control function is available if it not face any internal issue and if at least one of alternatives to estimate the requested parameters is available.

2.4   Physical Architecture

The functions presented above are implemented thanks to the physical architecture illustrated by Fig. 1b. The architecture mainly depicts the avionics added to the initial design of the YAMAHA FAZER-R. This avionics is based on three processors (MCUs) where: 1. Navigation MCU is in charge of nominal telecommunications, payload interface and navigation function implementation; 2. Piloting MCU is in charge of nominal acquisition of flight parameters from sensors, the implementation of piloting and guiding function for nominal and degraded control modes; 3. Safety MCU is in charge of backup acquisition of flight parameters from backup sensors, the implementation of piloting and guiding function for degraded control modes, the backup communications. The dependencies of the functions w.r.t. the physical equipment are specified thanks to dependency tables. For instance, Fig. 2a formalizes the dependencies between the available sources and the estimation of flight parameters. The altitude estimation function relies on three independent sources: the barometer, GPS, and inertial measurement unit (IMU).

3   ALTARICA Background

The development of complex avionic systems typically follows a tiered approach, wherein design and validation activities are iteratively performed at each stage,

Parameter	Resource
attitude	IMU
ground speed	IMU OR GPS
position	GPS OR IMU
altitude	barometer OR GPS OR IMU

(a) Physical dependencies for flight parameters acquisition

Functions	Parameters
piloting	attitude AND altitude
guiding	Position

(b) Example of control functions dependencies

Fig. 2. Dependency tables

with outputs informing subsequent stages. To ease these activities, architecture-aware formalisms have emerged among which ALTARICA [1] stands out as a particularly popular and widely applied language in both academia and industry. As a formal language, ALTARICA enables behavior simulation and automated safety assessment, as provided by approaches such as [20]. Therefore, the underlying language used in the models presented in this paper is the dataflow restriction of ALTARICA and their analysis is performed by the tool CECILIA-WORKSHOP [21] designed by Dassault Aviation and developed by SatoDev.

3.1 Failure Propagation Model

An ALTARICA-modeled system consists of interconnected components, where connections enforce constraints on the possible values of component inputs and outputs. An ALTARICA component contains: 1. *flow variables*: inputs and outputs interfacing the component with its environment; 2. *state variables*: internal variables encoding the component's functional or dysfunctional state (*e.g.* failure modes); 3. *events* triggers state transitions, which can be either deterministic (*e.g.* reconfiguration events) or probabilistic (*e.g.* failure events). The component's functional and/or dysfunctional behaviour is defined by: 1. *transitions*: specify the possible state evolutions, each transition written $g \vdash e \rightarrow a$ informally means "when the guard g (a condition over current state and flow variables) is true, upon event e triggering, action a is performed (*i.e.* assigning state variables)"; 2. *assertions*: the definition of output flows from the inputs flows and the state variables. For instance, the ALTARICA code in Fig. 3 models a function providing a digital output to the system without requesting any external information. So the source has no input flow. This source can produce either a correct data (Ok), no data (fail_loss failure mode) or an erroneous data (fail_err failure mode). So the output flow O can take a value in the totally ordered set OLE = [Ok, Lost, Err] (see Fig. 3, line 3) This means that we consider that Err is worst than Lost that is worst than Ok. The internal state of the source is encoded by the OLE state variable St (see Fig. 3, line 7). We also consider that this function may be implemented by a resource R that can be itself ok, lost or erroneous. Finally, the failure of the source can be activated or not depending on a Boolean input A.

```
 1  node source
 2  flow //interface flows
 3    O: OLE : out; //output
 4    R: OLE : in; //resource
 5    A: bool : in; //activate
 6  state
 7    S: OLE;
 8  event //one event per FM
 9    e_err, e_lost;
10  init //state initially ok
11    S:=Ok;
12  trans
13    //failures are permanent
14    S=Ok and A |-e_lost-> S:=Lost;
15    S=Ok and A |-e_err-> S:=Err;
16  assert
17    //O is the worst of R and S
18    O = worst(R,S);
19  end
20
```

Fig. 3. ALTARICA code of the source component

3.2 Analyses

The used ALTARICA tools can compute the sequences of events leading to the observation of a failure condition. The computation inputs are the model targeted observation and criteria to bound the sequence search. A common bound is the maximum number of events that are in each sequence. The tools extract sequences of events leading from the initial configuration to configurations where the observer of the failure condition holds. Let us consider a system made of two instances F1 and F2 of the source function and such that A inputs are true, R inputs are Ok and the failure condition FC_Err_CAT is that both F1 and F2 outputs are erroneous. In this case, <F2.fail.err; F1.fail.err> and <F1.fail.err; F2.fail.err> are the sequences of length 2 leading to FC_Err_CAT.

4   Safety Barrier Model

As introduced by [4], this model relates operational barriers to prevent the occurrence of hazardous events or mitigate the severity of their effects. These barriers leverage the risk reduction means offered by the operational environment and the fault tolerance of the drone. When the implementation of safety barriers are mandated by regulations, it becomes possible to refine the definition of scenario classes (minor, major, hazardous, catastrophic) as the progressive breach of safety barriers, culminating in the occurrence of a fatal accident. Several works such as [3,4] rely on barrier diagram formalism initially developed by EuroControl [19] to model and formalise the impact of such barriers. This model contains operational barriers such as Land As Soon As Practicable, with situations such as mitigated crash, or unmitigated crash, depicted by rounded boxes. When a barrier is applied (diamond node), it can be successful then the situation connected to the left of the diamond is the next situation; otherwise, the situation that is connected to the top of the diamond is the next situation. This formalism can also associate a level of hazard with each situation identified in the diagram. An example is provided by Fig. 5a wherein the classic severity scale has been used i.e.: Catastrophic (red), Hazardous (orange) and Major (yellow).

```
 1  node barrier application          11     // unapplicable or unavailable or
 2  flow //interface flows                      not applied
 3   hazardOut : bool : out;          12     hazardOut = (hazardIn and not (
 4   barrierPerformed : bool : out;             barrierApplicable and
 5   barrierApplied : bool : in;                barrierAvailable and
 6   barrierApplicable : bool : in;             barrierApplied));
 7   barrierAvailable : bool : in;    13     barrierPerformed = (
 8   hazardIn : bool : in;                       barrierAvailable and
 9  assert                                       barrierApplied);
10   //the hazard propagates if the   14  end
       barrier is
```

Fig. 4. ALTARICA code of the barrier application

4.1 Model Implementation

This section provides a method and an ALTARICA framework to model the safety barrier diagram. The first step involves identifying initiators based on pre-existing safety analyses, such as drone-level Failure Hazard Analyses (FHAs). Each initiator is encoded in the ALTARICA model as a component referred to as a *source* similar to the model provided by Fig. 3. To enable automatic system analysis, we formalize the effects of applying or not applying a safety barrier using four aspects: 1. Available: Is resource necessary for barrier application available? 2. Applied: Is the barrier applied for the considered initiator? 3. Applicable: Is the barrier effective in addressing the initiator? 4. Outcome: What is the resulting situation from successful/failed barrier application?

Consider the *MediDelivery*'s Land As Soon As Practicable. We can characterize this barrier by identifying the initiators for which it is available, applicable, and applied. Here we consider it available for communication, UTM transient/permanent loss and transient loss of localisation. It is applicable only for transient/permanent communication loss and transient localisation loss. It is applied for permanent communication loss or transient localisation loss.

In the model, a barrier is a specific ALTARICA component taking three Boolean input signals (availability, application, and applicability). These three information are the inputs of the diamond nodes that compute the local outcome of the barrier state and current outcome as specified by Fig. 4.

The last step is the assembly of safety barriers to form the diagram. This phase connects the initiators to the barriers to encode its applicability, application and availability. Moreover if one initiator is triggered then it initiates the bottom situation of the safety barrier diagram. Eventually, the barrier, situations and barrier application nodes are connected to build the diagram. Considering the *MediDelivery* uses modes to manage mission-related hazards presented in Sect. 2, an excerpt of the barrier diagram is described by Fig. 5a:

5 Procedure Model

This analysis centers on the formal definition of nominal and emergency procedures that implement the safety policy described by barrier diagrams.

5.1   Model Implementation

Each procedure is modeled by identifying its initiators, actors, tasks, dependencies and assignments, and potential errors during execution. The identification of initiators establishes a connection between the initiators of procedures and those identified in the barrier diagrams. These initiators and subsequent tasks are modelled by ALTARICA node whose definition is adapted from Fig. 3. In this case the enumeration is the true/false values (where true stands for the triggering of the initiator); and the worst between two Boolean value is the OR connective. For a given initiator, a procedure can be put in place to mitigate its effects, which typically involves one or more of the following types of tasks: 1. Detection Task: representing an actor's ability to identify the occurrence of an initiator (*e.g.* by analyzing its effects). This task is represented by a test component, with an output true if the triggering situation is observed, and false otherwise. 2. Action Task: representing an actor's capacity to implement a measure to mitigate the effects of an initiator. This task is represented by a function component, with an output true if the implementation is successful, and false otherwise. 3. Communication Task: representing the transmission of data between actors necessary for detection and/or implementation of the recovery action. This task is represented by a Boolean test component.

Task distribution is achieved by assigning each task to a *pool line*, which is a rectangle encompassing tasks handled by a single actor. An example assignment is illustrated in Fig. 5b, where detection tasks are distributed between the UAV and the ground station (denoted *PIC*). In the case of detection, this management can be as simple as triggering the action if either of the two actors consider it necessary. This choice is encoded in Fig. 5b by a logical *OR* gate located above

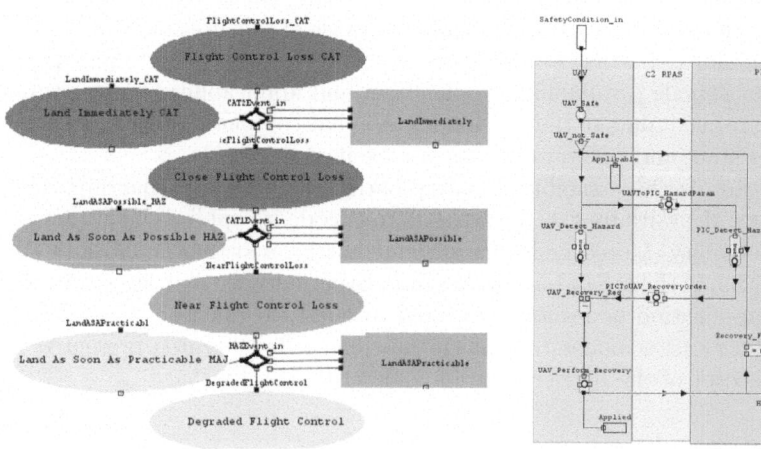

(a) Example of the ALTARICA model of the barrier diagram of *MediDelivery*

(b) ALTARICA model of *MediDelivery* procedure

Fig. 5. Barrier and procedure ALTARICA models (Color figure online)

the *UAV_Perform_Recovery* action. The situation triggering the procedure is modelled as a Boolean *SafetyCondition_in* input of Fig. 5b, when false, represents the generic hazard that is managed by the procedure.

The orchestration of procedures models the choices for applying these procedures in two scenarios: when multiple initiators are triggered simultaneously, and when a failure is detected in the execution of a given procedure. To successfully orchestrate procedures, we suggest using the same characteristic dimensions, namely: 1. Availability: indicates whether the resources for detecting and implementing recovery actions are available. 2. Application: determines whether the procedure should be applied for the considered initiator. 3. Applicability: assesses whether the procedure is effective in addressing the initiator's effects. It's worth noting that a procedure not initially intended for a given initiator can still be applied if the initial procedure fails (c.g., due to resource constraints), a phenomenon we term *procedure escalation*. The procedure prioritization/selection strategy is modeled as a function that takes the states of the procedures as input and outputs the applied procedure.

5.2   Interface with Safety Barrier Model

In this method, procedures are the implementations of the formalized ground and air risk management strategies, as represented by barrier diagrams. This implementation link is modeled by a set of ALTARICA functions that refine the concepts of initiator occurrence, applicability, availability, and application of barriers. These functions specify: 1. The connection between diagram initiators and procedure initiators is established. 2. The relationship between applied procedures and deployed barriers is defined, ensuring consistency between the barriers and the action tasks of the procedures. 3. The relationship between applicable procedures and applicable barriers is specified, maintaining consistency between the definition of applicability for a given initiator in both a barrier and a procedure utilizing that barrier.

6   Functional Model

The analysis of the functional architecture formalises the dependencies between functional elements and tasks contained within procedures, particularly highlighting the functions involved in detecting and mitigating procedure initiators.

6.1   Model Implementation

The modelling process is based on an adaptation of the UAV's functional architecture template provided by [4]. The adaptation effort has already be made when presenting the functional architecture of *MediDelivery* in Sect. 2. The next step is to model at a high level the impact of trajectory control issues and resource functions that will be detailed in the physical architecture analysis. To do so, the first step is to define the fault model of the functions. In our modelling framework, most functions can be erroneous (respectively lost) if it spontaneously produces incorrect values (respectively stops suddenly), or if at least one of the parameters required by the function is itself erroneous (respectively lost). This paradigm is used for acquisition, piloting, guiding and navigation functions listed in Sect. 2. The ALTARICA nodes of such function is still based on the code provided by Fig. 3, excepts that some functions may own an additional input I modelling the dependencies to other functions. This additional input is mandatory to model the trajectory control functions that perform control for each of the available modes for the UAV (*e.g.* LandASAPracticable or LandImmediatly modes).

Concerning monitoring functions, we encode the loss of the alarm (*i.e.* the alarm is not emitted when it should be); and the untimely triggering of the alarm (*i.e.* the alarm is emitted when it should not be). In this framework, error detection is considered as available if the means of observation (*e.g.* a sensor) is available and the monitored equipment or parameter is in an erroneous state.

6.2   Interface with Procedure Model

The link strategy is based on a mapping between the types of function and the types of task. More precisely, the UAV functions are linked to initiators, detection tasks, and mitigation tasks; communication functions are linked to transmission tasks; and ground functions are linked to detection tasks and mitigation tasks. The initiators of procedures are triggered by the failure or combination of failures of a subset of the functions of Data Acquisition and Trajectory control. Detection tasks on the drone are performed by the sub-functions of Monitoring and Alarm Management nodes. Reconfiguration tasks on the drone are performed by the On-board control model selection logic. Transmission tasks are performed by Ground-to-board and Board-to-ground communication functions.

7   Physical Model

This final level formalises the dependencies between physical equipments and the functions introduced during allocation, as well as the dependencies between physical equipments themselves, such as power supplies.

7.1   Model Implementation

To ease the link between functional and physical architecture we propose to identify physical equipments based on their role in the functional architecture. The physical equipments contributing to the data acquisition are typically sensors and data-buses that connect them to on-board processors. In our case the sensors contributing to the Data acquisition function are the GPS, IMU, magneto and altimeter. This set of sensors is duplicated for the Safety MCU. Concerning the trajectory control, the processors implementing command and control software, the actuators executing the resulting commands and the data-buses in charge of connecting them are considered. In our use case, nominal control modes rely on the Navigation and Piloting MCU, while the degraded modes can be executed either by the Piloting or Safety MCU. Last, the components implementing Monitoring and alarm management and Control mode selection logic must be identified, in our use-case the Piloting MCU and Safety MCU. There are no specific components dedicated to executing a degraded mode; instead, these modes are triggered via the actuators used by Piloting MCU and Safety MCU. The equipments involved in power supply (*e.g.* batteries) are provided, along with a precise description of the equipments powered by each of these sources.

The failure modes of physical components must be adapted to the type of component considered. In our case, we do not have fine-grained models of the different failure modes for each physical component. Therefore, we reuse the ALTARICA node of functions by specializing the set of failure modes for each kind of physical equipment. For digital components (calculators, sensors, communication modems) and electromechanical components (actuators, circuit breakers), we consider the lost/erroneous behaviours. For components involved in power supply, we propose performance levels for sources (High, Medium, Low, None) and cutoffs or short circuits for components responsible for energy transport.

7.2   Interface with Functional Model

Usually, the physical architecture of UAV is highly integrated, hence equipments may be involved in the implementation of several functions. Nevertheless, to avoid single point of failure, the physical architecture may implement redundancy patterns. Therefore, the relation between function and physical equipments is seldom a one-to-one relation, as illustrated by *MediDelivery*. This relation is encoded by a set of ALTARICA functions providing for each function the quality of their R input. This encoding formalizes the impact of the physical components' failure modes on the occurrence of a failure in a given function. For instance the control functions used to perform a Land As Soon As Practicable are available iff at least the Safety or Piloting MCU are available.

8   Supported Assessment

As identified in the introduction section, the SORA may require a Probable Failure Qualitative Assessment (PFQA). An acceptable approach to fulfill this requirement involves conducting an enriched Failure Mode, Effect and Criticality Analysis (FMECA) on the UAV's physical architecture. Specifically, for each probable failure mode of the physical architecture's components that is likely to occur at least once in the UAV's lifetime, the applicant must provide: 1. the means of detecting the effects of the failure mode, whether direct or indirect, if such detection exists; 2. the recovery actions in place to mitigate the effects of the failure mode, if applicable; 3. the high level failure condition that the resulting situation contributes to; 4. the criticality of this failure condition.

To streamline the creation of the PFQA table, we suggest leveraging the layered ALTARICA models introduced earlier to partially automate the generation of the table. The generation is based on a FMECA generation tool provided by CECILIA-WORKSHOP. This tools takes as input a set of failure events to triggers and observation points (*i.e.* variables of the model). For each failure event, the tool computes the values of the observation points and stores the results in an XML file. The combination of the FMECA generation tool and the structured ALTARICA model enables us to establish a direct and straightforward relationship between the elements required in the table and the corresponding ALTARICA variables within the model. More precisely, 1. for our use-case we considered that all the failure modes of the components within the ONERA built avionics and power supply are probable. 2. the detection means are encoded either at functional level by the alarms implemented in the Monitoring and Alarm Management function or by detection tasks of the procedures involving other actors (*e.g.* UTM, safety pilot). 3. the recovery actions are encoded either in the selection of a dedicated control mode in the Mode Selection Logic function or physical reconfigurations (*e.g.* primary to backup switch). 4. the high level failure conditions and their criticality are encoded by the safety barrier diagram.

Note that a PFQA table contains semantically coupled information that can be systematically checked to ensure consistency between the layers and their connection. For instance, the table enables to check that the safety outcomes computed by the safety barrier diagram is consistent with the Mode Selection Logic function. Another consistency check can be performed w.r.t. the observability of failures effects, indeed if a recovery action is triggered without any alarms being raised, then it might highlight an error in the functional layer. Conversely, the effects of some failures may not trigger any alarm or mitigation action since our framework does not enforce to monitor and isolate the effects of all possible failures. Such a lack of observability can raise a safety concern if its safety outcome is severe and may trigger a redesign of the system.

To facilitate analysis, we created a processing tool that converts the XML file generated by CECILIA-WORKSHOP into a CSV table. Table 1 provides an extract of the analysis result and illustrates that most single component failures most failures lead to a LandAsSoonAsPracticable outcome, resulting in a landing in a controlled area. Let us consider two distinct failure scenarios: 1. The loss of either the telemetry module or the Navigation MCU triggers the TelemetryFailed alarm, since the Navigation MCU is responsible for nominal telemetry functions. 2. A low battery condition activates the ElecLow alarm. In response to these alarms, both the on-board and on-ground Mode Selection Logic functions activate a LandAsSoonAsPracticable mode. This mode can be safely executed since it can tolerate a telemetry loss or a low battery level (thanks to an alternator providing alternative power supply).

9   Related Works

AltaRica language and tools were already used for aircraft certification, they can support the analysis of dynamic systems and do not require the availability of some other design models (e.g. Simulink, SysMl, AADL, ...). So this framework was selected for its maturity and compatibility with the lack of FAZER design models. The proposed modelling and analysis methodology could be implemented by similar frameworks (e.g. [5,7,18]) and the whole AltaRica model of the FAZER is proposed as a benchmark for the MBSA community.

The model and assessment methods presented in this paper supports the Probable Failure Qualitative Assessment requested by SORA to obtain flight approval. Some former works proposed other models and analysis to address other safety objectives.

For instance, bow-tie models are extensively used by [9,10] for analyzing Unmanned Aerial Systems (UAS). However, as noted by [4], these models lack the detail of our Safety Barrier Diagrams, instead considering a broader range of barrier types. Such barriers can relate to system reliability, exposure, entity response, and loss intervention barriers, many of which are already addressed in SORA assessments, such as Exposure barriers relating to population density and Ml mitigation. The bow-tie models high-level abstraction of technical capability failures, without distinguishing between erroneous, partial, or total loss, makes it less suitable for supporting Failure Hazard Assessment. Furthermore, the authors of [10] acknowledge that the bow-tie formalism does not account for the sequential or parallel application of barriers (or mitigation tasks).

Alternative formalisms based on ALTARICA, such as the one proposed by [17], have been developed to model procedures for safety analysis. This particular work introduces an ALTARICA library and a modeling methodology specifically designed for capturing both nominal and emergency procedures of UAVs. A notable aspect of this framework is its ability to manage dynamic interactions among tasks that unfold across multiple parallel procedures. However, this approach falls short in establishing a connection between task failures and the failures of the functions that implement them. This link is a crucial element in our framework, rendering the proposed framework unsuitable for our context.

[2] explores the use of dependable digital identity to monitor the occurence of complex basic events during the flight and to compute the remaining mean time to failure.

Finally, [16] explored various methods for implementing multi-layer models, revealing a key challenge: integrating ALTARICA models that consider different types of contributors to feared events. The paper presents a comparative analysis of several connection strategies, evaluating their expressiveness, ability to

Table 1. Extract of the PFQA table for *MediDelivery* (ALTARICA models, tools and results for the *MediDelivery* are available at https://w3.onera.fr/PHYDIAS/en/reference-case-study-fazer)

Equipment	Component	Failure mode	Detection mean(s)	Recovery Action	Failure condition	Criticality
Coms	Telemetry	Lost	TelemetryFailed	Land As Soon As Practicable	Landing in controlled area	MAJ
Navigation	MCU	Lost	TelemetryFailed			
Power Supply	Bat	Low	ElecLow			

encode dynamic failure propagation, and modeling effort required to connect functional to physical architectures. Flow-based connection offers the best balance between expressiveness, analytical capabilities, and modeling effort, which is why we adopted this approach in our proposed framework. Flow-based connections was also used in [8]. The layers introduced in this paper were tuned to better aligns with the requirements of SORA.

10 Conclusion

This paper outlines the principles employed to model procedural, functional, and physical aspects crucial for assessing safety objectives applicable to UAV-based operations. The primary focus of this paper lies in systematically identifying the effects of probable failures, as requested by the SORA for medium-risk drones. To do so, we developed a tool based on the CECILIA-WORKSHOP FMEA generator to verify that no single failure would result in a unmitigated Loss of Control. Such an approach has been used successfully within the SORA of an actual drone in 2024. To promote further research and development, we offer the *MediDelivery* example as a public case study. This resource is available for the scientific community to test alternative methods or tools. To further ease the conduct of the SORA for medium-risk operations, our current research investigates ways to document models and results for efficient authority review, ensuring seamless regulatory approvals. Eventually we are exploring alternative means of compliance for high-risk drones, such as exploiting the layered-model to perform an automatic identification of the sequences of failures leading to failure conditions.

Acknowledgement. The authors acknowledge the funding of PHYDIAS2 project by DGAC, France Relance 2030 and European Union NextGenerationEU and the Defense Innovation Agency (AID) of the French Ministry of Defense (research project CONCORDE N° 2019 65 0090004707501)

References

1. Arnold, A., Point, G., Griffault, A., Rauzy, A.: The Altarica formalism for describing concurrent systems. Fundamanta Informaticae **40**(2–3), 109–124 (1999)
2. Aslansefat, K., et al.: SafeDrones: real-time reliability evaluation of UAVs using executable digital dependable identities, pp. 252–266 (2022). https://doi.org/10.1007/978-3-031-15842-1_18
3. Bieber, P., Delmas, K., Blaye, P.L., Pizziol, S., Prosvirnova, T., Seguin, C.: Safety barrier diagrams for specific operations of drones. In: 2024 International Conference on Unmanned Aircraft Systems (ICUAS), pp. 858–864 (2024)
4. Bieber, P., Delmas, K., Pizziol, S., Prosvirnova, T., Seguin, C.: A generic approach for safety assessment of medium-risk drones. Eng. Proc. **90**(1) (2025)
5. Bittner, B., et al.: The xSAP safety analysis platform. In: Chechik, M., Raskin, J.-F. (eds.) TACAS 2016. LNCS, vol. 9636, pp. 533–539. Springer, Heidelberg (2016). https://doi.org/10.1007/978-3-662-49674-9_31

6. de Bossoreille, X., Delavault, S., Deschamps, F., Frazza, C., Prosvirnova, T., Seguin, C.: MBSA modelling guide and validation report. Technical report. LIV-S085L01-001, IRT Saint Exupéry (2023). https://sahara.irt.saintexupery.com/S2C/Public-Documents/src/branch/master/Guide
7. Delange, J., Feiler, P.: Architecture fault modeling with the AADL error-model annex. In: Proceedings - 40th Euromicro Conference Series on Software Engineering and Advanced Applications, SEAA 2014, pp. 361–368 (2014). https://doi.org/10.1109/SEAA.2014.20
8. Delmas, K., Seguin, C., Bieber, P.: Tiered model-based safety assessment. In: Model-Based Safety and Assessment, pp. 141–156 (2019)
9. Denney, E., Pai, G., Johnson, M.: Towards a rigorous basis for specific operations risk assessment of UAS. In: 2018 IEEE/AIAA 37th Digital Avionics Systems Conference (DASC), pp. 1–10. IEEE (2018)
10. Denney, E., Pai, G., Whiteside, I.: Modeling the safety architecture of UAS flight operations. In: Tonetta, S., Schoitsch, E., Bitsch, F. (eds.) SAFECOMP 2017. LNCS, vol. 10488, pp. 162–178. Springer, Cham (2017). https://doi.org/10.1007/978-3-319-66266-4_11
11. EASA: Cologne, G.: Means of Compliance with OSO#05/10/12 System Safety and Reliability (2023)
12. EUROCAE: ED279 – Generic FHA for RPAS/UAS (2020)
13. EUROCAE, SAE: Aerospace Recommended Practices 4761 - guidelines and methods for conducting the safety assessment process on civil airborne systems and equipment (2023)
14. EuropeanUnion: COMMISSION IMPLEMENTING REGULATION (EU) 2019/947 of 24 May 2019 on the rules and procedures for the operation of unmanned aircraft (2019)
15. JARUS: JARUS Guidelines on Specific Operations Risk Assessment (SORA), Edition Number 2.5 (2024)
16. Machin, M., Saez, E., Virelizier, P., Bossoreille, X.: Modeling functional allocation in AltaRica to support MBSE/MBSA consistency. In: Papadopoulos, Y., Aslansefat, K., Katsaros, P., Bozzano, M. (eds.) IMBSA 2019. LNCS, vol. 11842, pp. 3–17. Springer, Cham (2019). https://doi.org/10.1007/978-3-030-32872-6_1
17. Mathou, C., Delmas, K., de Saqui-Sannes, P., Chaudemar, J.C.: Safety-oriented dynamic procedure modeling. In: 2024 IEEE International Systems Conference (SysCon), pp. 1–8. IEEE (2024)
18. Papadopoulos, Y., et al.: Engineering failure analysis and design optimisation with hip-hops. Eng. Failure Anal. **18**, 590–608 (2011). https://doi.org/10.1016/j.engfailanal.2010.09.025
19. Perrin, E., Kirwan, B., Stroup, R.: A systemic model of ATM safety: the integrated risk picture. In: Proceedings of the 7th USA/Europe ATM R&D Seminar, Barcelona (2007)
20. Rauzy, A.: Mathematical foundations of minimal cutsets. IEEE Trans. Reliab. **50**(4), 389–396 (2001)
21. SatoDev: Cecilia Workshop Version 6.1 (2022)

Timed Models in AltaRica 3.0

Isabella Lanzani[1]([✉]) and Christel Seguin[2]

[1] Dipartimento di Elettronica Informazione e Bioingegneria, Politecnico di Milano,
Milan, Italy
isabella.lanzani@polimi.it
[2] ONERA, 2 Avenue Edouard Belin, 31055 Toulouse, France

Abstract. Model-Based Safety Assessment is a cornerstone of modern
safety-critical system design, providing formal verification techniques to
ensure compliance with stringent safety requirements. The AltaRica 3.0
modeling language offers a structured approach to model system behavior
and failures. The associated tools support qualitative and probabilistic
risk analysis. In addition, the language semantics and the simulator integrate timing constraints associated with thell probability of event occurrence. In this work, we explore the potentialities of AltaRica's semantics and tools to express and analyze the timed properties of critical
safety systems. To evaluate this approach, a case study involving two
autonomous drones performing an obstacle avoidance maneuver is used.
Our findings shed light on the strengths and limitations of using AltaRica
for time-sensitive verification and provide insights into its applicability
for real-world, time-critical safety assessments.

Keywords: Model-Based Safety Analysis · AltaRica · Formal
Methods · Timed failure propagation models

1 Introduction

AltaRica is a well known language created in the scope of Model-Based Safety
Assessment (MBSA). It supports the construction, through the AltaRica 3.0
language and its tools, of a specific event-transition automata from which it is
possible to extract scenarios of occurrence of failure events that lead to undesired
situations.

In industrial safety practice, static scenarios describe undesired situations in
the form of Minimal Cut Sets (MCSs) i.e. an unordered set of failure events.

In this scope, AltaRica static models are deemed detailed enough to provide
valuable results. A model is defined static if all the sequences of transitions which
starts from the same configuration and which are made up of permutation of a
same set of events leads to the same configuration of the reachability graph of
the model [1]. In other words, in a static model, the order in which a combination of events occurs does not influence the scenario's outcome. Consequently,
generating MCSs from the static model analysis yields a list of event sets where
the order of events within each set is irrelevant.

© The Author(s), under exclusive license to Springer Nature Switzerland AG 2026
P. Katsaros (Ed.): IMBSA 2025, LNCS 15755, pp. 398–412, 2026.
https://doi.org/10.1007/978-3-032-05073-1_26

Although not strictly required in industrial safety assessment, it is obvious that in real-case applications, the static assumption could be too restrictive. To overcome this, AltaRica 3.0 language allows for dynamic model description. Contrary to static, dynamic models contains at least one pair of sequences that are constituted with the same events and result in different configurations. Dynamic models provide valuable results in the form of critical sequences: a list of event sets generated by the dynamic model analysis where the order of events within each set is relevant. In other words, in a dynamic model, the order in which a combination of events is fired influences the occurrence of the scenario.

To further advance in the study, a new class of scenarios is defined: timed scenarios. A timed scenario is a dynamic scenario where one (or more) time stamps have been included. Similar to the previous definitions, we define timed models as models that are representative enough to describe timed scenarios. In other words, in a timed model, the order and the time at which the events are triggered play a role in the occurrence of the event.

This work uses AltaRica 3.0 language and AltaRica Wizard tool to create timed model to address timed scenarios. The results are studied in the same form of critical sequences, where one or more specific events are defined to keep track of the passage of time. Both a simple case study (formed by a timed switch system) and a more complex case study (formed by a drone in a collision trajectory path) are reported. Looking at the generated results, significant features of the timed models are addressed.

The article is structured as follow. Section 2 presents the formal semantics of AltaRica language and its associated tool, AltaRica Wizard. It includes considerations for static, dynamic, and timed models within AltaRica. Furthermore, in the same section, the timed switch system is modeled and analyzed to further illustrate the methodology underlying the proposed approach. Section 3 describes a more complex example involving a drone performing an avoidance maneuver while on a collision course with an intruder. Section 4 will delve into more details over current methodologies for timed automata description. Section 5 contains conclusions and future works.

2   AltaRica Language and Basic Timed Model

AltaRica 3.0 is an event-centric language designed to facilitate failure propagation modeling and safety analyses of complex technical systems [2]. Hence, it naturally allows to model the system's functional dynamics (change of control mode, reconfiguration of equipment, etc.) and failures (cascades of failures, hidden failures, etc.) [3]. Section 2.1 introduces how to write static AltaRica 3.0 models, while Sect. 2.2 explains dynamic models and the timed contribution. The timed switch example is reported in Sect. 2.3.

2.1 AltaRica Language

The AltaRica 3.0 modeling units are classes that describe the behavior of system components by Guarded Transition Systems (GTS) [4]. A class is defined by events, state variables, flow variables, transitions and assertions.

The initializations of variables are introduced by the keywords *reset* for flow variables and *init* for the state variables.

A transition has the following format: $name : guard \rightarrow effect$. The guard specifies when the transition is enabled, while the effect specifies how the values of some current state variables change after firing the enabled transition.

A *delay* attribute is associated with the events to calculate the firing dates of the enabled transitions.

An assertion specifies the value of a flow variable based on the current values of the state variables and the other flow variables.

Figure 1 presents a class that models a generic *agent*. This *agent* receives a boolean input I and it produces a boolean output O depending on its internal state s. This *agent* may fail and cannot be repaired. Moreover, the probability of firing *fail* event follows an exponential law with $\lambda = 3E^{-9}$ as the failure rate.

```
class AGENT
    Boolean s (init = true);
    Boolean I, O (reset = false);

    parameter Real Lambda=3e-9;
    event fail (delay=exponential(Lambda));

transition
    fail : s == true -> s := false;

assertion
    O := if s == true then I
            else false;
end
```

Fig. 1. AltaRica class of *agent* class

The value of the output variable O is defined by an assertion over the state variable s and the flow variable I. Following this assertion, the output O can either be false due to an internal loss or be equal to the input I.

AltaRica 3.0 is an Object-Oriented language. Generic classes can be instantiated and reused in other classes or block (the main instance of the project). For example, Fig. 2 presents a block model *DroneCommunication*, that uses two instances of the class *agent* and that connects these instances thanks to specific assertions.

Figure 3 provides a graphical view of the model topology.

The interested reader can find more details about the features of the AltaRica 3.0 language in other works [2,5].

2.2 Timed Simulation of AltaRica Models

GTS from an AltaRica 3.0 model specifies a reachability graph. Each node of this graph is a specific configuration of the model i.e. an assignment of values

```
block DroneCommunication
    AGENT transmit;
    AGENT pic_engage;

    Boolean O (reset = true);

    observer Boolean FailedCommunication = (O == false);

    assertion
    transmit.I := true
    pic_engage.I := transmit. O;
    O := pic_engage.O;
end
```

Fig. 2. AltaRica block of the *DroneCommunication* system

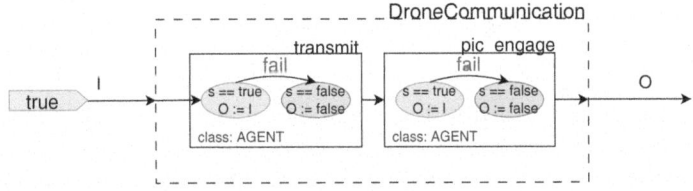

Fig. 3. Graphical representation of the AtaRica *DroneCommunication* system

to the state and flow variables that satisfies the rules defined by the parts *init*, *assertion* and *transition* in the model. Each edge from one configuration σ_i to σ_{i+1} is labeled by one event name e and it represents the transition e that is fired in σ_i and leads to σ_{i+1}. So σ_i shall satisfy the guard of e and σ_{i+1} shall satisfy the effects of e.

Moreover, the events of the model are characterized by different types of delays that add the following complementary constraints to the transition firing:

1. **Deterministic transitions** have a delay defined by the probability distribution named $Dirac(\delta)$, where δ is a fixed delay - an integer and non-negative number. If a deterministic transition becomes enabled at time t, then it must fire exactly at time $t + \delta$, where δ counts the number of fired transitions. A special case of deterministic transitions are immediate transitions, defined by $Dirac(0)$. They should be fired as soon as their guards become true (before any other transition)

2. **Stochastic transitions** have a delay defined by a stochastic probability distribution (for example, exponential, Weibull, etc.). If a stochastic transition becomes enabled at time t, it should be fired at time $t+\epsilon$, where ϵ is a random delay calculated according to the associated probability distribution.

Let us build the reachability graph for the example of a primary-backup system that mixes stochastic and deterministic transitions. This system can be modeled by two generic classes of *agent*, *c1* and *c2*, that model respectively a primary lane and a backup lane; the switch s engages the reconfiguration from the primary lane to the backup lane when *c1* fails. The reconfiguration can be inhibited on some external *StuckCondition*. At the moment, we assume that this condition is always false (see Fig. 4).

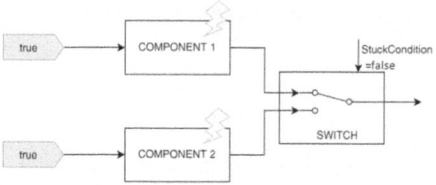

Fig. 4. Primary-backup system

The class *agent* is defined in Fig. 1 and it contains the stochastic transition *fail*. The class *switch* (see Fig. 5) contains two events with *Dirac(0)* delays. Initially the switch selects the input *I1*. The transition *select_latched* latches the selector position when the switch receives the *stuck* input. Event *select2* engages the commutation on *I2* input when the switch is not stuck and the input *I1* becomes false.

```
class SWITCH
    Boolean I1, I2 (reset = true);
    Boolean O (reset = true);
    Boolean StuckCondition (reset = false);

    Boolean select1 (init = true);
    Boolean stuck (init = false);

    event select_latched (delay = Dirac(0));
    event select2 (delay = Dirac(0));

    transition
    select_latched : not stuck and StuckCondition -> stuck := true;
    select2 : not stuck and not I1 and select1 -> select1 := false;
    assertion

    O := if select1 then I1 else I2;
end
```

Fig. 5. AltaRica class of the switch

Figure 6 shows the reachability graph of the primary-backup model. A symbolic date of arrival is associated to each configuration [6]. Symbolic dates define the date of arrival in each configuration. For instance, t_0 is the date in the initial configuration, $t_0 + \delta_1$ is the date of arrival in σ_1. It is worth noting that the firing of the event *select2* does not change the arrival date of the next configuration because the event is instantaneous (i.e., delay law is *Dirac(0)*). The paths $< \sigma_0; \sigma_1; \sigma_2; \sigma_3 >$ and $< \sigma_0; \sigma_4; \sigma_5; \sigma_6 >$ start from the same initial state and lead to the same configurations of variables in σ_3 and σ_6. However, the arrival dates in σ_3 and σ_6 are different and there is no variable that enables an access to this arrival dates. For this reason, it is hard to write observers that take into account timing constraints.

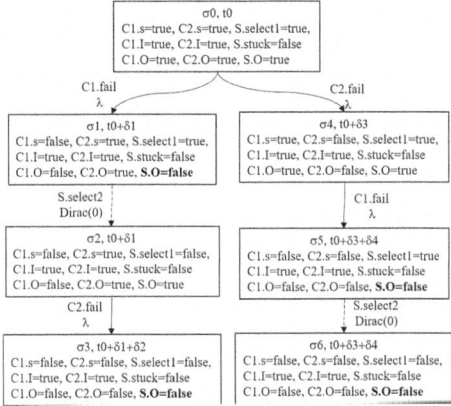

Fig. 6. Reachability graph of the primary back-up model

To overcome this difficulty, we introduce a *tick* transition with *delay = 1*, so that the event is always enabled (and not limited) to fire under all circumstances (except when the system is forced to fire a *Dirac*). The event *tick* will be used to represent a clock, giving us a measure to describe absolute time dependencies.

Our contribution revolves around this last transition definition: contrary to $Dirac(\delta)$, after each event transition, even if its guard is true, it is not mandatory for it to be fire.

With this new capability, the scope of timed observers will expand, enabling a broader application of time-related properties. This enhancement will allow for a more complete description of timed scenarios of real systems. It allows, for example, to check if a certain state of the system is achieved inside a certain time interval or to delay by a given time interval a certain transition.

2.3   Timed Switch System

As previously mentioned, AltaRica 3.0 tracks transition progression based on the number of fired events—for example, specifying that an event must occur as the second transition. This is achieved through the use of $Dirac(\delta)$ semantics, which model instantaneous and event-indexed behavior. However, progression based on absolute time—such as requiring an event to fire after two clock ticks—cannot be modeled in the same manner. To address this limitation and describe time-dependent behavior, the original Switch model of Fig. 4 is extended into a timed variant. The resulting timed primary-backup system (illustrated in Fig. 7) includes two sources, two functional components (instances of class *agent*), a *switch*, a *time monitor*, and an observer.

The *time monitor* in Fig. 7 is responsible for introducing timed considerations into the otherwise static system. Specifically, it operates within the time threshold specified by the *freeze* event (i.e., 2 ticks of the clock). If a failure of the first source is detected before this threshold, the monitor instructs the switch to

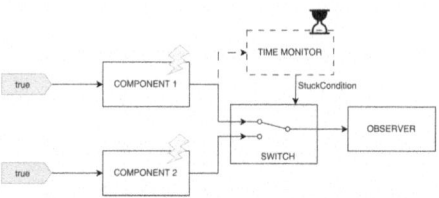

Fig. 7. Timed primary-backup system

select the second source. In any case, once the threshold has elapsed, the switch becomes stuck in its last valid position.

This simple example includes both stochastic events (i.e., the failures from the sources) and deterministic events (i.e., events in *switch* and *time monitor*).

AltaRica model for the *time monitor* is illustrated in Fig. 8a, while the overall *TimedSwitch* system is represented in Fig. 8b. The latter makes use of the same classes defined in the previous Sect. 2.2.

```
block TimedSwitch
    AGENT c1;
    AGENT c2;
    TIME_MONITOR tm;
    SWITCH s;

    Boolean O (reset = true);

    observer Boolean FailedTransmission = (O == false);
    assertion
    c1.I := true;
    c2.I := true;
    s.I1 := c1.O;
    s.I2 := c2.O;
    s.StuckCondition := tm.StuckCondition;

    O := s.O;
end
```

```
class TIME_MONITOR
    Boolean StuckCondition (reset = false);
    Boolean timeRunning (init = true);
    Integer t (init = 0);

    event Tick (delay = 1);
    event freeze (delay = Dirac(0));

    transition
    Tick : true -> t := t + 1;
    freeze : t >= 2 and timeRunning -> timeRunning := false;

    assertion
    StuckCondition := if timeRunning then false else true;
end
```

(a) AltaRica class of the Time Monitor

(b) AltaRica main block for the Timed Switch

Fig. 8. AltaRica instances

Observer *FailedTransmission* is defined as the unwanted situation in which the output from the switch is set to false.

The generated results (composed by string of ordered events) lacked general readability and did not emphasize absolute timing. To address this, a graphical representation was introduced, inspired by the prefix tree (or trie) data structure. A trie is specifically designed to store and manage a large number of ordered sequences efficiently: common prefixes among sequences are represented only once, allowing for compact visualization and clear identification of shared execution paths [7].

The most common use of the tree structure is for words retrieval, but for the article purpose, its structure was modified to better support time-based reasoning. In a classical trie, the nodes are structurally meaningful but semantically empty, while the transitions carry the elements of the stored sequences (e.g., characters or symbols). In this timed trie, however, the main nodes represent absolute time instances (specifically, *tick* events) thus anchoring the sequences to a global timeline. Graphically, these main nodes are displaced at the same position of the horizontal axis. The transitions instead carry the ordered events, preserving their temporal order. Additional intermediate nodes are introduced as needed to handle bifurcations, even though they do not correspond to specific events themselves. This approach reduces visual redundancy while preserving the logical structure of the execution paths. The trie for the timed switch described before is reported in Fig. 9.

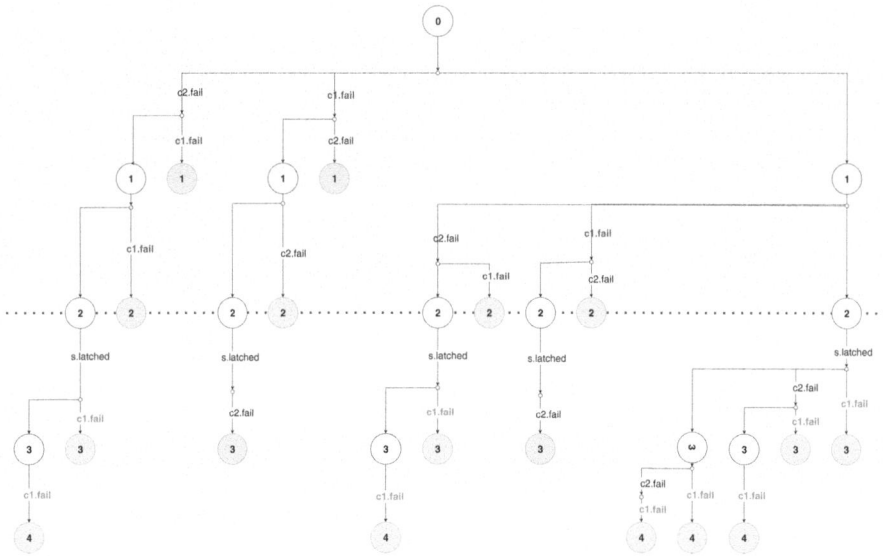

Fig. 9. Timed trie for the timed primary-backup system (Color figure online)

As expected, there is a dependency between the date in which stochastic failures have been fired and the observer activation. Observing the trie structure in Fig. 9, blue and orange colors describe a internal classification. Blue nodes represent the final node for those sequences where the failure of the first component happens before 2 ticks of the clock (the dotted red line). Here, it is necessary to have a second (not time-constrained) failure on the second component. In contrast, where the final nodes are orange, first component fails after 2 ticks of the clock. In this case, it is this failure alone that activates the observer. Nevertheless, as this generation computes all sequences, the presence of a second failure is evident. However, this is not a prerequisite for failure.

As expected, the event *tm. Tick* is an arbitrary event: any number of events can occur between one firing and the next. It creates an artificial time counter.

3   Experimental Validation

The purpose of this section is to validate the proposed approach on a significant case, inspired by real systems. In many applications, combining standard timed logic (such as delays) with failure events enables a more in-depth analysis. It is not at all trivial or uninteresting, for example, to reveal how the timing of failures would affect the system's overall fault resilience.

The following Section contains the description and the results of the proposed experiment.

3.1   Experiment Description and Model

Looking at Fig. 10, the proposed case study describes an air collision trajectory manoeuvre performed by a Unmanned Aerial System (UAS). UAS is divided into the Unmanned Aerial Vehicle (UAV) and the Pilot In Control (PIC) located on ground. The foreseen collision is always detected by onboard sensing, that generates *AirProximity* signal. The avoidance maneuver is engaged either by PIC or by the UAV autopilot system, following a certain priority defined below.

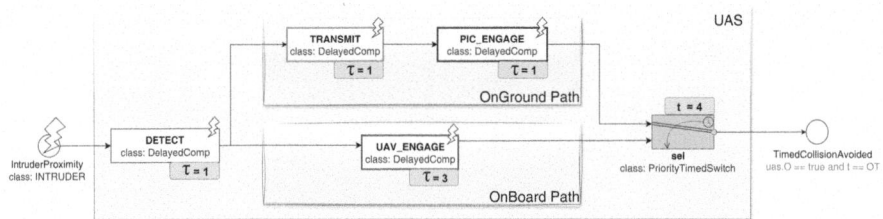

Fig. 10. Air Collision Avoidance

The four white functional blocks shown in Fig. 10 represent the elements responsible for the Air Collision Avoidance scenario. They are instances of the same class, *delayed agent*, characterized by the following events:

- *failure*—modeled by an exponential distribution; it inhibits the correct execution of the agent and it can be triggered before or after the function nominal execution.
- *request*—modeled as a deterministic instantaneous event; it captures the absolute time instant at which the agent is requested.
- *engage*—another deterministic instantaneous event; it triggers the correct execution of the agent a specified number of ticks of the clock after the request, if the system is in nominal conditions.

In this way, each agent exhibits two key behaviors: the possibility of a failure and a delay of the specified number of ticks of the clock from the request.

```
class Delayed_AGENT
    triplet s (init = notActive);
    Boolean countStarts (init = false);

    Boolean I (reset = false);
    Boolean O (reset = false);

    Integer t (reset = 0);
    Integer tg (init = 0);
    parameter Integer Delay = 1;

    event request (delay = Dirac(0));
    event engage (delay = Dirac(0));
    event failure (delay = exponential(0.5));

transition
    failure : not s == Failed -> s := Failed;
    request : I and not countStarts and
              not s == Failed ->
                        {countStarts := true,
                         tg := t;}
    engage : countStarts and s == notActive and
             t == tg + Delay -> s := Active;

assertion
    O := if s == Active then I else false;
end
```

```
class PriorityTimedSwitch
    Boolean waiting (init = true);
    Boolean Select1 (reset = true);

    Boolean I1 (reset = false);
    Boolean I2 (reset = false);
    Boolean O (reset = false);

    Integer t (reset = 0);
    parameter Integer Delay = 4;

    event timeout (delay = Dirac(0));

transition
    timeout : not I1 and t >= Delay
              and waiting == true -> waiting := false;
assertion
    Select1 := if waiting then true else false;
    O := if Select1 == true then I1 else I2;
end
```

(a) Delayed agent   (b) Priority timed switch

Fig. 11. AltaRica classes for UAS

This latter behavior models a known latency between engagement and nominal execution. AltaRica code is reported in Fig. 11a.

PriorityTimedSwitch implements the priority logic: if the pilot initiates the maneuver, it is executed immediately. However, if no request is received within a predefined time interval t, the UAV will autonomously initiate the maneuver, entering what is referred to as a "last-minute collision avoidance scenario".

3.2 Experiment Results

Figure 10 shows two automata: one describes the system, contained in the grey "UAS" area, while the other describes the property to be checked. This is defined by *IntruderProximity* and *TimedCollisionAvoidance*, and indicates the scenario in which a collision trajectory has been successfully avoided within a given time interval OT. OT is the maximum number of 'ticks' permitted for the manoeuvre to be performed. This is a bounded-time safety property. The generated critical sequences provide us with the complete set of ordered events that lead successfully to the scenario.

The timed system will be tested against OT = 4 and OT = 5.

Table 1 contain the interval of generated events for each row: it gives an approximate indication on the computational cost required for the analysis. To generate the sequence, a deterministic model with a unique initial configuration is required. The algorithms then perform an automated simulation, guided by the

Table 1. Generated sequences

Sequence Length	Number of	Sequences
11	2	
12	15	
13	36	
14	20	
15	24	
16	12	
	TOT = 109	

(a) OT = 4

Sequence Length	Number of	Sequences
12	2	
13	17	
14	40	
15	30	
16	32	
17	28	
	TOT = 149	

(a) OT = 5

search for configurations in which the observer is present. The automated simulation is stopped in one configuration either because the configuration satisfies the observer or because the maximum sequences length (set at 20) is reached. In terms of complexity, it took AltaRica approximately eight seconds to generate the 109 OT = 4 sequences and around ten seconds for the 149 OT = 5 sequences. The computational effort required is directly related to the maximum sequence length specified by the user, and it may be necessary to perform costly simulations to understand the order of magnitude of the results.

Post-processing operations over the sequence generated were made:

– removal of ".timed" events: they manage the agent guard activation, with no significant effect on the system behaviour
– removal of not-relevant instantaneous events after the last tolerate ".Tick"
– removal of duplicate sequences

Events labeled as ".failure" show the system resilience to faults, and from them results in Table 2 were extracted.

Table 2. Summary of results

OT	Admitted combination of failure events	Number of sequences (after post-process)
4	none	1
	uas.uav_engage.failure	3
		TOT = 4
5	none	1
	uas.uav_engage.failure;	5
	uas.pic_engage.failue;	9
	uas.trasmit.failure;	9
	uas.pic_engage.failure and uas.transmit.failure;	29
	uas.transmit.failure and uas.pic_engage.failure;	29
		TOT = 82

In Table 2, the column "Admitted combinations of failure events" lists the ordered combinations of ".failure" events (if any) appearing in the extracted sequences. The column "Number of sequences" counts, after post-process, how many combination of events lead to a positive outcome from the maneuver while including the specified ".failure" event(s).

From Table 2, it is cleat that, with OT = 4, the positive scenario is achieved only via the OnGround path, hence requiring the correctness from both uas.transmit and uas.pic_engage.

Imposing OT = 5 creates a system more robust to failures. In this case, the system is able to execute the manoeuvre by switching from the OnGround path to the OnBoard path. In fact, the system is tolerant to failures of one or both agents on the OnGround path, as well as tolerant against the failure of the OnBoard path. In both cases, it is confirmed that a failure of the agent "uas.detect" would not be mitigated and would lead to the collision scenario.

A sample from the generated sequence is reported below:

$$OT = 4$$
IntruderProximity.Trigger Tick uas.detect.del uas.uav_engage.failure Tick uas.transmit.del Tick uas.pic_engage.del Tick

$$OT = 5$$
IntruderProximity.Trigger Tick uas.detect.del uas.pic_engage.failure Tick uas.transmit.del uas.transmit.failure Tick Tick uas.uav_engage.del uas.sel.timeout Tick

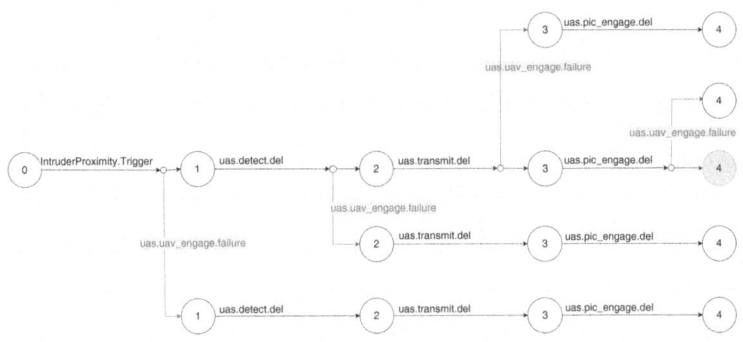

Fig. 12. Timed trie for OT = 4

Figure 12 contains a graphical representation of the generated sequences for OT = 4. The same trie structure for OT = 5 is present in GitHub for the interested reader [8]. Timed tries make use of the absolute time counting (namely, the event *tick*) to sort and represent all the sequences that lead to the defined observer. Event *tick* in this scenario represents the passing of time and it plays a fundamental role in system timed behavior.

4   State of the Art

A timed automaton is a finite-state automaton extended with a set of real-valued variables modeling clocks [9,10]. They could use local invariant conditions to restrict the behaviour of an automaton to enforce progress properties [11]. Unlike AltaRica's semantics, transitions in timed automata are neither purely stochastic nor fully deterministic, but they could be fired within a specified time interval. This is implemented by guards using clock constraints, which create equality or inequality functions of the clock current values. Timed automata are generally undecidable, but under certain assumptions they can be decidable. This case study represents one such case: we declared a unique and unresettable clock (used by timed transition guards and by the observer declaration), which enforces fully deterministic behavior [12]. Indeed, for timed considerations, guards are fired as soon as the associated *Dirac* allowed it.

In logic, any system of rules and symbols used to represent propositions qualified in terms of time is referred to as temporal logic. Temporal logic, particularly Linear Temporal Logic (LTL) and Computation Tree Logic (CTL), forms the foundation for reasoning about sequences of events in reactive and time-dependent systems [13]. These logics are widely used in verification tools to express time-based properties like "event A eventually follows event B" or "event C always holds after event D." Model checkers such as PRISM [14] and NuSMV [15] have been effectively used to model and verify time-dependent behavior, including in the context of safety analysis and assessment generation. These tools explore system executions to determine whether a given temporal property holds, and are particularly powerful in analyzing timed automata, probabilistic models, and hybrid systems. Model checkers are typically designed to verify or falsify specific properties over execution traces, often returning one or more counterexamples or witnesses. Consequently, they are not inherently suited for exhaustively collecting all relevant ordered sequences of events, a task more naturally addressed by AllSAT solvers [16], which aim to enumerate all satisfying assignments under given constraints.

Looking at past research, mixing model checkers with AltaRica models to reason about the correctness of temporal conditions is part of an ongoing research path. In [17]: here, a tool chain linking an AltaRica 2.0 Dataflow models to Tina model-checker was created to evaluate temporal properties. In [18] the formalism of AltaRica Dataflow has been reinterpreted in the HyDI [19] language, readable by the standard symbolic language SMV, and then processed using model checker NuSMV to address temporal properties. In both these researches, the analysis of time-related properties was demanded to an external (model-checker) tool.

5   Conclusions and Future Works

This study advances the current state-of-the-art in timed scenario description for AltaRica 3.0 by introducing absolute time modeling. By doing so, all language capabilities are preserved, including the description of degraded system behavior in terms of failure propagation rules. AltaRica Wizard is the only adopted tool, and its analyses do not rely on external model checkers or other tools. Timed observers were instantiated to address the effect of absolute time in the faulty system, using sequence generation and particularly modified trie structures to analyze the results. Although there is no direct connection with static probabilistic safety analysis, the same AltaRica model can nonetheless be reused to derive such analyses—as is commonly done. Within a broader methodological framework, the current analysis can be viewed as a complementary corollary to traditional safety assessments. However, it is important to emphasize that the focus here lies on timed behavioral properties, which are conceptually and methodologically distinct from quantitative probabilistic evaluations typically associated with static models.

For an industrial application, the approach is promising. AltaRica timed models are able to cover a wider range of system requirements, thus allowing for a dual purpose: ensuring a greater degree of similarity to the real system while collecting more system knowledge (e.g. estimated delays, time stamps, etc.) in the safety model. Indeed, addressing this timed scenarios could significantly improve system comprehension and safety results.

In AltaRica, it is possible to define structures based on classical Linear Temporal Logic (LTL), such as 'until', 'next', 'eventually', and 'globally'. One possible area for future research would be to extend the framework to support the definition of more complex timed properties.

Future work in this project will explore the use of timed AltaRica models for time parameter synthesis, with the aim of identifying the (absolute) time intervals within which a given operation can still be successfully completed, even in the presence of failures.

Furthermore, the computational cost for timed scenario description will be further investigated. Indeed, dynamic and timed considerations make use of instantaneous *Dirac* events, resulting in large order sequences and complexity in larger applications could be a bottleneck.

In addition, the graphical representation of the trie structure could be automated and integrated into the AltaRica Wizard tool, improving the interpretability of the analysis results and enhancing user comprehension.

References

1. Batteux, M., Prosvirnova, T., Rauzy, A.: AltaRica 3.0 language specification. AltaRica Association (2015)
2. Prosvirnova, T.: AltaRica 3.0: a Model-Based approach for Safety Analyses (2014)
3. Prosvirnova, T., et al.: Strategies for Modelling Failure Propagation in Dynamic Systems with AltaRica. IMBSA (2022)
4. Rauzy, A.B.: Guarded transition systems: a new states/events formalism for reliability studies (2008)
5. Arnold, A., Griffault, A., Point, G., Rauzy, A.: The AltaRica language and its semantics. Fundamenta Informaticae (2000)

6. Batteux, M., Prosvirnova, T., Rauzy, A.: Abstract executions of stochastic discrete event systems. https://doi.org/10.1504/IJCCBS.2022.121363
7. Fredkin, E.: Trie memory (1960)
8. Repository. https://github.com/Sabeast-4/TimedAltaRica-
9. Alur, R., Dill, D.L.: Automata for modeling real-time systems. In: Proceedings, Seventeenth International Colloquium on Automata, Languages and Programming (1990)
10. Alur, R., Dill, D.L.: A theory of timed automata. J. Theoret. Comput. Sci. (1994)
11. Henzinger, T.A., Nicollin, X., Sifakis, J., Yovine, S.: Symbolic model checking for real-time systems. J. Inf. Comput. (1994)
12. Bengtsson, J., Yi, W.: Timed automata: Semantics, algorithms and tools. Advanced Course on Petri Nets (2003)
13. Pnueli, A.: The Temporal Logic of Programs. FOCS (1977)
14. Kwiatkowska, M., Norman, G., Parker, D.: PRISM: probabilistic model checking for performance and reliability analysis. ACM SIGMETRICS Perform. Eval. Rev. (2009)
15. Bozzano, M., Cavallo, A., Cifaldi, M., Valacca, L., Villafiorita, A.: Improving Safety Assessment of Complex Systems: An industrial case study. FME (2003)
16. Toda, T., Soh, T.: Implementing efficient all solutions SAT solvers. JEA (2016)
17. Albore, A., Zilio, S.D., Infantes, G., Seguin, C., Virelizier, P.: A ModelChecking approach to analyse temporal failure propagation with altaRica. IMBSA (2017)
18. Bozzano, M., et al.: Safety Assessment of AltaRica models via Symbolic Model Checking (2015)
19. Cimatti, A., Mover, S., Tonetta, S.: HyDI: a language for symbolic hybrid systems with discrete interaction. EUROMICRO (2011)

Experience in Developing an Algorithm at the MBSA Level to Minimize the Complexity of Fault Trees During Automatic Generation from Design Data

Romain Roy[1]([✉]) [iD], Youssef Lahlou[2] [iD], Julien Blangis[2] [iD], and Ayoub Zeghari[2] [iD]

[1] EDF LAB, 7 bd Gaspard Monge, 91120 Palaiseau, France
`romain.roy@edf.fr`
[2] CentraleSupelec, 3 Rue Joliot-Curie, 91192 Gif-Sur-Yvette, France
`{mohamed-youssef.lahlou,julien.blangis,`
`ayoub.zeghari}@student-cs.fr`

Abstract. In EDF's probabilistic safety assessment (PSA) studies, sequence of events diagrams represent all scenarios identified during qualitative analysis following an initiating event. These diagrams trace all possible paths involving successful or failed missions of backup systems or human actions. System missions identified in reliability studies are modeled using fault trees, generated with an MBSA expert system-based tool [3]. A key challenge for analysts is the complex modeling of systems from mechanical diagrams, often in difficult formats.

[1] and [4] present a tool (CONFLUENT) capable of reading data from multiple sources (electrical, hydraulic, and control) while managing system boundaries through path definitions. It supports compression of control, hydraulic, and electrical systems helping reduce EPS model complexity, especially in the context of zoomable EPS [2]. Finally, the tool enables topological mapping of complex networks by displaying attributes like location, altitude, function, or support structures, which aids in redundancy analysis at the support level (e.g., panels).

This article is a continuation of this work aimed at automating the generation of fault trees with low complexity by directly utilizing design data specification and PSA mission specifications of backup systems. Two main objectives were pursued: first, to minimize the complexity of the fault tree as much as possible, and second, to streamline communication between the system designer and the safety analysis engineer. An algorithm has been developed to partition the system into subsystems in order to minimize the complexity of the fault trees linked to mission's specifications based on three criteria: the scope of the system, the operational configurations and the purpose of the circuit (for example: bringing water from point A to point B). The input data and visualizations at both the CONFLUENT and algorithm levels are strictly those provided by the system designer, which helps facilitate communication.

Keywords: MBSA · CAD · COMPLEXITY · KB3 · FAULT TREE

P. Katsaros (Ed.): IMBSA 2025, LNCS 15755, pp. 413–428, 2026.
https://doi.org/10.1007/978-3-032-05073-1_27

1 Context

In a roadmap document for the work of the U.S. Department of Energy Office of Nuclear Energy [5], there is a discussion about developing tools based on declarative modeling, which we are already implementing for our studies through MBSA-type tools like KB3, which is based on the FIGARO language [3]. Additionally, one of the objectives of this roadmap is to automate the reading and acquisition of data from the information system to help verify or construct logical structures of the systems in question with a view to integrating EPS models. EDF has developed a tool called CONFLUENT [1, 4] that enables this automation of data reading and acquisition. The purpose of this article is to present examples based on a fictional case with the main objective of reducing the complexity of models by cutting the system into subsystem via CONFLUENT.

2 State of Art

In [4], there is a state of art with a synthetic illustration of a vision using CONFLUENT in Fig. 1.

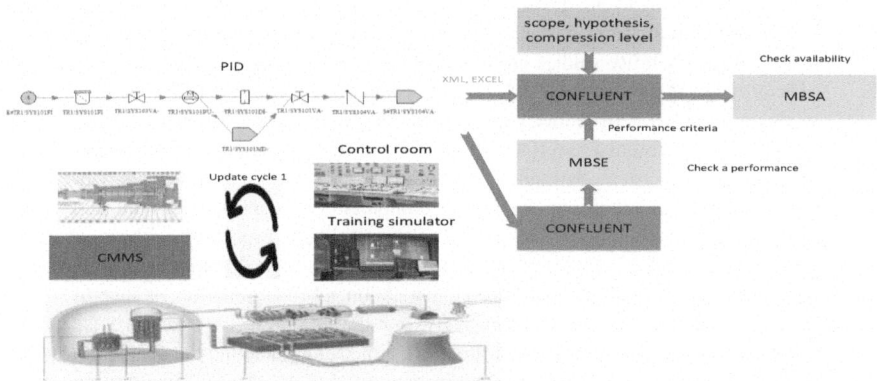

Fig. 1. Principle of creation of MBSE and MBSA directly from the PID by CONFLUENT

The P&ID (Piping & Instrumentation Diagram) serves as the functional diagram for the nuclear power plant. Each component of the PID is accompanied by a detailed plan that can be broken down into approximately a hundred referenced parts. The PID undergoes daily checks through maintenance (CMMS: Computerized Maintenance Management), operations (control room), training (simulator), and interventions (detailed plan). Keeping this information up to date enhances efficiency and minimizes human errors during operator training, operations, and preventive and corrective maintenance (Update cycle 1 of the diagram).

MBSE (Model-Based Systems Engineering) and MBSA (Model-Based Safety Assessment) are methodologies that define and verify the system's performance and availability [6], but they maintain a higher level of abstraction compared to the PID. In [6] and [7], there is a shared goal of achieving an MBSE and MBSA that are synchronized with reality, approached in two different ways. The first approach suggests generating the MBSA directly from the MBSE (performance model) through a table conversion, while the second emphasizes conducting successive synchronizations to ensure consistency between the PID and these two abstract models.

The approach in [4] is notably different, proposing a direct transition from the PID to the MBSA by automatically importing CAD data into the KB3 tool with CONFLUENT (translating objects using a dictionary for a target library containing MBSA knowledge (FIGARO Knowledge Base)). Furthermore, [7] suggests that the consistency between MBSE and MBSA is akin to the concept of a digital twin. Ultimately, MBSE, MBSA, CMMS, detailed plans, simulators, and PID all represent digital twins of the nuclear power plant, each with varying levels of detail and abstraction tailored to the needs of the user. Lastly, [6] highlights a strong interest in leveraging the performance data from MBSE to directly define undesirable events and the acceptance thresholds for unavailability.

Authors in [8] present updates to the AI tools, marking a significant advancement from the initial component-level FT creation to a more detailed failure mode level. This enhancement allows for the assessment of system changes resulting from individual component failures, represented as basic events in the FT. Additionally, the image recognition process for FT creation has been improved to include power supply systems alongside piping systems by extracting relevant components from single-line diagrams.

To what the authors are presenting in [9], the implementation of model-driven engineering for RAMST (Reliability, Availability, Maintainability, Safety, and Testability) assessment necessitates the development of large-scale, highly interconnected dynamic models that incorporate feedback loops typical of industrial systems. These complex models pose challenges for existing evaluation engines in efficiently delivering RAMST performance results within acceptable timeframes. To tackle this issue, simulation engines have been developed capable of managing such intricate models. It allows to reduce strongly the time of simulation.

These two articles still show the interest of generating Fault Trees starting from the design plan with AI while trying to reduce computation times. This is an objective that will be achieved in this article via CONFLUENT in different ways.

3 Fictional Case

The example below is a diagram represented in a CAD software (See Fig. 2). The associated data of the diagram (picture) exists in EXCEL format (See Fig. 3).

For the article, a fictional diagram was chosen, which is a circuit of four trains, each containing a pump to cool the water from a heat exchanger. The water comes from a tank. Each train has a zero-flow returning to the tank (SYSi05VA-), a filter (SYSi01FI-) , a flow sensor (SYSi01MD- and SYSi01DI-), and purge/vent valves (SYSi02VA- and SYSi06VA-). There are three configurations in the circuit for each train:

- Water Injection (INJ): injection configuration with START and ON.
- Min Flow (MF): configuration with zero flow on the pump.
- Purges / Vent (PU): configuration for the purge of the train.

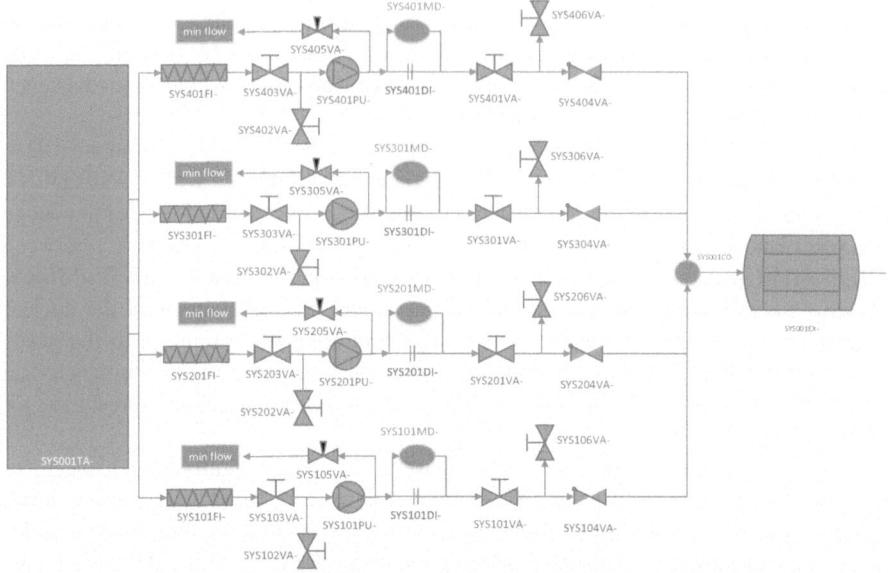

Fig. 2. Diagram of the fiction system

objet	type	page	x	y
SYS001EX-	exchanger	page_5	10	10
SYS001TA-	tank	page_6	5	5
SYS001CO-	node	page_5	5	10
SYS101VA-	valve	page_1	25	10
SYS102VA-	valve	page_1	12	15
SYS103VA-	valve	page_1	10	10
SYS104VA-	valve_stop	page_1	30	10
SYS105VA-	valve	page_1	10	5
SYS106VA-	valve	page_1	28	5

objet1	PtCoOut	PtCoIn	objet2	lien
SYS001TA-	out	in	SYS101FI	pipe_1
SYS101FI	out	in	SYS103VA-	pipe_2
SYS103VA-	out	in	SYS102VA-	pipe_3
SYS103VA-	out	in	SYS101PU-	pipe_4
SYS101PU-	out	in	SYS105VA-	pipe_5
SYS101PU-	out	in	SYS101DI-	pipe_6
SYS101PU-	out	in	SYS101MD-	pipe_7
SYS101DI-	out	in	SYS101VA-	pipe_8

Fig. 3. Excel table data

4   Confluent

The basic need of CONFLUENT is to redesign the schema structure with the same data as the input data (CAD), with a scope reduced to the needs of the study, based on the objects of a target knowledge base KB3.

CONFLUENT (Fig. 4) allows you to choose the target FIGARO knowledge base with these rules for the graphical management of objects. It enables the selection of multiple sources of different types (hydraulic, electrical, control-command, or support functions). For each source, it is necessary to define a conversion table. The tool allows for the merging of sources to trace a coherent set within the same study, concatenating the main function with, for example, the electrical circuit to power the pump and the ventilation to cool the area where the pump is located. Commands with an API developed for CONFLUENT allow for modifications to the diagram and the generation of a file readable by KB3. Finally, it is possible to define attributes that will link the sources together through links or interfaces. Common cause failures (CCF) are not considered in CONFLUENT but are defined at the calculation tool level (for EDF, this is Risk Spectrum or Andromeda).

[1] and [4] explain fully how to convert data, how to fix error on data and functionalities like managing system boundaries (scope), compression and topological mapping of complex networks by displaying attributes like location, altitude, function, or support structures.

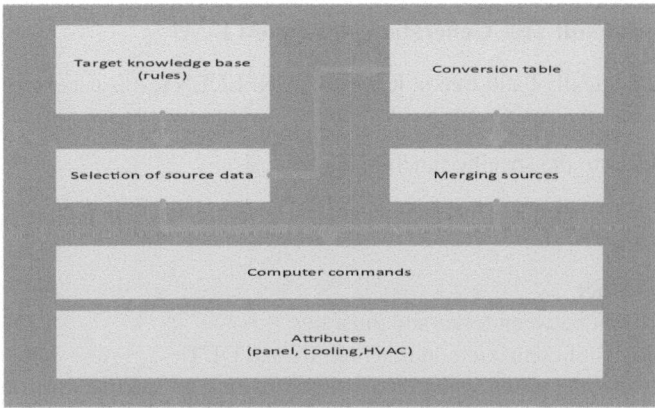

Fig. 4. Simplified visual of CONFLUENT.

Before this update, in [4] it is possible to trace only a specific function of the system by defining the inputs and outputs of the fluid of interest via a request in this form (See Table 1).

Table 1. Request to trace only train 1.

Name	Page	IN	OUT
TR1	PAGE_1	ISYS101FI-I	ISYS104VA-I

The diagram obtained after the construction of the paths via the request (Fig. 5):

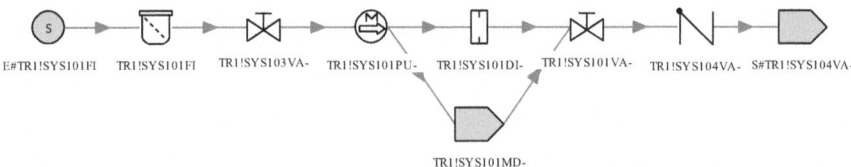

Fig. 5. System rendering only on train 1 under KB3.

This implemented function is very efficient because the request is minimalist in terms of attributes: only inputs and outputs (close to physics).

For the objective to generate Fault Tree easily with low complexity, it was necessary in CONFLUENT to improve the management of system boundaries (specific function) with 4 new modules and to develop a dedicated module for an algorithm to cut the diagram into subsystem. These modules are described in detail in Sect. 5.

5 New Modules in CONFLUENT

5.1 Module 1: Fault Tree Generation on Request Level

To create automatically Fault tree in KB3 via CONFLUENT, it is necessary to:

- Define the type of tester to link the top gate to the diagrams
- Link the tester to the specific function via request

CONFLUENT has a new module where it's possible to define a type of tester with this information:

- Type of the tester
- Type of the link between tester and diagrams
- Name of points of connexion on this link: IN and OUT
- Effect tested by the tester: water circulation, isolation or reduced flow rate

To illustrate the new module, we propose to trace the PUMP FUNCTION of the train_1 with one INPUT and two OUTPUTs (Table 2 and Fig. 6).

Table 2. Request to trace only train 1 without tester.

Name	Page	IN	OUT
PU_TR1	PAGE_1	ISYS103VA-I	ISYS101PU-I ISYS105VA-I

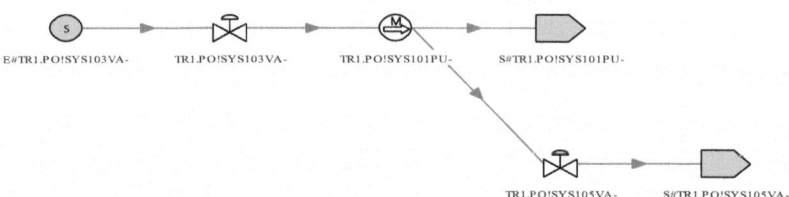

Fig. 6. System rendering of the PUMP FUNCTION under KB3.

This module allows CONFLUENT to draw the tester directly in the diagram without human gesture by completing the PUMP FUNCTION with the tester as follows (see Table 3. Request to trace only train 1 with tester.).

Table 3. Request to trace only train 1 with tester.

Name	Page	IN	OUT	Tester
PU_TR1	PAGE_1	ISYS103VA-I	ISYS101PU-I ISYS105VA-I	Hydraulic ITR1_PUI (HYD)

The new diagram contains the tester (Fig. 7):

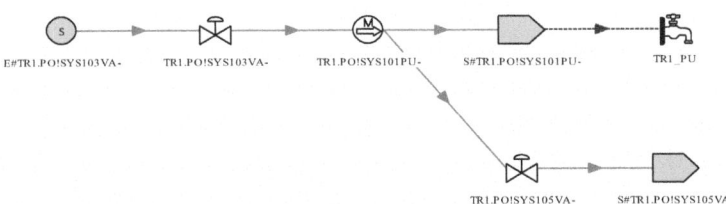

E#TR1.PO!SYS103VA-   TR1.PO!SYS103VA-   TR1.PO!SYS101PU-   S#TR1.PO!SYS101PU-   TR1_PU

TR1.PO!SYS105VA-   S#TR1.PO!SYS105VA-

Fig. 7. System rendering of the PUMP FUNCTION under KB3 with connector to Fault Tree (tester).

The Fault tree generated with KB3 (see Fig. 8) is based on the default operating profile (start a train). The valve 105VA- has no effect because no link with the tester. The Fault Tree contains Basic Event linked to 103VA- and 101PU- for solicitation and operation.

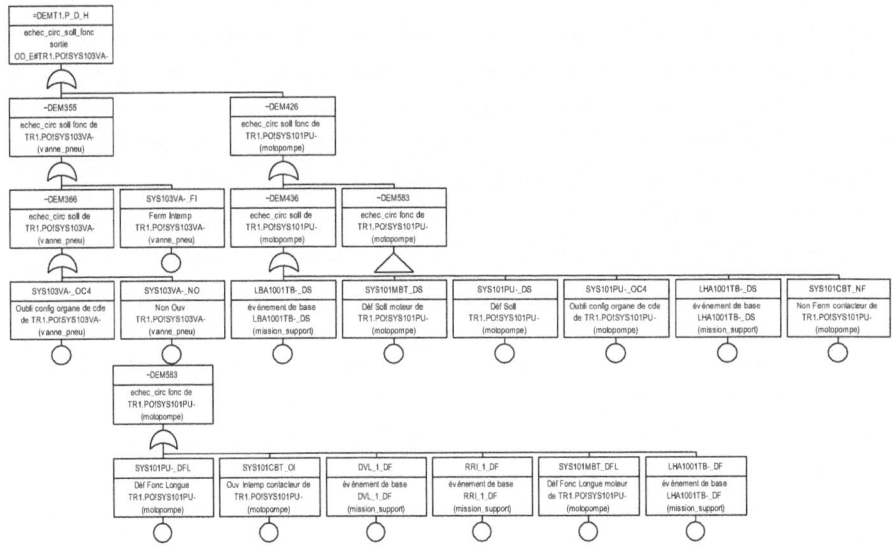

Fig. 8. Fault tree generated by KB3 from data of CONFLUENT for the PUMP FUNCTION

This new module allows CONFLUENT to move from just "defining a function with boundaries" to "generating a fault tree of the function with a default operating profile".

5.2   Module 2: Fault Tree Generation Containing Several Functions with Tester

With module 1, it's possible to generate Fault Tree which is the exact bijection of the diagram reduced to the function (see Table 3 and Fig. 8). In PRA, a Fault Tree is a combination of functions (little Fault Tree) with OR and AND gates. CONFLUENT contains a new module that allows the analyst to define the Fault Tree through a Boolean formula.

First, it necessary to name this low-level Fault Tree (exact bijection of the diagram reduced to the function) by adding a column with the possibility to define a name. The name "PU_TR1_HYD" is unique and explains the Fault Tree with a default operating profile (START).

Table 4. Request to trace only train 1 to 4 with tester and name.

Name	Page	IN	OUT	Tester	Name
PU_TR1	PAGE_1	ISYS103VA-I	ISYS101PU-I ISYS105VA-I	Hydraulic (HYD)	PU_TR1_HYD
PU_TR2	PAGE_2	ISYS203VA-I	ISYS201PU-I ISYS205VA-I	Hydraulic (HYD)	PU_TR2_HYD
PU_TR3	PAGE_3	ISYS303VA-I	ISYS301PU-I ISYS305VA-I	Hydraulic (HYD)	PU_TR3_HYD
PU_TR4	PAGE_4	ISYS403VA-I	ISYS401PU-I ISYS405VA-I	Hydraulic (HYD)	PU_TR4_HYD

It is possible to generate Fault Tree for the 4 trains with name (see Table 4).

The complete Fault Tree can be defined by a Boolean formula using these names as below:

$$\text{Total Fault Tree} = \text{OR (PU\_TR1\_HYD, PU\_TR2\_HYD, PU\_TR3\_HYD,}$$
$$\text{PU\_TR4\_HYD)}$$

In this case, we will obtain with CONFLENT four Fault Tree similar by train like the one presented in Fig. 8 and a TOP one making the connection between the TOP gate and these four low-level Fault Trees (see Fig. 9).

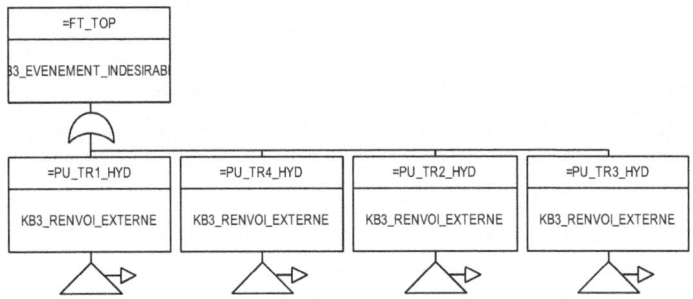

Fig. 9. Fault tree generated by KB3 from data of CONFLUENT for the TOP gate

This new module is very efficient because it is possible to define very complex Fault Tree like a "LEGO" in connecting TOP gate to small bricks. The next module will introduce operating profile in these bricks.

5.3 Module 3: Evolution of Module 1 and 3 by Adding Operating Profile

It is necessary to develop the module by adding the notion of operating profile in small bricks to build a very interesting "LEGO". The Table 5 defines how a class behavior for different operation profiles like: ON, OFF, START or STOP. For examples, a component "Valve" will move from "close" to "open" for the operating profile "START".

Table 5. Specification by class of operating profiles

Type	ON	OFF	START (STA)	STOP (STO)
Tank	debits / debits	does not debit / does not debit	does not debit / debits	debits / does not debit
Valve	open / open	close / close	close / open	open / close
Filter	debits / debits	does not debit / does not debit	does not debit / debits	debits / does not debit

Next, we need to add this information on the request tables like in Table 6.

Table 6. Request to trace train 1 to 4 with tester, profile and name.

Name	Page	IN	OUT	Tester	Profile	Name
PU_TR1	PAGE_1	ISYS103VA-I	ISYS101PU-I ISYS105VA-I	HYD	STA ON	PU_TR1_STA_HYD PU_TR1_ON_HYD
PU_TR2	PAGE_2	ISYS203VA-I	ISYS201PU-I ISYS205VA-I	HYD	STA ON	PU_TR2_STA_HYD PU_TR2_ON_HYD
PU_TR3	PAGE_3	ISYS303VA-I	ISYS301PU-I ISYS305VA-I	HYD	STA ON	PU_TR3_STA_HYD PU_TR3_ON_HYD

(continued)

Table 6. (*continued*)

Name	Page	IN	OUT	Tester	Profile	Name
PU_TR4	PAGE_4	ISYS403VA-I	ISYS401PU-I ISYS405VA-I	HYD	STA ON	PU_TR4_STA_HYD PU_TR4_ON_HYD

The boolean formula can be this one:

Total Fault Tree = OR (PU_TR1_ON_HYD, PU_TR2_ON_HYD,
PU_TR3_STA_HYD, PU_TR4_STA_HYD)

The bricks for TR3 and TR4 will be the same as Fig. 8 because the operating profile is "START": containing basic events for solicitation and operation. The bricks for TR1 and TR2 will be different of Fig. 8 because the operating profile is "ON": containing only basic events for operation.

The top gate Fault Tree will have this shape (see Fig. 10).

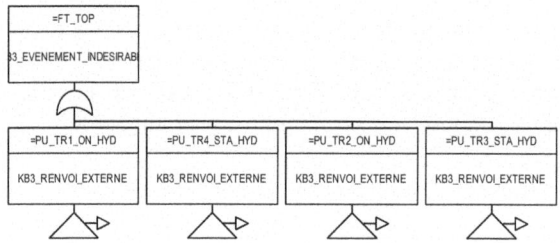

Fig. 10. Fault tree generated by KB3 from data of CONFLUENT for the TOP gate with profile

This module is very efficient because the analyze can create very complex Fault Tree by compiling bricks with possibly to take in account specific operation profile.

5.4   Module 4: Symmetrizes a Model Easily

With the module 3, it is possible to build very complex Fault Tree but boolean formula will be big to symmetrize a complete system with all redundancy configurations. To reduce the formula, CONFLUENT contains a combination generator. The boolean formula will be an association of combination with OR or AND gates.

A combination is defined like this: Comb_1 = [PU_TR1_HYD, PU_TR2_HYD, PU_TR3_HYD, PU_TR3_HYD] + [2: ON; 2: STA]. CONFLUENT will generate a TOP gate with four sub level with 2 bricks "ON" and 2 bricks "STA". (see Fig. 11).

This module is very efficient to build complex Fault Tree with all combinations to symmetrize completely a system with simple boolean formula.

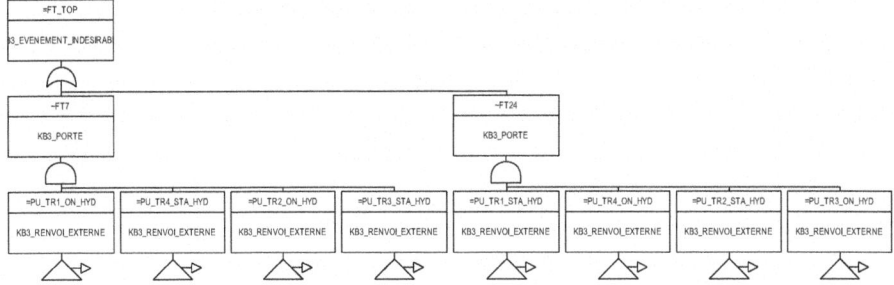

Fig. 11. Fault tree generated by KB3 from data of CONFLUENT for the TOP gate with profile and combinations

5.5 Module 5: Algorithm to Optimally Cut the Diagram into Subsystems

A system is defined on multi-level (see Fig. 12) system, train, function and component. The algorithm will take in account these four levels to define correctly the missions without implicit with a complete component table like Table 7 with the functions [1: store], [2: filter] and [3: measure].

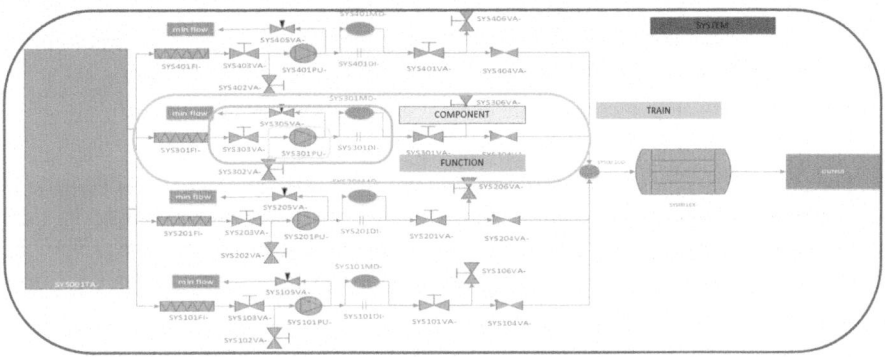

Fig. 12. Multi-level system.

Table 7. Component table of the system

Component	Type	Function	Operation profile	Train	System
SYS001TA	tank	1	ON	upstream common	SYS
SYSi01DI	diaphragm	3	ON	Train i	SYS
SYSi01FI	filter	2	ON	Train i	SYS
SYSi01MD	sensor	3	ON	Train i	SYS

To be possible to read the Mission_0 (The complete system with 4 necessary train and without the purge/vent function. All train are ON), it needs to shape these data in digital form.

The scope will define the system less the function of "PURGE/VENT". It is necessary to define profile, tested effect and the numbers of required trains to fulfill the need of the mission (Table 8).

Table 8. Mission_0 in digital form

Mission	Scope	Operation profile	Tested effect	required number of trains
Mission_0	SYS[1–4] – [PURGE/VENT]	ON	HYDRAULIC	4

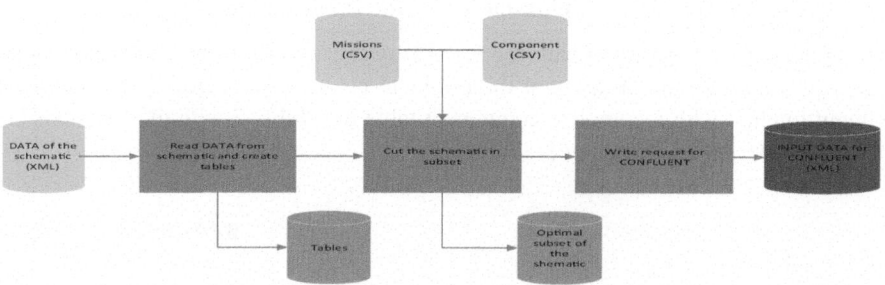

Fig. 13. Algorithm to cut system into subsystems.

The algorithm (Fig. 13) will read the diagrams to create tables, cut the schematic in subsystem with optimization to fulfill mission with the aim of reducing complexity (less number of gates, lesser depth of trees, smallest repetition of a basic event in the bricks) based on four levels (system, train, function and component). The final output are these subsystems in CONFLUENT specifications forms in request with tester and profile like in Table 6. The goal of the algorithm is to identify the largest subsystems with the same criteria: type, function and profile.

6   Fictional Case Example

In this section, we will use these new modules on the fictional case presented in Sect. 3 with theses missions to generate Fault Tree with low complexity:

- Mission_1: The complete system with only one sufficient train and without the purge/vent function. For each configuration, one train is ON and three trains have to START.
- Mission_2: Only train 2 and 4 with tank and exchanger and without the purge/vent function. Only one sufficient train. For each configuration, one train is ON and one train have to START.
- Mission_3: Only the tank and train 1 without the purge/vent function. It has to START.
- Mission_4: The complete system with 4 necessary trains without the purge/vent and filtering functions. All are ON.

The Table 9 is the "component table" for the fictional system in 4 levels (Type, Function, Train and System) with the profiles described in Table 5.

Table 9. "Component table" of the system

Component	Type	Function	Operation profile	Train	System
SYS001TA	tank	1	ON	common upstream	SYS
SYSi01DI	diaphragm	4	ON	Train i	SYS
SYSi01FI	filter	2	ON	Train i	SYS
SYSi01MD	sensor	4	ON	Train i	SYS
SYSi01PU	motor pump	3	ON / START	Train i	SYS
SYSi01VA	valve	4;6;5	ON / START	Train i	SYS
SYSi02VA	valve	5	ON / START	Train i	SYS
SYSi03VA	valve	2;4	ON / START	Train i	SYS
SYSi04VA	stop valve	6	ON / START	Train i	SYS
SYSi05VA	valve	3	ON / START	Train i	SYS
SYSi06VA	valve	9	ON / START	Train i	SYS
SYS001EX	exchanger	8	ON	common downstream	SYS
SYS001CO	barrel	7	ON	common downstream	SYS

Functions: [1: store], [2: filter], [3: pump], [4: measure], [5: min flow], [6: stop flow], [7: barrel], [8: exchange], [9: purge/vent].

In order of being processed by the algorithm, we shaped the missions in a digital form (see Table 10.).

Table 10. Missions in digital form

Mission	Scope	Operation profile	Tested effect	required number of trains
Mission_1	SYS[1–4] – [EVENT]	1 TRAIN[ON], 3 TRAIN[STA]	HYDRAULIC	1
Mission_2	SYS[2, 4] – [EVENT]	1 TRAIN[ON], 1 TRAIN[STA]	HYDRAULIC	1
Mission_3	SYS[1] – [VENT; EXCHANGE]	STA	HYDRAULIC	1
Mission_4	SYS[1–4] – [EVENT; FILTER]	ON	HYDRAULIC	4

The algorithm (module 5) transforms this INPUT data to CONFLUENT specification.

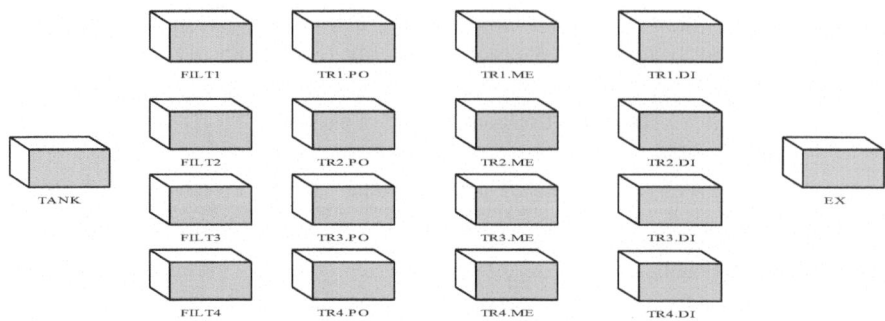

Fig. 14. Result of CONLUENT cutting system in subsystems

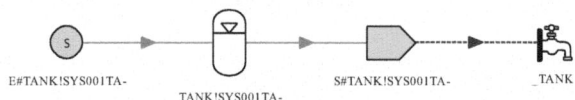

Fig. 15. Example of the subsystem "TANK"

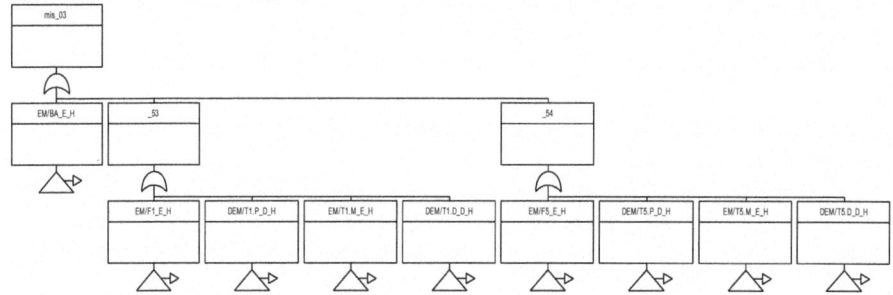

Fig. 16. TOP gate Fault Tree for mission3

CONFLUENT specifications will cut the system in subsystems like Fig. 14 and Fig. 15 with the tester and the profile (modules 1, 2 and 3). Each subsystem contains very few components and will generate a simple Fault Tree, easy to check. It will also generate the top gate boolean formula like in Fig. 16. For calculation test interest, it was necessary to transform the diagrams from 4 trains to 8 trains and had Common Cause Failure to have significant difference in time calculation. In Tables 11 and 12. Results are presented in two parts:

- metrics on fault tree shape
- data on calculations

Table 11. Metrics on Fault Trees (FT)

Case	Gates	Deepness of gates	Number of top gates	FT generator
With ALGO	177	6	54	6
Without ALGO	507	20	6	10

Table 12. Data on calculations

Case	Calculation time	Value	Cut off error	MCS
With ALGO	10 s	2E-02	1E-08	471300
Without ALGO	300 s	2E-02	2E-07	471300

There is a correlation between reducing the number of gates by 3, reducing the calculation time by 30 and the cut off error divided by 20. Indeed, optimizing the shape of the trees allows to reduce the number of gates which allows the quantification tool to calculate more quickly with less error. Each brick contains a very simple fault tree with almost the MCS because a basic event appears only one or two times. It is different from [9] where they optimize the quantification tool as we try to break complexity from the start at the system level.

7   Conclusion and Perspectives

This experiment is very interesting to demonstrate a reduction in complexity and analyst workload by analyzing design data at the system level. We will continue to test this modeling method in a larger system with common support systems such as panels, HVAC, and cooling water.

Acknowledgments. We would like to thank all the contributors to the project in EDF and CENTRALE-SUPELEC.

Disclosure of Interests. The authors have no competing interests to declare that are relevant to the content of this article.

References

1. Roy, R., Houbedine, J.-C., Hibti, M. : Ré-cupération automatique des données de conception des systèmes pour les études de fiabilité. LAMBDA-MU 23, SACLAY
2. Hibti, M., Hasseni, M., Villatte, N.: Zooming over PSA models: reducing psa models without loss of generality. 18th International Probabilistic Safety Assessment and Analysis (PSA 2023) Knoxville, TN (2023)
3. Bannelier, M., Bouissou, M., Villatte, N., Bouhadana, H. : Knowledge modeling and reliability processing: presentation of the figaro language and associated tools. SAFECOMP'91, Trondheim (1991)

4. Roy, R., Houbedine, J.-C., Hibti, M.: Illustration d'exemples de récupération automatique de données de conception pour les études de sûreté avec représentation compressée et/ou par attribut et/ou par multi configuration. Congrès Lambda Mu 24 « Les métiers du risque : clés de la réindustrialisation et de la transition écologique », Institut pour la Maîtrise des Risques (IMdR), Oct 2024, BOURGES, France
5. Miller, A., Hess, S., Smith, C.: R&D Roadmap to Enhance Industry Legacy Probabilistic Risk Assessment Methods and Tools. Tech. rep., U.S. Department of Energy Office of Nuclear Energy
6. Dumont, L.: Passerelles MBSE-MBSA : limites actuelles et propositions, LAMBDA-MU 23, SACLAY
7. Milcent, F. : Model-Based Safety Assessment : Comment renforcer la confiance dans les modèles ?,LAMBDA-MU 23, SACLAY
8. Futagami, S., Kondo, Y., Yamano, H., Kurisaka, K. : Automatic fault tree creation tools for failure mode level fault tree. 17th International Conference on Probabilistic Safety Assessment and Management (PSAM17&ASRAM2024), Japan
9. Clement, E. : System-Analyst : nouveau moteur d'évaluations de modèles MBSA dynamiques de grandes tailles S. Congrès Lambda Mu 24 « Les métiers du risque : clés de la réindustrialisation et de la transition écologique », Institut pour la Maîtrise des Risques (IMdR), Oct 2024, BOURGES, France

From Abstract to Action: Tailored Environment Taxonomies for More Complete ADS Safety Analyses

Daniel Hillen[1]([✉]), Jan Reich[1], Nishanth Laxman[1], Joshua Frey[1], Satoshi Otsuka[2], Takehito Ogata[2], and Donato Di Paola[3]

[1] Fraunhofer IESE, Kaiserslautern, Germany
{daniel.hillen,jan.reich,nishanth.laxman,joshua.frey}@iese.fraunhofer.de
[2] Hitachi Ltd, Tokyo, Japan
{satoshi.otsuka.hk,takehito.ogata.bs}@hitachi.com
[3] European Research and Development Centre, Hitachi Europe, London, England
donato.di-paola@hitachi-eu.com

Abstract. Different safety engineering processes of automated driving systems (ADS), such as hazard identification and risk assessment (HARA) or SOTIF analyses, require a model of the system's operational environment. Environment taxonomies like ISO 34503 and the "PEGASUS Six-Layer Model" can serve as a basis to derive such models. To ensure comprehensive coverage applicable for different ADS and operational design domains, these taxonomies must be defined at a generic abstract level. However, creating effective environment models relies on the engineer's ability to adapt a base taxonomy for a specific system, operational design domain, and safety analysis scope.

This study examines how a base environment taxonomy can be tailored to enhance a specific safety engineering process. Our proposed method involves deriving guide questions from the process's quality requirements. Engineers then use these questions to systematically refine a given taxonomy for use in the safety process.

We applied this method in a case study, adapting the ISO 34503 taxonomy to improve HARA quality for an autonomous last-mile delivery vehicle in urban intersection scenarios. The tailored taxonomy was compared with the generic baseline in identifying relevant situation elements for HARA. Industry experts interviewed post-study reported that the tailored taxonomy better structured the situation space exploration than the generic baseline. The detailed guide questions also revealed critical situation elements not identified with the generic taxonomy alone.

This paper argues that the developed taxonomy tailoring method improves the quality of safety engineering processes. The case study confirmed the hypotheses that engineers profit from a guided analysis approach, especially in complex situation spaces and that, in consequence, critical situation elements can be identified with less dependence on the engineer's experience. Thus, we conclude that although the approach cannot guarantee a complete coverage of the situation space, it evidently improves the quality of safety engineering processes.

Keywords: Ontology · ODD · Operational Design Domain

P. Katsaros (Ed.): IMBSA 2025, LNCS 15755, pp. 429–443, 2026.
https://doi.org/10.1007/978-3-032-05073-1_28

1   Introduction

Context. Modern standards such as ISO 21448 (SOTIF) for automated driving systems (ADS), require manufacturers to specify the operational area within which the system is intended to operate, commonly referred to as the operational design domain (ODD). This is necessary because these systems must be capable of handling various situations autonomously. These constraints are based on understanding the environment and are further consumed by safety analysis processes. The environmental aspects that are relevant for the safety engineering within the ODD highly depend on the safety analysis and the concrete system. For instance, risk assessment for an ADS focuses on elements on a higher abstraction layer than test scenario generation or cause-effect analysis.

Problem. In current practice, engineers identify these relevant environmental factors primarily based on their expert knowledge. They also use existing taxonomies or situation catalogs to manage the complexity of the environment. However, for automated driving functions, such standardized documents are usually either too generic or too detailed for a specific system, its operating environment, and its safety engineering process. While experienced engineers can leverage their expertise to deliver good results, less experienced engineers need more concrete guidance to effectively carry out these processes.

State-of-the-Art Deficiencies. In recent years, the industry recognized the benefit of taxonomies to ensure the safety of ADS. Therefore, standards like the ISO 34503 [9] or VDA 702 v2 [13], and research projects like the Pegasus successor VVM [2] published taxonomies for ADS. But no taxonomy can support all safety engineering tasks for all environments equally, because the level of abstraction and the categories can vary significantly depending on the activity the taxonomy is created for. A taxonomy that describes potential triggering events that cause perception systems to fail will define elements on a lower technical level compared to one that focuses on risk assessment like the VDA 702 v2 [13] for example. They further are described for any generic ADS and do not take into account one specific ODD. Other researchers identified the need of taxonomies for safety engineering like Kemmann [10] who proposed an ontology specifically for situations for the hazard analysis and risk assessment (HARA). This ontology however describes a way to formalize the situation but it does not describe which concrete elements of the environment are relevant. Another approach for streamlining the HARA is described by the SafeSpection [6] framework that uses guiding-questions to support the engineers. Although it focuses on identifying software-related hazards, the approach is applicable to different safety engineering methods. Some meta-questions might also be applicable for tailoring the taxonomy however the main focus of the framework is to identify hazards so that this approach could benefit from a taxonomy to generate concrete questions.

Therefore, a method is missing that tailors a base taxonomy to lower the dependency of safety engineers' expertise on the quality of safety artifacts.

Method. In this paper, we present a guide-question-based method to tailor a baseline taxonomy for the specific engineering process and system context. Guide-questions are derived based on the operational design domain, the system context and the concrete safety engineering activity to systematically tailor a baseline taxonomy. The resulting taxonomy should define these elements of the environment that are relevant for the process in the given context.

Contribution. With our method we propose a systematic approach to tailor taxonomies that can enhance safety engineering processes. We do not aim to provide a complete taxonomy but a taxonomy with increased coverage of those elements in the operational environment that are relevant to the engineering process.

Paper Structure. In Sect. 2 we briefly discuss the related work about taxonomies and systematic safety analysis. In Sect. 3 we propose our method to tailor the taxonomy for the needs of safety engineers. The application of this method is then demonstrated in Sect. 4 on an industry example where a base taxonomy is tailored for risk assessment in the automotive domain. Last, we discuss the limitation of our method and provide an outlook for future research in Sect. 5.

2 Related Work

Several taxonomies exist for different domains and different tasks in safety engineering. For verification and validation, ISO 34503 [9], defines a taxonomy of the public traffic environment for specifying the ODD, while VDA 702 v2 [13] describes a situation catalog for supporting the HARA. For other domains standardization activities define their own taxonomy like in the DIN SPEC 99004 [7] for trains. Another high-level taxonomy for specifying test scenarios is described with the 6-layer model [1].

Because standards must be applicable to a wide range of systems, they typically define elements at a higher level of abstraction. For a specific system, these standards require refining those elements and extending the taxonomy, yet they do not specify how to do so. As a result, when applying such taxonomies to safety analyses in a concrete system and ODD, engineers rely on their own expertise to identify the relevant elements on the fly.

Other researchers propose world models [4,5] which cover significantly more details than the aforementioned taxonomies. However, when taxonomies are overly detailed, it becomes difficult to filter for the elements that truly matter for a specific system, its ODD, and the analysis task. In such cases, the level of abstraction may be too low to cover the full situation space for a HARA, potentially leading to an underestimation of risk. Moreover, adapting these very detailed taxonomies to different tasks is not straightforward, and there is no established process yet for tailoring them.

The need for a more systematic HARA process is addressed by SAHARA [10]. This framework formalizes situations of a HARA with an ontology. The ontology describes the different categories to specify a hazardous event. These categories are high level and define internal system states, behavior and high-level aspects of the environment. However, which concrete elements of the environment are relevant for that system in its ODD are not further described.

All of the aforementioned taxonomies describe the environment targeting one concrete process or they are too generic. Taxonomies that are too detailed cannot easily be transferred to other activities and generic taxonomies rely on the expertise of the engineer to tailor them on-the-fly during the analysis.

In standards like the ISO 26262 [8] a common approach to ensure process quality is to use keyword based methods like Hazard Operability Studies (HAZOP). Applying the keywords commission, omission, too long/ too short, too early/too late enables engineers to systematically construct hazards. Such keywords are in particular used in the HARA, in System-Theoretic Process Analysis (STPA) and also in Failure Mode and Effect Analysis (FMEA). While they can ensure coverage of functional hazards, they are not directly applicable to analyze the environment. SafeSpection is a more advanced framework for creating guiding questions specifically for software-based hazard identification. While SafeSpection can enhance hazard analysis the guiding questions are not applicable for identifying environmental aspects. The guiding questions can rather benefit from a taxonomy that describes the concrete elements that are relevant for hazard analysis. Therefore, a good taxonomy can provide support by:

- Starting the creative part of the safety engineering process
- Controlling the focus and ensure that the scope of the process is not left
- Inspiring the engineer with new ideas
- Providing a termination criteria and a progress indicator
- Reducing the interpretation depth so that less experienced engineers can produce artifacts effectively

In summary, taxonomies become more and more relevant to enhance safety engineering for ADS systems. One taxonomy however, cannot support all safety engineering processes equally good and there is no method yet to tailor a taxonomy for the different ODDs and safety engineering processes.

3 Guide-Question-Based ODD Tailoring Method

In this section we present our method to systematically tailor a base taxonomy for the needs of safety engineers and their activities. An overview of the method is shown in Fig. 1.

3.1 Input

In tailoring a base taxonomy to a specific safety-engineering activity, both the taxonomy and the engineering process must be taken into account. In addition, the ODD and the feature design provide crucial input.

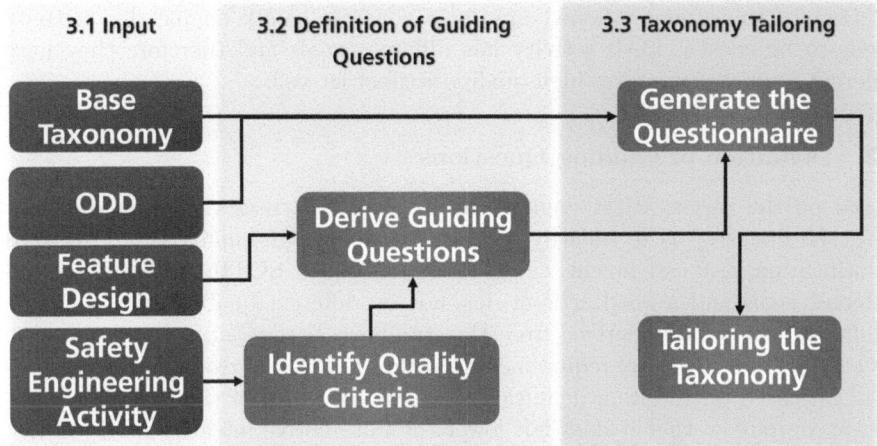

Fig. 1. Method overview

The base taxonomy is the starting point from which the whole process starts. Standardized taxonomies such as ISO 34503 [9] can be used as the base taxonomy because they will be further required for other safety engineering processes and therefore should exist. The method, however, also works with manufacturer-internal taxonomies or taxonomies from other domains such as the DIN SPEC 99004 [7] for railway.

The environment relevant to the safety engineering activity strongly depends on the ODD. The ODD explicitly or implicitly defines which environmental elements are relevant to the system. For example, a highway pilot does not need to consider elements that only occur in urban areas, such as zebra crossings. Therefore, the ODD can reduce the situation space of the operating environment and thus the set of elements that are relevant for the safety engineering process. The ODD itself is based on a taxonomy according to ISO 34503 and described in the standardized format ASAM OpenODD [3] which can provide a feasible base taxonomy. This method can also tailor the taxonomy with the goal to improve the ODD constraints when the taxonomy defined in standards are not sufficient for a concrete system.

Another important input is the feature design. Different kinds of feature may introduce different constraints that are not reflected in the ODD. For example the objective, system properties or functional constraints based on the use case. A system could be designed to only drive with a speed of maximum 10 km/h, or with special cargo etc. These constraints are not reflected in the ODD. This can lead to additional perspective and aspects of the system which can be relevant for safety engineering. For example a last-mile delivery vehicle will encounter different situations than a highway chauffeur. The system context is described further in the item definition which is demanded by ISO 26262.

Despite the aforementioned inputs, a concrete safety engineering activity needs to be chosen. Each activity has different goals and therefore they have different requirements for a high-quality artifact as well.

3.2 Definition of Guiding Questions

Based on the target safety engineering activity that uses the tailored taxonomy, the first step is to identify the criteria for a high-quality result. Hazard identification, risk assessment, cause-effect analysis or SOTIF analysis, have all different goals and a good artifact depends on different quality aspects. These quality criteria can be derived from the standards that require these processes. ISO 26262 defines several requirements for the HARA. For example the analysis shall be based on the item definition, the level of detail of the situations shall be appropriate so that it does not lower the automotive integrity level (ASIL), the risk should be based on the severity, exposure and controllability, and many more. In the next step, guiding questions are derived from the criteria. In the example, a guiding question could be: *"Which <element> can be harmed?"* or *"Which <element> have an unpredictable behavior?"*.

Another standard and activity define different requirements. For identifying factors that can cause foreseeable misuse according to ISO 21448, they need to cover different aspect such as loss of concentration or lack of understanding. Potential guiding questions could be: *"Which <element> can indicate loss of concentration of the driver?"*.

The two example show how different guiding question can look like as they focus on two very different analysis demanded by standards for ADS. The different guiding questions also focus on totally different aspects of the environment and come from very different perspectives. This is the case because the goal of the safety analysis is very different and so are the respective quality criteria.

The next step is to generate the questionnaire by concretizing the guiding questions.

3.3 Taxonomy Tailoring

After the guiding questions are derived, the questionnaire can be instantiated. Therefore, the guiding questions are combined with the base taxonomy considering the ODD and the feature design. For example *"Which vulnerable road user have an unpredictable behavior?"*. Systematically combining the guiding question with the base taxonomy generates a sophisticated questionnaire. However, not every combination between an element of the base taxonomy and a guiding questions leads to a meaningful question. For example *"Which roundabout can be harmed?"*. The engineer should therefore remove such questions or ensure that they are not generated.

Combining each guiding question with leaves of the taxonomy is not the most feasible option in all cases. Some taxonomies describe very detailed aspect in their lower branches. Then generating a question with the parent element can be the better option. For example, *"Which heavy snow, visibility less than*

0.5 km can impair the perception of the driver?" it could be better to ask *"Which level of snowfall can impair the perception of the driver?".* Which hierarchical level is the most feasible heavily depends on the guiding question and also the quality criteria. In general, asking the guiding questions for parent elements can lead to relevant elements that are not part of the base taxonomy at all. Instead of refining and increasing the elements, this approach can also lead to a more abstract taxonomy which describes a more suitable abstraction level for the given engineering activity.

After the questionnaire is prepared, the questions need to be answered by domain experts. This process requires a mixture of creativity and expertise. Ideally, several experts with different perspective would answer the questionnaire. A workshop setting could therefore be a good option to collectively brainstorm and to find many different elements.

The last step is then to document the tailored taxonomy and to use it during the targeted safety engineering activity. Standardized formats such as ASAM OpenODD [3] can be used to export the tailored taxonomy.

4   Demonstration

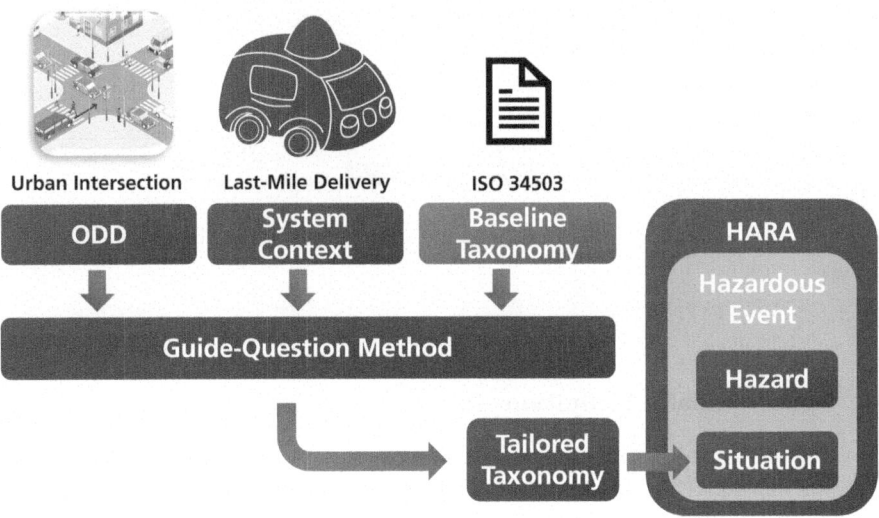

Fig. 2. Evaluation use cases with a last-mile delivery vehicle on urban intersections

We applied our method with industry experts to tailor the ISO 34503 [9] for risk assessment of an autonomous last-mile delivery vehicles. The ADS should only operate in a small urban environment that mainly consists of an urban intersection. As shown in Fig. 2 the question is, how can we tailor the taxonomy of ISO 34503 [9] for that use case.

The evaluation consists of 3 major phases:

1. **Questionnaire Definition:** Derive quality criteria and guiding questions.
2. **Taxonomy Tailoring:** Workshop with domain experts to tailor the last-mile delivery taxonomy
3. **Documentation:** Create a model instance of the taxonomy to enable traceability to the environment from other safety engineering artifacts
4. **Evaluation:** Feedback of the industry experts

Figure 3 shows the overall evaluation process. This means we first start to derive the guiding-question and criteria to generate a questionnaire. Afterward, we tailor the taxonomy using the questionnaire for our use case. The tailored taxonomy is then evaluated by our industry experts.

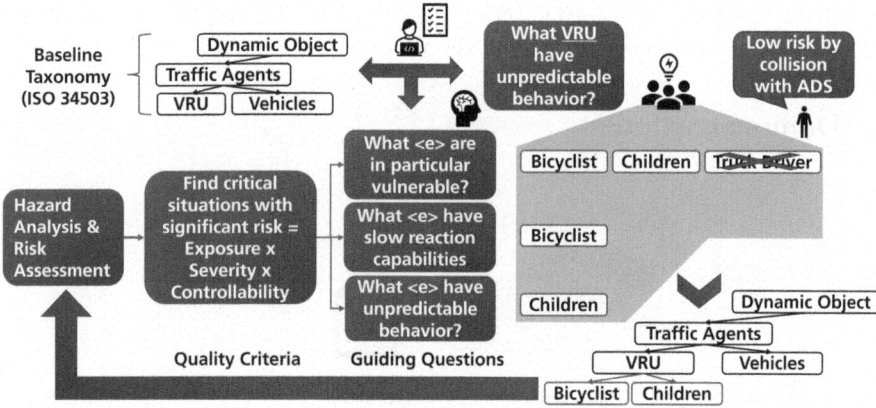

Fig. 3. Overview of the demonstration of our guide-question-based taxonomy tailoring method

4.1 Questionnaire Definition

First, before we can derive the guiding questions, we need to identify the quality criteria. For our case study the taxonomy should support engineers with the HARA and in particular identify critical situations. In the context of HARA, a situation is critical if a hazard can lead to an accident which causes damage. Accordingly, risk is defined through the severity, exposure and controllability. Based on this an engineer can ask themselves the following high-level questions:

– What are the severe situations?
– What are the situations with high accident probability?
– What are the situations with limited controllability?

These questions however are not too abstract to effectively analyze the situation space, especially when it is more complex.

Consequently, we came up with questions like *Who can be harmed?* and *What can cause harm?*. These questions are further enhanced by attributes like *Vulnerability*, *Predictable Behavior* and *Reaction Capabilities*. This leads to questions like *Who is in particular vulnerable and can be harmed?*.

These questions are then combined with the base taxonomy. An excerpt of the final questions then looked like:

- Which VRU is in particular vulnerable and can be harmed?
- Which VRU imposes rules to the ego vehicle?
- Which special location imposes rules to the ego vehicle?
- Which VRU has in particular high awareness of critical traffic situations?

4.2   Taxonomy Tailoring

After we generated the questionnaire, we organized a workshop with domain experts and safety engineers. We systematically iterate over the abstract taxonomy and asked the questionnaire to experts. Their responses are collected and harmonized into a more detailed taxonomy which is tailored towards the target operational area, risk assessment activity, and use case. The questionnaire and the base taxonomy help to a) kick start the brainstorming and b) stay focused on the quality aspects. This leads to generated taxonomy elements that are relevant for risk assessment.

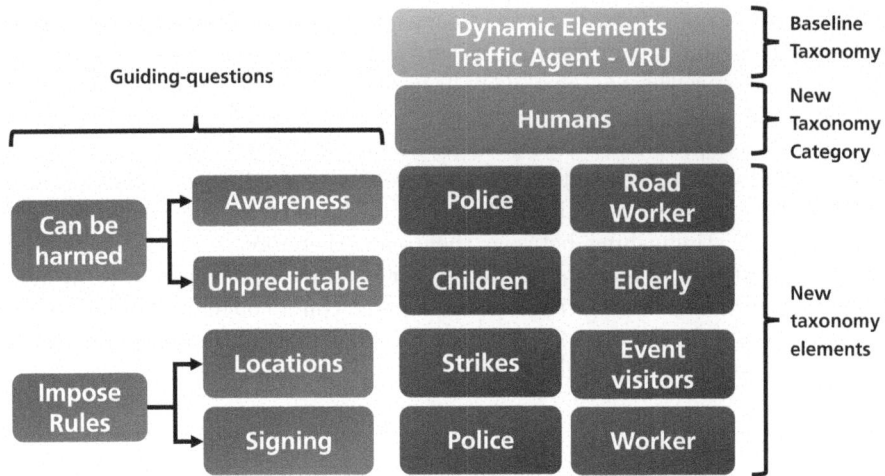

Fig. 4. Excerpt of taxonomy elements added to the baseline taxonomy

In Fig. 4 an excerpt of the workshop result is shown. The initial category *Dynamic Elements - Traffic Agents - VRU* is further refined. Instead of the high-level element *VRU* we identified various elements that influence the risk through different aspects. All of the added elements are humans so we first added a new sub-category *Humans*. The humans could be further categorized based on the guiding-question criteria. The criteria is closely bound to the way how the elements influences the risk. For example, trained humans that are more aware then other, such as policemen or construction workers can control critical situations better then the average human and significantly better than children. Especially children or elderly might behave unpredictable more often which could increase the risk in comparison to the average human. Therefore we added those people to the taxonomy. We could further categorize them within the *Humans* category based on the criteria. This means for example, *Awareness* as a child of *Humans* which describes the *Police* and *Road Worker*. Analogue for the other criteria and elements. This can also allow a traceability back to the original guiding question which led to the respective taxonomy element.

In Fig. 5 an excerpt from another set of questions is shown. The *subject vehicle* does only contain some basic attributes like weight and speed. For the risk assessment of an ADS also its behavior can introduce risk and lead to an accident. How can the subject vehicle behavior influence the behavior of other traffic participants (TP)? Not turning on the lighting in the darkness or the rear fog light in heavy fog can cause other TPs to not perceive our vehicle and lead ultimately to an accident. Similarly, driving through a puddle too fast could cause the subject vehicle to splash water onto pedestrians which could cause financial damage. Even though this might not introduce a significant risk in the classical meaning but it might be relevant for the company e.g. related to marketing, Furthermore, we considered here a last-mile delivery vehicle which will transport various goods to the customers. These goods might be poisonous or explosive. This aspect is probably irrelevant when considering robotaxis, but for our special use case this can be a likely hazard which requires suitable measures.

One could argue whether the level of granularity might be too high, i.e., that humans could already be sufficient. In the ISO 34503 [9] only VRUs are mentioned. However, different levels of awareness or predictable behaviors can lead to different behaviors of the ADS so that different safety requirements could be required. Distinguishing between them can, therefore, reveal open critical problems or identify irrelevant elements. For example, as VRU one could add beside bicyclists also truck drivers. However, one could conclude in a low speed collision, a small ADS cannot severely hurt a truck driver and thus assess those situations as low risk and neglect them.

4.3   Documentation

Our tailored taxonomy, hazards and safety requirements are documented by modeling in our modeling framework called digital dependability identities (DDI) [12]. The tailored taxonomy is modeled as an instance of the environment model [11]. We further extended the environment model so that guiding questions can be modeled and linked to elements of the environment model. We further added a reasoning element attached to taxonomy elements in order to provide additional

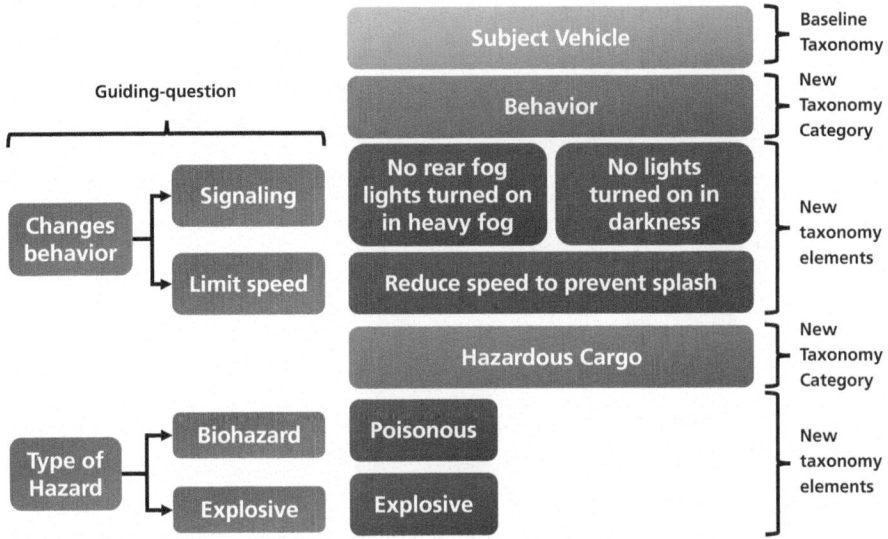

Fig. 5. Excerpt of taxonomy elements added to the baseline taxonomy

information why they were added. Then it is possible to trace back which guiding questions led to which taxonomy elements.

Modeling the taxonomy in the DDI we created the foundation to implement traceability between different artifacts and the taxonomy. Furthermore, we can run automated analysis and model-to-model transformations. For example, we implemented a script to request which taxonomy elements are linked to a given guiding question. An excerpt of the output is shown in Fig. 6. In the future it also enables us to implement the export of the taxonomy in standardized languages like OpenODD [3].

4.4   Evaluation

For evaluation of the method, we asked two industry experts for their subjective assessment of the approach after the moderated two-day workshop. Afterwards, the method was executed on a small warehouse use case within an industrial engineering team. Industry experts and the engineers think that the created taxonomy can support engineers to identify safety requirements more effectively. They highlighted that the tailored taxonomy contains elements that are not intuitive to them. This means, the base taxonomy provides not sufficient support to identify these elements. The new taxonomy elements are filling this gap so that this more sophisticated taxonomy can indeed support the engineers.

Furthermore, their trust increases into the quality of the artifact that is created using the tailored taxonomy. Several guiding questions led to the same element from different perspectives. That showcased the importance of some elements, and this redundancy also improved the confidence that the tailored tax-

```
Following context elements consider the guiding safety question "Who/what imposes ADS operation related rules?":
------------------------------------------------------------------------------------------------------------
- Bicycle lane markings:
            - Rule determination for other traffic participants but also relevant for ADS: Markings determine allowed
              area for bicycles, ego is not always allowed to cross markings
- Traffic regulating police officer:
            - Temporary rule altering object: Temporary traffic regulation
            - Dynamically rule altering object: Traffic regulating police officer often alter rules during their work
- Pedestrian Traffic Light:
            - Rule determination for other traffic participants but also relevant for ADS: Green pedestrian light on
              street where ADS wants to turn into, has to be considered
            - Dynamically rule altering object: Pedestrian lights can switch between different states indicating if
              pedestrians are allowed to cross street or not
- Traffic Light:
            - Dynamically rule altering object: Traffic lights can switch between different states indicating if
              traffic is allowed to pass traffic light or not
```

Fig. 6. Example script to query taxonomy elements based on the guiding question within the DDI

onomy can support the engineer to reach a sufficient situation coverage according to the quality criteria of the HARA. If there is only one path to identify a certain element, the probability that the engineer fail to describe it is significantly higher. The method is therefore more forgiving and acknowledges the fact that different people think differently and thus come to one elements over different paths. The performance tradeoff is less important than the robustness. While the method cannot ensure completeness the tailored taxonomy provides a more comprehensive set of elements.

For example, a policeman is identified through the guiding question about element that are imposing rules as also from the awareness perspective. This introduces redundancy of the element policemen which indicates its importance. Further, the different guiding questions also show different perspectives that can impact the risk assessment and how safety goals are derived accordingly. Different people have a different thinking process, while most people think immediately about children when it comes to people that are vulnerable, some other elements are less obvious. Strikes or other large groups of persons who do not follow the normal traffic rules are discovered based on individual interests and experience. For example, football fans that go regularly to games might experiences such situations and think about them easier than other engineers who are not familiar with it. Therefore, it is also beneficial to have guiding questions that refer to the same elements from different angles.

The method itself helped to start the creative process for identifying new elements because they asked concrete questions within our use cases. Engineers could better take different perspectives and focus on one aspect of the environment at a time. On the other hand, the guiding questions also ensured that the engineer mentally does not drift towards aspects that are less relevant to the concrete system or process. Whenever, some discussion started to go too far off track, the engineers were put back on track by following the guiding questions.

Also, after the whole questionnaire was answered the process finished. The experts highlighted that this finishing criteria is important because today the engineers rely only on their expertise to decide when it is good enough. Usually only vague requirements define the termination criteria such as "identify all critical situations". Under the assumption that the tailored taxonomy reflects relevant items, going through it defines a concrete termination criteria.

In summary, the tailoring method acknowledges multiple perspectives to ensure robust identification of safety requirements, that instills trust in the artifact's quality, and define a clear finishing criterion. This structured approach helps engineers prevent oversight and boosts confidence in the coverage of critical situations.

4.5 Discussion

The quality of the tailored taxonomy is tightly linked to the quality of the guiding-questions and its quality criteria. A complete set of guiding questions for most activities might not even be possible without specifying them too abstract which limits the practicality. Completeness of the taxonomy from a mathematical point of view is not the goal of the method. Our method should be applicable in industry and improve the current process. The tailored taxonomy can improve standardized taxonomies such as the ISO 34503, VDA 720 v2 [13] or DIN SPEC 99004 [7], which by their nature are created for a large number of systems while engineers can concentrate on one concrete system. With such a tailored taxonomy it is possible to improve the coverage of the most relevant aspects of the environment for the analysis. Furthermore, a high-quality taxonomy depends on the quality criteria, which are not trivial to identify. Further methodology is required for each engineering process to derive the quality criteria and the questions. Currently we are working on formalizing quality criteria to environment models from the perspective of different safety engineering processes.

While we showed the application of the method in the situation analysis in the context of HARA, other safety engineering processes can also benefit from a tailored taxonomy to improve their effectiveness. However, not every activity and not every concrete use case can benefit equally from a taxonomy. Some process may have already dedicated tool support or mature taxonomies and others may not depend as much on the environment. Further research is necessary to identify those activities that can benefit the most from a tailored taxonomy.

For traditional safety engineering processes engineers rarely use taxonomies and hence it is not clear how to integrate taxonomies most efficiently in the process. Even without clear integration, engineers can benefit from taxonomies that describe the relevant elements. It can be used for various cases such as inspiring for creative processes or to track the progress.

Another challenge is the scalability. When the number of elements in the base taxonomy is very high, then a combinatorial approach with the guiding questions might not be feasible. Not every element of the taxonomy can be combined with each guiding question and criteria. Further, it sometimes is more valuable to combine higher-level elements instead of leaves. Finding the most appropriate way is up to the engineer. In practice, it is rather an intuitive approach which question can be combined with which taxonomy element. A better guidance can be developed by testing the method on more use cases in the future. Automation is one approach to resolve this problem. Therefore, Large Language Models like ChatGpt can potentially support engineers to identify realistic combinations.

While the method also initially requires quite some effort, once the guiding-questions are derived, many of them can be reused for similar systems. Therefore, one manufacturer can reduce the effort required to execute the method for systems of the same product family. This also applies for the tailored taxonomy, especially if ODD and feature design remain similar. How to efficiently identify the reusability potential and to implement change management requires future research.

Our evaluation showed that the guiding-question approach can be very beneficial. In comparison to established keyword-based approaches like HAZOP our guiding-questions can be applied more intuitive on environmental elements. The tailored taxonomy describes concrete elements which can be used in the SAHARA or SafeSpection framework. In future research the integration of our approach into SAHARA and SafeSpection can be investigated.

5   Conclusion

This paper argues that the developed taxonomy tailoring method improves the effectiveness of safety engineering processes by reducing the dependency of safety engineering expertise to the artifact quality. Therefore, we presented a guide-question-based method, that systematically enhances existing base taxonomies based on quality criteria of the targeted safety analysis. Guiding questions are derived from these quality criteria to identify those environmental elements that are most relevant for the analysis of the concrete ADS.

We evaluated our method in a case study with industry experts. In our case study, we demonstrated our method on a last-mile delivery vehicle within urban intersections. The experts confirmed the hypotheses that engineers profit from a guided analysis approach especially in complex situation spaces. The tailored taxonomy can in particular reduce the dependency on the engineer's level of experience to find critical situation elements. Thus, we conclude that although the approach cannot guarantee a complete coverage of the situation space, it evidently improves the quality of ADS safety analyses significantly, eventually leading to safer systems than before.

In future research, the derivation of quality criteria for different safety analysis processes needs further refinement to ensure high-quality guiding questions, and thereby produce high-quality taxonomies.

In order to objectively quantify the benefit of the method, a case study is necessary that quantitatively evaluates the improvements of the effectiveness of novice safety engineers using the tailored taxonomy.

References

1. 6-layer model for a structured description and categorization of urban traffic and environment. IEEE Access **9** (2021). https://doi.org/10.1109/ACCESS.2021.3072739
2. VVM: Verification Validation Methods (2023). https://www.vvm-projekt.de/
3. ASAM: ASAM OpenODD: Concept Paper (2021). https://www.asam.net/standards/detail/openodd
4. Czarnecki, K.: Operational world model ontology for automated driving systems–part 1: Road structure. Waterloo Intelligent Systems Engineering Lab (WISE) Report, University of Waterloo (2018)
5. Czarnecki, K.: Operational world model ontology for automated driving systems–part 2: Road users, animals, other obstacles, and environmental conditions. Waterloo intelligent systems engineering lab (WISE) Report, University of Waterloo (2018)
6. Denger, C.: SafeSpection-A framework for systematization and customization of software hazard identification by applying inspection concepts. Ph.D. thesis, Fraunhofer IRB Verlag (2009)
7. DIN: DIN DKE SPEC 99004:2025-05: Specification of Operational Design Domain in Rail (2025). https://doi.org/10.31030/3610746
8. ISO: ISO 26262 Road vehicles - Functional Safety (2018)
9. ISO: ISO 34503 Road vehicles - Test scenarios for automated driving systems — Taxonomy for operational design domain (2023)
10. Kemmann, S.: SAHARA - A Structured Approach for Hazard Analysis and Risk Assessments. doctoralthesis, Technische Universität Kaiserslautern (2015). https://nbn-resolving.de/urn:nbn:de:hbz:386-kluedo-40270
11. Reich, J., et al.: Concept and metamodel to support cross-domain safety analysis for odd expansion of autonomous systems. In: Guiochet, J., Tonetta, S., Bitsch, F. (eds.) SAFECOMP 2023. LNCS, vol. 14181, pp. 165–178. Springer, Cham (2023). https://doi.org/10.1007/978-3-031-40923-3_13
12. Schneider, D., Trapp, M., Papadopoulos, Y., Armengaud, E., Zeller, M., Höfig, K.: Wap: digital dependability identities. In: 2015 IEEE 26th International Symposium on Software Reliability Engineering (ISSRE), pp. 324–329 (2015). https://doi.org/10.1109/ISSRE.2015.7381825
13. VDA: VDA 702 Situation catalog E-Parameter as per ISO 26262-3:2018 (06/2023) V2 (2023)

Author Index

The manufacturer's authorised representative in the EU is Springer
Nature Customer Service Centre GmbH, Europaplatz 3, 69115 Heidelberg,
Germany. If you have any concerns regarding our products, please
contact ProductSafety@springernature.com

Printed and bound by CPI Group (UK) Ltd, Croydon, CR0 4YY
29/04/2026
02099461-0016